ASPEN PUBLISHERS

Understanding the AMA Guides in Workers' Compensation
Fourth Edition

by Steven Babitsky and James J. Mangraviti, Jr.

The American Medical Association's *Guides to the Evaluation of Permanent Impairment* (or *AMA Guides*) is mandated for use in many workers' compensation systems and the Longshore and Harbor Workers' Compensation Act and is commonly used in personal injury cases. Aspen's *Understanding the AMA Guides in Workers' Compensation* explains the key issues and problems regarding the adoption and use of the *AMA Guides* and provides the practitioner with tools, resources, and the legal background to successfully argue cases involving use of the *AMA Guides*.

Highlights of the Fourth Edition

Understanding the AMA Guides in Workers' Compensation, Fourth Edition provides up-to-date coverage of the following:

- Key points in the new sixth edition of the *AMA Guides* (published January 2008)

- Red flag issues under the new sixth edition such as inconsistencies, major changes, areas of most likely challenge, and unratable conditions

- Sample cross-examinations under the fifth and sixth editions

- Difficult cross-examination questions under the *AMA Guides*

- Analysis and explanations of the latest case law relating to workers' compensation

- Updated list of state and federal statutes and regulations dealing with the *AMA Guides*

- Annotated sample proofs showing how a well-prepared physician can excel at deposition

- Legal analysis of the sixth edition

- Comparison and contrasts of provisions under the fourth, the fifth, and the sixth editions of the *AMA Guides*

Wolters Kluwer
Law & Business

The Fourth Edition includes a number of appendixes, a table of cases, and a detailed index.

8/08

For questions concerning this shipment, billing, or other customer service matters, call our Customer Service Department at 1-800-234-1660.

For toll-free ordering, please call 1-800-638-8437.

ASPEN PUBLISHERS

UNDERSTANDING THE AMA GUIDES IN WORKERS' COMPENSATION

Fourth Edition

Steven Babitsky

SEAK, Inc.
Falmouth, Massachusetts

James J. Mangraviti, Jr.

SEAK, Inc.
North Reading, Massachusetts

 Wolters Kluwer

Law & Business

AUSTIN   BOSTON   CHICAGO   NEW YORK   THE NETHERLANDS

Printed in the United States of America

1 2 3 4 5 6 7 8 9 0

Library of Congress Cataloging-in-Publication Data

Understanding the AMA guides in workers' compensation.—4th ed. / Steven Babitsky, James J. Mangraviti, Jr.
    p. cm.
    Includes index
    ISBN 978-0-7355-7427-4 (alk. paper)
    1. Workers' compensation—Law and legislation—United States. 2. Disability Evaluation—Law and legislation—United States. I. Babitsky, Steven. II. Mangraviti, James.

    KF3615.B33 2008
    344.7302'1—dc22

                                                                      2008029514

About Wolters Kluwer Law & Business

Wolters Kluwer Law & Business is a leading provider of research information and workflow solutions in key specialty areas. The strengths of the individual brands of Aspen Publishers, CCH, Kluwer Law International and Loislaw are aligned within Wolters Kluwer Law & Business to provide comprehensive, in-depth solutions and expert-authored content for the legal, professional and education markets.

CCH was founded in 1913 and has served more than four generations of business professionals and their clients. The CCH products in the Wolters Kluwer Law & Business group are highly regarded electronic and print resources for legal, securities, antitrust and trade regulation, government contracting, banking, pension, payroll, employment and labor, and healthcare reimbursement and compliance professionals.

Aspen Publishers is a leading information provider for attorneys, business professionals and law students. Written by preeminent authorities, Aspen products offer analytical and practical information in a range of specialty practice areas from securities law and intellectual property to mergers and acquisitions and pension/benefits. Aspen's trusted legal education resources provide professors and students with high-quality, up-to-date and effective resources for successful instruction and study in all areas of the law.

Kluwer Law International supplies the global business community with comprehensive English-language international legal information. Legal practitioners, corporate counsel and business executives around the world rely on the Kluwer Law International journals, loose-leafs, books and electronic products for authoritative information in many areas of international legal practice.

Loislaw is a premier provider of digitized legal content to small law firm practitioners of various specializations. Loislaw provides attorneys with the ability to quickly and efficiently find the necessary legal information they need, when and where they need it, by facilitating access to primary law as well as state-specific law, records, forms and treatises.

Wolters Kluwer Law & Business, a unit of Wolters Kluwer, is headquartered in New York and Riverwoods, Illinois. Wolters Kluwer is a leading multinational publisher and information services company.

ASPEN PUBLISHERS SUBSCRIPTION NOTICE

This Aspen Publishers product is updated on a periodic basis with supplements to reflect important changes in the subject matter. If you purchased this product directly from Aspen Publishers, we have already recorded your subscription for the update service

   If, however, you purchased this product from a bookstore and wish to receive future updates and revised or related volumes billed separately with a 30-day examination review, please contact our Customer Service Department at 1-800-234-1660, or send your name, company name (if applicable), address, and the title of the product to:

ASPEN PUBLISHERS
7201 McKinney Circle
Frederick, MD 21704

Important Aspen Publishers Contact Information

- To order any Aspen Publishers title, go to *www.aspenpublishers.com* or call 1-800-638-8437.
- To reinstate your manual update service, call 1-800-638-8437.
- To contact Customer Care, e-mail *customer.care@aspenpublishers .com*, call 1-800-234-1660, fax 1-800-901-9075, or mail correspondence to Order Department, Aspen Publishers, PO Box 990, Frederick, MD 21705.
- To review your account history or pay an invoice online, visit *www .aspenpublishers.com/payinvoices*.

ABOUT THE AUTHORS

Steven Babitsky, Esq. is the president of SEAK, Inc., a medical/legal publishing and seminar company located in Falmouth, Massachusetts. Mr. Babitsky was the senior managing partner of the law firm of Kistin, Babitsky, Latimer & Beitman in Falmouth, Massachusetts. A graduate of Boston College Law School, Mr. Babitsky concentrated his practice in representing clients injured as a result of industrial injury or disease and other personal injuries. His cases involved back and neck injuries, heart attacks, hearing loss, cancer claims, multiple sclerosis, death claims, amputations, and most other occupational diseases and injuries. Mr. Babitsky is the seminar leader of the Annual National Expert Witness Seminar and has directed SEAK's National Workers' Compensation and Occupational Health Seminar for the past 28 years. He is a co-founder of the American Board of Independent Medical Examiners, is the founder of the National Association of Social Security Claimants' Representatives, and is co-author of *Litigating a Workers' Compensation Stress Case*. He has a strong interest in independent medical examinations and is the co-author of *Writing and Defending Your IME Report: The Step-by-Step Guide with Models*.

James J. Mangraviti, Jr., Esq. currently serves as vice-president and general counsel of SEAK, Inc. a medical/legal publishing and seminar company located in Falmouth, Massachusetts. Mr. Mangraviti received his B.A. degree in mathematics *summa cum laude* from Boston College and his J.D. degree *cum laude* from Boston College Law School. Mr. Mangraviti has written and presented extensively on expert witnessing and independent medical examinations. His publications include the following texts: *Litigating Stress Cases in Workers' Compensation*; *Writing and Defending Your IME Report: The Step-by-Step Guide with Models*; *The A-Z Guide to Expert Witnessing*; *Depositions: The Comprehensive Guide for Experts*; and *How to Become a Dangerous Expert Witness*.

CONTENTS

Chapter 5
AMA GUIDES, SIXTH EDITION 5-1

Chapter 6
DIRECT EXAMINATION: USING THE *AMA GUIDES* TO PROVE PERMANENT IMPAIRMENT 6-1

Chapter 7
FOURTH EDITION CROSS-EXAMINATION GUIDE 7-1

Chapter 8
SAMPLE CROSS-EXAMINATIONS UNDER THE FIFTH EDITION 8-1

Chapter 9
SAMPLE CROSS-EXAMINATIONS UNDER THE
SIXTH EDITION **9-1**

Chapter 10
SAMPLE PROOFS **10-1**

Chapter 11
JUDICIAL INTERPRETATION OF THE *AMA GUIDES* 11-1

PREFACE

It has been an eventful six years since the publication of the third edition of *Understanding the AMA Guides in Workers' Compensation.* In this fourth edition of *Understanding the AMA Guides,* we review significant changes that have occurred in the field. The most notable development that gives impetus to the new edition is, of course, the American Medical Association's publication of the all-new sixth edition of its *Guides to the Evaluation of Permanent Impairment* in January 2008.

The fourth edition of *Understanding the AMA Guides in Workers' Compensation* provides a detailed guide to cross-examination of impairment ratings under the *AMA Guides* (6th ed. 2008) and includes a new chapter summarizing the most important changes made in the sixth edition. This volume also provides summaries and analyses of key new appellate cases dealing with the *Guides.*

As was the case with the earlier editions, the fourth edition of *Understanding the AMA Guides in Workers' Compensation* is in no way intended to be used in place of the *AMA Guides* themselves. Copies of the *Guides* may be ordered by calling the American Medical Association at 1-800-621-8335. We have written this work to give attorneys and others access to the key information needed to represent their clients effectively when workers' compensation issues arise under the *AMA Guides.* We sincerely hope you find this volume a valuable resource.

Steven Babitsky
Falmouth, Massachusetts

James J. Mangraviti, Jr.
North Reading, Massachusetts

Spring 2008

ACKNOWLEDGMENTS

We are deeply grateful to **Christopher R. Brigham, MD** for his contributions to preceding editions of this publication and for contributing to Chapter 4 in this edition. Dr. Brigham is the Founder and President of Brigham and Associates, Inc. He is the Senior Contributing Editor for the AMA *Guides to the Evaluation of Permanent Impairment* (6th ed. 2008), and serves on the Advisory Committee. He was a contributor/author for several chapters, including those on Upper Extremities, Lower Extremities, and Spine.

For the Fifth Edition of the *Guides,* Dr. Brigham served on the Advisory Committee and as a contributor. For the Sixth Edition, Dr. Brigham served as Senior Contributing Editor. Dr. Brigham is Board-Certified in Occupational Medicine (ABPM), Founding Director of the American Board of Independent Medical Examiners (ABIME), a Certified Independent Medical Examiner (CIME), a Certified Impairment Rater (CIR), a Fellow of the American Academy of Disability Evaluating Physicians (FAADEP) with Certification in Evaluation of Disability and Impairment Rating (CEDIR), a Fellow of the American College of Occupational Environmental Medicine (FACOEM), and a graduate of Washington University School of Medicine in St. Louis. He is the Editor of the AMA's publications *The Guides Newsletter* and the *The Guides Casebook.*

Dr. Brigham has written more than 100 published articles on impairment and disability evaluation and other texts. He chaired the Medical Advisory Board for the *Medical Disability Advisor*, Fourth Edition. He is featured in several video, audio, and Web-based productions in the medico-legal field, and has trained thousands of physicians, attorneys, claims professionals, and fact finders throughout the United States, Canada, and overseas. More information about Dr. Brigham is available on his Web site: *www.impairment.com.*

HISTORICAL DEVELOPMENT

§ 1.01   INTRODUCTION

The year 2008 marks the 97th anniversary of the beginning of state workers' compensation programs.[1] Each program is intended to be a mechanism for providing cash-wage benefits and medical care to victims of work-related injuries, and for placing the cost of these injuries ultimately on the consumer, through the medium of insurance, by passing the premiums on to the consumer in the cost of the product.[2] An underlying principle of workers' compensation is that industrialization benefits everyone in society, and, because injury and death are inevitable in industrial activity, society should help bear the economic consequences of industrialization.[3] Workers' compensation statutes were enacted to provide efficient, dignified, and certain financial and medical benefits to the victims of work-related injuries.[4] The quid pro quo of workers' compensation is, of course, the worker's right to sue the employer in tort. The worker gives up this right in exchange, it is to be hoped, for a simple and summary recovery of medical expenses and lost income due to occupational injuries, regardless of who is at fault.[5]

Before workers' compensation, the injured workers had to use common-law tort remedies to recover damages for work-related injuries. Injured workers had to prove both that the employer was negligent and that the employer's negligence resulted in damages. Employers had a host of defenses at law, including the defenses established by contributory negligence, the assumption of risk, and the fellow servant rule doctrine. These defenses posed major stumbling blocks to injured workers. Substantial delays in the civil courts and medical, legal, and other expenses only compounded the injured workers' problems and often consumed substantial portions of the award.[6] Also, the injured worker faced the dilemma caused by the reality that suing one's employer is not conducive to keeping one's job.

As criticism mounted, the courts began to chip away slowly at some of the employer defenses.[7] The so-called employers' liability statutes abrogated some of the traditional defenses and made recovery somewhat easier for workers. Ultimately, however, these statutes proved unsatisfactory to both employers and workers. The worker lost or was uncompensated in 80 percent of the cases. Even in the

---

[1] Price, *Workers' Compensation: Coverage, Benefits, and Costs*, 1986, 49 Soc. Security Bull., at 5, 6 (Feb. 1986) (10 states passed workers' compensation legislation in 1911).

[2] 1 A. Larson, The Law of Workmen's Compensation § 1.00, at 1 (1985).

[3] J. Rasch, Rehabilitation of Workers' Compensation and Other Insurance Claimants 37 (1985).

[4] 1 A. Larson, The Law of Workmen's Compensation § 2.20, at 5 (1985).

[5] National Commission on State Workmen's Compensation Laws, Compendium on Workmen's Compensation (1973) (hereinafter Compendium) at 23. *See also* A. Larson, *Basic Concepts & Objectives of Workmens' Compensation*, 1 Supplemental Studies for the National Commission on State Workmens' Compensation Laws 36 (1973).

[6] S. Horovitz, Current Trends in Workmen's Compensation (1947) (hereinafter Horovitz) at 467.

[7] Report of the National Commission on State Workmen's Compensation Laws (1972) (hereinafter National Commission Report) at 34.

20 percent of the cases that were successful, litigation costs, delays, and uncertainty plagued the process. Employers, on the other hand, were faced with the threat of having to pay very large awards, as well as substantial defense costs, which were common even in successful cases.[8] Not surprisingly, friction often resulted between the employer and the employee.

In response to pressure from organized labor and employers, the first workers' compensation statutes were passed in the early 1900s. In 1910, New York became the first state to adopt a compulsory workers' compensation act. The New York law was later held unconstitutional.[9] In 1911, Wisconsin's Workmen's Compensation Act became the first law to remain effective.[10] Even though 24 jurisdictions had enacted similar legislation by 1925, workers' compensation was not provided in every state until Mississippi passed such a law in 1948.[11] The passage of workers' compensation statutes throughout the United States made subsistence benefits available and ameliorated many of the prior problems but created many new concerns, including the adequacy of workers' compensation benefits, their fairness, and the increasing delays in obtaining them.

At present there are workers' compensation programs in all 50 states, the District of Columbia, and six territories. There are also two federal programs[12]—the Federal Employees' Compensation Act,[13] enacted in February 1993, and the Longshore and Harbor Workers' Compensation Act,[14] initially passed in 1927.

In 2006, there were 4.1 million nonfatal occupational injuries and illnesses among private industry employers.[15] The rate of workplace injuries and illnesses was 4.4 per 100 full-time workers.[16] Mining experienced the lowest incident rate in 2006 among goods-producing industries with 3.5 cases per 100 full-time workers. Approximately 2.1 million injuries and illnesses involved cases with days away from work, job transfer, or restrictions.[17] Manufacturing accounted for 36 percent of the total number of injuries and illnesses, but the rate at which injuries occurred was more than double the national average.[18] Transportation and warehousing reported the highest rate of injury among service sector jobs, although there was a significant decrease in the rate from the previous year.[19]

---

[8] Compendium, at 13, 14; *see also* Horovitz, at 467.

[9] Ives v. South Buffalo Ry. Co., 201 N.Y. 271, 94 N.E. 431 (1911).

[10] Wis. Stat. Ann. §§ 102.01 *et seq.*

[11] Compendium, at 18.

[12] National Commission Report, at 32.

[13] 5 U.S.C. §§ 8101 *et seq.*

[14] 33 U.S.C. §§ 901 *et seq.*

[15] U.S. Department of Labor Bureau of Labor Statistics, Survey of Occupational Injuries and Illnesses Summary (2006); *see http://www.bls.gov/news.release/osh.nr0.htm.*

[16] *Id.*

[17] *Id.*

[18] *Id.*

[19] *Id.*

It has been estimated that, as of 2005, workers' compensation laws covered more than 128 million employees.[20] Benefits paid in the United States in 2005 totaled $55.3 billion.[21] Of that amount, medical expenses were $26.2 billion and workers' compensation benefits were $29.1 billion.[22]

The most severe industrial injuries result in permanent partial or permanent total impairment. The term *permanent* means lasting the rest of the claimant's life.[23] Permanent impairment claims are the most costly claims in the workers' compensation system, accounting for approximately 80 percent of the indemnity costs, even though they make up only 35 percent of the cases.[24] The determination of what a permanent impairment is frequently involves substantial litigation.

Workers' compensation cases often hinge on medical testimony and often become battles of medical experts. It is extremely important that physicians present competent medical testimony. The differences in medical opinions, or the manner in which the opinions are expressed, frequently determine whether the claimant receives benefits. One commentator states:

> Even though the medical evidence is often conflicting, and sometimes evenly divided, the issue over the cause of the disability and the physical impairment must be finally resolved by the hearing tribunal and disposed of in a clear-cut fashion.[25]

In part, the *American Medical Association's Guides to the Evaluation of Permanent Impairment* (hereinafter *AMA Guides*) represent an effort to provide clear-cut solutions to very complex problems. In the words of the editors, the *AMA Guides* were designed to provide a standard framework and method of analysis through which physicians can evaluate, report on, and communicate information about the impairments of any human organ system.[26] This purpose is echoed by the courts and the various state legislatures. New Hampshire adopted the *AMA Guides* to reduce litigation and to establish more certainty and uniformity in the rating of permanent impairments.[27] Tennessee's legislature stated that its reason for adopting the *AMA Guides* was to provide uniformity and fairness to all parties.[28] The New Mexico Supreme Court recognized the legitimacy of relying on the *AMA*

---

[20] National Academy of Social Insurance, Workers' Compensation: Benefits, Coverage, and Costs 2005, Aug. 2007.

[21] *Id*

[22] *Id.*

[23] 2 A. Larson, The Law of Workmen's Compensation § 57.13, at 10–42 (1985).

[24] National Academy of Social Insurance, Workers' Compensation: Benefits, Coverage, and Costs 2005, Aug. 2007.

[25] E. Cheit, Injury and Recovery in the Course of Employment (1961) (hereinafter E. Cheit) at 161.

[26] AMA, Guides to the Evaluation of Permanent Impairment (4th ed. 1993) (hereinafter *AMA Guides* (4th ed. 1993)) at 1.

[27] N.H. Rev. Stat. Ann. § 281-A:23.

[28] Tenn. Code Ann. § 50-6-204.

Guides, as the state legislature could have concluded that it lacked the resources to develop independent standards.[29] The purpose of adopting the *AMA Guides* has been described by the courts as "to standardize the compensation to be awarded for substantially identical injuries"[30] and "to promote uniform procedures and evaluation criteria."[31]

The *AMA Guides* are a recent manifestation and extension of the same trend toward standardization that led to scheduled awards in workers' compensation. The *AMA Guides* are a vast improvement over the statutory schedules because they are far more comprehensive, and they are updated more regularly.

§ 1.02 ORIGINS OF SCHEDULED AWARDS

In 1911, New Jersey enacted the first workers' compensation statute with scheduled awards.[32] The concept of a fixed or scheduled award for a specific loss was (and remains) at odds with the concept that workers' compensation consists of only wage replacement or wage loss payments. Larson explains:

> The schedule was never intended to be a departure from or an exception to the wage loss principle. The typical schedule, limited to obvious and easily provable losses of members, was justified on the grounds that the gravity of the impairment was supported by a conclusive presumption that actual wage loss would sooner or later result; and, the conspicuousness of the loss guaranteed that awards would be made with no controversy whatever.[33]

The states adopted scheduled awards for several reasons. The following rationales explain the almost universal acceptance of scheduled awards:

1. The loss ensuing from the personal injury detracts from the former efficiency of the worker's body in the ordinary pursuits of life.[34]
2. A workers' compensation award for a permanent impairment is one for the rest of the claimant's life.[35]
3. It is fundamentally unfair for claimants who suffer permanent impairment, but lose little or no time from work, to be left without benefits after having surrendered any rights they had under common law.

The issue arises as to whether the *AMA Guides* apply to scheduled injuries. The courts are divided on the issue. An Oklahoma court, in *Oklahoma Tax*

---

[29] *See* Madrid v. St. Joseph, 928 P.2d 250 (N.M. 1996).

[30] Gomez v. Industrial Comm'n, 716 P.2d 32 (Ariz. Ct. App. 1985).

[31] Javins v. Workers' Comp. Comm'n, 320 S.E.2d 119 (W. Va. 1984).

[32] 1911 N.J. Laws ch. 95.

[33] 2 A. Larson, § 57.14(c), at 10–54 (1985).

[34] Everhart v. Newark Cleaning & Dyeing Co., 119 N.J.L. 108, 194 A. 294 (1937).

[35] Kurschner v. Industrial Comm'n, 40 Wis. 2d 10, 161 N.W.2d 213 (1968).

Commission v. Evans,[36] found that the *AMA Guides* do extend to combining the impairment to scheduled members for the purposes of evaluating the impairment to the body as a whole. The Oklahoma Supreme Court, in *TRW/REDA Pump v. Brewington,*[37] found that the statute does not require use of the *AMA Guides* when an injury is to a scheduled member. The Oklahoma Supreme Court has gone further and held that where an injury is to a scheduled member, the combined values chart in the *AMA Guides* is not to be used.[38]

Despite the almost universal acceptance of scheduled awards, some commentators and self-styled reformers have pushed to do away with them and return to a conceptually pure workers' compensation system based only on wage loss. Larson forcefully states:

> There are two main motives behind the present movement to restore the wage loss principle. The first is reducing waste of the compensation dollar on non-disabling losses. The second is reducing waste of administrative, legal and judicial time and resources. As to the first, the beginning-point is that the fund available for compensation payments is finite. If for example 80 percent of the compensation dollar is frittered away on small schedule awards for conditions that are in no sense disabling inevitably the ability of the system to do its real job, that of taking adequate care of the really disabled, is damaged.[39]

The rationale for adopting and retaining scheduled awards remains clear. Fairness to the maimed or the permanently injured workers requires such awards.

Under most acts, if an injury has left the claimant with a permanent bodily impairment, compensation is payable for a specified number of weeks, without regard to wage loss, during that period. For the loss (or sometimes the loss of the use) of members, arbitrary schedules spell out the number of weeks for which compensation is payable; for other partial permanent impairments, a calculation of the percentage of the total permanent disability is made.[40]

The definitions, procedures, and maximum benefit amounts for scheduled injuries vary widely from jurisdiction to jurisdiction. Against this background, it is not hard to understand why state legislatures have attempted to achieve a degree of standardization by adopting the *AMA Guides.*

The Colorado Supreme Court decided the issue of what to do when a claimant suffers both a scheduled and a nonscheduled injury. In *Mountain City Meat v. Oqueda,*[41] the court held that in these cases the scheduled injury should first be converted to a whole-person impairment and then combined with the nonscheduled impairment. A Colorado court also held that the *AMA Guides* themselves are not

---

[36] 827 P.2d 183 (Okla. Ct. App. 1992).

[37] 829 P.2d 15 (Okla. 1992).

[38] Special Indem. Fund v. Choate, 847 P.2d 796 (Okla. 1993).

[39] 2 A. Larson, The Law of Workmen's Compensation § 57-14(J), at 10–78, 10–79 (1985).

[40] *Id.* § 58.00 at 10–164, 10–174.

[41] 919 P.2d 246 (Colo. 1996).

competent evidence to determine which injury is scheduled or nonscheduled.[42] It has also been held that the *AMA Guides* are not relevant in determining whether the situs of loss falls within the statutory schedule.[43]

§ 1.03   DEVELOPMENT OF THE *AMA GUIDES*

The *AMA Guides* first appeared in the *Journal of the American Medical Association* (*JAMA*) as 13 separate articles on rating physical impairment. The following list includes the medical topic of the physical impairment as well as the issue and date of publication of the original *JAMA* article:

- Extremities and Back—*JAMA*, Special Edition (Feb. 15, 1958)

- Visual System—*JAMA*, No. 169:475–485 (Sept. 27, 1958)

- Cardiovascular System—*JAMA*, No. 172:1049–1060 (Mar. 5, 1960)

- Ear, Nose, Throat, and Related Structures—*JAMA*, No. 177:489–501 (Aug. 19, 1961)

- Central Nervous System—*JAMA*, No. 185:24–35 (July 6, 1963)

- Digestive System—*JAMA*, No. 188:159–171 (Apr. 13, 1964)

- Peripheral Spinal Nerves—*JAMA*, No. 189:128–142 (July 13, 1964)

- Respiratory System—*JAMA*, No. 194:919–932 (Nov. 22, 1965)

- Endocrine System—*JAMA*, No. 198:195–208 (Oct. 10, 1966)

- Mental Illness—*JAMA*, No. 198:1284–1296 (Dec. 19, 1966)

- Reproductive and Urinary Systems—*JAMA*, No. 202:624–636 (Nov. 13, 1967)

- Skin—*JAMA*, No. 211:106–112 (Jan. 5, 1970)

- Hematopoietic System—*JAMA*, No. 213:1314–1324 (Aug. 24, 1970).[44]

---

[42] Strauch v. PSL Swedish Healthcare Sys., 917 P.2d 366 (Colo. Ct. App. 1996). The court held that the determination of the situs of any functional impairment due to an injury may be distinct from the situs of the initial harm. As a result, an injury to the shoulder may only impair use of the arm and thus become an injury for which benefits under the schedule are provided. The court further concluded that while the rating system for physical impairment under the *AMA Guides* may be considered in resolving the location of the permanent impairment, the *AMA Guides* are not determinative. *See* Morris v. Industrial Claim Appeals Office of the State of Colo., 942 P.2d 1343, 1344 (Colo. 1997). *Morris* held that a nonscheduled injury must be ratable under the *AMA Guides* before the benefits provided under Colo. Rev. Stat. Ann. § 8-42-107(8) may be awarded. *Id.*

[43] Walker v. Jim Fuoco Motor Co., 942 P.2d 1390 (Colo. 1997). *See also* Getson v. WM Babcorp, 694 A.2d 961 (Md. 1997).

[44] AMA, Guides to the Evaluation of Permanent Impairment (1st ed. 1971) (hereinafter *AMA Guides* (1st ed. 1971)), at 1. (The 1971 edition is a compilation and "updated" version of a series of individual articles on rating physical impairments.)

The *AMA Guides* were mentioned in workers' compensation literature as early as 1961:

> Although experts admit scientifically accurate disability rating is an impossibility, much credit must go to the medical and administrative personnel who have developed many meaningful, practical approaches to rating, i.e., the American Medical Association's committee on Medical Rating of Physical Impairment.[45]

In 1971, an American Medical Association (AMA) committee on rating physical impairment assembled the first *Guide to the Evaluation of Permanent Impairment*.[46] This first edition was released again in 1977. In 1980, the AMA Council on Scientific Affairs formed 12 separate committees to review the *AMA Guides*. Each committee reviewed a single chapter, resulting in the 12 chapters of the second edition in 1984.[47] The preface to the second edition states:

> A permanent impairment rating that is derived from use of the *AMA Guides* may serve as a *starting point* for determinations about the consequences of the impairment, such as a disability rating or a legal entitlement, which is based on the most advanced and comprehensive application of current medical knowledge. The approach that has been taken in the AMA's Guides will provide for standardized communications of medical information about the impact of medical impairment on an individual's activities of daily living.[48]

The editors of the third edition of the *AMA Guides* in 1988[49] expanded the preface into two chapters. The first chapter explains the concepts of impairment evaluation, and the second chapter deals with medical records and reports. For cross-examination purposes and from a legal perspective in general, these chapters may be the most important chapters in the *AMA Guides*. As a result, these two chapters were expanded upon in the fourth edition of the *AMA Guides* (hereinafter *AMA Guides* (4th ed. 1993))[50] and each subsequent edition.

The fifth edition of the *AMA Guides* (hereinafter *AMA Guides* (5th ed. 2000)) was published in November 2000. A summary of the features of that edition is the topic of Chapter 4 in this volume. The most important features of the sixth edition of the *AMA Guides*, published in January 2008, are discussed in Chapter 5.

---

[45] E. Cheit, at 161.

[46] *AMA Guides* (1st ed. 1971).

[47] Telephone interview with Dr. Alan Engelberg, Director, Department of Public Health Policy, AMA (June 27, 1986).

[48] AMA, Guides to the Evaluation of Permanent Impairment (2d ed. 1984) (hereinafter *AMA Guides* (2d ed. 1984)), at vii (emphasis added).

[49] AMA, Guides to the Evaluation of Permanent Impairment (3d ed. 1988) (hereinafter *AMA Guides* (3d ed. 1988)).

[50] *See* Appendix 3 and Appendix 4 in this volume for details concerning the *AMA Guides* (4th ed. 1993).

§ 1.04   THE CRUCIAL DISTINCTION BETWEEN IMPAIRMENT AND DISABILITY

One distinction between impairments and disabilities must remain clear. The *AMA Guides* are designed to aid in the assessment of physical impairment, which is a medical determination. The *AMA Guides* were never intended to be used for rating disability, which is a nonmedical determination.[51] An impairment rating is merely one factor in determining disability (the one most amenable to physician determination) and must be placed in context with psychological, social, vocational, and avocational issues.[52]

Impairment and disability, while distinct from each other, are nonetheless related concepts. The proper use of medical information to assess impairment depends on the recognition that disability arises out of the interaction between impairment and external demands. Consequently, as used in the *AMA Guides:*

> Impairment is defined in the Guides as an alteration of an individual's health status. Impairment, according to the Guides, is assessed by medical means and is a medical issue. An impairment is a deviation in a body part or organ system and its functioning. Disability must be defined as an alteration of an individual's capacity to meet personal, social or statutory demands, or statutory or regulatory requirements, because of an impairment. Disability refers to an activity or task the individual cannot accomplish. A disability arises out of the interaction between impairment and external requirements, especially those of a person's occupation. Disability may be thought of as the gap between what the individual can do and what the individual needs or wants to do.[53]

In other words, a physician's evaluation of impairment under the *AMA Guides* is a medical evaluation of an individual's health status. Numerous courts have commented on the definitions of impairment and disability. Impairment is generally a question of medical fact.[54] Disability is a question of law.[55] It has been held that it is up to the workers' compensation board to translate the percentage of functional impairment into occupational disability, if any.[56] That is, impairment is a medical determination, whereas disability is an administrative evaluation.[57] It has also been held that it is a reversible error to conclude that a physician's testimony that there was no permanent disability equated to a conclusion that there was no permanent impairment.[58]

---

[51] *AMA Guides* (4th ed. 1993) at 1, 317.

[52] *AMA Guides* (6th ed. 2008) at 6.

[53] *Id.* at 1, 2.

[54] Cassey v. Industrial Comm'n, 731 P.2d 645 (Ariz. Ct. App. 1987).

[55] Alsbrooks v. Industrial Comm'n, 578 P.2d 159 (Ariz. Ct. App. 1978).

[56] Cook v. Paducah Recapping Serv., 694 S.W.2d 684 (Ky. Ct. App. 1985).

[57] Northwest Carriers v. Industrial Comm'n, 639 P.2d 138 (Utah 1981).

[58] Kessler v. Community Blood Bank, 621 So. 2d 539 (Fla. Dist. Ct. App. 1993). *See also* Farm Fresh, Inc. v. Bucek, 895 P.2d 719 (Okla. 1995).

The distinction between impairment and disability was correctly drawn in *Foxx v. American Transportation.*[59] In *Foxx*, the court held that in determining impairment, the workers' compensation commission had incorrectly given weight to the fact that the claimant was not disabled. In *Rosser v. S.I.I.S.*[60] the Nevada court held that the *AMA Guides*, although relevant, should not be the only resource used for determining a claimant's permanent total disability. The *Rosser* court noted that the *AMA Guides* themselves state that they are ill-equipped to rate such subjective factors as a claimant's age, training, or education.

In *Whittaker v. Johnson,*[61] the court held that the Kentucky workers' compensation statute's use of the terms *impairment* and *disability* was a distinction without a practical difference. In *Colwell v. Dresser Instrument Division,*[62] the Kentucky court held that an increased *impairment* rating was not required for a claimant to show increased *disability* under the applicable statute even where the statute required "objective medical evidence of a worsening . . . of impairment." The court reasoned that a worsening of impairment may or may not result in an increased impairment rating.

§ 1.05   USING THE *AMA GUIDES* FOR DIRECT FINANCIAL AWARDS TO CLAIMANTS

The physician's evaluation of an impairment should not be used to make direct financial awards or direct estimates of disabilities.[63] The *AMA Guides* emphatically state:

> It must be emphasized and clearly understood that impairment percentages derived according to the Guides criteria should not be used to make direct financial awards or direct estimates of disabilities.[64]

The critical problem is that there is no known formula by which knowledge about a medical condition can be combined with knowledge about other factors to calculate the percentage by which the employee's industrial (i.e., work) use of the body is impaired.[65] An evaluation under the *AMA Guides* may provide much important information that is useful in determining disability, but the *AMA Guides* cannot provide complete and definitive answers.[66] Despite the explicit and emphatic prohibition contained in the *AMA Guides*, states continue to award compensation solely on the basis of a permanent impairment rating under the *AMA*

---

[59] 924 S.W.2d 814 (Ark. Ct. App. 1996).

[60] 113 Nev. 1125, 946 P.2d 185 (1997).

[61] 987 S.W.2d 320 (Ky. 1999).

[62] 2006 Ky. LEXIS 297 (2006).

[63] *AMA Guides* (4th ed. 1993) at 5.

[64] *Id.* at 5.

[65] *Id.*

[66] *Id.* at 4.

Guides.[67] A criticism of the use of impairment ratings, as opposed to lost-earning capacity, to determine benefits is contained in the special concurrence of *McLane Western Inc. v. Industrial Claim Appeals Office.*[68]

The *AMA Guides* (6th ed. 2008) recognizes what the legal system has been doing and likely will continue to do with impairment ratings (i.e., using them to make direct financial awards). The sixth edition states that the primary purpose of the *AMA Guides* is "to assist adjudicators and others in determining the financial compensation to be awarded to individuals."[69]

§ 1.06   ADOPTING THE *AMA GUIDES*

In 1972, the National Commission of State Workmen's Compensation Laws called for the use of the *AMA Guides* in workers' compensation cases. The commission's report stated:

> Almost every workmen's compensation statute contains a schedule for the listed impairments. These schedules in some cases may provide a short-cut to the determination of the benefits to be paid, but that is not an adequate justification for their use. Present schedules include only a small proportion of all medically identifiable permanent impairments. Also, some schedules have not been revised for many years, despite considerable progress in the understanding of the relationship between specific injuries and extent of functional impairment. A basis for a rational evaluation of injury or disease is the recently published American Medical Association's *Guides to the Evaluation of Permanent Impairment.* Use of the AMA publication instead of statutory scheduling appears desirable.
>
> It must be stressed, however, that the *AMA Guides* are relevant for evaluation of impairment, not disability; and disability should be the primary basis for awarding permanent partial benefits. Use of the *AMA Guides* to help establish the impairment rating, and then use of the impairment rating in conjunction with other information, such as the worker's age, education, and previous experience, to establish the extent of disability seems most appropriate. It is hard to see how any statutory schedule could substitute effectively for this process.[70]

Most of the state legislatures that did adopt the *AMA Guides* did so in a haphazard manner. Initially, they simply added a few words or sentences to their states' scheduled award statutes, stating that the *AMA Guides* should now be used. For example, Alaska added the sentence "Permanent impairment ratings must be based upon the American Medical Association Guides to the Evaluation of

---

[67] *See, e.g.,* Alaska Stat. § 23.30.190; N.D. Cent. Code § 65-05-12.2.

[68] 996 P.2d 263 (Colo. Ct. App. 1999).

[69] *AMA Guides* (6th ed. 2008) at 20.

[70] National Commission Report, at 69.

Permanent Impairment (1977)."[71] This language not only failed to anticipate future editions of the *AMA Guides* but also conflicted with administrative regulations that stated: "The Board shall adopt and use a schedule for determining the existence and degree of impairment consistent with the American Medical Association Guides to the Evaluation of Permanent Impairment."[72] In addition, no attempt was made to amend the scheduled award section to make it consistent with the *AMA Guides.* Not surprisingly, this has led to litigation.[73]

Georgia is another state that simply grafted sentences onto its existing scheduled award legislation. Georgia practically invited litigation when it initially adopted the *AMA Guides* by providing that:

> (5) In all cases arising under Chapter 9 of Title 34, any percentage of disability or bodily loss ratings shall be based upon *Guides to the Evaluation of Permanent Impairment* published by the American Medical Association or any other recognized medical books or guides.[74]

The language was then amended to read:

> In all cases arising under this chapter, any percentage of disability or bodily loss ratings shall be based upon *Guides to the Evaluation of Permanent Impairment* published by the American Medical Association.[75]

The amended Georgia language still failed to take into account the various editions of the *AMA Guides*. The Georgia legislature addressed this deficiency by mandating a specific edition:

> In all cases arising under this chapter, any percentage of disability or bodily loss ratings shall be based upon *Guides to the Evaluation of Permanent Impairment*, fifth edition, published by the American Medical Association.[76]

Massachusetts, a state without a whole-person scheduled award provision, adopted legislation providing, "where applicable, losses under this section shall be determined in accordance with standards set forth in the American Medical Association's *Guides to the Evaluation of Permanent Impairment*."[77] No edition is specified and no provision is made for future editions.

Hawaii adopted the *AMA Guides* by providing only that "[i]mpairment rating guides issued by the American Medical Association, American Academy of

---

[71] Alaska Admin. Code tit. 8, § 45.120K(a).

[72] Alaska Workers' Compensation Act, Alaska Stat. § 23.30.095.

[73] Yoder v. Alaska, No. 4FA-84-1315 (Alaska Super. Ct. Jan. 30, 1985).

[74] Ga. Code Ann. § 34-9-1 (Michie).

[75] Ga. Code Ann. § 34-9-1.

[76] Ga. Code Ann. § 34-9-263(d).

[77] Mass. Gen. Laws Ann. ch. 152, § 36 (West).

Orthopedic Surgeons, and any other such guides which the director deems appropriate and proper may be used as a reference or guide in measuring a disability."[78]

Another consistent problem was how to deal with subsequent editions of the *AMA Guides*. After years of litigation, the states have become more careful and specific when adopting the *AMA Guides*. This advance over earlier attempts is encouraging. Many state statutes mandate the adoption of the most recent edition of the *AMA Guides*.[79]

The Alaska Administrative Code now states:

(a) The board will give public notice of the edition of the American Medical Association *Guides to the Evaluation of Permanent Impairment* and effective date for using the edition by publishing a notice in a newspaper of general circulation in Anchorage, Fairbanks, and Juneau as well as issue a bulletin for the "Workers' Compensation Manual," published by the department.

(b) It is presumed that the American Medical Association (AMA) *Guides to the Evaluation of Permanent Impairment* address the injury. If the board finds the presumption is overcome by clear and convincing evidence and if the permanent impairment cannot, in the board's opinion, be determined under the AMA guides, then the impairment rating must be based on The State of Minnesota, Department of Labor and Industry, Permanent Partial Disability Schedule, effective July 1, 1993, or the American Academy of Orthopedic Surgeons (AAOS) *Manual for Evaluating Permanent Physical Impairments*, first edition (1965). If a rating under the Permanent Partial Disability Schedule or the AAOS is not of the whole person, the rating must be converted to a whole person rating under the AMA guides.

(c) A rating of zero impairment under AMA guides is a permanent impairment determination and no determination may be made under the Permanent Partial Disability Schedule described in (b) of this section or the AAOS.[80]

The language in the Alaska statutes is also much more specific. The statute now provides:

(b) All determinations of the existence and degree of permanent impairment shall be made strictly and solely under the whole person determination as set out in the American Medical Association *Guides to the Evaluation of Permanent Impairment*, except that an impairment rating may not be rounded to the next five percent. The board shall adopt a supplementary recognized schedule for injuries that cannot be rated by use of the American Medical Association Guides.

(c) The impairment rating determined under (a) of this section shall be reduced by a permanent impairment that existed before the compensable injury.

---

[78] Haw. Rev. Stat. § 12-10-21.

[79] *See, e.g.*, Alaska Stat. § 23.30.190.

[80] Alaska Admin. Code tit. 8, § 45.122.

If the combination of a prior impairment rating and a rating under (a) of this section would result in the employee being considered permanently totally disabled, the prior rating does not negate a finding of permanent total disability.

(d) When a new edition of the American Medical Association Guides described in (b) of this section is published, the board shall, not later than 90 days after the last day of the month in which the new edition is published, hold an open meeting under AS 44.62.310 to select the date on which the new edition will be used to make all determinations required under (b) of this section. The date selected by the board for using the new edition may not be later than 90 days after the last day of the month in which the new edition is published. After the meeting, the board shall issue a public notice announcing the date selected. The requirements of AS 44.62.010-44.62.300 do not apply to the selection or announcement of the date under this subsection.[81]

Alaska's well-written rules and statutes address many of the problems associated with adopting the *AMA Guides.* Among these problems is what to do when the *AMA Guides* do not cover a specific injury and how to deal with the *AMA Guides'* position on rounding off impairment ratings.

The use of the *AMA Guides* before their legislative adoption may be problematic.[82] In some cases, however, the use of the *AMA Guides* before their enactment has been permitted. One state held that the use of the *AMA Guides* to reach a decision about an unscheduled loss is permitted under the broad discretionary powers granted to a workers' compensation commissioner.[83]

In some circumstances, the *AMA Guides* may be only partially adopted. This is in direct contradiction of the *AMA Guides* themselves. For example, in *Baker v. Bethlehem Steel Corp.,*[84] the court ruled that monaural hearing loss was to be computed under the *AMA Guides* but that this rating was not to be converted to binaural hearing loss.

Specific statutory provisions have been held to override portions of the *AMA Guides.* For example, Colorado does not allow an impairment rating for chronic pain without anatomic or physiologic correlation.[85] The Arkansas Appeals Court has stated:

The American Medical Association Guides must give way to the statutory definition of objective findings as defined by the General Assembly. Although subjective criteria may be included in the *AMA Guides* when determining a permanent physical impairment rating, clearly the portions of the impairment rating guide that are based upon subjective criteria cannot supersede the statutory definition provided by the General Assembly. Thus, to the extent that

---

[81] Alaska Stat. § 23.30.190.

[82] Reeder v. Rheem Mfg. Co., 832 S.W.2d 505 (Ark. Ct. App. 1992).

[83] Piscitelli v. Connecticut Coke/Eastern Gas & Fuel Assocs., 575 CRD-3-87 (Workers' Comp. Comm'n Jan. 1989).

[84] 24 F.3d 632 (4th Cir. 1994).

[85] Colo. Rev. Stat. § 8-42-101.

there is a conflict, the General Assembly's statutory definition takes precedence over any subjective criteria included in the *AMA Guides*.[86]

A divided West Virginia Supreme Court held in *Repass v. Workers' Compensation Division*[87] that the diagnosis-related estimate (DRE) model of the fourth edition of the *AMA Guides* conflicts with West Virginia's Workers' Compensation statute and is thus invalid.

Some courts have held that benefits may be given based on monaural hearing loss.[88] It has also been held that awards for psychological benefits are not available, despite the contrary position of the *AMA Guides*,[89] and that a band impairment of 100 percent under the enabling statute supersedes a rating of 92 percent under the *AMA Guides*.[90] Alaska's enabling statute specifically precludes rounding off even when rounding off is allowed by the *AMA Guides*.[91] A Colorado court held that eye disfigurement is not a "permanent medical impairment" under that state's workers' compensation statute, even assuming the disfigurement would constitute an impairment under the *AMA Guides*.[92]

It has been held that once a state has adopted the *Guides*, the applicable workers' compensation authority may not issue rules or advisories contradicting the *Guides* without the statutory authority to do so. For example, in *Texas Department of Insurance v. Lumbermen's Mutual Casualty Co.*,[93] the court ruled invalid a Workers' Compensation Division Advisory that (contrary to what is allowed by the fourth edition of the *Guides*) allowed raters to use their medical judgment or experience to take into account surgery or the effect of surgery when assigning impairment ratings under the injury model of the fourth edition.

§ 1.07   FAILURE TO FOLLOW THE *AMA GUIDES*

Where the *AMA Guides* have been mandated by law, they should be used, and used properly. If the rating physician fails to follow the *AMA Guides*, the rating may be successfully challenged.[94] For example, in *Fireman's Fund Insurance v. Weeks*, the court discounted a rating where the physician used his medical judgment and factored in surgery and the effect of surgery—factors not permitted by the edition of the *AMA Guides* in question.[95]

---

[86] Mays v. Alumnitec, 64 S.W.3d 772, 774 (Ark. Ct. App. 2001).

[87] 569 S.E.2d 162 (W. Va. 2002).

[88] Tanner v. Ingalls Shipbuilding, Inc., 2 F.3d 143 (5th Cir. 1993); Rasmussen v. General Dynamics, 993 F.2d 1014 (2d Cir. 1993).

[89] Maxwell v. SIIS, 849 P.2d 267 (Nev. 1993).

[90] Jacob v. Columbia Ins. Group, 511 N.W.2d 211 (Neb. Ct. App. 1994).

[91] Alaska Stat. § 23.30.190.

[92] Advanced Component Sys. v. Gonzales, 935 P.2d 24 (Colo. Ct. App. 1996).

[93] Texas Dep't of Ins. v. Lumbermen's Mut. Ins. Co., 212 S.W.3d 870 (Tex. App.—Austin 2006).

[94] *See* Clark v. State *ex rel.* Workers' Div., 934 P.2d 1269 (Wyo. 1997).

[95] 2007 WL 4460608 (Tex. App.—El Paso).

In *Russell v. Bill Heard Enterprises, Inc.*,[96] the claimant injured a shoulder and a surgeon removed the distal clavicle and repaired the rotator cuff. The surgeon assigned a permanent impairment rating of 10 percent to the right upper extremity, which he equated with a 6 percent whole-person impairment rating, using appropriate guidelines. The surgeon testified that the *AMA Guides* provide a rating for the removal of the distal clavicle but not for acromioplasty. An independent medical examination (IME) physician then estimated the claimant's permanent impairment at 10 percent for the resection of the distal clavicle and opined that the acromioplasty should result in higher rating. The higher rating was based on the IME physician's own guidelines. On the basis of the IME physician's opinion, the trial court awarded benefits based on a 20 percent whole-body rating. The appellate court, noting that a physician's testimony concerning the extent of a claimant's permanent medical impairment must be based on the most recent edition of the *AMA Guides* (or the *Manual for Orthopaedic Surgeons in Evaluating Permanent Physical Impairment*), held that the trial court was in error to consider the IME's estimate of 20 percent permanent medical impairment, and it reduced the award based on the surgeon's 6 percent rating.

In *Jackson v. Goodyear Tire & Rubber Co.*,[97] the trial court determined that the plaintiff had suffered a 20 percent permanent partial disability to her right arm and a 30 percent permanent partial disability to her left arm as the result of bilateral carpal tunnel syndrome. The appellate court disallowed the testimony of an IME physician due to his failure to use the *AMA Guides* in determining grip-strength loss. Just because a physician uses the *AMA Guides* in evaluating impairment does not mean that the impairment is work related.[98]

In *In re Compensation of Clemons*,[99] the court held that under the Oregon Administrative Rules,[100] if a finding of impairment does not comply with the AMA criteria, it may not be used to rate a claimant's impairment.[101]

In *LTV Steel Co. v. W.C.A.B. (Mozena)*,[102] the court held that the use of a non-*AMA Guides* standard to determine an impairment rating for hearing loss was improper under the workers' compensation statute.

In *Phillips v. Marvin Windows*,[103] one of the ratings was challenged on appeal. The employer claimed that the rating was based on the wrong table in the *AMA Guides*, and was thus invalid, thereby rendering it erroneous for the court to award disability. The court stated that it was unable to determine whether the

---

[96] No. W2000-00965-WC-R3CV, 2001 WL 721062 (Tenn. Spec. Workers' Comp. App. Panel June 26, 2001).

[97] 2001 WL 303508 (Tenn. Spec. Workers' Comp. App. Panel Mar. 29, 2001).

[98] Washington Steel Corp. v. W.C.A.B., 734 A.2d 81 (Pa. Commw. Ct. 1999).

[99] 169 Or. App. 231, 9 P.3d 123 (2000).

[100] Or. Admin. R. 436–035–0007(27) (1996).

[101] 169 Or. App. at 234.

[102] 562 Pa. 205, 754 A.2d 666 (2000).

[103] 2000 WL 987312 (Tenn. Spec. Workers' Comp. App. Panel July 18, 2000).

IME relied on the appropriate table in the *AMA Guides*, and declared that even if the doctor did not use the proper table, the opinion of permanent impairment should not be totally rejected as "invalid": "Numerous awards have been affirmed on appeal even though reliance on the *AMA Guides* was imprecise, once causation and permanency are established by expert testimony."[104]

In *Tennessee Roofing Corp. v. Lloyd*,[105] the appellate court found that the trial court's reliance on a rating that did not include range-of-motion testing, as set out in the *AMA Guides*, was misplaced. Another physician had rated the claimant in accordance with the *AMA Guides*, and the appellate court modified the award to an amount that reflected this rating.

In *Wal-Mart Stores, Inc. v. Williams*,[106] the court upheld an impairment rating as being made pursuant to the *AMA Guides* (as required by statute) even though the physician did not specifically refer to the *AMA Guides*. The evidence in *Wal-Mart* demonstrated the accuracy of the rating under the *AMA Guides*.[107]

In *Shaffer v. Lourdes Hospital*,[108] the administrative law judge (ALJ) found other evidence supporting disability, but the appeals court refused to ignore the plain language of the statute that required the disability rating to be based on an impairment rating and affirmed the denial of income benefits. In *Lanoue v. All Star Chevrolet*,[109] the court held that a physician's rating under the "orthopedic surgeon's manual" was insufficient to award benefits and remanded the case for a rating under the *AMA Guides*. However, the court in *Chapman v. Bekaert Steel Wire Corp.*[110] held that it was an error to exclude a rating physician impairment rating based on the *Manual for Orthopedic Surgeons* because this manual is named in the workers' compensation statute. The court in *Cabatbat v. County of Hawaii, Department of Water Supply*[111] held that it was an error to rely solely on the *AMA Guides* where there was reliable, probative, and substantial evidence on the record that the *Recommended Guide to the Evaluation of Permanent Impairment of the Temporomandibular Joint* (hereinafter referred to as *Recommended Guide*) appropriately addressed the claimant's TMJ impairment. The court in *Wilson v. Industrial Claim Appeals Office of State of Colorado*[112] held that whether or not an IME physician correctly applies the *AMA Guides* is a question of fact, not of law.

In the case of *Williams v. FEI Installation*,[113] the ALJ chose to accept the rating of the *employer's* physician, who referenced the *Guides* in general over the

---

[104] 2000 WL 987312, at *3.

[105] 2000 WL 365656 (Tenn. Spec. Workers' Comp. App. Panel Apr. 11, 2000).

[106] 2000 WL 528252 (Ark. Ct. App. 2000).

[107] *Id.* at *4.

[108] 2000 WL 1763242 (Ky. Ct. App. 2000).

[109] 867 So. 2d 755 (La. Ct. App. 1st Cir. 2003).

[110] 2003 Tenn. LEXIS (Tenn. Spec. Workers' Comp. App. Panel Oct. 16, 2003).

[111] 78 P.3d 756 (Haw. 2003).

[112] 81 P.3d 1117 (Colo. Ct. App. 2003).

[113] 2005 WL 3488386 (Ky. Ct. App. Dec. 22, 2005).

rating provided by the *employee's* physician; the employer's physician admitted he deviated from the *Guides*. In *Brasch-Barry General Contractors, Inc. v. Jones*,[114] the court held that an ALJ's acceptance of a rating that deviated from the *Guides* was a question of law, not of fact.

The court in *Pekala v. E.I. DuPont de Nemours & Co.*[115] found that substantial evidence to deny permanent impairment benefits existed where the rating physician did not articulate the effect on the claimant's activities of daily living as required by the *AMA Guides*.

§ 1.08   THE IMPORTANCE OF USING THE MOST RECENT EDITION

The question arises regarding which edition of the *AMA Guides* to use. In the fourth edition, the AMA strongly discourages the use of any but the most recent edition:

> The American Medical Association strongly discourages the use of any but the most recent edition of the Guides, because the information in it would not be based upon the most recent and up-to-date material.[116]

The fifth edition contains similar language in which it is "strongly recommended" that physicians use the fifth edition as it is the most current.[117] The sixth edition implicitly recommends its own use by being highly critical of previous editions. According to the sixth edition, problems in the fifth edition included "adherence to antiquated and confusing terminology, limited validity and reliability of the ratings, lack of meaningful and consistent application of functional assessment tools, and lack of internal consistency."[118]

Due to the drafting of certain state laws, some workers' compensation professionals are forced to use an outdated or soon-to-be-outdated edition of the *AMA Guides*. This problem was avoided in Wyoming simply by adding the phrase "the most recent edition of" to the adoptive language.[119] Similarly, the federal Longshore and Harbor Workers' Compensation Act allows for future editions of the *AMA Guides*, promulgated and modified from time to time by the AMA.[120] Other states have also adopted legislation mandating the latest edition of the *AMA Guides*.[121] One

---

[114] 175 S.W.3d 81 (Ky. 2005), *on remand*, 2006 WL 572815 (Ky. Ct. App. Mar. 10, 2006).

[115] 2007 WL 1653496 (Del. Super. Ct.).

[116] *AMA Guides* (4th ed. 1993) at 5.

[117] *AMA Guides* (5th ed. 2000) at 2.

[118] *AMA Guides* (6th ed. 2008) at 2.

[119] Wyo. Stat. § 27-14-405(g).

[120] 33 U.S.C.A. § 902 (West).

[121] These states include Kentucky (Ky. Rev. Stat. Ann. § 342.316 (Baldwin) ("latest edition available"); Louisiana (La. Rev. Stat. Ann. § 1221(4) ("most recent")); Montana (Mont. Code Ann. § 39-71-703 ("latest edition")); Nevada (Nev. Rev. Stat. 616C.110(1) ("most recently published")); New Hampshire (N.H. Rev. Stat. § 281-A:32 ("most recent edition")); New Mexico (N.M.

court held that the proper edition to use is the most recent edition at the time of the evaluation, not at the time of the injury.[122]

In *George Humfleet Mobile Homes v. Christman*,[123] the Kentucky Supreme Court held that the edition of the *AMA Guides* to be used is the latest edition that has been certified as being available on the date that proof closes. The Hawaii Supreme Court held in *Duque v. Hilton Hawaiian Village*[124] that a claimant's rating was *not* required to be made under the latest edition of the *Guides*, and that rating physicians should draw on their medical expertise and judgment to select the most appropriate guide to use in assessing an individual's impairment.

The court in *Blanton v. CVS Tennessee Distribution, Inc.*[125] allowed a physician to cite numerical ratings from the second edition regarding a mental impairment (the second edition provides impairment numbers, whereas the fifth edition does not). The court allowed this because the issue at hand was vocational disability and not anatomical disability.

Some states, however, continue to adopt explicitly specific editions of the *AMA Guides*. For example, South Dakota[126] and Pennsylvania[127] explicitly adopted the fourth edition of the *Guides* (1993). Utah specifically adopted the fourth edition (1993), but it is to be used only for conditions not found in *Utah's 1997 Impairment Guides*.[128] Colorado continues to mandate the use of the third edition of the *Guides*.[129] Georgia explicitly adopted the fifth edition of the *Guides*[130] as has North Dakota.[131] Some states, such as Massachusetts, do not specify which edition should be used.[132]

The use of an edition different from the mandated edition has resulted in litigation. The Tennessee Supreme Court, in *Harness v. CNA Insurance Co.*,[133] found that the use of an outdated edition of the *AMA Guides* was not fatal, as the permanency of the impairment had already been established. A Florida court held that it was permissible for rating physicians to change their testimony to find permanent impairment when none was found previously if the new testimony

---

Stat. Ann. § 52-1-24 (Michie) ("most recent edition")); Oklahoma (Okla. Stat. tit. 85, § 3 ("latest publication")); Rhode Island (R.I. Gen. Laws § 28-29-2 ("most recent edition")); Tennessee (Tenn. Code Ann. § 50-6-102 ("most recent")); and Vermont (Vt. Stat. Ann. ch. 9, § 648 ("most recent edition")).

[122] Ransier v. State Indus. Ins. Sys., 766 P.2d 274 (Nev. 1988).

[123] 125 S.W.3d 288 (Ky. 2004).

[124] 98 P.3d 640 (Haw. 2004).

[125] 2006 Tenn. LEXIS 197 (2006).

[126] S.D. Codified Laws Ann. § 62-1-1.2.

[127] Pa. Stat. Ann. tit. 77, § 25.5. However, 77 P.S. § 511.2 and 34 Pa. Code § 123.105 mandate the use of the "most recent edition."

[128] Utah Admin. Code R612-6-3.

[129] Colo. Rev. Stat. § 8-42-107.

[130] Ga. Code § 34-9-263(d).

[131] N.D. Cent. Code § 65-05-12.2.6.

[132] Mass. Gen. Laws ch. 152, § 35.

[133] 814 S.W.2d 733 (Tenn. 1991).

was based on a newly released edition of the *AMA Guides*.[134] The Texas Supreme Court has even suggested in dicta that the mandated use of an out-of-print early edition of the *AMA Guides* could be unconstitutional.[135]

Some courts have taken a commonsense approach to the "current edition" problem. The Oklahoma Supreme Court, in *Tulsa County v. Roberts*, dealt with this issue forcefully:

> The employer's next complaint was that the impairment percentage given by the claimant's expert was invalid because the edition of the *AMA Guides* he used was more current than the 1977 edition specified by Workers' Compensation Court Rule 20 and 23. The complaint appears on its face to be an overindulgence in legalistic surrealism. If it is the intent and purpose of the rules to require the testimony of an expert in the *AMA Guides* where possible in evaluating consequences of work-related injuries, and an expert draws on the latest edition because an earlier edition offers no help, to deny the expert the right to do so would manifest ultimate contempt for common sense. Moreover, Rule 20(i) provides that adherence to the first edition of the *AMA Guides* is not required if the reason for deviating is stated, which the expert did in this case.[136]

By contrast, in *Thompson v. U.S.D. No. 512*, a Kansas court ruled that the rating physician must use an outdated version of the *Guides* because that edition is specified in the state statute:

> While Kansas only recognizes the fourth edition, Poppa relied on the fifth and sixth editions of the *AMA Guides*, which address the deficiencies in the fourth edition regarding assessment of impairment for RSD. . . . As indicated by the administrative law judge, the fourth edition of the *AMA Guides* specifically indicates the manner in which a physician may derive an impairment rating for RSD. Moreover, Poppa concedes RSD is contained within the fourth *AMA Guides*, but . . . the impairment rating is not to his liking. While it is unfortunate that a physician may be bound by an outdated version of the *AMA Guides*, this court is obligated to read the statute as written. Allowing a physician to rely on more recent editions of the *AMA Guides* and other publications would open the door to what the proper guide is and should be. No doubt evaluating physicians would seek a reference providing the most favorable rating for their patient or client. The statute was clearly enacted to avoid just that and provide clear standards for calculating consistent impairment ratings.[137]

---

[134] McCabe v. Bechtel Power Corp., 510 So. 2d 1056, 1059 (Fla. 1987).

[135] Texas Workers' Comp. Comm'n v. Garcia, 893 S.W.2d 504, 526 (Tex. 1995).

[136] 738 P.2d 969, 971 (Okla. Ct. App. 1987).

[137] 2007 WL 2580530, at *3, *6–*7 (Kan. Ct. App.).

At least one court recognizes the constitutional validity of adoption of new editions of the *AMA Guides*.[138] The court in *McCabe v. North Dakota Workers' Compensation Bureau*[139] held that statutory language requiring use of the "most current" or "most recent edition" of the *AMA Guides* should be interpreted to mean the most recent edition at the time of the statute's enactment. The court reasoned that this construction was necessary to avoid "significant constitutional conflicts" concerning the delegation of law-making authority from the legislature to the American Medical Association.

In the Longshore and Harbor Workers' Compensation Act case of *Rosa v. Director, Office of Workers' Compensation Programs*,[140] the court held that it was permissible for an ALJ to rely on the fourth edition of the *AMA Guides*, even when such reliance resulted in a lower disability percentage than had been stipulated to from a previous injury. In *Turbitt v. Blue Hen Lines, Inc.*,[141] however, the court held that the board could not reject an evaluator's use of an outdated version of the *AMA Guides* without specific references in its findings as to why the evidence prompted disbelief. The court in *Turbitt* reinstated a rating based on the third edition of the *AMA Guides*.

The use of an earlier edition of the *Guides* may be permitted where the earlier edition provides numerical ratings that a subsequent edition lacks. In *Gates v. Jackson Appliance Co.*,[142] the plaintiff was assigned no permanent impairment rating for a strained groin because the fourth edition of the *AMA Guides* did not assign an impairment rating for chronic muscle strain. However, the plaintiff complained of emotional problems and was examined by a psychologist, who described the plaintiff as "significantly depressed" and rated the disorder in the moderate range caused by the chronic pain from his work injury. The psychologist explained that the fourth edition does not provide a numerical rating for mental impairment but classifies disorders as mild, moderate, or severe. Under the second edition of the *AMA Guides* (1984), however, a moderate impairment is rated as a 25 percent to 50 percent impairment to the body. The court in *Gates* awarded benefits based on this rating. The appeals court affirmed the award based on second edition ratings. It can be argued that, under the reasoning of *Gates*, a *newer* edition of the *AMA Guides* may be used when an older edition does not provide for rating the plaintiff's condition or does not provide numerical ratings.

§ 1.09   THE *AAOS MANUAL*

It should be noted that the *AMA Guides* has not been the only manual available for evaluating permanent impairment. In 1965, the American Academy of

---

[138] *See* Madrid v. St. Joseph, 928 P.2d 250 (N.M. 1996).

[139] 567 N.W.2d 201 (N.D. 1997).

[140] 1998 U.S. App. LEXIS 7171 (9th Cir. Apr. 8, 1998).

[141] 711 A.2d 1214 (Del. 1998).

[142] 2001 WL 720624 (Tenn. Spec. Workers' Comp. App. Panel June 27, 2001).

Orthopaedic Surgeons (AAOS) published its *Manual for Orthopaedic Surgeons in Evaluating Permanent Physical Impairment* (hereinafter *AAOS Manual*). From the timing of its publication, the *AAOS Manual* appears to have been considered a supplement to the *AMA Guides* then published. Although the *AAOS Manual* is no longer in print, it is still accepted for use in some jurisdictions.[143]

The *AAOS Manual* limits its scope to musculoskeletal impairments, which, then as now, accounted for a large share of industrial injuries. The percentage ratings set forth in the *AAOS Manual* are presented as guiding examples of approximately what impairment ratings should be in corresponding individual cases. The authors of the *AAOS Manual* emphasize that no matter what rating guide the physician consults, the final rating should be the physician's personal opinion based on the physician's knowledge, experience, and consideration of the nature and importance of any anatomical damage, the clinical findings, and the patient's personality reactions.

In comparison to the *AMA Guides*, the *AAOS Manual* requires much less mathematical computation and is faster to use. Perhaps this accounts for the fact that many orthopedists continue to prefer the *AAOS Manual* over the *AMA Guides*.

Because of differences in terminology, it is difficult to compare impairment ratings between these two systems. However, it is clear that ratings under the *AAOS Manual* are in general higher (i.e., more generous to claimants), when compared with ratings under the *AMA Guides*. An excellent example of this difference in ratings found under the *AAOS Manual* and the *AMA Guides* is set forth in *Alien v. Natrona County School District One*,[144] a case in which a claimant with bilateral epicondylitis (tennis elbow) had a 20 percent impairment rating under the *AAOS Manual* but a 0 percent rating under the *AMA Guides*.

§ 1.10 COMPARING THE *AMA GUIDES* TO SCHEDULED AWARDS

For 80 years, workers have received scheduled awards for permanent impairments. The rationale for such awards has been that it would be fundamentally unfair for a worker to suffer a permanent impairment and receive either token benefits or no benefits at all under the Workers' Compensation Act.

The North Dakota Supreme Court expressed another reason for scheduled awards:

> [I]n addition to affecting earning power, parts of one's body serve personal and social purposes as well, and . . . a worker should be compensated to some extent for those effects, other than occupational, from an injury which impairs a part of his body.[145]

---

[143] *See, e.g.*, Alaska Admin. Code tit. 8, § 45.122; Tenn. Code Ann. § 50-6-204; Haw. Admin. R. § 12-10-21.

[144] 811 P.2d 1 (Wyo. 1991).

[145] Kroeplin v. North Dakota Workmen's Comp. Bureau, 415 N.W.2d 807, 809 (N.D. 1987).

Awards under the *AMA Guides* differ from awards under the statutory schedules in several ways. For example, awards under the *AMA Guides* are combined instead of added. In addition, some permanent impairment ratings that were available under the schedules are not rated under the *AMA Guides*, and still other impairments are rated differently. In general, however, the *AMA Guides* are far more comprehensive than the statutory schedules.

In *Coffman v. Kind & Knox Gelatine, Inc.*,[146] the claimant tried to obtain the higher benefits of an unscheduled award by arguing that an injury to his eyes (a scheduled award) "spilled over" to his body as a whole by causing dizziness, headache, and a headache effect. The appellate court in *Coffman* never ruled on this issue.

§ 1.11   THE WHOLE-PERSON CONCEPT, ROUNDING OFF, AND THE COMBINED VALUES CHART

Impairment ratings under the *AMA Guides* are traditionally based on the *whole-person concept*. The examinee's loss is rated as a percentage loss of the whole person.[147] This concept applies even when the examinee has injured only one organ system. When more than one organ system is impaired, the physician calculates the whole-person impairment for each organ system[148] and combines the impairments into a total impairment by using the combined values chart in the *AMA Guides*.[149] The sixth edition of the *AMA Guides* recognizes that some impairments need not be converted to whole-person impairment if either the jurisdiction or the referring source requests otherwise.[150]

It is important to note that the fourth edition allows the final impairment rating, whether based on one or several organ systems, to be rounded to the nearer of the two values ending in 0 or 5.[151] Under the fifth and sixth editions of the *AMA Guides*, impairment ratings are rounded to the nearest whole number.[152]

Combining impairment ratings always results in a lower figure than merely adding the ratings. This is because the combined values chart uses the following formula: $A + B (1 - A) =$ the combined value of A and B, where A and B are decimal equivalents of percentage ratings. The combined values chart has been termed illogical by at least one court because the use of the chart results in a lower rating than if the impairments were added up.[153] The combined values chart need not be used where the injury is to a scheduled member.[154] One advantage of

---

[146] 2006 Iowa App. LEXIS 784 (2006).

[147] *AMA Guides* (4th ed. 1993) at 8.

[148] *Id.*

[149] *Id.* at 322–24.

[150] *AMA Guides* (6th ed. 2008) at 21.

[151] *AMA Guides* (4th ed. 1993) at 9.

[152] *AMA Guides* (5th ed. 2000) at 20; *AMA Guides* (6th ed. 2008) at 24–25.

[153] Norwood v. Lee Way Motor Freight, Inc., 646 P.2d 2, 4 (Okla. Ct. App. 1982).

[154] Special Indemn. Fund v. Choate, 847 P.2d 796 (Okla. Ct. App. 1993).

combining rather than adding impairments is that it is impossible for the level of combined impairments to exceed 100 percent.[155]

The *AMA Guides* (5th ed. 2000) retained the combined values chart found in the *AMA Guides* (4th ed. 1993). The fifth edition, however, recognized that other approaches for dealing with multiple impairments exist, and noted that other approaches will be considered for future editions of the *AMA Guides* "when published in scientific, peer-reviewed literature."[156] Yet the new sixth edition did not adopt a different method; in fact, it has retained the combined values chart.[157]

Many workers' compensation statutes do not have scheduled awards based on the whole-person concept. Unlike the *AMA Guides*, most scheduled awards run from the general to the specific. Thus, the general pain or loss of use expressed by the claimant is translated to a specific body part and compensated based on the statutory schedule. When the maximum medical improvement is reached, the claimant receives compensation based on the schedule without regard to any wage loss sustained. For example, the complete loss of a hand, arm, leg, or foot would entitle the claimant to a specific amount of workers' compensation benefits. The loss of hearing, vision, or bodily functions would also entitle the claimant to a specific amount of compensation. To use the state schedules, the claimant must express the loss of use in terms of the specific body part or function. Few states have any provisions for translating the loss of use of the whole person into a specific award of workers' compensation benefits.

The dilemma is this: If a physician rates an impairment according to the *AMA Guides*, based on the whole-person concept, attorneys and judges are left with a percentage loss that does not coincide precisely with their specific loss schedule. These problems should be resolved by the various state legislatures adopting payment systems compatible with impairment ratings under the *AMA Guides.*

Some courts have attempted to resolve this issue on their own. The Vermont Supreme Court, citing an earlier decision, stated:

> The amount of compensation for back injuries must be assessed based on the percentage of loss of the back's function rather than on the degree of impairment of the whole person. Because the *AMA Guides* are premised on a whole person standard, their use in assessing back injuries is inconsistent with section 648, as interpreted in [case name] making the Commissioner's rejection of them in his calculation of disability appropriate.[158]

The court in *Dillard v. Industrial Claim Appeals Office*[159] held that because of the wording of Colorado's statute, mental impairment cannot be combined with physical impairment to exceed the state's 25 percent threshold. This ruling

---

[155] *AMA Guides* (5th ed. 2000) at 9.

[156] *Id.*

[157] *AMA Guides* (6th ed. 2008) at 604–05.

[158] Stamper v. University Apartments, Inc., 522 A.2d 807, 809 (Vt. 1986).

[159] 134 P.3d 407 (Colo. 2006).

demonstrates the imperative of checking the applicable state's statute and regulations to see how they require the *Guides* to be applied.

§ 1.12   INJURIES NOT COVERED BY THE *AMA GUIDES*

The *AMA Guides* do not specifically cover all injuries, so it may be difficult to use the *AMA Guides* for rating some impairments. The *AMA Guides* (4th ed. 1993) acknowledged this fact:

> [T]he Guides does not and cannot provide answers about every type and degree of impairment, because of the considerations noted above and the infinite variety of human disease, and because the field of human medicine and medical practice is characterized by constant change in understanding disease and its manifestations, diagnosis, and treatment. Further, human functioning in everyday life is a dynamic process, one that presents a great challenge to those attempting to evaluate impairment.[160]

The *AMA Guides* (5th ed. 2000) recognized that the *AMA Guides* is not comprehensive because of the "range, evolution and discovery of new medical conditions."[161] Where impairment ratings are not provided, the *AMA Guides* (5th ed. 2000) suggests that physicians use "clinical judgment" based on similar conditions with similar impairment of function.[162] The methodology in the *AMA Guides* (6th ed. 2008) is to rate by analogy "if the Guides provides no other method for rating objectively identifiable impairment."[163]

The issue of injuries not covered by the *AMA Guides* has generated substantial confusion and litigation. What should a court do when the statute says to use the *AMA Guides* but the *AMA Guides* do not cover or rate an impairment? If the *AMA Guides* are to be used exclusively for rating permanent impairments, but they do not cover a specific loss, is the injured employee to be denied benefits? Most courts and some legislatures have said no. One court stated:

> As a practical matter, over four years of experience have shown the futility of attempting to view the *AMA Guides* as a comprehensive all-inclusive schedule of permanent impairments. This valuable treatise, viewed by the division as the best available, is, nevertheless, according to much credible medical testimony, reflected in the cases coming before us, incomplete and unsuited to the determination of permanent impairment resulting from certain types of injuries.[164]

---

[160] *AMA Guides* (4th ed. 1993) at 3.
[161] *AMA Guides* (5th ed. 2000) at 11.
[162] *Id.*
[163] *AMA Guides* (6th ed. 2008) at 23.
[164] Trindade v. Abbey Road Beef 'N Booze, 443 So. 2d 1007 (Fla. Dist. Ct. App. 1983). *See also* Okla. Stat. Ann. tit. 85, § 3(11) (West).

Many states have explicit safety valve provisions in their statutes or regulations whereby impairments may be rated under a different method if they are not addressed by the *AMA Guides*. In Alaska, it is presumed that the *AMA Guides* will apply. If this presumption is overcome by clear and convincing evidence, the alternatives that should be used are the State of Minnesota Department of Labor and Industry Permanent Partial Disability Schedule or the *AAOS Manual*.[165] In New Hampshire and Arizona, the *AMA Guides* apply only "where applicable."[166] Vermont has ordered that its workers' compensation commissioner adopt a supplementary schedule for those injuries that are not rated by the *AMA Guides*.[167] New Mexico has also recognized its workers' compensation commission's discretion to deviate from the *AMA Guides*.[168]

It has been held that a physician exercising competent professional skill and judgment who finds that the recommended procedures in the *AMA Guides* are inapplicable to estimate impairment may use other methods not otherwise prohibited by the *AMA Guides*.[169] For example, the *AMA Guides* (4th ed. 1993) requires that the injury model be used whenever possible to assess permanent impairment.[170] In *In re Wal-Mart Stores*,[171] a neurosurgeon explained that the preferred injury model did not apply to the claimant's injury; the physician provided a full evaluation and analysis justifying his use of the range-of-motion (ROM) model to assess permanent impairment of the claimant's shoulder. The court noted:

> The *AMA Guides* expressly allows a physician to deviate from the guidelines if the physician finds it necessary to produce an "impairment rating more accurate than the recommended formula can achieve." [Citations omitted.] In this case, there is record evidence to show that deviation from the guidelines was necessary to evaluate accurately the impairment suffered by the respondent.[172]

In *Cantalope v. Veterans of Foreign War Club of Eureka*,[173] a case involving a worker with subcutaneous pneumomediastinum (a pulmonary impairment not specifically ratable under the fourth edition of the *AMA Guides*), the court affirmed the rating physician's 10 percent to 15 percent impairment. It stated that whether a rating outside the *AMA Guides* is proper, credible, and permissible is a question of fact.

---

[165] Alaska Admin. Code tit. 8, § 45.22.

[166] N.H. Rev. Stat. Ann. § 281-A:23; Ariz. Admin. Code R20-5-113.

[167] Vt. Stat. Ann. tit. 21, § 648.

[168] *See* Madrid v. St. Joseph, 928 P.2d 250 (N.M. 1996).

[169] *See* Appeal of Rainville, 1999 N.H. LEXIS 6 (N.H. Feb. 8, 1999). *See also* Knott Floyd Land Co. v. Fugate, 2007 WL 4462301 (Ky.), where a doctor was permitted to use his clinical judgment for a hearing impairment circumstance not covered under the *Guides*.

[170] *See AMA Guides* (4th ed. 1993) § 3.3i at 108, § 3.3j at 112.

[171] 765 A.2d 168 (N.H. Dec. 28, 2000).

[172] *Id.* at 172.

[173] 674 N.W.2d 329 (S.D. 2004), *reh'g denied*, 2004 SD 4 (S.D. 2004).

Some claimants with injuries not ratable under the *AMA Guides* have challenged the constitutionality of the adoption of the *AMA Guides*. To date, these challenges have all been ultimately unsuccessful. However, at least one trial court has found the mandated use of the *AMA Guides* to be an equal protection violation when applied to those claimants whose injuries are not ratable under the *AMA Guides*.[174] Constitutional challenges to the adoption of the *AMA Guides* are discussed in detail in Chapter 3.

The question arises about how to determine whether the *AMA Guides* apply to a particular claim. The Arizona court of appeals has ruled that whether a certain condition is ratable under the *AMA Guides* is a purely medical question.[175] The Colorado court of appeals has held that expert medical opinion that the *AMA Guides* are inapplicable to a particular case supported deviation from the *AMA Guides*.[176]

The courts have held the *AMA Guides* inapplicable in numerous cases. A Colorado appellate court found the *AMA Guides* inapplicable to a claimant's noise-induced hearing loss claim.[177] Another Colorado court, in *City of Aurora v. Vaughn*,[178] found that where the claimant had lost the ability to distinguish and comprehend sounds across the frequencies of human hearing, the *AMA Guides* need not be used to rate the impairment.

The Florida Supreme Court found that the degree of impairment from contact dermatitis should not be determined by the *AMA Guides* because the *AMA Guides* do not rate skin conditions that do not affect daily living. The court stated:

> Under the terms of the *AMA Guides*, there is no impairment if the injury does not affect the employee's daily living. In the case sub judice, the claimant's skin condition does not affect his daily living as long as he does not work in his job. Essentially as long as claimant does nothing, there is no impairment.[179]

In another case involving acute contact dermatitis, the Florida Supreme Court stated:

> Economic loss is an indispensable requisite of the wage-loss concept. Therefore the *AMA Guides* are inapplicable when as here, they preclude a finding of permanent impairment where the claimant suffered a disability due to an occupational disease which permanently impairs his ability to work and results in economic loss but does not affect his activities of daily living.[180]

---

[174] Harless v. Huntsville Manor Nursing Home, CA No. 7258 (Ch. Ct. for Scott County, Tenn., Aug. 31, 1994).

[175] Department of Corr. v. Industrial Comm'n, 894 P.2d 726 (Ariz. Ct. App. 1995).

[176] City of Aurora v. Vaughn, 824 P.2d 825 (Colo. Ct. App. 1991).

[177] Jefferson County Sch. v. Headrick, 734 P.2d 659 (Colo. Ct. App. 1986).

[178] 824 P.2d 825 (Colo. Ct. App. 1991).

[179] OBS Co. v. Freeney, 475 So. 2d 947 (Fla. 1985).

[180] Dayron Corp. v. Morehead, 509 So. 2d 930 (Fla. 1987).

The courts have found that subjective pain can constitute a permanent impairment despite the express language of the *AMA Guides*.[181] In *Gainesville Coca Cola v. Young*,[182] the court rejected a 1 percent impairment rating based on subjective pain and remanded the case for a consideration of a 0 percent impairment rating.

An Arizona appellate court, in a case dealing with a chronic back strain and the inability of the physician to rate the impairment under the *AMA Guides*, stated:

> Thus in pain cases, the line between the medical question and the legal question is blurred. Because of the intertwined issues when pain is the only residual permanent injury, the claimant must be allowed to introduce evidence of disability to show impairment. During the first stage, the claimant meets his burden of proof in showing the existence of a permanent impairment if he shows that the pain is caused by his industrial injury and results in his permanent inability to return to his former work.[183]

Other courts have found the loss of strength,[184] knee injuries,[185] neck injuries,[186] thumb injuries,[187] bronchial hypersensitivity,[188] prior surgery in the same area,[189] hematomas,[190] and back injuries[191] not to be covered by the *AMA Guides*.

The Arizona Supreme Court has held that where the *AMA Guides* do not apply, they should not be used to limit the percentage of impairment to that portion which is rated therein.[192] The general rule followed is that although the percentages established in the *AMA Guides* are conclusive for rating specific impairments that fall within their provisions, they are not conclusive when there is medical evidence that the *AMA Guides* do not cover the specific impairment adequately.[193] Arizona

---

[181] Smith v. Industrial Comm'n, 552 P.2d 1198 (Ariz. 1976). *Contra* Maggard v. Simpson Motors, 451 So. 2d 529 (Fla. Dist. Ct. App. 1984); Cassey v. Industrial Comm'n, 731 P.2d 645 (Ariz. Ct. App. 1987); Sutton v. Quality Furniture Co., 381 S.E.2d 389 (Ga. Ct. App. 1989).

[182] 596 So. 2d 1278 (Fla. Dist. Ct. App. 1992).

[183] Cassey v. Industrial Comm'n, 731 P.2d 645 (Ariz. Ct. App. 1987).

[184] Mountain Shadows Resort Hotel v. Industrial Comm'n, 710 P.2d 1066 (Ariz. Ct. App. 1985); Dutra v. Industrial Comm'n, 659 P.2d 18 (Ariz. 1983).

[185] Trindade v. Abbey Road Beef 'N Booze, 443 So. 2d 1007 (Fla. Dist. Ct. App. 1983); Mathis v. Kelly Constr. Co., 417 So. 2d 740 (Fla. Dist. Ct. App. 1982).

[186] Desert Insulations, Inc. v. Industrial Comm'n, 654 P.2d 296 (Ariz. Ct. App. 1982); Deseret Ranches v. Crosby, 461 So. 2d 295 (Fla. Dist. Ct. App. 1985).

[187] Cavco Indus. v. Industrial Comm'n, 631 P.2d 1087 (Ariz. 1981).

[188] Hunter v. Industrial Comm'n, 633 P.2d 1052 (Ariz. Ct. App. 1981).

[189] Chavez v. Industrial Comm'n, 575 P.2d 340 (Ariz. Ct. App. 1978).

[190] Quality Petroleum Corp. v. Mihm, 424 So. 2d 112 (Fla. Dist. Ct. App. 1982).

[191] Martin County Sch. Bd. v. McDaniel, 465 So. 2d 1235 (Fla. Dist. Ct. App. 1984); Coca-Cola Co. Foods Div. v. Hawk, 451 So. 2d 1025 (Fla. Dist. Ct. App. 1984); Florida Sheriffs Youth Fund v. Harrell, 438 So. 2d 450 (Fla. Dist. Ct. App. 1983).

[192] Adams v. Industrial Comm'n, 552 P.2d 764 (Ariz. 1976). *See also* Peck v. Palm Beach County Bd. of County Comm'rs, 442 So. 2d 1050 (Fla. Dist. Ct. App. 1983); Peabody Galion Corp. v. Workman, 643 P.2d 312 (Okla. 1982).

[193] Gomez v. Industrial Comm'n, 716 P.2d 32 (Ariz. Ct. App. 1985).

has also recognized that in such cases as those involving chronic pain, where the *AMA Guides* do not permit an accurate assessment of the claimant's opinion, the claimant may establish his or her impairment through other means.[194] In *Rogers v. Morales*,[195] a claimant suffering from fibromyalgia attempted to have the Texas workers' compensation statute declared unconstitutional because the condition was not listed in the *AMA Guides*. The federal court dismissed the case without prejudice under the abstention doctrine, as the matter was more properly decided in a Texas state court.

Alaska's regulations provide for using alternative guides if the permanent impairment cannot be determined under the *AMA Guides*.[196] A board may not be able to decline assigning a rating only because the condition is not specifically mentioned in the current edition of the *AMA Guides*.[197]

Where impairment percentages are not available under the current edition of the *AMA Guides*, at least one court has held that the percentages may be obtained from a previous edition. This avoids the "absurdity" of the claimant being rated as impaired under the *AMA Guides* but being denied benefits because no numerical rating for the impairment is provided. In *Knott County Nursing Home v. Wallen*,[198] the claimant claimed psychiatric impairment as a consequence of a work-related lower back injury. A psychologist, using the *AMA Guides* (4th ed. 1993), assessed a class 3 impairment, then translated the injuries into a 25 percent impairment rating. The ALJ awarded a 35 percent whole-person impairment rating, 25 percent of which was attributable to claimant's psychological impairment and 10 percent of which was attributed to claimant's lower back injury. The appellate court affirmed the award, noting that the psychologist assessed the mental impairment as class 3, according to the fourth edition of the *AMA Guides*, then turned to the second edition of the Guides to assign a percentage. The psychologist had reasoned that because a class 3 impairment corresponded to moderate impairment, and because the second edition, when dealing with a moderate impairment, provided for estimating whole-body impairment in a range of 25 percent to 50 percent, the claimant's impairment could be estimated at 25 percent. The appeals court writes:

> We believe that the argument raised by counsel in this case highlights the fact that often the legal community and the medical community are simply not operating on the same page. In order for there to be an award of permanent partial disability, the ALJ is bound to the formula contained in KRS 342. In order to accomplish this, the ALJ must have in hand a functional impairment rating. The current edition of the *AMA Guides* on the other hand, state [sic] that there is no empiric evidence to support any method for assigning a percentage of impairment of the whole person. It seems to us it would border on absurdity

---

[194] Simpson v. Industrial Comm'n of Ariz., 942 P.2d 1172 (Ariz. Ct. App. 1997).

[195] 975 F. Supp. 856 (N.D. Tex. 1997).

[196] Alaska Admin. Code tit. 8, § 45.122.

[197] Butler v. Ryder M.L.S., 1999 Del. Super. LEXIS 29 (Del. Super. Ct. Feb. 1, 1999).

[198] 2001 WL 629401 (Ky. Ct. App. June 8, 2001).

to allow an ALJ to award permanent total disability in an injury case where there is also a psychiatric/psychological component wherein the medical expert testifies as to classification of impairment as opposed to percentages of impairment, and to deny another claimant a permanent partial disability award because there is a classification of impairment but no corresponding finding of a percentage of impairment. What remains is that we are left with clinical judgments which may not be based on empirical evidence but made of necessity.[199]

§1.13 THE *AMA GUIDES* AND APPEALS

The number of reported appellate cases discussing the *AMA Guides* is increasing. How to deal with mistakes in using the *AMA Guides* is a frequently litigated issue. In one case, a Florida court found that an error in the use of the *AMA Guides* was, for the purposes of the appeal, a harmless error.

The Oklahoma courts have rendered many appellate decisions on the use of the *AMA Guides*. One of the chief problems faced by the Oklahoma courts has been what to do when medical reports are not in strict compliance with the *AMA Guides*.

Due to the volume of litigation, in *Gaines v. Sun Refinery & Marketing*,[200] Oklahoma enunciated the rule (the Oklahoma Rule) that the state will follow in future cases.

> Henceforth the appellate courts of this state will not reverse for failure to follow Rule 20 or the A.M.A. Guidelines unless an objection is made in compliance with Rule 21 that also states the specific grounds under Section 2104. The objection may be either for lack of competency or lack of probative value, but an objection with a mere reference to lack of A.M.A. Guidelines will not suffice for specificity. A party must state the specific provision of Rule 20 and/ or the A.M.A. Guidelines which is the basis of the objection. For example, if a party would ask this Court to reject a report for failure to administer the single breath D_{co} test, he must have initially asked the trial court to reject the report for the doctor's failure to have administered that particular test. If he would ask this Court to disqualify a report for inadequate history in that the claimant's history of exposure to other toxic chemicals was not included, he must first have made that substantially identical request to the trial court. We will make like requirements with respect to alleged errors in computations, uses of ratios, percentages of disability, and so forth. Absent objections to medical reports made with such specificity the appellate courts hereafter will rely on a reporting physician's Rule 20-required assertion that his report substantially complies with A.M.A. Guidelines, and appealing parties in Compensation Court cases will not be heard to advance arguments thereon at this level that were not expressed at the trial of the case.[201]

---

[199] 2001 WL 629401, at *2.
[200] 790 P.2d 1073 (Okla. 1990).
[201] *Id.* at 873.

The Oklahoma Rule may be followed by other jurisdictions. Thus, counsel desiring to preserve an *AMA Guides* issue for appeal should specify all objections to the *AMA Guides'* reports, testimony, computations, and so forth, at the trial level.

Of course, many an appellant will face the heavy burden of showing that the original decision was not supported by substantial evidence.[202] If a litigant wants the option of including the *AMA Guides* in an appeal, he or she should submit the *AMA Guides* into evidence at the time of the hearing or trial. Failure to do so could result in the appellate court's failure to consider the *AMA Guides* on appeal for lack of a proper record.[203] However, in *Polk County v Jones*,[204] the court held that the Workers' Compensation Commission may refer to the *AMA Guides*, even if not in evidence, to decide an issue in dispute because the use of the *AMA Guides* is mandated by law. Similarly, in *Appeal of Fournier*,[205] the court held that the *AMA Guides* are not "evidence" because their use is required by administrative rule as authorized by statute. The court in *Wilson v. Industrial Claim Appeals Office of State of Colorado* held that whether or not an IME physician correctly applies the *AMA Guides* is a question of fact, not of law.[206] In *Brasch-Barry General Contractors v. Jones*,[207] the court held that an ALJ's acceptance of a rating that deviated from the *Guides* is a question of law, not of fact.

---

[202] Robbennolt v. Snap-On Tools Corp., 555 N.W.2d 229 (Iowa 1996).

[203] Durham v. Cessna Aircraft Co., 945 P.2d 8 (Kan. Ct. App. 1997), *review denied*, No. 96-77514-AS (Kan. Dec. 23, 1997).

[204] 47 S.W.3d 904 (Ark. Ct. App. 2001).

[205] 786 A.2d 854 (N.H. 2001).

[206] 81 P.3d 1117 (Colo. Ct. App. 2003).

[207] 175 S.W.3d 81 (Ky. 2005), *on remand*, 2006 WL 572815 (Ky. Ct. App. Mar. 10, 2006).

CHAPTER 2

USE OF THE *AMA GUIDES* FOR MEDICAL EVALUATIONS

§ 2.01   WHEN TO EVALUATE PERMANENT IMPAIRMENT

It is axiomatic that the degree of permanent impairment should not be determined until the claimant has reached an end result or maximum medical improvement (MMI). The second edition of the *AMA Guides* referred to "maximum medical rehabilitation."[1] The third edition replaced the concept of maximum medical rehabilitation with the concept of *permanent impairment*—that is, impairment that has become "static, or will stabilize with or without medical treatment, or is not likely to remit despite medical treatment."[2] A claimant need not show a minimum of six months of medically documented pain before MMI to be rated under the third edition of the *AMA Guides* (1988).[3]

The appropriate time to determine permanent impairment has been described by the courts as when the medical condition reaches an end result,[4] becomes stationary,[5] and reaches MMI.[6] As with other aspects of the *AMA Guides*, specific statutory provisions can override the definition of permanency in the *AMA Guides*. For example, in *Municipality of Anchorage v. Leigh*,[7] the Alaska Supreme Court rejected the medical stability definition of the *AMA Guides* and used Alaska's own statutory presumption on the definition of medical stability. Indeed, the sixth edition of the *AMA Guides* now explicitly recognizes that when to rate impairment and what to call this time will vary according to the jurisdiction.[8]

The fourth edition of the *AMA Guides* dictated that "it must be shown that the problem has been present for a period of time, is stable, and is unlikely to change in future months in spite of treatment."[9] The fourth edition also states that an impairment should not be considered permanent until the clinical findings, determined during a period of months, indicate that the medical condition is static and well stabilized.[10] The glossary in the fourth edition of the *AMA Guides* contains perhaps the most precise definition of permanent impairment:

> Permanent impairment is impairment that has become static or well stabilized with or without medical treatment and is not likely to remit despite medical treatment. A permanent impairment is considered to be unlikely to change

---

[1] AMA, Guides to the Evaluation of Permanent Impairment (3d ed. 1988) (hereinafter *AMA Guides* (3d ed. 1988)) at 8.

[2] *Id.*

[3] McLane W. Inc. v. Industrial Claim Appeals Office, 996 P.2d 263 (Colo. Ct. App. 1999).

[4] Rainville v. Kings Trucking, 448 A.2d 733 (R.I. 1982).

[5] Sandoval v. Industrial Comm'n, 559 P.2d 688 (Ariz. 1976).

[6] Azwell v. Franklin Assocs., 374 So. 2d 766 (Miss. 1979).

[7] 823 P.2d 1241 (Alaska 1992).

[8] AMA, Guides to the Evaluation of Permanent Impairment (6th ed. 2008) (hereinafter *AMA Guides* (6th ed. 2008)) at 612.

[9] AMA, Guides to the Evaluation of Permanent Impairment (4th ed. 1993) (hereinafter *AMA Guides* (4th ed. 1993)) at 3.

[10] *Id.* at 9.

substantially and by more than 3% in the next year with or without medical treatment.[11]

The fifth edition of the *AMA Guides* defines permanent impairment as an impairment that has reached "maximum medical improvement."[12] It describes *maximum medical improvement* as a condition that "is well stabilized and unlikely to change substantially in the next year, with or without medical treatment."[13]

In the sixth edition of the *AMA Guides*, Chapter 2 ("the constitution") describes *maximum medical improvement* of examinees in terms of being "as good as they are going to be" or reaching "a date from which further recovery or deterioration is not anticipated, although over time (beyond 12 months) there may be some expected change."[14]

It has been held that a permanent impairment evaluation may be made even after the patient has died. The case in question involved a person who was assigned a 40 percent permanent impairment four months after dying from unrelated causes.[15] After an accident, the patient had seen the rating physician on several occasions. The court reasoned that there was no reason to exclude the rating simply because the underlying data had not been expressed in the form of an *AMA Guides* compliance report until after the patient's death.[16] The court in *Martinez v. Excel Corp.*[17] held that the *AMA Guides* require that a patient with severe bilateral carpal tunnel syndrome who refused release surgery be rated as she was, without having the surgery and not based on speculation about results after a successful surgery.

§ 2.02   THE PROCESS OF EVALUATING IMPAIRMENT

[A] *AMA Guides,* Fourth Edition

AMA Guides (4th ed. 1993) used a three-step approach to rating permanent impairment.[18] The fourth edition contains a helpful Report of Medical Evaluation Form, which physicians can use to follow the three-step process discussed in this section.[19]

Step 1 is the medical evaluation of the examinee. This evaluation includes a narrative history of the medical condition(s) with specific references to the onset and the course of the conditions, symptoms, findings on previous examination(s),

---

[11] *Id.* at 315.

[12] AMA, Guides to the Evaluation of Permanent Impairment (5th ed. 2000) (hereinafter *AMA Guides* (5th ed. 2000)) at 602.

[13] *AMA Guides* (5th ed. 2000) at 601.

[14] *AMA Guides* (6th ed. 2008) at 26.

[15] Sears, Roebuck & Co. v. Ralph, 666 A.2d 1239 (Md. 1995).

[16] *Id.* at 243.

[17] 79 P.2d 230 (Kan. Ct. App. 2003).

[18] *AMA Guides* (4th ed. 1993) at 14.

[19] *Id.* at 11–12.

treatments, and responses to treatments, including the adverse effects. The results of the most recent clinical evaluation, including diagnostic studies and physical examination, are also analyzed. Step 1 concludes with the current clinical status, a statement of plans for future treatment, the diagnoses, and the expected date of full or partial recovery.[20]

Step 2 is an analysis of the findings from the first step. The impact of the medical conditions on the examinee's life activities should be given. The medical basis for the physician's conclusion regarding permanency should also be given.[21] Also explained are the conclusions that the examinee is not likely to suffer further impairment by engaging in usual activities and that accommodations or restrictions related to the impairment are (or are not) warranted.[22]

Step 3 is a comparison of the results of the analysis with the impairment criteria found in the *AMA Guides*.[23] The comparison should describe the specific clinical findings related to each impairment, with reference to how the findings relate to and compare with the criteria described in the applicable *AMA Guides* chapter.[24]

Finally, the physician provides an explanation of each estimated impairment (with reference to the applicable criteria of the *AMA Guides*), a summary list of all impairment percentages, and an estimated whole-person impairment percentage.[25] It has been held that a clerical error committed by a rating physician in computing impairment was not grounds to keep evidence of the impairment rating from the jury.[26]

[B] *AMA Guides,* Fifth Edition

AMA Guides (5th ed. 2000) focuses on the elements that should be included in all impairment evaluation reports.[27] These elements are: (1) clinical evaluation, (2) a calculation of the impairment rating, and (3) a discussion of how the impairment rating was calculated.[28] Each report should include specifics such as narrative history, current clinical status, diagnostic studies, the medical basis for determining MMI, diagnoses, prognosis, and other related items, as provided in Section 2.6. Reports that do not meet the requirements spelled out in Section 2.6 may be open to effective cross-examination.

---

[20] *Id.* at 10.

[21] *Id.*

[22] *Id.* at 14.

[23] *Id.* at 10.

[24] *Id.*

[25] *Id.* at 10, 14.

[26] Old Republic Ins. Co. v. Rodriguez, 966 S.W.2d 208 (Tex. App. 1998).

[27] *AMA Guides* (5th ed. 2000) at 21-22.

[28] *Id.*

[C] *AMA Guides,* Sixth Edition

In *AMA Guides* (6th ed. 2008), the three-step process for evaluating impairment is contained in Section 2.7.[29] This section is required reading for counsel, as it contains many important requirements for the impairment rater.

Step 1 is clinical evaluation, which requires a review of medical records and documenting inconsistencies.[30] The examinee should be encouraged to give full effort in the physical examination, and the physician should review diagnostic studies.[31]

Step 2 is analysis of findings, including diagnoses, MMI status, current abilities for activities of daily living (ADLs), and flagging of missing data.[32]

Step 3 is a specific discussion of how the impairment rating was calculated, and the discussion should cite the pages and tables in the *AMA Guides* that are used and how they are used.[33]

§ 2.03 THE EVALUATOR'S QUALIFICATIONS

Questions have arisen about the competence of non-physicians, such as physical therapists and chiropractors, to evaluate impairment and testify concerning the *AMA Guides.* The first and second editions of the *AMA Guides* spoke exclusively in terms of physicians. The fourth edition continued to speak of "physicians" with one notable exception. According to the fourth edition, "any knowledgeable person" may compare the results of a medical analysis performed by a physician with the criteria in the *AMA Guides* for the particular body part, system, or function.[34] The fifth edition states that impairment evaluations are performed by "licensed physicians."[35] This terminology may be problematic when an evaluation is performed by a psychologist or chiropractor.

The sixth edition is self-contradictory as to who can perform ratings. Page 20 in Chapter 2 ("the constitution") states that ratings "must" be performed by a licensed physician, but page 23 in the same chapter states that "mostly" physicians (MDs, DCs, and DOs) "use" the *AMA Guides.*[36] This contradictory language leaves open the question of whether, absent contrary law, psychologists and chiropractors are allowed to rate patients under the *Guides.* In terms of legal requirements, the sixth edition now explicitly recognizes that each jurisdiction is "best suited" to determine the definition of the doctor to make ratings.[37]

---

[29] *AMA Guides* (6th ed. 2008) at 28.

[30] *Id.*

[31] *Id.*

[32] *Id.*

[33] *Id.*

[34] *AMA Guides* (4th ed. 1993) at 8.

[35] *AMA Guides* (5th ed. 2000) at 15.

[36] *AMA Guides* (6th ed. 2008) at 20, 23.

[37] *AMA Guides* (6th ed. 2008) at 23.

AMA Guides (6th ed. 2008) is noteworthy for its bias against treating physicians' performing ratings, since treaters are not "independent."[38] Evaluations of patients by their treating physicians are allowed, but these evaluations are to be given greater scrutiny.[39] This bias is even more remarkable given that under the guidelines, impairments are mostly diagnosis based. The sixth edition makes no mention of evaluations bought and paid for by employers or insurers being suspect for lack of independence. It also makes no mention of the long tradition of fact finders' giving greater weight to the testimony of the treating physician or of legal presumptions in favor of the treating physician.[40]

The courts have addressed the question of who is competent to evaluate impairment under the *AMA Guides*. The Tennessee Supreme Court, in *Elmore v. Travelers Insurance Co.*,[41] found that a physical therapist was not qualified to rate permanent impairment. The Tennessee court had previously found, in *Bolton v. CNA Insurance Co.*,[42] that a physical therapist was not competent to assess permanent disability or impairment by using the *AMA Guides* because a physical therapist's testimony must be limited to objective findings and cannot encompass an opinion on ultimate disability. Another court held that a chiropractor is competent to testify as an expert using the *AMA Guides* if the testimony is both in accordance with the *AMA Guides* and within the scope of the chiropractor's expertise and licensure.[43]

A number of statutes and regulations address the issue of who is legally competent to evaluate permanent impairment under the *AMA Guides*. For example, Montana allows a chiropractor to evaluate impairment if the claimant's treating physician is a chiropractor and the chiropractor is certified as an evaluator under Montana law.[44] In New Mexico, an evaluation may be performed by an "MD, DO or DC."[45] Pennsylvania requires evaluators to receive training in the *AMA Guides*.[46] In *Thomas v. Magna Seating Systems of America, Inc.*,[47] the court of appeals held that the trial court was within its discretion in accepting the testimony of an independent medical examination (IME) physician. The court of appeals had made note of the fact that the IME physician was board certified in the use of the *AMA Guides*. In *Brown v. Nissan North America, Inc.*,[48] the Tennessee State Supreme Court at Nashville, in a de novo review, implicitly gave more weight to an IME physician's rating because the IME physician had training in use of the

---

[38] *Id.*

[39] *Id.*

[40] *See, e.g.*, Conaghan v. Riverfield Country Day Sch., 163 P.3d 557 (Okla. 2007).

[41] 824 S.W.2d 541 (Tenn. 1992).

[42] 821 S.W.2d 932 (Tenn. 1991).

[43] Humphrey v. David Witherspoon, Inc., 734 S.W.2d 315, 318 (Tenn. 1987).

[44] Mont. Code Ann. § 39-71-711.

[45] N.M. Admin. Code § 11.4.7.

[46] 34 Pa. Code § 123.103.

[47] 2003 Tenn. LEXIS 711 (Tenn. Spec. Workers' Comp. App. Panel Aug. 15, 2003).

[48] 2006 Tenn. LEXIS 1138 (Dec. 18, 2006).

Guides. The court specifically cited the IME physician's certification by the American Academy of Disability Evaluating Physicians.

One court was asked to decide whether an industrial commission may use the *AMA Guides* under its own motion and without expert testimony to support the use. The court avoided deciding the issue by finding that the commission had used the *AMA Guides* for only a limited purpose.[49] Another case involved an administrative law judge (ALJ) who had recalculated a claimant's pulmonary impairment because the rating physician had used improper norms for the claimant's age and height. In this situation, the court approved, reasoning that the ALJ had not performed any function that required medical expertise and that the action was administratively efficient.[50] In *Newberg v. Price*,[51] the court held that an ALJ could not choose the height of a claimant when four different physicians had measured the claimant at four different heights. However, in *Polk County v. Jones*,[52] the court upheld the Workers' Compensation Commission's assignment of an 8 percent impairment rating based on the medical records in evidence and the board's use of the *AMA Guides.*

The question has arisen whether a physician requires formal training to rate permanent impairment under the *AMA Guides.* In *Pacific Power & Light v. Heermann*,[53] the court held that formal training in the *AMA Guides* is not required for a physician to rate impairment under the *AMA Guides.* In Nevada, a chiropractor may not rate impairment unless the chiropractor has completed an advanced course in rating disabilities under the *AMA Guides.*[54] This rating course needs to be approved by the state.[55] Impairment evaluations in Colorado must be performed by physicians who have been accredited to do so under state rules.[56]

A New Mexico court stated that a workers' compensation judge (WCJ) was not capable of assigning an impairment rating where the issue was impairment of the lungs.[57] However, a Montana court has held that when an impairment evaluation is made by a medical evaluator according to the *AMA Guides*, a judge is not prohibited from translating that evaluation into a percentage so the injured worker may be compensated; under this particular state's statute, there was no requirement that the medical evaluator express impairment as a percentage.[58] The court in *Appalachian Racing, Inc. v. Blair*[59] held that it was not an error for an ALJ to

---

[49] Pomerinke v. Excel Trucking Transp., 859 P.2d 337 (Idaho 1993).

[50] Beale v. Highwire, Inc., 843 S.W.2d 898 (Ky. Ct. App. 1993).

[51] 868 S.W.2d 92 (Ky. 1994).

[52] 47 S.W.3d 904 (Ark. Ct. App. 2001).

[53] 872 P.2d 1171 (Wyo. 1994).

[54] Nev. Rev. Stat. § 616C.105.

[55] *Id.*

[56] Colo. Rev. Stat. Ann. § 8-42-101.

[57] Yeager v. St. Vincent Hosp., 973 P.2d 850 (N.M. Ct. App. 1998).

[58] S.L.H. v. State Comp. Mut. Ins. Fund, 15 P.3d 948, 954 (Mont. 2000).

[59] 2003 WL 21355872 (Ky. June 12, 2003).

adjust an impairment rating using the tables in the *AMA Guides* after the ALJ found that the physician had misapplied the *AMA Guides.*

In *Thornton v. Volt Services Group,*[60] the court held that an ALJ may not disregard uncontradicted medical evidence on the *Guides.*

Nonmedical (lay) testimony may be considered in determining loss of use of an arm.[61] An ALJ is not free to simply choose any functional impairment rating assigned by physicians unless the specific procedures and directions contained in the *AMA Guides* are undertaken.[62] The court in *In re Pohl*[63] upheld a "paper review" impairment rating by a physician who did not examine the claimant personally. Similarly, an employer's expert's rating has been upheld even where the expert never physically examined the claimant.[64]

Psychologists' ratings of permanent impairment have been accepted.[65] However, use of a psychologist to testify regarding a mental injury may not be allowed. In *Gates v. Jackson Appliance Co.,*[66] discussing the testimony of a psychologist, the court wrote:

> This panel is mindful of the decisions which require expert medical evidence and not that of a psychologist to establish causation and permanency of a mental injury. Cigna Property & Casualty Ins. Co. v. Sneed, 772 S.W.2d 422, 424 (Tenn. 1989); Henley v. Roadway Exp., 699 S.W.2d 150, 155 (Tenn. 1985); Freeman v. VF Corp., Kay Windsor Div., 675 S.W.2d 710, 711 (Tenn. 1984). However, once causation and permanency of a mental injury have been established by medical testimony, vocational experts such as Dr. Kennon may express an opinion as to the extent of vocational disability.[67]

Some systems specify that the *AMA Guides* are to be used to rate injuries to nonscheduled members. In that case, some courts will take it upon themselves to make the conversion to a whole-person rating. In *Light v. Frontier Health, Inc.,*[68] the trial court based an award to the body on an impairment rating for the upper extremity, a nonscheduled member. The appellate court converted the rating to a whole-person rating and adjusted the award.

---

[60] 2005 WL 1412530 (Ky. June 16, 2005).

[61] Christensen v. Snap-On Tools Corp., 602 N.W.2d 199 (Iowa Ct. App. 1999).

[62] Ball v. Big Elk Creek Coal Co., 1999 WL 1086306 (Ky. Ct. App. Nov. 19, 1999).

[63] 980 P.2d 816 (Wyo. 1999).

[64] Appeal of Cote, 781 A.2d 1006 (N.H. 2001).

[65] Knott County Nursing Home v. Wallen, 2001 WL 629401 (Ky. Ct. App. June 8, 2001) (Tenn. Spec. Workers' Comp. App. Panel June 27, 2001); S.L.H. v. State Comp. Mut. Ins. Fund, 15 P.3d 948, 2000 MT 362 (Mont. 2000).

[66] 2001 WL 720624 (Tenn. Spec. Workers' Comp. App. Panel June 27, 2001).

[67] *Id.* at *5.

[68] No. E1999-00256-SC-WCM-CV, 2000 Tenn. LEXIS 671 (Tenn. Spec. Workers' Comp. App. Panel Dec. 5, 2000).

CHAPTER 3

CHALLENGES TO THE ADOPTION AND USE OF THE *AMA GUIDES*

§ 3.01   INTRODUCTION

In the preceding chapters, the development of the American Medical Association's *Guides to the Evaluation of Permanent Impairment* (hereinafter *AMA Guides*), their adoption to varying extents by state and federal lawmakers, and their use by the medical community are examined. This chapter examines the challenges to the validity of the *AMA Guides,* their reliability, their scope, and their application to the various workers' compensation systems.

§ 3.02   ARE THE *AMA GUIDES* VALID AND RELIABLE?

The *AMA Guides* have been judicially recognized as an "authoritative treatise."[1] Challenges have, however, been brought against the *AMA Guides* on the grounds that they are not scientifically valid and reliable. These challenges raise the question of whether the *AMA Guides* even purport to be scientifically valid and reliable. Generally, they do not. The fourth edition of the *AMA Guides* used scientific data accepted and derived from normal functioning for those systems for which such data are available.[2] Those systems include the respiratory, cardiovascular, visual, auditory, endocrine, hematologic, and digestive systems.[3] The *AMA Guides* (4th ed. 1993) does not purport to be scientifically valid and reliable regarding other systems of the body. The authors of the *AMA Guides* (4th ed. 1993) were not able to identify objective data on the normal functioning of musculoskeletal, neurological, pain, psychiatric, skin, and other systems.[4] Instead, for those systems where objective data were not available, the authors of the *AMA Guides* (4th ed. 1993) "estimated" the extent of the impairments based on "clinical experience, judgment, and consensus."[5] All users of the *AMA Guides* (4th ed. 1993) must remember that impairment ratings under the *AMA Guides* are merely "*estimates*" of impairment.[6]

The fifth edition of the *AMA Guides* also addresses its own reliability and validity. The *AMA Guides* (5th ed. 2000) states that much of the impairment percentages contained therein are "estimates" based on the "consensus of the chapter authors and not on scientific evidence."[7] The fifth edition promised, however, that subsequent editions would incorporate evidence-based studies when such research becomes available.[8] The *AMA Guides* (5th ed. 2000) recognizes that research is

---

[1] Battista v. United States, 889 F. Supp. 716 (S.D.N.Y 1995).

[2] AMA, Guides to the Evaluation of Permanent Impairment (4th ed. 1993) (hereinafter *AMA Guides* (4th ed. 1993)) at 3.

[3] *Id.*

[4] *Id.*

[5] *Id.*

[6] *Id.* at 315 (emphasis in original).

[7] AMA, Guides to the Evaluation of Permanent Impairment (5th ed. 2000) (hereinafter *AMA Guides* (5th ed. 2000)) at 4.

[8] *AMA Guides* (5th ed. 2000) at 10.

limited on the reproducibility and validity of the *AMA Guides* and that only "anecdotal" evidence has indicated that adoption of the *AMA Guides* has resulted in "a more standardized impairment assessment process."[9]

For criticism of past editions of the *Guides*, one need look no further than Section 1.2a of the sixth edition, which contains a candid list of explicit criticisms of previous editions of the *Guides*. The criticisms include charges that previous editions were not comprehensive, were not based on evidence, and did not have accurate ratings. Chapter 1 even quotes an article in the *Journal of the American Medical Association*, which stated that the numerical ratings in the *Guides* were more "legal fiction than medical reality."[10] Section 1.2a of *AMA Guides* (6th ed. 2008) goes on to suggest that the fifth edition used "antiquated and confusing terminology"[11] and had "limited validity and reliability of the ratings."[12] The sixth edition further states that impairment ratings in the fifth edition are estimates and are based on consensus (as opposed to evidence).[13]

§ 3.03   ARE THE *AMA GUIDES* COMPREHENSIVE?

Do the *AMA Guides* apply to "every type and degree of impairment"?[14] No, they do not. According to the *AMA Guides* (4th ed. 1993), such a goal is impossible due to "the infinite variety of human disease, and because the field of medicine and medical practice is characterized by constant change in understanding disease and its manifestations, diagnosis, and treatment."[15] According to the *AMA Guides* (5th ed. 2000), "[g]iven the range, evolution, and discovery of new medical conditions, the *Guides* cannot provide an impairment rating for all impairments."[16] In *AMA Guides* (6th ed. 2008), chapter 2 ("the constitution") states that rating by analogy is allowed where the *Guides* provides no other method for rating an objectively identifiable impairment.[17] However, various chapters in the sixth edition state that certain conditions (such as psychiatric reaction to pain) are explicitly not ratable under the *Guides*.[18]

Various challenges have been made to statutes adopting the *AMA Guides* on the basis that these statutes unfairly discriminate against those whose conditions are not covered by the *AMA Guides*. The issue of whether the statute in question contains an

---

[9] *Id.*

[10] *AMA Guides* (6th ed. 2008) at 2 (quoting E.A. Spieler, P.S. Barth, J.F. Burton et al., *Recommendations to Guide Revision of the* Guides to the Evaluation of Permanent Impairment, 283 JAMA 519–23 (2000)).

[11] *AMA Guides* (6th ed. 2008) at 2.

[12] *Id.*

[13] *Id.* at 5, 9.

[14] *AMA Guides* (4th ed. 1993) at 3.

[15] *Id.*

[16] *AMA Guides* (5th ed. 2000) at 11.

[17] *AMA Guides* (6th ed. 2008) at 23.

[18] *Id.* at 349.

"escape clause" to allow rating by another method when the *AMA Guides* do not cover the injury is an important consideration when these challenges are decided.

§ 3.04   CONSTITUTIONAL AND OTHER LEGAL CHALLENGES

Numerous challenges have been made to the *AMA Guides* as used in various workers' compensation systems. The *AMA Guides,* when used properly, serve their main purpose very well; that is, they provide uniformity, fairness, and predictability.[19] Statutes that not only recognize that the *AMA Guides* do not purport to be comprehensive but also do not misuse the *AMA Guides* by using the percentages to make direct financial disability awards to claimants should be able to withstand further constitutional challenges.

Texas has been the locus of an important challenge to the constitutionality of the wording of the Texas Workers' Compensation Act[20] adopting the *AMA Guides.* In 1993, in the case of *Texas Workers' Compensation Commission v. Garcia,*[21] the Texas Court of Appeals found certain portions of the Texas Act relevant to the *AMA Guides* to be unconstitutional.[22] The trial court made several findings of fact, including that

> [t]he Act adopts an improper use of the Guides . . . and that such use of the Guides as the determining factor to compensate injured workers for losses occasioned by their injuries is unreasonable and arbitrary and is not reasonably related to any individual or societal interest of the State of Texas;
>
> The impairment ratings generated from use of the Guides have no adequate scientific base and have no reasonable relationship to true impairment;
>
> 1. the 15% threshold as a qualification for supplemental benefits is arbitrary in and of itself and further that it is based upon an arbitrary use of the Guides; and
> 2. a significant number of workers . . . who sustain disabling injuries will have less than 15% impairment based on the Guides and thus will be totally denied access to supplemental income benefits under the Act.[23]

Under the federal Equal Protection Clause, the Texas Court of Appeals found unconstitutional the Texas Workers' Compensation Act's misuse of the *AMA Guides* in requiring a 15 percent impairment threshold to collect impairment benefits. The court reasoned that under the Act:

> There is no opportunity for workers who cannot qualify as impaired under the *AMA Guides* to show that they have in fact lost wage earning capacity; workers

---

[19] Brown v. Campbell County Bd. of Educ., 915 S.W.2d 407, 416 (Tenn. 1995).

[20] Tex. Lab. Code Ann. § 408.124.

[21] 862 S.W.2d 61 (Tex. App.—San Antonio 1993).

[22] *Id.*

[23] Texas Workers' Comp. Comm'n v. Garcia, 893 S.W.2d 504, 519–20 (Tex. 1995).

with unlisted impairments, no matter how severe or disabling, are ineligible for any benefits; workers with injuries not severe enough to rise to the presumptively severe level of 15 percent might, due to individual factors, actually be more severely disabled. Most significantly, the Act does not allow any adjustment for individualized factors relating to loss of wage earning capacity.[24]

The Texas Supreme Court reversed the court of appeals and held that the Texas Workers' Compensation Act's use of the *AMA Guides,* albeit imperfect, was not invalid under the equal protection clause.[25] The Texas Supreme Court applied the "rational basis" test in upholding this Act. The Texas Supreme Court also favorably referred to testimony that stated that even though the *AMA Guides* may not be entirely based on broad epidemiological studies, they are a product of a thorough state-of-the-art analysis and are the reference of choice for evaluating impairment.[26]

The Texas Supreme Court noted two challenges in dicta that were not raised by the plaintiffs.[27] The first challenge was whether the Texas Workers' Compensation Act[28] was constitutional as it applied to workers who were not ratable under the *AMA Guides.*[29] The court noted that, unlike other states, the Texas statute made no provision for a different rating system to be used when the *AMA Guides* do not apply.[30] The court also intimated that the legislature's mandating the use of the *AMA Guides* (3d ed. 1988),[31] which is now out of print, could possibly be the basis for a constitutional challenge.[32]

At least one member of the Oklahoma Supreme Court was prepared to hold the adoption of the *AMA Guides* to be an unconstitutional delegation of power by the legislature.[33] The *Davis* court stated:

> Section 3(11) vests in a purely private organization, the American Medical Association, the unbridled authority to set standards for permanent impairment which govern an employee's right to collect compensation for on-the-job injuries. This delegation is made *without guides, restrictions, or standards. . . .* The Legislature may not delegate the legislative power to a privately controlled national organization. Section 3(11) is unconstitutional because it vests the American Medical Association with the authority to determine the standards for the evaluation of permanent impairment—a power reserved to the Legislature acting in its lawmaking capacity.[34]

---

[24] Texas Workers' Comp. Comm'n v. Garcia, 862 S.W.2d 61, 88 (Tex. App.—San Antonio 1993).

[25] Texas Workers' Comp. Comm'n v. Garcia, 893 S.W.2d 504, 524 (Tex. 1995).

[26] *Id.* at 525–26.

[27] *Id.* at 504.

[28] Tex. Lab. Code Ann. § 408.124.

[29] Texas Workers' Comp. Comm'n v. Garcia, 893 S.W.2d 504, 526 (Tex. 1995).

[30] *Id.*

[31] AMA, Guides to the Evaluation of Permanent Impairment (3d ed. 1988) (hereinafter *AMA Guides* (3d ed. 1988)).

[32] Texas Workers' Comp. Comm'n v. Garcia, 893 S.W.2d 504, 526 (Tex. 1995).

[33] Davis v. B.F. Goodrich, 826 P.2d 587 (Okla. 1992).

[34] *Id.* at 599.

The Tennessee Supreme Court has also addressed the constitutionality of Tennessee's adoption of the *AMA Guides* as a result of a lower court's decision. The trial court in *Harless v. Huntsville Manor Nursing Home*[35] had held the Tennessee Workers' Compensation Act's[36] use of the *AMA Guides* to be unconstitutional. The trial court had made several findings of fact, including the following:

1. The condition of low back syndrome or chronic back syndrome is not adequately addressed in the *AMA Guides.*

2. The Tennessee statute is unconstitutional and unfairly discriminates between workers whose medical conditions are recognized by the *AMA Guides* and those whose problems are not, such as workers with mental trauma and chronic pain syndrome.

3. The ratings in the *AMA Guides* have nothing whatever to do with the inability to work.[37]

The Tennessee Supreme Court reversed and held that the Tennessee Workers' Compensation Act's adoption of the *AMA Guides* was constitutional. The court applied the reduced scrutiny of the rational basis test and reasoned that "our recognition that [the workers' compensation] system is imperfect does not mean that it is unconstitutional."[38] The court concluded that the uniformity, fairness, and predictability provided by the *AMA Guides* represented a reasonable and legitimate state interest.[39] "If the *Guides* were not used, medical opinions would be more subjective, and perhaps arbitrary. It is no surprise that most states mandate, recommend, or frequently use the *Guides* in workers' compensation cases."[40] The Tennessee Supreme Court further found that the argument that the adoption of the *AMA Guides* was unconstitutional because the *AMA Guides* are not comprehensive was without merit. The court reasoned that the escape clause written into the statute—that when the injury is not covered by the *AMA Guides,* the rating is to be based on "any appropriate method used and accepted by the medical community"—meant that those persons whose injuries are not covered by the *AMA Guides* are not discriminated against.[41]

Colorado has also seen a constitutional challenge to the way the *AMA Guides* were adopted. The Colorado statute[42] provided for a statutory schedule to be used for the partial loss of hands, arms, feet, legs, sight, or hearing. Compensation for total

---

[35] C.A. No. 7258 (Ch. Ct. Scott County, Tenn., Aug. 31, 1994).

[36] Tenn. Code Ann. § 50-6-204.

[37] Harless v. Huntsville Manor Nursing Home, C.A. No. 7258, at 2, 3 (Ch. Ct. Scott County, Tenn., Aug. 31, 1994).

[38] Brown v. Campbell County Bd. of Educ., 915 S.W.2d 407, 415 (Tenn. 1995).

[39] *Id.*

[40] *Id.* at 416.

[41] *Id.*

[42] Colo. Rev. Stat. § 8-42-42-107(2).

loss was provided from the definition of whole-person impairment under the *AMA Guides*. Under the statute, a worker with a 100 percent impairment of the arm could receive 300 percent more benefits than could a worker with a 95 percent impairment of the arm. The Colorado court upheld the statutory system and reasoned that although the legislative distinctions between partial and total injuries are imperfect, the classification is reasonably related to a legitimate governmental interest.[43]

A later, more specific constitutional challenge to the Colorado statute was also rejected. In the portion of the statute providing that when an injury causes a "partial loss of use of any member" as specified in the schedule, the statutory phrase "partial loss of use of any member" is not void for vagueness.[44] Rather, the court held, the phrase "loss of use" is sufficiently precise to permit persons of common intelligence to understand its meaning, especially since the *AMA Guides* may be used to assist in understanding "loss of use."[45]

The Wyoming Supreme Court, in *Allen v. Natrona County School District One*,[46] also upheld the constitutionality of Wyoming's adoption of the *AMA Guides*. The plaintiff in *Allen* had epicondylitis (tennis elbow), which did not rise to the level of an impairment under the *AMA Guides*. The court held that the adoption of the *AMA Guides* did not violate the equal protection clause as "it is reasonable for the Wyoming State Legislature to pass a statute that does not allow compensation for subjective pain, when such pain does not rise to the level of an impairment."[47]

In *McCabe v. North Dakota Workers' Compensation Bureau*,[48] the court held that statutory language requiring use of the "most recent" or "most current" edition of the *AMA Guides* should be interpreted to mean the most recent edition at the time of the statute's enactment. The court reasoned that this construction was necessary to avoid "significant constitutional conflicts" concerning the delegation of lawmaking authority from the legislature to the American Medical Association. A similar constitutional challenge to adoption of the *AMA Guides* was rejected in New Mexico.[49] The court held that adoption of the *AMA Guides* was not an unlawful delegation of legislative authority and did not violate the due process clause.

It has also been held that mandated use of the *AMA Guides* in evaluating hearing-loss claims does not violate the equal protection clause.[50]

In *Rogers v. Morales*,[51] a claimant suffering from fibromyalgia attempted to have the Texas workers' compensation statute declared unconstitutional because

---

[43] Duran v. Industrial Claim Appeals Office, 883 P.2d 477 (Colo. 1994).

[44] Walker v. Jim Fuoco Motor Co., 942 P.2d 1390, 1393 (Colo. Ct. App. 1997) (interpreting Colo. Rev. Stat. Ann. § 8-42-107(7)(b)).

[45] *Id.*

[46] 811 P.2d 1 (Wyo. 1991).

[47] *Id.* at 4.

[48] 567 N.W.2d 201 (N.D. 1997).

[49] *See* Madrid v. St. Joseph, 928 P.2d 250 (N.M. 1996).

[50] Green v. Glass, 920 P.2d 1081 (Okla. Ct. App. 1996).

[51] 975 F. Supp. 856 (N.D. Tex. 1997).

the claimant's condition was not listed in the *AMA Guides*. The federal court dismissed the case without prejudice under the abstention doctrine as the matter was more properly decided in a Texas state court.

A due process challenge to Pennsylvania's workers' compensation provision dealing with the *AMA Guides* was dismissed because it was not ripe for adjudication.[52] An equal protection challenge to the Pennsylvania workers' compensation provision addressing the calculation of hearing loss and the *AMA Guides* was rejected. The court held that the application of the binaural hearing test set out in the *AMA Guides* to a claimant who suffered work-related hearing loss in one ear did not deprive claimant of his equal protection rights. The claimant asserted that the application of the test unconstitutionally distinguished between two types of monaural hearing loss; however, the court found the use of the binaural test was neither arbitrary nor unreasonable, especially in light of the fact that the Pennsylvania Workers' Compensation Act addressed the different causation for monaural and binaural loss.[53]

The Arkansas Court of Appeals has held that range-of-motion testing under the *AMA Guides* can be invalidated if it can be shown that such testing can come under the voluntary control of the patient.[54]

The Texas Division of Workers' Compensation published advisories to deal with problems in the diagnosis-related estimate (DRE) spinal method mandated in the fourth edition of the *Guides*. These were held invalid because they contradict the *Guides* and thus the statute that enacted the *Guides*.[55]

A sharply divided Supreme Court of Appeals in West Virginia had held invalid the DRE method used in the fourth edition of the *Guides*.[56] The *Repass* court reasoned that the DRE method conflicted with the applicable statute in several areas, including the proper time for making an impairment rating, the proper treatment of progressive injuries, the procedure for reopening of a claim, and the consideration of a second injury.

The sixth edition of the *Guides* warns physicians that the *Guides* and their opinions are challengeable under *Daubert v. Merrell Dow Pharmaceuticals*[57] and Federal Rule of Evidence 702.[58] Notably, no arguments or talking points in defense of the admissibility of the *Guides* are provided. Concluding advice regarding such challenges is given by the sixth edition as follows:

> What does this all mean to the independent medical examiners offering medical expert testimony in legal proceedings? The U.S. Supreme Court said it best

---

[52] Philadelphia Fed'n of Teachers v. Ridge, 150 F.3d 319 (3d Cir. 1998).

[53] Kerstetter v. W.C.A.B. (Steel Tech.), 772 A.2d 1051, 1053–154 (Pa. Commw. Ct. 2001).

[54] Department of Parks & Tourism v. Helms, 959 S.W.2d 749 (Ark. Ct. App. 1998).

[55] Texas Dep't of Ins. v. Lumbermen's Mut. Ins. Co., 212 S.W.3d 870 (Tex. App.—Austin 2006).

[56] Repass v. Workers' Comp. Div., 569 S.E.2d 162 (W. Va. 2002).

[57] 509 U.S. 579 (1993).

[58] *AMA Guides* (6th ed. 2008) at 29.

in General Electric vs. Joiner: "The court need not accept testimony of an expert which is connected to data only by the *Ipse Dixit* of the expert."[59]

This is yet another remarkable statement in the *Guides* for two reasons. First, it shows the bias of the sixth edition toward IME physicians and against treating doctors (who are not even mentioned). Second, and most important, the statement agrees that unsupported assertions (*ipse dixit*) need not be accepted by courts of law. One could certainly argue that the *Guides* continue to be based, as past editions have been, not on science but on "legal fiction," "consensus," and other unsupported assertions.

---

[59] *Ibid.*

CHAPTER 4

AMA GUIDES, FIFTH EDITION

Christopher R. Brigham, MD[*]

---

* The authors wish to thank Christopher R. Brigham, MD, the original author of this chapter.

§ 4.01   INTRODUCTION

The fifth edition of the American Medical Association's *Guides to the Evaluation of Permanent Impairment* (hereinafter *AMA Guides,* 5th ed. (2000)) contained numerous changes that affected systems that use the *AMA Guides,* claimants, evaluators, and attorneys. Nearly twice the size of the preceding edition (613 pages versus 339 pages) and containing 18 chapters rather than 15 chapters, the fifth edition split the discussion of the musculoskeletal system into three chapters and the cardiovascular system into two. This chapter examines the major changes, focusing in particular on the assessment of musculoskeletal pain, neurological, mental, and behavioral disorders, and pain—the problems most frequently encountered in workers' compensation cases.

Linda Cocchiarella, MD, and Gunnar B.J. Andersson, MD, PhD, served as editors of the fifth edition of the *AMA Guides,* and development was performed in conjunction with numerous organizations and individuals. In mid-1997, Steering and Senior Advisory Committees were established. Some members of these committees expressed their concerns about the *AMA Guides* and offered recommendations that were published in the *Journal of the American Medical Association* (hereinafter *JAMA*) on January 26, 2000.[1] The committees' criticisms focused on two areas:

1.   Internal deficiencies, including the lack of a comprehensive, valid, reliable, unbiased, and evidence-based system for rating impairments; and

2.   The way in which workers' compensation systems use the ratings, resulting in inappropriate compensation.

The committees suggested that, to maintain wide acceptance of the *AMA Guides,* the authors needed to improve the *Guides'* ratings, validity, internal consistency, and comprehensiveness; document reliability and reproducibility of the results; and make the *AMA Guides* easily comprehensible and accessible to physicians.

The committees' primary concerns were that the *AMA Guides* failed to provide a comprehensive, valid, reliable, unbiased, and evidence-based system; offered impairment ratings that did not reflect loss of function; and provided numerical ratings that represented legal fiction, not medical reality. The committees also were concerned about how the *AMA Guides'* ratings were used. The authors did, however, recognize that the *AMA Guides* play an essential role in rating impairment, as well as the need for a valid and reliable system for rating impairment. The authors of the *JAMA* article made the following specific recommendations:

1.   The *AMA Guides* should provide a system to rate permanent impairments, including functional limitations.

---

[1] E.A. Spieler, P.S. Barth, J.F. Burton, J. Himerstein, L. Rudolph, *Recommendations to Guide Revisions of the* Guides to the Evaluation of Permanent Impairment, 283 JAMA 519–23 (2000).

2. Impairment ratings should be based on scientific evidence.
3. Impairment ratings should be based on a valid whole-person impairment (WPI) scale that accurately reflects functional loss.
4. The impairment ratings should be reliable.
5. The *AMA Guides* should be comprehensive.
6. The *AMA Guides* should be internally consistent.
7. The *AMA Guides* should be comprehensible.
8. The system for ratings should be accessible.
9. The *AMA Guides* should be acceptable.

The editors of the fifth edition of the *AMA Guides* responded to the impairment evaluation challenges.[2] Although the fifth edition addressed some shortcomings of earlier editions, problems remained.

§ 4.02 CHAPTER 1: PHILOSOPHY, PURPOSE, AND APPROPRIATE USE OF THE *AMA GUIDES*

The first two chapters in the fifth edition present the philosophy and key principles involved in assessing impairment. Therefore, anyone using the fifth edition must understand this content before performing an impairment evaluation. Because many evaluating physicians appear to be unfamiliar with the content of the first two chapters, key principles and rules for evaluation are often not followed, giving rise to numerous lawsuits that challenge the ratings. Chapter 1 in the fifth edition is longer than Chapter 1 in the fourth edition (16 versus 10 pages), contains further detail, and incorporates content that had been provided in the Appendix of the fourth edition.

The stated purpose of the *AMA Guides* is to "update the diagnostic criteria and evaluation process used in impairment assessment, incorporating available scientific evidence and prevailing medical opinion."[3] The first printing of the fifth edition does contain a number of errors that are to be corrected in the second printing.

Readers are advised, "It is strongly recommended that physicians use this latest edition, the fifth edition, when rating impairment."[4] This is similar to the statement in the fourth edition that "[t]he AMA strongly discourages the use of any but the most recent edition of the *Guides*."[5] It is probable some physicians and

---

[2] L. Cocchiarella, M.A. Turk, G.B.H. Andersson, *Improving the Evaluation of Permanent Impairment, Recommendations to Guide Revisions of the* Guides to the Evaluation of Permanent Impairment, 283 JAMA 532–33 (2000).

[3] AMA, Guides to the Evaluation of Permanent Impairment (5th ed. 2000) (hereinafter *AMA Guides* (5th ed. 2000)) at 1.

[4] *Id.* at 2.

[5] AMA, Guides to the Evaluation of Permanent Impairment (4th ed. 1993) (hereinafter *AMA Guides* (4th ed. 1993)) at 5.

AMA Guides users were unaware of the availability of the fifth edition for some time. State statutes that deal with the *AMA Guides* may or may not specify which edition to use and how they are to be used. Several jurisdictions stipulate use of a specific edition of the *AMA Guides,* and they undoubtedly analyzed the fifth edition to determine its impact before adopting it as the basis for rating impairment.

[A] Impairment in the *AMA Guides*

Impairment continues to be defined as "the loss of, loss of use of, or derangement of any body part, system or function."[6] Impairment is no longer defined as a condition that interferes with an individual's ability to perform activities of daily living (ADLs). It may, however, lead to functional limitations or the inability to perform ADLs. If an impairment does not interfere with an ADL, it is not ratable. If it does interfere, it qualifies for an impairment rating. ADLs are specified in Table 1-2, Activities of Daily Living Commonly Measured in Activities of Daily Living (ADL) and Instrumental Activities of Daily Living (IADL) Scales,[7] and include self-care, communications, physical activity, sensory functions, nonspecialized hand activity, travel, sexual function, and sleep. ADLs no longer include social activities, recreational activities, and work.

[B] Maximum Medical Improvement

Impairment is considered permanent when it reaches *maximum medical improvement* (MMI), meaning the impairment is well-stabilized and unlikely to change substantially in the next year with or without medical treatment. In the fourth edition of the *AMA Guides,* an impairment was also considered permanent if it was unlikely to change by more than 3 percent in the next year. This criterion is omitted from the fifth edition.

The fifth edition compared definitions and interpretations of impairment and disability, including those promulgated by the World Health Organization (1999), the Social Security Administration (1995), and typical state workers' compensation laws. This information is presented in Table 1-1, Definitions and Interpretations of Impairment and Disability,[8] which also explains the physician's role.

The fifth edition emphasized objective assessment, necessitating a medical evaluation. Impairment may lead to functional limitations or the inability to perform ADLs and reflects a change from normal or "preexisting" status. Some chapters placed a greater emphasis on either anatomic loss or functional loss.

Anatomic loss refers to measurable loss of a body structure or organ system, whereas functional loss refers to change in function.

---

[6] *AMA Guides* (5th ed. 2000) at 2.

[7] *Id.* at 4.

[8] *Id.* at 3.

[C]   Normal

Normal refers to a range that represents healthy functioning; it varies with age, gender, and other factors. Normal is defined from either an individual or a population perspective, depending on the pre-injury or pre-illness information that is available and the physician's clinical judgment. Normal for the individual may be determined by comparison to pre-injury or pre-illness status or, for example, comparison of an injured extremity to the contralateral uninjured extremity. This clarification is a significant change from the position taken in the fourth edition. The fifth edition advises, "Where population values are not available, the physician should use clinical judgment regarding normal structure and function and estimate what is normal for the individual based on the physician's estimate of the individual's preinjury or preillness condition."[9] The fifth edition also states that "if an individual has previous measurements of function that were below or above average population values, the physician may discuss that prior value and any subsequent loss for the individual, as well as compare it to the population normal."[10]

[D]   Impairment Criteria

Impairment criteria were designed to "provide a standardized method for physicians to use to determine medical impairment" and "were developed from scientific evidence as cited and from consensus of chapter authors or of medical specialty societies."[11] Although the fifth edition of the *AMA Guides* uses objective and scientifically based data when available, the degree of impairment often remains based on the clinical experience and consensus of the contributors to the fifth edition.

[E]   Impairment Percentages and Impairment Percentage Changes

The fifth edition stated that impairment percentages are "consensus-driven estimates that reflect the severity of the medical condition to which the impairment decreases an individual's ability to perform common activities of daily living (ADL), *excluding work.*"[12] This explicit exclusion for work was new and was potentially problematic because some workers' compensation jurisdictions use impairment rating as a proxy for inability to work. The fifth edition stated that work is not included in the clinical judgment for impairment because (1) it involves many activities and is highly individualized; (2) work and occupations change; and

---

[9] *Id.* at 2.
[10] *Id.* at 4.
[11] *Id.*
[12] *Id.* (Emphasis in original.)

(3) impairment interacts with such other factors as the worker's age, education, and prior work experience to determine the extent of occupational disability.

Some workers' compensation jurisdictions use impairment ratings from the fifth edition of the *AMA Guides* as a direct correlation with work capability. Although such ratings are not direct determinates of occupational disability, the fifth edition states that it is "appropriate for a physician knowledgeable about the work activities of the patient to discuss the specific activities the worker can and cannot do, given the permanent impairment."[13]

Impairment percentages in the fifth edition are largely unchanged from those in the fourth edition because the majority of ratings are currently accepted, there is limited scientific data to support changes, and ratings should not be changed arbitrarily. However, "some percentages have been changed for greater scientific accuracy or to achieve consistency throughout the book."[14] Among the most significant changes are spinal impairment ratings, now only performed at MMI, and the assessment of impairment for pain. With the spine, the diagnosis-related estimate (DRE) method now considers treatment outcomes. The whole-person impairment for each remaining category may be adjusted within a range of 3 percent. "If residual symptoms or objective findings impact the ability to perform ADL despite treatment, the higher percentage in each range should be assigned."[15] The fifth edition also recognizes that motion at a spinal segment may be abnormally decreased (fusion), as well as increased (instability), and references alteration, not just loss, of motion segment integrity. Hence, DRE Category IV now includes a single-level spinal fusion. In Chapter 18, titled "Pain," it is stated that under certain circumstances, a further impairment of up to 3 percent whole-person permanent impairment may be provided; however, this incremental impairment cannot be given in addition to the 3 percent impairment range for the spine.

[F]   Range of Ratings

Ratings vary from 0 percent to 100 percent whole-person permanent impairment. Zero percent whole-person rating implies no significant organ or body system functional consequences and no limitation of the performance of common ADLs. A 90 percent to 100 percent whole-person impairment rating reflects very severe organ or body system impairment and requires the individual to be fully dependent on others for self-care, approaching death.

[G]   Disability

Disability continues to be defined as "an alteration of an individual's capacity to meet personal, social, or occupational demands or statutory or regulatory

---

[13] *Id.* at 5.

[14] *Id.*

[15] *Id.* at 381.

requirements because of an impairment."[16] The use of the term *activity limitations* as opposed to *disability* avoids the stigma and labeling associated with the former, and emphasizes the person's residual ability. Impairment evaluation is only one aspect of disability determination, which also includes information about the individual's skills, education, job history, adaptability, and age, as well as environmental requirements and modification availability.

Impairment ratings are designed to reflect the severity of an organ or body system impairment and resulting functional limitations. Regional musculoskeletal impairments are provided with various weights and are converted to whole-person impairments. For example, loss of a hand is equivalent to 90 percent upper extremity impairment, complete loss of the upper extremity is equivalent to 60 percent whole-person permanent impairment, and complete loss of the lower extremity is equivalent to 40 percent whole-person permanent impairment. These conversion factors remain the same in the fifth edition of the *AMA Guides.*

[H]   Combining Impairments

Most impairments are not added but combined, so multiple impairments are equal to or less than the sum of all the individual impairment values. The process of combining reflects that, when considering two impairments, the combined impairment is equal to the first impairment plus the second impairment as it relates to the remaining portion that is unimpaired. The values are derived from the formula $A + B (1 - A)$, where A and B are the decimal equivalents of the two ratings. To simplify the process, values are provided in the Combined Values Chart.[17] The fifth edition recognizes that a scientific formula has not been established to indicate the best way to combine multiple impairments and that some impairments together may result in greater loss than by just adding them.

In general, regional impairments are combined before combining the regional impairment rating with that from another region. There are a few exceptions to combining impairments, for example, joint impairments at the same joint, impairments of the thumb, and digit impairments reflected as hand impairments are added.

The fifth edition states, "[T]he *Guides* uses objective and scientifically based data when available and references these sources. When objective data has not been identified, estimates of the degree of impairment are used, based on clinical experience and consensus."[18]

---

[16] *Id.* at 8.

[17] *Id.* at 604–06.

[18] *Id.* at 10.

[I] Subjective Complaints

Subjective complaints, such as fatigue or pain, when not accompanied by demonstrable organ dysfunction, clinical signs, or other independent, measurable abnormalities, are generally not ratable. These unratable disorders include fibromyalgia, chronic fatigue syndrome, and multiple chemical sensitivity. The Arkansas Appeals Court has held that straight-leg raising and range-of-motion (ROM) testing are not "objective findings" under Arkansas's Workers' Compensation Act despite any language to the contrary in the *Guides.*[19]

[J] Pain

A significant change in the fifth edition is that pain may be ratable under certain circumstances; for example, when there is an underlying organic cause and the conventional impairment rating does not adequately reflect the extent of functional loss. Pain evaluation is performed as outlined in Chapter 18. "If the patient appears to have pain-related impairment that has increased the burden of his or her condition *slightly,* the examiner may increase the percentage . . . by up to 3%."[20] Furthermore, "[I]f the examiner performs a formal pain-related impairment rating, he or she may increase the percentage . . . by up to 3%; *and* . . . should classify the individual's pain-related impairment into one of four categories: mild, moderate, moderately severe, or severe. In addition, the examiner should determine whether the pain-related impairment is ratable or unratable."[21] A pain-related impairment score can be determined; however, this is not an impairment rating.

[K] Clinical Judgment

The fifth edition recognizes that research on the reproducibility and validity of the *AMA Guides* is limited and that this is an opportunity for improvement in future editions. It is also recognized that the *Guides* cannot provide a framework for evaluating all conditions, including new or complex conditions:

> In situations where impairment ratings are not provided, the *Guides* suggest that physicians use clinical judgment, comparing measurable impairment resulting from similar conditions with similar impairment of function in performing activities of daily living. The physician's judgment, based upon experience, training, skill, thoroughness in clinical evaluation, and ability to apply the *Guides* criteria as intended, will enable an appropriate and reproducible assessment to be made of clinical impairment.[22]

---

[19] *See* Mays v. Alumnitec, 64 S.W.3d 772, 774–75 (Ark. Ct. App. 2001).

[20] *Id.* at 573.

[21] *Id.*

[22] *Id.* at 11.

[L]   Causation and Apportionment

The assessment of causation is critical in determining the extent of impairment that is attributable to a specific event. The fifth edition provides greater discussion of this topic and the analysis of apportionment. Before determining apportionment, the physician must be able to first document a prior factor, then determine that the current permanent impairment is greater as a result of the prior factor, and finally determine that the prior factor caused or contributed to the impairment.

The New Hampshire Supreme Court dealt with apportionment in the case *Appeal of Fournier.*[23] In *Fournier,* the claimant had developed carpal tunnel syndrome in her right wrist in May 1992. Both the treating physician and the independent medical examination (IME) physician gave the claimant a 10 percent impairment rating of the right upper extremity under the fourth edition of the *Guides.* Previously, in 1986, the claimant was diagnosed with a work-related thoracic outlet syndrome and was awarded 25 percent permanent partial disability for her right upper extremity. The court held that the proper way to deal with the previous injury to a different area of the upper extremity was to combine the impairment percentages for the two injuries and then subtract the previous 25 percent impairment. This resulted in an additional 8 percent impairment.

[M]   Use of the *AMA Guides* in Legal Proceedings

Many states require the use of the *AMA Guides* in their workers' compensation systems. State statutes that deal with the *AMA Guides* may or may not specify which edition to use and how the *Guides* are to be used. In any case, it is the ultimate responsibility of the courts to interpret these statutes and determine which edition of the *Guides* is to be used and how that edition is to be used. The fifth edition references a survey completed in 1999 that indicated that 41 of 51 jurisdictions in the United States make use of the *AMA Guides,* in addition to jurisdictions in Canada, Australia, New Zealand, and South Africa.

[N]   Impairment Percentages/Financial Awards

The fifth edition provides a brief overview of impairment evaluations in workers' compensation. The fourth edition contains only the following statement in boldface type:

> **It must be emphasized and clearly understood that impairment percentages derived according to the *Guides* criteria should not be used to make direct financial awards or direct estimates of disabilities.**[24]

---

[23] 786 A.2d 854 (N.H. 2001).
[24] *AMA Guides* (4th ed. 1993) at 5.

The comparable statement in the *AMA Guides* (5th ed. 2000) is as follows:

> **Impairment percentages derived from the *Guides* criteria should not be used as direct estimates of disability. Impairment percentages estimate the extent of the impairment on whole person functioning and account for basic activities of daily living, not including work. The complexity of work activities requires individual analyses. Impairment assessment is a necessary *first step* for determining disability.**[25]

[O]   Work Disability and Future Employment

The fifth edition notes that "there is no validated formula that assigns accurate weight to determine how a medical condition can be combined with other factors, including education, skill, and the like to calculate the effect of the medical impairment on future employment."[26] The fifth edition is a tool for evaluating permanent impairment, not disability.

Although the *AMA Guides* only assess impairment, "physicians with the appropriate skills, training, and knowledge may address some of the implications of the medical impairment toward work disability and future employment."[27] Combining medical and nonmedical information, including detailed information about essential work activities, is required for understanding the degree to which an impairment may affect an individual's work ability.

A brief summary of the Federal Employer's Liability Act (FELA) is provided in the fifth edition, as was done in the fourth edition. The fifth edition also provides an overview of the Americans with Disabilities Act (ADA), presenting key definitions.

§ 4.03   CHAPTER 2: PRACTICAL APPLICATION OF THE *AMA GUIDES*

Chapter 2 in the fifth edition describes how to use the fifth edition for "consistent and reliable acquisition, analysis, communication, and utilization of medical information through a single set of standards."[28] The goal is that two physicians following the methods defined in the fifth edition should reach similar conclusions. As in the fourth edition, it is noted, "If the clinical findings are fully described, any knowledgeable observer may check the findings with the *Guides* criteria."[29]

---

[25] *AMA Guides* (5th ed. 2000) at 13.

[26] *Id.*

[27] *Id.*

[28] *AMA Guides* (5th ed. 2000) at 17.

[29] *Id.*

The fifth edition contrasts impairment evaluations and independent medical evaluations. *Impairment evaluation* is defined in Section 2.1 as "a medical evaluation performed by a physician, using a standard method as outlined in the *Guides* to determine permanent impairment associated with a medical condition."[30] A treating physician or a nontreating physician may perform impairment ratings. An independent medical evaluation is performed by a physician who does not provide care for the individual. Independent medical evaluations are usually more comprehensive.

[A] New Responsibilities of Evaluator

Section 2.3 discusses the impairment evaluator's role and responsibilities, which include understanding regulations applicable to workers' compensation or personal injury evaluations, providing the necessary medical assessment to the party requesting the examination with the examinee's consent, and ensuring the examinee understands the evaluation is for assessment, not treatment. The statement that the "physician's role in performing an impairment evaluation is to provide an independent, unbiased assessment of the individual's medical condition including its effect on function, and identify abilities and limitations to performing activities as listed in Table 1-2"[31] provides an opportunity to challenge many ratings. In addition, it states, "[I]f new diagnoses are discovered, the physician has a medical obligation to inform the requesting party and individual about the condition and recommend further medical assessment."[32] This statement has interesting implications, because it does not establish clear boundaries between an evaluating and consultative role.

[B] Maximum Medical Improvement

Permanent impairment ratings are performed when the individual is at MMI. The fifth edition recognizes that an individual's condition is dynamic. MMI is defined as the "date from which further recovery or deterioration is not anticipated, although over time there may be some expected change."[33]

[C] Which Chapter to Use

"Generally, the organ system where the problems originate or where the dysfunction is the greatest is the chapter to be used for evaluating impairment."[34]

---

[30] *AMA Guides* (5th ed. 2000) at 18.
[31] *Id.*
[32] *Id.* at 18.
[33] *Id.* at 19.
[34] *Id.*

The fifth edition states that "whenever the same impairment is discussed in different chapters, the *Guides* tries to use consistent impairment ratings across the different organ systems." There are still inconsistencies between chapters. For example, there are significant inconsistencies in the rating of reflex sympathetic dystrophy (RSD), causalgia, and complex regional pain syndrome (CRPS), depending on whether the rating is performed using Chapter 13, "The Central and Peripheral Nervous System," Chapter 16, "The Upper Extremities," or Chapter 18, "Pain."

[D]   Rules for Evaluation

Section 2.5, "Rules for Evaluation," provides key content relating to confidentiality; combining impairment ratings; consistency; interpolation, measurement, and rounding off; pain; using assistive devices in evaluations; adjusting for effects of treatment or lack of treatment; and for changes in impairment from prior ratings. The fifth edition now includes a discussion of confidentiality, specifying "prior to performing an impairment evaluation, the physician obtains the individual's consent to share the medical information with other parties that will be reviewing the evaluation."[35]

When combining impairment ratings, evaluators are advised to "begin with an estimate of the individual's most significant (primary) impairment and evaluate other impairments in relation to it."[36]

[E]   Consistency

Consistency is a critical issue in the rating of impairment, for if clinical examination data are either invalid or unreliable, the rating will be erroneous. As in the fourth edition, it is noted that, "if in spite of any observation or test result, the medical evidence appears insufficient to verify that an impairment of a certain magnitude exists, the physician may modify the impairment rating accordingly and then describe and explain the reason for the modification in writing."[37] The same guidelines for interpolating, measuring, and rounding off apply, but instructions now indicate the final rating should be rounded to the nearest whole number. The fourth edition stated the final impairment "may be rounded to the nearer of the two nearest values ending in 0 or 5";[38] however, this would introduce error that could have significant impact on how ratings are used.

---

[35] *Id.*
[36] *Id.*
[37] *Id.*
[38] *Id.*

[F] Pain

Although the fifth edition states that "the impairment ratings in the body organ system chapters make allowance for any accompanying pain,"[39] as explained previously, there may be further pain-related impairment. "If an examining physician determines that an individual has pain-related impairment, he or she will have the additional task of deciding whether or not that impairment has already been adequately incorporated into the rating the person has received on the basis of other chapters of the *Guides*."[40] Advice on using assistive devices and adjustments for treatment or lack of treatment remains unchanged.

[G] Apportionment

Section 2.5h, "Changes in Impairment from Prior Ratings," provides a clearer discussion of apportionment. For example, "the physician should assess the current state of the impairment according to the criteria in the *Guides*. If an individual received an impairment rating from an earlier edition and needs to be reevaluated because of a change in the medical condition, the individual is evaluated according to the latest information pertaining to the condition in the current edition of the *Guides*."[41] In *Kentucky River Enterprises, Inc. v. Elkins*,[42] the court upheld a rating of 9.5 percent for a back injury occurring in 2000 even though a previous 1989 back injury had been rated at 14 percent. The court reasoned that it is possible that the claimant had recovered from the 1989 injury and that the appellant failed to raise the argument that apportionment was calculated contrary to the directives of the *AMA Guides*.

[H] Preparing Reports

In the fifth edition, Section 2.6, "Preparing Reports," is divided into three steps:

1. Clinical evaluation;
2. Calculation of impairment; and
3. Discussion of how the impairment rating was calculated.

In the fourth edition, Section 2.4, the three steps were:

1. Medical evaluation;
2. Analysis of findings; and
3. Comparison of the analysis results with the impairment criteria.

---

[39] *Id.* at 20.
[40] *Id.* at 570.
[41] *Id.* at 20.
[42] 107 S.W.3d 206 (Ky. 2003).

Again, the fifth edition states that a "clear, accurate, and complete report is essential."[43] Section 2.6 differentiates between items included in all impairment reports (in bold) and those that are commonly found in independent medical examinations or may be requested for inclusion (in italics). This is illustrated in Table 3, Preparing Reports.

§ 4.04   CHAPTERS 3–14: OTHER SYSTEMS

Most impairment evaluations deal with painful disorders involving the spine, upper extremities, or lower extremities; therefore, Chapters 15 through 18 are used most frequently. Chapters 3 through 13 deal with other organ systems, and Chapter 14 focuses on mental and behavioral disorders. With the notable exception of Chapter 12, "Vision," these chapters have not fundamentally changed. For the most part minor changes to the text and tables have been made, medical approaches have been updated, and further case examples have been included.

[A]   The Cardiovascular System

In the fifth edition, the cardiovascular system is presented in two chapters: Chapter 3, "The Cardiovascular System: Heart and Aorta," and Chapter 4, "Cardiovascular System: Systemic and Pulmonary Arteries," as opposed to a single chapter in the *AMA Guides* (4th ed. 1993), Chapter 6, "The Cardiovascular System." Chapter 3 reflects new information about valvular disease, the important prognostic impact of left ventricular function on individuals with coronary artery disease, and the inclusion of silent ischemia and coronary artery spasm with regard to impairment, as well as information about cardiomyopathy, including the impact of human immunodeficiency virus (HIV)—related conditions on cardiac function. Chapter 4 incorporates new guidelines on hypertension and expands the section on pulmonary hypertension.

[B]   The Respiratory System

Chapter 5, "The Respiratory System" (also Chapter 5 in the fourth edition), was revised to include criteria for asthma impairment based on guidelines published by the American Thoracic Society and includes a section on sleep apnea. Respiratory impairment criteria now incorporate the lower limits of normal for forced vital capacity (FVC), forced expiratory volume in the first second (FEV1), and the diffusing capacity for carbon monoxide (DCO). Respiratory impairments, such as a limited pleural plaque, that do not affect lung function or ADLs, although considered an impairment, are not given an impairment rating. Section 5.3

---

[43] *AMA Guides* (5th ed. 2000) at 21.

provides a discussion of tobacco use and environmental—occupational exposure associated with respiratory disease. In *Excelsior Hotel v. Squires*,[44] the appeals court found that there was substantial evidence to support a 30 percent lung impairment secondary to fractured ribs.

[C] The Digestive System

Chapter 6, "The Digestive System," is similar to Chapter 10 in the fourth edition; however, changes in impairment ratings have occurred to reflect improvements in treatment, for example, permanent impairment for ulcer disease has essentially been eradicated due to new treatment approaches. There is more consistency among impairments as they relate to impact on the ability to perform ADLs. Weight loss is an essential criterion.

[D] The Urinary and Reproductive Systems

Chapter 7, "The Urinary and Reproductive Systems" (Chapter 11 in the fourth edition), includes revisions of criteria for upper and lower urinary tract impairment, the process for rating bladder impairment by incorporating results of urodynamic studies, and reproductive system sections. All the tables were revised to eliminate overlap in ratings.

[E] The Skin

Chapter 8, "Skin," provides the same approach to rating impairment as does Chapter 13 in the fourth edition. New sections on contact dermatitis and natural rubber latex allergy are provided.

[F] The Hematopoietic System

Chapter 9, "Hematopoietic System," is similar to Chapter 7 in the fourth edition; however, there is a new table providing a functional classification of hematologic disease, and there are expanded sections on HIV and thrombotic disorders.

[G] The Endocrine System

Chapter 10, "Endocrine System," updated from the fourth edition's Chapter 12, provides descriptions of endocrine gland function and nomenclature of test

---

[44] 2005 WL 2375225 (Ark. Ct. App. Sept. 28, 2005).

procedures and of disease entities, including diabetes mellitus. The criteria for percentage of impairment have remained the same.

[H]   Ear, Nose, and Throat and Related Structures

Chapter 11, "Ear, Nose, Throat, and Related Structures" (Chapter 9 in the fourth edition), added a new section on voice impairment, added a new table on vestibular disorders, and combined facial disorders and disfigurements. The Supreme Court of Kentucky has held that statistical evidence of age-related hearing loss does not rebut a statutory presumption that a binaural hearing impairment that converts to 8 percent or more under the *AMA Guides* is entirely work related.[45]

[I]   The Visual System

Chapter 12, "Visual System," has been totally revised from the fourth edition's Chapter 8. The assessment of visual system impairment is now based on a functional approach, reflected by a functional acuity score (FAS) and a functional field score (FFS). Chapter 12 is designed to be used by ophthalmologists.

[J]   The Central and Peripheral Nervous System

Chapter 13, "The Central and Peripheral Nervous System," was expanded considerably (from 13 pages in the fourth edition), where it appeared as Chapter 4, to 51 pages in the fifth edition. The fundamentals of rating conditions affecting the nervous system remain largely unchanged.

There are some changes in the criteria for rating impairment due to central nervous system disorders, as explained in Section 13.2, "Criteria for Rating Impairment Due to Central Nervous System Disorders,"[46] and Section 13.3, "Criteria for Rating Cerebral Impairments."[47] Section 13.3f, "Emotional or Behavioral Impairments," now explicitly states that "psychiatric manifestations and impairments that do not have documented neurological impairments are evaluated using the criteria in the chapter on mental and behavioral impairments."[48] Much of the expansion in Chapter 13 was due to inclusion of additional cases to illustrate each area of impairment. Chapter 13 also included a new section discussing criteria for rating impairments related to chronic pain.

---

[45] AK Steel Corp. v. Johnston, 153 S.W.3d 837 (Ky. 2005).
[46] *AMA Guides* (5th ed. 2000) at 308.
[47] *Id.* at 309–27.
[48] *Id.* at 325.

[K] Mental and Behavioral Disorders

Taking the same approach as in the fourth edition, the fifth edition does not provide numeric ratings for psychological disorders in Chapter 14, "Mental and Behavioral Disorders." Revisions include a discussion of the *Diagnostic and Statistical Manual of Mental Disorders* (*DSM-IV*), the removal of the discussion on Social Security disability, the addition of more case examples, and the inclusion of a summary template of factors to be included in psychiatric assessment. *Lanter v. Kentucky State Police*[49] affirmed a finding by an administrative law judge that a person with behavioral symptoms following physical brain damage should be evaluated only under Chapter 13, not under Chapter 13 in combination with Chapter 14.

§ 4.05 CHAPTER 15: SPINE

Spinal impairment evaluation is the most frequent application of the *AMA Guides*, and the fifth edition contains several changes to this process. In the fourth edition, all musculoskeletal evaluation and rating was described in one chapter, Chapter 3. In the fifth edition, such evaluation and rating are divided into three chapters: Chapter 15, "Spine," Chapter 16, "The Upper Extremities," and Chapter 17, "The Lower Extremities." In the fourth edition, "Spine" was Section 3.3.

[A] Models and Methods for Rating Spinal Impairment

The "models" for rating spinal impairment are called "methods" in the fifth edition. In the fourth edition, the injury or DRE model labeled the spinal regions cervicothoracic, thoracolumbar, and lumbosacral. However, the ROM model used conventional nomenclature: cervical, thoracic, and lumbar. The fifth edition reverted to standard terminology for spinal regions in the DRE method, and both rating techniques now refer to cervical, thoracic, and lumbar. In *Adams v. Coastal Coal Co.*,[50] an appeals court affirmed an ALJ's decision to choose to accept the employer's physician's rating based on DRE, as opposed to the employee's physician's rating based on ROM.

[B] Which Methods to Use

The language requiring the use of the DRE, rather than the ROM, method is strengthened in the fifth edition; however, the decision-making process may result in controversies about which method to use. The process of determining the appropriate method is described in Section 15.2, "Determining the Appropriate Method

---

[49] 171 S.W.3d 45 (Ky. 2005).
[50] 2005 WL 2674978 (Ky. Oct. 20, 2005).

for Assessment."[51] Although the fourth edition required use of the DRE method for rating spinal injuries, the language was confusing, and many physicians continued to employ the ROM approach. Instructions in the fifth edition are to use the DRE method in any patient having sustained an injury, except for the specific conditions of multilevel or recurrent radiculopathy in the same spinal area or multilevel fractures or loss of structural integrity in the same spinal area. The ROM method is to be used only for those patients with those conditions, and patients being evaluated for administrative purposes, such as for retirement. The use of ROM method may also be mandated by certain jurisdictions.

In the fourth edition, the spinal impairment rating per the injury model (DRE) was based only on the results of the injury, not on the final outcome.

In the fifth edition, the rating is based on the findings when the individual is at maximum medical improvement, as explained in Section 15.3, "Diagnosis-Related Estimates Model." Findings that were described in the record but that have disappeared by the time of the rating examination are not considered, with the exception of an individual with radiculopathy. If a patient had an objectively diagnosed radiculopathy that resolved with nonsurgical intervention, the rating would be at least a DRE Category II, minor impairment (5 percent to 8 percent whole-person permanent impairment); if surgery was required for this radiculo-pathy, the rating would be at least a DRE Category III, radiculopathy, even if the objective signs of the radiculopathy have resolved.

[C]   Range of Impairment 3 Percent

Each category now includes a range of impairment ratings of 3 percent. For instance, a patient in Lumbar Category III can be given a rating from 10 percent to 13 percent whole-person impairment. The higher rating requires some objective evidence that a definite residual remains. A complaint of continuing pain does not in itself justify increasing the rating because this is expected with spinal injuries. A rating higher in the range is given if there is more significant interference with ADLs. A higher rating within a category cannot be given simultaneously to the 3 percent whole-person permanent impairment provided in Chapter 18, "Pain."

[D]   Clinical Objective Findings

"Clinical objective findings" are used to assist in placing patients in cate-gories and are presented in Box 15-1.[52] The term *differentiator* was abandoned, and for the most part objective findings were defined more precisely. If a patient has no objective findings at the time of the evaluation, there is no ratable impairment, unless there had been a previously documented significant radiculopathy or a

---

[51] *AMA Guides* (5th ed. 2000) at 379–81.
[52] *Id.* at 382–83.

fracture. In *Earls v. Sompo Japan Insurance Co. of America*,[53] the court accepted a physician's DRE Category II rating based on the "objective" evidence of decreased range of motion and guarding in the examination.

[E] Whiplash

A patient who sustains a hyperextension cervical injury, that is, "whiplash," and has documented guarding historically but who has no objective findings at the time of the impairment rating will have a nonratable impairment. In the past, if this patient had documented guarding, he or she would have been categorized as a DRE Cervicothoracic Category II and rated at 5 percent whole-person permanent impairment.

[F] Radiculopathy and Imaging Studies

In the fifth edition of the *AMA Guides,* to make a diagnosis of radiculopathy, an imaging study (e.g., a computed tomography [CT] scan, magnetic resonance imaging [MRI] scan, or myelogram) demonstrating a herniated disk concordant with the clinical findings is required.

[G] Spinal Fusions

Ratings for spinal fusions are dramatically increased. "Alteration of motion segment integrity" replaces the phrase "loss of motion segment structural integrity." In the fourth edition, by the criteria provided, it was rare to encounter "loss of motion segment structural integrity." In the fifth edition, this now includes acquired arthrodesis. This means that anyone who has had a single-level fusion qualifies for at least a Category IV rating, that is, at least a 20 percent whole-person permanent impairment (or 25 percent whole-person permanent impairment if it involves the cervical spine). If an individual had an objectively documented radiculopathy and underwent a single-level fusion, he or she would be classified as Category V with an impairment rating of 25 percent to 28 percent whole-person permanent impairment. According to the fourth edition, this same person would have been rated as a DRE Lumbosacral Category III at 10 percent whole-person permanent impairment. If the fusion involves multiple levels, they are rated using the ROM method, not the DRE method.

[H] Spinal Cord Injuries

There are significant changes in the evaluation of patients with spinal cord injuries. In the fourth edition, the patient with a spinal cord injury was assigned to

---

[53] 2006 Tenn. LEXIS 295 (Tenn. Spec. Workers' Comp. App. Panel at Nashville Apr. 11, 2006).

Category VI, VII, or VIII, as appropriate, and the rating was combined with one of the lower categories. In the fifth edition, a patient with a spinal cord injury is evaluated by the functional approach based on methods in Chapter 13, "The Central and Peripheral Nervous System," as explained in Section 15.7, "Rating Corticospinal Tract Damage."[54] Table 15-6[55] defines impairment due to loss of use of one or both upper extremities; the station and gait disorders; and loss of bladder, urinary, bowel, sexual, and respiratory functions. Ratings from each of these areas are combined with ratings from Categories II through V.

[I]   Range of Motion Method

The process of assessing impairment by the ROM method remains the same as in the fourth edition and is presented in Section 15.8, "Range of Motion Method."[56] Impairment is based on the combined impairment due to a specific spine disorder (Table 15-7 in the fifth edition; Table 75 in the fourth edition), reproducible spinal motion deficits, and objectified neurological deficits.

[J]   Changes in Spinal Ratings

Some spinal ratings performed using the fifth edition of the *AMA Guides* will be higher than those rated under the fourth edition. However, because the fifth edition takes into account treatment outcomes, the ratings for cases where there has been resolution of the symptoms and signs will often be lower than under their predecessor. With poor treatment outcomes, the converse will likely be true, particularly because the range of ratings now provided starts with the percentages used for the fourth edition categories and goes up by 3 percent. Furthermore, loss of motion segment integrity as defined in the fourth edition did not include fusions. However, in the fifth edition, *alteration* of motion segment integrity does. The newer, more inclusive term means more patients will be rated using the higher Categories IV and V. For example, lumbar radiculopathy treated with a fusion that would have been rated Category III with the fourth edition will now be Category V, with a rating at least 150 percent higher. Also, injuries at more than one level in the same spinal region, including multilevel radiculopathies, as well as recurrent or bilateral radiculopathy, are now rated using the ROM model, again resulting in higher impairment ratings.

---

[54] *AMA Guides* (5th ed. 2000) at 295–398.
[55] *Id.* at 396–97.
[56] *Id.* at 398–426.

§4.06   CHAPTER 16: THE UPPER EXTREMITIES

The changes in Chapter 16, "The Upper Extremities," appear minor compared to those in Chapter 15, "Spine." The primary approach to assessing upper extremity impairment is still anatomic, as it was in the fourth edition in Section 3.1, "The Upper Extremity," as opposed to functional. The most significant changes are the more rigorous standards for upper extremity evaluation, the mandate to compare motion findings to the contralateral extremity, entrapment neuropathies evaluation, and strength assessment.

[A]   Principles of Clinical Assessment

The principles of clinical assessment are essentially unchanged. The fifth edition of the *AMA Guides,* however, emphasizes in Section 16.1b, "Impairment Evaluation: Documentation and Recording," that "[e]valuation of the upper extremities requires a sound knowledge of the normal functional anatomy and would be incomplete without assessment of the general condition of the whole person. It must be thorough and should include several elements: status of activities of daily living; careful observations; both local and general physical examinations; appropriate imaging evaluation; laboratory tests; and preferably, a photographic record."[57] These "standards" are more comprehensive than what typically has been included in an upper extremity impairment evaluation report and do provide an opportunity for questioning the rating physician. Figure 16-1, Upper Extremity Impairment Evaluation Record,[58] should be completed, especially for digit and hand ratings.

[B]   Combining

Section 16.1c[59] clarifies the process of combining. Items must be combined at the unit (e.g., finger or thumb) before converting to the next larger unit (e.g., hand). If the evaluator must combine three percentages, the two lowest values are combined first. The evaluator then combines their combined value with the third. In most cases, however, the same final percentage will be obtained whether one begins combining the largest or smallest values. In the fourth edition of the *AMA Guides,* adding upper extremity impairments was limited to motion deficits at the same joint, thumb joint motion impairments, and total hand impairment derived from the converted hand impairment for each digit.

---

[57] *Id.* at 434.

[58] *Id.* at 436–37.

[59] *Id.* at 438–40.

[C] Amputations

In the fifth edition, thumb amputations proximal to the metacarpophalangeal (MP) joint level are given a 37 percent to 38 percent upper extremity (not digit or hand) impairment rating according to the level, and this percentage is added to any other upper extremity impairment.[60] There are no substantial changes in rating upper extremity amputation, as explained in Section 16.2, "Amputations," other than adding the impairment for thumb amputations proximal to the MP joint to any other upper extremity percentage.

[D] Digital Nerve Lesions

Rating digital nerve lesions using the fifth edition of the *AMA Guides* is described in Section 16.3, "Sensory Impairment Due to Digital Nerve Lesion," and is similar to doing such ratings using the fourth edition. The fifth edition, however, differentiates sensation and sensibility and includes a more detailed discussion of assessment. New to the fifth edition is a process for rating impairment due to digital neuromas. The severity of pain is graded using Table 16-10, Determining Impairment of the Upper Extremity Due to Sensory Deficits or Pain Resulting from Peripheral Nerve Disorders.[61] A percentage selected from the range for the appropriate grade is multiplied by the maximum digit impairment for the digital nerve under the columns for total longitudinal loss (ulnar or radial) in Table 16-6 or 16-7.[62]

[E] Abnormal Motion

In Section 16.4, "Evaluating Abnormal Motion," there is more direction on how to measure motion, but the values for motion deficits remain the same. Motion measurements falling between those shown in a pie chart may be adjusted or interpolated. "The examiner should first observe what an individual can and cannot do by asking him or her to move each joint of the extremity, from the shoulder down, through its full range of motion. Both extremities should be compared."[63] If active motion is incomplete, assisted active and/or passive motion measurements are made. However, "[m]easurements of active motion take precedence in the *Guides.*" New to the fifth edition are instructions permitting apportionment of diminished joint motion:

> If a contralateral "normal" joint has a less than average mobility, the impairment value(s) corresponding to the uninvolved joint can serve as a baseline and

---

[60] *Id.* at 440, 442.

[61] *Id.* at 482.

[62] *Id.* at 448.

[63] *Id.* at 451.

are subtracted from the calculated impairment for the involved joint. . . . A loss of motion in a zone beyond normal values does not as a rule represent a loss of function or impairment. . . . In rare cases . . . an impairment percent not to exceed 2% of the maximum regional impairment value of a unit of motion could be given.[64]

[F] Peripheral Nerve Impairment

There are several changes in rating peripheral nerve impairment, as presented in Section 16.5, "Impairment of the Upper Extremities Due to Peripheral Nerves." The most significant of these are grading sensory deficits, rating entrapment neuropathies, and evaluating complex regional pain syndrome. There are significant discrepancies between this chapter and Chapter 13, "The Central and Peripheral Nervous System," and Chapter 16, "The Upper Extremities." Sensory grading is reversed in the fifth edition's upper extremity chapter, compared to the upper extremity section in Chapter 3 of the fourth edition. The descriptions of sensory deficit or pain grades in Table 16-10 and those for motor deficits in Table 16-11[65] have been slightly modified in the fifth edition, which also contains a more extensive explanation regarding grading. These changes may result in some confusion. "The examiner must use clinical judgment to estimate the appropriate percentage . . . within the range of values shown for each severity grade. The maximum value is not applied automatically."[66] The new edition also acknowledges the wide range of weakness included in grade 4, from minimal to severe, and indicates it "should be rated from 1% to 25% depending on the degree within this grade."[67] .

[G] Entrapment Neuropathies

The fourth edition of the *AMA Guides* offered two means for rating entrapment neuropathies, the method applicable to all peripheral nerve disorders using Tables 11 and 12, or Table 16, Upper Extremity Impairment Due to Entrapment Neuropathy.[68] Although Table 16 was simpler to use than Tables 11 and 12, ratings depended on whether the entrapment was considered mild, moderate, or severe, and no criteria were listed for these three categories. Hence reliability among raters was low. For this and other reasons, no equivalent table appears in the fifth edition, and examiners are instructed to rate entrapment neuropathies as they would any peripheral nerve disorder. To minimize duplicative ratings, the new edition specifically states, "In compression neuropathies, additional impairment values are

---

[64] *Id.* at 453–54.

[65] *Id.* at 484.

[66] *Id.* at 482.

[67] *Id.* at 484.

[68] *AMA Guides* (4th ed. 1993) at 57.

not given for decreased grip strength."[69] If a patient has a carpal tunnel release and has no objective findings postrelease, there is no ratable impairment, unless this person has abnormal electrodiagnostic studies, in which case a rating of up to 5 percent upper extremity impairment may be given.

[H]   Causalgia, Reflex Sympathetic Dystrophy, and Complex Regional Pain Syndromes

The section on causalgia and reflex sympathetic dystrophy (RSD) in the fourth edition[70] was retitled in the fifth edition as "Complex Regional Pain Syndromes (CRPS), Reflex Sympathetic Dystrophy (CRPS I), and Causalgia (CRPS II)." Ratings are based on loss of motion, sensory deficits and pain, and, for causalgia, motor deficits. Both the fourth and the fifth editions emphasize that manifestations of peripheral nerve lesions, such as diminished motion, atrophy, or reflex changes, are taken into account in the impairment values listed. The fifth edition notes that CRPS I (RSD) can cause motion loss or other changes not due strictly to a peripheral nerve lesion. Different processes for rating CRPS are provided in Chapter 13, "The Central and Peripheral Nervous System," and Chapter 18, "Pain." Chapter 13 contains a new Section 13.8, "Criteria for Rating Impairments Related to Chronic Pain." This retains the older terminology for these conditions (RSD and causalgia). It also provides a different method for rating them, depending on ability to perform ADLs and whether the dominant or nondominant limb is involved.[71] A third approach to rating CRPS is presented in Chapter 18. These inconsistencies are likely to be problematic for the rating physician and provide opportunities for ratings to be challenged.

[I]   Impairment Due to Other Disorders

There are several changes in assessing impairment due to other disorders, as explained in Section 16.7, "Impairment of the Upper Extremities Due to Other Disorders." The most noteworthy are more explicit directions on how to rate these other disorders, the elimination of rating for joint crepitation, the inclusion of new radiographic criteria for rating carpal instability, and the introduction of a new process for rating shoulder instability. The section "Other Musculoskeletal System Defects" in the fourth edition states, "[I]f an examiner determines that the estimate for the anatomic impairment does not sufficiently reflect the severity of the patient's condition, the examiner may increase the impairment percent."[72] This does not appear in the fifth edition.

---

[69] *AMA Guides* (5th ed. 2000) at 494.
[70] *AMA Guides* (4th ed. 1993) at 56.
[71] *AMA Guides* (5th ed. 2000) at 343.
[72] *AMA Guides* (4th ed. 1993) at 63.

[J]   Cumulative Trauma Disorders

The discussion of cumulative trauma disorders in the fourth edition states that an individual whose symptoms are reduced by alteration of daily activities or work tasks "should not be considered to be permanently impaired."[73] This instruction is also absent in the successor edition. However, a similar statement appears in Section 16.7d, "Tendinitis." Epicondylitis, fasciitis, and tendinitis "are not given a permanent impairment rating unless there is some other factor that must be considered."[74]

[K]   Strength Evaluation

The discussion of strength evaluation is expanded in the fifth edition in Section 16.8, and a process for rating weakness of shoulder and elbow motions is now provided. Strength deficits for the shoulder and elbow are obtained from clinical assessment and based on ranges derived from unit of motion values. The ratings are presented in Table 16-35, Impairment of the Upper Extremity Due to Strength Deficit from Musculoskeletal Disorders Based on Manual Muscle Testing of Individual Units of Motion of the Shoulder and Elbow.[75] A rating for weakness could be combined with other impairments, but only if due to an unrelated cause. The fifth edition states strength loss "cannot be rated in the presence of decreased motion, painful conditions, deformities, or absence of parts."[76] Such a list of exclusions makes it unlikely an examiner would be able to justify a strength loss rating.

§ 4.07   CHAPTER 17: THE LOWER EXTREMITIES

Anatomic, diagnostic, and functional means are used to assess impairment in Chapter 17, "The Lower Extremities." These approaches are reflected in the same 13 methods provided in the fourth edition. This permits the examiner to match the approach to each patient's physical impairment, with usually a single method being selected. This chapter is very similar to Section 3.2, "The Lower Extremity," in the fourth edition; however, it provides clarification when the different evaluation methods should be used, includes a new table, Guide to the Appropriate Combination of Evaluation Methods (Table 17-2), and provides a lower extremity worksheet that may be used as a template to simplify making the assessment and recording the evaluation.

---

[73] *Id.* at 19.
[74] *AMA Guides* (5th ed. 2000) at 507.
[75] *Id.* at 510.
[76] *Id.* at 508.

[A]   History and Examination

The components of the history and a lower extremity physical examination are provided in Section 17.1, "Principles of Assessment."[77] The physician records lower extremity–related physical findings, such as range of motion, limb length discrepancy, deformity, reflexes, muscle strength and atrophy, ligamentous laxity, motor and sensory deficits, and specific diagnoses, such fractures and bursitis.

[B]   Methods of Assessment

Section 17.2, "Methods of Assessment,"[78] explains the methods of assessment in further detail than provided in Section 3.2 of the fourth edition. Anatomic changes, including range of motion, limb length discrepancy, arthritis, skin changes, amputation, muscle atrophy, nerve impairment, and vascular derangement, are assessed in the physical examination and supported by clinical studies. Specific fractures and deformities are usually evaluated by diagnosis-based estimates. This methodology tends to be objective, reliable, and specific. Diagnosis-based estimates are also commonly used for ligamentous instability, bursitis, and various surgical procedures. Functional methods, such as range of motion, gait derangement, and muscle strength, are assessed last, because they are generally not as objective, reliable, or specific as other approaches.

[C]   Choosing a Method to Rate Impairment

A new worksheet, Figure 17-10,[79] is provided in the fifth edition to record abnormal motion, and to be used as guidance to most common regional impairments with corresponding tables. Usually, one method adequately characterizes the impairment and its impact on the ability to perform ADLs. If more than one method can be used, the method that provides the higher rating should be adopted. In some cases, more than one method needs to be used to accurately assess all features of the impairment. The cross-usage chart, Table 17-2, Guide to the Appropriate Combination of Evaluation Methods,[80] is new and provides guidance on what can and cannot be combined. The evaluator should explain in writing why a particular method(s) to assign the impairment rating was chosen. The fifth edition explains that, when there are multiple impairments involving different regions of the lower extremity (e.g., thigh and foot), these impairments are combined as a whole-person value. When there are multiple impairments within a region (e.g., the toes and the ankle), the impairments are first combined as regional impairments

---

[77] *Id.* at 524–25.
[78] *Id.* at 525–54.
[79] *Id.* at 561.
[80] *Id.* at 526.

and then converted to whole person. Impairment values in Chapter 17 of the fifth edition are unchanged from those in the fourth edition in Section 3.2.

[D] Limb Length Discrepancy

Section 17.2b, "Limb Length Discrepancy,"[81] includes a statement that in the case of shortening due to overriding or malalignment or fracture deformities, but not including flexion or extension deformities, a value of up to 20 percent of the lower extremity (for a discrepancy of 3.75 to 5.0 cm) is combined with other functional sequelae.

[E] Gait Derangement

Section 17.c, "Gait Derangement,"[82] is essentially unchanged in the fifth edition. However, to emphasize that this is not the preferred method for assessing impairment, the statement "whenever possible, the evaluator should use a more specific method" is now italicized, and the evaluator is advised, "when the gait method is used, a written rationale should be included in the report."[83]

[F] Muscle Atrophy and Weakness

Section 17.2d, "Muscle Atrophy (Unilateral),"[84] explains that "the method that most accurately and objectively reflects the individual's impairment" should be used. When there is atrophy of both the thigh and leg (calf), the impairments are determined separately and the whole-person impairment is combined. Section 17.2e, "Manual Muscle Testing,"[85] is unchanged.

[G] Range of Motion

Section 17.2f, "Range of Motion,"[86] notes, "If it is clear to the evaluator that a restricted range of motion has an organic basis, three measurements should be obtained and the greatest range measured should be used." Findings that are inconsistent by a rating class between two observers, or by the same observer on separate occasions, are considered invalid. Guidance is now provided on how to approach range of motion deficits in multiple directions in the same joint. These values are added to determine the total joint range of motion

---

[81] *Id.* at 528.
[82] *Id.* at 529.
[83] *Id.*
[84] *Id.* at 530.
[85] *Id.* at 531.
[86] *Id.* at 533.

impairment. Section 17.2g, "Joint Ankylosis,"[87] advises the "values listed [in the tables] are for the maximum end of the deformity range," and "[s]pecific deformities should be rated using interpolation of the ranges in the tables. . . ." By contrast, with joint motion deficits, a range of values is included in one class having a single impairment estimate without interpolation. Section 17.2h, "Arthritis,"[88] is essentially unchanged and emphasizes that roentgenographic grading is a more objective and valid method for assigning impairment estimates than are physical findings, such as range of motion or joint crepitation. The approach to Section 17.2i, "Amputations,"[89] is the same as in the fourth edition.

[H] Lower Extremity Impairments

Section 17.2j, "Diagnosis-Based Estimates,"[90] is also the same. Table 17-33, Impairment Estimates for Certain Lower Extremity Impairments,[91] is identical to Table 64, Impairment Estimates for Certain Lower Extremity Impairments, in the fourth edition.[92] There had been discussion about new diagnosis-based estimates being provided for full thickness articular cartilage defects, un-united osteochondral fracture, anterior cruciate ligament (ACL) repair without laxity, and severe cavus deformity of the foot; however, these were not provided in the first printing of the fifth edition.

[I] Peripheral Nerve Injuries

In Section 17.2*l*, "Peripheral Nerve Injuries,"[93] Table 17-37, Impairments Due to Nerve Deficits,[94] provides the same values for motor, sensory, and dysesthesia impairments as appeared in Table 68 in the fourth edition.[95] Specific guidance on how to approach both sensory and dysesthesia deficits in the same individual are not offered in either the text or case examples. The evaluator is advised to grade sensory deficits according to Table 16-10, Determining Impairment of the Upper Extremity Due to Sensory Deficits or Pain Resulting from Peripheral Nerve Disorders;[96] however, in this table and in Section 16.5, "Impairment of the Upper Extremities Due to Peripheral Nerve Disorders," sensory and dysthesia impairments are not dealt with separately. In Chapter 13, "The Central

[87] *Id.* at 538.

[88] *Id.* at 544.

[89] *Id.* at 545.

[90] *Id.* at 545.

[91] *Id.* at 546–47.

[92] *AMA Guides* (4th ed. 1993) at 85–86.

[93] *AMA Guides* (5th ed. 2000) at 551–52.

[94] *Id.* at 552.

[95] *AMA Guides* (4th ed. 1993) at 89.

[96] *AMA Guides* (5th ed. 2000) at 482.

and Peripheral Nervous System," examples of lower extremity peripheral nerve impairment are given; however, these rate only sensory and motor deficits, not dysthesias, and use Table 13-23[97] and Table 13-24[98] for grading sensory and motor losses, rather than Table 16-10[99] and Table 16-11.[100]

[J] Causalgia and Reflex Sympathetic Dystrophy

Section 17.2m, "Causalgia and Complex Regional Pain Syndrome (Reflex Sympathetic Dystrophy),"[101] states, "The evaluator should use the method described in Chapter 13, The Central and Peripheral Nervous System." However, earlier Chapter 17 states, "Causalgia and complex regional pain syndrome (reflex sympathetic dystrophy) are evaluated using a combination of ROM and peripheral neurologic evaluation techniques."[102] This advice is contrary to that provided in Section 13.9,[103] which does not use the phrase "complex regional pain syndrome" and rates impairment based on functional classes, not on range of motion and peripheral neurological findings.

[K] Vascular Disorders

Section 17.2n, "Vascular Disorders,"[104] uses Table 17-38, Lower Extremity Impairment Due to Peripheral Vascular Disease,[105] to place the individual in classes of impairment in the same manner described in the fourth edition in Table 69.[106] Table 17-38 is the same as Table 4-5, The Cardiovascular System: Systemic and Pulmonary Arteries,[107] which appears in Chapter 4.

In summary, the process of assessing lower extremity impairment in the fifth edition of the *AMA Guides* is similar to that in the fourth edition.

§ 4.08   CHAPTER 18: PAIN

Chapter 18, "Pain," has been completely revised. An overview of pain and a discussion regarding the complexity of assessing the impact of pain have been

---

[97] *Id.* at 346–47.
[98] *Id.* at 348–49.
[99] *Id.* at 482.
[100] *Id.* at 484.
[101] *Id.* at 553.
[102] *Id.* at 525.
[103] *Id.* at 343.
[104] *Id.* at 533.
[105] *Id.* at 534.
[106] *AMA Guides* (4th ed. 1993) at 89.
[107] *AMA Guides* (5th ed. 2000) at 76.

added, as reflected in Section 18.1, "Principles of Assessment,"[108] and Section 18.2, "Overview of Pain."[109] The chapter reviews situations in which pain is a major cause of suffering, dysfunction, or medical intervention, rather than a part of injuries to or illnesses of specific organ systems.

[A] Chronic Pain

Section 18.3, "Integrating Pain-Related Impairment into the Conventional Impairment Rating System,"[110] provides a qualitative method for evaluating impairment due to rating chronic pain. The pain of individuals with ambiguous or controversial pain syndromes is considered unratable. If an individual appears to have pain-related impairment that has increased the burden of his or her condition slightly, the examiner may increase the percentage up to 3 percent whole-person permanent impairment. If the examiner performs a formal pain-related impairment rating, he or she may increase the percentage by up to 3 percent and classify the individual's pain-related impairment into one of four categories: mild, moderate, moderately severe, or severe. This 3 percent range may not be used in conjunction with the 3 percent range provided for rating spinal impairment using the diagnosis-related estimates method.

[B] Formal Pain-Related Impairment Rating

The performance of a formal pain-related impairment rating is done if the individual appears to have pain-related impairment that is substantially in excess of the conventional impairment rating, if the individual has a well-recognized medical condition that is characterized by pain in the absence of measurable dysfunction, or if there is a syndrome with the following characteristics: "(a) it is associated with identifiable organ dysfunction that is ratable according to other chapters in the *Guides*; (b) it may be associated with a well-established pain syndrome, but the occurrence or nonoccurrence of the pain syndrome is not predictable; so that (c) the impairment ratings provided in step A do not capture the added burden of illness borne by the individual because of his or her associated pain syndrome."[111] A pain-related impairment score is obtained from a point system derived from information obtained from the patient and the physician. Using Table 18-4, Ratings Determining Impairment Associated with Pain, the individual completes information about his or her pain, activity limitations or interference, and mood. Each section results in a score, totaling to a maximum of 60. The physician assesses global pain behavior (whether it supports or questions pain complaints)

---

[108] *Id.* at 566.

[109] *Id.* at 566–69.

[110] *Id.* at 569–81.

[111] *Id.* at 573.

and makes a clinical judgment on credibility, each of which two areas results in an adjustment of minus to plus 10. The resulting score, which is not an impairment rating, places the patient in a pain impairment class. It is probable that this process will result in challenges; however, the amount of quantitative impairment is relatively small, that is, 3 percent whole-person permanent impairment.

[C]   Behavioral Confounders

The discussion of behavioral confounders presented in Section 18.4[112] is useful in understanding and challenging impairment ratings. Assessing behavioral reliability includes analysis of congruence with established conditions, consistency over time and situations, consistency with anatomy and physiology, observer agreement, and inappropriate illness behavior. Section 18.5[113] summarizes the steps in performing a rating. The chapter concludes with a discussion of psychogenic pain in Section 18.6[114] and malingering in Section 18.7.[115]

§ 4.09   SUMMARY

In summary, the fifth edition of the *AMA Guides* is similar to the fourth edition, with a few notable exceptions, such as the assessment of spinal, pain, and visual impairment. There are numerous minor changes, and many more case examples have been added. The fifth edition is more complex than the fourth, and therefore it has been more challenging and probably not as comprehensible. There continue to be many opportunities for improvement, including developing a process of rating impairment that is based on functional loss and supported by scientific evidence. There are internal inconsistencies and errors that are likely to result in conflict and interfere with the reliability of ratings. Regardless of these challenges, the *AMA Guides* are still the standard for assessing impairment.

---

[112] *Id.* at 581–83.
[113] *Id.* at 583–84.
[114] *Id.* at 585.
[115] *Id.* at 585–86.

EXHIBIT 4-1   **Difficult Cross-Examination Questions Under the Fifth Edition of the *AMA Guides***

Q 1. Because medicine is not an exact science, what is your margin of error in doing this impairment rating?
Comment. Counsel is trying to get the examiner to play a numbers game; for example, Could it be 1 percent? What about 2 percent? Is that plus or minus?

Q 2. Why do you use the fourth edition of the *Guides* when the *Guides* say: "Since this [fifth] edition encompasses the most current criteria and procedures for impairment assessment, it is strongly recommended that physicians use this latest edition [the 5th edition] when rating impairment?[116]
Comment. Some states still mandate that practitioners use the fourth (or an even earlier) edition to rate permanent impairment. In those states, counsel will use this inconsistency to examine physicians.

Q 3. Doctor, can you point to the impairment criteria for evaluating sexual dysfunction in the fifth edition, and increasing the percentage by 50 percent for men younger than 40 and decreasing the percentages by 50 percent for men older than 65?
Comment. Here counsel is trying to get the examiner to admit that he or she does not know what criteria were used, what they said, and how they came up with the seemingly arbitrary increase and decrease of the impairment rating depending on the age of the examinee.

Q 4. Are the impairment ratings using the *Guides* valid and reproducible?
Comment. Counsel is using the uncertainty raised by the *Guides* themselves in this question: "Research is limited on the reproducibility and validity of the *Guides*."[117] A look at the footnotes cited shows only three articles on this key issue, one being 21 years old (footnotes 18–20, page 16, 5th ed.).

Q 5. Did you consider the examinee's fatigue and inability to concentrate when you performed your impairment rating?
Comment. In Q 5, counsel is pointing out that the *Guides* admit that the ratings do not normally include consideration of fatigue and inability to concentrate.

> Subjective concerns, including fatigue, difficulty in concentrating, and pain, when not accompanied by demonstrable clinical signs or other independent measurable abnormalities are generally not given separate impairment ratings.[118]

Q 6. How do you explain the fact that three different physicians each came up with different impairment ratings for this examinee?
Comment. In Q 6, counsel is using the words of the *Guides* to cross-examine the physician: "Two physicians following the methods of the *Guides* to evaluate the same patient should report similar results and reach similar conclusions."[119]

---

[116] The *AMA Guides* (5th ed. 2000) at 2.
[117] *Id.* at 10.
[118] *Id.*
[119] *Id.* at 17.

EXHIBIT 4-1   UNDERSTANDING THE AMA GUIDES

Q 7. Since your impairment report is not consistent with the *AMA Guides* Section 2.6, why should the fact finder accept your impairment ratings?

Comment.   Here, counsel is using the strict requirements of Section 2.6 to question the validity of the report and impairment ratings. Section 2.6 provides in part:

> A clear, accurate, and complete report is essential to support a rating of permanent impairment. The following elements in bold type should be included in all impairment evaluation reports. Other elements listed in italics are commonly found within an IME or may be requested for inclusion in an impairment evaluation.
>
> 2.6a A. Clinical Evaluation
>
> 2.6a.1 Include a **narrative history** of the medical condition(s) . . .
>
> 2.6a.2 *Include a work history with a detailed, chronological description of work activities.* . . .
>
> 2.6a.3 Assess **current clinical status**, . . .
>
> 2.6a.4 List **diagnostic study results** and outstanding pertinent **diagnostic studies** . . .
>
> 2.6a.5 Discuss the medical basis for determining whether the person is at **MMI.**
>
> 2.6a.6 Discuss **diagnoses, impairments** . . .
>
> 2.6a.7 *Discuss causation and apportionment, if requested* . . .
>
> 2.6a.8 **Discuss impairment rating criteria, prognosis, residual function, and limitations** . . . [120]

Q 8.   When you rated the impairment in this examinee, which chapters of the *Guides* did you use?

Comment. Counsel is trying to elicit one of two responses:

 a. Chapter 15—Spine.

Counsel is then free to ask the examiner about all of the chapters the examiner missed, which may impact the impairment rating, for example, Chapter 14—Mental and Behavioral Disorders, Chapter 16—Upper Extremities, and Chapter 18—Pain.

 b. The entire text.

Counsel is then free to ask questions from any chapter to test the truthfulness of the examiner's response.

Q 9.   Why is your impairment rating inconsistent with *The Guides Casebook*, published by the AMA?

Comment.   Here, counsel is utilizing the AMA's own publication, which was developed "to ensure the correct application of the *Guides* principles in the clinical setting."[121] Physicians who are not familiar with *The Guides Casebook* will be at a distinct disadvantage.

Q 10.   Which ambiguous or controversial pain syndromes are not ratable under the fifth edition?

Comment.   The fifth edition is less than instructive on this point. As noted earlier, the distinctions between well-recognized conditions and ambiguous or controversial ones are subtle, so that no definitive list of ambiguous or controversial conditions

---

[120] *Id.* at 21–22.

[121] AMA, *Foreword*, The Guides Casebook (2d ed. 2002).

can be given. The examining physician can, however, identify ambiguous or contro-versial syndromes by asking the following questions.

Q 11. On what scientific evidence are impairment criteria in the *Guides* based?
Comment. According to the *Guides,* these criteria "were developed from scientific evidence as cited and from consensus of chapter authors or of medical specialty societies."[122] This is a potential area of challenge in terms of the reliability of the *Guides.*

Q 12. You like to get injured workers back to work as soon as possible, don't you?
Comment. This question helps to establish bias.

Q 13. What percentage of your 24-page report is standardized computer-gener-ated boilerplate language?
Comment. Many physicians who perform impairment ratings use standard form reports. This can be used against the rater.

Q 14. Because you saw the claimant only once, for 30 minutes, but the treating physicians saw him dozens of times over the past four years, isn't the treating phy-sician in a much better position to evaluate the claimant's impairment?
Comment. This can be a strong line of attack.

Q 15. On page 1 of your report, you state that you explained to my client that you have no doctor-patient relationship with him. However, 15 times in your report you refer to my client as "the patient." There are 15 mistakes in your report, are there not?
Comment. Referring to the claimant or examinee as "the patient" is a common mistake of independent medical examiners, and this mistake should be taken advantage of during cross-examination.

Q 16. Doctor, would it be fair to say that, as a busy surgeon, you have a lot on your plate and that you haven't completely mastered proper use of the *Guides?*
Comment. This question may result in an admission of lack of mastery of a com-plicated book.

Q 17. Doctor, when was the last time you made a mistake in an impairment rating?
Comment. This is a potential win-win question for counsel. If the doctor admits making a mistake, that can be used against the doctor. A doctor who denies ever having made a mistake may not be believable.

Q 18. Doctor, did you follow the ethical guidelines of the American Board of Independent Medical Examiners when conducting this examination?
Comment. Whether the response is yes or no, this is an effective question. If the answer is yes, a good follow-up would be to ask the doctor to recite, list, or describe the standards. [Note: To date the authors have not found an IME physician who can do so.] Good lead-in questions include: Are you an ethical doctor? What would you think of an unethical physician's opinions?

---

[122] *AMA Guides* (5th ed. 2000) at 4.

EXHIBIT 4-1   UNDERSTANDING THE AMA GUIDES

Q 19.   Please describe all the training you have had in the use of the *Guides*.
Comment.   The fact finder may give greater weight to the testimony of a rating physician who has had significant training in the use of the applicable edition of the *Guides*.

CHAPTER 5

AMA GUIDES, SIXTH EDITION

§ 5.01   KEY POINTS FOR COUNSEL

The AMA published the long-awaited sixth edition of its *Guides to the Evaluation of Permanent Impairment* (hereinafter *AMA Guides*, 6th ed. 2008) in January 2008. This chapter is intended to alert counsel to various important issues, changes, and concepts presented in the sixth edition.

1. The impairment rating system is now based for the most part on diagnoses. Ranges of impairment, which allowed the physician to choose a number within a range, are generally no longer used. Now the physician will use non-key factors, such as clinical signs, physical examination, and functional status, along with a mathematical formula, to determine the precise impairment rating within a given class.

2. For the most part, the chapters in the sixth edition use a rating method (by key and non-key factors) similar to that in the previous editions.

3. The sixth edition is extremely critical of previous editions. The criticisms could be used to challenge the accuracy and effectiveness of older editions and even of the sixth edition itself.

4. The impairment numbers in the sixth edition are based on consensus, not on evidence.

5. Examiners are told to ignore and not use unreliable, subjective reports.

6. The sixth edition is not clear and precise on what the examining physician should do when the examinee's organ system can be rated in multiple ways. Should the examiner rate all the impairments and combine them or simply rate the worst impairment?

7. Diagnoses that are not included in the *AMA Guides* can be rated by analogy.

8. Numerous conditions that the *AMA Guides* explicitly state are non-ratable include the following:
   - abnormal segmentation
   - annular tears
   - conjoined nerve roots
   - disk degeneration
   - dissociative disorders
   - excessive lordosis
   - facet arthropathy
   - factitious disorders
   - fibromyalgia

- kyphosis
- mental retardation
- personality disorders
- psychosexual disorders
- scoliosis
- somatoform disorders
- spina bifida occulta
- spondylolysis
- spondylolisthesis (some forms)
- substance abuse disorders
- tension headaches

9. Ratings are supposed to be performed only by a physician. It is not clear, however, whether a psychologist is allowed to perform a mental impairment evaluation.

10. The sixth edition is prejudiced against treating physicians, and, remarkably, states that ratings by treating physicians should undergo greater scrutiny due to the physicians' lack of independence.

11. The sixth edition emphasizes that examiners must be cognizant of cultural differences among examinees. This point raises many potential areas of inquiry.

12. Examiners must use qualified interpreters and not family members.

13. If an examinee refuses treatment, the examiner is to rate the examinee as is and estimate the rating that would have been assigned had the examinee complied with treatment recommendations.

14. Add-on impairments for pain are not allowed under the sixth edition. Chronic pain conditions that cannot be rated under any other chapter of the *Guides* are ratable up to 3 percent, using Chapter 3, "Pain-Related Impairment."

15. Many of the ratings in the sixth edition have been lowered, but examiners are now encouraged to rate other affected systems and combine the resulting impairments.

16. Migraine headaches are now ratable.

17. Only a very few DSM-IV Diagnoses are ratable. All others are not.

18. Under the sixth edition, psychological distress associated with a physical injury is not ratable as the stress is presumed to be included in the physical rating.

19. The instructions in the sixth edition on when to use the range of motion model for the upper and lower extremities are inconsistent and unclear.

20. Musculoskeletal surgery does not result in additional impairment percentages.

21. Complex Regional Pain Syndrome is rated under Chapter 15, Chapter 16, or Chapter 3.

22. Chapter 15 in the sixth edition encourages examiners to in effect spy on examinees to validate functional assessment.

23. The sixth edition emphasizes that examiners should review the actual clinical studies and not just reports on the studies.

24. The sixth edition allows the use of additional functional assessment instruments but does not list which instruments can be used or how they should be converted to a grade modifier.

25. The instructions on which grade modifier to use are sometimes vague and imprecise or contradictory.

26. Each chapter in the sixth edition contains important information about what the physician should be doing and how to do it. Counsel should carefully read all applicable chapters.

§ 5.02   PREFACE TO THE SIXTH EDITION

The *AMA Guides* (6th ed. 2008) admits that it is only partially evidence-based. It states in the Preface that an evidence-based process was used to develop the new edition where possible and, otherwise, was built on "consensus."[1] The exact extent to which the sixth edition is or is not evidence-based, and the evidence upon which it is based, are potentially problematic.

The sixth edition is implicitly and explicitly critical of past editions of the *Guides*. The sixth edition's stated purposes include "to enhance the relevance of impairment ratings, improve internal inconsistencies, promote greater precision, and standardize the rating process."[2]

Many jurisdictions can be expected to continue to use older editions of the *Guides* for years to come. In those jurisdictions, statements such as those made by the American Medical Association (AMA) certainly can be used to call into question the validity of previous editions. It can be argued that the next edition of the *AMA Guides* will be critical of the sixth edition. Indeed, one of the stated purposes of the sixth edition is to "provide a solid basis for future editions of the *Guides.*"

---

[1] AMA, Guides to the Evaluation of Permanent Impairment (6th ed. 2008) (hereinafter *AMA Guides* (6th ed. 2008)) at iii.
[2] *Id.*

Impairment evaluation for many important chapters in the sixth edition, such as the musculoskeletal chapters, is based fundamentally on diagnosis. The emphasis in the sixth edition is expanding the diagnoses that are covered by the *AMA Guides.*

§ 5.03   METHODOLOGY OF THE SIXTH EDITION

The methodology used in the sixth edition is consistent in each chapter. Each diagnosis places an impairment in one of five classes: (1) no problem; (2) mild; (3) moderate; (4) severe; or (5) complete. Each class (decided by the key factor— usually the diagnosis) provides for a range of impairment percentages. The impairment percentage is then adjusted within the class by "severity grade" factors (the non-key factors), which could include:

- functionally based history

- physical findings

- clinical test results

Unlike previous editions of the *AMA Guides*, the sixth edition determines the exact percentage of impairment within the class by a simple mathematical formula determined by the applicable non-key factors. The rating physician generally no longer has discretion to adjust the rating within an impairment class. The purpose of this change is to make impairment ratings more consistent, so that different persons with the same condition would receive the same ratings.

§ 5.04   CHAPTER 1: CONCEPTUAL FOUNDATIONS AND PHILOSOPHY

Section 1.2a in Chapter 1 contains a list of candid and explicit criticisms of previous editions of the *AMA Guides.* These criticisms leveled at previous editions could be used eventually to challenge the sixth edition itself. Previous editions are criticized for (1) not being comprehensive; (2) not being based on evidence; and (3) not having accurate ratings.

Chapter 1 even quotes the *JAMA* article that states that the numerical ratings in the *AMA Guides* are more a representation of "legal fiction than medical reality."[3] Section 1.2 goes on to suggest that the fifth edition of the *AMA Guides* used "antiquated and confusing terminology,"[4] and its ratings had "limited validity and reliability. . . ."[5]

---

[3] *AMA Guides* (6th ed. 2008) at 2 (quoting E.A. Spieler P.S. Barth, J.F. Burton et al., *Recommendations to Guide Revision of the* Guides to the Evaluation of Permanent Impairment, 283 JAMA 519– 23 (2000)).

[4] *Id.* at 2.

[5] *Id.*

Section 1.3d provides definitions of impairment and disability that differ from those contained in the fifth edition. The sixth edition states that impairment ratings are estimates and are based on consensus as opposed to evidence.[6] The sixth edition reminds the reader that *impairment* does not equal *disability* and that the *AMA Guides* should not be used to directly determine a person's ability to work.[7]

Section 1.4d, "Measurement Issues," states that "precision, accuracy, reliability, and validity are critical issues in defining impairment."[8] This is a good passage to quote to a sloppy or careless physician at a deposition or hearing. Section 1.4d also stresses examiner training as an important factor in accuracy.[9] The training of a physician in the use of the *AMA Guides* has often been cited by fact finders evaluating the credibility of conflicting impairment ratings. An examiner's training should be explored at deposition.

Section 1.8c, which describes the system used in the sixth edition for calculating impairment, should be required reading for counsel. This section notes that some of the non-key factors in some chapters are based on self-reporting tools from the examinee. In those cases, the *Guides* proscribe that the rater is to judge the consistency and credibility of the results and justify the judgments.[10] Whether and how these checks have been performed can be explored by counsel at deposition.

Section 1.8c also notes that "Burdens of Treatment Compliance" (how an examinee's treatment regimen impacts activities of daily living) are already built into the functional history in some chapters,[11] including all the musculoskeletal chapters.[12] For those chapters, there is therefore no longer justification to add to a final rating for "the impact of medication or treatment side effects, or pain."[13] When "Burdens of Treatment Compliance" are not included in the impairment rating in the chapter in question, additional impairment according to the point system may be allowed (e.g., in Chapter 6 on the digestive system).[14] These points are assigned for medication usage, dietary modifications, frequency of routine procedures, and history of prior operative procedure or radiation therapy.[15]

Section 1.8g seems to give physicians some discretion to adjust ratings within a class where the key factor is objective test results/clinical studies and where a "suitable rationale is provided."[16] The language is ambiguous; it is not clear if this refers to adjustments through non-key factors or adjustments based on the

---

[6] *Id.* at 5 and 9.

[7] *Id.* at 5–6.

[8] *Id.* at 7.

[9] *Id.* at 8.

[10] *Id.* at 14.

[11] *Id.* at 9.

[12] *Id.* at 16.

[13] *Id.* at 14.

[14] *See* Appendix B in *AMA Guides* (6th ed. 2008) at 607–08.

[15] *Id.* at 607–08.

[16] *AMA Guides* (6th ed. 2008) at 15.

discretion of the physician. It can certainly be argued that this language gives physicians authorization to adjust ratings based on discretion.

Section 1.8h, "Functional Assessment," states that whether and how a rater should adjust a grade within a class depends on the jurisdiction in question.[17] This suggests that the rating physician's knowledge of legal requirements outside the scope of the *AMA Guides* is necessary for rating impairment. It also can be read to explicitly anticipate and approve the situation whereby the use of the *AMA Guides* is modified in particular jurisdictions.

§ 5.05   CHAPTER 2: PRACTICAL APPLICATION OF THE *GUIDES*

One of the AMA's goals in issuing its sixth edition of the *Guides* is the elimination of internal inconsistencies. To help effectuate this, the authors of the sixth edition made Chapter 2 the "constitution" of the *Guides*.[18] Anything that is conflicting in the *Guides* is preempted by Chapter 2.[19] What actually conflicts and how precisely conflicts are resolved are likely to be issues as the sixth edition is used. Apparently, the authors recognized there are conflicts and wanted a consistent mechanism for resolving them. All attorneys who deal with the *AMA Guides* should read Chapter 2.

All attorneys also should study Table 2-1 on page 20 of the sixth edition. Table 2-1 provides an excellent executive summary of the 14 key points in the *AMA Guides*.

Under the sixth edition, most impairment ratings are converted to whole-person ratings.[20] Certain impairments (such as hearing loss or impairments of upper extremities or lower extremities) may be left as regional impairments if requested by the referring source or if required in the particular jurisdiction.[21] As in previous editions of the *Guides*, multiple impairments are not added but combined using the combined value chart.[22]

A potential problem arises when an examinee can be rated under separate organ systems or can be rated separately within an organ system chapter. In this circumstance the examining physician is directed to rate separately and combine the separate ratings unless "criteria for the second impairment are included in the primary impairment."[23] The examining physician is specifically warned to avoid increasing the rating by duplication, by considering the "underlying pathophysiology."[24] The sixth edition further provides that if the *AMA Guides* provide more

---

[17] *Id.*
[18] *AMA Guides* (6th ed. 2008) at 19.
[19] *Id.*
[20] *Id.* at 21.
[21] *Id.*
[22] *AMA Guides* (6th ed. 2008) at 23.
[23] *Id.*
[24] *Id.*

than one method of rating an impairment, the method that produces the higher rating must be used.[25]

Rating by analogy (choosing a similar diagnosis and basing the rating on that diagnosis) is permissible "only if the *Guides* provides no other method for rating objectively identifiable impairment."[26] Several of the chapters dealing with organs list specific conditions that are not ratable under the *Guides*. Those conditions include fibromyalgia and tension headaches. Because Chapter 2 is "the constitution" of the sixth edition, it could be argued that the analogy provision conflicts with the conditions that are later stated to be unratable. One could then argue that for those conditions the rater *could* rate using an analogous diagnosis.

Because ratings under the sixth edition are largely based on diagnoses, the sixth edition emphasizes the importance of making the correct diagnosis.[27] The sixth edition states that although impairment ratings will usually be performed by MDs, DOs, and DCs, the jurisdiction in question determines which doctors may rate impairment.[28] The sixth edition also stipulates that the rater must have knowledge of Chapters 1 and 2 and a thorough understanding of the chapters dealing with the organ systems that are evaluated,[29] which is fair warning that rating physicians are likely to be closely questioned on Chapters 1 and 2 at depositions or hearings. Since Chapter 2 also states that an impairment evaluation must be performed by a licensed physician, it could be argued that psychologists may not rate mental impairment.[30]

The sixth edition also states that although treating physicians may perform ratings under the *Guides*, such ratings should be subject to greater scrutiny due to the physicians' lack of independence.[31] No mention is made of giving extra scrutiny to "independent" medical examiners paid for by the employer or insurer (i.e., examiners for the defense). Because the sixth edition is diagnosis-based, it can be argued that the treating physician would be in the best position to rate the subject. Indeed, in many cases the independent medical examiner (IME) physician strongly considers the diagnoses of the treating physicians after reviewing the medical records. Finally, fact finders and some statutes and regulations give preference to treating physicians, who are regarded as being more objective and credible.

The sixth edition of the *Guides* states that rating for permanent impairment does not create a physician-patient relationship between the examinee and the rating physician.[32] The authors of this work concur. It is interesting to note, however, that throughout the *Guides* the person being rated is referred to as "the patient."

---

[25] *Id.* at 20.

[26] *Id.* at 23.

[27] *Id.*

[28] *Id.*

[29] *Id.*

[30] *AMA Guides* (6th ed. 2008) at 20.

[31] *Id.* at 23.

[32] *Id.* at 24.

Impairments are rated only if they are permanent and when the examinee reaches maximum medical improvement (MMI).[33] Various definitions and explanations of MMI are found in the sixth edition. These definitions should be carefully studied by counsel. Instruction is provided on the circumstances where the examinee is either noncompliant or refuses treatment. In those circumstances the examinee can still be rated, but the examiner is asked to write an addendum to the report addressing the noncompliance or refusal of treatment and to include an estimate of what the rating would have been had there been optimal treatment.[34] The speculative nature of such an estimate is likely to be an issue when such an estimate is made.

Examinees using less than full effort are covered in Section 2.4b. The sixth edition instructs raters to "appropriately discount" symptom magnification behavior such as unjustified self inhibition of effort.[35] How to detect the symptom magnification and appropriately discount it are not explained.

Rounding off is covered in Section 2.4c. Intermediate or final ratings are to be rounded to the nearest whole number.[36] Numbers ending in .5 are to be rounded up.[37]

"Most" allowances for pain are contained in the underlying diagnoses in the relevant organ chapters.[38] What does and does not contain these allowances is not specifically stated. Physicians are referred to Chapter 3, "Pain-Related Impairments," but they are not told exactly when to use this chapter.

Where an assistive device (such as a hearing aid, eyeglasses, or a prosthesis) is easily removable, the impairment rating should be made both with and without the device, and both ratings should be reported.[39]

Apportionment requires the physician to determine the current rating and estimate the rating from a previous injury.[40] Accurate information is required for apportionment;[41] however, no explicit instruction is given for situations where accurate information regarding previous impairments is not available. In addition, the sixth edition contradicts itself when it states that where a previous rating was not assigned, the rating must be estimated based on available information.[42] Unclear instructions are provided in Section 2.5c for dealing with situations where a previous impairment was based on an older edition of the *AMA Guides*. Such situations are likely to generate substantial confusion and litigation.

If the condition of a person who was rated for permanent impairment unexpectedly worsens, the person may be rated for permanent impairment again. If the person was rated originally under an earlier edition of the *Guides*, the updated

---

[33] *Id.* at 23.
[34] *Id.*
[35] *AMA Guides* (6th ed. 2008) at 24.
[36] *Id.*
[37] *AMA Guides* (6th ed. 2008) at 25.
[38] *Id.*
[39] *Id.*
[40] *Id.*
[41] *AMA Guides* (6th ed. 2008) at 26.
[42] *Id.*

rating must be done under the sixth edition.[43] This edict creates some interesting potential problems. Suppose a person who receives a 12 percent impairment rating under an earlier edition worsens and, when rated again under the sixth edition, receives a lower impairment rating for a worsened condition. Is the person owed a refund? Is this a fair and reasonable outcome?

Section 2.5g in the sixth edition is all new. This section states that cultural differences can "greatly increase the risk of the examiner misinterpreting the patient's responses."[44] Raters are instructed to use qualified interpreters and not family members.[45] This statement makes the qualifications of the interpreter an even more important issue.

The sixth edition states that Waddell's signs are invalid in non-Anglo cultures as they have been tested only on English and North American patients.[46] Does this statement mean that any method of testing for symptom magnification that has not been tested on a particular culture is invalid when used on that culture? Are the *AMA Guides* as a whole invalid because their reliability has not been tested?

The sixth edition states that the examiner must be cognizant of cultural differences.[47] However, no instruction is provided on exactly how to implement this. Are examiners supposed to treat people differently based on their culture? Does this mean that an examiner who is not cognizant of cultural differences cannot rate impairment? Nowhere is it explained what the examiner who is cognizant of cultural differences is supposed to do with this knowledge.

The sixth edition provides examples of cultural differences among Asians, Native Americans, and Hispanics. No other cultures are mentioned. The examples on page 27 of the sixth edition provide extremely broad generalizations that may be controversial or considered by some to be offensive.

The examinee's medical records, diagnostic studies, and lab reports must be reviewed prior to rating for impairment.[48] Evaluations of impairment of the extremities should be performed bilaterally, with an uninjured extremity as the baseline.[49] Also required is a precise discussion of how the guidelines are applied, citing the appropriate tables and pages in the *AMA Guides*.[50] A sample report template is provided on page 30 to "ensure that all essential elements are included in the impairment evaluation report."[51] This template is for entering whatever reason or reasons that are clearly inconsistent with the requirements stated above. Surprisingly, the template does not contain a field for the impairment rating or a field for indicating how the rating was calculated.

---

[43] *Id.*
[44] *Id.* at 27.
[45] *AMA Guides* (6th ed. 2008) at 27.
[46] *Id.*
[47] *Id.*
[48] *AMA Guides* (6th ed. 2008) at 28.
[49] *Id.*
[50] *Id.*
[51] *Id.*

§ 5.06   CHAPTER 3: PAIN-RELATED IMPAIRMENT

Chapter 3 contains a new approach to the evaluation of pain-related impairment. The authors of the sixth edition clearly struggled with whether a chapter on pain should be included, and, if so, how pain should be rated. Neither proponents nor opponents of rating pain are likely to be satisfied with the system for rating pain set forth in the sixth edition.

Ratings for pain can be performed only in the limited circumstances where the examinee's condition cannot be rated using other chapters in the *AMA Guides*. In those circumstances, an impairment rating up to 3 percent (and no higher) may be given for chronic pain, based on the examinee's responses to a 15-question Pain Disability Questionnaire, which is accompanied by precise instructions (literally down to the millimicron).[52] How accurately the rating physician follows these instructions will no doubt become an issue in many cases.

The tentative rating achieved on the basis of the Pain Disability Questionnaire may be reduced (or increased) by examiners who suspect the examinee's credibility, but the rating may never exceed 3 percent.[53] Pain impairments are stand-alone; add-on impairments for pain are explicitly prohibited.[54]

There is a practical, logistical problem with this approach. In the sixth edition, the Pain Disability Questionnaire is reprinted, with the permission of its copyright owners, on page 43. Nowhere is permission given for a user of the *AMA Guides* to copy that information from the *AMA Guides*. There are no instructions given regarding where to go to obtain copies of the questionnaire or where to seek permission to reproduce the questionnaire published in the sixth edition.

The problems with this system of rating pain are obvious. The rating is based on the subjective self-report of the examinee and can be easily overreported. On the other hand, for persons experiencing chronic pain, the 3 percent cap on impairments may not be indicative of the person's true level of impairment. This system is based on judgment and not empirical data.[55] Indeed, the 3 percent cap was determined by precedent, as that was the amount used in the fifth edition of the *AMA Guides*.[56]

Chapter 3 contains a long discussion of both sides of the debate over including ratings for pain. Included as part of this debate is a candid statement regarding the impairment numbers contained in the *AMA Guides* as a whole. An argument against rating for pain is the lack of empirical evidence. The *AMA Guides* themselves admit that "most of the conventional ratings in the Guides are not validated by empirical research."[57] It can be anticipated that this admission will be used in future legal and political challenges to the *AMA Guides*.

---

[52] *AMA Guides* (6th ed. 2008) at 43, 44.

[53] *Id.* at 40.

[54] *Id.* at 39, 581.

[55] *Id.* at 37.

[56] *Id.* at 45.

[57] *Id.* at 37.

§ 5.07   CHAPTER 4: THE CARDIOVASCULAR SYSTEM

Chapter 4 in the sixth edition has been redesigned for greater internal consistency. The key factor (determining impairment class) for cardiovascular impairments is objective testing. This key factor determines the class of impairment. The non-key factors that can serve to adjust an impairment rating within the class are the history and physical findings. Table 4-15 in the sixth edition[58] serves as a useful tool for counsel as it indexes by diagnoses (such as stroke, MI, angina pectoris) the tables to be used to evaluate impairment.

§ 5.08   CHAPTER 5: THE PULMONARY SYSTEM

The key factor used in Chapter 5 is objective testing.[59] The non-key factors are history and physical examination.[60] Most impairments are rated under Table 5-4.[61] Asthma is rated under Table 5-5.[62] No additional impairment should be added for burdens of treatment, as such burdens are already factored into the ratings in the tables of the chapter. Sections 5.1 ("Assessing the Pulmonary System"), 5.3b ("Occupational History"), and 5.4A ("Physical Examination") provide details on what the rating physician should be doing, and these sections could be useful for cross-examination.

§ 5.09   CHAPTER 6: THE DIGESTIVE SYSTEM

Many of the ratings under the sixth edition have been revised downward, because the ratings in previous editions took into account the effect of impairment on other organ systems.[63] The sixth edition encourages raters to rate the other organ systems separately and combine the resulting impairments.[64] Chapter 6 permits additional ratings of Burdens of Treatment Compliance (BOTC) according to the point system contained in Appendix B of the sixth edition on pages 607 and 608.[65] The rationale for this is the increasing use of parenteral nutrition programs.[66]

The key factor for most digestive impairments is history.[67] The key factor for hernias is physical findings.[68] Successful hernia repairs usually result in a 0 percent

---

[58] *AMA Guides* (6th ed. 2008) at 74–75.
[59] *AMA Guides* (6th ed. 2008) at 86.
[60] *Id.*
[61] *Id.* at 88.
[62] *Id.* at 90.
[63] *AMA Guides* (6th ed. 2008) at 102.
[64] *Id.*
[65] *Id.* at 102.
[66] *Id.*
[67] *Id.*
[68] *Id.* at 122.

rating.[69] Table 6-11[70] provides information on which table to use for common digestive diagnoses.

§ 5.10   CHAPTER 7: THE URINARY AND REPRODUCTIVE SYSTEMS

Many of the ratings under Chapter 7 are lower than the ratings made under previous editions because the previous ratings reflected the impact of impairment on secondary organ systems.[71] Raters using the sixth edition are encouraged to rate the other affected systems separately and then combine the resulting impairments.[72] For example, a person with a spinal cord impairment resulting in urinary dysfunction should be rated under both Chapter 7 and Chapter 17, with the two impairment ratings combined.[73] Similarly, for an individual with a penile impairment the physical aspects are to be rated under Chapter 7 and the rating combined with the rating under Chapter 14 for mental and behavioral disorders such as loss of libido, or interest or orgasm.[74] The key factors used in Chapter 7 ratings vary. BOTC (especially dialysis) are already built into the impairment ratings.[75]

§ 5.11   CHAPTER 8: THE SKIN

The key factor in rating skin impairments is the history, especially medically documented interference with activities of daily living.[76] BOTC (e.g., applying topical medications frequently) are included in the history. The maximum impairment rating in Chapter 8 is 58 percent because it is assumed that persons with severe skin impairments will also have impairments ratable under other chapters, and that those other impairments will be combined with the skin impairment.[77] Facial scarring is rated under Table 11-5 and then combined with other ratings in Chapter 8.[78]

§ 5.12   CHAPTER 9: THE HEMATOPOIETIC SYSTEM

Chapter 9 in the sixth edition contains new tables for rating leukemia, lymphoma, metastatic disease, neutropenia, thrombocytopenia, and bleeding

---

[69] *AMA Guides* (6th ed. 2008) at 121.
[70] *Id.* at 124–27.
[71] *AMA Guides* (6th ed. 2008) at 129.
[72] *Id.*
[73] *Id.* at 131.
[74] *Id.* at 143.
[75] *Id.* at 129–30.
[76] *AMA Guides* (6th ed. 2008) at 167.
[77] *Id.* at 161.
[78] *Id.* at 167.

disorders.[79] The key factors in Chapter 9 vary according to each regional disorder.[80] Many of the ratings in this chapter as in other chapters have been reduced, and the rater is instructed to rate other affected organ systems, if appropriate, and combine the resulting ratings.[81] Additional percentages of impairment may be added for BOTC pursuant to Table 9-3.[82] BOTC include anticoagulant therapy, chronic oral corticosteroids, and transfusions.[83] The additional rating for chronic anticoagulation therapy has been reduced from 10 percent to 5 percent with the (non-evidence-based) explanation that 5 percent "would seem more appropriate."[84] Examiners are warned that because interpretation of symptoms and signs in this area is largely subjective and open to misinterpretation, examiners should obtain objective data.[85] This stipulation may become an issue in ratings under Chapter 9. Table 9-14[86] provides a good overview of the appropriate tables to use for key diagnoses and the other organ systems to check for additional impairment.

§ 5.13   CHAPTER 10: THE ENDOCRINE SYSTEM

The key factor in endocrine impairments is usually the history.[87] Due to the nature of endocrine disorders, physical examination and objective tests are often of limited or no value.[88] Impairments of other organ systems should be rated separately under their respective chapters and then combined with the rating for a Chapter 10 impairment.[89] The BOTC in this chapter are determined via the point system described at pages 216 to 218 of the sixth edition. The BOTC are based on medication use, dietary modification, and procedure-based impairment and are generally then used to determine the grade within the appropriate impairment class.[90]

§ 5.14   CHAPTER 11: EAR, NOSE, AND THROAT AND RELATED STRUCTURES

The most commonly used impairment covered under Chapter 11 is hearing loss. Impairment from hearing loss must be measured with any assistive devices

---

[79] *AMA Guides* (6th ed. 2008) at 184.
[80] *Id.* at 187.
[81] *Id.* at 183–84.
[82] *Id.* at 186.
[83] *Id.*
[84] *Id.*
[85] *Id.* at 184.
[86] *See Id.* at 210–11.
[87] *AMA Guides* (6th ed. 2008) at 214.
[88] *Id.* at 215.
[89] *Id.* at 214.
[90] *Id.* at 216.

removed.[91] Each ear is tested with a pure tone audiometer, and Table 11-1 is used to calculate the impairment.[92] Up to 5 percent impairment may be added to a measurable impairment for tinnitus.[93] The sixth edition notes that tinnitus is subjective and difficult to verify.[94] No correction is made for age-related hearing loss.[95] Chapter 11 also provides tables for rating vertigo, facial disorders and disfigurement, air passage defects, and speech impairment.

§ 5.15   CHAPTER 12: THE VISUAL SYSTEM

The impairment rating system in Chapter 12 does not take into account eye disfigurement.[96] Impairments are rated by measuring visual acuity (blurriness) and visual field (peripheral vision) in both eyes.[97] All impairment ratings must be based on measuring both eyes, as the impairment ratings in the *AMA Guides* are functionally based, and one cannot ignore the function of a "good" eye.[98] Detailed impairment instructions for contrast sensitivity, light sensitivity, color vision defects, and diplopia are not provided in the sixth edition.[99] Where these defects exist, the examiner may adjust the impairment scores pursuant to the guidelines discussed on page 305 of the sixth edition.

§ 5.16   CHAPTER 13: THE CENTRAL AND PERIPHERAL NERVOUS SYSTEM

Chapter 13 does not follow the sixth edition's system for selecting a class with a key factor and then a grade within a class according to non-key factors. As the authors of the sixth edition state, their goal was a chapter that is "evolutionary, but not revolutionary."[100]

Another goal of Chapter 13 was to provide single values rather than ranges for impairment ratings.[101] The stated reason for having single values was that "ranges implied a level of impairment rating validity that does not exist."[102] (This is yet another self-criticism.) The statement also causes some confusion. Almost all of the rating tables in Chapter 13 actually do provide ranges (e.g., 1 percent to

---

[91] *AMA Guides* (6th ed. 2008) at 248.
[92] *Id.* at 250.
[93] *Id.* at 249.
[94] *Id.*
[95] *Id.*
[96] *AMA Guides* (6th ed. 2008) at 282.
[97] *Id.*
[98] *Id.* at 305.
[99] *Id.*
[100] *AMA Guides* (6th ed. 2008) at 321.
[101] *Id.*
[102] *Id.*

10 percent). However, in each example presented, the highest permissible rating under the table is assigned. This raises a number of questions:

1. Are the ranges in the tables a misprint?

2. Are examiners allowed to select a rating within the category lower than the maximum value?

3. Why wasn't Chapter 13 written to be consistent with the other chapters of the sixth edition in terms of key and non-key factors and precise impairment ratings?

4. Are the criticisms of previous editions regarding lack of precise ratings equally applicable to Chapter 13 in the sixth edition?

Complex Regional Pain Syndrome (CRPS), also known as Reflex Sympathetic Dystrophy (RSD), is not ratable under Chapter 13.[103] It is ratable however under Chapter 15 (Upper Extremities) and Chapter 16 (Lower Extremities).

For the first time, a procedure is provided for rating migraine headaches. This procedure, described in Section 13.11, allows for a maximum impairment rating of 5 percent. In addition to migraine, Chapter 13 rates disorders of the cerebral function, disorders of spinal cord function, craniocephalic pain, trigeminal neuralgia, glossopharyngeal neuralgia, miscellaneous nerves of the head and trunk, disorders of the neuromuscular junction, peripheral neuropathy, and myopathic disorders.[104]

Chapter 13 emphasizes that many if not most problems involving nerves are rated under other chapters. For example, radiculopathy is rated under Chapter 17 (Spine) and plexus injuries are rated under both Chapter 15 (Upper Extremities) and Chapter 16 (Lower Extremities).

Table 13-1 on page 323 of the sixth edition provides a quick reference for finding which problems are rated under which chapter(s).

§5.17   CHAPTER 14: MENTAL AND BEHAVIORAL DISORDERS

The only major mental illnesses (as defined in DSM-IV) that are ratable under Chapter 14 are:

*   Mood disorders (including major depressive disorder and bipolar affective disorder);

*   Anxiety disorders (including generalized anxiety disorder, panic disorder, phobias, posttraumatic stress disorder, and obsessive compulsive disorder); and

*   Psychotic disorders (including schizophrenia).[105]

---

[103] *Id.* at 321–22.

[104] *Id.* at 323.

[105] *AMA Guides* (6th ed. 2008) at 349.

Conditions that are not ratable under the sixth edition are:

- Somatoform disorders

- Dissociative disorders

- Personality disorders

- Psychosexual disorders

- Factitious disorders

- Substance use disorders, and

- Mental retardation.

Since ratability is dependent on diagnosis, the diagnosis is a crucial component of a rating under Chapter 14.

The sixth edition states that the psychiatric distress associated with a physical injury is not ratable because the distress has already been included in the rating for the physical injury.[106] Example 14-4[107] is consistent with this mandate. However, on page 349 of the sixth edition, it is stated: "[I]n *most* cases of a mental and behavioral disorder accompanying a physical impairment, the psychological issues are encompassed within the rating for the physical impairment, and the mental and behavioral disorder chapter *should not* be used."[108] No guidance on exceptions is provided. This sentence makes the sixth edition internally inconsistent and provides some justification for assigning additional impairment under Chapter 14 for a physical injury.

Another question is what happens when one of the recognized disorders (such as major depressive disorder) *results from* a physical injury (say the worker hurt his back and then suffered major depression as a result). Is this ratable or not ratable? Is the depression associated with the physical impairment and thus not separately ratable, or is it caused by it and thus presumably ratable? Chapter 17 does not help to clarify the situation; "Under *most* circumstances, however, impairment rating for mental health disorders related to the stressors that often accompany a chronic disabling musculoskeletal disorder, is captured within the rating for the musculoskeletal disorder itself."[109]

Sections 14.2 and 14.3 contain detailed recommendations and information on how to conduct a psychiatric IME. These sections should be carefully studied as they provide counsel with a wealth of information to be used in challenging an examiner's evaluation. The information may include discussions on the limitations of psychological testing in a medical-legal context, faking psychological testing, proper record review techniques, interview techniques, the limitations of definitive

---

[106] *Id.*

[107] *Id.* at 363–64.

[108] *Id.* at 349 (emphases added).

[109] *Id.* at 581.

testing to confirm most major illnesses, and malingering. In the case of malingering, the sixth edition states that "under ordinary circumstances, the health care provider rarely gets a sufficient insight into patient illness behaviors to obtain evidence for such definitive labeling."[110] The sixth edition further states that, because of bias issues and because "mental health clinicians align themselves closely with their patients," professionals who treat mental health patients "should" avoid serving as an expert witness for their patients.[111] Although the sixth edition recognizes the risk of *examinee* exaggeration to obtain monetary awards,[112] no mention is made of the risk of bias or understatement from examiners paid for by employers or insurers.

Chapter 14 uses a system different from the standard key factor/non-key factor system used in most other chapters. First, the examiner must determine by diagnosis whether the impairment is ratable under the *AMA Guides* (most of the 300-plus diagnoses in DSM-IV are not). If the diagnosis is ratable, the examiner will then score three scales: (1) the Brief Psychiatric Rating Scale, (2) the Global Assessment of Functioning Scale, and (3) the Psychiatric Impairment Rating Scale.[113] Instructions for each scale are provided in the sixth edition of the *Guides.* The score for each scale is then converted to an impairment score in accordance with Table 14-9, Table 14-10, or Table 14-17.[114] The examinee's impairment rating is the median (i.e., middle) value of the three impairment scores generated.

§5.18   CHAPTER 15: THE UPPER EXTREMITIES

At 110 pages, Chapter 15 is by far the longest chapter in the sixth edition of the *Guides.* This chapter now uses a diagnosis-based key factor impairment system for most impairments. If a diagnosis is not included in the sixth edition, the examiner is allowed to use a similar condition to determine impairment, as long as the rationale for the analogy is fully explained.[115] The reader is told that range of motion is used as a physical examination grade adjustment and is used to determine impairment in rare cases where definition of impairment is otherwise impossible.[116] These include severe crush injuries, multiple tendon lacerations, and residual compartment syndromes.[117] The reader is then told that conditions in the grid followed by a asterisk *may* be assessed by loss of range of motion if such loss is present.[118] These two contradictory statements are not reconciled. If

---

[110] *Id.* at 353.
[111] *AMA Guides* (6th ed. 2008) at 351.
[112] *Id.* at 353.
[113] *Id.* at 355.
[114] *Id.,* Tables 14-9, 14-10, and 14-11.
[115] *AMA Guides* (6th ed. 2008) at 385.
[116] *Id.* at 387.
[117] *Id.* at 461.
[118] *Id.* at 390, 394.

an examinee has a ratable diagnosis, then it would seem possible to rate the examinee using the diagnosis-based method. Does the examiner have discretion to rate under range of motion for these conditions? When range of motion is used as a primary method, it is not combined with other methods, except in the case of amputation.[119] The instructions on page 461 do not settle the inconsistency when they state that range of motion is to be used when the grid refers the reader to the range of motion section or when no other diagnosis-based impairments are applicable.[120]

Surgery to a joint does not result in additional impairment.[121] Impairments in Chapter 15 may be expressed as of the digit, hand, upper extremity, or whole person using the conversion formulas in the *Guides*.

The grade of impairment within each class is primarily adjusted with the non-key factors of functional status, physical examination, and clinical test results. The non-key factors are only considered if the examiner determines they are reliable and associated with the diagnosis.[122] For example, examiners are instructed to disregard an examinee's self-reports of functional status that do not correlate with the underlying diagnosis. If the non-key factor is primarily used to determine class, it may not be used to determine grade (e.g., an X-ray to determine carpal instability).[123]

A strict protocol for rating CRPS impairments is provided in Chapter 15. Vascular conditions are not rated under Chapter 15 but are rated under Section 4.8.[124] Impairment based on cervical spine pathology is rated under Chapter 17.[125] Some of the impairment values presented in the sixth edition are different from those in previous editions.[126]

The authors of Chapter 15 in the sixth edition are candidly self-critical. They recognize that, despite their intention to "provide a solid basis for future editions of the *Guides*," the process presented in the chapter is "far from perfect."[127]

Section 15.1—a section that would be useful on cross-examination—provides a list of things an examiner should watch for when taking and reporting a history. The non-key factor of functional history is discussed at page 386. The examiner is authorized to use a functional assessment tool to assist in determining functional history, and the *Quick*DASH is recommended.[128] The *Quick*DASH is a shortened version of the DASH Outcome Measure. Instead of 30 items, the *Quick*-DASH uses 11 items to measure physical function and symptoms in people with any or multiple musculoskeletal disorders of the upper limb.

---

[119] *Id.* at 387.

[120] *Id.* at 461.

[121] *AMA Guides* (6th ed. 2008) at 389.

[122] *Id.* at 385, 406.

[123] *Id.* at 405.

[124] *Id.* at 384.

[125] *Id.* at 386.

[126] *Id.* at 384.

[127] *Id.*

[128] *AMA Guides* (6th ed. 2008) at 386.

The examiner is given the option of not considering functional history as a grade modifier if the examinee's subjective complaints are inconsistent with the underlying diagnoses.[129] If the grade for functional history differs by more than one grade from the diagnosis, the examiner should assume the functional history is unreliable and should not use it as a grade modifier.[130]

In determining functional assessment, the examiner is encouraged to basically spy on the examinee ("observe" is the word used; "casually observed" is the euphemism used in Example 15-5 on page 415) to determine how well the examinee performs a function such as writing.[131] The examiner is asked to note inconsistencies.[132] Two functions that are suggested for "observation" are changing into a hospital gown and dressing after the examination.[133]

The examiners who follow these recommendations in the sixth edition could be subjected to a devastating cross-examination, and those who do not follow the recommendations could be challenged for not following the *AMA Guides.*

Appendix 15.9 in the sixth edition discusses the *Quick*DASH in some detail. Appendix 15.9 also lists a Web site from which the examiner may access the *Quick*DASH Outcome Measure.[134] The examiner is instructed to attach the examinee's answer to the evaluation report.[135] The *Quick*DASH cannot be used unless the examinee answers at least 10 of the 11 questions.[136] Examiners using the *Quick*-DASH are required to correlate for consistency (and, thus, symptom magnification) the information provided to activities of daily living.[137] The *AMA Guides* recognize that inconsistency can be caused by poor language proficiency or organic brain injury.[138]

Appendix 15.9 also explains why the *Quick*DASH was adopted. The endorsement is less than ringing. The sixth edition of the *Guides* states that "[a]t this time the *Quick*DASH *appears to be* the most acceptable functional assessment measure."[139] The sixth edition also acknowledges that *Quick*DASH has "a few deficiencies," although there are no details about those deficiencies.[140]

Instructions for conducting detailed physical examinations are provided on pages 386 and 407. These sections should be read carefully by counsel as they provide a checklist of things the examiner should do and how to do it. The

---

[129] *Id.*
[130] *Id.* at 406–07.
[131] *Id.* at 386.
[132] *Id.*
[133] *Id.*
[134] *AMA Guides* (6th ed. 2008) at 482.
[135] *Id.*
[136] *Id.*
[137] *Id.*
[138] *Id.*
[139] *Id.* at 486 (emphasis added).
[140] *Id.*

unaffected extremity is used as a baseline to determine normalcy.[141] Objective findings (e.g., atrophy) are given greater weight over findings within the control of the examinee (e.g., active range of motion, strength, reports of tenderness).[142]

Clinical studies are discussed on page 386. The examiner is instructed to personally review the actual studies and the findings from the studies.[143] In cases where this was not done (e.g., because the films were not provided), the examiner will be vulnerable on cross-examination.

Examiners are asked to include all of the information in Figure 15-2 in their reports.[144] Only one diagnosis is to be used in most cases.[145] In cases where the examinee has two significant diagnoses, the examiner should use the higher one.[146] The sixth edition goes on to say that in cases of more than one diagnosis, the more specific diagnosis should be used.[147] These two inconsistent instructions are not clearly reconciled. Further discussion is made in Section 15.3f. Here the examiner is instructed to rate the highest impairment in a region (shoulder, elbow, wrist, digits/hand), but is given discretion to rate multiple impairments within a region if the most impairing diagnosis does not adequately reflect loss.[148] When the evaluator is uncertain whether to rate separately and choose the highest rating or to combine impairments, the instructions are to rate both ways and then "choose the method or combination of methods that gives the most clinically accurate impairment rating."[149] This instruction provides little objective guidance on what to do. If the examiner does choose to combine, he must explain in writing his rationale for choosing to do so.[150]

Chapter 2, "the constitution" of the sixth edition, does not help to resolve this inconsistency. It states that "related but separate conditions are rated separately and impairment ratings are combined unless criteria for the second impairment are included in the primary impairment."[151] It also states that "[i]f the Guides provides more than one method to rate a particular impairment or condition, the method producing the higher impairment *must* be used."[152]

The sixth edition expresses a remarkable credibility judgment regarding examiners who routinely use multiple diagnoses without supporting data.[153] With such examiners the validity and reliability of their evaluations may be questioned.[154]

---

[141] *AMA Guides* (6th ed. 2008) at 386.
[142] *Id.*
[143] *Id.* at 386, 407.
[144] *Id.* at 387.
[145] *Id.*
[146] *Id.*
[147] *AMA Guides* (6th ed. 2008) at 389.
[148] *Id.* at 419.
[149] *Id.*
[150] *Id.*
[151] *Id.* at 25.
[152] *Id.* at 20 (emphasis added).
[153] *AMA Guides* (6th ed. 2008) at 387.
[154] *Id.*

This statement injects the sixth edition into determining the credibility of expert witnesses and can be seen as another thinly veiled preference for ratings by medical examiners for the defense over ratings by treating physicians. It also brings into question under the *Guides* an examiner's past history. Of note is that no mention is made of the credibility of examiners who routinely find no impairment.

Since impairments are based upon diagnosis, accuracy of the diagnosis is essential.[155] This requires "judgment and experience."[156] Counsel may be able to argue that for many defense medical examiners, recent clinical experience is lacking.

Peripheral nerve impairments are rated under Section 15.4. Peripheral nerve impairments may be combined with diagnosis-based impairments of upper extremities if the DBI did not encompass the nerve impairment.[157] Deficits must be permanent and unequivocal in order to be rated.[158] Sensory defects are acknowledged to be challenging to rate since they are based on the patient's subjective reports.[159] Motor deficits are based on strength testing, which is also subjective.[160] Manual muscle testing is very challenging in examinees who are in pain or who fear pain.[161] Sensory defects on the dorsal thumb and fingers are not considered to be impairing.[162]

Entrapment neuropathy is rated under Section 15.4f. It uses its own system as described on pages 448 and 449. The most common conditions covered are carpal tunnel syndrome and focal compromise of the ulnar nerve at the elbow. To be ratable under this section they must be documented by sensory and motor nerve conduction studies and/or needle EMG.[163] If, due to test results, the entrapment is not ratable under Section 15.4f, it may be rated as a Diagnosis-Based Impairment for nonspecific pain.[164] Detailed instructions on diagnosing entrapment neuropathy and electrodiagnostic studies are contained in Chapter 15 and in Appendix 15-B. The examiner is instructed to suspect symptom magnification if the examinee has a *Quick*DASH score of 60 or greater and refuses surgery.[165]

Very mild nerve entrapments exist, but may not be ratable under the *Guides*.[166] Other conditions that are typically not ratable under the *Guides* include tension pattern headache, dysmenorrhea, irritable bowel syndrome, and fibromyalgia.[167]

---

[155] *Id.* at 389.

[156] *Id.*

[157] *Id.* at 419.

[158] *Id.* at 423.

[159] *AMA Guides* (6th ed. 2008) at 424.

[160] *Id.* at 425.

[161] *Id.*

[162] *Id.* at 426.

[163] *Id.* at 445.

[164] *Id.* at 433.

[165] *AMA Guides* (6th ed. 2008) at 447.

[166] *Id.*

[167] *Id.*

Complex Regional Pain Syndrome (CRPS) impairments of the upper extremities are rated under Section 15.5. The *Guides* state that CRPS has not been scientifically validated as a specific and discrete heath condition and that the diagnostic process is unreliable, but CRPS is ratable nonetheless.[168]

A CRPS rating depends on four requirements: (1) confirmation by objective parameters; (2) diagnosis present for one year; (3) diagnoses verified by more than one physician; and (4) comprehensive ruling out (differential diagnosis) of other diagnoses.[169] The differential diagnosis must rule out somatoform disorders, factitious disorders, and malingering.[170] (This raises the question whether a mental health professional needs to be involved in differential diagnosis.) The process used to determine impairment from CRPS-I differs from the process used for determining impairment under other sections of the *Guides.* Impairment class is determined by objective diagnostic criteria points (e.g., skin color changes, nail changes, etc.).[171] The grade within the class is determined not by a mathematical formula as in other sections but rather by the physician's clinical judgment.[172] Examinees who do not qualify for CRPS impairment may be rated under Chapter 3 for pain.[173] CRPS-II involves a specific nerve and is rated under Table 15-21 after severity is determined by Table 15-26.[174]

Amputation impairment is determined under Section 15.6. Of note is the information on which the impairment percentages are based. It is incomprehensible that many percentages in the sixth edition, which boasts it contains the latest information, come from an article published in 1964!

Range of motion is discussed in Section 15.7. The methods for measuring range of motion employed in past editions of the *AMA Guides* have been retained in the sixth edition. Provisions for rounding, warming up, detecting pain behavior, and obtaining usable measurements are all provided and should be carefully read by counsel in an applicable case (i.e., where range of motion is used as a grade modifier or a stand-alone method). A warning on relying on active range of motion is made as active range of motion is under the control of the examinee.[175] Where applicable, the unaffected upper extremity is used to define normal.[176] Impairment percentages are based directly on the range of motion. The greater the range, the less the impairment.

---

[168] *Id.* at 451.
[169] *Id.*
[170] *Id.*
[171] *AMA Guides* (6th ed. 2008) at 452–53.
[172] *Id.* at 452.
[173] *Id.*
[174] *Id.* at 451.
[175] *Id.* at 461.
[176] *Id.*

§5.19 CHAPTER 16: THE LOWER EXTREMITIES

Chapter 16 adopts a methodology that is generally consistent with Chapter 15. The diagnosis-based impairment method (with diagnosis as the key factor and functional history, physical examination, and clinical studies as non-key factors) is the primary and preferred method used.[177] As in Chapter 15, the non-key factors are only considered if they are determined to be reliable and associated with the diagnosis.[178]

Vascular problems in the lower extremity are rated under Section 4.8 of the *AMA Guides.* Peripheral nerve disorders are rated under Section 16.4. CRPS is rated under Section 16.5, and amputation is rated under Section 16.6. If problems in the lower extremities are related to a spinal problem, they are generally assessed under Chapter 17.[179]

The impairment values have been adjusted in some cases from previous editions.[180] If a specific diagnosis is not listed in the applicable grids, the examiner is asked to use a similar condition and then explain the rationale for the analogy.[181] The examiner is also instructed to use the range of motion model where no diagnosis-based sections are applicable.[182] The potential conflict between these statements is not resolved. If the diagnosis is not included in the grids, should the examiner use range of motion or an analogous similar diagnosis? Page 529 seems to suggest that the examiner can use either method as long as the ratings are done both ways and "the most clinically accurate impairment rating" is selected. No instructions are provided on judging clinical accuracy. Note that range of motion is also used in some of the diagnosis grids to place an examinee in a class and as a factor in the physical examination grade modifier (Table 16-7, page 517).

If an examinee has multiple diagnoses, each diagnosis should be rated.[183] On page 497 of the sixth edition, it is stated that in the case of two significant diagnoses the examiner should use the highest score and that examiners who routinely rate multiple diagnoses should be suspect.[184] Page 499 states that if more than one diagnosis can be used, the examiner should use the one that is most clinically accurate. On page 552, however, it states that in the case of more than one ratable diagnosis, the impairment values should be combined at the lower extremity level.

These conflicting statements give rise to the following question: When is it appropriate to combine multiple impairments of the lower extremity?

---

[177] *AMA Guides* (6th ed. 2008) at at 495.
[178] *Id.*
[179] *Id.* at 496.
[180] *Id.* at 494.
[181] *Id.* at 495.
[182] *Id.* at 543.
[183] *AMA Guides* (6th ed. 2008) at 497.
[184] *Id.*

Page 529 seems to leave it to the examiner's discretion whether to rate multiple impairments and either combine the ratings or just take one rating per region. The test on page 529 is duplication and which rating is most clinically accurate. The examiner is instructed to rate both ways when in doubt and explain the rationale for the rating chosen. Chapter 2, "the constitution" of the *Guides*, does not help to resolve this inconsistency. Chapter 2 states that "[r]elated but separate conditions are rated separately and impairment ratings are combined unless criteria for the second impairment are included in the primary impairment."[185] However, Chapter 2 also states that "[i]f the *Guides* provide more than one method to rate a particular impairment or condition, the method producing the higher impairment *must* be used."[186]

Chapter 16, like other sections of the *Guides*, is candidly self-critical. The authors of the sixth edition state that this chapter is far from perfect yet provides a solid basis for presumably improved future editions.[187]

Section 16.1a contains a laundry list of things the physician must and should do in terms of taking a history, drafting the report, examining records, and so forth. It should be read carefully by counsel and can provide a good outline for direct or cross-examination of a physician.

The diagnosis that is "most applicable" should be selected.[188] This requires judgment and experience.[189] There is no additional impairment percentage per se for surgery.[190]

If a non-key factor was used as a primary criterion for class assignment, it cannot be used again as a grade modifier.[191]

The examiner may use outcome instruments and assessments when assessing functional history.[192] The AAOS Lower Limb instrument contained in Appendix 16-A may be used for this purpose.[193] The *Guides* do not, however, provide instructions on how to score the AAOS instrument. Functional history is assumed to be unreliable and is not considered if it differs by more than one grade from physical examination and clinical studies.[194]

In physical examinations, greater weight is given to objective findings.[195] Specific instructions for measuring limb circumference and limb length discrepancy are found on page 518. Examiners are instructed to review actual clinical

---

[185] *Id.* at 25.

[186] *Id.* at 20 (emphasis added).

[187] *Id.* at 494.

[188] *Id.* at 499.

[189] *Id.*

[190] *Id.*

[191] *AMA Guides* (6th ed. 2008) at 516.

[192] *Id.*

[193] *Id.*

[194] *Id.*

[195] *Id.* at 517.

studies whenever possible.[196] Specific instructions for how imaging studies of lower extremity joints should be taken are set forth on page 518.

There is some ambiguity on determining proper grade. The *Guides* states that where there are multiple components to a grade (e.g., a physical examination could include range of motion, stability, knee, and so forth), the examiner is to choose "the most objective grade modifier with the highest value."[197] This instruction raises questions. What if the most objective grade modifier does not have the highest value? Who is to say which is the most objective grade modifier? Did the authors of the sixth edition mean to say the highest value *from* the most objective grade modifier? Example 16-4 seems to suggest that the examiner would just take the highest value.

Peripheral nerve impairment is rated according to Section 16.4. When there is a nerve lesion, no other rating method is also applied.[198] The sixth edition of the *Guides* recognizes that sensory deficits are subjective and difficult to grade.[199] The same is true of motor defects.[200]

Complex Regional Pain Syndrome (CRPS-1 and CRPS-II) is rated in a way analogous to that described in Chapter 15 discussed above. Amputation is rated under Section 16.6.

Range of motion is discussed in Section 16.7. Range of motion is primarily used in some of the diagnosis grids to place an impairment in a class and as a factor in the physical examination grade modifier (Table 16-7, page 517). It is also used as a stand-alone when no diagnosis grids are applicable.[201] The circumstances include burns or other severe scarring, complex flexor or extension tendon or multiple laceration injuries, severe crush injuries, and residual compartment injury.[202] Detailed instructions on measuring range of motion are provided. Impairment is based directly on the range of motion and is calculated via Table 16-25. Functional history may in certain circumstances be used as a modifier.[203]

§ 5.20   CHAPTER 17: THE SPINE AND PELVIS

Impairments of the spine and pelvis are now diagnosis-based, with impairment adjustments made for the non-key factors of functional history, physical examination, and clinical studies. In the sixth edition, the authors state that range of motion is no longer used because current evidence does not support its

---

[196] *Id.* at 518.

[197] *AMA Guides* (6th ed. 2008) at 521.

[198] *Id.* at 531.

[199] *Id.* at 532.

[200] *Id.* at 533.

[201] *Id.* at 543.

[202] *Id.*

[203] *AMA Guides* (6th ed. 2008) at 544.

reliability.[204] Interestingly, no citation to this current evidence is provided. Also, no mention is made of the reliability of range of motion for the upper and lower extremities where this method is retained in some circumstances. As in other musculoskeletal chapters the authors admit that their new process is "far from perfect."[205]

The categories of diagnoses covered include nonspecific pain, disk and motion segment pathologies, stenosis, fractures, and dislocations.[206] As in the other musculoskeletal chapters, Chapter 17 instructs the examiner to use a similar condition as a guide, if the diagnosis in question is not listed, and then fully explain the analogy.[207] Because diagnosis is the key factor in rating impairment, reliability of the diagnosis is essential. And to determine the reliability of the diagnosis requires judgment and experience.[208]

The instructions for multiple diagnoses are once again vague and somewhat contradictory. Where more than one diagnosis can be used, the examiner is told to select the most clinically accurate one, generally the most specific.[209] Examiners are also told to select the highest causally related diagnosis.[210] Section 17.3h only adds to the confusion. It instructs examiners to determine whether multiple diagnoses should be considered or if they are duplicative.[211] For multiple diagnoses within a region of the spine, the examiner should select the most serious injury unless that injury does not adequately reflect the loss.[212] If there is any doubt, the examiner should calculate all the impairments and choose the one that is most clinically accurate.[213] No guidance is given on how to make these determinations. Chapter 2 ("the constitution") in the *AMA Guides* does not help to resolve this inconsistency. Chapter 2 states that "related but separate conditions are rated separately and impairment ratings are combined unless criteria for the second impairment are included in the primary impairment."[214] However, Chapter 2 also says that "[i]f the *Guides* provide more than one method to rate a particular impairment or condition, the method producing the higher impairment *must* be used."[215]

There is a specific list of conditions not ratable under the *Guides*. Those conditions include annular tears, facet arthropathy, disk degeneration, spina bifida occulta, abnormal segmentation, conjoined nerve roots, spondylolysis, some forms

---

[204] *Id.* at 558.
[205] *Id.* at 559.
[206] *Id.*
[207] *Id.*
[208] *Id.* at 562.
[209] *Id.*
[210] *Id.*
[211] *AMA Guides* (6th ed. 2008) at 592.
[212] *Id.*
[213] *Id.*
[214] *Id.* at 25.
[215] *Id.* at 20 (emphasis added).

of spondylolisthesis, kyphosis, excessive lordosis, and scoliosis.[216] Chronic sprain/strain is rated at 1 to 3 percent whole-person impairment.[217]

Functional history may be measured with functional assessment tools.[218] Specifically listed as being acceptable are the Pain Disability Questionnaire and the Oswestry Disability Index.[219] The Pain Disability Questionnaire (PDQ) is reproduced in Appendix 17-A of the sixth edition, along with scoring instructions and a grid to translate scores into grades. Examiners are told to reproduce the questionnaire,[220] but permission to do so is not explicitly granted on page 600 where the PDQ appears. No instruction is provided on what other assessments are reliable or how to convert the scores of other assessments to grades for use in the *AMA Guides*. Functional histories that differ by more than one grade from clinical studies and physical examination are deemed unreliable and are not to be used.[221]

Fairly specific instructions on what to look for on physical exam are provided.[222] Table 17-7 contains inconsistent instructions concerning the use of grade modifiers. On page 568, examiners are instructed to use the highest grade. On page 582, they are instructed to use the highest modifier that is objective and is associated with the rated diagnosis. On page 590, Example 17-14 seems to suggest that the examiner should use the highest modifier he or she considers reliable.

In terms of clinical studies, examiners are once again directed to look at the actual studies.[223] Surgery does not result in add-on impairment.[224] Detailed instructions on how the studies should be conducted and interpreted, and what these tests can and cannot show are found on pages 577 to 580 of the sixth edition.

---

[216] *Id.* at 563.

[217] *Id.*

[218] *AMA Guides* (6th ed. 2008) at 560.

[219] *Id.* at 572.

[220] *Id.* at 599.

[221] *Id.* at 572.

[222] *Id.* at 560, 572–76.

[223] *Id.* at 560.

[224] *AMA Guides* (6th ed. 2008) at 562.

EXHIBIT 5-1   UNDERSTANDING THE AMA GUIDES

EXHIBIT 5-1.   **Difficult Cross-Examination Questions Under the Sixth Edition of the *AMA Guides***

Q.   Are you an expert in the sixth edition of the *AMA Guides*, Doctor?

Comment. Counsel here it trying to "lock down" the expert by getting her to commit to the degree of her expertise. If she says she is not an expert, counsel could move to exclude her testimony or rating. If the doctor says she is an expert, then counsel can cross-examine her on anything and everything in the text.

Q.   What don't you agree with in the sixth edition of the *Guides*?

Comment. Counsel is trying to get the physician to either say that he agrees with everything in the 634-page book or start to list points of disagreement with the book. If the physician testifies that he is familiar only with portions of the *Guides*, the question becomes which portions/chapters has he read?

Q.   Are you saying under oath that the impairment rating numbers in the sixth edition are precise, accurate, reliable, and valid?

Comment. Counsel is attempting to put the rating physician on the defensive about his testimony. Physicians may be reluctant to testify to a reasonable degree of medical certainty about these aspects of the sixth edition. In addition, if an affirmative response is given, counsel can then utilize section 1.4 and the definitions of these four terms to impeach the physician.

Q.   Sometimes you are a treating physician and other times an independent medical examiner. Do you agree with the sixth edition that you cannot be trusted to give an independent impairment rating for patients you have treated?

Comment. Here counsel is attacking a fundamental weakness of the sixth edition—namely, the statement that treating physicians cannot be trusted to give an honest impairment rating on their patients. A doctor who treats patients and occasionally performs impairment ratings during an IME will be hard pressed to say that he himself cannot be trusted to fairly and independently rate his patients.

Q.   Doctor, our Workers' Compensation statute and case law provide that the psychological distress that flows directly from a physical injury is compensable, but you did not rate it when you arrived at your impairment rating. Why did you flaunt the Workers' Compensation law?

Comment. Counsel is contrasting the workers' compensation statute with the sixth edition of the *AMA Guides*. In cross-examination, counsel will be able to use the contradictory language on page 349: "In most cases of a mental and behavioral disorder accompanying a physical impairment, the psychological issues are encompassed within the rating for the physical impairment. . . ."

Q.   Which chapters of the sixth edition did you use to rate the claimant, Doctor?

Comment. Counsel is trying to back the physician into a corner by forcing him to name the chapters he used/considered in his rating. If the physician fails to mention chapter 1, 2 (the constitution), 3, 14, or other applicable chapters, counsel can attack the validity of the rating and the care, accuracy, and thoroughness of the physician.

Q. As the sixth edition explicitly states that the impairment numbers are estimates, what is the margin of error in the numbers and your impairment rating doctor?

Comment. Counsel is attempting to start the doctor down the slippery slope of margin of error. Counsel can then take the margin of error for each number and combine them to point the range of possible ratings.

Q. You are required under Section 1.8c(7) to score the self-report tool and assess the results for consistency and credibility, and provide your rationale. Where is that in your report, Doctor?

Comment. Counsel here is putting the rating physician to one of the numerous tasks that the sixth edition requires her to do. Physicians may not appreciate this and may be caught off guard. The reliability of the rating itself may be called into question by counsel.

Q. Tell me, Doctor, how you used your knowledge, skill, and ability generally accepted by the medical scientific community when you took a number from the sixth edition and swore under oath that it was accurate and reliable?

Comment. Counsel here is utilizing the 14 fundamental principles of the guides set forth on page 20. The physician may be hard pressed to justify using numbers from a book that may or may not be based science or medicine.

Q. Doctor did you consider the "burden of treatment compliance" and assign points on the basis of medication use, dietary modifications, frequency of routinely performed procedures, and history of prior operative procedures as set forth in Appendix B on page 607?

Comment. Counsel here is attacking the physician's knowledge of the entire text and the fact that in most chapters, the burden of treatment compliance, or BOTC, is already built into the ratings. To answer this type of question confidently and correctly, the physician would have to know which chapters include BOTC and which do not.

Q. Did you consider the subjective complaints of the examinee in arriving at your impairment rating?

Comment. Counsel here can utilize at least two confusing sections of the sixth edition: Section 1.8 (page 15) requires the physician consider subjective reports when arriving at his functional assessment. Fundamental principle 13 (page 20) says that subjective complaints alone are generally not ratable under the guides. (*See* Chapter 3, "Pain," for potential exceptions.) Forcing the physician to talk about the subjective complaints of the examinee may help both with the impairment rating and the claim for disability and lost time.

Q. Doctor, can you explain when and how physicians under the sixth edition are supposed to rate permanent impairment by analogy?

Comment. The guides provide a cryptic statement on page 23 about "rating permanent impairment by analogy only if the guides provide no other method for rating objectively identifiable impairment." Counsel can utilize this as a catchall question to put the physician on the defensive and also use it when she claims no other methods are identified in the guides for rating the impairment.

Q. Doctor, Section 2.4d states: "the impairment ratings in the body organ system chapters make allowance for most of the functional losses accompanying pain." Which losses are not covered, and do you consider them in your rating?

Comment. Counsel here is utilizing an ambiguity in the guides to call into question the rating performed by the physician. As there is no apparent answer in the book, the physician will be on his own in trying to honestly answer the question under oath.

Q. What are the five new axioms of the sixth edition?

Comment: This is a purely factual question based on Section 1.2b (page 2). If the doctor is not familiar with the axioms (or even what the word means), he may be hard pressed to impress the finder of fact with his knowledge of the sixth edition.

Q. Doctor, since the claimant was initially rated under the fourth edition, his condition has worsened. Your rating is based on the fifth edition, as is required by our statute. The sixth edition states in Section 2.4d (page 26) that in these circumstances the latest edition (i.e., the sixth) should be used to rate the condition. Are you not using the wrong text to rate this injured claimant?

Comment. With the numerous harsh criticisms of the fifth edition (page 2), this text calls into question the reliability and validity of any and all ratings being performed using a prior edition. Counsel may have solid grounds to challenge these ratings.

Q. Doctor, can you explain why this claimant with chronic, severe, unremitting pain should only receive 3 percent for his pain?

Comment. Counsel here is attempting to get the doctor to justify the arbitrary 3 percent maximum he is permitted to award for chronic severe pain. The more the doctor tries to explain or justify it, the more he will sound like he is just bound by some unreasonable book.

Q. Doctor, the pain disability questionnaire in Appendix 3-2 talks about a milli-micron in scoring the questionnaire. What is a millimicron?

Comment. The more counsel can show that the physician is just blindly following a book without even knowing what it means, the more vulnerable and suspect the ratings become.

Q. Doctor, in rating the claimant under Chapter 13 for her neurological impairment, you are required under Section 13.1 to note if the report of ADL loss is consistent with the impairment evident in your office. Can you explain how you were able to do this with regard to sexual function and money management?

Comment. Counsel is pointing out the difficulty of assessing certain ADLs in his office, as required under Section 13.1 (page 322).

Q. Doctor, in rating the claimant's upper extremity you used the diagnosis-based method. Why did you not perform the rating as required by the range of motion method?

Comment. Counsel here is pointing out a possible inconsistency in this chapter. On page 387 physicians are told to use the diagnosis method, but on pages 390 and 394 the text says that conditions in the grid followed by an asterisk "may be" assessed by a range of motion if such loss is present.

Q. Doctor, when rating the claimant's spinal permanent impairment, did you use the eight steps set forth in the *Guides?*

Comment. Counsel is again questioning the physician's familiarity with the sixth edition. The steps are set forth on page 597. If the physician testifies he used the steps, he will then have to explain the eight steps themselves and how he used them.

CHAPTER 6

DIRECT EXAMINATION: USING THE *AMA GUIDES* TO PROVE PERMANENT IMPAIRMENT

§ 6.01   INTRODUCTION

To learn how to prove permanent impairment using the American Medical Association's *Guides to the Evaluation of Permanent Impairment* (hereinafter *AMA Guides*), claimant's counsel must (1) know precisely what must be proven under the *AMA Guides*; (2) lay a detailed foundation with the claimant's testimony; and (3) prepare the physician to testify. These tasks are examined in detail in the following sections.

§ 6.02   KNOWING WHAT MUST BE PROVEN

In permanent impairment cases, it is extremely important for counsel to know precisely what must be proven under the *AMA Guides*. If counsel is unfamiliar with the specific provisions of the *AMA Guides*, he or she may lose not only additional compensation for permanent impairment but also the underlying workers' compensation case.

The case of *Zebco v. Houston*[1] illustrates this point. In this case, a claimant is exposed to air pollutants in the workplace that impair his breathing functions. A medical opinion is obtained that concludes that the medical condition resulted from exposure to spray, mist, or various respiratory particulates emitted by the machinery that the claimant operated. The physician rates the claimant's lung impairment under the *AMA Guides* at 15 percent. The claimant is also given a 20 percent impairment rating for the loss of function to the upper respiratory system and a 35 percent impairment rating for the whole body.

Before the adoption of the *AMA Guides*, such a finding would be sustained routinely under the substantial evidence rule. In this instance, however, the award was set aside for noncompliance with the *AMA Guides*. The Supreme Court of Oklahoma set aside the award because the physician

1. Failed to comply with the *AMA Guides*.

2. Formed an opinion from an incomplete history; and could not, during the deposition, identify or describe the nature, concentration, or source of the air pollutants to which the claimant had been exposed at the claimant's workplace.[2]

In the AMA's *Guides to the Evaluation of Permanent Impairment* (3d ed. 1988) (hereinafter *AMA Guides* (3d ed. 1988)), the task of the physician (and counsel) in a respiratory impairment case is specified. The third edition calls for evaluation of:

environmental exposure, tobacco usage and chronological occupational data.

---

[1] 800 P.2d 245 (Okla. 1990).
[2] *Id.*

A detailed history of the individual's employment, in chronological order, should be obtained. It is easiest to begin with the most recent job and work back to the earliest job. The examiner should ask about the specific activities in each job, rather than about only the job title. The individual should be questioned about exposure to dusts, gases, vapors, and fumes. The specific information required includes:

1. The year [the individual] was first exposed to an agent,

2. The extent of the exposure,

3. The total number of years of exposure,

4. [The individual]'s estimate of the hazard that the agent posed, and

5. The number of years since exposure ceased.

The physician should be aware that hobbies that generate dust, such as woodworking, may cause lung disease as well.[3]

The courts have started to undertake long, hard reviews of the medical examinations and the medical reports to see if they specifically comply with the *AMA Guides.* Many courts have set aside awards due to computation errors,[4] inadequate medical testing,[5] inadequate medical history,[6] and deviation from the *AMA Guides* without an adequate explanation.[7] Failure to rely on the *AMA Guides* at all can also result in the invalidation of a rating.[8] In *Reece v. J.T. Walker Industries, Inc.,*[9] the judge discounted the opinions of two physicians who did not follow the tests of anatomical impairment required by the *Guides.* In *Pekala v. E.I. DuPont De Nemours & Co.,*[10] the Board emphasized that the rating physician did not articulate the detailed effects on the claimant's activities of daily living as required by the *Guides.* Thus, counsel who provides a workers' compensation judge with an inadequate medical report or inadequate medical testimony risks the loss or the delay of permanent impairment benefits.

---

[3] AMA, Guides to the Evaluation of Permanent Impairment (hereinafter *AMA Guides* (3d ed. 1988)) at 108.

[4] Whitener v. South Cent. Solid Waste Auth., 773 P.2d 1248 (Okla. 1989); Tulsa County v. Roberts, 738 P.2d 969 (Okla. Ct. App. 1987).

[5] Gaines v. Sun Refinery & Mktg., 790 P.2d 1073 (Okla. 1990).

[6] Houston v. Zebco, 821 P.2d 367 (Okla. 1991); Gaines v. Sun Refinery & Mktg., 790 P.2d 1073 (Okla. 1990); LaBarge v. Zebco, 769 P.2d 125 (Okla. 1988).

[7] Wheat v. Heritage Manor, 784 P.2d 74 (Okla. 1989).

[8] Simmons v. Delaware State Hosp., 660 A.2d 384 (Del. 1995).

[9] 2007 WL 4322003 (Tenn. Workers' Comp. Panel).

[10] 2007 WL 1653496 (Del. Super.).

§ 6.03   LAYING THE FOUNDATION WITH THE CLAIMANT'S TESTIMONY

The claimant's testimony is the foundation on which an award for permanent impairment must be crafted. The testimony must include information about the background of the claimant in the following areas:

1. Education and schooling

2. Military service

3. Work experience

4. Hobbies

5. Prior medical problems

6. Job description

7. Description of the incident, injury, accident, or disease

8. Subsequent work attempts

9. Chronological recitation of medical care

10. Description of the claimant's medications and their effects

11. Attempts at returning to work or rehabilitation

Counsel should focus on the impairment(s) in question and obtain detailed information about the claimant's limitations and pain, as well as the effects on the claimant's personal, social, and occupational demands (i.e., functional assessment[11]). It is also useful to explore the treatment regimen the claimant is required to follow because, under some chapters of the sixth edition of the *Guides*, additional impairment may be given for Burdens of Treatment Compliance.[12]

Form 6-1 is a sample trial sheet, presented as an outline. The trial sheet can help counsel lay a solid foundation for proving individual impairments.

---

[11] *See* Section 1.8h of *AMA Guides* (6th ed. 2008) at 15.

[12] *See* Appendix B of *AMA Guides* (6th ed. 2008) at 607.

EXHIBIT 6-1   UNDERSTANDING THE AMA GUIDES

EXHIBIT 6-1   SAMPLE TRIAL SHEET

Direct Examination of Claimant
   Please state your name.
   Your address.
   Your marital status.
   Your spouse's name.
   Your spouse's occupation.
   How many years have you been married?
   Please state your children's names and ages.

Education and Schooling
   Please tell us how far you went in school (highest grade you actually completed).
   Do you have any problems reading or writing, or with learning disabilities?

High School
   Did you attend high school?
   Which one?
   Did you graduate?
   When?
   What kind of degree did you obtain (GED, vocational)?

Further Education
   Did you obtain further education?
   Where?
   When?
   What degree, if any, did you obtain?

Special Training
   Have you received any additional special training?
   If so, when and where?
   What did the training consist of?

Military Service
   Were you ever in the military?
   When?
   What branch?
   What special training, if any, did you receive?

Work Experience
   After you finished school, did you obtain employment? Please describe the job(s) that you have held, including employer, dates of employment, and a brief description of your job, title, and duties starting with the first job you held.

Hobbies

Prior to (date of injury), what hobbies or recreational activities, if any, did you participate in?

Have you been involved in any civic activities (describe)?
Church or synagogue activities (describe)?
Sports (describe)?

Prior Medical Problems

Prior to (date of injury) what physical and/or emotional problems, if any, did you suffer from?
Please describe the condition and the treatment you received.
Have you had any recent auto or work-related accidents?
What problems, if any, were you left with as a result of the prior accident?

Incident

On the date of injury, by whom were you employed?

Average Weekly Wage

How much were you making per week, gross?

Job Description

What was your job title?
What did you do on your job?
What, if anything, happened on the date of injury?
How did you feel after the accident?

Report of Accident

What, if anything, did you do next (describe whom accident was reported to)?
Was an accident report completed?
By whom?

Work Attempts

After the date of injury, did you return to work the next day?
If not, why not?
If so, how were you feeling?
Were you able to continue working?
If not, why not?
What additional attempts, if any, did you make to return to work?
What was the last date that you worked?
How were you feeling at that time?
What specific problems were you having?

Medical Attention

As a result of your accident at work did you seek medical attention?
Please describe the doctors that you saw, when you saw them, and what, if anything, they did for you.

EXHIBIT 6-1   **UNDERSTANDING THE AMA GUIDES**

Hospitalization(s)

Did there come a time when you were treated at a hospital for this condition?

How were you feeling just prior to your admission?

Please describe when you were treated, where you were treated, and what, if anything, was done for you.

How were you feeling after your discharge?

Have you undergone any diagnostic testing?

Describe the test(s) and where and when they were done.

Medications

What medications, if any, have been prescribed for you?

Did you take these medications?

Did they help you?

What problems (side effects), if any, have you had with these medications?

Return to Work

Have you returned to your old job since (last day worked)?

If not, why not?

Have you been able to return to any job?

If not, why not (describe in detail the limitations as a result of the impairment)?

Rehabilitation

What, if anything, have you done in the way of rehabilitation?

What have they done for you?

Have you completed the evaluation process?

What, if anything, remains to be done?

Physical Therapy

What, if anything, have you done in the way of physical therapy?

Where were you treated?

How often did you go?

Did it help?

Are you still going?

Other Income

Other than workers' compensation, what income, if any, do you have (Social Security disability, long-term disability insurance, and so forth)?

Current Status

How are you feeling now (describe in detail pain, sleeping problems, inability to function as a result of permanent impairment, and so forth)?

Pain

Do you still have pain?

Where is the pain?

How often do you have it?

Can you describe the pain (dull, shooting, constant, intermittent, and so forth)?

Continuing Medical Care
Are you still under active medical care?
If so, by whom?
How often do you see a doctor or therapist?
What does the doctor or therapist do for you?

Medication
Are you currently on medication?
If so, describe the medication, who prescribed it, how often you take it, and for what condition you take it.

Hobbies and Recreation
Are you currently able to partake in your usual hobbies and recreational activities, sports, and so forth?
If not, why not?

Average Day
Would you describe what you normally do during the day?
What about sleeping?
What about pain?

Work
Are you currently able to return to your old job?
If not, why not?
Are you able to return to any work?
If not, why not?

§ 6.04   PREPARING THE PHYSICIAN TO TESTIFY

It is not uncommon for physicians to reveal, during their testimony, that they are not familiar with the claimant's occupational history, the claimant's medical records, or even the *AMA Guides*.[13] On one occasion, a doctor, qualified as a board-certified dermatologist, testified as follows:

Q.   Doctor, do the *AMA Guides to Permanent Physical Impairment* have any guidelines as to contact dermatitis?
A.   I will have to look into it. I don't know.

On another occasion, a doctor, qualified as an orthopedic surgeon, testified in the following manner:

Q.   Doctor, are you familiar with the *AMA Guides*?
A.   No, I'm not.

In these instances, the attorney is responsible for the lack of adequate preparation and the failure to properly vet the physician to ensure that the latter is

---

[13] Philpot v. City of Miami, 541 So. 2d 680 (Fla. Dist. Ct. App. 1989).

competent in the application of the *Guides*. When vetting a physician on competency with the *Guides*, counsel should seek to obtain the following information:

1. Whether the physician is certified by the American Board of Independent Medical Examiners

2. Whether the physician has been trained in the use of the *Guides* (and which editions), and how many ratings the physician has performed.

3. The physician's reputation among his colleagues.

4. Previous impairment reports prepared by the physician or the physician's responses to some general questions concerning the *Guides*.

Before the date of the physician's testimony, counsel should provide the physician with a summary of the testimony that the claimant has already given. This summary should include the information from the trial sheet (shown in Exhibit 6-1). In addition, counsel should provide the physician with an outline of the information that the medical report should contain. According to the AMA's *Guides to the Evaluation of Permanent Impairment* (4th ed. 1993) (hereinafter *AMA Guides* (4th ed. 1993)), the report should include the following information:

A. Medical evaluation

1. History of medical condition
2. Results of most recent clinical evaluation
3. Assessment of current clinical status and statement of further medical plans
4. Diagnoses

B. Analysis of findings

1. Impact of medical condition on daily activities
2. Explanation for concluding that the condition is stable and stationary and unlikely to change
3. Explanation for concluding that the individual is or is not likely to suffer further impairment by engaging in usual activities
4. Explanation for concluding whether accommodations or restrictions related to the impairment are or are not warranted

C. Comparison of analysis with impairment criteria

1. Description of clinical findings and how these findings relate to the *AMA Guides* criteria
2. Explanation of each estimated impairment
3. Summary list of all impairment percentages
4. Estimation of the whole-person impairment percentage[14]

---

[14] *See AMA Guides* (4th ed. 1993) at 14.

The AMA's *Guides to the Evaluation of Permanent Impairment* (5th ed. 2000) (hereinafter *AMA Guides* (5th ed. 2000)) also specifies the information that should be included in all impairment evaluation reports.[15] These are a clinical evaluation, a calculation of the impairment rating, and a discussion of how the impairment rating was calculated.[16] Specifics of what each of these sections should include, such as narrative history, current clinical status, diagnostic studies, the medical basis for determining maximum medical impairment (MMI), diagnoses, and prognosis, are provided in Section 2.6 of the *AMA Guides* (5th ed. 2000). Physicians using the *AMA Guides* (5th ed. 2000) should be reminded that their reports and subsequent testimony must comply with the requirements of Section 2.6.

The required information in physicians' reports is described in the *AMA Guides* (6th ed. 2008), Section 2.7, on page 28. The three-step process described in Section 2.7 is applicable to *all* impairment ratings and should be carefully studied by counsel and the rating physician.[17] The physician's failure to follow precisely the instructions listed can lead to disaster. These instructions include:

1. A review of the medical records before the rating is performed (with documentation of inconsistencies);

2. A physical examination at which the examinee is encouraged to give full effort;

3. A review of clinical studies, diagnoses, rationale for finding MMI;

4. A reference to the activities of daily living the examinee can and cannot perform; and

5. A specific reference to how the rating was performed (citing page numbers, tables, and criteria).[18]

Counsel should provide the physician with not only a copy of the pertinent section of the *AMA Guides* but also the language of the relevant workers' compensation statute or rule adopting the *AMA Guides*. The physician must know whether the use of the *AMA Guides* is mandatory, or if they are considered to be guidelines, and whether the physician's judgment and discretion can be utilized in arriving at an impairment evaluation.

Counsel should note that, in certain states, a specific reference to the *AMA Guides* may be necessary to prove impairment.[19] Some courts have been more

---

[15] *See AMA Guides* (5th ed. 2000) at 21–22.

[16] *Id.*

[17] *AMA Guides* (6th ed. 2008) at 28.

[18] *Id.*

[19] Toynbee v. Mimbres Mem'l Nursing Home, 833 P.2d 1204 (N.M. Ct. App. 1992). *See also* Landry v. Graphic Tech., Inc., 2 P.3d 758 (Kan. 2000).

lenient. For example, the New Hampshire Supreme Court has upheld an impairment rating despite the fact that the medical report violated the statutory requirement of referring to the *AMA Guides*.[20] The court stressed the evaluating physician's testimony that the physician's report was generated from a computer program based exclusively on the *AMA Guides*.[21]

It is good practice to remind physicians using computerized programs to verify that their equipment is in conformity with the proper edition of the *AMA Guides*.[22] Finally, it is important for counsel to note that total compliance with the *AMA Guides* is not necessarily a prerequisite to the admissibility of the physician's expert testimony.[23] However, practitioners should take note of the ruling in *Napier v. Middlesboro Appalachian Regional Hospital*,[24] in which the Supreme Court of Kentucky held that the claimant failed to satisfy her burden of proof because her physician did not specifically mention the *AMA Guides* when assigning a 10 percent impairment to the "whole body."

---

[20] Petition of Blake, 623 A.2d 741 (N.H. 1993).

[21] *Id.*

[22] Lacy v. Schlumberger Well Serv., 839 P.2d 157 (Okla. 1992).

[23] Special Indem. Fund v. Choate, 847 P.2d 796 (Okla. 1993). *See also* Phillips v. Marvin Windows, 2000 WL 987312 (Tenn. Spec. Workers' Comp. App. Panel July 18, 2000).

[24] 2004 WL 538123 (Ky. Mar. 18, 2004).

CHAPTER 7

FOURTH EDITION CROSS-EXAMINATION GUIDE

§7.01   INTRODUCTION

With the widespread use of the American Medical Association's *Guides to the Evaluation of Permanent Impairment* (hereinafter *AMA Guides*) in workers' compensation cases, physicians must be prepared to answer questions posed by attorneys, judges, and other professionals regarding their use of, and compliance with, the *AMA Guides* in their reports and testimony. Conversely, attorneys must familiarize themselves with the *AMA Guides* before undertaking the examination of a physician.

Once familiar with the *AMA Guides*, attorneys will realize their single most important secret is that the *AMA Guides* themselves provide a wealth of material for an effective cross-examination of the evaluating physician. For example, counsel should be familiar with the specific chapter of the applicable edition of the *AMA Guides* that deals with the impairment in question. Counsel should also be able to use effectively the concepts set forth in the applicable edition of the *AMA Guides*. For a probing and detailed cross-examination, counsel should be particularly familiar with the *Guides'* first two chapters (which deal with all impairment ratings) and the glossary.

This chapter illustrates several areas of inquiry pertaining to the use of the fourth edition of the *AMA Guides* during cross-examination, the most widely used edition at the time of this writing. Specific sample cross-examinations relevant to the fifth edition of the *AMA Guides* are discussed in Chapter 8. Attorneys should be prepared to inquire about, and physicians should be prepared to answer, all relevant issues and aspects of the proper use of the *AMA Guides*, and to preserve these issues properly so they can be raised either during cross-examination or on appeal.

§7.02   WERE THE *AMA GUIDES* USED?

If the state in which the case is heard requires, encourages, or permits the use of the *AMA Guides*, it is important for counsel to ask whether the physician used the *AMA Guides*. A good example of such a question is as follows:

Q.   Doctor, in formulating your opinion on the evaluation of permanent impairment in this case, did you use and comply with the *AMA Guides to the Evaluation of Permanent Impairment?*

If the answer to this question is negative, then a motion to strike the complete testimony of the doctor should be filed. The proposed testimony will most likely be found to be without probative value and stricken.[1] If the answer to this question is affirmative, the physician can be questioned at length about his or her compliance with the *AMA Guides*.

---

[1] *See* Zebco v. Houston, 800 P.2d 245 (Okla. 1990), in which the testimony under these circumstances was completely stricken.

§ 7.03   WHICH EDITION WAS USED?

Different state legislatures have required that specific editions of the *AMA Guides* be used for evaluating permanent impairment. Two basic inquiries are presented as a result of these requirements:

1. Was the correct edition of the *AMA Guides* used?

2. If not, and since a new edition of the *AMA Guides* has been adopted, is the testimony invalid?

An example of the first inquiry follows:

Q. Doctor, which edition of the *AMA Guides* did you use to arrive at your evaluation of permanent impairment?

Note that if the edition used is other than the edition required in the statute, a motion to strike the question should be made. If the judge overrules the motion, allowing the physician to testify further, counsel should note the objection and proceed with the following questions:

Q. You used the third edition of the *AMA Guides* in arriving at your opinion, isn't that correct?

Q. Are you aware that the AMA replaced the third edition with the fourth edition in 1993, doctor?

Q. Doctor, are you aware of the substantial changes made in the fourth edition of the *AMA Guides?*

§ 7.04   EXAMPLES OF SPECIFIC CHANGES BETWEEN EDITIONS

Because there are now six editions of the *AMA Guides*, and because some state legislatures have required the use of specific editions, counsel may need to ask about the changes from one edition to another. The following questions reflect the changes from the AMA's *Guides to the Evaluation of Permanent Impairment* (3d ed. 1988) (hereinafter *AMA Guides* (3d ed. 1988)) to the *AMA Guides* (4th ed. 1993). For specific suggested questions dealing with changes made between the publication of the fourth edition and the fifth edition, see Chapter 8.

Q. What is the difference in the definitions of permanent impairment found in the third and fourth editions of the *AMA Guides?*

The third edition defined *permanent impairment* as an impairment for which the clinical findings determined over a period of time, usually 12 months, indicate that the condition is "static and well stabilized."[2] The fourth edition defines

---

[2] AMA, Guides to the Evaluation of Permanent Impairment (hereinafter *AMA Guides* (3d ed. 1988)) at 6.

permanent impairment as "an adverse condition that is stable and unlikely to change."[3]

Q. Are physicians allowed to express an opinion regarding disability when using the *AMA Guides* (4th ed. 1993)?

The third edition carefully avoided the issue of whether a physician could express an opinion on the ultimate topic in many workers' compensation cases— namely, disability. The third edition used the term *employability* and then concluded that disability results when the individual lacks the characteristics of employability.[4]

The fourth edition recognizes that physicians may, under certain circumstances, directly express an opinion about disability. It specifically states, "If the physician is well acquainted with the patient's activities and needs, he or she may also express an opinion about the presence or absence of a disability or handicap."[5]

Q. Did you include in your report all the information required under the fourth edition of the *AMA Guides?*

The *AMA Guides* (4th ed. 1993) make several changes to the Model Report Form[6] found in the *AMA Guides* (3d ed. 1988). These changes include:

1. Requiring the date of the report

2. Changing the language in item 4b from "The degree of impairment is not likely to change by more than 3 percent within the next year"[7] to "The degree of impairment is not likely to change substantially within the next year"[8]

3. Adding the words *including occupation* to the list of daily activities and asking the doctors to list the types of daily activities affected in item no. 5

4. Including the following sentence in item 6: "Each organ system impairment estimate should be expressed in terms of percent impairment of the whole person and by adding a column for percent impairment of the whole person"[9]

5. Adding items no. 7 through no. 9, "Requiring the final estimated whole person impairment, the dates of treatment or evaluation and a statement of consistency or inconsistency in the history, physical examination and laboratory findings."[10]

---

[3] AMA, Guides to the Evaluation of Permanent Impairment (hereinafter *AMA Guides* (4th ed. 1993)) at v.

[4] *AMA Guides* (3d ed. 1988) at 2.

[5] *AMA Guides* (4th ed. 1993) at 2.

[6] *AMA Guides* (3d ed. 1988) at 11–12.

[7] *Id.* at 8.

[8] *AMA Guides* (4th ed. 1993) at 11.

[9] *Id.* at 12.

[10] *Id.*

Q. Did you use the injury model to rate spinal impairment?

The previously used range of motion (ROM) model is now out of favor and can be used only in limited circumstances.

Q. Did your evaluation reflect the changes in rating lower extremity impairment under the fourth edition of the *Guides*?

The third edition based impairment evaluation of the lower extremity on range of motion and amputation. The fourth edition uses "anatomic, diagnostic, and functional methods" to evaluate permanent impairment of the lower extremity.[11] The crucial innovation of this edition is that the physician is given the discretion to select the appropriate method of evaluation. A physician may select from among the following evaluation methods:

1. Limb length discrepancy

2. Gait derangement

3. Muscle atrophy

4. Manual muscle testing

5. Range of motion

6. Joint ankylosis

7. Arthritis

8. Amputation

9. Diagnosis-based estimates

10. Skin loss[12]

Q. Doctor, did your administration of spirometric testing conform to the requirements of the *AMA Guides* (4th ed. 1993)?

The *AMA Guides* (4th ed. 1993) contains specific directions to follow in order to ensure acceptable spirometry.[13] The measurements are to be performed at least three times.[14] The results of the two best forced vital capacity (FVC) efforts should be within 5 percent of each other.[15] Special instructions are provided when wheezing is heard or when the FEV_1/FVC ratio is below .70.[16]

---

[11] *Id.* at 75.
[12] *See id.* at 75–78.
[13] *Id.* at 159–60.
[14] *Id.* at 159.
[15] *Id.* at 159–60.
[16] *Id.* at 160.

Q. Are you aware of the change in predicted normal spirometry values for non-whites?

The *AMA Guides* (4th ed. 1993) contains information concerning the average or predicted spirometry values used in the impairment evaluation process.[17] It is important to note that adjustments in the spirometry values need to be made for non-whites. For example, the predicted spirometry values for white males and females are provided in Tables 2, 3, 4, 5, 6, and 7. However, counsel should note that because blacks have lower spirometric values than corresponding whites, an adjustment must be made to the predicted values in Tables 4, 5, 6, and 7 when a black patient is evaluated for pulmonary impairment.[18] Under the *AMA Guides* (3d ed. 1988), a similar adjustment is made for Asians. This adjustment is made by multiplying the predicted FVC and the predicted forced expiratory volume (hereinafter FEV_1) by .88 and multiplying the predicted diffusing capacity by .93. The *AMA Guides* (3d ed. 1988) further notes that evidence exists that Hispanics, Native Americans, and Asians have lower lung function than whites from North America.[19] Because the cause and magnitude of this difference is not well established yet, no adjustment for this difference is made in the *AMA Guides* (4th ed. 1993).[20]

Q. Are you aware of and did you implement the changes in the *AMA Guides* (4th ed. 1993) for rating skin disfigurement?[21]
A. Yes, I followed Chapter 13 on this point, Table 2, page 280.
Q. Are there any new sources of documentation that the *AMA Guides* (4th ed. 1993) allows a rating physician to rely upon when rating mental impairment?

The *AMA Guides* (4th ed. 1993) permits the documentation of a mental disorder by the use of reports of new sources, that is, psychiatric nurses, psychiatric social workers, and health professionals in hospitals and clinics.[22]

Q. Are the impairment criteria and percentages in the *AMA Guides* (4th ed. 1993) identical to those contained in the *AMA Guides* (3d ed. 1988)?

The answer to this question is no. Many of the organ systems of the *AMA Guides* (4th ed. 1993) are rated for impairment through criteria that have been modified from the criteria found in the *AMA Guides* (3d ed. 1988). Also, in the *AMA Guides* (4th ed. 1993), many of the categories of impairment for the various organ systems contain different ranges of impairment than were found in the *AMA Guides* (3d ed. 1988).[23]

---

[17] *See AMA Guides* (4th ed. 1993) ch. 5.
[18] For the tables containing the spirometry values, *see id.*
[19] *See id.*
[20] *See id.*
[21] *See id.*, ch. 13.
[22] *Id.* at 293.
[23] *See id.*

§ 7.05   TRAINING AND THE *AMA GUIDES*

Few physicians are familiar with the nuances in the *AMA Guides*, and even fewer physicians have received formal training in the use of the *AMA Guides*.[24] A physician's level of training in the *AMA Guides* can be a fruitful area of inquiry. The following questions are useful in ascertaining this information:

Q.   Were you trained to use the *AMA Guides* in medical school?

Q.   Were you trained to use the *AMA Guides* during internship or residency?

Q.   Did you receive any formal training with regard to the use of the *AMA Guides*? (Insist on specifics.)

Q.   How did you get your copy of the *AMA Guides?*

Q.   Did the *AMA Guides* come with any instructional information?

Q.   Have you studied the *AMA Guides* in entirety with all the charts and tables?

Q.   Do you claim to understand fully how to use the *AMA Guides?*

Q.   Do you consider yourself an expert in the use of the *AMA Guides?*

Q.   Are you certified as an independent medical examiner by the American Board of Independent Medical Examiners?

§ 7.06   THE GENERAL PRINCIPLES BEHIND THE *AMA GUIDES*

A physician should be able to explain both the general principles behind the *AMA Guides* and how they are applied. If the physician demonstrates an inability either to understand or to explain the basic concepts of the *AMA Guides*, then the fact finder should exclude the testimony or, at minimum, give little weight to the physician's testimony. The physician's knowledge of these principles can be elicited by the following questions:

Q.   Doctor, you have rated the claimant's impairment under the *AMA Guides*, have you not? How is *impairment* defined in the *AMA Guides*? (*Impairment* is an alteration in an individual's health status; it is a medical issue assessed by medical means.[25]).

Q.   When you talk of disability, what do you mean? (*Disability* is defined as "an alteration of an individual's capacity to meet personal, social, or occupational demands, or statutory or regulatory requirements, because of an impairment."[26])

Q.   What is the combined values chart? (It is a chart that must be used to combine all impairment ratings to be expressed as the impairment of the whole person.)

Q.   Where is the combined values chart found? (The chart is found on pages 322–24 of the *AMA Guides* (4th ed. 1993).)

Q.   Can you explain how you use the combined values chart?[27]

Q.   There is a three-step approach to rating impairment, is there not? (Yes, there is.)

---

[24] For a discussion of the legal requirement of training by an evaluator, see § 2.03 in this volume.

[25] *AMA Guides* (4th ed. 1993) at 1.

[26] *Id.* at 3.

[27] For an explanation of how to use the combined values chart, *see id.* at 322.

Q. Would you explain the three steps?[28]

Q. Would you explain apportionment and how you do it? (*Apportionment* is the estimate of the degree to which each of various occupational or nonoccupational factors has contributed to a particular impairment.[29])

Q. What are some of the activities of daily living?

Q. What is the significance of the activities of daily living in estimating impairment?

Q. What is rounding off and how does it work? (Rounding off allows the final impairment value to be expressed in terms of the nearest 5 percent.[30])

Q. Are there occasions when the impairment values are added and not combined? (Yes.)

Q. When is that? (For example, when evaluating impairment of the hand, the impairment values of the involved digits are added and not combined.[31])

Q. How do you test for range of motion? (The *AMA Guides* recommend using a goniometer to examine the extremities; for examining the spine, either two mechanical inclinometers or a single, computerized inclinometer is needed.[32])

Q. Are there impairment percentages for pain in the *AMA Guides*? (No.)

Q. How do you arrive at an impairment rating for pain?

Q. Are you familiar with the terms describing the frequency of symptoms?

Q. Would you please define the terms *intermittent, occasional, frequent,* and *constant*?

Q. Are you familiar with the terms describing intensity of symptoms?

Q. Please define the terms *minimal, slight, moderate,* and *marked*.

Q. Can superficial disfigurement result in impairment? (Yes.)

§7.07 WHEN TO RATE PERMANENT IMPAIRMENT

The physician should be questioned on whether the claimant's medical condition is stable. The physician should be allowed to testify as to the degree of permanent impairment only if the claimant's medical condition is stable. The answers to the following questions allow for a determination of stability:

Q. When do you define a condition as a permanent impairment? (A permanent impairment is "an impairment that has become well stabilized with or without medical treatment and is not likely to remit despite medical treatment."[33])

Q. What does the term *maximum medical improvement* mean? (This term is typically defined by statute or rule.)

Q. Is the claimant's condition likely to progress and get worse?

---

[28] *Id.* at 10.

[29] *Id.*

[30] *Id.* at 9.

[31] *AMA Guides* (4th ed. 1993) at 66.

[32] *Id.* at 114.

[33] *Id.* at 315.

§ 7.08   THE PHYSICIAN'S REPORT

The *AMA Guides* suggest, and arguably require, that the physician's report address several important areas. The *AMA Guides* (4th ed. 1993) contains a model report for physicians to follow.[34] If a medical report omits one or more of these areas, the following questions can lay a foundation for excluding the report.

Q.   Do you consider your report complete and valid?

Q.   Does your report contain all of the information suggested by the *AMA Guides*?

The *AMA Guides* (4th ed. 1993) suggests that all of the following areas of information are included in the physician's reports:

- History of the medical condition

- Results of the most recent clinical evaluation.
  —Assessment of current clinical status and statement of further medical plans
  —Diagnosis
  —Impact of the medical conditions on daily activities
  —Explanation for concluding that the condition is stable and stationary and unlikely to change
  —Explanation for concluding that the individual is or is not likely to suffer further impairment by engaging in usual activities
  —Explanation for concluding that accommodations or restrictions related to the impairment are or are not warranted
  —Description of clinical findings and how these findings relate to *AMA Guides* criteria.
  —Explanation of each estimated impairment
  —Summary list of all impairment percents
  —Estimated whole-person impairment percent[35]

Another area to address in the report is the individual's employability:

Q.   Did you make a determination as to employability?

Q.   What factors did you consider in making the employability determination?[36]

---

[34] *Id.* at 11–12.

[35] *Id.* at 14.

[36] The *AMA Guides* (4th ed. 1993) uses the following definition for the term *employability determination*: Employability determination is an assessment by management of the individual's capacity, with or without accommodation, to meet the demands of a job and the conditions of employment. The management carries out an assessment of performance capability to estimate the likelihood of performance failure and an assessment of the likelihood of future liability in case of human failure. If either likelihood is too great, then the employer may not consider the individual employable in the job. *Id.* at 318.

Q. Is the claimant an increased risk to himself or herself and/or the employer because of this medical condition?

An Oklahoma court held that a physician's report need not be in substantial compliance with the *AMA Guides* if the physician has determined that the impairment in question is not work-related.[37]

§7.09   THE WHOLE-PERSON RATING CONCEPT

Even though the *AMA Guides* espouse the whole-person rating concept, many workers' compensation statutes do not recognize this concept despite having adopted the *AMA Guides*. A suggested line of inquiry dealing with this problem follows:

Q. You rated the claimant's impairments and then combined them to determine a whole-person rating, did you not?

Q. That whole-person rating concept is based on the philosophy of the *AMA Guides* that all physical and mental impairments affect the whole person and therefore all physical and mental impairments should be combined to be fair and accurate. Is that correct?

Q. The values and percentages expressed in the *AMA Guides* are based in part on the assumption that they will be combined in the end to reach a whole-person impairment rating, correct?

Q. Are you aware that this state's workers' compensation statute does not provide for ratings of the whole person in its scheduled award section?

Q. Are you aware that in this state the whole-person rating concept cannot be used in determining the amount of any award made to the claimant?

Q. Do you agree that using the impairment ratings you reached before combining and arriving at a whole-person impairment would be inconsistent with the underlying philosophy of the *AMA Guides*?

§7.10   PAIN

There are no criteria in the *AMA Guides* (4th ed. 1993) for measuring impairment related to pain. As a result, close questioning in this area is almost always fruitful.

Q. Did you consider the employee's complaints of pain in rating the impairment?

Q. What method did you use to rate the pain?

Q. Did you classify the pain as acute, recurrent acute, or chronic?[38]

Q. Did you consider the duration of the pain, dramatization of pain, use of drugs, despair, disuse, and dysfunction?[39]

---

[37] Moore v. Uniroyal Goodrich, 935 P.2d 1193 (Okla. Ct. App. 1997).

[38] For the definitions of the different pain classifications, see *AMA Guides* (4th ed. 1993) at 306.

[39] For an explanation of these terms, *see id.* at 308.

Q.   How did the pain interfere with the claimant's performance of the activities of daily living?

Q.   Did the pain follow defined anatomical pathways?

Q.   Did you take into consideration the intensity of the pain?

Q.   Did you take into consideration the frequency of the pain?

Q.   How did you use the *AMA Guides* to rate the frequency of the pain?

Q.   Did you take into consideration all subjective complaints of the employee's pain?

Q.   Did you rate only the complaints of pain that could be medically substantiated?

§ 7.11   MENTAL AND PSYCHIATRIC IMPAIRMENTS

In a similar manner to their treatment of pain, the *AMA Guides* avoid making any direct link between medical findings on mental and behavioral disorders and any percentage of impairment. This is an extremely subjective area. The following questions can highlight these problems:

Q.   Did you rate the mental or psychiatric aspects of the claimant's disability?

Q.   How did you rate the impairment?

Q.   How did you take into account the diagnosis, motivation, history, treatment, and attempts at rehabilitation?[40]

Q.   Are you trained as a psychiatrist?

Q.   How does the claimant's mental condition affect the claimant's ability to carry on the activities of daily living?[41]

Q.   Did you make the general observations of the claimant required by the *AMA Guides*?[42]

Q.   What is the claimant's personal and family mental history?

Q.   Did you provide a description of the claimant's mental status as is required by the *AMA Guides*?[43]

Q.   What other special considerations did you consider as called for in the *AMA Guides*?

Q.   Did you consider the effects of structured settings, medication, and rehabilitation?[44]

Q.   Are you familiar with the five classes of mental impairment in the *AMA Guides*?

Q.   Would you describe and explain them? (The classes are categorized in the following way: Class 1–no impairment; Class 2–mild impairment; Class 3–moderate impairment; Class 4–marked impairment; Class 5–extreme impairment.[45])

Q.   Please explain how you used the prior factors in reaching your psychiatric impairment rating.

---

[40] *See id.* at 292.

[41] *See id.* at 294.

[42] *See id.* at 299.

[43] *Id.* at 300.

[44] *Id.* at 295–96.

[45] *Id.* at 301.

§7.12   FOCUSING ON ALL OF THE IMPAIRMENTS

It is not at all uncommon for physicians to focus on what they view as the principal impairment, without adequately considering all of its ramifications. Perhaps this is due to the time pressures under which most physicians work. Regardless of the reason, the cross-examiner should probe the following areas to uncover additional impairments that might have been overlooked.

Q.   Did you consider the claimant's prior medical impairments?

Q.   How did this affect your rating?

Q.   Did you rate all the impairments, including prior surgeries, abnormal range of motion, muscle weakness, motor impairment, sensory impairment, loss of strength, headaches, psychiatric impairment, and disfigurement impairment?

CHAPTER **8**

SAMPLE CROSS-EXAMINATIONS
UNDER THE FIFTH EDITION

§8.01 INTRODUCTION

The many changes made in the American Medical Association's *Guides to the Evaluation of Permanent Impairment* (5th ed. 2000) (hereinafter *AMA Guides* (5th ed. 2000)) have left those using that edition vulnerable to cross-examination. Examples of potentially fertile areas of inquiry follow.

§8.02 MISREFERENCES TO THE *AMA GUIDES*

Q. Doctor, according to your report, you performed this evaluation according to the "AMA Guidelines to the Evaluation of Permanent Disability." Is that correct?

A. Yes, as stated on the first page of my report.

Q. You did not specify the edition or printing of the book, did you?

A. No.

Q. You are familiar with the use of this resource?

A. Yes.

Q. Is this publication routinely used to assess disability?

A. Yes, it is used to assess permanent disability.

Q. Doctor, is it your experience that if a colleague misreferences the title of a commonly used medical text, that physician may be less familiar with the text than another colleague who currently references the title?

A. Yes.

Q. Is this the publication you used to assess disability? [Shows physician copy of the *AMA Guides to the Evaluation of Permanent Impairment* (5th ed. 2000).]

A. Yes, that is the book.

Q. Doctor, can you read the name of the book?

A. Yes.

Q. Please read the name of the book aloud.

A. *AMA Guides to the Evaluation of Permanent Impairment,* fifth edition.

Q. Is that the name you referenced in your report?

A. No.

Q. Your report states "Guidelines," not "Guides," isn't that correct?

A. Yes.

Q. It uses the term *disability* in the title, not *impairment,* isn't that correct?

A. Yes.

Q. Doctor, did you misreference the title in your report?

A. Yes, apparently my transcriptionist made a mistake.

Q. Doctor, did you read the report before you signed it?

A. Yes.

Q. As you didn't even know the correct name of the book, Doctor, would it be fair to say you really are not familiar with this text?

Comment. Misnaming the *AMA Guides* in an impairment rating is a mistake that can and will make the physician appear ill-informed, sloppy, and uncaring. This mistake is routinely made and is completely avoidable.

§ 8.03   USE OF THE *AMA GUIDES* TO ASSESS PERMANENT PARTIAL DISABILITY

Q. Doctor, you used the *AMA Guides* to assess disability, isn't that correct?

A. Yes.

Q. Doctor, what you really did was perform an impairment rating?

A. Yes, I guess; however, that is the same as a permanent partial disability rating.

Q. Doctor, you have read Chapters 1 and 2 of the *AMA Guides?*

A. Yes, quickly.

Q. Doctor, doesn't the fifth edition state on page 4, "The whole person impairment percentages listed in the *AMA Guides* estimate the impact of the impairment on the individual's overall ability to perform activities of daily living, excluding work," and on page 5 that "impairment ratings are not intended for use as direct determinants of work disability"?

A. I do not know.

Q. Doctor, so you rated disability, even though the *AMA Guides to the Evaluation of Permanent Impairment* is used only to assess impairment?

A. Yes, I guess I did.

Q. Doctor, you do not regard yourself as an expert on assessing impairment, do you?

A. No, I am a very capable orthopedic surgeon; however, I am not an expert on assessing impairment.

Q. Are you an expert in assessing disability?

A. Well, I see a lot of disabled people in my practice.

Q. Doctor, do you have special skills, training, and knowledge in vocational assessment and functional job analysis?

A. No.

Q. Doctor, did you perform an assessment of occupational demands, your patient's education, skills, and motivation, and the state of the job market?

A. No.

Q. Doctor, wouldn't you agree with me, therefore, that you are not capable of assessing disability?

Comment. Physicians who use the terms *impairment* and *disability* interchangeably will be closely cross-examined about their knowledge and their specific training and experience in rating disability. Chapters 1 and 2 of the *AMA Guides* (5th ed. 2000) provide substantial ammunition for effective cross-examination of the physician evaluator.

§ 8.04   EXAMINERS' ROLES AND RESPONSIBILITIES

Q. Doctor, you have cared for your patient over a period of five years, isn't that correct?

A. Yes, we have a long-standing physician-patient relationship.

Q. You have seen your patient many times and have helped her through some times that she has found difficult?

A. Yes.

Q. You have tried to assist her with her problems as best you could, correct?

A. Yes.

Q. Here, Ms. Jones had a new problem, didn't she?

A. I do not follow you.

Q. She wanted to get as much money as possible for her permanent impairment, correct?

A. I guess so.

Q. She asked for your help again, didn't she?

A. Actually, it was her lawyer.

Q. You agreed to help her?

A. Yes.

Q. Doctor, in your role as her treating physician, therefore, wouldn't you agree with me that it would be difficult to provide an independent, unbiased assessment of her condition?

A. Well, I . . . I told the truth.

Q. Doctor, do the *AMA Guides* state in the first sentence under Section 2.3, "Examiners' Roles and Responsibilities," that the "physician's role in performing an impairment evaluation is to provide an independent, unbiased assessment of the individual's medical condition including its effect on function, and identify abilities and limitations to performing activities as listed in Table 1-2"?

A. Yes.

Q. Doctor, wouldn't you agree with me that an independent, unbiased evaluator, skilled in the assessment of impairment, would be in a better position to assess impairment than a long time treating physician who is fond of his patient and has "helped her out many times before"?

Comment. Here, counsel turns the tables on the attack that independent medical examinations (IME) physicians usually undergo—that is, since the treating physician has seen the patient more often, the physician is in a better position to impartially assess impairment. As can be seen by the previous questioning, the treating physician is vulnerable because he or she is dealing with a long-standing patient.

§8.05   EXAMINERS' ETHICAL OBLIGATIONS

Q. Doctor, you identified the diagnoses of "somatization disorder, depression, and deconditioning" in your report?

A. Yes.

Q. These were new diagnoses, isn't that correct?

A. Yes.

Q. You performed this evaluation according to the *AMA Guides to the Evaluation of Permanent Impairment*, fifth edition?

A. Yes.

Q. Are you familiar with Chapter 2, "Practical Applications of the *AMA Guides*"?

A. Yes.

Q. Doctor, did you inform the requesting party and individual about these conditions and recommend further medical assessment?

A. I put it in my report.

Q. Did you notify the examinee and recommend further medical assessment to the examinee?

A. No.

Q. Doctor, could you read the following sentence, which I have highlighted from page 18 in the *AMA Guides*? It is in the last sentence in the second column.

A. "If new diagnoses are discovered, the physician has a medical obligation to inform the requesting party and individual about the condition and recommend further medical assessment."

Q. You had this medical obligation according to the *Guides*. Isn't that correct?

A. Yes.

Q. You didn't do that, did you?

A. No.

Q. Is that because you didn't really believe the examinee had these conditions, or because you made a mistake?

Comment. The *AMA Guides* (5th ed. 2000) placed a new ethical obligation on the examining physician. Few physicians are likely to fulfill this obligation, due to ignorance or to fear of creating additional legal liability for themselves by becoming a treating physician. This is an important area of cross-examination.

§ 8.06 UPPER EXTREMITY IMPAIRMENT EVALUATION PROTOCOL

Q. Doctor, you performed this rating using Chapter 16 of the fifth edition, "The Upper Extremities." Is that correct?

A. Yes.

Q. Doctor, you followed the principles of assessment as explained in Section 16.1, "Principles of Assessment," on pages 434 to 440 of the fifth edition. Is that correct?

A. Yes.

Q. Doctor, did your examination include measurements of wrist motion?

A. Yes.

Q. You evaluated motion as explained in Section 16.4a, "Clinical Measurements of Motion." Is that correct?

A. Yes.

Q. You did not perform an assessment of the general condition of the whole person?

A. No, I did not. I am a hand surgeon.

Q. You do not document the status of activities of daily living, as listed in Table 1-2 on page 4 of the fifth edition, did you?

A. No, I did not.

Q. You did not perform a general physical examination, did you?

A. No, I did not. That is not what I do.

Q. You did not do any laboratory testing, did you?

A. No.

Q. Doctor, you did not obtain a photographic record, did you?

A. No.

Q. You did not assess motion of the opposite wrist, did you?

A. No, it was not injured.

Q. You did not observe motion of each joint of the extremity, did you?

A. No.

Q. Please read this highlighted text from Section 16.1b, "Impairment Evaluation: Documentation and Recording," which appears on page 434 of the fifth edition, the bottom of the second column.

A. "Evaluation of the upper extremities requires a sound knowledge of the normal functional anatomy and would be incomplete without assessment of the general condition of the whole person. It must be thorough and should include several elements: status of activities of daily living; careful observations; both local and general physical examinations; appropriate imaging evaluation; laboratory tests; and preferably, a photographic record."

Q. Doctor, wouldn't you agree that your evaluation did not follow those guidelines?

A. No, it did not.

Q. Please read this highlighted text from Section 16.4, "Evaluating Abnormal Motion," starting at the top of the first column on page 451 of the fifth edition.

A. "The examiner should first observe what an individual can and cannot do by asking him or her to move each joint of the extremity, from the shoulder down, through its full range of motion. Both extremities should be compared."

Q. Wouldn't you agree that your evaluation did not follow those guidelines?

A. I agree that it did not.

Q. As your evaluation was not done in accordance with the *AMA Guides*, it was incomplete and in error, was it not?

Comment. Many physicians and specialists are unfamiliar with the specific requirements set forth in the *AMA Guides* (5th ed. 2000) and are vulnerable to cross-examination.

§8.07   DIFFERENT RATINGS UNDER DIFFERENT EDITIONS

Q. Doctor, you found in the examinee an objectively documented radiculopathy and a single-level fusion, correct?

A. Yes.

Q. Under the fifth edition of the *AMA Guides*, you arrived at an impairment rating of 25 percent?

A. Yes.

Q. Under the fourth edition of the *AMA Guides*, you rated examinees with similar conditions as a diagnosis-related estimate lumbosacral Category III at 10 percent, correct?

A. Yes.

Q. If a sixth edition of the *AMA Guides* comes out and says rate them at 35 percent, you will do so?

A. Yes.

Q. What about 40 percent?

A. Yes.

Q. What about 50 percent?

A. Well, I don't know.

Q.   Is there any number that the *AMA Guides* could put in the book that you would not follow?

Comment. The disparity between different editions of the *AMA Guides* for the exact same condition is an excellent area for cross-examination. Counsel can attempt to show that the physician is not really rating permanent impairment but is merely plugging in numbers from the latest edition of the *AMA Guides*.

§ 8.08   FAILURE TO RATE PAIN

Q.   Doctor, the examinee's major complaint was pain, correct?
A.   Yes.
Q.   In your report, you stated that he reported on a scale of 0, no pain, to 10, excruciating pain, that his pain averaged a 6 to 7 and would increase to 9 with certain activities. Is that correct?
A.   Yes.
Q.   He reports his pain as constant?
A.   Yes.
Q.   Doctor, he is taking medications—anti-inflammatories—on a regular basis?
A.   Yes.
Q.   You rated him on the basis of Chapter 16, "The Upper Extremities," correct?
A.   Yes.
Q.   You based the impairment on shoulder motion impairment, according to Section 16.4i, using Figure 16-40, Figure 16-43, and Figure 16-46?
A.   Yes.
Q.   You found the range of motion methods reproducible?
A.   Yes.
Q.   Did you not document any unusual illness or pain behavior?
A.   No, I did not. In fact, my observations during the examination reinforced the fact that he has significant pain from his rotator cuff disease.
Q.   You reported that he was pleasant and cooperative?
A.   Yes.
Q.   You found him credible?
A.   Yes.
Q.   You do not believe that he is exaggerating his difficulties with pain?
A.   Correct.
Q.   You did not document any unusual illness or pain behavior?
A.   No, I did not.
Q.   Does this problem with his shoulder have at least a moderate impact on his activities of daily living, such as self-care—reaching up to comb his hair or to dress—physical activity, hand activities, such as lifting above shoulder level, and his sleep?
A.   Yes, it interferes with all of these.
Q.   Has it affected his mood?
A.   Yes, he said he was depressed.

Q. So you would agree that he has significant pain, interference in activities of daily living, and appears depressed?

A. Yes.

Q. Wouldn't you also agree that you found he was credible and that there was no unusual pain behavior?

A. Yes.

Q. Would you agree that this particular patient has more pain than most patients with rotator cuff disease?

A. Yes.

Q. Did you also evaluate him by Chapter 18, "Pain"?

A. No, I am an orthopedic surgeon.

Q. Doctor, are you familiar with the changes in the fifth edition of the *AMA Guides* concerning the evaluation of pain?

A. No, I have not yet studied that chapter because it is at the end of the book.

Q. Doctor, could you read the instructions in Section 16.3d, "How to Rate Pain-Related Impairment: Overview," at this time?

A. Yes. [Reads section.]

Q. Doctor, wouldn't you agree with me that he should have been rated for pain?

A. Yes.

Q. Wouldn't you agree that, based on your findings, according to the fifth edition of the *AMA Guides* you should increase his impairment by 3 percent whole person, due to the severity and frequency of his pain, its interference with activities of daily living, and its impact on his mood, as well as your own findings that he was credible and had no unusual pain behavior?

A. Yes.

Q. So his impairment would now be 11 percent whole-person permanent impairment, based on the 8 percent whole-person permanent impairment you found for his motion deficits, and 3 percent whole-person permanent impairment for his pain difficulties?

A. Yes, it is 11 percent whole-person permanent impairment according to the fifth edition of the *AMA Guides*.

Comment. The *AMA Guides* (5th ed. 2000) provide for a rating of up to 3 percent whole-person permanent impairment for pain in certain circumstances. Counsel should be thoroughly familiar with Chapter 18, "Pain," because pain is a frequent complaint in an impairment evaluation.

§ 8.09 COMBINATION VERSUS ADDITION

Q. Doctor, you found this person to have both a right shoulder and hand injury?

A. Yes.

Q. I would like to review your report with you.

A. Okay.

Q. You did not complete Figure 16-1, Upper Extremity Impairment Evaluation Record, found on pages 436 and 437 of the fifth edition of the *AMA Guides*, did you?

A. No. It is all in my report.

Q. Doctor, you rated the hand and stated that the person had a 24 percent digit impairment for his thumb, which converted to a 10 percent hand impairment and a 52 percent digit impairment for his index finger, which converted to 10 percent hand impairment, as well. You also stated that for the amputation of the rest of his fingers, there was a 20 percent hand impairment for the loss of middle finger, a 10 percent hand impairment for the ring finger, and a 10 percent hand impairment for the little finger.

A. Yes.

Q. You combined these, using the Combined Values Chart on page 604?

A. Yes.

Q. You got a combined impairment of 47 percent hand? And you converted this 47 percent hand to a 42 percent upper extremity impairment using Table 16-2 on page 439?ss

A. Yes.

Q. You based the impairment on shoulder motion impairment, according to Section 16.4i, using Figure 16-40, Figure 16-43, and Figure 16-46?

A. Yes.

Q. You combined the deficits of motion of shoulder, that is, the values of 12, 2, 9, 1, 2, and 1 using the Combined Values Chart on page 604?

A. Yes.

Q. You got a 24 percent upper extremity?

A. Yes.

Q. You then combined the 42 percent upper extremity from the hand with the 24 percent upper extremity from the shoulder and got 55 percent upper extremity? Doctor, are you familiar with Section 16.1d, "Principles for Adding Impairment Values"?

A. Yes. I have read all of this chapter.

Q. Please read the first item on page 440.

A. "The total hand impairment rating is determined by adding the hand impairment values contributed by each digit."

Q. You did not do that, did you?

A. No.

Q. Doctor, you made a mistake, didn't you?

A. Yes.

Q. If you added the hand impairment values contributed by each digit—10, 10, 20, 10, and 10—what do you get?

A. Sixty percent hand.

Q. And what does this convert to in terms of upper extremity?

A. Fifty-four percent upper extremity.

Q. Doctor, please review item 4 at the top of page 441.

A. Yes.

Q. Doctor, you should have added, not combined, the values at the shoulder, isn't that correct?

A. Yes.

Q. If you added these values for the shoulder, wouldn't you agree you would get 27 percent, not 24 percent?

A. Yes.

Q. Doctor, the 54 percent upper extremity impairment for the hand should be combined with the 24 percent upper extremity impairment for the shoulder. Isn't that correct?

A. Yes, I think so. . . . The book is so confusing.

Q. Doctor, referencing the Combined Values Chart, this results in 65 percent upper extremity impairment. Isn't that correct?

A. Yes.

Q. Doctor, so the actual impairment is 65 percent upper extremity, not 55 percent upper extremity. That is 10 percent higher than you reported. Isn't that correct?

A. Yes, it should be 65 percent upper extremity impairment.

Q. Doctor, would it have been useful for you to complete Figure 16-1, "Upper Extremity Impairment Evaluation Record," in this case?

A. Yes.

Comment. Most values are combined in the upper extremity; however, values are added for the total hand impairment derived from the digit components. Thumb amputations proximal or at the MP (metacarpophalangeal) joint are added, thumb ray joint values are added, range of motion deficits at the same joint are added, and certain other disorders of the upper extremity are added (as discussed in Section 16.7 of the *AMA Guides* (5th ed. 2000)). There may be little, if any, difference for smaller values (e.g., 6 and 6 combined is 12); however, there are significant differences for larger values (e.g., 60 and 60 combined is 84). On page 438 of the fifth edition, the *Guides* advise, "If three or more values are to be combined, the lowest two values are first selected and their combined value is found." Counsel should be familiar with the process of combining versus adding and should request evaluating physicians to complete Figure 16-1, "Upper Extremity Impairment Evaluation Record," for upper extremity cases.

§8.10 SPINAL IMPAIRMENT

Q. Doctor, this patient had a recurrent radiculopathy?

A. Yes.

Q. You rated the patient by the Diagnosis-Related Estimate Method as a diagnosis-related estimate lumbar Category III and gave him 12 percent whole-person permanent impairment?

A. Yes.

Q. He has had two surgical procedures for his disk at L4–L5?

A. Yes.

Q. He also had substantial loss of motion?

A. Yes.

Q. He also continues to have a radiculopathy?

A. No, his neurological examination was normal following his second surgery.

Q. Doctor, if he had been rated by the range of motion method, his rating would have been higher?

A. Yes.

Q. In fact, he would have received 12 percent whole-person permanent impairment alone on the basis of having a surgically treated disk lesion (IIE) and a second operation (IIG1) according to Table 15-7 on page 404 of the fifth edition of the *AMA Guides?*

A. Yes.

Q. According to the data in your report, it appears he would also have a 10 percent whole-person permanent impairment due to his motion deficits.

A. Let me check. Yes, that is correct.

Q. So by that model, his rating would have been the combined value of 12 percent and 10 percent, or 22 percent whole-person permanent impairment?

A. Yes.

Q. Doctor, Section 15.2 on pages 379 to 381 discusses the process of determining the appropriate method for rating spinal impairment, isn't that true?

A. Yes.

Q. Under the listing of when to use the range of motion method, doesn't item number 4 state, "When there is recurrent radiculopathy caused by a new (recurrent) disk herniation or a recurrent injury in the same spinal region"?

A. Yes.

Q. Wouldn't you agree that according to these explicit directions, the range of motion method must be used in this case?

A. Yes.

Q. So, the correct rating is not 12 percent whole-person permanent impairment; it is 10 percent whole-person permanent impairment.

A. Yes.

Comment. Most ratings are performed using the diagnosis-related estimate model; however, in certain circumstances, the range of motion method is used. Counsel should be very familiar with when certain models should be used and consult with an expert if this is unclear.

§ 8.11   RADICULOPATHY RATINGS

Q. Doctor, this examinee had a radiculopathy and was treated with surgery?

A. Yes.

Q. He had a single-level fusion?

A. Yes.

Q. He has ongoing difficulties with pain and interference with daily activities?

A. Yes.

Q. You found there was no longer evidence of a radiculopathy at the time of the examination?

A. Yes, it had resolved.

Q. You rated him by the diagnosis-related estimate method as a DRE Lumbar Category II and gave him 8 percent whole-person permanent impairment?

A. Yes. I gave him the higher score in the range of 5 percent to 8 percent, because of his difficulties.

Q. Why did you rate him Category II?

A. Because his radiculopathy resolved. The surgery made him better. The goal of surgery is to improve function; therefore, we would expect to have lower impairment.

Q. Referring to *AMA Guides* Section 15.4, "DRE: Lumbar Spine," and specifically Table 15-3, "Criteria for Rating Impairment Due to Lumbar Spine Surgery," on page 384, did he have surgery for radiculopathy?

A. Yes.

Q. Therefore, wouldn't he meet the criteria for at least a DRE Lumbar Category III?

A. Yes, I guess so.

Q. He had a fusion, a surgical arthrodesis?

A. Yes.

Q. Therefore, wouldn't he meet the criteria for at least a DRE Lumbar Category IV?

A. Yes.

Q. Isn't DRE Lumbar Category V for those individuals who meet the criteria of DRE Categories III and IV?

A. Yes, that is what it says.

Q. He has marked interference in his activities; therefore, wouldn't he be rated in the higher range?

A. Yes.

Q. Doctor, the correct rating is therefore 28 percent whole-person permanent impairment, not 5 percent whole-person permanent impairment.

A. Yes. I stand corrected.

Comment. Ratings are markedly higher for spinal fusions in the *AMA Guides* (5th ed. 2000) versus the *AMA Guides* (4th ed. 1993). Improved function following a surgical procedure may be reflected in a higher as opposed to a lower rating. Counsel should be thoroughly familiar with the criteria for placing an individual in an appropriate category.

Q. Doctor, you rated this person for her radiculopathy as the result of a herniated disk, on the basis of your clinical skills as a chiropractor?

A. Yes.

Q. This was on the basis of her complaints of shooting pain and entire leg numbness? There was no documented weakness and loss of sensation fitting consistent with a specific radiculopathy?

A. No.

Q. Significant atrophy of 1 centimeter or greater of the leg or 2 centimeter of the thigh?

A. No.

Q. Any objective evidence of radiculopathy?

A. No.

Q. Abnormal electrodiagnostic verification of a radiculopathy?

A. No, we did only surface EMG studies. They revealed spasm.

Q. You did not perform any imaging studies, such as a CT scan or MRI scan?

A. No, we did periodic plain X-rays to document the subluxations.

Q. You cannot see herniated disks on plain X-rays, can you?

A. No, just the narrowing of the spaces.

Q. You did not substantiate your diagnosis of a radiculopathy due to a herniated disk using a imaging study?

A. No, I am a superb clinician, and that was not necessary.

Q. Doctor, doesn't the fifth edition of the *AMA Guides* state in Box 15-1 that "the diagnosis of herniated disk must be substantiated by an appropriate finding on an imaging study"?

A. Yes.

Q. Doctor, therefore, according to the fifth edition, that is not objective evidence of a radiculopathy or of a herniated disk.

A. The book was written by medical doctors, not chiropractic experts.

Q. Doctor, according to the fifth edition, she would not meet the classification of a DRE Lumbar Category III?

A. No, she would not.

Comment. Radiculopathy must be substantiated clinically and by imaging studies. Counsel must be familiar with the criteria set forth in the *AMA Guides* (5th ed. 2000).

§ 8.12   WHIPLASH

Q. Doctor, you diagnosed this examinee as having a whiplash injury?

A. Yes.

Q. You rated her as a DRE Cervical Category II at 5 percent whole-person permanent impairment?

A. Yes.

Q. Can you explain the basis for this?

A. Yes.

Q. What was the basis?

A. She had marked tenderness on the examination and has had problems with muscle spasm.

Q. Are you aware that with the fifth edition of the *AMA Guides*, the rating is based on current, not historical, findings?

A. That would be a difference from the fourth edition, wouldn't it?

Q. Doctor, please read the first full sentence in the second column of page 383 of the fifth edition of the *AMA Guides*.

A. "The impairment rating is based on the condition once MMI is reached, not on prior symptoms or signs."

Q. Doctor, did this examinee have documented findings of spasm?

A. She complained of pain.

Q. Doctor, did she have objective findings of spasm that you were able to independently determine and verify?

A. No, I guess not.

Q. Did, she have objective findings of muscle guarding?

A. No.

Q. Asymmetry of spinal motion?

A. No.

Q. Nonverifiable radicular root pain?

A. No.

Q. Abnormal reflexes?

A. No.

Q. Objective, documented weakness and loss of sensation fitting consistent with anatomic findings?

A. No.

Q. Significant atrophy of 1 centimeter or greater of the arms?

A. No.

Q. Objective evidence of radiculopathy?

A. No.

Q. Abnormal electrodiagnostic verification of a radiculopathy?

A. No.

Q. Alteration of motion segment integrity as explicitly defined in the fifth edition of the *AMA Guides*?

A. No.

Q. Cauda equina syndrome?

A. No.

Q. Abnormal urodynamic tests?

A. No.

Q. Any clinical finding listed in Box 15-1?

A. No.

Q. This patient whom you diagnosed as having whiplash has no significant clinical findings, no observed muscle guarding or spasm, no documentable neurological impairment, no documentable alteration in structural integrity, no other indication of impairment related to injury or illness, and no fractures, correct?

A. She complains of pain.

Q. Other than that complaint, isn't this the description for a DRE Lumbar Category I?

A. Yes.

Q. What impairment is this associated with?

A. Zero percent.

Q. Doctor, wouldn't you agree that whiplash is a controversial pain syndrome?

A. Yes.

Q. Doctor, isn't it true that you cannot use Chapter 18, "Pain," to rate controversial pain, according to the explicit directions provided in Section 18.3b, "When the Chapter Should Not Be Used to Rate Pain-Related Impairment"? Isn't that correct?

A. Yes, you could not use Chapter 18 to rate whiplash. You must use Chapter 15.

Q. By the fourth edition, her rating would have been 5 percent whole-person permanent impairment for a DRE Cervicothoracic Category II classification?

A. Yes.

Q. You must rate her by the most current edition, which is the fifth edition?

A. Yes.

Q. According to the fifth edition, she would have no ratable impairment, not 5 percent whole-person permanent impairment.

A. Yes, by the current edition, she has no ratable impairment; however, I do feel she is in pain.

Comment. With the *AMA Guides* (5th ed. 2000) categorization, the diagnosis-related estimate (DRE) model is based on current findings, with the exception of radiculopathy. If the person has objective radiculopathy and it resolved without surgery, there is a DRE Category II rating. If surgery was required, there is at least a DRE Category III rating. There is no ratable impairment for controversial pain syndromes. Counsel should be familiar with these changes.

§ 8.13 CARPAL TUNNEL SYNDROME

Q. Doctor, your patient had a carpal tunnel release two years ago, and she has ongoing complaints. Isn't that correct?

A. Yes.

Q. Electrophysiological studies performed by your technician one month ago were reported to reveal some minor sensory findings involving the median nerve?

A. Yes.

Q. You rated her on the basis of Chapter 16, "The Upper Extremities," correct?

A. Yes.

Q. Did her neurological examination reveal any objective evidence of median nerve sensory or motor losses?

A. Yes, she complained of pain; however, she had no neurological deficits.

Q. So after an optimal recovery time, she continues to complain of pain, paresthesias, and difficulties in performing certain activities. She also had normal sensibility and opposition strength with abnormal sensory and motor latencies or abnormal EMG testing of the thenar muscles?

A. Yes, that is an accurate description.

Q. You rated her at 10 percent upper extremity impairment for a mild carpal tunnel syndrome?

A. Yes.

Q. This would be consistent with Table 16, "Upper Extremity Impairment Due to Entrapment Neuropathy," in the fourth edition of the *AMA Guides*.

A. Yes.

Q. This table does not appear in the fifth edition, does it?

A. No.

Q. Doctor, on page 495 of the fifth edition, first column, item 2 states, "Normal sensibility and opposition strength with abnormal sensory and/or motor latencies or abnormal EMG testing of the thenar muscle: a residual CTS is still present, and an impairment rating not to exceed 5 percent of the upper extremity may be justified," correct?

A. Yes, it does.

Q. Doctor, therefore her rating could not exceed 5 percent according to the fifth edition. Isn't this correct?

Comment. The process for rating carpal tunnel syndrome, a common disorder, changed between the fourth edition of the *AMA Guides* and the fifth edition. Counsel should be familiar with these significant differences.

§8.14 COMPLEX REGIONAL PAIN SYNDROME (REFLEX SYMPATHETIC DYSTROPHY)

Q. Doctor, you rated this patient for reflex sympathetic dystrophy.

A. Yes.

Q. She complained of severe pain involving her entire right arm and was reluctant for you to touch her?

A. Yes.

Q. She had no changes to skin color or skin temperature, nor any edema?

A. Correct. She did not have these findings.

Q. Her skin was not overly dry or overly moist?

A. No, it did not appear to be.

Q. There were no abnormal findings of skin texture, were there?

A. No.

Q. There was no objective evidence of atrophy?

A. No.

Q. She had no objective evidence of decreased passive motion?

A. No.

Q. She had no nail or hair changes, did she?

A. No.

Q. On her X-rays, she had no evidence of osteoporosis, did she?

A. No.

Q. Her bone scan was normal, isn't that correct?

A. Yes.

Q. You rated her on the basis of Chapter 13, "The Nervous System," and the use of Table 13-22, correct?

A. Yes.

Q. You also rated her as a high Class 3 impairment, and because this involves her dominant hand, rated at 39 percent impairment of the whole person?

A. Yes.

Q. Did you consider Section 16.5e, "Complex Regional Pain Syndromes," in Chapter 16, "The Upper Extremities"?

A. No.

Q. Her problem involved her upper extremity?

A. Yes.

Q. It would have been appropriate to consider this, correct?

A. Yes.

Q. Referencing Table 16-16, "Objective Diagnostic Criteria for CRPS," on page 496, does she have a single sign that supports the diagnosis of CRPS?

A. No, she has pain.

Q. Does it state that if there are fewer than eight criteria, there is no CRPS?

A. Yes.

Q. Therefore, according to this standard, she does not have CRPS?

A. Yes.

Q. Therefore, she has no ratable impairment according to Chapter 16?

A. Yes.

Q. Doctor, wouldn't you agree she has a controversial pain syndrome, and despite her subjective complaints' there are no true objective findings?

A. Yes.

Q. According to Chapter 18, "Pain," are controversial pain syndromes ratable?

A. No.

Q. Doctor, in consideration of the information in Chapters 16 and 18, wouldn't you agree that the diagnosis of complex regional pain syndrome is not supportable, and she has no ratable impairment?

Comment. The evaluation and rating of complex regional pain syndrome (CRPS) is dealt with in different ways in Chapter 13, "The Nervous System," Chapter 16, "The Upper Extremities," and Chapter 18, "Pain." Counsel should be familiar with the differences between these chapters.

§ 8.15   TENDINITIS

Q. Doctor, this patient has tendinitis, and the complaint is discomfort?

A. Yes.

Q. You rated him on the basis of Chapter 16, "The Upper Extremities," correct?

A. Yes.

Q. You rated him for strength loss, finding a 40 percent strength loss index and, therefore, according to Table 16-34 on page 509, 20 percent upper extremity impairment.

A. Yes.

Q. You performed measurements in one position, two times during the visit?

A. Yes.

Q. You did not perform these three times, in all five positions on the Jamar, and compare this to rapid alternating grip measurements?

A. No.

Q. Did he complain of discomfort while doing grip testing?

A. Yes.

Q. Did he have any reproducible motion deficits, neurological deficits, or ratable disorders other than strength loss?

A. No.

Q. Does Section 16.7d, "Tendinitis," on page 507, state, "Although these conditions may be persistent for some time, they are not given a permanent impairment rating unless there is some other factor that must be considered"?

A. That's what it says.

Q. Would you consider this case of tendinitis a "rare" case?

A. No, it is a very common problem.

Q. Doctor, doesn't Section 16.8a, "Principles," on page 508, discuss the use of strength loss in a rare case?

A. Yes.

Q. It gives an example of someone with a severe muscle tear and a palpable muscle defect. Did this patient have a severe muscle tear and a palpable muscle defect?

A. No.

Q. The fifth edition of the *AMA Guides* states on page 508, "Decreased strength cannot be rated in the presence of decreased motion, painful conditions, deformities, or absence of parts (e.g., thumb amputation) that prevent effective application of maximal force in the region being evaluated," correct?

A. Yes.

Q. Therefore, because this is not a rare case and is a painful condition, wouldn't you agree that by explicit language in the fifth edition, it was not appropriate to rate him for strength loss?

A. Yes. However, I do believe he has a significant disability.

Q. Do the *AMA Guides* rate impairment, or do they rate disability?

A. They rate impairment.

Q. In terms of impairment, does he have any ratable impairment according to the fifth edition for his upper extremity problems, according to Chapter 16?

A. No.

Comment. Tendinitis usually does not result in ratable impairment, although it may be disabling. It is possible that there would be up to 3 percent whole-person permanent impairment if the claimant's pain was rated by the physician using Chapter 18, "Pain." Counsel should be familiar with the controversies involved in assessing cumulative trauma disorders, such as tendinitis, and the rating of strength loss.

§ 8.16 MUSCLE ATROPHY

Q. Doctor, you used Section 17.2d of the fifth edition of the *AMA Guides* when evaluating the muscle atrophy in the examinee, correct?

A. That is correct.

Q. Section 17.2d, "Muscle Atrophy (Unilateral)," provides as follows:

> In evaluating muscle atrophy, the leg circumference should be measured and compared to the opposite leg at equal distances from either the joint line or another palpable anatomic structure. For example, thigh atrophy may involve measuring the thigh circumference with a tape measure 10 cm above the patella and comparing it to a similar measure on the other leg. Calf circumference is compared at the maximum level bilaterally. Neither limb should have swelling or varicosities that would invalidate the measurements. Diminished muscle function can be estimated using four different methods. Only one should be used; that is, use only one method for assessing muscle function. Atrophy ratings should not be combined with any of the other three possible ratings of diminished muscle function (gait derangement, muscle weakness, and peripheral nerve injury). When muscle dysfunction is present, assess the condition with all four methods. Use the method that most accurately and objectively reflects the individual's impairment. Atrophy at both the thigh and calf is evaluated separately, and the whole-person impairment combined. Impairment ratings from atrophy are provided in Table 17-6.

How closely did you follow Section 17.2d when rating the impairment?

A. I followed it exactly.

Q. Despite the obvious inconsistent measurement instructions in the text?

A. I just followed the book. What inconsistent instructions?

Q. When the text says, "The leg circumference should be measured and compared to the opposite leg at equal distances from either the joint line or another palpable anatomic structure," isn't this actually reference to the thigh circumference measurement?

A. I think . . . yes, it appears to be.

Q. Would you agree with Drs. Brooks and Talmage writing in the *Guides Newsletter* "September/October 2002 Impairment Tutorial" page 10, that "[t]he *Guides* sometimes means thigh when it states leg, and means leg when it states calf"?

A. Looking at the section again, I would say yes.

Q. These doctors recommend replacing the *Guides'* sometimes vague and inconsistent measurement instructions with a simple, unambiguous one: "Thigh and leg circumferences are measured 15 centimeters superior and inferior to medial joint line of the knee, respectively." Doctor, did you follow this recommendation with this examinee?

A. No, I did not.

Q. Are you aware, Doctor, that the AMA has published a 16-page errata for all of the mistakes in the text?

A. No, I was not aware of that.

Q. Let's go over the errata and see which errors impact the impairment evaluation you did on this examinee.

Comment. Attorneys using the *AMA Guides* (5th ed. 2000) should familiarize themselves with the 16-page errata and the "Impairment Tutorials" available in the *AMA Guides Newsletter* and the *AMA Guides Casebook*. These resources provide a treasure trove of cross-examination material.

CHAPTER 9

SAMPLE CROSS-EXAMINATIONS UNDER THE SIXTH EDITION

§9.01 INTRODUCTION

This chapter provides examples of potentially fertile areas of cross-examination under the new sixth edition of the AMA's *Guides to the Evaluation of Permanent Impairment*, released in January 2008.

§9.02 READING AND UNDERSTANDING CHAPTERS 1 AND 2 AND THE GLOSSARY AS REQUIRED

Q. Doctor, are you familiar with the sixth edition of the *AMA Guides*?
A. Yes, I am.
Q. What are the five new axioms described in this edition?
A. I am not sure.
Q. The *Guides* are based on the "ICF" model, correct?
A. Yes, that's true.
Q. What does "ICF" stand for?
A. International . . . I am not sure of the rest of the acronym.
Q. When you rated the impairment here, did you take into account "precision, accuracy, reliability, and validity" as required by the *Guides*?
A. Yes, I did.
Q. How exactly did you do that, Doctor?
A. Well, I . . . I assume that was built into the ratings and I followed the book.
Q. You would agree that reliability should not vary significantly between instruments for a given rater and between raters for a given instrument?
A. Yes, I do.
Q. Would you read the highlighted portion from page 9 of the *Guides*, Doctor?
A. "Reliability can vary significantly between instruments for a given rater and between raters for a given instrument . . ."
Q. Which functional tasks did you observe the patient perform to determine if her self-report was indeed accurate?
A. Are you reading that from the *Guides* as well? Where is that located?
Q. Which chapter is the constitution of the sixth edition, Doctor?
A. I am not sure—I know it is in the beginning of the book.
Q. If anything conflicts with the constitution, that is preempted by the constitution, correct?
A. Right.
Q. But you are not sure which one is the constitution?
A. I think it is in Chapter 1 or 2.
Q. You are, of course, familiar with the 14 fundamental principles of the sixth edition?
A. Somewhat . . . it is pretty new.
Q. Doctor, do you still maintain you are familiar with the sixth edition?

Comment. All examiners are instructed at the beginning of each chapter in the *Guides* to familiarize themselves with Chapters 1 and 2 and the Glossary. This requirement can be easily challenged on cross-examination, especially because

Chapter 2 is the "constitution" of the sixth edition and preempts anything that conflicts with it. How can the physician know if there is a conflict if he or she is not thoroughly familiar with Chapter 2?

§ 9.03   CHALLENGING THE VALIDITY OF THE *AMA GUIDES* PAST AND PRESENT

Q.   Doctor, is the sixth edition of the *AMA Guides* scientifically valid?
A.   Yes, it is.
Q.   Is it evidence-based?
A.   Some parts are.
Q.   Which parts are evidence-based, Doctor?
A.   That's hard to say . . . . I guess you would have to look at the footnotes?
Q.   Are not the impairment ratings themselves consensus-derived percentages?
A.   Yes—but that does not make them wrong.
Q.   What exactly does "consensus-derived" mean in English?
A.   Well, a group of leading physicians presumably reviewed the literature and agreed on the percentages.
Q.   So they made up the numbers?
A.   I wouldn't put it that way.
Q.   How many examinees did you rate under the fifth edition, Doctor?
A.   I don't have an exact number—hundreds.
Q.   Did you do these ratings with the same care and accuracy as you are doing under the sixth edition?
A.   Absolutely.
Q.   So when the sixth edition of the *Guides* says that the fifth edition contained "deficiencies, antiquated and confusing terminology, limited validity and reliability, lack of internal inconsistency, and a higher error rate," this is the text that you used to rate those hundreds of injured workers?
A.   Yes—but . . . I was just following . . .
Q.   Orders, doctor?

Comment. The candid admissions in the *AMA Guides* (6th ed. 2008) on its flaws can be used should counsel choose to make a frontal assault on the *Guides*.

§ 9.04   CULTURAL DIFFERENCES

Q.   Doctor, where did you do your formal training in cultural sensitivity?
A.   I have no such training, Counsel.
Q.   Do you agree with the sixth edition of the *Guides* where it says: "Cultural differences between the examiner and the patient can greatly increase the risk of the examiner misrepresenting the patient's responses"?
A.   Where are you reading from, Counsel?
Q.   Page 27, Doctor. Now that you see it in "the book," do you agree with that statement?

A. Yes, I do.

Q. You utilized the Waddell signs when rating Mr. Sanchez, correct?

A. Yes, of course. I do it with all my examinees.

Q. Are you aware that Waddell signs are not valid in non-Anglo cultures?

A. If that is what it says.

Q. Now doctor, as you are required to understand and respect Mr. Sanchez's background, what is his background?

A. Well, he is Hispanic, I assume, but he speaks English.

Q. What about his religious beliefs?

A. Catholic?

Q. Is that a question or your answer?

A. I don't ask examinees about their religious beliefs. If I did, I am sure I would get in some kind of trouble for asking.

Q. What about Mr. Sanchez's ability to assimilate medical information?

A. No idea.

Q. Did you in fact consider cultural differences when you found Mr. Sanchez was a malingerer?

A. Is this a trick question?

Q. No, Doctor, that is what the sixth edition requires. No tricks.

A. Well, I took into consideration he was Hispanic—I know these people . . . enough said.

Q. Are Hispanics less likely to disagree with physicians out of respect for the physician's education and experience?

A. Counsel, I am surprised at you—that is a racist and stereotypical statement—you should be ashamed.

Q. I am reading from the sixth edition, Doctor, the one you said you followed when you rated Mr. Sanchez.

Comment. The instructions in Chapter 2 of the sixth edition regarding cultural differences raise many potential issues.

§9.05   REQUIRED COMPONENTS OF IMPAIRMENT EVALUATION REPORTS

Q. Doctor, did you follow the sample report form provided in the sixth edition?

A. What page is that on, Counsel?

Q. Doctor, that's on page 30.

A. Generally, I did follow the form.

Q. What portions did you not follow?

A. Well, the narrative history for one.

Q. Did you obtain an occupational history?

A. Generally—but a full occupational history could take hours.

Q. So you just cut short this part?

A. I did not obtain a full occupational history.

Comment. The requirements in Section 2.7 of the sixth edition can serve as a good guide for cross-examination.

§ 9.06   ACCURACY OF DIAGNOSIS

Q.   Doctor, you would agree that if the medical diagnosis here is incorrect the impairment rating is incorrect as well?

A.   Not necessarily.

Q.   Would you read the highlighted portion of page 23, Section 2.3, for us, Doctor?

A.   Sure.

Q.   Out loud, if you would, Doctor?

A.   "The *Guides* is of value only if the medical diagnosis is correct; an incorrect diagnosis leads to an incorrect impairment rating."

Q.   Do you agree with the *AMA Guides* on this point, Doctor?

A.   No, I do not.

Q.   Why is that, Doctor?

A.   Well, if I used the incorrect diagnosis and rated the examinee at 3 percent and the right diagnosis would also result in a 3 percent rating, then I would have the incorrect diagnosis and the correct rating.

Q.   What are the chances of that happening, Doctor?

A.   I am not a math major, but since most of the ratings are under 20 percent . . . I would say . . . maybe one in twenty.

Q.   I ask you again: If you used the wrong diagnosis here, your impairment rating is likely incorrect as well, is it not, Doctor?

Comment. As much of the sixth edition of the *Guides* is diagnosis-based, making an accurate diagnosis is essential for properly rating an examinee.

§ 9.07   PREJUDICE AGAINST THE TREATING PHYSICIAN

Q.   The sixth edition of the *Guides* provides that the physician performing an impairment evaluation should be independent, correct?

A.   That's true.

Q.   You are not independent, are you?

A.   I certainly am.

Q.   Do you still treat patients?

A.   No.

Q.   You work exclusively or almost exclusively doing IMEs for insurance carriers?

A.   Yes—but that does not mean I am not independent.

Q.   You are completely dependent on the same insurance carriers that continue to feed you IME after IME?

A.   I resent the implication.

Q.   It's not an implication, but a fact of life for you, Doctor?

A.   No.

Q.   You are also unbiased, correct?

A.   Absolutely.

Q.   How many unfavorable IMEs would it take before the insurers would stop using you?

A.   I am not sure.

Q. The 850,000 treating doctors in the United States are not independent and not trustworthy?

A. Well, I would not say that.

Q. Does the *AMA Guides* not say treating physicians "are not independent and therefore may be subject to greater scrutiny"?

A. Yes—that is what it says.

Q. You don't agree with that broad indictment of the medical profession and your colleagues, do you?

A. No, I do not.

Comment. The sixth edition of the *Guides* is consistently prejudiced against evaluations by treating physicians. The reasons for this prejudice can be used against IME physicians as well.

§ 9.08   RATING UNLISTED DIAGNOSES BY ANALOGY

Q. Doctor, you assigned a rating of 7 percent impairment for this upper extremity condition even though the diagnosis in question is not covered by the *Guides*?

A. Yes, that is correct.

Q. You never followed the instructions for rating by analogy on page 385 of the sixth edition of the *AMA Guides*, did you?

A. I believe I did. I chose a similar condition and used that.

Q. The sixth edition of the *Guides*, on page 385, requires that you fully explain in your report your rationale; do you see that?

A. Yes, I do.

Q. You didn't do that, did you?

A. I believe I did. I said I rated by analogy.

Q. You didn't provide any specific reasons in your report justifying the analogy, did you?

A. Not specifically.

Q. Can you do so now for us?

A. Well, let me see. . . .

Comment. Rating unlisted conditions by analogy is allowed in the sixth edition of the Guides. The justification for doing so must be well documented and can be challenged on cross-examination.

§ 9.09   USING A FUNCTIONAL ASSESSMENT, ALLOWED BY THE *AMA GUIDES*, THAT DOES NOT HAVE INSTRUCTIONS ON HOW TO SCORE OR CONVERT SCORE TO GRADE MODIFIER

Q. Doctor, you rated this examinee who has C8 disk herniation with C8 radiculopathy at 12 percent whole-person impairment?

A. That is correct.

Q. And that rating is based on the diagnosis of intervertebral herniation with radiculopathy, which placed him in Class 2?

A. Yes.

Q. Now for a grade modifier on functional history, you determined that to be grade 3?

A. Yes.

Q. And that grade modifier resulted in an increased impairment rating?

A. Yes, it moved it up one grade in Class 2 to Grade D 12 percent whole-person impairment.

Q. And you based that on the Oswestry Disability Index?

A. Yes, that is explicitly allowed under the *Guides*, at page 572.

Q. And you determined a score for the ODI?

A. Of course.

Q. And you translated that score into a grade modifier according to the *Guides*?

A. Yes. I mean, no. I guess not exactly. The *Guides* doesn't explain how to do that, so I used my clinical judgment.

Q. You looked at the score and, based on your experience, decided it should translate to a grade 3 functional assessment modifier?

A. Yes.

Q. You can't point to anything in the *AMA Guides* or anywhere else that supports this method, can you?

A. Aside from my experience, no.

Comment. The chapters in the sixth edition dealing with musculoskeletal disorders are permissive in terms of which functional assessments to use. For example, Chapter 17, "The Spine and Pelvis," allows the use of the Oswestry Disability Index but provides neither instructions on how to score the impairment nor instructions on how to convert the score to a grade modifier.

§ 9.10   FAILURE TO REVIEW ACTUAL CLINICAL STUDIES

Q. Doctor, prior to rating the examinee's complex regional pain syndrome, did you review the radiographs?

A. Well, I saw one set—I believe there were a few others.

Q. Why didn't you review the other two sets, Doctor?

A. They were not sent with the file.

Q. Did you ask for them?

A. No. The examinee presented herself—I didn't want to delay . . . the short answer: no, I did not.

Q. So you did not determine if they were unavailable?

A. Well, I didn't have them, but I am sure someone does.

Q. What about the bone scan?

A. Well, I saw the results of the scan, not the films themselves.

Q. So you didn't review the scan either?

A. Not as such—but the report was pretty clear.

Q. Are you aware, Doctor, that Section 2.7A requires the rating physician to "review all available diagnostic studies and laboratory data" as a critical step to the correct rating?

A. I did the best I could with what I had, Counsel.

Q. If you had to do it again, Doctor, would you ask to see all three sets of radiographs and the actual bone scan films?

Comment. The sixth edition of the *AMA Guides* repeatedly instructs examiners to review the actual films in question. This can be a fertile area for cross-examination because, in practice, these films are often not provided to the rating physician.

§9.11   SPYING ON EXAMINEE

Q. Doctor, you rated the 21-year-old examinee for permanent impairment, correct?

A. Yes, I did.

Q. You used the five categories of incremental impairment?

A. Correct—she fell into category #2.

Q. Did you cross-validate your findings of impact on ADL by observing her?

A. Yes, I did.

Q. Did you follow the recommendations of the *AMA Guides* on page 386 for your observation?

A. In fact I did.

Q. So when she was taking off her clothes, you stood in front of her to observe her ADLs?

A. No, of course not. She was behind a privacy screen.

Q. You surreptitiously observed this young woman while she was dressing and undressing, without her permission, Doctor?

A. I don't like the way that sounds.

Q. I understand completely, Doctor . . . . Do you do this with all your examinees or just the young and attractive ones?

Comment. The sixth edition encourages treating physicians to spy on the examinees. On page 386, it even suggests they observe examinees changing into and out of their robe. This instruction provides fruitful opportunities for cross-examination.

§9.12   FOLLOWING CHAPTER-SPECIFIC INSTRUCTIONS

Q. Doctor, you rated the examinee under Chapter 14, "Mental and Behavioral Disorders," correct?

A. Yes—that is correct.

Q. Did you follow the 11 recommendations of the *Guides* for performing an M&BD IME?

A. I followed my usual protocol.

Q.   Did you obtain and evaluate the examinee's legal history?

A.   Well, I asked him about this case.

Q.   Where is the information in your IME about prior lawsuits, work-related injuries, incarcerations, and bankruptcies?

A.   It is not in the report.

Q.   Where is the examinee's military history, his service overseas, adjustment to service, type of discharge, and pay grade?

A.   It is not in there—I only have so much time.

Q.   What about your assessment of the influence of the litigation process on his return to work?

A.   Not in there—Counsel, I only get $800 for an M&BD IME, . . . there is just so much time I can spend.

Q.   How many of the recommendations set forth in Table 14-4 on page 352 did you actually comply with, Doctor?

Comment. Many of the chapters in the *AMA Guides* contain specific instructions as to how the examiner should conduct the examination in terms of physical examination, functional assessment, and so forth. These instructions can be fertile grounds for cross-examination.

§ 9.13   APPORTIONMENT

Q.   Doctor, this examinee suffered three separate and distinct workers' compensation injuries, correct?

A.   Yes—that is my understanding.

Q.   She initially suffered a cervical sprain and was rated under the fourth edition of the *Guides* at 5 percent?

A.   That's correct.

Q.   She subsequently had a second cervical injury with radicular complaints and was rated under the fifth edition of the *Guides* at 8 percent?

A.   That is accurate.

Q.   Now you are rating her for her third cervical injury, an intervertebral disk with herniation at C5–6 and an anterior fusion at C5–6 with intermittent arm pain?

A.   Yes—that is what we have.

Q.   How did you apportion the injuries and arrive at your final rating, Doctor?

A.   Well—I attempted to use [Section] 2.5C. I took the total rating—I assigned her to Class 1—Grade modifier 1 (based on motor strength)—clinical studies Grade modifier 2—net adjustment +1—impairment Class 1—Grade D—for a total impairment of 7 percent.

Q.   What about the apportionment, Doctor?

A.   I took the all-inclusive rating (7 percent) and tried to subtract off the prior rating of 8 percent, but that did not work. I then went to plan B and tried to convert the ratings from the fourth and fifth editions. That did not work either.

Q.   What did you finally do, Doctor?

A.   I used my best clinical judgment and determined that the prior cervical injuries did leave the examinee impaired to a certain extent (e.g., 3 percent) and subtracted the 3 percent from the 8 percent, leaving 5 percent.

Q. Could you tell us, Doctor, where you got the 3 percent from?
A. Experience.
Q. Did you compare the fourth, fifth, and sixth editions of the *Guides* to assess their similarity as required by [Section] 2.5c?
A. Are you kidding?
Q. Was it possible to convert the earlier ratings under the fourth and the fifth editions to a rating under the sixth edition before you did your apportionment?
A. I don't know.
Q. Are you aware that is also required by Section 2.5c on page 26?

Comment. The sixth edition of the *Guides* contains instructions on apportionment that are less than precise and can be problematic in some circumstances.

§9.14 UNDERSTANDING THE DEFINITION OF MAXIMUM MEDICAL IMPROVEMENT

Q. You rated permanent impairment here, Doctor. Correct?
A. Yes, I did.
Q. Was the examinee at MMI?
A. Yes.
Q. What exactly is MMI?
A. Well—his condition was stabilized.
Q. The *Guides* define MMI as "where patients are as good as they are going to be from the medical and surgical treatment available to them." Is that correct?
A. May I see your copy of the book? What page are you referring to?
Q. Page 26—is that correct, Doctor?
A. Yes—that is what I meant.
Q. Is that the same as "the point at which a condition has stabilized and is unlikely to change (improve or worsen) substantially in the next year with or without treatment"?
A. No—it is not the same.
Q. Doctor, that is the glossary definition provided by the sixth edition of the *Guides* on page 612.
A. Well, it's pretty much the same.
Q. In this case the examinee refused therapy, correct?
A. Yes, she did.
Q. Did you take this into account in your rating?
A. Absolutely.
Q. Did you comment in your report addressing the therapeutic value of the therapeutic approach?
A. Am I required to do that also?
Q. Yes, you are, doctor—here, look at [Section] 2.3c.
A. That is what it says.
Q. Will this examinee get worse in the future?
A. Well—I don't think so—but medicine is not an exact science.

Q. So he might get worse during the next year?

A. Well . . . yes, I suppose.

Q. In that case, he has not reached MMI, has he?

Comment. The sixth edition of the *Guides* rates permanent impairment at maximum medical improvement. Whether or not an examinee was at MMI, as defined in the *Guides*, is a potential area of inquiry.

SAMPLE PROOFS*

* The authors gratefully acknowledge the assistance of the following attorneys in the preparation of this section of the book: O. John Alpizar, Palm Bay, FL; William E. Farmer, Lebanon, TN; John T. Fryback, Bradenton, FL; Michael D. Galligan, McMinnville, TN; Edward H. Hurt, Jr., Orlando, FL; Rex A. Hurley, Orlando, FL; Gary M. Israel, Tucson, AZ; Chris Lackmann, Albuquerque, NM; Merton E. Marks, Phoenix, AZ; George E. Mundy, Cedartown, GA; John L. Myrick, Pensacola, FL; Michael J. Paduda, Jr., Bogalusa, LA; Thomas L. Root, Council Bluffs, IA; John Sprowls, Pauls Valley, OK; Mark L. Zientz, Miami, FL; Daniel E. Gershon, Santa Fe, NM; Pepe J. Mendez, Denver, CO; Wayne Harris, Fort Smith, AR; Anthony Fabrizio, Wilmington, DE; Michael V. Tichenor, Memphis, TN; Gary S. Nitsche, Wilmington, DE; Susan K. Bradley, Murfreesboro, TN; Marc Sorin, Memphis, TN; James M. Glascow, Jr., Union City, TN.

§ 10.01   INTRODUCTION

This chapter presents examples of actual testimony given by both claimants and physicians that was used to establish permanent impairment in workers' compensation proceedings. These examples are representative of some of the medical problems that would be involved in workers' compensation proceedings. Sections 10.2 through 10.08 reproduce portions of actual trial transcripts from recent workers' compensation decisions.

§ 10.02   LOWER BACK INJURY**

The claimant in the following case was an auto body painter who injured his lower back at work. Doctor F. was selected by the Workers' Compensation Bureau to perform an impairment evaluation. He determined that the claimant did not have a cauda equina syndrome diagnosis and rated the claimant's impairment under the Range of Motion Model of the fifth edition of the *AMA Guides* at 28 percent. Claimant's treating physician, Dr. E., testified that the claimant did in fact have a diagnosis of cauda equina syndrome and used the fifth edition's DRE model to rate the claimant at 50 percent impairment. The workers' compensation judge held that the treating physician's testimony was more credible. The depositions of Dr. F. (IME) and Dr. E. (treating physician) and a portion of the workers' compensation judge's decision in this matter follow.

Direct Examination of Treating Physician by Claimant's Counsel

Qualifications of Physician

Q.   Doctor, you've been kind enough to provide us with a copy of your curriculum vitae, and you've testified in workers' compensation proceedings before.

[**Ms. Dempsey**]. We'll mark this as Claimant's Exhibit No. 1.

[At this time Claimant's Exhibit No. 1 was marked for identification.]

Q.   If called upon to testify, would you testify in conformity therewith?
A.   Yes.
Q.   Doctor, are you licensed to practice medicine in this Commonwealth?
A.   Yes.
Q.   And what boards are they?
A.   The American Board of Physical Medicine and Rehabilitation, the American Board of Independent Medical Examiners, the American Board of Electrodiagnostic Medicine, and the American Board of Pain Medicine.
Q.   And, Doctor, do you presently have an active clinical practice of at least 20 hours a week, and have you had an active clinical practice for the last two years at a minimum?

** The authors wish to acknowledge the contribution of Mary Walsh-Dempsey, Esq., and Todd J. O'Malley, Esq., of Scranton, PA, to this section.

A.   Yes.

[Ms. Dempsey]. I have no further questions for the doctor. I'd ask that he be admitted as an expert in the fields that he was listed as board certified in and submit him to cross-examination.

[Mr. Wyatt, Employer's Counsel]. I have no objection.

[By Ms. Dempsey]

History as Treating Physician

Q.   Doctor, you're the claimant's treating physician, is that correct?
A.   Yes.
Q.   And you've been his treating physician since January 22, 1999, is that correct?
A.   Yes.
Q.   Who referred _____ to you?
A.   His family physician, Dr. Davis.
Q.   Doctor, since you've treated him so often over the years, we're going to highlight a lot of your records, but I'd like to at least start with your initial evaluation of him and the history of a work-related injury that he relayed to you.
A.   Yes. I had originally seen _____ for that injury on January 22, 1999. There was a history of a work injury from January 6, 1999. He was lifting an item at work, had back pain going down the back of his right thigh and calf. He had seen Dr. Davis. He was referred to Dr. Presper. He had an MRI done, which showed a herniated disk at his lumbar spine at L5–S1 with a free fragment. He had surgery by Dr. Presper on January 18, 1999, and was discharged the next day.

     I had seen him on January 22, 1999, which was four days later. He had reported continued back and posterior thigh symptoms. He wasn't sure whether he had had any improvement from the surgery at that point.
Q.   Doctor, did you have any treatment recommendations at that point in time?
A.   Yes.
Q.   And what were they?
A.   I recommended a follow-up with Dr. Presper and when he was cleared for therapy, to come back and I would be happy to set up the therapy at that time.

[Ms. Dempsey]. I'm going to move for the admission of Claimant's [Exhibit] 2, which is the operative report from Dr. Presper dated January 18, 1999.

[At this time Claimant's Exhibit No. 2 was marked for identification.]

[By Ms. Dempsey].

Q.   When was your next follow-up with the claimant?
A.   February 5, 1999.
Q.   And his subjective complaints at that point in time?
A.   He had continued back pain, he had some numbness in his right groin, the back and side of his right thigh and buttocks.
Q.   And, Doctor, your physical exam on that date?

A. It showed a negative straight leg raise. There was good trunk range in all directions. There was discomfort when he would bend from side to side and when he bent forward. The surgical scar was healing well. There was some tightness in his back. His neurologic exam was normal.

Q. And your treatment recommendations at that point?

A. I recommended physical therapy.

Q. And, Doctor, your next follow-up with him?

A. February 19, 1999.

Q. And, Doctor, on that visit, he was complaining of dysuria symptoms; is that correct?

A. Yes.

Q. What exactly is that?

A. Pain when he would urinate.

Q. Is that consistent at all with postsurgical course?

A. Sometimes it can be.

Q. And what treatment recommendations did you make on that date?

A. I recommended continued physical therapy, a urinalysis. I put him on an antibiotic in case he had a urinary tract infection.

Q. And, Doctor, what was your working impression as of that date?

A. Improving from his hemilaminectomy from the L5–S1 ruptured disk.

Q. Doctor, your next visit with the claimant?

A. February 26, 1999.

Q. And just summarize that for us, if you would.

A. He was having normal bowel and bladder movements at that time. He had a sense that there was still fullness in his belly such that he could not urinate—I'm sorry—such that he was urinating frequently. I had placed him on an oral prednisone wean at that time.

Q. And, Doctor, your impression at that point in time?

A. Unchanged.

Q. And, Doctor, did you have an opportunity either on that date or thereafter to review a February 26, 1999, MRI report—for your convenience, I'll show you a copy—and if so, the impression on that report and whether it was consistent with your subjective findings and physical exam?

A. The MRI was read as showing the surgery at L5–S1, that at that time there was no evidence of a recurrent disk herniation. There was a disk protrusion at L4–L5, as well as 1, at T12–L1. There was epidural fibrosis at L5–S1. The MRI findings were consistent with subjective complaints and the objective findings.

Q. And, Doctor, the level that he had the surgery at was what?

A. L5–S1.

Q. And that is where the epidural fibrosis was?

A. Yes.

Q. What is that specifically?

A. Scarring around the area of where the spinal cord is.

Q. And, Doctor, your next visit with the claimant?

A. March 3, 1999.

Q. And the subjective complaints on that date?

A. Continued back discomfort, numbness in the buttocks, groin, and scrotum, all on the right side. Once or twice he had a sense that he was leaking urine. His bowel movements were normal.

Q. And, Doctor, did your impression remain the same?

A. Yes.

Q. Was there any discussion about returning to work at that point in time?

A. There was.

Q. And what transpired?

A. _____ wanted to try things back at work at his preinjury job as an auto mechanic, and I cleared him for doing such.

Q. And your next follow-up with the claimant?

A. March 19, 1999.

Q. And did his subjective complaints remain the same?

A. Yes.

Q. And what was your impression on that date?

A. Status postsurgery of L5–S1 disk herniation with a diskectomy, laminectomy, and the continued numbness.

Q. And, Doctor, at that point you had discussed a cauda equina syndrome?

A. Yes.

Q. What is that?

A. It's when the spinal cord gets injury at the thoracolumbar junction such that there's _____ and/or bladder and/or erectile or ejaculatory dysfunction as a result of a nerve injury at the spinal cord.

Q. And, Doctor, your next visit with the claimant?

A. April 14, 1999.

Q. And just a brief summary.

A. He had a functional capacity evaluation at that time. He had continued symptoms. His exam was the same. He continued to have the occasional leakage of urine. I had made a referral for urology.

Q. And your next visit with the claimant?

A. May 14, 1999.

Q. His subjective complaints on that date?

A. They were unchanged.

Q. And, Doctor, up until this point, were you continuing him on a course of medication?

A. Yes.

Q. And had he also undergone physical therapy?

A. Yes.

Q. Had you heard back from the urologist at all?

A. Yes.

Q. Number one, what doctor sent you back a report?

A. Dr. Stefanelli.

Q. And he's a urologist?

A. Yes.

Q. Did you have an opportunity to read that report as the treating physician and rely on it in making treatment recommendations?

A. Yes.

Q. And, Doctor, I'm going to show you what is a May 12, '99, report from Dr. Stefanelli, as well as a January 19, 2000, report. Having had the opportunity to review these in the past, what basically were Dr. Stefanelli's findings regarding the urology consult?

[Mr. Wyatt]. Before you answer, Doctor, I'm going to object on two bases: Number one, the reports of Dr. Stefanelli have not been provided in this matter. I've never seen them.

In addition, Dr. Stefanelli's comments would not be relevant at this point in time because we're dealing solely with a low back injury under the Notice of Compensation Payable issued in this matter, and there's never been any adjudication that claimant had any injury other than a low back injury; and, therefore, I would also object on the basis of relevance.

You may answer, Doctor, in light of the parties' stipulation.

[Ms. Dempsey]. In light of your objection? You said "parties' stipulation."

[Mr. Wyatt]. Well, the stipulation that he can answer over an objection.

[Ms. Dempsey]. Okay.

[The Witness]. The notice indicates an assessment of voiding dysfunction, as well as painful ejaculation and decreased erectile firmness. It indicated that there may have been—or it says, certainly may have urologic impairment at the bladder. A voiding diary had been recommended, as well as voiding urodynamics.

The second note from January 2000 indicated that an ultrasound of the rectum had been done to rule out any prostate abnormalities. There was decreased anal sensation noted, decreased sensation to the right thigh. It was noted from the voiding dysfunction that it may be from a combination of outlet obstruction at the bladder, as well as a neurologic component.

[By Ms. Dempsey].

Q. Doctor, are those findings at all consistent with this cauda equina syndrome that you spoke of?
A. Yes.

[Ms. Dempsey]. I'm going to admit that as Claimant's Exhibit No. 3.

[At this time Claimant's Exhibit No. 3 was marked for identification.]

[By Ms. Dempsey].

Q. When was your next visit with the claimant, Doctor?
A. May 28, 1999.
Q. And just review that for us, please.
A. His symptoms were unchanged. The exam was unchanged. There was a recommendation at that time for an epidural injection, and the patient was going to be seen by Dr. Presper for consideration for that.
Q. And your next visit with the claimant?
A. June 18, 1999.
Q. And, again, just summarize for us.

A.   There was [sic] continued symptoms. There was some improvement in the _____ work hardening. He had the epidural. It didn't help at all. His symptoms were unchanged. His exam was unchanged.

Q.   And, Doctor, at that point, what type of medication regimen did you have him on?

A.   He was on Ativan, OxyContin, Ultram, and Neurontin.

Q.   And, Doctor, your next visit with the claimant?

A.   July 14, 1999.

Q.   And, again, just review that for us.

A.   His symptoms were unchanged. A TENS unit was tried, which _____ had to turn up very high to get any sort of effect. He had seen Dr. Presper. A spinal cord stimulator had been recommended. An MRI of the pelvis was done, which was normal. The exam was essentially unchanged.

Q.   And, Doctor, did you see him again on August 25th of 1999?

A.   Yes.

Q.   Number one, did your medication regimen change at all at that point?

A.   Yes.

Q.   And what was the change?

A.   I had started weaning him from the Neurontin and the OxyContin and put him on Dilaudid.

Q.   And what type of medication is that, Doctor?

A.   That's a narcotic pain medicine.

Q.   Was [sic] there any other treatment recommendations?

A.   Yes.

Q.   And what were they?

A.   An MRI of the lumbar spine, consideration for a repeat epidural, the recommendation for a spinal cord stimulator was also made, the continued TENS unit, as well as specific massage therapy treatments in the form of shiatsu.

Q.   Doctor, on September 10th of 1999, did you refer him for a pain management consult?

A.   Yes.

Q.   And to which doctor did you refer him?

A.   Dr. Achecar.

Q.   Doctor, I'm going to show you a report that was authorized by yourself, which we'll mark as Claimant's 4. Just a summary of what you were hoping to obtain by sending him for a pain management consult.

A.   Where he'd be a candidate for a spinal cord stimulator, morphine pump, or a long-standing epidural catheter.

Q.   Thank you.

[**Ms. Dempsey**]. I'll move for the admission of that as Claimant's 4.

[At this time Claimant's Exhibit No. 4 was marked for identification.]

[By Ms. Dempsey].

Q.   Doctor, when was the next time you saw the claimant?

A.   September 15, 1999.

Q.   And, again, just a summary, please.

A. He re-saw Dr. Presper. There was a recommendation against the spinal cord stimulator. He was referred to Dr. Bell. An epidural was recommended. _____ decided to have that done, but in Honesdale as opposed to Dr. Bell's office down in Kingston.

   There was noted to be a recurrent disk herniation at L5–S1 on the recent MRI that had been reordered. The exam was unchanged. He continued with his positive seated straight leg raise. He actually had some slight weakness of his right ankle and toe at that time. That's it.

Q. Doctor, what was his ambulation at that point in time? Were there any problems with it?

A. Well, he was leaning to one side when he walked, and he would limp on his right side when he walked.

   [Ms. Dempsey]. I would move for the admission of Claimant's 5, the September 3rd, '99 MRI that the doctor just discussed in his note.

   [At this time Claimant's Exhibit No. 5 was marked for identification.]

[By Ms. Dempsey].

Q. Doctor, when was the next time you saw the claimant?

A. October 6, 1999.

Q. And just a summary, please.

A. He continued with positive straight leg raise. His limp remained unchanged. His pain was unchanged. He was going to be seen by Dr. Moore in Englewood, New Jersey, for a second opinion regarding his back surgery. He continued on his pain medicines.

Q. And your next visit, please.

A. November 3, 1999.

Q. And a summary, again.

A. Symptoms were unchanged. He saw Dr. Moore. He was scheduled for a repeat L5–S1 diskectomy with lysis of the epidural fibrosis, and that was scheduled for November 16, 1999. Exam was unchanged. Pain medicines were continued.

Q. Doctor, was this the same level he had the first surgery at?

A. Yes.

Q. And your next follow-up with him?

A. December 22, 1999.

Q. And his chief complaints at that point in time?

A. He had the surgery. There was continued pain. It was unchanged from what it was preoperatively. There was actually an increase in his right groin, buttocks, and scrotal pain postoperatively, as well as an increase in numbness of his right foot.

Q. And your physical exam on that date, if it changed at all?

A. It was essentially the same.

Q. Doctor, did you notice anything regarding claimant's mood at that point in time?

A. Yes, he was depressed.

Q. And did he have any other complaints at that point in time?

A. Yes.

Q. And what were they?

A.   He had some itchiness, which he related to the OxyContin.

Q.   Was he having any difficulty with sleeping?

A.   Yes.

Q.   And, Doctor, your medication regimen at that point?

A.   Celexa, Xanax, Neurontin, a Duragesic patch.

Q.   And your next visit with the claimant?

A.   January 24, 2000.

Q.   Did his subjective complaints remain the same?

A.   Yes.

Q.   And what were your recommendations at that point in time?

A.   The Xanax was increased. The Celexa was continued. The Dilaudid was increased. He followed up with Dr. Davis and was referred to Dr. Yoo, who's a psychiatrist.

Q.   And did you agree with that referral, Doctor?

A.   Yes.

Q.   When was your next visit with the claimant?

A.   March 3, 2000.

Q.   And a summary at that point in time, please.

A.   Symptoms were unchanged. He had seen Dr. Davis. The Celexa dose was increased. He was seen by both psychiatry and psychology. He was noted to be using a cane at that time. He was noted to have difficulty getting in and out of bed. He remained with some weakness of his right lower extremity. The tightness of his back remained. His straight leg raise remained positive.

Q.   And, Doctor, any treatment recommendations at that time?

A.   He was seeing Dr. Stefanelli, the urologist; his family physician, Dr. Davis; the psychologist; and the psychiatrist. He was noted to be on Celexa, Dilaudid, MS Contin, Xanax, Benadryl for the itchiness, Neurontin, doxycycline, and Flomax.

I had recommended that he continue the MS Contin, but that if he still had nausea from it, then we would just put him back on the Dilaudid. The recommendation for the spinal cord stimulator was remade, and _____ decided to hold off on that.

[At this time Claimant's Exhibit 6 was marked for identification.]

[By Ms. Dempsey].

Q.   Doctor, I'm going to show you what we've had marked as Claimant's Exhibit No. 6. It's a March 20, 2000, psychiatric evaluation from Dr. Yoo. Being the treating physician, have you ever had the opportunity to review that in the past?

A.   I don't think so.

Q.   Oh, okay. Would you take an opportunity to review that now for me, please?

A.   **[Witness complies.]** Okay.

Q.   Having had an opportunity to review that, what, if anything, did you find significant on that?

[Mr. Wyatt]. Doctor, before you address that question, I would make the same objection as I did in reference to Dr. Stefanelli's reports; that being, it hasn't been produced prior to the deposition. The only accepted injury is the claimant's lumbar spine. Moreover, given the fact that Dr. Epstein has stated that he didn't see or rely upon the report prior to today, it doesn't meet the hearsay exception. For all those reasons, I object.

[By Ms. Dempsey].

Q. You can answer, Doctor.
A. A diagnosis of major depression was made. There was noted to be anxiety as well, and there were findings on exam that were consistent with those diagnoses.
Q. Doctor, did you feel that was consistent with his presentation to you upon your office visits as well?
A. Yes.
Q. And, Doctor, when was the next time you saw the claimant?
A. April 7, 2000.
Q. And, again, his subjective complaints, did they remain the same?
A. Yes.
Q. Any further treatment recommendations?
A. Yes.
Q. And what were they?
A. That he follow up with the surgeon, Dr. Moore, that he continue with the psychologist and psychiatrist. He was going to try acupuncture. He was continued on the present medications. He was noted to also be on Valium and Zoloft. He was noted to have a coincidental finding of a breast mass on his right side, and I had recommended a mammogram, as well as follow-up with his family physician for that.
Q. And, Doctor, when was the next time you saw the claimant?
A. June 9, 2000.
Q. And his subjective complaints at that point, did they remain the same?
A. Yes.
Q. And your physical exam on that date, did that remain the same?
A. Yes.
Q. And, again, any further treatment options?
A. We had, again, discussed the morphine pump and spine stimulator. He had seen Dr. Moore. He was felt not to be a candidate for that. _____ decided to hold off on that recommendation.
Q. And your next visit with the claimant?
A. June 30, 2000.
Q. And, again, just a summary, please.
A. His subjective complaints were unchanged. There was a history of having a pseudoseizure. He was referred to Dr. O'Boyle from neurology at that point, and an EEG [electroencephalogram] was recommended at that point. His exam was unchanged.

[At this time Claimant's Exhibit No. 7 was marked for identification.]

[By Ms. Dempsey].

Capability to Work

Q. Doctor, I'm going to show you what we've marked as Claimant's 7, which is an Injury Status Report. Would you just confirm that this is your signature and your opinion on claimant's ability to work at that point in time?

A. That is my opinion. It was my opinion that he was not capable of working.

Q. And, Doctor, did that basically remain the same since the point in time when he had had the second surgery?

A. Yes.

Q. And, Doctor, your next visit with the claimant?

A. July 21, 2000.

Q. And a summary of your subjective findings at that time.

A. Subjective complaints were unchanged. He had needed a scooter or a wheelchair for long-distance mobility. He was using a cane for short-distance mobility. His exam was unchanged. He actually was noted to have more limited range of motion on that date.

Q. Your impression at that point, Doctor?

A. L5–S1 disk herniation with L5–S1 radiculopathy, the laminectomy and decompression at L5–S1, and he remained with chronic pain.

Q. Doctor, when you use the term *free fragment* in your impression, what does that refer to?

A. That means a piece of disk that has essentially popped off.

[At this time Claimant's Exhibit No. 8 was marked for identification.]

[By Ms. Dempsey].

Q. Doctor, I'm going to show you what we've marked as Claimant's Exhibit No. 8. Is this a copy of the prescription you gave claimant for a wheelchair?

A. Yes.

[At this time Claimant's Exhibit No. 9 was marked for identification.]

[By Ms. Dempsey].

Q. I'm going to show you what we've marked as Claimant's Exhibit No. 9, which is another Injury Status Report that you filled out on July 21st after you saw the claimant. Would you be kind enough to summarize the treatment and prognosis?

A. The treatment was the wheelchair and scooter for long-distance mobility. It was noted that the EEG urodynamics was negative. His Dilaudid dose was increased. The other meds were unchanged.

   The prognosis was that he was at maximum medical improvement with a permanent impairment and a permanent disability of not being able to work.

[At this time Claimant's Exhibit No. 10 was marked for identification.]

[By Ms. Dempsey].

Q. And, Doctor, I'll show you what has been marked as Claimant's 10. Would you just confirm that's the prescription you gave to claimant for a scooter for mobility?

A. It is.

Q. And, Doctor, your next visit with the claimant?

A. August 16, 2000.

Q. And, again, just summarize, please.

A. Complaints were unchanged. The dose of the Dilaudid was increased. The exam was unchanged. Impressions were unchanged.

Q. Now, Doctor, for the rest of 2000, I do not have your notes, but if you would be kind enough to just look through them and summarize your treatment, including whether the subjective complaints changed at all, any significant positive findings and any referrals to other physicians, just to give us a general idea of the treatment.

A. I had seen _____ subsequently on 9/8/2000, 9/29/2000, 10/20/2000, 11/17/2000, 11/20/2000, 12/20/2000, 2/21/01, 3/21/01, 6/27/01, 10/31/01, and 3/13/02. Complaints were essentially unchanged.

> **[Mr. Wyatt].** I believe counsel's question was to the end of 2000. To the extent that you're going to comment upon any treatment after February 9, 2001, I must object.
>
> The impairment rating was done by Dr. F. on 2/9/2001; therefore, any visits subsequent to that time would not be relevant to this matter by virtue of a prior order of Judge Hall at the December 27, 2001, pretrial conference.
>
> Therefore, to the extent that your opinion relies upon any of the reports beyond February 9, 2001, I would object, and I would further object because I don't have the reports, but go ahead and answer.

> **[Ms. Dempsey].** Just in response. At this point in time, I'm not asking the doctor any opinion questions. I'm asking him to be kind enough to detail his medical records for the judge so the judge has a basic idea of the treatment that claimant has received.

[By Ms. Dempsey].

Current Status

Q. And, Doctor, you can do it from 2000 and 2001 and up to the present for me to make things quicker and easier for us.

A. Thank you. His pain complaints were unchanged. He had a repeat MRI of his lumbar spine on 10/20/2000, which showed recurrent scar formation at L5–S1 impinging on the nerve root. The medicines were essentially unchanged.

He was referred to Dr. K. Davis, who's a pain management doctor in Wilkes-Barre, for a referral. There was a recommendation to try a medicine called Kadian. I did try him on that. _____ had some nausea from that. We discontinued that medicine.

He was continued on the Dilaudid and the other medications that he was on. He was also on various antianxiety, antidepressant medicines, and he was on

Flomax, as well, for his bladder. He was subsequently tried on a lidoderm patch, which he continues on.

Q. And, Doctor, when was the last visit you had with the claimant?
A. March 13, 2002.
Q. And did everything remain the same up until that point in time?
A. Yes.

Opinions

Q. Doctor, to begin with, I'm going to ask a series of questions that are going to call for your opinion within a reasonable degree of medical certainty, and then I'm going to switch over to your May 17, 2001, report.

Number one, based on the extensive treatment you've had with the claimant over the period of the last three years, including physical exams, review of diagnostic tests, and coordination of his treatment, what is your final diagnosis of claimant's condition as it relates to his work injury?
A. L5–S1 disk herniation with L5–S1 radiculopathy, status postlaminectomy, and decompression of the free disk fragment at L5–S1, epidural fibrosis at L5–S1, cauda equina syndrome.
Q. And, Doctor, again, to be more specific regarding the cauda equina syndrome, what does that entail or encompass?
A. It encompasses an injury to the spinal cord such that there is resultant bowel, bladder, and/or sexual dysfunction.
Q. And, Doctor, within a reasonable degree of medical certainty, the diagnoses that you've just rendered, do you feel they were causally related to claimant's January 6, 1999, work-related injury?

[**Mr. Wyatt**]. I would object on this basis: The sole injury accepted is a low back injury, and there's been no petition to review or request for any other change in the Definition of Injury in the Notice of Compensation Payable; therefore, the doctor's opinion at this point in time is irrelevant on the other issues unrelated to the back injury.

[By Ms. Dempsey].

Q. You can answer, Doctor.
A. Yes.
Q. And, Doctor, from the point of the second surgery with Dr. Moore in New Jersey, do you have an opinion as to claimant's ability to return to work?
A. Yes.
Q. What is that?
A. That he's not capable of substantial gainful employment.
Q. Doctor, do you feel he'll be capable of that in the future at all?
A. No.
Q. Doctor, you were kind enough at my request to review an IRE [impairment rating evaluation] that was performed by Dr. F. on February 9, 2001, is that correct?
A. Yes.

Q. Having an opportunity to review that, did you also author for me a May 17, 2001, report that I'll mark as Claimant's Exhibit No. 11?

A. Yes.

[At this time Claimant's Exhibit No. 11 was marked for identification.]

[By Ms. Dempsey].

Impairment Rating

Q. I'm going to give you pretty much freedom here to go through this report and explain for us, if you will, number one, your review of the doctor's report; number two, any differences you may have; and, number three, your final conclusions.

A. Dr. F. had done an IRE on 2/9/01. It's important to note that in doing impairment ratings for the lower back, the *AMA Guides*, under the fifth edition, allows the doctor essentially two different ways to rate someone's back.

One is . . . called the DRE, or Diagnosis Related Estimate model, and the second is called the ROM, or Range of Motion model.

The DRE model is to be used for patients who have single-level back problems, single-level disks, single-level root injuries. When there's more than one disk or nerve root involved, then the Range of Motion model is the one to be utilized. . . .

I could go through all the other calculations in detail, but essentially that's what it came to, so it was my opinion that _____'s whole-person impairment based on his diagnosis was 50 percent.

Q. Doctor, if called upon to testify in more detail in conformity with your report that was authored on May 17, 2001, would you do so?

A. Yes.

Q. Doctor, utilizing the *AMA Guidelines of Permanent Impairment,* more specifically the fifth edition, within a reasonable degree of medical certainty, do you have an opinion as to whether claimant has an impairment that's equal to or greater than the 50 percent that's required by Section 306-A22 of the Workers' Comp Act?

[Mr. Wyatt]. I would just object, Doctor, on this basis: Again, the fact that it's clear from Dr. E.'s testimony a few moments ago that he was relying upon a percentage impairment for injuries that have not been accepted as part of the work injury in this matter; therefore, I would object to his opinion on the basis of relevance since it's including injuries that have not been accepted or adjudicated as part of the January 6, 1999, injury date. You may answer, Doctor.

[The Witness]. Yes.

[By Ms. Dempsey].

Q. And, Doctor, is it equal to 50 percent or greater than 50 percent?

A. Equal.

Q. Doctor, would that opinion have been as of the date of your report, May 17, 2001?

A. Yes.

Q. Now, I want to go back just briefly. You had spoken about the claimant's back injury at L5–S1. The cauda equina syndrome that you discussed, does that emanate from the L5–S1 level?

A. Yes.

Q. And is that part of the back injury?

A. Yes.

Q. And the L5–S1 radiculopathy, again, does that emanate from the back injury?

A. Yes.

Q. And the epidural fibrosis, is that part of the back injury?

A. Yes.

Q. Are they just all different diagnoses relating back to the disk herniation and what emanates from it?

A. Yes.

Q. Doctor, your prognosis for the claimant?

A. He's at maximum medical improvement.

Q. Will he ever get any better?

A. No.

Q. Doctor, throughout the three years that you had treated him and your review of the medical records of various physicians to which you referred him, did he continuously have the bowel and bladder problems?

A. Subsequent to the surgery, yes.

Q. Was that the first or second surgery . . . ?

A. He had some bladder complaints after the first surgery.

Q. And, Doctor, throughout that period of time, as well, did he have complaints of sexual impairment?

A. Yes.

[Ms. Dempsey]. That's all I have for the Doctor. I would just reserve the right—I don't have it with me now . . . —but to make copies of the specific tables and the specific sections of the *AMA Guides* to submit them at the hearing for the judge so he can see the sections that the doctor relied upon, and other than that, I have no further questions.

Cross-Examination of Treating Physician by Employer's Counsel

[By Mr. Wyatt].

Missing Records

Q. Doctor, I have a few questions. Dr. Stefanelli's reports, first set of reports, did you actually have those?

A. Yes.

Q. Then the second report you were asked to look at was a psychiatrist's report. I understand you did not have that one?

A. I don't think so.

Critical of Other Physician's Rating Methodology
(Used ROM and Not DRE)

Q. Okay. Doctor, looking at the AMA issue, if you will, if I understand what you're telling us, you don't disagree with the percentage that Dr. F. reached. You just disagree with the method that he used to reach it?

A. That's fair.

Q. And at least based on the method that he did use, recognizing that you don't agree with it, he did reach the correct impairment rating?

A. Well, he reached a wrong impairment rating because he used the wrong method, but if you're asking me if he came up with an impairment rating that was accurate based on his wrong method—

Q. Well, let's look at Paragraph No. 1 of your May 17th report, the last sentence—and I'll quote it—Based on this data, Dr. F. obtained the percentage of impairment that was determined was accurate using that formula, meaning the range of motion formula, correct?

A. Well, if one were to use the range of motion formula, the number he came up with would have been correct, using the range of motion formula; however, he used the wrong formula.

Q. Well, there's something to be determined, but using the formula that he did—all I'm trying to establish, rather than getting into an argument here, is that based on the formula he did use, whether it was right or wrong, appreciating your opinion that it was wrong, he at least applied the formula in the correct fashion to come out with the percentage that he did, and I think that's what you're saying in Paragraph No. 1?

A. I'm saying that if I used the Range of Motion model, I would have come up with the same number he did.

Q. Okay.

A. But if I used the Range of Motion model, I would have been wrong.

Q. Now, it's your opinion today that the reason Dr. F. erred is because he should have used the DRE because you were dealing with only one disk level—

A. That's correct.

Q. —correct?

A. Yes.

Q. Now, in your testimony, you've indicated that he had an L5 disk herniation, and I guess he was operated at the same level on two occasions?

A. Correct.

Q. You also indicated at some point in 2000, I believe, that there was an MRI that showed that in addition to having the herniation and fragment at L5–S1, there was an MRI that showed a protrusion or some defect at L4–L5; is that correct?

A. Yes.

Q. And you also mentioned that there was some problem in the thoracic versus lumbar area?

A. Yes.

Q. So there were multiple levels of pathology, at least radiographically?

A. Yes; however, the injury was to only one level, as noted in my reports, as well as by Dr. F.'s.

Q. But the radiographic evidence tells us that there was more than one level involved?

A. But only one level was active.

Q. Only one level operated on?

A. That's true, as well.

Q. And in this particular instance, the IRE that you evaluated from Dr. F. was done on February 9, 2001, so by definition of the IRE, he would only have had available to him whatever records, reports, diagnostic studies, etc., were available at that point in time.

A. That makes sense.

Q. So he would not have seen any of your records, at least, that postdated February 9, 2001?

A. Well, that wouldn't have existed.

Doctor Combined Spinal Problem with Other Problems to Reach Final Percentage

Q. That's my point. And in your report of May 17th, to get to the 50 percent level that you've told us about, you've included percentages of impairment for conditions other than a lumbar disk herniation?

A. Well, they're conditions and symptoms which in my opinion emanate from that disk herniation.

Q. I recognize that, but they are—and I think you made that opinion on direct—to get to the 50 percent that you reached, you took into account all of those other symptoms, other than the L5–S1 disk herniation, and you combined them to reach a total of 50 percent?

A. Yes.

Q. If you take only the L5–S1 disk herniation as opposed to the other things that you talked about here today, the percentage would be less than 50 percent, would it not?

A. Yes.

[Mr. Wyatt]. Okay, that's it.

[Ms. Dempsey]. I have no further questions. Thank you.

[At this time the deposition in the above-captioned matter was concluded.]

Direct Examination of IME Physician by Defense Counsel

[By Mr. Notarianni]

Qualifications as an Impairment Rater

Q. Doctor, are you board certified in any area of medicine?

A. Yes, emergency medicine.

Q. I'd like you to take a look at a document which we've marked as F. Exhibit Number 1. Do you recognize that?

A. That's my curriculum vitae.

Q. And does that accurately address and set forth your background, both education experience and qualifications?

A. Yes, sir.

Q. It's accurate and up to date?

A. It's accurate, not up to date. I've been recertified as of November 2002.

Q. And during the course of your practice, have you been called upon to perform impairment rating evaluations?

A. Yes, sir.

Q. And you've been requested to perform those by whom?

A. They are requested typically by the Department of Labor and Industry in Harrisburg.

Q. And what does that involve, Doctor?

A. Basically, you're asked to perform what they call an impairment rating evaluation to determine the percentage of impairment for a particular injury, which in these cases are [sic] due to work-related injury. It's different than the typical medical evaluations that are done for treatment or, say, for an independent medical evaluation.

Q. Can you estimate how many times you've done that in the past, Doctor?

A. The impairment rating evaluations?

Q. Yes.

A. As far as for the Department of Labor and Industry, I would assume somewhere in the vicinity of 10 or 15. There's not—there have not been very many in the last couple years. Recently they seem to be requesting more.

[Mr. Notarianni]. I move for the admission into evidence of Dr. F.'s curriculum vitae.

[Whereupon, Exhibit F-1 was offered into evidence.]

[Ms. Dempsey]. I have a few questions.

[By Ms. Dempsey].

Training in Rating Impairment

Q. Doctor, what type of training have you received, if any, regarding the performance of IREs?

A. The training primarily are [sic] courses we attend with the American Academy of Disability Evaluating Physicians as well as a course given by the American Board of Independent Medical Examiners. The requirements basically were that an individual be board certified, have attended those classes, taken an exam.

Q. Are you board certified in IMEs?

A. Yes.

Q. And emergency medicine you said, is that correct?

A. Yes.

Q. When you first saw _____, and that was on February 9, 2001—how many IREs had you performed at that point?

A. I honestly don't know. I never quantified it.

Q. Would that have been one of the first ones for workers' comp purposes in Pennsylvania under Act 57?

A. I don't know.

[**Ms. Dempsey**]. That's all I have.

[**Mr. Notarianni**]. Subject to that cross-examination, I would offer Dr. F. as an expert in this matter.

Q. Doctor, did there come an occasion when you performed an impairment rating evaluation regarding the claimant in this case?

A. Yes, sir.

Q. And, again, do you know at whose request that was performed?

A. I don't recall the woman's name. Our office would have that, but that, again, was at the request of the Department of Labor and Industry in Harrisburg.

Q. And what was the date of that impairment rating evaluation?

A. February 9, 2001.

Q. At that time, you examined _____?

A. Yes, sir.

Q. And he appeared at your office?

A. Yes.

Impairment Rating

Q. And at that examination, did he provide you with a history as it related to his injury?

A. Yes, sir.

Q. What did he indicate to you, Doctor?

A. He stated on January 6, 1999, he was seated on a small stool placing a jack under a car using one hand. He stated he was trying to secure it in place when he felt, quote unquote, something happen. This was to his lower back. From then on, he noted that he experienced progressive lower back pain which eventually began radiating down the right leg. Thus he sought medical treatment.

Q. In conjunction with this evaluation, Doctor, did you obtain a history as it related to _____'s treatment?

A. Yes, sir.

Q. And what did that involve?

A. Well, the history primarily is to be taken from the review of medical records that are submitted for review as well as from the individual, which in this case was _____. Once the evaluating physician determines the course of events, the treatment rendered, and diagnoses, the physical examination is performed, and then the impairment ratings are quantified according to the guides.

Q. In conjunction with your impairment rating evaluation, did you have the opportunity to author a written report?

A. Yes, sir.

Q. I'd like to show you what's been marked as F. Exhibit Number 2. Do you recognize that, sir?

A. Yes, sir, that's my report dated February 9, 2001.

Q. And in that report, Doctor, do you detail the records which you reviewed in conjunction with your impairment rating evaluation?

A. Yes, sir.

Q. And is what is stated in that report accurate as far—as best as you can tell, Doctor?

A. Yes, sir.

Q. And it accurately reflects the medical records which you reviewed?

A. Yes, sir.

Q. Did _____ provide to you a history of his present complaints?

A. Yes.

Q. And what did he indicate to you, Doctor?

A. He primarily noted right-sided lower back pain which would radiate into the right leg. He had some numbness, I believe, at the right buttock, the leg, as well as the fourth and fifth toes. He specifically denied any dysuria or urinating or increased frequency. At times, he stated his bladder would, quote unquote, leak when getting out of a chair.

  He also stated on occasion he may have some difficulty starting his urinary stream and maintaining it, particularly if he was not concentrating. He was able to sustain an erection. More importantly, when he is awoken and when he awakes in the morning, he does have an erection which basically showed that he was capable.

  Beyond that, he noted no increase in pain, particularly of the legs, when coughing or sneezing, which is an important concept when looking at radicular type pain.

Q. Did Mr.—I'm sorry.

A. Then he also noted what his medications were.

Q. And that's what I was going to ask you, Doctor. What medications did _____ indicate that he was currently taking?

A. He was taking Dilaudid for pain; Serzone, which may have been prescribed for depression; Benadryl for sleep; Xanax, which may have been—Xanax and diazepam, which both may have been utilized for anxiety; Excedrin, which is aspirin, which I'm unsure why he was taking that at this time; Flomax, which was prescribed typically for what we call a urinary bladder outlet obstruction from prostrate problems; and I believe that was all of his medications.

Q. Did he provide you with a past medical history?

A. Yes, sir.

Q. Anything significant there, Doctor?

A. He had a history of gall bladder stones. More importantly, there was notation in the past records, I believe, of neuropathy of the upper and lower extremities. I was uncertain as far as his diagnosis so—what the particulars were. He stated he was treated by a physician in the past for problems with the arms and legs.

Q. Did he indicate past surgical history?

A. Yes, sir.

Q. And what did he indicate with regard to that?

A. He had several surgeries unrelated to the purpose of the IRE. Those surgeries, which were pertinent to the IRE, were hemilaminectomy and decompression of the S1 nerve root. This was at the L5–S1 level as well as a second surgery which involved an L5–S1 diskectomy, foraminotomy with excision of scar tissue.

Q. You had the opportunity to perform a physical examination of the claimant?

A. Yes, sir.

Q. Aside from the examination regarding his back, Doctor, anything significant which you would like to indicate with respect to that physical examination?

A. Not particularly.

Q. You had the opportunity as part of the physical exam to examine _____'s back?

A. Yes, sir.

Q. What did that indicate, Doctor?

A. Well, I noted there was a well-healed lumbar surgical scar. He felt there was some tenderness to palpation primarily over the muscles in the right paralumbar region as well as over the sacroiliac joint and sciatic notch. In other words, he noted tenderness in a diffuse area to the right upper lower lumbar spine. I found no evidence of spasm nor what we call trigger points. He was able to bend forward or flex reaching his digit as far as his knees before noting some pain. He found extension less painful. Side bending was pain free.

The supine straight leg raising test caused posterior leg pain on the right; however, on the left, he noted no pain to correlate this particular maneuver with a seated knee extension. I noted that it was without what we call a flip sign, which would state that he had a specific tension sign or radicular component to his leg pain. In other words, the supine straight leg raising test tries to stretch the lower nerve roots. The correct response would be production of leg pain.

He then performed a seated knee extension, which tries to correlate, in other words, reproduce, the same complaint. He did state the right leg was painful; however, he did not produce a flip sign, which would give it a positive test. And a flip sign primarily refers to the individual leaning back to remove pressure off the pulling of that nerve root. Therefore, it was what we call an equivocal response as to whether the two correlated.

I examined his hips, his sacroiliac joints, piriformis muscles, all of which were normal. It did not appear to cause back pain.

The neurologic portion of the exam, I tested all the muscles, and initially he stated he had some difficulty with walking on his toes on the right, noting some discomfort or weakness. However, when I had him lying supine, I found no weakness in these particular muscles.

Those were the main areas that I was concerned with as far as motor strength. Ultimately, I did not feel he showed evidence of true weakness, but, again, I noted that he did mention he had weakness with that one particular maneuver.

As far as sensation, when I utilized a pinwheel, he stated he had decreased sensation over the entire right lower leg as well as the entire right foot. This also included the buttock and sacral region. Unfortunately, I was unable to determine a specific dermatomal pattern, which is very important for the guide's purpose.

Q. How so, Doctor?

A. When you're rating an individual, you're essentially attempting to isolate a specific region to be certain that what you are rating is as objective as possible. Therefore, the guides ask that you make an attempt to find specific dermatomes to determine whether an individual falls within certain categories, such as radiculopathy. The reflexes I found to be somewhat symmetrical. I did find the left ankle was depressed and the right ankle was absent. The remainder of the neurologic exam was relatively normal.

Q. If I can stop you there just for a second. Earlier when you were describing your examination of the back, you described one finding as equivocal. Is that correct?

A. Yes.

Q. What was that?

A. The straight leg raising test.

Q. Is that significant with respect to applying that finding to the guide?

A. As you'll see later, one of the criteria you're trying to assess is whether an individual has radiculopathy, and when looking at radiculopathy, there are certain objective signs that we utilize in determining whether true radiculopathy is present. Although I feel that he has evidence of radiculopathy, it was very difficult stating that all the objective criteria were actually met.

In other words, the straight leg raising would have to be empirically positive, or it would have to be definitely positive, In other words, if I raised the leg up, and he had shooting pain all the way down the leg, and then I performed the seated knee extension and got the same response, or if I have a cross straight raising leg maneuver whereby I raise the opposite leg and pain on the right side again, then these would fit into the classification for tension signs causing radiculopathy. Because I didn't feel as though they are correlated, I felt it was a soft sign for radiculopathy. Other objective signs would be if there was atrophy or muscle wasting.

Q. Did you find that here?

A. No, I didn't. But again, muscle weakness would be another clinical sign. Although he noted muscle weakness with the toe walking, when I had him lie supine, I couldn't assess true weakness with the same muscle tested. Although, you know, he had a lot of areas that were kind of equivocal or gray, one still has to make a determination whether one actually feels radiculopathy is present; and therefore, these are the reasons why I kind of refer to one versus the other. Oftentimes you're dealing with more than one maneuver to attempt to objectify whether the specifics are there to classify into one category versus another.

We performed his actual range of motion measurements and then subsequently did flexion/extension views of the lumbar spine with x-rays.

Q. And what did that indicate, Doctor?

A. I found no evidence of instability or malalignment, and that's essentially why we were performing the flexion/extension views. Typically, if he had any evidence of malalignment or instability on these types of x-rays, then that might qualify for a specific category in the rating.

Q. Were diagnostic studies performed?

A. Just the flexion/extension views of the lumbar spine.

Q. That was the extent of it?

A. Yes, sir.

Opinion as to Impairment Percentage

Q. Now, based upon the information that you gathered and the methods that you've explained here, Doctor, did you come to a conclusion with respect to a

reasonable degree of medical certainty as to the whole-person impairment rating with respect to _____?

A.   Yes, sir.
Q.   And what conclusions did you come to?
A.   The final rating was 28 percent.

How Doctor Arrived at 28 Percent Impairment Rating

Q.   And how did you calculate—or how did you arrive at that figure, Doctor?
A.   When attempting to determine a lumbar spine injury, there are certain methods
and categories utilized according to the *AMA Guides to Evaluation of
Permanent Impairment.* This is the fifth edition. Typically, we review the history
provided by the patient, review the medical records, particularly all the pertinent data, and then perform the physical examination. And once we've compiled all of that information, we then determine the method as well as the
categories that we will eventually provide the rating for. In this particular situation, I went to the guides using Chapter 15, which is entitled "The Spine."
Q.   Let me just stop you there, Doctor, just so the record is clear. You are reading
from a book which is in front of you, and again, the title of that book is what?
A.   It's called *Guides to the Evaluation of Permanent Impairment,* fifth edition.
Q.   And I believe now you are referring to a specific section of the guide?
A.   Yes, Chapter 15.

   [Mr. Notarianni]. I believe I've provided counsel with a copy of the specific
   section to which Dr. F. is referring to right now.

[By Mr. Notarianni].

Q.   And it's section—is it Chapter 15?
A.   Chapter 15.
Q.   And what is that entitled, Doctor?
A.   Chapter 15 is entitled "The Spine."
Q.   All right. And is this a subsection of the chapter, I presume?
A.   There are subsections which I then went to once I began to utilize this chapter,
realizing that we were dealing with the lumbar region. I then had to determine
the appropriate method for assessment. There are specifically two methods that
one can utilize when rating the lumbar pain. One is called DRE, which stands for
diagnosis related estimate method, and the second or alternative method is the
range of motion method or oftentimes referred to as the ROM method.
Q.   Now, which method did you employ in this matter, Doctor?
A.   Well, I actually utilized both methods, both the DRE and the range of motion,
and then awarded it the highest percentage.
Q.   If you can, explain exactly the calculations that you made whatever process you
used?
A.   The eventual method I utilized was the range of motion method, and I guess I'll
need to explain why I used the range of motion method, because typically we
would require that a physician utilize the DRE method. Therefore, any time a
physician decides to utilize an alternative method from the one that's most

utilized, then it's important that we support it. So I'll first need to explain to you why I used the range of motion method because this is the first premise upon my calculations—

Q. Let's even—

A. —or would you prefer that I just give you the rating?

Q. Let's even go back further. Did you employ at some point the diagnosis related estimate?

A. Yes, sir.

Q. Okay. And did you do that first?

A. Yes.

Q. Okay. Explain what that involved, Doctor.

A. Well, with the diagnosis related estimate, there are five separate categories, and the physician must first determine which category, if any, the patient falls in. When reviewing the five categories, I had used Table 15.3, which is on page 384, of the guides. The appropriate category or at least the category which I felt _____ most closely resembled was DRE lumbar category 3.

Using this category, an impairment is allowed upwards of 10 to 13 percent. And given the fact that he had an L5–S1 disk herniation with a subsequent recurrent disk herniation at the same level, he was given the upper percentage of impairment, which was 13 percent.

Q. How did you place _____ in category 3?

A. Well, if one looks at the criteria, there are several different criteria. Essentially, I utilized the criteria that referred to his presurgery diagnoses regarding radiculopathy as well as, I believe, his history of a herniated disk that was associated with radiculopathy.

There was an additional category which you can utilize, an individual who has had surgery for radiculopathy but was asymptomatic. He was not asymptomatic, but nevertheless, this was the category which most closely paralleled his particular case.

Category 2, which is the category before 3, deals with individuals who have no radiculopathy, are just primarily have—I'm sorry, who have no radiculopathy after surgery or have had radiculopathy following conservative treatment.

Category 4, which is the category beyond category 3, primarily deals with individuals who have lost their segment integrity due to fusion, or a successful or unsuccessful surgical attempt at fusion. He obviously did not fall into that category; so, therefore, category 3 was the one that most closely paralleled his particular diagnoses and findings.

Q. And by placing _____ into category 3, you arrived at a whole-person impairment rating of what, Doctor?

A. Thirteen percent.

Q. Upon obtaining this result, what did you next do?

A. I then placed him into the range of motion—I'm sorry. Then I placed him into a range of motion method which derived a different percentage of impairment.

Q. Exactly what did you do?

A. Well, to be able to utilize a range of motion method, one has to determine whether that particular individual can fall into that method, and there are certain criteria that would allow it.

Therefore, utilizing the text, I then returned to certain pages. And I made certain that he actually fell within those categories to be able to utilize a range of motion method.

Q. And applying the facts of this particular case to those categories, what did you find, Doctor?

A. He, indeed, qualified for the range of motion method, and because of that qualification, I then went ahead and performed his impairment rating utilizing the range of motion method.

Q. I'll guess we'll ask the question now. How did you determine that the range of motion method fit in this particular case?

A. Once again, utilizing the guide, if we look at Chapter 15, specifically under 15.2, which is entitled "Determining the Appropriate Method for Assessment," there are several situations—approximately five—which are numbered under that section. On page 380 of the guide, number 4, which is essentially in the first column on the left, it states where there is recurrent radiculopathy caused by new and in parentheses recurrent disk herniation or recurrent injury in the same spinal region.

In other words, _____ originally had an L5–S1 disk herniation with radiculopathy and then had a recurrent radiculopathy again at the same level, i.e., the L5–S1, and in the same spinal region, that being the lumbar region. So he had a recurrent radiculopathy caused by a recurrent disk herniation in the same spinal region. That allows one to go ahead and use the range of motion method.

Now, if one goes over to Figure 15-4, again on page 380, there is a diagram which outlines the spinal impairment evaluation process. And again, if we follow that diagram, we can see that of the two middle boxes, the bottom one states permanent impairment due to injury or illness. And again, I felt he fell into that box category and then went to the left, which shows injury. And if it says yes, you go down to the next box, which says single level.

Now, he was a single level. If you recall, he had an L5–S1 disk herniation. He had a recurrent injury, but again was at the same level. So we were dealing with a single level. So now the next box, if you follow from the single-level box, it says first injury, but again . . . was at the same level. So we were dealing with a single level. So now the next box, if you follow from the single-level box, it says first injury or repeat injury different region. If it was a different region, you would continue on down to use the DRE method. However, we were not dealing with different regions. We were dealing with the same region. True, we have a second injury or repeat injury, but we're dealing with the same region. Therefore, if you follow the arrow that says no, it now refers you back to the range of motion method.

Q. And that's how you made your determination—

A. Correct.

Q. —that the range of motion method applies in this case?

A. Yes. Now, if we look directly under that diagram, under 15.2, number 4, subsection D, [it] essentially states, use the ROM, which is the range of motion method, if in D there is recurrent disk herniation, which _____ had recurrent disk herniation at L5–S1, at the same or different level in the same spinal region, and that's exactly what he had.

He had a recurrent disk herniation at the same level, which was L5–S1, in the same spinal region, which was the lumbar region. And then it goes on to state in this case, combine the ratings using the range of motion method. So this is how I was capable of using the range of motion method.

Now, I refer you back on the same page again in the left-hand column, I believe the third paragraph. It states, in the small number of incidents in which the ROM and DRE methods can both be used, evaluate the individual with both methods and award the higher rating. So in an attempt to give _____ the highest rating I possibly can, I elected to use the range of motion method, which was a perfectly valid method, and so award him 28 percent.

Q. So you did employ the range of motion method, correct, Doctor?

A. Yes, sir.

Q. And you've indicated that you arrived at the impairment rating of 28 percent?

A. Correct.

Q. And if you could explain exactly how you arrived at that 28 percent figure?

A. Well, when utilizing the range of motion method, again, we have to go back to the guides and we remain within the same chapter, which is 15, entitled "[The] Spine." Range of motion starts in section 15.8 on page 398, and this sets up the criteria for using the range of motion method, and that's how it's done.

Again, to be certain that we were utilizing the range of motion method, I refer you to page 398, section 15.8, entitled "Range of Motion Method," the third paragraph in the right-hand column, number 4; it states, the ROM method should be used only—and, again, number 4—if there is recurrent radiculopathy caused by a new or recurrent disk herniation or recurrent injury in the same spinal region. So, therefore, we know we're in the right category.

Now, to rate range of motion, there are certain categories for which we derive our percentage of impairment. We perform range of motion measurements in flexion, extension, lateral flexion, or side bending, as well as, again, the extension. We take the actual measurement, and then we go to page 407, Table 15.8, and based upon those measurements, we are given certain percentages for each of those motions.

Once those percentages are tallied, they are added, and we get a resulting impairment for the range of motion measurement only, in other words, for the degrees of motion. Then we take the actual diagnosis which is found on page 404, Table 15.7, and here we have four categories according to diagnosis utilizing the ROM method.

I had determined _____ fell into category 2, subsection E, where it is noted as surgically treated disk lesion, which he had, with residual medically documented pain and rigidity. If you recall, he had surgery on the L5–S1 disk, and he continued to complain of pain within the same region. So, therefore, I felt he qualified for that subsection E, a certain amount of percentage given for that particular category.

However, I went one step [further], and subsection G refers to multiple operations with or without residual signs or symptoms. And number 1 under that subsection is second operation. If you recall, he had two operations. So, therefore, I was able to award him an additional 2 percent. Thus, I had determined his percentage based upon diagnosis.

So now we had two percentages: one for range of motion measurement, and a second for the diagnosis. Then the method requires a third category to be utilized. This was a calculation of impairment due to motor and sensory loss. I refer you now to page 424, which is Table 15.15. In this particular section, we rated the sensory deficit as well as motor impairment or motor deficit for the S1 nerve roots. Those were the nerve roots that were affected by the L5–S1 disk. Percentages were given for both the sensory loss as well as the motor deficit.

Once both of those were determined, they were combined, and that gave us a third percentage of impairment. Now, we took all three final percentages of impairment, i.e., the percentage for the range, the percentage for the diagnosis, and the percentage for the motor and sensory nerve loss. We utilize what they call the combined values chart on page 604 and determined the whole-person impairment. The whole-person impairment was 28 percent. And this was the method I utilized.

Q.   You arrived at a 10 percent range of motion figure, is that correct, Doctor?

A.   Yes.

Q.   And specifically, what were the figures that you put in to get to that percentage?

A.   Well, for the altered range of motion, it was 10 percent impairment; for the diagnosis, it was 12 percent; and for the sensory and motor loss, it was 9 percent. These three numbers were then utilized to arrive at the final percentage of impairment, which was 28 percent.

Q.   I was asking how you arrived at the 10 percent range of motion figure in the first place. Exactly what figures were put in to get that result?

A.   Well, I had to utilize Table 15.8 on page 407. They request what the actual measurements of the individual were in flexion, extension, and side bending. Those we had determined during the physical examination.

Q.   That was my question. So you plugged those figures in that you determined in the physical exam?

A.   Correct, and rather [than] just having him bend forward one time, we actually had him do it three times and then take the highest degree that he bends forward and extends and side bends. So it's not just taking one measurement, but we take the total of three and award the highest. Therefore, the range of motion is determined by measuring the actual range of motion in each of the planes so noted and then apply[ing] them to the table where specific numbers are given for the ranges that were measured.

Q.   So again, Doctor, in employing the range of motion method, you arrived at a whole-person impairment rating of what?

A.   Twenty-eight percent.

Q.   And in employing the DRE method, you arrived at a whole-person impairment rating of what?

A.   Thirteen percent.

Q.   And as far as what you submitted to the Department of Labor or whomever you were doing this rating for, what did you indicate the impairment rating as?

A.   Twenty-eight percent.

Critical of Treating Physician's Rating

Q. Doctor, subsequent to your completing the evaluation, are you aware of another evaluation that was done with respect to _____?

A. Yes, sir.

Q. Do you know who that was performed by?

A. Dr. Scott E.

Q. Did you have a chance to review that evaluation authored by Dr. E.?

A. Yes, sir.

Q. Subsequent to that review, did you have the opportunity to, yourself, author a report regarding your review of Dr. E.'s report?

A. Yes, sir.

Q. And I show you a document which we've previously marked as F. Exhibit Number 3. And if you could identify that, please, for the record?

A. This was the subsequent report.

Q. And that was authored by you on what date, Doctor?

A. April 16, 2002.

Q. Now, let me back up. You had a chance to review Dr. E.'s evaluation?

A. Yes, sir.

Q. And first of all, with respect to your April 16, 2002, report, Doctor, is there anything at this point that you'd like to clarify other than what's stated therein?

A. No. I primarily tried to give reasons behind what—or how I determined my method and what I felt appropriately applied and what did not apply. I would make one note, however. On the day I authored this, I was trying to catch a plane and was actually doing several IREs at one time, and I discussed whether or not radiculopathy was a consideration.

   I would like to note that I did feel _____ had symptoms and signs of radiculopathy and thus the reason that I did use radiculopathy when ultimately determining his percentages. There were some mistakes made in that determination, but ultimately the percentages derived and how they were derived and the reasons for which they were derived were very accurate.

Q. Now, if you could specify exactly what Dr. E. indicated with regard to your evaluation.

A. Essentially, I believe after reading Dr. E.'s letter, he basically was of the opinion that the use of the range of motion method was incorrect and that the DRE or diagnosis related estimate method was that which should have been utilized. The basis for his assumption was that we were dealing with recurrent radiculopathy due to recurrent disk herniation in the same spinal region. And if one were to refer to the figure I had noted on 15.4, page 380, it was his assumption that following that figure, that one would end up using the DRE model. Unfortunately, as I had shown earlier, he was incorrect in making that assumption.

Q. And how was he incorrect in your opinion, Doctor?

A. Well, again, based upon—his opinion is that had we—and if I may reread his quote so I don't misquote him, he stated that according to the figure, should the injury be to a single level, then the DRE model should be utilized. If you look at 15.4 in the box where single level is noted, if it's single level and it says no, then you go to the range of motion model. If it's single level and it's yes, then you go on to the DRE method, okay.

Now, if you go below that and it says first injury or repeat injury at different regions, then you go ahead to DRE method. If you have a repeat injury, which is what we were dealing with, and if it were at the same level, then no, we would go—we'd follow the arrow that says no to the range of motion model.

I think what was happening is that he was becoming confused. And actually, in reality, we did have a single level, but we had a repeat injury. Since it was not at a different region, then we could not use the DRE method. In other words, if we have a repeat injury and it incorporated a different region such as cervical or thoracic, then we would continue on and use the DRE method.

However, since we do not deal with different regions on the repeat injury, then we have to go to the range of motion method; and therefore, the basis of his assumption that the range of motion model was incorrect would be false. And again, I think not only is it according to the figure, but to the direct statements which I had noted on page 380.

Q. As you've already testified to?

A. Correct. Now, if one wanted to use the DRE lumbar category, [one] would utilize category 3, which is the same category that I cited.

Q. And you arrived at what type of impairment rating?

A. Thirteen percent, and that is maximum for category three.

Q. In addition in this evaluation performed by Dr. E., did he provide his own rating evaluation?

A. Yes.

Q. And what figure did he arrive at, Doctor?

A. Well, curiously, he arrived at exactly 50 percent. Unfortunately, the basis upon which he derived that 50 percent would not be valid.

Q. Why do you say that, Doctor?

A. Because he also gave an additional percentage for what was termed cortico-spinal tract damage. Corticospinal tract damage was not—was never diagnosed, whether it was based upon review of the records, and more importantly after—not only having reviewed the records but examining _____, there was no corticospinal tract damage.

Q. And how are you able to say that, Doctor?

A. Well, specifically, to have corticospinal tract damage, one has to have damage to the corticospinal tract, which is essentially the spinal cord. The spinal cord ana-tomically ends at the L1–L2 level of the lumbar spine. The disk herniation that was noted was at the L5–S1 level and, therefore, is virtually impossible from an ana-tomic standpoint to cause corticospinal tract damage unless the lesion were anywhere from the cervical or thoracic or even the upper lumbar L1–L2, you cannot have corticospinal tract damage. He then went on to state the additional percen-tages were based upon a neurogenic bladder, which there was no objective evidence from diagnostic studies to substantiate—to diagnosis and unfortunately—

Q. Why is that important, Doctor?

A. Well, the guides require that only objective evidence be utilized when deter-mining percentage of impairment. If the objective evidence were present, then it makes it very easy to assign it; but since we do not have objective evidence, it's very difficult to assign that, particularly in this case, where he's referring to a neurogenic bladder. I believe he had performed an EMG and nerve conduction study in 1999 and specifically stated, according to that study, there was no evidence of a neurogenic bladder.

Q. Is that the kind of study or is that the study that would be utilized for making such a diagnosis?

A. One of them, yes, and then there are additional criteria that I have looked at when trying to determine the symptoms noted by _____ with respect to his bladder and urinary output. And truthfully, the weight of evidence falls upon what we call outlet obstruction or problem with the outflow of urine from the bladder primarily due to prostate problems and not the spinal cord. And these were determined after reviewing Dr. Stefanelli's, a urologist, records.

Q. So as far as a causal relationship between these two, Doctor, what is your opinion?

[Ms. Dempsey]. Objection.

[The Witness]. There is no—

[Mr. Notarianni]. Objection noted.

A. **[The Witness].** There is no urologic basis as far as his work injury pertaining to an L5–S1 disk herniation and that of an assumed diagnosis of neurogenic bladder. If you recall the gentleman was on Flomax prescribed by Dr. Stefanelli. This is a medication for bladder outlet obstruction typically secondary to benign prostatic hypertrophy or prostate problem. Urinary problems from a neurogenic bladder with those characteristics would not be treated with Flomax.

Additionally, I believe Dr. E. had also given him an impairment percentage based upon sexual impairment. Again, we do not have any objective evidence of sexual impairment that would fill criteria for the guides. I believe Dr. Stefanelli had noted _____ had painful erections due to what he termed was prostatic calcifications after having performed a transrectal ultrasound.

Again, prostatic calcifications would not be due to the L5–S1 disk herniation. Therefore, additional percentages or points were given to _____, which would be invalid. I think at best one could perform the DRE method utilized category, give a maximum 13 percent; or utilize the range of motion method and get a—find a maximum of 28 percent, and then give him or award him the higher of the two. But I don't believe that anatomically or pathophysiolog[icall]y we were dealing with corticospinal tract damage, which would allow for additional points.

[By Mr. Notarianni].

Opines That Treating Physician's Rating Is Invalid

Q. So, in conclusion, then, Doctor, do you have an opinion to a reasonable degree of medical certainty as to the impairment rating evaluation reached by Dr. E. in this matter?

A. It's invalid.

Q. Doctor, I'd also like to show you what we have had marked prior to the start of the deposition as F. Exhibit Number 4. Do you recognize that?

A.   Yes, sir.

Q.   Can you identify that, please, for the record?

A.   These are copies of page 379 and page 380 from the *Guides to Evaluation of Permanent Impairment,* fifth edition, and it primarily refers to the situations in which one can utilize the range of motion method in place of the DRE or diagnosis related estimate. I felt it was imperative that it be understood as to how and why I use the range of motion method as opposed to the DRE method.

Q.   And you referred specifically to the section and flow chart and other items during the course of your direct examination here today; is that correct?

A.   Yes.

Q.   I also note there's some notations—markings, I should say—

A.   Yes, sir.

Q.   —on the copies of this document, Doctor. Do you know how they got there?

A.   They were from my textbook, and oftentimes, I underline or make notations in areas that I feel are important. Some pertain to this case; some do not. The majority do, I believe.

[**Mr. Notarianni**]. With that, I'd move for the introduction into the evidence—I believe I already moved the DV into evidence—Exhibits F.-2, F.-3, F.-4.

[**Ms. Dempsey**]. I have no objection.

[Whereupon, Exhibits F.-2 through F.-4 were offered into evidence.]

[**Mr. Notarianni**]. And I offer Dr. F. for cross-examination.

Cross-Examination of IME Doctor by Claimant's Counsel

[By Ms. Dempsey].

Presence of Radiculopathy

Q.   Doctor, do you or do you not feel there's radiculopathy present in this case?

A.   That's a good question. Most definitely the gentleman had radiculopathy prior to surgery—first surgery and, again, the second surgery. After the second surgery, he was still noted to have leg pain; therefore, the question is whether or not he had radiculopathy or not. For the purpose of the guides when establishing radiculopathy, we utilize certain objective signs, as I stated earlier. Some of which seem to fit that diagnosis of radiculopathy; others don't. And thus the reason for using more than one type of maneuver on physical exam was to try to remove gray zones. Bottom line is I felt he had symptoms that were consistent with radicular pain or radiculopathy. That's why I had noted that when I discussed my subsequent report.

Q.   And you had an opportunity to review the records of Dr. Presper, who was the first operating neurosurgeon. Is it fair to say that he agreed with that as well, that there was lower extremity radicular pain which was a residual from the herniated disk?

A.   Well, radicular pain is different from radiculopathy. I mean, radicular pain describes leg pain. That's all. It doesn't necessarily state it's radiculopathy.

Q.   Did he or did he not feel there was radiculopathy present?

A. You would have to refer me to—what you're stating here, what you're referring to.

Q. Do you have his records in front of you, Doctor, or not?

A. Is there a certain date? You're referring to postoperative period, I assume.

Q. Correct.

A. What is the date?

Q. They seem to have some reference to it. You could review them, and tell me if you agree or disagree. Did you have an opportunity to review them prior to writing your report?

A. I have records of Dr. Presper's prior to my report. But I'm not sure what you're asking me. You're asking me at a time, I assume, after the surgery?

Q. Correct.

A. All I noted is that, based upon the records that I have, Dr. Presper noted improvement of numbness and pain which had been below the right knee, which refers to radicular-type pain. He states above the knee pain persisted.

Q. Okay. You can review the records I'm providing you. It is a report which was following the surgery.

[Pause]

A. He refers to radicular pain as opposed to a specific radiculopathy. He performed surgery for the radiculopathy which apparently had improved. So he refers to again, as I stated, radicular pain, which is a descriptive term for pain in the leg.
    As far as true radiculopathy, I can't state he necessarily makes a diagnosis of true radiculopathy. He mentions about performing an EMG/nerve conduction test by Dr. E., but I can't say otherwise anything more beyond that.

Q. Now, when the claimant presented to you, he was utilizing a cane to ambulate; is that correct?

A. Yes.

Unaware That Examinee Had Been Prescribed a Wheelchair

Q. And did your review of Dr. E.'s records show you that he had also been prescribed a scooter and/or a wheelchair for further distance mobility?

A. I'm not sure if I had seen that or not.

Q. Doctor, your initial exam was performed on February 9; is that correct?

A. Yes.

Forgot Things in Initial Exam of Claimant

Q. Was there a period in time after that you had contacted my office and had indicated that _____ needed to come back down because certain things were forgotten in that initial exam?

A. The range of motion—I believe his range of motion measurements.

Q. Okay. What happened there?

A. I have to look back through my records. Let's see if I recall what happened at that time. Whether he felt he was too uncomfortable or if he had to be somewhere and then would come back, I honestly don't recall at this point. I do recall, though, that we did ask him to come back, and he said he would. Unless you recall.

Q.   Was it that you had initially done it under the DRE method and had come up with the 13 percent and needed to do the range of motion method to get better readings?

A.   You know, it may or may not have been. I honestly don't recall. Either way, it's perfectly reasonable.

Did Not Rate for Depression

Q.   Doctor, did you pay any attention or give any credence to the fact that _____ suffered from depression and was treating with a psychiatrist and was medicated for the depression?

A.   As far as?

Q.   The ratings under the *AMA Guides*?

A.   No. I rated primarily what the diagnosis had been.

Q.   Do the *AMA Guides* at all address depression?

A.   There's a section for depression.

Q.   Does it actually put any type of a rating on, or is it an arbitrary rating?

A.   There are ratings in there, but that would have to be done by a psychiatrist.

Q.   So your report did not address that issue at all?

A.   No, depression was not considered a diagnosis.

Was Pain Considered?

Q.   And, at all, did you consider the chronic pain or any type of pain that he would have been suffering relevant to his conditions?

A.   Yes, pain was factored into it.

Q.   Is there a provision under the *AMA Guides* where you're allowed to give up to 3 percent additional for certain pain that's associated with certain conditions?

A.   Yes, and if you look at the DRE method, category 3, it spans from 10 to 13 percent; given the upper percentage, which is 13 percent, would have allowed that pain.

Q.   Okay. Did you do that?

A.   I gave him 13 percent.

Q.   Okay. Now, Doctor, with regard—it seems to me your basic problem with Dr. E. is that he added in bladder problems, he added in sexual dysfunction, and he added in radiculopathy; would that be correct?

A.   No.

Disagrees with Bladder Dysfunction Finding

Q.   Okay. Do you have a problem with him saying that there is bladder dysfunction when he's doing his ratings?

A.   Yes.

Q.   Okay. Now, did your review of the records indicate that claimant suffered from a neurogenic bladder?

A.   No.

Q.   And for the judge, what is a neurogenic bladder?

A.   It's a bladder condition typically caused by excessive compression of the spinal cord, more particularly the sacral nerve roots and not necessarily the spinal cord. It can occur from cauda equina syndrome or specifically a neurogenic bladder would actually have to occur from the compression [of] the sacral nerve roots and not the lumbar area.

Q.   What is cauda equina syndrome?

A.   Cauda equina is a severe compression of the spinal cord.

Q.   Did you find that in this case at all?

A.   No. In fact, I believe Dr. E. also had noted it was not present.

Q.   Was _____ prescribed Viagra at all for sexual dysfunction?

A.   I don't recall.

Q.   Is it fair to say that in your review of the records, he did—was able to obtain an erection, but did have difficulty continuing with one?

A.   I believe he stated that he was capable of obtaining an erection but may have had difficulty. I'd have to go back through the physical—through his complaints. You see, he can have these problems, but it doesn't necessarily mean it's due to a neurogenic cause. And I think that's where you're becoming confused. Because an individual has other complaints, you're automatically attributing it to a neurogenic cause.

Unless you have objective evidence or basis for it, you cannot rate it according to [the] guides, and the guides are typically based upon objective findings only. I would have been more than glad to give him additional percentages, but since it's not noted, you cannot give it. And I think you're confusing how you do your ratings just for the purpose of obtaining 50 percent.

Causation

Q.   Did he have any of these problems prior to his work injury, and by that I mean—

A.   I don't know.

Q.   Okay. Were you asked to review that?

A.   He did not note it.

Q.   Is that important for you in determining causation at all?

A.   I was not performing my evaluation for the purpose of causation. This was not an independent medical evaluation, and, again, I think that's where you've confused what I was doing with what other physicians may do regarding IMEs. IMEs are typically performed to determine how an individual is performing at the time of the evaluation. It may address causation, i.e., whether something is related to a specific event, i.e., motor vehicle accident or work injury, but the purpose of my exam had nothing do with causation. It had nothing do with whether he can or cannot work. It was solely to determine what his percentage of impairment was.

Q.   Doctor, without determining causation, how do you determine which diagnoses get rated and which diagnoses don't?

A.   Based upon the objective evidence in the records.

Q.   The medical records?

A.   Correct.

Q. Okay. And who provides you with those?
A. The state.
Q. Okay. Now, the 28 percent impairment that you gave the claimant, that's forever; that's permanent. Is that correct?
A. Yes.
Q. He'll never fully recover from that?
A. Well, again, it depends on when you use the term *recovered*. If you want to state an individual is half dead, but to say recovered, you make it sound as if you're laying a drape over the individual. But again, it is a permanent injury, and that's a permanent rating.

No Gait Impairment Rating Given

Q. Now, Dr. E. had discussed an impairment due to station in gait?
A. Yes.
Q. And what is that in reference to? Did you pay any attention to that in your range of motion method?
A. No. Again, he determined station gait based upon corticospinal tract damage. There is no verification of corticospinal tract damage, and that's what I've been trying to explain to you. If you have corticospinal tract damage, then you could add additional percentages for sexual impairment, bladder dysfunction, station and gait, but unfortunately, we do not have corticospinal tract damage. I can give you additional percentage points for a number of diagnoses and symptoms and so on and so forth. But again, unless it is verified by objective evidence, I am not allowed to do that according to the *AMA Guides*.

Length of Exam

Q. Doctor, how long did your exam take?
A. Minimum of one hour.
Q. And on one occasion?
A. Yes, other than for him returning for the range of motion.

Did Not Personally Perform Range of Motion Testing

Q. Did you actually perform the range of motion?
A. No, I had one of our physical therapists who is certified.
Q. And is that done using any type of meter, or is that done—
A. Yes.
Q. . . . visually?
A. No. That's done with a machine.

Questioning on AMA Guides

Q. Now, in general, a few questions on the *AMA Guides*. Is it or would you agree that, in general, they're not to be used in determining or in directing financial awards to claimants?

A. That's a loaded question because, unfortunately, they are used as you well know, and I assume that's what you're utilizing it for. But the *Guides* specifically state it's [sic] not intended to be utilized for financial award. But again, it's subject to interpretation of attorneys. I am merely performing a medical evaluation regarding impairment rating and nothing more.

Q. Doctor, in the foreword of that book as well, does it also say that it's not to be used to determine disability status?

A. Correct.

Q. And it also says—or would you agree that the *Guides* are not and cannot provide answers of every type and degree of impairment; in addition, human functioning in everyday life is a highly dynamic process, and that presents a great challenge to those attempting to evaluate impairment?

A. And that is why only certain physicians will perform these impairment ratings.

Q. Is it also correct that the physician's judgment in his or her experience, training, and skill and thoroughness in examining the patient and applying the *Guides'* criteria will be a factor in estimating the degree of a patient's impairment according to the *AMA Guides'* foreword?

A. I believe so. Again, I assume you're reading from the *Guides.*

Justification for Not Using DRE Method Not Made in Report

Q. Now, Doctor, in your report, did you specifically explain why you disallowed the DRE method? You said you're supposed to, and I know you did today. But in your report, was a specific reference made to that fact?

A. I believe I noted although the DRE method would normally be utilized to an injury, it was decided to use the ROM method to establish his impairment. I then noted that he would fall into lumbar category if we used the DRE, and then I went on to state, however, the ROM or range of motion model was utilized as it was felt to better represent his true impairment. And I specifically noted this was based upon the fact he has had recurrent radiculopathy due to recurrent disk herniation in the same spinal region. Therefore, this would allow utilization of the range of motion method versus the DRE method.

Q. Now, Doctor, in your second report which was dated August—April 16, 2002, in the second paragraph, you go through the two options—the DRE and the ROM and basically state [the] DRE method is the primary method utilized to evaluate individuals?

A. Yes, I routinely utilize the DRE method when I'm evaluating individuals for lumbar problems.

Q. And only when an individual's condition is not well represented by a DRE, then do you go to the range of motion?

A. Yes.

Q. And you and Dr. E. agree on at least one thing, that if you were to use the DRE method, category 3 would be the best?

A. Yes, if you were to use the DRE method. However, in [an] attempt to give _____, who I assume is your client, a greater percentage, I opted for the ROM method.

Q. Now, you have started to say something about you're catching a plane, and the second page of your report has inaccuracies about radiculopathy. What were you referring to?

A. When looking at the DRE category 3, one of the criteria is based upon whether there's true radiculopathy. When I performed my physical examination of _____, I was trying to attempt to objectify with clarity that, indeed, radiculopathy was present as opposed to just pain in general. The objective signs are abnormal sensation or pain in specific dermatomal patterns.

Unfortunately, neither his pain nor his sensation specifically follows the S1 dermatome. There's been several dermatomes. So now we were hitting gray zones. I did feel he had a loss reflex at the S1 which was appropriate. However, he also had a depressed reflex in the opposite side which is ineffective, and I could not explain this.

He had no measurable atrophy, which if he had atrophy greater than two sonometers, this also makes it more objectified. If his EMG had stated there was evidence of radiculopathy, this would have made it much easier, but that performed by Dr. E. did not note radiculopathy.

So I originally had felt that he had radiculopathy. Then, when I was reviewing it to—for the second letter, I stated that his pain mimics dermatomal distribution but does not satisfy sufficient criteria for true radiculopathy, when in reality my gut feeling is he has radiculopathy. Whether he did or he doesn't, the manner in which the percentage is derived still stands [at] 13 percent for DRE, 28 percent for the range of motion.

Bladder Issue

Q. Doctor, is it also fair to say at one point _____ was using, which I believe is a strong narcotic, Dilaudid?

A. Yes.

Q. And that that can be known to either cause or aggravate a neurologic component to a bladder problem?

A. Well, Dilaudid, as you well know, and if you don't know, causes [an] anti-coenergic effect on the bladder and can be responsible for dysuria or difficulty with your stream. Therefore, being on Dilaudid can mimic problems with the bladder; and therefore, when _____ was evaluated for bladder problems, it was determined by Dr. Stefanelli that the Dilaudid was contributing to those problems and not specifically neurogenic—a neurogenic bladder. There's a difference between side effects from a medication causing symptoms and having neurogenic bladder.

Q. Was the Dilaudid being taken for the chronic pain following the surgery?

A. Yes.

Additional Medical Records from Urologist Do Not Change Doctor's Opinion on Bladder Dysfunction

Q. Doctor, did you have an opportunity to review medical report forms that were submitted to Workers' Compensation by Dr. Stefanelli, the urologist, in order to get paid for his treatment?

A. Yes.

Q. Does that in any way change your opinions today regarding the neurogenic bladder or the bladder findings, that they are not related to the work injury?

A. No, in fact, if anything, I felt it did not demonstrate neurogenic bladder, or at least I did not feel there was sufficient objective criteria for the diagnosis of neurogenic bladder.

Decision of Workers' Compensation Judge

The claimant testified that he was injured on January 6, 1999, while placing a jack underneath a car. The claimant described the pain in his back as burning, numbness, and deep pain that spread down his right leg. In January 1999 he had surgery on his back. Following this surgery, the claimant testified that he began having urinary problems and sexual dysfunction. He underwent a second surgery on his back in November 1999.

The claimant testified that he attempted to return to work after the first surgery but lasted only half a day. After the second surgery, the claimant had pain and total numbness in the right leg from his hip down to his foot. As a result, he was prescribed a cart and used a cane to assist with walking. He also built a ramp onto his home so the cart could go up it. The claimant has been prescribed Flomax by Dr. Stefanelli for bladder dysfunction, which continues to date. The claimant testified that he also had bowel dysfunction after the surgery.

The claimant testified he was referred to a psychiatrist for depression due to the problems caused by the injury, including weight gain and sexual problems. The claimant's current medications include Dilaudid, Flomax, Lidoderm, and Benadryl/Claritin. The claimant testified that his sexual dysfunction problems are caused by the pain and numbness in his groin, and he stated that he did not have this problem prior to the work injury. The claimant testified that he was prescribed Viagra at one time, but it did not help. The claimant testified that he continues to have problems with his back, right leg, bladder dysfunction, depression, and chronic pain and that he continues to use a cane.

The claimant presented the testimony of Dr. Scott E. He is board certified in physical medicine and rehabilitation, independent medical exams, EMGs, and pain medicine. Dr. E. has an active clinical practice of at least 20 hours a week for at least a two-year minimum. Dr. E.'s name also appears on a list promulgated by the Bureau of Workers' Compensation listing the doctors approved in the Commonwealth to perform impairment rating evaluations (IREs).

Dr. E. has been the claimant's treating physician since January 22, 1999. The claimant was referred to Dr. E. by his family physician, Dr. Bill Davis. The claimant first saw Dr. E. on January 22, 1999, and the doctor obtained a history from the claimant of a work injury on January 6, 1999. The claimant indicated he was lifting an item at work and had back pain going down the back of his right thigh and calf. The claimant had an MRI done, which showed a herniated disk at the lumbar spine at L5–S1 with a free fragment. The claimant had surgery by Dr. Presper on January 18, 1999, and was discharged the next day.

Dr. E. saw the claimant approximately four days later, on January 22, 1999. The claimant reported continuing back and posterior thigh symptoms. Dr. E. recommended a follow-up with Dr. Presper and physical therapy. Dr. E. continued to treat the claimant and in February 1999 noted that the claimant's chief complaints were of continued back pain, numbness in the right groin, the back and side of his right thigh, and into his right buttocks. Dr. E. recommended physical therapy and saw the claimant again on February 19, 1999. On that visit, the claimant had symptoms of dysuria. Dr. E. explained that dysuria is when you have pain when you urinate and indicated that this could be consistent with the postsurgical course.

Dr. E. recommended continued physical therapy and a urinalysis. Dr. E. also put the claimant on an antibiotic in case the claimant's problem was caused by a urinary tract infection. On that day, Dr. E. had a working impression of "improving from hemilaminectomy from the L5–S1 ruptured disk."

On his February 26, 1999, visit with Dr. E., the claimant had a sense that there was still fullness of his belly and that he was urinating frequently. At that point, Dr. E. placed claimant on oral prednisone. Dr. E. also reviewed an MRI, postsurgery, which showed the surgery at L5–S1 and no evidence of recurrent disk herniation; however, there was a disk protrusion at L4–L5 as well as S1 and at T12–L1. There was also epidural fibrosis at L5–S1.

Dr. E. opined that the MRI findings were consistent with the claimant's subjective complaints and objective findings. Dr. E. explained that the claimant's surgery at the L5–S1 level was the same level where the claimant had "epidural fibrosis," which he described as "scarring around the area of the spinal cord."

Dr. E. saw the claimant again on March 3, 1999. His subjective complaints included continued back discomfort and numbness in the buttocks, groin, and scrotum, all on the right side. The claimant had a sense that he would leak urine. At that point, the claimant wanted to try things back at work at his pre-injury job as an auto mechanic, and Dr. E. cleared him for doing such.

Dr. E. saw claimant again on March 19, 1999, and his subjective complaints remained the same. At that point, Dr. E. noted cauda equina syndrome. Dr. E. explained that this is when the spinal cord is injured at the thoracolumbar junction such that there is bowel and/or erectile or ejaculatory dysfunction as a result of a nerve injury at the spinal cord.

On April 14, 1999, Dr. E. noted the claimant had a functional capacity evaluation and continued to have occasional leakage of urine. Dr. E. referred him for a urology consultation. During this time as well, Dr. E. continued the claimant on a course of medication and physical therapy.

Dr. E. stated that he had referred the claimant to Dr. Stefanelli, a urologist, and received a report back from Dr. Stefanelli, upon which he relied in making treatment recommendations.

Dr. E. testified that Dr. Stefanelli noted a history from the claimant of voiding dysfunction as well as painful ejaculation, decreased erectile firmness, and urologic impairment of the bladder. A second note, from January 2000, indicates that an ultrasound had been done to rule out prostate abnormalities. This note also referenced decreased anal sensation and also decreased sensation in the right thigh. Dr. Stefanelli noted that the voiding dysfunction may be a combination of outlet obstruction at the bladder and a neurological component. Dr. E. opined that the findings of Dr. Stefanelli are consistent with cauda equina syndrome.

When Dr. E. saw the claimant on May 28, 1999, his symptoms remained unchanged, and the exam remained unchanged. He made a recommendation at that time of an epidural injection, and the claimant was going to be seen by Dr. Presper for consideration of surgery. The claimant remained on medication, including Ativan, OxyContin, Ultram, and Neurontin.

On July 14, 1999, the claimant was seen again by Dr. E., at which time a TENS unit was tried. The claimant had seen Dr. Presper, and a spinal cord stimulator had been recommended. In August 1999, Dr. E. started weaning the claimant from the Neurontin and the OxyContin and put him on Dilaudid, a narcotic-type pain medication. Dr. E. also recommended an MRI of the lumbar spine, consideration of repeat epidural, recommendation for spinal cord stimulator, continuation with the TENS unit, and specific massage therapy treatments in the form of shiatsu.

Dr. E. saw the claimant on September 15, 1999. The claimant had seen Dr. Presper, who recommended he not have the spinal cord stimulator. The claimant was referred to Dr. Bell. A recent MRI noted a recurrent disk herniation at L5–S1. The claimant continued with a positive seated straight leg raise and had some slight weakness of his right ankle and toe at that time. He was leaning to one side when he walked and limped on his right side. Dr. E. next saw the claimant on October 6, 1999. The claimant's pain was unchanged, and he was going to be seen by Dr. Moore in Englewood, New Jersey, for a second opinion regarding back surgery. The claimant was scheduled for a repeat L5–S1 diskectomy with incision of the epidural fibrosis on November 16, 1999.

Dr. E. saw the claimant following his surgery on December 22, 1999. The claimant told him he had the surgery and continued to have pain. The pain was unchanged from what it was preoperatively. There was actually an increase in the right groin pain, buttock pain, and scrotal pain postoperatively, as well as an increase in the numbness in the right foot. Dr. E.'s physical exam on that date was essentially the same. He also noted that the claimant was depressed. The claimant was also having difficulty sleeping. Medications at that time were Celexa, Xanax, Neurontin, and the Duragesic patch. Dr. E. testified he saw the claimant on January 24, 2000. The claimant's subjective complaints remained the same. Dr. E.'s recommendation included an increase in Xanax and a continuation of Celexa. Dilaudid was increased, and the claimant was instructed to follow up with Dr. Davis, his family physician; he also was referred to Dr. Yoo, who is a psychiatrist.

Dr. E. next saw the claimant on March 3, 2000, and noted that his symptoms were unchanged. The claimant had seen Dr. Davis. The Celexa dose was increased. The claimant was seen by both psychiatry and psychology. He was noted to be using a cane at that time and to have difficulty getting in and out of bed. The claimant continued to have weakness in his right lower extremity. The tightness in his back remained. The claimant did have positive straight leg raise. He continued to see Dr. Stefanelli, the urologist; his family physician, Dr. Davis; the psychologist; and the psychiatrist.

Dr. E. testified he reviewed a report from Dr. Yoo, the claimant's psychiatrist, dated March 20, 2000, and noted a diagnosis of major depression and anxiety. Dr. E. felt that this diagnosis was consistent with the claimant's presentation to him at his office visits.

Dr. E. saw the claimant again on April 7, 2000. The claimant's subjective complaints remained the same. He was to follow up with his surgeon, Dr. Moore, and continue with the psychologist and psychiatrist. He also was going to try acupuncture. The claimant was continued on his medications. He was also noted to be on Valium and Zoloft.

Dr. E. continued to treat the claimant throughout the summer of 2000. The doctor opined that the claimant was not capable of working. As of July 21, 2000, the claimant's subjective complaints were unchanged. The claimant needed a scooter or a wheelchair for long-distance mobility. He was using a cane for short-distance mobility. The physical exam was unchanged. The claimant was noted to have more limited range of motion on that date.

Dr. E.'s impression at that time was L5–S1 disk herniation with L5–S1 radiculopathy, including laminectomy and decompression at L5–S1, and the claimant remained with chronic pain.

Dr. E. explained that the term *free fragment* actually means a piece of disk that has essentially popped off. Dr. E. authenticated prescriptions, including one for a wheelchair and scooter for the claimant's long-distance mobility. During the summer of 2000, Dr. E. felt that the claimant's prognosis was that he was at maximum medical improvement with a permanent impairment and a permanent disability.

Dr. E. continued to treat the claimant throughout 2000, seeing him on a monthly basis. He also treated the claimant throughout 2001 and 2002. Asked to summarize these visits, Dr. E. noted the claimant's complaints were essentially unchanged. The claimant did have a repeat MRI of his lumbar spine on October 20, 2000, which showed recurrent scar formation at L5–S1 impinging on the nerve root. Medications were essentially unchanged. The claimant was referred to Dr. Kara Davis, who is a pain management doctor in Wilkes-Barre. He was continued on Dilaudid and other medications. The claimant was also on antianxiety and antidepressant medications, as well as Flomax for his bladder dysfunction.

At the time he testified, Dr. E. had last seen the claimant on March 13, 2002. Dr. E. noted that the claimant's subjective complaints, physical exam, and treatment remained the same.

Dr. E. opined that the claimant's work-related condition consisted of L5–S1 disk herniation with L5–S1 radiculopathy, status postlaminectomy, and decompression of the free disk fragment at L5–S1, epidural fibrosis at L5–S1, and cauda equina syndrome. Dr. E. explained that cauda equina encompasses an injury to the spinal cord that results in bowel, bladder, and/or sexual dysfunction. Further, Dr. E. opined that these diagnoses were causally related to the claimant's January 6, 1999, work-related injury. In addition, Dr. E. opined that the claimant is not capable of any substantial gainful employment.

Dr. E. did have an opportunity to review the IRE that was performed by Dr. Patrick F. on February 8, 2001. Dr. E. testified that in performing an IRE for the low back, the *AMA Guides,* under the fifth edition, allow the doctor essentially two different ways to rate. One model is known as the DRE, and the second is the ROM model. The DRE is to be used with patients who have single-level back problems or a single-level disk injury. When there is more than one disk involved, the ROM model is normally used. Dr. E. explained that there are certain caveats to that rule. One is that when someone [presents] with a spinal cord injury or cauda equina syndrome, in addition to a single disk level, the physician is to use the DRE model. Dr. E. stated that Dr. F., in doing his report, noted that there was a single disk lesion but opted not to use the DRE criteria. Instead, Dr. F. opted to use the ROM criteria and came up with an impairment percentage based on the ROM model. Dr. E. opined, however, that the ROM model should not have been used in this case. The DRE should have been used because there was a single-level lesion and there was evidence of bladder, rectal, and neurological sexual dysfunction in this case. The *Guides* (page 498) provide that these additional impairments need to be calculated and added into the impairment based solely on the DRE. Dr. E. testified he did this in deciding his impairment rating.

Dr. E. testified that he took the diagnosis of radiculopathy and his findings based on all his previous exams. Using the DRE model, the claimant's impairment for the radiculopathy diagnosis was 13 percent. For the corticospinal tract impairment, that is, the bowel, bladder, and sexual dysfunction, his impairment was 40 percent, with 3 percent additional for pain. After using the combined value chart on page 604 of the *Guides,* Dr. E. found the claimant's whole-person impairment was 50 percent. Dr. E. opined that in using the *AMA Guidelines [sic] of Permanent Impairment,* more specifically the fifth edition, the claimant has an impairment rating that is equal to 50 percent, as required by section 306 of the Workers' Compensation Act.

Dr. E. explained that the diagnosis of cauda equina syndrome does emanate from the L5–S1 level and that this diagnosis is part of the claimant's back injury. The L5–S1 radiculopathy also emanates from the claimant's back injury, as does the epidural fibrosis. These are just different diagnoses relating to the disk herniation and what emanates from the disk herniation. Dr. E. further opined that through the three years he treated the claimant, including his review of the medical records of other physicians, to whom he referred the claimant, the claimant did continuously have bowel and bladder problems subsequent to his surgeries. The claimant also submitted a report dated May 17, 2001, authored by Dr. E., admitted as Claimant's Exhibit No. 11, where Dr. E. further explained that based on Figure 15-4, page 380, of the *Guides,* fifth edition, should the injury be to a single level (whether it be the first injury or a repeat injury), then the DRE model should be used.

Dr. E. specifically explained that the claimant's impairment rating of 50 percent was calculated using Table 15-6 for rating corticospinal tract impairments.

A review of the table reveals that the claimant has evidence of three impairments listed in the table: (1) impairment due to station and gait disorders (15-6c), (2) neurological impairment of the bladder (15-6d), and (3) neurologic sexual impairment (15-6f). Using Table 15-6c, Dr. E. found the claimant would fall under class 2 given the claimant's limited walking distance and use of an adaptive device, which would yield a rating of 19 percent. Using Table 15-6d, given the urologic findings documented by Dr. Stefanelli, would yield a rating of 9 percent. Using Table 15-6f, a class 2 impairment, given claimant's history, painful erection/ejaculation, and Dr. Stefanelli's findings, would yield a 19 percent impairment. Because more than one rating has been given, reference to the combined value chart yields a 40 percent rating from the impairments listed in Table 15-6.

Dr. E. explained that the rating from Table 15-6 must be combined with the rating for the DRE lumbar category 3 for radiculopathy, Table 15-3, which yields a 13 percent impairment. Because the claimant's condition is a pain-related impairment, using Figure 18-1, Dr. E. opined that the claimant would be entitled to an additional 3 percent for pain. When the ratings for corticospinal tract impairment from Table 15-6, radiculopathy from Table 15-3, and pain from Figure 18-1 are combined, the combined value chart yields a whole-person impairment of 50 percent.

Dr. E. concluded that the DRE model was the correct method to be used to calculate the claimant's impairment rating and that it yielded a whole-body impairment rating of 50 percent. Dr. E. did agree, however, that under the ROM model, the claimant would be found to have a 28 percent whole-body impairment, as rated by Dr. F.

The employer/insurer presented the testimony of Dr. Patrick J. F. Dr. F. is board certified in emergency medicine and was appointed by the bureau to perform the claimant's IRE [impairment rating evaluation], which took place on February 9, 2001. At that time, Dr. F. took a history from the claimant that on January 5, 1999, the claimant was seated on a small stool placing a jack under a car and using one hand. The claimant stated that he was trying to secure the jack in place and "felt something happen" to his lower back. From then on, the claimant noted progressive lower back pain that began radiating down the right leg. His chief complaints at that time were primarily right-sided lower back pain, which would radiate into his right leg. The claimant had some numbness at the right buttock and the leg, as well as in the fourth and fifth toes. Dr. F. testified that the claimant denied any dysuria or increased frequency. At times, the claimant stated, his bladder would leak when getting out of a chair. The claimant also stated that, on occasion, he would have some difficulty starting a urinary stream and maintaining it, particularly if he was not concentrating. Dr. F. stated that the claimant was able to sustain an erection. The claimant was taking Diluadid for pain, Serzone for depression, Benadryl for sleep, Xanax and diazepam for anxiety, and Flomax. Dr. F. also noted that the claimant underwent a hemilaminectomy and decompression of the S1 nerve root and that the claimant also had a second surgery, which involved an L5–S1 diskectomy foraminotomy with incision of scar tissue.

Dr. F. performed a physical examination of the claimant, which noted a well-healed lumbosacral scar. There was some tenderness to palpation, primarily over the muscles in the right paralumbar region, as well as over the sacroiliac joint and the sciatic notch.

Dr. F. found no evidence of spasms or trigger points. The claimant was able to bend forward or flex, reaching his digit as far as his knees before noting pain. Neurologically, Dr. F. tested the claimant's muscles, and the claimant stated he had some difficulty walking on his toes on the right, noting some discomfort or weakness. Dr. F. had the claimant lie supine and stated he found no weakness in those particular muscles. With regard to sensation, Dr. F. noted that the claimant had decreased sensation over the entire right lower leg as well as the entire right foot. This also included the buttock and sacral region. Left ankle reflex was depressed, and right ankle reflex was absent.

Dr. F. opined that the claimant's whole-person impairment rating was 28 percent. Dr. F. explained that when attempting to determine a lumbar spine injury, there are certain methods or categories used according to *AMA Guides to Evaluation of Permanent Impairment,* fifth edition. Dr. F. explained that typically, "we review the history provided by the patient, review the medical records, particularly all the pertinent data, and then perform the physical examination. Once we compile all that information, we then determine the method, as well as the categories that we will eventually provide the ratings for." In this particular situation, Dr. F. went to the *Guides* using Chapter 15, entitled "The Spine." Dr. F. further explained that he used both the DRE and ROM methods, then awarded the highest percentage.

Dr. F. explained that first he used the DRE, which states there are five separate categories. The physician first must determine in which category, if any, the patient falls. When reviewing the five categories, Dr. F. used Table 15.3, which is on page 384 of the *Guides*. The appropriate category or at least the category that Dr. F. felt the claimant most closely resembled was DRE lumbar category 3. Using this category, an impairment is allowed upward of 10 to 13 percent. Given the fact that the claimant had an L5–S1 disk herniation with a subsequent recurring disk herniation at the same level, the claimant was given the upper percentage of impairment, which was 13 percent. Dr. F. explained that he placed the claimant in category 3 as he referred to the claimant's presurgery diagnosis regarding the radiculopathy, as well as his history of herniated disk that was associated with radiculopathy.

Dr. F. explained that his rating under the DRE method differed from Dr. E.'s rating because Dr. E. included elements of the claimant's anatomy, which were not part of the compensable injury per the Notice of Compensation Payable and were outside the purview of Section 306(8) of the Workers' Compensation Act.

Dr. F. explained that he believed the ROM method was appropriate for the claimant. The claimant qualified for the ROM method because utilizing the *Guides,* Chapter 15, specifically 15.2, which is entitled "Determining the Appropriate Method for Assessment," there are several situations, approximately five, which are numbered under that section allowing one to go ahead and use the ROM method. Dr. F. explained that he used the ROM to award claimant the 28 percent impairment rating. Dr. F. explained that the ROM measurements are performed in flexion, extension, lateral flexion, or side bending. For the actual measurements, certain percentages are given for each motion. Once those percentages are tallied, they are added, producing a resulting impairment for the ROM measurement only, in other words, for the degrees of motion. Then you take the actual diagnosis, which is found on page 404, Table 15.7, and there are four categories according to diagnosis utilizing the ROM method.

Dr. F. determined that the claimant fell into category 2, subsection E, noted as surgically treated disk lesion with residually medically documented pain and rigidity. Dr. F. noted that the claimant had surgery on the L5–S1 disk and he continued to complain of pain in the same region. Therefore, Dr. F. felt the claimant qualified for subsection E. Dr. F. then went to subsection G, which refers to multiple operations, with or without residual signs or symptoms. Number one under that section is second operation. Since claimant had two operations, Dr. F. was able to award claimant an additional 2 percent.

Dr. F. determined his percentage based upon diagnosis. At that point, Dr. F. had 2 percentages, one for range of motion measurement, and a second for diagnosis. The ROM method required a third category to be utilized, a calculation of impairment due to motor and sensory loss. Dr. F. then referred to Table 15.15. He rated the sensory deficit as well as the motor impairment or the motor deficit for the S1 nerve root, which was affected by the L5–S1 disk. Percentages were then given for both the sensory loss and the motor deficit. These percentages were combined. This third percentage of impairment was combined with the other two for range and diagnosis and based on the combined values chart, and Dr. F. determined the whole-person impairment rating of 28 percent.

Rationale

The parties have presented expert medical opinion testimony from two equally qualified impairment raters approved by the Bureau of Workers' Compensation who have differing opinions as to the percentage of claimant's whole body impairment from his work injury. A close examination of the testimony of both doctors reveals that the reason for the differing opinions and the main issue in dispute between the parties in this case is whether or not the diagnosis of a "cauda equina syndrome" with its resultant abnormalities can be included within the calculation of the claimant's impairment.

Dr. F., who was selected by the bureau to perform an IRE evaluation, chose not to include a cauda equina syndrome diagnosis in his impairment calculations. Dr. E., claimant's treating physician, did include the cauda equina syndrome in his calculations.

The *AMA Guides to Evaluation of Permanent Impairment* provides a tool for evaluation of permanent impairment.

The *AMA Guides to Evaluation of Permanent Impairment,* fifth edition, allows for the determination of a claimant's impairment using two rating models. The Range of Motion (ROM) model, is to be utilized when more than one disk level is involved in the injury. The Diagnostic Related Estimate (DRE) model, is to be used when only one disk level is involved in the injury. However, the DRE model is also to be used if the patient has a spinal cord injury.

Dr. F. initially calculated the claimant's impairment rating utilizing both methods. However, since Dr. F. did not include a cauda equina syndrome diagnosis, Dr. F. did not provide a rating for a spinal cord injury. Dr. F.'s evaluation solely using the diagnosis of a radiculopathy without a spinal cord injury would yield the claimant a higher rating using the ROM model. The ROM model would yield the more favorable rating for the claimant given the lack of a rating for a spinal cord injury diagnosis. Dr. E., however, utilizing a "cauda equina syndrome" diagnosis, used the DRE model, which included the spinal cord injury diagnosis, which gave the claimant a higher rating than the ROM model did without recognizing a spinal cord injury. Therefore, the issue in this case comes down to whether or not the claimant had a spinal cord injury related to the work injury.

Dr. F. did not find sufficient evidence to document a spinal cord injury from his review of the records. However, Dr. E.'s testimony provides credible and convincing evidence that the claimant has had a spinal cord injury as a result of his work injury. Dr. E. has long documented the claimant's bladder, bowel, and sexual dysfunction as related to the work injury and surgeries the claimant has had for the injury. This documentation goes back to 1999, long before the claimant was faced with the IRE ratings issue. The Notice of Compensation Payable lists the claimant's work injury as only a sprain. However, both doctors agree that the claimant's work injury was something more than a sprain. Both Dr. F. and Dr. E. had, at least in part, utilized a diagnosis of an L5–S1 radiculopathy in calculating their impairment ratings. The credible medical evidence of record, particularly the testimony of Dr. E., clearly establishes the claimant's work injury extended beyond that set forth in the Notice of Compensation Payable and did involve a spinal cord injury in the nature of a cauda equina syndrome, encompassing bowel, bladder, and sexual dysfunction. The diagnosis of a cauda equina syndrome should have been included within the impairment rating. The only impairment rating that included the diagnosis of cauda equina syndrome with its encompassing bowel, bladder, and sexual dysfunction was the rating provided by Dr. E. Dr. E.'s rating should be accepted as both credible and convincing. Dr. E. rated the claimant as having a whole body impairment of fifty (50) percent, which would meet the requirement of the [Workers' Compensation] Act for the claimant to be considered permanently totally disabled.

Conclusions of Law

1. All parties to these proceedings are bound by the provisions of the Workers' Compensation Act, as amended.

2. Claimant has met his burden of proving that the impairment rating evaluation of twenty-eight (28) percent whole body impairment is incorrect and that claimant's permanent whole body impairment is fifty (50) percent.

3. Claimant's work injury consisting of an L5–S1 disk herniation with L5–S1 radiculopathy, status postlaminectomy and decompression of the free disk fragment at L5–S1, epidural fibrosis at L5–S1 and cauda equina syndrome would require the use of the Diagnostic Related Estimate, DRE, method for calculating Claimant's impairment rating. Table 15-6 for rating corticospinal tract impairments reveals that Claimant has evidence of three (3) impairments listed on the Table. Claimant has evidence of impairment due to station and gait disorders (15-6c). Claimant would fall under Class 2 given claimant's limited walking distance and use of an adaptive device. Claimant would have a rating of nineteen (19) percent due to his impairment due to station and gait disorder. Claimant also has a neurological impairment of the bladder under 15-6d. Claimant's neurologic findings would yield a rating of nine (9) percent impairment. Under Table 15-6f Claimant has evidence of neurologic sexual impairment, a Class 2 impairment, given Claimant's history of painful erections/ejaculation and other similar findings. Claimant's neurologic sexual impairment under Table 15-6f would yield a rating of nineteen (19 percent). Since more than one rating or one Table has been utilized in determining Claimant's rating, reference must be made to the combined value chart which yields a rating of forty (40) percent from the impairments listed on Table 15-6. In addition to these impairments found from reviewing Table 15-6, Claimant also had a lumbar category three (3) impairment for radiculopathy from Table 15-3, which would yield an impairment rating of thirteen (13) percent. Figure 18-1 would also call for Claimant to receive an additional three (3) percent rating for pain since his condition is a pain-related impairment. When the rating for the corticospinal tract impairment from Table 15-6, the radiculopathy from Table 15-3 and pain from Figure 18-1 are combined, the combined value chart would yield a whole-person permanent impairment of fifty (50) percent. Claimant had a whole-body permanent impairment of fifty (50) percent from his work injury of January 6, 1999.

§ 10.03 HERNIATED L4–L5 DISK INJURY

The claimant in this case, Richard D., was a 37-year-old factory worker who had suffered a herniated disk at L4–L5 and underwent a diskectomy. Mr. D. claimed that a postoperative coughing and sneezing fit caused him to herniate a second disk at L5–S1. The following deposition is by Dr. B., a second opinion orthopedic surgeon, who rated the claimant at 13 percent impairment for the two disk injuries under the fourth edition of the *AMA Guides* (1993).

Deposition of Second Opinion Orthopedic Surgeon

[By Ms. Estes].

Qualifications

Q. Dr. B., what kind of practice do you have?

A. I'm an orthopedic surgeon, and I restrict my practice to lumbar spine disorders.

Q. Doctor, I'm handing you what has been marked as Defendant's Exhibit A. Can you identify that document?

A. It's my CV [curriculum vitae].

Q. How long have you been practicing as an orthopedic surgeon?

A. I graduated from medical school in 1979, so I've been in the practice of medicine for 20 years. I've been an orthopedic surgeon, having completed residency, since 1984.

Q. And you maintain a private practice in orthopedic surgery?

A. Yes.

Q. What do you specialize in your practice?

A. Lumbar spine disorders.

Q. Can you estimate for me approximately how many patients you've treated for lumbar spine disorders in the course of your practice?

A. I could say thousands, but I can't give an accurate estimate.

Evaluation and Report

Q. Doctor, are you familiar with the plaintiff in this lawsuit, Mr. D.?

A. I don't have a personal recollection of Mr. D., but I did evaluate him on May 4, 1998, according to my records.

Q. Did you issue a report as a result of your evaluation of Mr. D. of May 4, 1998?

A. Yes.

Q. I am handing you what has been marked as Defendant's Exhibit B. Can you identify that document, please?

A. This is a copy of my report issued on May 4, 1998.

Q. Doctor, when you saw Mr. D. on May 4, 1998, did you take a history from him?

A. Yes.

Q. What was the history given to you at that time?

A. Mr. D. at that time was a 37-year-old gentleman employed in factory work for Raybestos. He had been referred to me by H.B., a nurse with _____ Company, for the purpose of a second opinion. Mr. D. stated that he had suffered an injury on June 1, 1997, resulting in a disk herniation and subsequent surgery on February 4, 1998. That surgery was performed at L4–L5 on the right. In early March of 1998, Mr. D. developed insidious onset left lower extremity pain. He stated that at this time his pain radiated from the left buttock down the posterior thigh into the posterior calf to the sole of his foot. He rated his pain at level 10 on a scale of zero to 10. He had been off work since January 22, 1998. He had failed to obtain adequate relief with an epidural steroid injection. He noted that his symptoms were becoming worse.

Examination and Findings

Q. Did you conduct an examination of Mr. D. on that date as well?

A. Yes.

Q. What were your findings?

A. Mr. D. ambulated with a limp on the left side. There was limitation to forward bending and extension. He located symptoms originating in the left posterior iliac crest region. His straight-leg raising exam was positive on the left, and there was a positive cross-straight-leg raising exam on the right. There was numbness in the S1 dermatome on the left.

Q. Did you make a diagnosis as a result of your examination of Mr. D.?

A. I then reviewed radiographs, including an MRI of the lumbar spine obtained March 27, 1998, which revealed a herniated disk at L5–S1 on the left, compressing the S1 root. It was my impression that Mr. D. was suffering a herniated nucleus pulposus or ruptured disk at L5–S1 on the left.

Causation

Q. Do you have an opinion, Dr. B., as to what caused the herniated disk at L5–S1?

A. According to the history provided to me by Mr. D., the pain developed in early March of 1998. And the pain was insidious without any precipitating event described.

Q. What do you mean by the term *insidious*?

A. It developed without incident. It occurred with no dramatic event.

Q. Is it your opinion then that you cannot identify the cause of Mr. D.'s herniated disk at L5–S1?

A. That's correct.

Q. Or at least cannot identify an activity that precipitated the herniation of that disk?

A. Correct.

Q. I believe your testimony was that Mr. D. gave you the history that his left leg pain began in early March of 1998?

A. Yes.

Q. Was your conclusion that the left lower extremity pain was of an insidious onset, also based upon what was told to you by Mr. D. when you saw him on May 4, 1998?

A. Yes.

Inconsistent History from Claimant

Q. You are aware, Doctor, that Mr. D. is alleging that his herniated disk at L5–S1 was caused by a coughing or sneezing spell related to postoperative respiratory problems subsequent to his surgery at L4–L5 with Dr. Dietz [treating physician]?

A. Yes.

Q. Did Mr. D., when you saw him on May 4, 1998, report to you that his left leg pain began after a coughing and sneezing spell?

A. No.

Q. Did he report to you that his left lower leg pain began within two days of his surgery on the L4–L5 disk?

A. No.
Q. Did Mr. D. report to you that he was lying down at the time his left leg pain began?
A. No.

Plausibility of Plaintiff's Causation Theory

Q. You have performed back surgeries in the past, Dr. B., have you not?
A. Yes.
Q. And utilized general anesthesia performing those surgeries?
A. Yes.
Q. Could you explain to me what kind of respiratory problems might follow with a person who has had the kind of back surgery that Mr. D. had on his L4–L5 disk?
A. With a general anesthetic an endotracheal tube is placed. And once the endotracheal tube is removed sometimes patients have secretions that need to be cleared, and will cough. Sometimes there will be some upper extremity airway irritation, some increased secretion production, which can lead to drainage and coughing.
Q. Is this a common occurrence in patients who have had a general anesthesia with an endotracheal tube?
A. I wouldn't state that it is common with this surgery, but it is not uncommon either.
Q. Have you seen this in the course of your practice?
A. Yes.
Q. When a person does have respiratory problems after the general anesthesia, do these problems typically, if not exclusively, manifest themselves within a short period of time after the surgery?
A. Yes.
Q. What period of time would that be?
A. Generally, they will occur within a day, perhaps two days, after the anesthetic.
Q. And what kind of symptoms would you see?
A. Generally, the coughing is prolonged. It's usually not one episode. Generally, it resolves within a short period of time unless it progresses to pneumonia.
Q. When you say the coughing resolves within a short period of time, what period of time after surgery on a lumbar disk would it take for a patient to recover from that kind of respiratory distress?
A. It's very rare that any of our patients report problems with coughing or upper respiratory problems, but on occasion someone will. And it's usually—within a couple of days it will resolve. And any problems beyond that period of time have usually been when a patient develops pneumonia.
Q. Are you aware of any history of pneumonia with Mr. D. with respect to his surgery on the L4–L5 disk?
A. No.
Q. Would you expect Mr. D. to have been suffering from respiratory problems related to his previous back surgery as late as March of 1998?
A. That would be extremely unlikely.
Q. That would have been approximately one month after the surgery on his back, would it not?

A. That's correct.

Q. Is it your testimony that it would be extremely unlikely that he would be continuing to suffer from respiratory problems related to the back surgery at that time?

A. Unless he had pneumonia.

Q. If there were some kind of respiratory problems that followed the original back surgery, would you expect to see coughing or sneezing, or one or the other, or both?

A. I would expect to see coughing, and I would expect that it would have been an ongoing problem. If he was coughing in March, then I would expect he would have been coughing through February as well.

Q. Would sneezing be an unlikely symptom?

A. I believe so.

Q. And would that be because sneezing has no effect on clearing of the respiratory passages?

A. Sneezing, in my impression, is an upper nasal passage problem, whereas coughing would reflect a tracheal or lung condition.

Q. You have noted, Dr. B., and I believe Mr. D.'s records confirm, that he suffered from asthma. Is that correct?

A. That is my understanding.

Asthma

Q. Are you familiar with the nature and extent of his asthma?

A. I've reviewed records reflecting Mr. D.'s previous history of asthma problems.

Q. These records reflect, do they not, a rather severe case of asthma?

A. I'm not really qualified to judge severity of asthma.

Q. Fair enough. If I could, let me refer you to Dr. N.'s report of June 17, 1996. Are you familiar with that report, Dr. B.?

A. I believe I reviewed it along with other materials.

Q. That report indicates that Mr. D. suffers from coughing spells related to his asthma, does it not?

A. Yes.

Q. And does Dr. N. comment on the nature and extent of those coughing spells?

A. He states, quote, he has coughing spells so severely that he passes out. In fact, he's passed out twice, hitting his head, unquote.

Causation

Q. It is entirely possible, is it not, Dr. B., that Mr. D.'s herniated disk at L5–S1 as a result of a coughing incident, that that coughing incident was related to his severe asthma?

[Mr. Ayers]. To which I'll object. There is no foundation for that.

A. I'm really not qualified to address that question.

Q. Do you see anything in Mr. D.'s medical records, Dr. B., that would indicate to you that his herniated disk at L5–S1 was in any way related to his work injury?

A. I do not.

Q. Would you therefore look to other possible causes of this herniated disk?

A. Yes.

Q. There has been a suggestion in some of the medical records, or perhaps it was by Mr. D. himself, that Dr. Dietz told him the disk at L5–S1 was weakened by the surgery on L4–L5. Can you comment on that?

A. There would be no basis for that statement.

Q. Why is that?

A. Diskectomy surgery at L4–L5 would not affect L5–S1.

Disability

Q. Had you been the doctor performing the surgery on Mr. D., could you estimate for me the length of disability that would be reasonably associated with the surgery?

A. Disability is variable. My routine would be for the procedure to be done as an outpatient. And I allow patients to return to normal activities as soon as they're able. There's no evidence that restriction of activities is beneficial or the return to activity is harmful. Some patients return to work within a day or two. Some patients return to work within a few weeks. Some patients return to work longer. It depends partly on motivation, partly on residual pain complaints.

Q. And would this be true with respect to both the surgery at L4–L5 and L5–S1?

A. Yes.

Impairment

Q. Could you also estimate permanent partial impairment that would be attributable to both of those surgeries?

A. Typical impairment rating for diskectomy surgeries is in the range of 10 percent. It can vary a point or two either direction.

Q. And that would be for both disks combined?

A. I believe when a second diskectomy is performed that there is an additional two points. I'd have to pull out the *AMA Guides* to verify that.

Q. What would be your best estimate then as to the amount of impairment that you would attribute to the injury to Mr. D.'s disk at L4–L5 and L5–S1?

[Mr. Ayers]. To which I'll object. There's no foundation. The doctor obviously didn't do an examination with that in mind. I take it this is all hypothetical to Mr. D.

[Ms. Estes]. The doctor is entitled to give his best estimate.

A. Typical impairment rating for the diskectomy would probably be in the range of 10 to 12 percent.

Q. And would that be taking into consideration both diskectomies?

A. I'd have to retrieve the book to verify. If you'd like me to I could.

Degenerative Disk Disease

Q. Doctor, does your review of Mr. D.'s medical records indicate that he suffers from degenerative disk disease in the lumbar spine?

A. Mr. D. did have degenerative disks at L4–L5 and L5–S1, as confirmed by an MRI of the lumbar spine on December 24, 1997.

Q. And have you seen any diagnostic testing indicating degeneration at other levels of the lumbar spine?

A. According to my notes on review of the MRI from March 27, 1998, there was level disk dehydration over the lower three lumbar levels.

Q. Did you take notes, Dr. B., when you saw Mr. D. on May 4, 1998?

A. Yes.

Q. Are those notes contained in your file?

A. Yes.

Q. What, if any, reference is contained in those notes to the history of the onset of Mr. D.'s left leg pain?

A. My notes reflect exactly my dictation, that the related onset occurred in early March 1998.

Q. Could you show me the specific notes you're referring to?

[Witness hands documents to defense counsel.]

[Defendant's Deposition Exhibit D is marked for identification.]

Q. Dr. B., did you review and rely upon Mr. D.'s medical records, in part, in forming your opinions in this case, and giving your testimony here today?

A. Yes.

Q. I'm handing you what's been marked as Defendant's Exhibit C, which is the report from Dr. N. that we referred to previously. Was that part of the records that you reviewed in preparation for today's deposition?

A. Yes.

Q. I'm also handing you what's been marked Defendant's Deposition Exhibit D. Could you please identify that document?

Doctor Questioned on His Notes

A. These are my rough notes that were prepared on May 17, 1998, at the time of the evaluation of Mr. D.

Q. There is a section on Exhibit D, halfway down the page, labeled "physician use only." What does that indicate?

A. This section is reserved for me to make notes during my history of Mr. D.

Q. And are the notes that were written on this section, written by you at the time you were taking a history from Mr. D. on May 4, 1998?

A. Yes.

Q. With regard to date of onset, what did you enter?

A. Early March 1998.

Consistency of Plaintiff

Q. I am now handing you what has been marked Defendant's Exhibit E, which contains a reference to the onset of left leg pain on March 10, 1998. Is this a record contained in your patient file on Mr. D.?

A. Yes.

Q. Did you also review Mr. D.'s deposition prior to giving your testimony today?

A. Yes.

Q. With regard to the contention that Mr. D. was having respiratory distress after the surgery on his L4–L5 disks, Mr. D. testified in his deposition that he was suffering from no respiratory distress at the time he had his coughing or sneezing spells, did he not?

A. I believe so.

Q. Referring you to page 52 of Mr. D.'s deposition, lines 7 through 10, would you read that question and that answer, Dr. B.?

A. Question: Were you having any respiratory problems when you had this sneezing fit at home that caused your left leg pain? Answer: Not that I recall. No.

Q. Would Mr. D.'s own testimony be consistent with the history that you took from him in your office on May 4, 1998, that it does not reference a coughing and sneezing spell due to respiratory distress as precipitating the onset of his left leg pain?

[**Mr. Ayers**]. To which I'll object. A lack of the reference is not a positive support for diagnosis.

[**Ms. Estes**]. You may certainly try to bring that out on cross-examination, Counsel, but the doctor can still answer my question as posed.

A. Correct.

Q. Do you find Mr. D.'s deposition testimony to also be consistent with your opinion that Mr. D.'s herniated disk was not caused by postoperative respiratory distress?

A. Correct.

[**Ms. Estes**]. Those are all the questions I have. Thank you, Doctor.

Cross-Examination of Second Opinion Surgeon by Employer's Counsel

[By Mr. Ayers]

Coughing Fit

Q. Dr. B., what position was Mr. D. in when he had the coughing or sneezing fit that he related to the onset of pain?

A. I'd have to review the records. I thought he said he was in bed, but I'm not sure without looking at the records.

Q. I believe in an earlier question you said he was not lying down.

[**Ms. Estes**]. I believe the doctor's testimony was that he did not relate to him that he was lying down at the time of his symptom onset.

[**Mr. Ayers**]. That's what I said.

A. That is correct. He did not relate to me.

Q. What did he relate to you then about his position, or did you ask?

A. He related that his pain occurred in March with no apparent reason.

Q. What did he relate to you in terms of his position when the sneezing fit occurred?

A. Well, he didn't describe any sneezing fit to me.

Q. Did he describe a coughing fit?

A. No.

Q. Assuming that there was a sneezing or a coughing fit sometime, assume that with me.

A. Okay, I'll assume that.

Q. Do you have anything—

[Ms. Estes]. For purposes of this question only?

Q. Do you have anything in the record that indicates to you what his position was?
A. Not from my personal records.

Records Reviewed

Q. Tell me, please, what records you were given to review before coming to your professional opinions in this case?
A. Are you asking about the records that I had available as of May 4, or the records that I've had available as to today?
Q. Both.
A. As of May 4th. I had an MRI report from March 27, 1998. I had an office note of Dr. Dietz from April 13,1998, and an office note of April 21, 1998.
Q. And what, if anything, did the office notes of Dr. Dietz on April 13 and April 21 indicate that Dr. Dietz had concluded in terms of etiology?
A. Dr. Dietz addressed that issue on April 21, 1998, in the third paragraph of his office notes. Would you like me to read that pertinent part?
Q. Yes.
A. "The next question that was brought up was whether the disk herniation is related to the lifting injury that occurred at work. This is extremely difficult to determine with certainty. His coughing and sneezing episode immediately after surgery is probably the reason for the disk herniation. And whether that is related to the surgery as a complication of surgery is arguable."
Q. Would it be fair to say that Mr. D., at least in his history at that time, had a coughing or sneezing fit as part of his history?
A. Yes.
Q. Were you ever provided Dr. Dietz's notes of February 2, 1998?
A. Yes. I was provided with at least one note.
Q. What note is that?
A. The note of February 20, 1998.
Q. As to Dr. Dietz's note of February 20, when did you receive that note?
A. I saw it for the first time yesterday.

[Mr. Ayers]. Mark the note of February 20 as an exhibit.

[Plaintiff's Deposition is marked as Exhibit 11.]

Q. I'll hand you Claimant's [Exhibit] 11 and ask you whether there's reference in Dr. Dietz's note of February 20 to such an occurrence?
A. Yes.
Q. And would you read that note?
A. This is a follow-up note for Mr. D. two weeks' status post an uncomplicated microdiskectomy done at St. Vincent's Hospital at L4–L5 on the right. He had a severe sneezing spell two days after surgery and had a good deal of problems since then with leg pain, although now his leg pain is resolved down to his knee, but he is having severe leg pain in his calf. On physical examination, he noted the calf pain is in the lateral aspect.

Q. Does the note from Dr. Dietz indicate to you that the symptoms that Mr. D. was experiencing were waxing and waning to some extent?

[Ms. Estes]. Which symptoms are you referring to?

[Mr. Ayers]. The ones described in the . . .

[Ms. Estes]. In the February 20 note?

[Mr. Ayers]. The February 20 note.

A. I note two things in the note of February 20. First of all, Dr. Dietz does not state which leg. He simply uses the word "leg." And we don't know whether or not he is referring to recurrent right leg pain or a new onset of left leg pain. By his physical examination, however, he describes the calf pain as in the lateral aspect. The lateral aspect is typical L5 dermatomal distribution, which would be more compatible with his surgery at L4–L5 on the right. Because he decompressed the L5 nerve root. The disk herniation at L5–S1 was on the left, which would have affected the S1, which is posterior calf instead of lateral calf. So as I read the note it's unclear, but I would suspect he was talking about right leg pain as a result of coughing rather than left leg pain.

Q. And the right leg pain then that you assume he's talking about would have gotten worse after this sneezing incident?

A. It's not uncommon. Patients have irritation of the nerve following surgery. Any trivial incident can aggravate discomfort on a temporary basis.

Q. And in this case the surgery that was on February 4, is that correct?

A. I believe so.

Q. Would you give Dr. Dietz's report the weight of establishing an incident of severe coughing and/or sneezing a few days after surgery?

[Ms. Estes]. I'm sorry, Counsel, I don't understand that question. Could you repeat it?

[Mr. Ayers]. Well, the doctor does.

A. Dr. Dietz establishes by history that there was an episode of coughing and sneezing two days post-op.

Q. And is it also the case that the history of February 20 was not made available to you until just before this deposition?

A. That's correct.

Q. Let's go back to the April note of Dr. Dietz—April 14th, was it?

A. There was one, I believe, on April 24 and on April 21.

Q. Go back to the one you were reading before and would you read me the rest of that entry?

A. I quoted from the April 21st note. The rest of that paragraph, is that what you're considering?

Q. Yes.

A. In my estimation the disk herniation was not present at the first MRI scan and so it was extremely likely it was due to his coughing and sneezing episode two days after the surgery. The real question would be whether postoperative respiratory problems can be related to the surgery and that is the connection that I see between the two of those.

History Taken by Treating Physician

Q. And Dr. Dietz's opinion as expressed there is that there is a relationship to the surgery and the second herniation, is that correct?

A. That would appear to be the case.

Q. Dr. Dietz was the treating physician?

A. Yes.

Q. And had seen Mr. D. several times during this time period?

A. Yes.

Q. Do you have any reason to doubt Dr. Dietz's observations and his recording of basic history of events?

A. Well, the only issue that I see in that regard is that Mr. D. returned in February and we have an inaccurate recording as to whether it was right leg pain or left leg pain. The physical examination description would be more compatible with right leg pain. And then the next note occurs in April. And whether Dr. Dietz discerned at that time whether he was referring to right leg pain or left leg pain two months earlier is unknown.

Q. What are you saying? Do you think Dr. D. misread his own file?

A. If he read his own file it does not say whether it was right leg pain or left leg pain—

Q. I understand that. So the February 20th note just says he had a coughing fit and now he [claimant]'s in distress and he's had a lot of pain since the coughing fit. Okay. Now, in April he says I think that the second herniation is caused by the coughing fit, does he not?

A. Yes.

Q. My question is: Do you have any reason to doubt Dr. Dietz's evaluation of his own treatment and his own care?

A. Well, I have reason to doubt his conclusion in there as to which leg he was referring to two months earlier. I'm sure he sees lots of patients.

Q. You don't think Dr. Dietz knew that he was talking about the second herniation?

A. I believe that part of this could be cleared up if there are further records in Dr. Dietz's office where Mr. D. would have called and talked to a nurse. Because somebody scheduled an MRI scan in March. Mr. D. must have notified the office he is having problems in March. And perhaps there's a nurse's note about what happened, why the MRI was scheduled, and that is consistent with patient calling and still having left leg pain. Then I believe Dr. Dietz is referring to the left leg. But unfortunately, the reporting here is just not complete enough to draw an accurate conclusion.

Q. Is it the reporting that is not complete, or you haven't been given a full copy of the file?

A. I may not have a full copy of the file.

Permanent Impairment Rating

Q. When you assess PPI ratings, what method do you use?

A. I use the *AMA Guides to Evaluation of Permanent Impairment,* fourth edition.

Q. There are different methods with any *AMA Guides.* Which one do you use? DRE?

A. I do not use that one. I use the chart.

Q. And by the chart, what are you referring to?

A. I could produce the chart for you. It's a guide for impairment rating based upon diagnosis and procedure performed.

Q. Okay. I think that's what I'm referring to, diagnosis related estimates [DRE], as opposed, for instance, to range of motion [ROM].

A. That's correct. Range of motion is not taken into consideration.

Q. If it's not too much trouble, could you refer to the book and the chapter . . . so we've got a single reference?

A. Okay.

[Witness gets book and returns.]

A. This is the table I use.

Q. We're working with Table 75, page 113. And that's in the fourth chapter?

A. Yes.

Q. I take it from your earlier testimony that your diagnosis was, as your second opinion, that claimant did need surgery?

A. Yes, that it was appropriate.

Q. And if you had—did you have a procedure that you would have recommended and do you know what was done?

A. I would have done a microdiskectomy at L5–S1 on the left as performed by Dr. Dietz.

Q. Same procedure that was performed?

A. Yes.

Work History

Q. Do you have a record or any information on when Mr. D. did in fact return to work?

A. It may be contained in the records reviewed, but I did not specifically study that aspect.

Q. Who was it that you had contact with about this case originally?

A. H. B. was a rehabilitation nurse who referred Mr. D. to me for the second opinion. I sent her a copy of the report. And the only other communication I had is a notification of the desire to take my deposition, copies of the medical records, and then today.

Q. Did you ask H. B. for a more complete copy of I. O. records or . . . ?

A. No, I didn't.

Q. Do you know whether the I. O. treatment of the first surgery was all done for Workers' Comp? Do you have any idea?

A. I probably did at the time, although this would have to be reconstructed from my notes.

Q. Do you have any recollection at all or any indication that there was any problem with getting your records from I. O.?

A. No.

DRE Rating

Q. You have referred to the *AMA Guides.* Let me ask you, does double diskectomy fall within the chart on page . . . on chart number 75 on page 331?

A.   Under the category of intervertebral disk surgery, Mr. D. by my estimate would be placed in the category of surgically treated disk lesion with residual medically documented pain and rigidity. That category would receive a 10 percent whole-body permanent physical impairment, and also physical function to the whole body. Multiple operations—that is, a second operation—would add 2 percent. Multiple levels add 1 percent.

Q.   So then if we take these two, it would be 10 plus 2, plus 1?

A.   Which would be 13 percent whole-body physical impairment.

Q.   And that's under the *Guides* of . . . ?

A.   Yes.

Q.   And do you have a translational standard that you use, if any, to transfer the *Guides'* numbers to Indiana's statutory system?

A.   No, I wasn't aware that that takes place. I don't know anything about that.

[**Mr. Ayers**]. No other questions.

Redirect Examination of IME Physician

[By Ms. Estes].

Q.   Doctor, I believe you testified that Mr. D. was referred to you initially by H. B., a rehabilitation nurse?

A.   Yes.

Q.   And was it your understanding at that time that you were to evaluate Mr. D. and make a diagnosis and render an opinion regarding the cause of his medical condition as there was a dispute over that?

A.   Yes.

Q.   Do you feel that you had sufficient information at the time that you saw Mr. D. on May 4, 1998, to make that diagnosis and issue the report that you issued at that time?

A.   I relied upon the history given to me by the patient, which, if accurate, supports the conclusion that I derived.

Q.   You also had the benefit of some of Dr. B.'s reports at that time, did you not?

A.   Yes.

Q.   Reports which made reference to some kind of a coughing or sneezing fit?

A.   Yes.

Q.   So you were aware as early as the very first time you saw Mr. D. that there was a dispute involving causation relative to the second herniated disk, were you not?

A.   Yes.

Q.   And your opinion was, in fact, that that second herniated disk was not related?

A.   Mr. D. told me it occurred in March, and there was no inciting incident according to Mr. D.

Q.   The additional medical records that I provided to you after a lawsuit was filed and we realized that we would have to take your deposition in this case, were provided to you sometime within the past couple of weeks, were they not?

A.   Yes.

Q.   Did those records in any way change any of your opinions in this case?

A.   No.

Q. Doctor, you have been handed what has been marked Defendant's Exhibit F. Can you identify that document?

A. This is a note by Dr. Dietz dated March 24, 1998.

Q. And is there a history contained in that note?

A. Yes.

Q. What does that history say with regard to the onset of symptoms in Mr. D.'s left leg?

A. Quote, beginning two weeks ago he began to have left leg pain radicular in nature. Unquote.

Q. That would place the onset of Mr. D.'s left leg pain at approximately what date?

A. Early March of 1998.

Q. Is that consistent with the history that Mr. D. gave to you when he saw you on May 4, 1998?

A. Yes.

Q. Doctor, I am handing you Defendant's Exhibit G. Can you identify that document, please?

A. This is a back history form dated January 6, 1998, from the office of Dr. Dietz.

Q. Regarding Mr. D.?

A. Yes.

Q. Referring you to page 3 of that form, is there a section that identifies certain activities which cause a worsening of Mr. D.'s pain?

A. Yes.

Q. And what activities are checked as causing a worsening of Mr. D.'s pain?

A. Sneezing, standing, and walking, and in the morning.

Q. Would that indicate to you, Doctor, that Mr. D. had sneezed prior to the time the history was completed, certainly well prior to the time of the L5–S1 herniation, and had experienced pain as a result?

A. Yes.

Q. One last question, Doctor. I understand from the rehabilitation nurse that assisted Mr. D., H. B., you communicated your findings and opinions after your examination of May 4, 1998, to her. You have no reason to dispute that, do you?

A. No.

Recross-Examination of IME Physician by Employer's Counsel

[By Mr. Ayers]

Q. A couple of questions. You said earlier, Doctor, that this was an insidious condition.

A. Insidious by my history.

Q. And does "insidious" mean to you the same as "spontaneous"? Or does "insidious" mean that it's been there a while and it's just now being discovered?

A. When I use the term, perhaps it is being used loosely here. I'm referring to pain that develops for no apparent reason.

Q. Yes, but in this case you found a reason? You found a herniated disk?

A. Let me amend that.

Q. Okay.

A. A herniated disk that developed insidiously would be a herniated disk wherein there was no inciting factor identified.

Q. So you didn't figure out or you didn't find from the history, et cetera, the triggering event?

A. Correct.

Q. Would there be a triggering event in the case of a disk herniation?

A. Not necessarily. Most disk herniations occur for no apparent reason.

Q. Does that mean they occur without any trauma or—

A. Correct.

Q. That most times you don't know what the trauma or impact or force was?

A. Most of the time they occur without trauma or force.

Q. Then you're saying that most disk herniations are spontaneous?

A. Right.

Q. They just happen—not that you can't tell which particular thing caused them, but that nothing really caused them. They just happened because a person now is 43 instead of 42?

A. A herniated disk only occurs in a degenerative disk. It is not an isolated event. A disk herniation can be one final event occurring in a degenerative disk and it may occur for absolutely no identifiable reason at that time.

Q. What I want to do is distinguish between identifiable reason and no reason whatever. Is it fair to say that something happened that caused the disk to herniate between the time of the MRI that said it was okay and the MRI that said it was now herniated?

A. A pre-herniation MRI, the one obtained in December of 1997, showed that the disk was degenerative and protruding toward the left. Simply as a natural process of further deterioration . . . , the disk could herniate. And many patients report that they were doing nothing. They just got up out of bed; they were just sitting there; there was no inciting event when the pain developed.

Q. Got up out of bed. And do some patients report that they happen when they have sneezing fits or coughing fits?

A. I believe that I've had an occasional patient report that. Generally with sneezing, but I believe the disk pressure, the intradiscal pressure, is increased with sneezing or coughing. So that would be reasonable.

Q. So that is an event that could cause this?

A. Yes.

Q. When the injury occurs, when it involves a herniation, what is the course . . . typical course of symptomatology?

A. The typical course can be anything from a gradual onset of pain beginning in the buttock and extending distally over time to acute and severe incapacitating pain, all the way down the leg to the foot.

Q. So it is not atypical for someone to have an event and then for the discomfort to increase over time.

A. That's correct.

[**Mr. Ayers**]. I have no other questions.

[Whereupon, the deposition was concluded.]

§ 10.04 BILATERAL UPPER EXTREMITY INJURY*

The claimant in this case, R. Stephens, was a 49-year-old female material handler who developed pain and numbness in both hands. The worker was evaluated by a family physician who was not board certified. The rating doctor rated the impairment as 27 percent whole person under the fifth edition of the *AMA Guides.* This rating was the major issue in the following deposition. The rating doctor was critical of the *Guides* for being contradictory; he admitted he did not strictly follow the instructions in the *Guides* and based his opinion in part on his 35 years of experience.

Direct Examination of IME Physician by Claimant's Attorney

Preliminary Information

Q. Would you please state your name for the record.
A. D. B. Gibson, M.D.
Q. Are you a licensed, practicing physician in the state of Tennessee?
A. Yes.
Q. Doctor, do you have a curriculum vitae that shows your educational background, training, and experience?
A. Yes.
Q. I'll ask that a copy of that curriculum vitae be made the next numbered exhibit or the first numbered exhibit to your testimony.
A. I have it and I'm handing it to the court reporter.

[Ms. Bishop]. No objection.

[Exhibit No. 1 was marked for identification.]

IME and Impairment Rating

Q. Doctor, at the request of Attorney C. F., did you have occasion to do an independent medical evaluation on R. Stephens?
A. Yes.
Q. And I believe you did that on February 1, 2001?
A. That's right.
Q. I'm looking at a report dated February 10, 2001, that appears to encompass the scope of that evaluation: The history she gave you, your physical examination, your assessment of major life activities and daily living, and your impairment rating. It's composed of eight pages. Did you prepare that report in connection with your independent medical evaluation?
A. Yes.
Q. I ask that a copy of that document be made Exhibit No. 2 to your testimony.

[Ms. Bishop]. No objection.

---

*The authors wish to acknowledge the assistance of Linda J. Himilton Mowles, Esq., of Knoxville, Tennessee, in the preparation of this section.

[Exhibit No. 2 was later copied and marked for identification.]

Q.   Doctor, if you will, just tell us the scope of your examination.

A.   This was a neuromuscular and orthopedic examination of a 49-year-old lady who said that on September 20, 2001, she developed pain and numbness in both hands while working as material handler for _____ Company in Etowah, Tennessee.

She was subsequently, within a day or two as I understand it, seen by Dr. J. Killeffer, specialist in Knoxville. The records that I reviewed indicated that she did have problems in both wrists, although she had had carpal tunnel release, by Dr. Killeffer, I believe, from a 1999 injury.

My scope was to have her complete what is called a Patient Pain Drawing, which has a legend for marking on parts of the body pain or discomfort or any type of abnormal sensations, and she marked aching pains on the back of her neck and also across both shoulders. She put aching pains on the front of the wrists and palms and numbness across the palms and the fingertips.

After that I had her complete a two-page questionnaire called "Workplace Accident," on which she gave the answers to these questions that carry the patient through the chronology of what happened to her, what she said she had, and how she was treated, a review of her prior health, that is, prior to the September 2001 date, and the inquiry into her work history before she went to work for Johns Manville.

Also she gave me a brief resume of her treatment. However, it related primarily to Dr. Killeffer. I then went ahead before I saw her and after I saw her and read the records from Dr. Killeffer with respect to what he had done for her with respect to treatment.

Then I proceeded with a neuromuscular and orthopedic examination with particular attention to both upper extremities, and I included grip strength testing using the Jamar Dynamometer on both hands. I then looked at the *AMA Guides* in various sections that I considered to be pertinent with respect to her weakness in her hands and the tendinitis of both forearms, the loss of sensation in the fingertips of both hands.

An assessment of activities of daily living was made where [it was determined] that 16 activities, 15 or so, were interfered with or prevented apparently by these injuries. In other words, I looked at those activities that the injured parts depend upon. She had ranges of difficulty with respect to the arms, hands, and shoulders from "Some difficulty" to "Unable to do." The bearing of the weight on the hands was "Unable to do." The vast majority of the activities of daily living that she had trouble with were very difficult. That is, they were performable, but she had a great deal of difficulty.

Then as I went to the *AMA Guides*, fifth edition, . . . I found those areas in the *Guides* that pertained to her problems that I had found clinically and also with respect to the history, and I added them up according to the Combined Values. After getting them from the page citations, I used the Combined Values on page 604 and came up with an impairment rating of 27 percent whole person.

Q.   All right. Doctor, on page 5 of your report you list your impressions. Are those the impressions or diagnoses that you made after your examination?

A. That's right.

[**Ms. Bishop**]. I'm sorry, I couldn't hear you.

[**Mr. Moss**]. I asked him if the impressions listed on page 5 of his report were his diagnoses or impressions after his evaluation.

[**Ms. Bishop**]. Okay.

Q. [**Mr. Moss**]. Doctor, the opinions that you have expressed in this deposition and in your report, are those opinions within a reasonable degree of medical certainty?

A. They are.

Q. And I believe, as the report and your testimony indicates, your impairment rating was based upon the fifth edition of the American Medical Association's *Guides to Evaluation of Permanent Impairment.*

A. That's right.

[**Mr. Moss**]. That's all I have.

Cross-Examination by Defense Attorney

Qualifications of Physician

Q. Dr. Gibson, unfortunately, I don't have the ability to look at your CV, so I have a couple of questions. Do you have any sort of board certification, Doctor?

A. I am not board certified. I am a fellow of the American Academy of Family Physicians and now a life member of the American Academy of Family Physicians. I'm also a life member of the AMA.

Q. Okay. Do you currently have an active practice?

A. Yes. I do family practice and disability evaluations at _____, Cleveland, Tennessee, where I am at the moment.

Q. Okay. I understand that you do the disability evaluations, but you also maintain an active family practice?

A. That's right.

Q. Have you ever been sued for malpractice, Dr. Gibson?

A. No.

Q. I would like to, in order to clarify and clean up the record, make the pain drawing and the questionnaire the next collective exhibit to your evaluation.

A. All right.

Past Medical History

Q. Doctor, did you look at any diagnostic testing which had been performed by Dr. Killeffer?

A. I looked at the results and the interpretations of testing that had been done. I also looked at records that related to his statement concerning this lady's left wrist after the 1999 event, when he did carpal tunnel release. Then I also noted that he had statements that he made on January 16, 2001, on a page called Neurosurgical Follow-up. And I noted that there were differences of language in the two statements, that is, the 1999 impression versus the 2001 impression concerning the left wrist.

Q.   What were the differences, Doctor?

A.   In the 1999 neurosurgical follow-up—and I'm reading from June 15 (it's crossed out and says June 8, 1999)—by J. A. Killeffer, M.D., there is a paragraph where he gives an impairment rating. I only saw that this morning. I was given this by Mr. Moss, but I did not have this in my records. But I'm reading from the fact that in his last paragraph he does refer to how he arrived at a 10 percent mild impairment to the left upper extremity, and he made the statement, "I have no restrictions." And this is a reference to the left wrist.

Then when I compared it to the January 16, 2001, follow-up, I noted in the next to the last paragraph that the doctor, the same doctor, stated, "I suggested to her that she permanently avoid work that involves pressure on the left palm. She has symptoms of carpal tunnel syndrome on the right that are exacerbated by her work."

My question is why there were no restrictions placed in 1999, although the patient in her history says that she has repetitive pushing of a horn button with the left hand as she drives the forklift truck, so that there appeared to have been more activity involving the left palm after he gave her the 10 percent rating.

Q.   Are those the only two records of Dr. Killeffer's that you've looked at?

A.   There are some other statements here by him and I think that they have primarily to do with his clinical impression of both wrists. It's just the fact that, even though I saw the 10 percent rating here, I never did understand exactly why that there were no restrictions placed on her after the carpal tunnel release in 1999. And then historically, according to her testimony, she is working this left wrist, and, of course, the right wrist with the pulling of levers and pushing and so forth, I did not understand why she appeared to perform on the job or was required to perform on the job without any limitations.

Q.   Okay. So you're talking about after the 1999 injury.

A.   Yes. So that the question is, the 10 percent has been brought to my attention. Mr. Moss gave me this, and then I compared this to his statements. So I don't know really what the basis of the 10 percent [rating] was. I know that Dr. Killeffer in his letter here refers to a certain section in the *Guides* at that particular time. I believe that the burgundy book, as we called edition four, was being used at that particular time. There was no limitation put on her, apparently because she had no limitations. But if she had a 10 percent rating, I didn't understand why—unless he had second thoughts—he would go back on January 16, 2001, and say that she should be avoiding pressure on the left hand.

Effect of Previous Impairment Rating Under Fourth Edition

Q.   Does your impairment rating that you have given her include the 10 percent for the prior carpal tunnel surgery?

A.   It does not include it because I could not find a basis for it. And I really question whether or not he used a functional basis, that is, a performance basis. In my particular approach I use performance basis—that is, what activities do the injured parts depend upon. This lady had limitations in activities of daily living that she cannot do well because these activities depend on the injured parts.

Q. I'm not sure you understand my question, Doctor. So in your impairment rating you're assuming that she had no preexisting permanent partial impairment rating or award of vocational disability; is that correct?

A. That's correct. And it's also based on the fact that since she had no limitations placed on her at the worksite, as far as I can tell, she overrode any rating that she was given unless one says that she wasn't performing well with the left hand.

Job Requirements

Q. Did you go actually visit the job site or review a video of the job that Ms. Stephens was performing?

A. No, I didn't, so I'm depending on the accuracy of her statements as to what her job routine was.

Q. And in the event that those are different than what she revealed to you, your opinion could necessarily be very different. Is that correct?

A. Only if we look at the statements in the pages that were provided to me by someone who has a Ph.D., and apparently this was put in the records here, and it's a series of statements that describe the activities that she was apparently engaging in. There is a statement in here by a Ph.D. that has to do with the work scenario. If I found out that she was not indeed repeatedly using the left hand, the base of the hand, to push that horn and not repeatedly pulling with the right hand, as she said that she was, if I find that she was not doing that, that would change my opinion.

How Specifically the Doctor Performed His Rating

Q. All right. Now, the—I guess what you might refer to as the "green book" or fifth edition of the *AMA Guides*, can you explain to the Court please where you came up with your impairment rating for her? Let's go one by one. You've got sensory deprivation, page 482, Grade 4, for the left upper extremity.

A. Yes.

Q. Okay. I'm looking at that now, Doctor, and you refer to Table 16-10, Grade 4?

A. Yes.

Q. That talks about determining impairment for upper extremity due to sensory deficits or pain resulting from peripheral nerve disorders. Why was it more appropriate to use that than it was to use the section of the *AMA Guides* specifically dealing with carpal tunnel?

A. Because these nerves that are involved come out of the neck. And although the neck is not singled out, we know that the neck is involved. And the brachial plexus, which supplies the fingertips and the hand grip, come out of the neck at the mid level, C5 and C6 and C7, and course all the way through the shoulder. . . . The shoulders are sore, all the way down through the forearms, where she has tendinitis on each side, to the hand grips, which are diminished, and also the fingertips. So I felt that we should use the entire upper extremity, which is described in Table 16-10 on page 482.

Q. So does that rating that you've given include anything for carpal tunnel, Doctor?

A. It includes that portion of the nerve function that is related to carpal tunnel, especially on the right. In my report I said that she did not clinically have a positive Tinel's sign and negative on the left. But she did have a positive Tinel's sign, which means on the right. I am of the opinion that she does have carpal tunnel syndrome.

I use Grade 4 because if one looks at Table 16-10 one will find that this chart is inverted. This means that Grade 5 is the best on the left, Grade 0 is the worst. So when I'm giving her a Grade 4, I'm not giving her a heavy rating. I'm giving her a light rating because Grade 5 is zero deficit. So I'm only giving her the next to the best [rating], which is 1 to 25 percent, and I selected the number from that range and put it in the report.

Doctor Doesn't Follow Instructions in the Guides

Q. Okay. Did you follow the procedure for utilizing this chart as indicated on page 482?

A. No. I used what I consider the severity based on this ladder diagram. Since this ladder diagram goes from zero deficit to 100 percent deficit, I felt that she had mild impairment. And that's what Grade 4 would be, and that would be consistent with the language that Dr. Killeffer has used in the past.

Q. I'm looking, Doctor, at page 482, and it appears that Table 16-10 has a section classified as Section B, which utilizes a procedure for you to come up with an impairment rating under Table A using the Grade. Is that correct?

A. Yes. But procedure 4 refers to the brachial plexus, and I've already said that the brachial plexus supplies the entire hand and the entire upper extremity. So it is not necessary to delineate every nerve in the brachial plexus because the entire brachial plexus of this lady is involved, from the neck to the shoulders all the way down to the hand and fingertips. This is Grade 4, brachial plexus.

Q. So if I understand you, you did not utilize the procedure as set out in Table 16-10. Is that correct?

A. Sure. I used the brachial plexus. It says under Grade 4, for example, brachial plexus, so we have the brachial plexus. We can go to [Table] 16-14 if you want to, but it is not necessary to delineate the nerves in the brachial plexus that are going all the way to the fingertips because we know they run all the way from the last half of the neck all the way to the fingers and the thumb.

Q. I'd like to make this chart—Table 16-10, page 482, of the *AMA Guides,* fifth edition—the next exhibit, please.

A. All right.

[Page 482 was later marked Exhibit 4 for identification.]

Q. Would your testimony be the same then, Doctor, for the right upper extremity that you used again this Table 16-10 and did not use the procedure as set out in Table 16-10 in coming up with the 15 percent right upper extremity?

A. Yes, page 482, because I did refer to sensory deprivation in the right hand. That motor impairment, under the left upper extremity, should be page 509, because I'm referring to grip strength. So I said page 508. Under left extremity, my second statement should read "page 509." But it still comes out to be 20 percent upper extremity.

I also used the same table for the poor handgrip of the right hand. I showed in my chart that her handgrip is one-fourth to one-third of that expected, so that I get the 20 percent from page 509; the table that has to do with the middle grade of index of deficit is Table 16-34.

Q. Now, I'm going back to the motor impairment of the left upper extremity. I was just trying to utilize everything you used from one chart initially, Doctor.

A. That should read page 509.

Q. Okay. So going to page 509, this section specifically deals with the strength valuation, correct?

A. That's correct. There's no reference, though, to the strength of the shoulders or the upper arms. It only has to do with grip strength. That's what the reference is, so that's the reference that I went to.

Q. And you combined this with the page 482, 16-10 loss?

A. Yes, ma'am. The combination is allowable through page 604, Combined Values.

Q. Where did you come up with what her grip strength should be?

A. Based on 60 pounds, as the average grip strength for a lady of her age should be about 60 pounds, and that is in the Jamar chart that comes with the device.

Q. Do you have any idea what her grip strength was after her carpal tunnel surgery in the left hand?

A. Not unless Dr. Killeffer knows that. And I would also ask whether he included grip strength in his 10 percent? That is a valid question. I wonder if he included any loss of grip strength in his 10 percent.

Prior Loss of Grip Strength

Q. Well, my question to you, Doctor, is: Do you have any idea whether she suffered a loss of grip strength after undergoing carpal tunnel surgery on the left hand?

A. I have no information that she did suffer a loss.

Q. You don't know that she had an average grip strength in the left hand of a woman of her age after her left carpal tunnel surgery, right?

A. Not unless Killeffer said so.

Q. And the last page of your impairment rating, Doctor, has to do with the loss of her ability to function in her daily life. Is that correct?

A. Activities of daily living are delineated on page 583. As far as the importance of it, I might have made a reference here to page 582, but really I believe it's—

Q. I've got [page] 572 in your—

A. It's page 573. . . . My reference was to [page] 572. Section 18.3d, which I referred to, is really on page 573, and the key statement there is that the ADL [activities of daily living] deficits are given the greatest weight in considering the pain factor as impacting function.

Q. Okay. So you're now saying it should be [page] 572, paragraph 18.3d?

A. Well, Section 18.3d is on page 573. That is my error . . . referring to 572. It's page 573. There is also a reference, though, to other sections, and I did refer to page 578. But Section 18.3d is on page 573.

Probing for Potential Bias

Q. Doctor, do you do any disability ratings for employers?

A. We have in the past. They're very few.

Q. How many cases on an annual basis, just average, does the law firm of _____ submit to you?

A. We probably do about 15 to 25 per year.

Q. And how many do you do on an annual basis?

A. Fifteen to 25 per year.

Q. So all of the disability ratings that you do come from the law firm of _____?

A. Oh, no. We evaluate injured persons that come from various legal representatives and sources, and I have actually been asked to do impairment ratings for carriers.

Q. What percentage of your business comes from _____'s law firm?

A. Oh, probably a third.

Q. And what were you paid for performing this IME?

A. I believe I charged $650. I would have to verify that. That is, that is what I charge. I don't know whether that's been paid or not.

Activities of Daily Living

Q. Page 573, Section 18.3d, specifically says that the system relies specifically on self-reports by individuals. Correct?

A. That's right. But my ADL assessment is challengeable because these are performance activities, and therefore I delineate subjective versus objective. If a person says "I have a headache," I cannot demonstrate that with a performance. If a person says, "I can't twist off a jar lid," the person can be challenged to perform that.

Q. Well, how many performance things did you have her do?

A. I did not have her do all of the things, but just some of them, in the grip strength testing. Most of these I did not, but these are challengeable. And all of the ADL assessments here are challengeable if one wants to observe the patient in the life routines.

Q. But you did not challenge any of them, correct?

A. Well, I can't challenge [the carrying of] the bag of groceries and the bag of garbage because I am not at her house. I did have her shake hands with me, and I noticed that she could not shake hands in a normal manner with her right hand.

Q. All of these are self-reported limitations in the ADL on the chart that you had her fill out, correct?

A. That's right. But as far as bearing weight on her hands, I say she is unable to do that. It means she could be placed on her stomach, on her abdomen, on the floor and asked to do one, two, or three push-ups. But she cannot do that because of the soreness of her hands and wrists.

Q. But you did not ask her to do that, did you, Doctor?

A. Well, I don't want to tort the patient.

Q. So again, this is all subjective reporting. Although it can be challenged, you did not challenge or confirm it by any mechanism, did you?

A. That is correct. One who challenges it should be very wise so as to not injure the patient.

Q. I'd like to make a copy of page 573 and the corollary where it refers back to Table 18.1, and make that page the next exhibit to your deposition, Doctor.

[**Mr. Moss**]. No objection.

A. All right.

[Pages 571 and 573 were later marked Exhibit 5 for identification.]

Conversion to Whole-Person Impairment

Q. If I understand the pain impairment, Doctor, this should be to the body as a whole. Is that not correct?

A. It is, yes, ma'am.

Q. But you've got it listed as 25 percent to the upper extremity, correct?

A. No. On the last page I have it converted according to page 439, if one wants to go there. But actually what I did was I took the upper extremity values and combined them, getting a total upper extremity rating. And then after that I converted it to the body as a whole.

Q. I understand that you combined all your ratings to the body as a whole utilizing the combined values chart.

A. Yes.

Q. But the chronic pain factor that you list under No. 3, where did you get that rating to the upper extremity? You say page 572, Section 18.3d. I don't see a chart and table there.

A. There is not a chart or a table. It's based on my training and experience.

Q. Does it not say . . . Where are you getting the 25 percent to upper extremity?

A. I'm sorry, I didn't understand that. The 27 percent whole person is from the conversion factor.

Q. Where are you getting the 25 percent listed for chronic pain, Doctor?

A. That's based on interference with or prevention of 16 activities of daily living and the pain in these areas related to those activities. Those activities depend on the injured parts, and I estimate that as 25 percent impairment.

Q. Okay. But there is not a chart or a table in the *AMA Guides* that gives you that number, is there?

A. That's correct. But the ADL deficits are given the greatest weight and therefore I stand on that.

Q. And again, those were all subjective, correct?

A. Well, they're challengeable. Also, I'd like to make the statement that if you look at the ADL assessments, it takes motor activity to reach overhead or bend over and pick up objects off the floor. That might have to do with the grip strength, but it might not. But the reaching of the arms and the shoulders, some of these ADLs are not verified nor substantiated by grip strength testing. The bearing of the weight on the hands and twisting off a jar lid would relate to hand strength, but the carrying of groceries and a heavy load would relate to the entire arm strength and the pull on the shoulder.

So that all of these things that are in the ADLs, some of them overlap with the grip strength, but many of them have to do with the part of the arm above the wrist, have to do with the tendinitis and also the soreness that she has in her shoulders.

Q. If I'm reading Section 18.3d correctly, Doctor, it appears that the *Guides* say that you should increase the impairment rating up to 3 percent.

Doctor Criticizes the Guides *and Deviates from Them*

A. That's using their algorithm, which is a labyrinthine approach, very ambiguous and has nothing to do with performance. They even make the statement that pain is subjective and is self-reporting. I say that 15 to 16 of these activities that I have pointed out are challengeable because they are activities that the patient either can or cannot perform.

Q. Even though the *Guides* say that you can increase the impairment rating by up to 3 percent, you opted to give an additional 25 percent to the upper extremity. Is that correct?

A. Yes. Because I disagree with the fact that the *Guides* contradict themselves by saying that pain is subjective, and then link it to ADLs. If they're going to link it to ADLs in Section 18.3d, then the pain impacts function. And I say that her activities, 15 to 16 of them, depend on the injured part and therefore they are pain related.

Q. So is it a fair statement to say that some of the numbers that you've relied on in your report do not agree with the *AMA Guides*?

A. I don't agree with their contradiction. I do not believe that pain is totally subjective if in 18.3d they say that ADL deficits are given the greatest weight. If ADL deficits, what the patient cannot do, are given greater weight, they are performance deficits, and performance deficits are not totally subjective because they're challengeable.

Q. You opted not to use the number set out by the *Guides* and rely instead on your own. . . .

A. I say that the *Guides* are contradictory and that's—I don't believe I'm under a mandate to follow contradictions in the *Guides*.

[**Ms. Bishop**]. Thank you very much, Doctor.

[**Mr. Moss**]. Ms. Bishop, can we agree that the activities of daily living that have been discussed are a part of Dr. Gibson's report that was Exhibit 1?

[**Ms. Bishop**]. I want a copy of his whole chart and that's going to be the workplace accident, the pain drawing, his report, and this ADL assessment.

Q. [**Ms. Bishop**]. Doctor, this ADL assessment is something that you utilize. It's not something that's come out of the *Guides*. Is that right?

A. Well, I derived it from the *Guides,* because when I first got this book I read it from cover to cover. And since they put the emphasis on the ADL deficits, I asked myself what deficits are they talking about. I looked at all the parts of the body that they allow, some of them come from my 35 years of experience, and I came up with a two-page list.

Q. Again, that's something you created, correct?

A. I created out of experience and also out of the *Guides*.

Q. Created by yourself, though, right? It's not something that has come out of a treatise or anything else; it's something that you've created on your own.

A. No. It's not de novo. All I am doing is extracting and deducing what is in the *Guides* plus my experience. All these things here I already knew. I didn't know whether the *Guides* would allow some of these things. There are places in the *Guides* where you can find out what arms and legs and necks and shoulders and hands do, and I came up with it that way.

[**Ms. Bishop**]. Okay. That's fine. . . . Whatever is in his chart can be made an exhibit. If you want to just do one collective exhibit of everything that's there, that's fine.

[**Mr. Moss**]. All right. I just wanted to make sure we had everything.

[**Ms. Bishop**]. That's fine.

§10.05 ULNAR NERVE INJURY[*]

In this deposition, the employer's counsel was successful in getting the claimant's physician, Dr. Auerbach, to admit that he had deviated from the *Guides*. In the end, the administrative law judge chose not to accept the employee's physician's rating and accepted, instead, the 0 percent rating provided by the employer's physician. See digest of the case *Williams v. FEI Installation*, 2005 WL 3488386 (Ky. Ct. App. Dec. 22, 2005), in §11.14 of this volume. Portions of the deposition are reproduced below.

Preliminaries

[By Mr. Brown].

Q. Dr. Auerbach, my name is B. Brown, and I'm representing the employer of R. Williams in his workers' compensation claim. . . . Have you had the opportunity to see Mr. Williams as part of your practice here?

A. Yes, sir.

Q. Okay, and at whose request was that?

A. At Mr. Jennings' request.

Q. And do you recall the date of that examination?

A. The 2nd of March of this year.

Missing Medical Records

Q. Okay. And did you prepare a report as a part of that examination?

A. Yes, I did.

Q. Okay. That has already been filed into evidence. At the end of that report, it says: "I have none of his medical records, but once I have reviewed them—received and

---

[*] The authors wish to acknowledge the assistance of Chad Jennings, Esq., in the preparation of this section.

reviewed them, I will make additional comments and complete the questionnaire that was provided." Have you now completed that questionnaire, as well?

A. Yes, sir.

Q. And that has also been filed into evidence. My question to you is: What medical records did you receive in between making the two reports?

A. The only report I have is the report of February 6, 2004, by his—by Dr. Kilambi.

Q. When did you receive that?

[Dr. Auerbach examines documents.]

A. I don't know. I have May 5th.

Q. Okay.

A. . . . That must have been the date that it was sent.

Q. Okay. Could I see that report, sir? [Report is passed to Mr. Brown.] Thank you.

A. That was the last. . . . They sent a lot of other information for my review on that. I can give you that, too.

Q. Did all of it come together?

A. Yes.

Q. So you have all of Dr. Kilambi's records?

A. Yes.

Q. Okay. Are those the only—

A. Well, these—

Q. I'm sorry. Go ahead.

A. These are still all his records. These are all Kilambi's records.

Q. Okay.

A. May 5th.

Q. Okay. What specifically was it in the records that you received from Dr. Kilambi's records that allowed you to make that supplemental report?

A. I didn't have anything. I just wanted to know exactly. . . . My information, at the time, came primarily from the patient. And from my examining him. I know what his history is. I could see his incision, and so I knew the nature of the surgery. . . . But I want to know exactly what he did.

History Received from Claimant

Q. Okay. What history did you receive from Mr. Williams as far as what type of work he performed?

A. Well, he said he did construction work. And he was working for a millwright, I gather. And from what he told me, that was a pretty physical type of work.

Impairment Rating

Q. Now, you've directed us to Table 16-15 in the fifth edition of the *AMA Guides,* as far as your impairment rating is concerned.

A. Okay.

How Did Physician Come Up with Number?

Q. Could you explain to me and the judge how you came about—I believe you gave—a total of a 7 percent impairment rating.

A. Well, this decision was which way to go, and I probably—I just reread my records today—I may be a little bit on the low side. I used the number one, you understand, he had an injury involving the ulnar nerve.

Q. Yes, Doctor.

Unconvincing Explanation

A. And it had to be moved. It was a pretty serious procedure. You then transfer the nerve anteriorly, and it remains severely vulnerable, because it's no longer in its usual protected area.

But I still chose to use Table 16-15, which probably isn't that accurate for this kind of thing. But you could use that for—where you have a sensory impairment. . . . Actually, he [Mr. Williams] has residual weakness of the hand grasp. But I thought it was maybe a little early; that with time, maybe he would recover additional strength. Because by the Jamar measurements that I gave, you'll note that he's a dominant—right-hand—person, but the left hand is stronger than the right side.

It might have been even more appropriate to go to the other section of the *AMA Guidelines,* where the loss of grip strength could be done, but it happens that I used 5 percent for the upper extremity, for the involvement of the ulnar nerve. But to not use the combined motor sensory, which would have—I'd given him a higher rating, because I didn't think he was that weak. But anyway, I did [give] the 7 percent [rating] to the upper extremity, which translated to 4 percent to the body as a whole. And I thought he had enough discomfort to give him, from the pain thing, the added 3 percent.

Q. Doctor, is 7 percent the maximum amount that Table 16-15 allows?

A. No. If I had plugged into this the—the weakness—now, if this exam had been, let's say, six—years, right—years after the—the injury, with his weakness, I would have probably gone to the 50 percent to the upper extremity.

Q. Okay. And then as far as the sensory, is 7 percent the highest that Table 16-15 allows?

A. All I'm allowed, yes.

Witness Asked to Refer to Instructions in the Guides

Q. Okay. Does Table 16-15 direct you to—I believe it's Table 16-10—to determine what the sensory deficit is?

A. Well, if you use this enough that you get a—you—you can do things this way, as well. And I thought he had, you know, a deficit. He didn't have total loss.

Q. Okay.

A. So that—this is a judgment call.

Q. How much loss—under Table 16–10 on page 482—would you say Mr. Williams demonstrated?

A. I'd have probably put it in class 2, and not at 1 or zero.

Q. Okay. Class 2. Would that be 1 to 25 percent?

A. No, that'd be 61 to 80 [percent].

Q. 61 to 80? And based on what physical findings would you put him at 61 to 80 percent?

A.   Well, now, initially he was totally numb. Then he recovered. But by the time I saw him, he said that the numbness wasn't . . . I'm looking at Table 16-15. And so that I hadn't weighed it all together. I just went to the 7 percent.

Q.   But doesn't Table 16-15 direct you to this table so that you can then take the percentage you get from Table 16-10 and multiply it by the 7 percent?

Doctor Concerned That Following the Guides Would Result in Underrating

A.   Yeah, I agree with that. But I was concerned that I was underrating him for the seriousness of his injury and the surgery.

Q.   Okay. My question wasn't whether you could have done it that way. It was whether the *AMA Guides* send you there to do that?

A.   I could have.

Extent of Pain

Q.   Okay. Was his pain preventing any activities at that time—at the time of your examination?

A.   I always thought he would not be able to do the kind of work that he did before.

Q.   In your report, did you not say that he should give it a try?

A.   Well, he has to make a living, and that's the only thing he's trained to do. And he's 54 years of age, and if he could do it, you know, that's fine. Sometimes, employers can be helpful and make some allowances and keep the [employees] away from doing the repetitive heavy lifting.

Work History of Claimant

Q.   Did Mr. Williams tell you about the supervisory positions that he has held as a millwright?

A.   He told me he did construction; it varied. Sometimes he worked with conveyors; sometimes he did overhead work. And [he] once worked for the fire department.

Close Questioning on the Guides

Q.   Okay. Going back to Table 16-15. That sensory deficit—that also takes into account pain. Is that correct?

A.   . . . That is a sensory, and the 3 percent of pain is a judgment. . . . Under the section on pain, the—it's a little bit more specific in the spine, where the ratings allow—give—you a very close choice.

Q.   Going back to the very last medical record you have on Mr. Williams from Dr. Kilambi, did it indicate that he was experiencing any extensive amount of pain?

[Dr. Auerbach examines documents.]

A.   No, it said that his hypersensitivity is much improved. And of course, I saw him after this report. I saw him a month later.

Doctor Admits Not Following "Complicated" Guides but Using "Own Judgment" Instead

Q. And under what section of the *AMA Guides* and table did you assess the 3 percent pain rating, Doctor?

A. Under the pain section, I've allowed up to 3 percent. [Examines documents.] It has a formula that is very complicated. . . . I tried using the scoring system and using . . . I just used my own judgment. Overall, it was in my judgment that this was probably an acceptable rating, thinking in terms that his strength would improve. . . . But I have some concerns that I maybe have undervalued what his rating probably should be.

Doctor Makes Powerful Admission

Q. Okay. So, Doctor, are you kinda just throwing the 3 percent impairment rating for pain in to get to where you think you should be, or . . . ?

A. Probably.

Q. Okay.

A. I've been doing this a long time.

Doctor Again Questioned on Following the Guides

Q. Sure. Going back to the section of the *Guides* that you gave your rating in. . . . In order to make a diagnosis of entrapment or compression, it requires the examiner [one], to have a history of the symptoms; two, objective clinical signs and findings on detailed examination; and three, documentation by electroneuromyographic studies. Did you have any studies performed, or have any studies at your disposal to look at?

A. Are you asking me . . . whether I questioned the need for the surgery?

Q. No, I was just—

A. Because I don't want to get into that.

Q. No, I'm not questioning the need for the surgery. I'm just citing to you what the *Guides* say in order to make the diagnosis, because the *Guides* then go on to say: To have an impairment rating, you have to have the diagnosis.

A. Well, he had studies done originally that I'm sure satisfied Dr. Kilambi that he was justified in doing the movement of the ulnar nerve out of its position—to transfer it inferiorly.

Q. Did you review those studies, Doctor?

A. I really don't remember. I wasn't questioning that the man had enough of an injury that it warranted moving it. I know that there was a referral to the EMG studies, but I don't see that I have a copy of those that were made. I'm not questioning if the surgery was necessary.

Basis for Opinions on Restrictions

Q. Okay. Doctor, looking at your restrictions, you've checked that he should never crawl. What prevents him from being able to crawl?

A.   Well, it's a lot of . . . depends, you know, on your arm. I'm not always happy with the questions that I'm asking . . . , but rather than make a federal case out of it—and just like when you ask me: "How much weight can a guy lift?" Well, I put in the numbers to satisfy whoever is asking, because they obviously don't really understand that if you don't tell me how they are lifting, or what they are lifting, what I'm telling you isn't worth anything anyway. You may be able to lift 50 pounds safely if it's in front of you and you lift with your legs, with your back straight; on the other hand, if you're lifting things that weigh two pounds, repetitively, where you have to reach in for them with your knees straight, then you're going to get into trouble if you're someone who has a back problem. So if you don't tell me exactly what you're doing, I take a guess at some numbers that I think will make you happy and then you'll leave me alone.

Q.   These restrictions you put on bending, twisting, turning, sitting, standing, walking—you've limited that to two to four hours per day. Is that due to the injury to his elbow?

A.   Well, sometimes it's a matter of just common sense. Usually, in things like this it's a little more applicable in someone with back injuries, where anyone who's had spine surgery, for example, no matter how good the outcome is, if the job is heavy lifting or repetitive bending, they're going to get in trouble sooner or later. Maybe not this year, but it'll happen again in the next year or two. And here you've got an ulnar nerve in an abnormal place. And I have to tell you that, in my experience, the transfer of the ulnar nerve usually isn't this successful. And when you flex your elbow, you're gone—if you flex it all the way, you're going to compress the nerve anteriorly and you may irritate it, so that you have to be careful of what you're doing.

Q.   Okay.

A.   Or you may find that your—that it's not been particularly successful.

Wrap Up

Q.   Okay. Doctor, have all your answers to my questions today been within the realm of reasonable medical probability?

A.   I really believe so.

Q.   Is that your signature, Doctor?

A.   Yeah.

   [Mr. Brown]. Okay, Thank you very much.

§ 10.06   BACK INJURY*

   The following is a portion of the testimony of the plaintiff's physician in the case of *Brasch-Barry General Contractors v. Jones*, 175 S.W.3d 81 (Ky. 2005). (See case summary in § 11.14 in this volume.) Dr. Reasor, the plaintiff's treating doctor, testified that the plaintiff received a category IV, 26 percent impairment

---

* The authors wish to acknowledge the assistance of attorney Kenneth Nevitt in the preparation of this section.

rating. On cross-examination, Dr. Reasor admitted that he did not follow the "textbook definition" provided by the *Guides* in assigning the impairment rating. The ALJ in this case awarded 26 percent impairment, and the employer appealed, without first requesting a rehearing. At issue in the case was whether the ALJ's acceptance of the 26 percent rating, which deviated from the *Guides,* was a question of law that allowed for direct appeals to the board or a question of fact that prohibits appeals unless a motion for rehearing is made. The Kentucky Supreme Court held that the ALJ's acceptance of a rating that deviated from the *Guides* was a question of law, not of fact. Therefore, the board's throwing out of the 26 percent impairment rating was affirmed.

Preliminaries

[By Mr. Harding].

Q. Please state your name for the record.
A. It's G. L. Reasor.
Q. Doctor, you have had the opportunity to treat J. Jones, is that correct?
A. Yes, it is.
Q. And did you write a letter on November 4, 2002, to S. Lilly setting out your thoughts as to the extent of Mr. Jones' functional impairment?
A. Let me find that. I am sure if you have got a copy, I did. What is the date on that letter?
Q. November 4, 2002.
A. Yes, I did.
Q. And in that letter you set out your thoughts as to this gentleman's functional impairment, is that correct?
A. Yes. That is in the second full paragraph.

Questioned on Written Report

Q. Okay. I would like to ask you a couple of questions with regard to that. I would like to direct your attention to Table 15.3 appearing on page 384. This gentleman had what type of surgical procedure?

Doctor Not Wholly Familiar with Medical History

A. I will have to look at my chart. Let me go back and look at his initial H and P. I apologize. It looks like this chart has been taken apart and put together a couple of times. Things are kind of out of order.

Now, his initial H and P occurred on May 22, 2000, and at that time he was seen just for a lumbar strain. He eventually underwent surgery with Dr. Guarnaschelli. Let's find the date of that surgery. It looks like November 7, 2001. What I have on my note dated November 27, 2001, is that he . . . that is a procedure we did. . . . Yes, we had seen him on October 16, 2001. . . . He was seen in July 2000, and we kind of lost the follow-up. He came back in

October 16, 2001, stating that he had a two-level lumbar laminectomy and diskectomy done by Dr. Guarnaschelli, and I am not sure I have a copy of his op note in my chart. But in any event, that is what he told me that he had had.

Which DRE Category Should Worker Have Been Placed In?

Q. Okay. Doctor, under Table 15.3 of the DRE, if you have a back surgery of that sort, doesn't that fit under DRE lumbar category III—as opposed to IV?

[Mr. Harding hands Dr. Reasor the text.]

A. Yes. Let's look at this. Okay. DRE section III, or category III, states . . . and there are three categories here . . . the second category says high history of herniated disk with a level and onset would be expected to have objective findings. It says radiculopathy or individuals who had surgery for radiculopathy, but are now asymptomatic, and [when] you look at DRE category IV, the last part of the first paragraph says [individuals that] have had successful or unsuccessful attempts at surgical arthrodesis. Okay, so your question is whether or not he fits into category III or category IV?

Q. Yes. It looks like category IV is referring to a fusion, which he did not have. Category III is referring, it seems—and I am just a lawyer, that is why I am asking you—to more of this gentleman's condition, and I realize you have got some other aspects that go into your impairment [rating], but just as a baseline are we talking about . . . 10 to 13 percent, plus whatever pain factors fit on top of that?

A. Maybe. But if you look at category III, it talks about people who have had their disks repaired and are now asymptomatic, and he is still symptomatic for back and leg pain.

Q. No. It says here significant signs of radiculopathy, such as dermatomal pain and/or dermatomal distribution, sensory loss, loss of relevant reflexes, loss of muscle strength, et cetera, so category III is contemplating a symptomatic individual.

A. Well, I guess we would have to look at—

Q. Is that correct?

A. Well, look, you read this second paragraph here—

Q. The second paragraph says "or." It's preceded by "or." So that is the second category, but he fits definitely within the situation of significant signs of radiculopathy, such as dermatomal pain and/or dermatomal distribution, sensory loss, loss of relevant reflexes, loss of muscle strength or major unilateral atrophy above or below the knee, doesn't he? In fact, he is better than that?

A. Yes, but he is still symptomatic because of pain.

Q. Right, but you've got another category for pain. I am going to get to that in a minute. But in terms of the baseline we are looking at, the Claimant didn't have a fusion, did he?

A. No, not that I know of.

Q. Okay. And have you reviewed any flexion/extension radiographs?

A. Let me see if I looked at those. I don't recall if we have got those on there or not. No, I don't have any flexion/extension radiographs on that chart.

Q. Did he have a compression fracture?

A. No. He has disk problems.

Q. All right. So basically what we have just described, a fusion or a compression fracture greater than 50 percent, falls under DRE category IV—is that correct?

A. Yes.

Q. Okay. DRE Category III, though, encompasses a person who has symptoms as a result of having undergone a diskectomy or surgery such as that experienced by the Claimant, isn't that correct?

A. It's one way for us to be able to judge it, correct, but I still look at that when it says "or." That means we have to look at the other situation, too, where in the second paragraph it says the Claimant has a history of a herniated disk, had the surgery, but now is asymptomatic, and he still—

Q. Well, no, it doesn't say. Well, if you look here at the whole thing, it says history of herniated disk at the level on the site that would be expected from an objective clinical finding that would be associated with radiculopathy or individuals within that phrase or individuals who have had surgery for radiculopathy that are now asymptomatic. So he has had surgery for a herniated disk, and under the first part of that he is still having problems?

A. He is still symptomatic.

Doctor Holds Ground on Category, Then Offers to Split the Difference

Q. Yes, so he would fit under DRE lumbar category III, wouldn't he?

A. [No response.]

Q. He doesn't fit under IV?

A. If we could do III and a half, I will split the difference with you.

Q. Well, then my analysis—

A. Unfortunately, they don't have that in the book.

Q. Right, but your baseline is category III, wouldn't you agree?

A. Oh, I just—

Q. In fact, he could fit under category II, couldn't he?

A. Oh, only because he, in my opinion, is at least a category IV. So, if that is the case then, if you look at the hierarchy, then I, II, and III fit under IV.

Q. Well, but IV encompasses a fusion?

A. Um-hmm, or he has had attempts at surgical arthrodesis, that is true.

Q. And he has not had that?

A. No, he hasn't had that.

Doctor Again Refuses to Budge on Category

Q. Okay. So we are looking at lumbar category III or less?

A. [No response.]

Doctor Testifies That the **Guides** *Are "Flawed"*

Q. The book perhaps is flawed?

A. Yes.

Q. And I understand you are sitting here, and you are struggling with that concept like many physicians do. . . . But, if you just look at the black-and-white text here it would seem to suggest that your baseline for developing an impairment falls under lumbar category III, doesn't it?

A. Yes.

Activities of Daily Living

Q. Okay. Now, let's discuss this gentleman's activities of daily living. Did you record some of his activities of daily living?

A. I think initially he states on the last—the last office visit was October 29—when he said that standing and walking aggravate the pain. As far as being able to feed himself, and dress and take care of personal hygiene, he does not appear to be significantly impaired with that.

Q. Okay. He is able to travel?

A. Um-hmmm.

Q. He is able to have a relatively normal sexual function, assuming he is in a relationship?

A. I have not asked him if he is having problems with his sexual activity.

Q. Communication. Is he able to write, type, see, hear, speak?

A. Yes.

Q. Okay. He didn't tell you, and I don't mean while attempting to work—but, outside of work, is he able to stand or sit?

A. For limited periods of time, yes.

Q. Recline, walk, climb stairs?

A. Yes.

Q. Okay. Has he made any modifications that you have recorded in his housing that would indicate a limitation?

A. No. Not that he reported.

Q. What about—did you record anything about his sleep?

A. Not recently.

Q. And if he had come in. . . . You take a history from people when they come in?

A. Yes.

Q. So if he had continued to have a sleeping disorder or a problem, you would have recorded that?

A. We would have talked about that, yes.

Q. Okay. Does he have any problem with grasping with his hands, lifting, tactile discrimination with his fingers at all?

A. Not with his upper extremities, no.

Current Status

Q. Have you had a good result from your surgery from what you can tell?

A. We have been able to take care of some of his pain. Still, if you look at that office note dated October 2002, he still rates his pain as 8 out of 10, but he says he is improved some.

Psychological Testing

Q. Did you take him through or have him undergo any psychological or psychiatric testing or refer him out for any prior to installation of your therapeutic advice?

A. Yes, we did.

Q. And what type of examination did you give him or where was he sent?

A. Let me see if I can find that. Here we go. Let's go off the record while I try to find this again.

[A discussion off the record was had.]

A. Here we go. Yes, he was seen by Dr. B. Monsma, who is a licensed clinical psychologist. The date of his exam was December 19, 2001.

Q. Could I see a copy of that, please?

A. I don't have a copy. You can see the original.

Q. Or original. I can see right off the bat that this psychologist Monsma took an inaccurate history of surgery as set out under his Axis 3. Did you provide him with any medical notes as to this gentleman's actual problem?

A. Typically, we make the referral. I don't usually send all of my notes over, but we do let the psychologist know that we are contemplating either a spinal cord stimulator or pain implant, and then the psychologist gets the history from there and makes his decisions.

Diskectomy Versus Fusion

Q. He recorded that this gentleman underwent a lumbar fusion and, as you pointed out by the records of Dr. Guarnaschelli, he did not undergo a fusion. There is a difference between the type of surgery that Dr. Guarnaschelli performed, between that and a fusion, is there not?

A. Yes. We just did a diskectomy. That is different from a fusion.

Q. And a fusion has a significantly longer period of recovery, doesn't it? It is a much more involved procedure and sometimes can involve multiple procedures, because you have to harvest donor grafts and things of that nature?

A. It's more complicated. But since I don't do fusions, I can't give you all of the specific details on that.

Psychological Contraindication to an Implanted Pain Device

Q. Okay. And basically did you ask him to address the question as to whether or not this individual could handle receiving morphine?

A. Well, actually, he wanted to know if there was any sort of psychological contraindication to an implanted device.

Q. And what type of problems are you looking for?

A. We are looking for problems with untreated depression, unrecognized—other unrecognized—mental illnesses, problems with substance abuse that have either been untreated or treated in the past that might pose problems with what we are talking about doing.

Q. Do you know how he verified whether or not this gentleman has any type of substance abuse?

A. I am assuming he went through the history, and it has been a while since I read the report.

Q. Okay. Do you recall if Mr. Jones had a history—a family history of alcoholism?

A. I don't recall. I don't recall Mr. Jones having any personal problems. I don't recall the family history. Typically, family history, if it doesn't affect the individual, is not going to come into a great deal of play when we make our decisions.

Q. Dr. Monsma says that he performed a Minnesota Multiphasic Personality Inventory. Do you know whether or not he had him undergo that test within the protocol of the MMPI test?

A. No, I don't know how he had the test.

Q. Did you have this gentleman undergo any type of psychiatric examination—that is, a medical examination that could ascertain the presence or absence of chemical insufficiencies, conditions of that nature that only a psychiatrist, as opposed to a psychologist, would be able to determine?

A. No. We just did a psychological evaluation.

Pain Rating Under the Guides

Q. Did you do the pain protocol as set out by the *AMA Guides?*

A. You are talking about the guidelines in the fifth edition?

Q. Yes, sir.

A. I would have to review those guidelines in particular, but as far as us asking the usual questions of location, intensity, things that aggravate, things that relieve, and how the pain interferes with his activities, I think we [were] fairly comprehensive in our approach initially and also when we worked him up for his pump.

Q. Doctor, let me attach a copy of that psychologist's report.

[The report was marked Defendant Employer Exhibit 1 for identification and was offered in evidence.]

Doctor Admits to Not Using Guides *Pain Protocol*

Q. My question is, did you use the pain protocol as set out in the fifth edition of the *AMA Guides?*

A. Specifically, no, I did not.

Q. Did you do any Waddell testing of this gentleman?

A. I think in the original time I saw him, but that was prior to his surgery, we may have done some, but as far as the specific axial loading, and checking for non-dermatomal pain, things of that nature, no, I did not.

Q. All right. Do you actually look for clinical findings when you examine a patient such as Mr. Jones?

A. Well, my clinical findings—what exactly do you mean?

Failed Back Surgery Syndrome

Q. You have made a diagnosis of him—chronic lumbar radiculopathy and failed back surgery syndrome. Let me back up a second and ask you a couple of questions. The diagnosis of failed back surgery syndrome—does that refer to the fact that an individual has undergone a back surgery and for whatever reason is experiencing an inordinate amount of pain afterward?

A. Yes.

Q. Okay. And what is lumbar arachnoiditis?

A. That is where you have a scar formation that occurs in the arachnoid layer, and, if you look at the way the tissues surround the thecal sac and also the spinal cord, the arachnoid layer lays between the pia mater and the dura mater, and typically that should be very loose, very flexible, and with arachnoiditis becomes scarred down and can cause the individual pain because nerve roots are not freely movable at that time.

Q. Now, in this gentleman's case, were you able to actually observe that? Did he have that Gelidium test, or is there just basically a diagnosis by exclusion?

A. That is usually done with—

Q. An injection of dye?

A. Injection of dye with an MRI, and I don't see in my notes a copy of that particular MRI, although we did—well, I will take that back. This was—yes, I guess we based that on our MRI dated August 17, 2001, where it talks about an L4–L5 surrounding epidural fibrosis. . . . So, I guess, technically, it shouldn't be arachnoiditis. It should be more epidural fibrosis.

Q. Okay, because they didn't do a Gelidium dye study, did they?

A. They did, with and without IV [intravenous] contrast.

Q. But that should be a fibrosis instead of arachnoiditis?

A. That should be epidural fibrosis.

Q. Okay. Now, chronic lumbar radiculopathy—what does that mean?

A. Someone has chronic leg pain in a dermatomal or nondermatomal distribution.

Q. Okay. So, in other words, if this gentleman came in to see you and he said, "Doctor, I feel great, I don't have any pain," then he would no longer have the failed back surgery syndrome, and the chronic lumbar radiculopathy and the third condition that we were talking about, the fibrosis?

A. Well, you are talking—if he had successful surgery with no complaints?

Q. Right.

A. Right.

Many Patients with Worker's Condition Get Better

Q. Okay. . . . . I realize that you are in the business of treating pain, so you probably observe a skewed population, you don't get the healthy patient necessarily, but is it your understanding that a lot of people do have that surgery and make an excellent recovery?

A. Anywhere from 60 to 85 percent, depending on the literature you read.

Q. And Dr. Guarnaschelli, as far as you know, is an eminently well-qualified physician?

A. As far as I know.

Diagnosis Based upon Subjective Complaints of Pain

Q. All right. Are his clinical findings in your office—what kind of clinical findings do you have, which would give further evidence to this condition, or is this basically a diagnosis that is based upon his subjective complaints of pain?

A. Well, it's based upon his subjective complaints, and also upon when we finally do the exam, and, of course, his exam has improved since he has had his pump implanted. Prior to that, going back to that visit when he came in after we had lost him to follow-up—let's go back and look at that here. For example, that office note dated October 16, 2001, when I came into the room, it was noted that he was sitting in the chair, but leaning off toward the right side, because he had problems with any sort of pressure on his left buttocks. He at that point in time had a well-healed surgical scar that went from L3 down to the sacral region, and he had tenderness all along that scar, he had tenderness over both of his S1 joints when I palpated them, and his knee reflexes were okay. They were one plus and equal, but then when we went to do a straight-leg raise, where we basically just extended his leg at the knee, he did have pain, with pain going down below the calf in what I felt was a radicular distribution on that left side, and then when we did the straight-leg raise on the right side he had pain that stopped at the knee. So it was more, I guess, coming from the back and not from the nerve root irritation itself. He had difficulty getting in a seated position. He was very stiff, and he could not stand erect. When he started to walk, he finally, after three or four steps, was able to become more erect and then he had difficulty with range of motion, particularly with forward flexion and extension.

Q. Okay. Now, that was before you put the pump in, is that right?

A. Yes.

Q. Now, your most recent test—you said he is improved?

A. Yes, he is.

Work Capacity

Q. Would you encourage him to try to do some type of remunerative activity with his restrictions?

A. If he is able to. We always encourage patients to try to get back and do some sort of work. I mean that is a question if he is able to.

Q. And would you leave that to an orthopedic or a neurosurgery physician?

A. To make the determination—

Q. If he physically is able to—

A. Well, no. I would probably end up getting a functional capacity evaluation to see what kind of limits he would have to have permanently.

Q. All right. His present condition—he is able to carry out more activities of daily living now than he was when he first saw you—is that correct?

A. He is able to do a little more, yes.

Q. In your mind, has the surgery been worth it—that is, the procedure that you had performed?

A. The one that we did?

Q. Yes.

A. I think it has helped him control his pain, yes.

Q. Are his conditions, his clinical findings, now atypical of his conditions or are they consistent with it?

A. You mean with the failed back?

Q. Um-hmm.

A. No. I think everybody responds a little differently to the pump. He has done okay. We would like to see him with a pain scale much lower than what he rates.

Q. Okay. . . . Would you say then that his—or, I mean, typically when you do this procedure, don't you reduce pain a lot more than what he is complaining of?

A. When we initially put the pump in we had really good resolution of his pain. That has returned some and we are making some adjustments with the pump. Some folks after a while build up tolerance to the pain medication, which requires some change of that medicine that we haven't done yet, but overall he is doing okay for a pump patient.

Poor Result Because Claim Is Pending?

Q. Did you usually, though, have a better result? And I am thinking in the sense of we have got a workers' compensation claim here, and traditionally the prognosis is poor, the complaints of pain last longer than in those identical injuries where there is no litigation or workers' compensation claim, and I am just wondering—

[Mr. Nevitt]. Well, note an objection to testimony by counsel.

Q. I mean that is what the literature shows, doesn't it?

A. Well, I haven't done an extensive review of the literature, but I have read where there may be some difference in outcome, but I am not an expert and can't really make a comment on that.

Q. Okay. So are you saying that you really aren't in a position to determine whether or not his particular findings are typical or atypical of those individuals who have had this morphine pump implanted?

A. He is not the most typical. I mean, we have folks that do better, but everyone has some small variation in the way they respond. Would we like to see them become more pain free? Yes. Is he an average patient? No, because he has had some breakthrough pain that we are still dealing with.

Adding an Additional 3 Percent to Guides Rating

Q. Now, I guess your assessment of this gentleman, if we used the fifth edition of the *AMA Guides* and we talk about him being under category III, then you are saying you would rate him under that, you would have a range of 10 to 13 percent?

A. Using category III, yes.

Q. Okay. And under that category it appears to refer that you get the extra three points, taking it from 10 to 13 percent, if there is a problem with a person carrying out the activities of daily living?

A.   Well, with the pain—and I will be the first to say that the chapter on pain is not the best in the world, but it does allow us to add an additional 3 percent for people with complaints of chronic refractory pain, which is, I think, what he has when he is untreated.

Q.   When he is treated, though, does he have it?

A.   No, but I don't think that that three percent rating disappears. You know, it just means that we have treated it appropriately. It's like saying about someone who has high blood pressure, put him on appropriate medication and his blood pressure goes to normal, [he] will still have hypertension, but only because [he is] treated [he is] normal tensive.

Range of Motion Versus DRE

Q.   Did you record his range of motion?

A.   Exactly with degree, no. The last time I saw him I did not.

Q.   Okay. The *AMA Guidelines* addresses that question when to use a range of motion versus the DRE, and I realize you are in the business of trying to treat pain, as opposed to trying to quantify numbers from a two-inch thick textbook. This book, though, does indicate that if you have a multilevel involvement, you use the range of motion finding, isn't that correct? I am looking here at page 380, Figure 15-4.

A.   If that is what the algorithm says, yes, then that is what you do.

Doctor States That the Guides Provide Latitude for Him to Deviate

Q.   So then his functional impairment you would agree—and I realize that it is reluctant on your part because you have some questions about the text itself—would be 10 to 13 percent under the fifth edition of the *AMA Guides?*

A.   Using the strict interpretation, but then I do agree wholeheartedly with the name of the textbook, that it is "Guidelines," and guidelines means there is hopefully some latitude at least on my part what I can write down, hence the reason for the meeting today.

Q.   Okay. Well, I appreciate you taking your time out and I thank you very much.

A.   Okay.

Examination of Doctor by Claimant's Counsel

Preliminaries and Restrictions

[Mr. Nevitt].

Q.   Doctor, we have just met today. My name is K. Nevitt. I represent J. Jones. You had, I believe, sent a letter to me dated November 18, 2002, and I am not sure if this was the first time, but you had written in there the permanent restrictions for Mr. Jones?

A.   Yes.

Q. And those are permanent restrictions that you feel are a result of the work injury, is that correct?

A. Well, the work injury—also, I think, because of his current treatment with the pain pump.

Q. You were asking earlier about some activities of daily living, and when you look at the activities of daily living . . . , one of these listed for physical activity is standing, sitting, reclining, walking, climbing stairs. I believe you have found that he has permanent restrictions in pretty much all of those areas: standing, sitting, climb, reclining, walking and climbing stairs—is that correct?

A. Well, I did put down the standing, the walking, the crawling, and the fear of unprotected heights, and then climbing of ladders, and twisting and bending.

Q. Now, would that also be true as far as his ability to perform activities excluding work? Would he also be limited in doing those kinds of things even when he is not working?

A. I think so.

Q. I couldn't find it today, but I was thinking somewhere in my notes I saw where you had given him medication, and he was complaining of problems with sleeping and I am not sure about the time period of that. Do you recall or if I look today what medications—

A. Well, briefly going over the medications we have got him on and we still have him on—some Zyprexa, and some Topamax. We tried Remeron, and I did mention in some of my past notes that he did have problems with sleep, that it was interrupted and he didn't feel completely rested.

Category III Versus Category IV

Q. Going to the disability rating that you had given, you had placed him in category IV, and you have looked at that today and been asked some questions about it. Looking at this today, do you feel that Mr. Jones fits more into a category IV, DRE lumbar category IV, rather than a category III?

A. My own personal gestalt is, yes, I think he fits more a category IV than a category III.

Q. And that is the 20 to 23 percent impairment to the body as a whole?

A. That is correct.

Q. Okay. And you have then in the past given your rating of 26 percent, and you were talking earlier about a 3 percent for pain, so I take it you are putting it at the top of category IV and then an additional three percent for the pain, is that correct?

A. That is what I tried to do, yes.

Doctor Admits Deviating from Literal Interpretation of the Guides

Q. And is that your opinion still, today, that you feel he has 26 percent whole-person impairment?

A. Again, yes, that is my personal feeling—although there is some disagreement with the official interpretation, or the literal interpretation, of the text.

Q. Okay. And when you say "some disagreement," you mean—

A. That the DRE category, and the textbook as a whole, is somewhat difficult to agree with just because of the way the text had to be written.

Q. And your opinions today have been based upon reasonable medical probability?

A. Yes.

[**Mr. Nevitt**]. Those are all the questions I have.

Examination of Treating Physician by Counsel

Doctor Feels Claimant Needs a Higher Number than Guides *Provide* [By Mr. Harding].

Q. Doctor, your disagreement with the text is simply that you feel he needs a higher number, as opposed to a different definition—isn't that correct?

A. Yes. That is basically it.

Q. Okay. You would agree that from a textual standpoint, if we ignore the impairment ratings, he fits within DRE lumbar category III—is that correct?

A. As I said, if we give it a III and a half—but there is no such thing.

Counsel Goads Witness into Making Admission

Q. So you would agree that he fits within the category III, you know, and for the purposes of my question I am saying excluding the quantification numbers, okay, the definition that most closely fits this gentleman is category III? Sometimes it could be a catharsis just to say yes.

A. By the strict definition—he, I would suppose, lean more toward a III than a IV, but if you ask me to give you a hard and fast "yes, he does," I just don't feel comfortable doing that.

Diagnoses of Claimant

Q. But you agree he did not have a fusion?

A. He didn't have a fusion.

Q. And he didn't have a fracture or a compression greater than 50 percent?

A. No, he did not, but he is not asymptomatic after the surgery.

Q. Right, but under the first category of DRE III, they say significant signs of radiculopathy, et cetera, and they talk about a symptomatic gentleman, don't they?

A. Well—

Q. I mean do they or do they not?

A. Yes, but he had surgery and he is still symptomatic.

Q. And they don't say that this is before or after surgery, do they?

A. No, but that second section talks about being symptomatic, asymptomatic—

Q. Well, that says "or," so that is another type of condition he could have and fit under III? That is what "or" means? "Or" is different from "and"?

Doctor Is Pressed and Starts to Joke

A. I will treat myself as a hostile witness, and I will say: Well, I am going to—gee, I mean this is such a hard one for me to say.

Q. You are not a grammarian are you? I mean you are just trying to practice medicine?

A. No. I'm a Republican, but even then there is some debate about that. I understand. I mean if you look at the strict, strict definition and without—just looking at the Guidelines—if you actually, if you exclude the Guidelines and say, "Okay, here are the limits," he is a category III. But, if you say the Guidelines is a guide to help you move toward an impairment rating, then I think he still fits better under IV, although he has not had a fusion. I should be a politician.

Doctor Again Explains Reason for Deviation

Q. And you say that he fits under IV just simply because you like the higher numbers? You think the higher numbers are more appropriate for him?

A. I think he fits under IV, because I don't think III addresses his condition appropriately. But I also understand, you know, the book is written trying to take people and categorize them as a whole, and it's difficult to try to write a book that teaches or treats each person individually.

Doctor Pressed on Symptoms

Q. Let me ask you this: Is he an individual who has a clinically significant radiculopathy and an ongoing imaging study that demonstrates a herniated disk?

A. Well, not now. Well, the last one, I mean . . . if we go by his last MRI, the one that shows the epidural fibrosis.

Q. And would that be something expected on the basis of previous radiculopathy?

A. Well, he doesn't have that now, because that was surgically removed. So then it goes back to saying, does someone have a history? Well, if they have cancer, just because the cancer is excised, are they completely cancer free? We don't know. Or if they have blood pressure problems, and they are treated appropriately and the blood pressure is normal, do they still have blood pressure problems? I know it is tough, but, no, I ain't no grammarian.

Doctor Unfamiliar with Key Tenet of the Guides

Q. All right. But the fifth edition of the *AMA Guides* talks about evaluating people at MMI [maximum medical improvement], isn't that correct?

A. Well now, that I am not sure about. I would have to go back and read the text on that.

Q. All right. If this gentleman showed up to see you on several occasions and was pain-free on those occasions, then his impairment rating would drop, wouldn't it, within that hypothetical?

A. Only if he was appropriately treated, which I think he is, but then you are still faced with what are the long-term manifestations and then you would have to

Q.   do—like I said before—have to do a fairly rigorous functional capacity evaluation to see what he could then do.

Q.   But I mean just from the standpoint of the *AMA Guides*, though, his functional impairment would drop perhaps to category II or lower?

A.   Oh, I won't even go there.

Q.   I mean that is possible, isn't it?

A.   Well, only if we could reverse the surgery he has had.

Q.   Well, a person can have a herniated disk, though, and actually come out with a five percent impairment, under the AMA [*Guides*], isn't that right?

A.   Once you have had a surgery, I think—I am not sure you can go down that low, but again it's—

Counsel Ends on a High Note; Doctor Admits Not Having Gained Mastery of the Guides

Q.   Would it be safe to say that you have a lot of things on your plate and one of them is not gaining a mastery of the fifth edition of *AMA Guides*? You are trying to treat people? Would that be a fair statement?

A.   Yes, I think so.

§ 10.07   DRE VERSUS ROM MODEL IN SPINAL IMPAIRMENT[*]

This succinct rating physician deposition transcript is instructive in three main ways. First, it shows that physicians struggle on a daily basis to follow the *AMA Guides* and that a well-trained and well-prepared physician will produce the most credible, defensible impairment ratings. In this case, one can easily get the impression that the lawyers were more familiar with the *Guides* and better prepared than the testifying physician. The effectiveness of both lawyers can be traced in part to their familiarity with the *Guides*. This case also shows how an opinion can be easily torn apart when the information on which the expert based his or her opinion is brought into question (in this case, the diagnostic studies that were not personally reviewed by the rating physician). Finally, it illustrates the vast difference between impairment ratings based on the DRE method (5 to 8 percent) and those based on the ROM method (28 to 32 percent).

Preliminaries

[By Mr. Jones (on behalf of employer)].

Q.   Doctor, my name is G. Jones. I represent the employer of S. Adams in Mr. Adams' claim for workers' compensation. If you would, Doctor, please state your name for the record.

A.   J. Smith.

Q.   And what is your occupation?

---

[*] The authors wish to acknowledge Thomas W. Moak, Esq., of Prestonsburg, KY, for his assistance in the preparation of this section.

A. Physician.
Q. And what is your specialty area?
A. Occupational medicine and pain management.
Q. Now, how long have you been doing this?
A. Approximately 20 years.

Impairment Evaluation

Q. Okay. During the course of your employment here, have you had the opportunity to evaluate Mr. Adams?
A. Yes, sir, I have.
Q. What was the date of your evaluation?
A. April 4, 2002.
Q. Okay. Looking at your report—and we'll just jump right into this and make this as short and sweet as possible—I see you gave for the lumbar spine two different impairment ratings. First, 5 percent to the whole man due to a DRE lumbar category II with asymmetrical loss of range of motion, with clinical history— or . . . whole person with clinical history in examination that's compatible with a specific injury together with asymmetrical loss of range of motion, nonverifiable radicular complaints. And a 5 percent rating to the whole man due to a compression fracture of the L2 vertebral body of less than 25 percent.
A. Yes, sir.

Diagnostic Studies

Q. Now, on what did you base the 5 percent compression fracture?
A. That was based on a report of a CT scan dated October 9, 2001, and an MRI scan dated October 6, 2001.
Q. Now, Doctor, I see the CT scan here, and the date of the CT scan was October 9, 2001.
A. Yes, sir.
Q. Could you explain a CT scan and what it's used for?
A. Yes, sir. It's a computer tomography, and it's an advanced objective study, advanced in comparison to an X-ray, showing more tissue, more of the disks, more of the pathology than we would be able to obtain with an X-ray.
Q. Okay. I'm reading the CT scan of October 9, and the impression is: "There is a hairline fracture of the L2 vertebral body with slight compression. This appears to be a stable fracture. Incidental notice made of multiple kidney stones."

   Now, you had a CT scan on October 9 at the referral of Dr. Soto. I see Dr. Brown. . . . Dr. Brown was the treating physician of this patient for a while?
A. Yes, sir.

Difference Between CT and MRI

Q. I see Dr. Brown recommended an MRI, which was subsequently performed on November 6, 2001. Why would a physician request an MRI after a CT scan had already been performed?

A.   The MRI scan can show more pathology than the CT scan can. I'm not absolutely sure why Dr. Brown ordered that, other than possibly to determine if there was any nerve impingement or entrapment. Sometimes a CT scan will not show the clarity obtained in looking at the nerves themselves.

Q.   Okay. Now, I'm looking at the MRI, the radiologist's report dated November 6, 2001, and the second paragraph of the report says: "At L1–L2, there's decreased signal in the disk spaces consistent with this degenerative disk disease. The patient had a previous hairline fracture of L2, but no abnormal signal changes can be seen other than a slight indentation of the superior end plate." . . . Now, it doesn't appear that the MRI scan actually showed a fracture.

"Previous" Fracture Noted on MRI

A.   Well, the MRI scan, as you noted, says "previous hairline fracture of L2 and with a slight indentation of the superior end plate." The date of injury was October 9, 2001, and the date of the—

Q.   The CT scan was on October 9, 2001. The injury date was . . . oh, you're right. Actually, October 9 was when he actually went through the CT also. Yeah, that's right.

A.   Okay.

Q.   Good. Sorry.

A.   And the date of the MRI scan was November 6, 2001. Normally, when they say a "previous" hairline fracture, I usually think they may be referring to an older fracture, and I'm really not sure in this particular case if [the radiologist] is referring to an old [fracture] when he used the word "previous." I'm just not sure what the radiologist is referring to.

Q.   So you don't know if this would be causally work related or not, then?

A.   With the use of the word "previous" there, I'm not sure. I'm hedging because I'm just not sure.

Doctor Did Not Personally Review Films

Q.   Okay. Now, did you personally review the CT scan or the MRI films?

A.   No, sir, I did not.

Q.   Okay. Now, are you familiar with Dr. J. Brown?

A.   Yes, sir, I am.

Q.   Now, Dr. Brown, as we discussed earlier, was the treating physician. We have filed into evidence Dr. Brown's report dated October 29, 2001. This was just after the CT scan and just prior to the MRI scan.

A.   Yes, sir.

Treating Doctor Did Not Find Fracture

Q.   I'm looking at the second paragraph of the October 29 report of Dr. Brown where Dr. Brown states: "X-rays of the lumbar spine were done. He [Mr. Adams] was told he had a hairline fracture at L2. I reviewed these x-rays and the CT. What he has is degenerative disk change at L2–L3, which gives the impression of a pseudo fracture. He also has significant degenerative change at L4–L5 with deformity of the superior plate of L5, but again not evidence of fracture." Doctor, I'm just looking at this, and I know Dr. Brown has a pretty good reputation in the community.

A. Yes, sir.

Witness Gives Ground and Makes Admission

Q. He personally reviewed the CT scan and determined that it was not a fracture but, rather, a DDD, which gave the impression of a pseudo fracture. He then recommended the MRI scan of November 6, 2001. Hypothetically, based on Dr. Brown's report—if you were to stick solely to Dr. Brown's report—would the additional 5 percent you gave for the compression fracture still be a valid assessment?

A. No, sir.

Q. Okay. Now, based on your review of this information today. . . . I don't know, did you have this available to you when you made your report?

A. I do not recall.

Doctor Asked to Back Off His Opinion

Q. Okay. Now, based on what we've seen here today, would you still conclude that Mr. Adams should be entitled to an additional 5 percent impairment due to a compression fracture of the L2 vertebral body?

A. I do respect Dr. Brown. I do not know Dr. Buck personally, but he is a radiologist and he's making his determination off two different studies, a CT scan and an MRI scan. Without looking at them myself, I would have a difficult time making a choice between two different individuals. And even in that case, individuals can differ on interpretations of studies like MRI scans and CT scans. Clearly, Dr. Brown believes that there is a change there, but he believes it's due more to the degenerative changes, given the impression of a fracture, whereas Dr. Buck believes that both studies indicate that there's a fracture. Obviously, in this case it's not a large compression fracture or it's not a large change, and even if it were . . . I really wouldn't want to make that call. It looks like Dr. Brown was looking at the CT scan—

Q. Only. Yes.

A. But then he orders the MRI scan.

Q. Yes.

A. Do you know what he stated after he reviewed the MRI scan?

Q. Let me see. Mr. Jones, we can go off [the record] just a second.

[Discussion off the record is held.]

[**Mr. Jones.**] Okay. Back on the record.

Q. Now, I'm looking at Dr. Brown's November 19, 2001, medical record. He states: "Scott Adams came in for a follow-up MRI scan, was reviewed. There is a degenerative disk with central herniation and a right-sided paracentral herniation at L4-5 producing moderate stenosis." Otherwise, I do not see any evidence of a compression fracture based upon Dr. Brown's interpretation of the MRI report.

And, now, Doctor, what I want to ask you too is to refer to the radiologist's MRI report. The MRI report itself did not reveal a hairline fracture, did it? If it did, it's not noted in the Impressions section, because it says he [Mr. Adams] had a previous hairline fracture. And this was the same radiologist who performed a CT scan and who concluded that the CT scan revealed a hairline fracture.

Vaguely Worded Radiology Report Causes Problems

A.   Correct. That's what I referred to earlier. When he uses the words "previous hairline fracture," I'm not sure exactly what he's referring to. The confusion in my mind is that he had reviewed the CAT scan earlier—that was on October 9— and then reviews or interprets the MRI scan and uses the word "previous." He doesn't use it initially, but then he uses it, and I'm not sure if he's referring to the hairline fracture that was present a month earlier when he uses the word "previous," or if it's some older hairline fracture when he uses the word "previous." I'm just not sure.

Q.   Okay. But in your interpretation of the radiologist's report, did the MRI itself reveal a hairline fracture of L2?

A.   Well, it says he had a previous hairline fracture of L2.

Q.   So would that have been visible on the MRI of the lumbar spine? When he said [Mr. Adams] had a previous hairline fracture, a prior hairline fracture, would it still be visible on an MRI a month later?

A.   It could. Yes, sir, it could be.

Q.   So you would think, then—

A.   I'm thinking that he's referring to the compression fracture. . . . What I believe you're referring to—and I do so myself when I say "hairline fracture"—it's something that you would see some healing at that point. But he doesn't mention that. So I'm just not sure.

Cervical Disorder and Asymmetrical Range of Motion

Q.   All right, Doctor. We've discussed this about as much as we can today. Let me go back to your report. I see that you ascribed a 5 percent also for a cervical disorder, and it's based on an asymmetrical loss of range of motion and non-verifiable radicular complaints. What is asymmetrical loss of range of motion, and how did you verify this?

A.   Yes, sir. The range of motion was determined using the methodology set forth in the *AMA Guides.* That includes using an instrument called an inclinometer to determine the exact range of motion, the number of degrees, doing three separate measurements of each range of motion, be it flexion, extension, lateral bending or rotation, and making sure that all three measurements were within 5 degrees of each other to have a valid test. So those were the methods used, as set forth in the *AMA Guides.*

Q.   I'm more concerned with the asymmetrical aspect of it, the asymmetrical loss of range of motion. Looking at your range of motion scores, how do you determine that it is asymmetrical?

Doctor Admits Range of Motion Differences Were "Small"

A.   Well, you can compare the scores one to the other—in other words, right side to the left side—otherwise, you have to make the comparison to a standard range of motion. Here, forward flexion was 50 degrees, which is normal; and extension was 43, 41, 40 degrees, which is abnormal as that extension normally is 60 degrees. But there was a very small variation between the three measurements. Of course, if it [the variation] had been more than that, then you would have been outside the validity factor. So the validity factor holds you within a 5-degree range.

On lateral bending, we had 36 degrees to the right, and 31 degrees to the left. So you can measure or compare the right to the left side. And then on rotation to the right, we have 58 degrees, and to the left, 52 degrees. So again, you can make that comparison. These are small differences, but they are different and consistent with the right and the left, and I believe they would be consistent too with his [Mr. Adams'] complaints.

Description of Range of Motion Testing Under the **AMA** **Guides**

Q.   Okay. Could you take me through how you do these range-of-motion studies? When a patient comes in right before you do it, what are the steps?

A.   Well, the first thing you would do is tell the patient what you're going to do. You have the patient go through that particular range of motion to make sure he understands. Then I do the three separate measurements concurrently. I do not wait 20 minutes or 5 minutes and do the next. I do them concurrently. And I would go through forward flexion and tell the patient to attempt to touch his chin to his chest, and then look at the ceiling, et cetera.

Q.   What is the patient required to do prior to this examination?

A.   Well, the patient is asked to get limber, to move his neck, to make sure that there's some suppleness. And . . . if the patient were real cold, then I wouldn't do the test. I never do anyway, because it comes at the end of the examination. So there's usually a 40- to 45-minute time frame between that time. But you would want to make sure that the patient is fairly limber. Or, if not, it's an excellent time to observe the patient, looking for muscle spasms, looking for that type of thing.

Fifth Edition of the **Guides**

Q.   Okay. Now, Doctor, I want to go back just for a second to the lumbar spine criteria, and I'm looking at the *AMA Guides,* fifth edition, page 384, with which you're quite familiar, I'm sure, as we all are.

A.   Yes, sir.

Q.   Now, I'm looking at your criteria for rating impairment due to lumbar spine injury, and in particular at the 5 percent for the DRE II with the asymmetrical loss of range of motion and nonverifiable radicular complaints, and also the 5 percent due to a compression fracture. Would both of these fall under a DRE II?

A.   Well, the compression fracture would be less than 25 percent because it's very minor, so it would [fall under a DRE II]. The interesting thing that has come out today was when you read the report from Dr. Brown—I am not sure if I had that or not—the second report, where he indicated there was a herniation. I don't remember seeing exactly everything he said. . . . I'm varying off a little bit.

Q. That's all right. No problem.

No Verifiable Radiculopathy

A. Mr. Adams did indicate that he was having radicular symptoms, but I do not have an EMG/nerve conduction study to verify actual radiculopathy. I don't believe I knew at that time that there was a herniation and—but the reason I chose [to rate it] II was because of that fact . . . that I could not verify a radiculopathy, but I believe that he would fall within the rest of the criteria.

Q. Doctor, when I'm looking at the DRE lumbar category II . . . and the first section has to do with the nonverifiable—actually, it has to do with loss of range of motion—nonverifiable radicular complaints, et cetera, I see an "or"—

A. Uh-huh. (Affirmative)

Q. ". . . had clinically significant radiculopathy," then "or fractures less than 25 percent." By using the disjunctive "or," it would appear to me that you could only place a 5 percent to 8 percent on one of these, rather than two, as you have done.

A. No. If there's more than one component. . . . If there is more than one condition that you feel that the individual is being affected by within a specific section, for instance, if there is more than one compression fracture, although it falls within this one category, you can give an additional impairment rating for that particular condition. Now, let me make—let me see if we have an example where I can show you that.

Q. Sure.

[A pause occurred in the proceedings.]

Doctor Cannot Find Support for His Position in the Guides

A. I'm not finding—

Q. I didn't see it either. I looked through it and couldn't find—couldn't make a determination one way or the other, and that's why I was hoping maybe you could clarify it a little bit.

A. Well, I guess I forget. It may have been they had an example in one of the previous editions. But I do not see it here, so I can only tell you that I believe I am correct in that that was the analogy that I utilized in making that . . . degenerative disk and a herniation—I'm sorry—a compression fracture—

Q. Sure.

A. But in the example that I remember, there were multiple compression fractures and they [the *Guides*] indicated that you would give the impairment rating for each one. But I don't see it in here, so that may be out of another book. And you could argue, and maybe correctly, that it's not applicable if it's not in this one.

Work Restrictions

Q. All right. The last thing, Doctor, on the restrictions—

A. Uh-huh. (Affirmative)

Q. How do you derive these restrictions?

Doctor Relies in Part on Patient's Self-Reporting for FCEs

A. Primarily on two methods: One is what the patient tells me he can or cannot do. Two, if we were to have a formal FCE [functional capability evaluation], I would utilize that if I felt it was consistent. And number three, based on historically what I have found to be fairly consistent with the patients I have treated under a similar condition.

Q. So an objective FCE would be a good standard to determine restrictions?

A. Yes. The problem I have with FCEs is that many patients indicate to me that they do not receive callbacks the next day to see actually what their response has been. In other words, this individual, Mr. Adams, and I think many more, may be able one day to perform certain activities, but were they to do that over a consecutive five-day week, they would not be able to. So there are questions, and what I normally attempt to do is I use the words, in my opinion, these are advisements. I tell the patient and I would want to tell an employer. And if an employer and the patient were to say, we want to do this, I would allow that. I just believe that if the individual engages in these activities, he or she—in this case, Mr. Adams—will experience increased pain.

Q. Now, when you refer someone for an FCE, where do you typically refer them to?

A. Usually to a physical therapist. . . . I know at _____ we use both a physical therapist and an occupational therapist. There are facilities, I believe, that use more of the automated machines.

Q. Like the ERGOS system maybe?

A. Yes, sir. So any of those would—I'm not sure if one is better than the other. They are professionals, and you have to give credibility and respect to those findings.

[Mr. Jones]. Okay. Thank you, Doctor. I have nothing further.

[The Witness]. Yes, sir.

Examination

[By Mr. Washington (on behalf of claimant)].

Q. Doctor, a couple of follow-up questions real quick. You've supplied the court with your report, and I think that's introduced. But would you attach a copy of the report to the deposition?

A. Yes, sir.

[Said document is filed with this deposition and marked as Smith Exhibit No. 1 for purposes of identification.]

Doctor Details His Objective Findings

Q. Okay. Physically, was there objective finding that supported your diagnosis here?

A.   Yes, sir. Well, one, a chronic low-back pain syndrome. There was subjective find-
       ing—that is, midline tenderness in the lower back. There was subjective/objective
       [finding] in range of motion. What I mean by that is, it is a subjective test, but the
       Guides attempt to make it more objective by utilization of the inclinometer, doing
       three separate tests, and making sure they meet the validity factor. But it still is
       subjective. There was decreased sensation to pinprick noted in the legs bilaterally
       in a dermatomal pattern consistent with L5, positive straight leg raise bilaterally. But
       those—all of these findings—have a subjective component. And there's the
       decreased sensation to pinprick with the individual's eyes closed, sitting and/or
       lying, which is considered objective as long as they meet the dermatomal pattern.
       But again, it has a subjective component. Now, if we look at the neck, the same
       things would be applicable. There is subjective tenderness; there are no muscle
       spasms; there's the decreased range of motion; there's the degenerative lumbar
       disk disease in the diagnosis that was confirmed on X-rays, MRI scans; and the
       focal annular disk bulge. Those were confirmed. And actually, I apologize, I can't
       remember if Dr. Brown's review was of the lumbar sacral or the cervical—

       [Mr. Jones]. It was the lumbar.

A.   Okay, lumbar. Then he interpreted it as showing a herniation. I don't believe
       I made that diagnosis. . . . There's the chronic cervical pain syndrome—again,
       we went through that. . . . Degenerative cervical disk disease—again, the find-
       ings objectively on the X-rays and MRI scans. . . . And the cervical disk bulge,
       C5–C6, C6–C7, that again was confirmed on the cervical MRI scan.

Diagnostic Studies Support the Objective Findings

Q.   Okay. And going back to the chronic pain syndrome and the diagnosis, there is
       objective testing in the record that support those complaints, correct, going back
       to the CT scans and MRI scan?
A.   That is correct, yes, sir.
Q.   And those are consistent with his complaints?
A.   I believe they are, yes, sir.
Q.   Now, would it make a difference if you assume, based upon Dr. Brown's inter-
       pretation, that there is herniation? What you saw—well, not what you saw, but
       at the time you saw the records, I believe there was only a bulge.

Doctor Won't Agree with Category III DRE

A.   Well, it would give credibility to the radicular symptoms, but I still would not have
       the EMG/nerve conduction study to confirm a radiculopathy. What we would
       have, where we would have an objective finding that would be consistent, but it
       does not—I'm not sure if—I don't believe he said it showed a nerve entrapment or
       impingement, and I'm pretty sure of that. So we would still need to have an EMG/
       NCV study to jump to the Category III, confirming a radiculopathy.
Q.   Okay. Now, in the Category II, there's a range of 5 to 8 percent.
A.   Yes, sir.
Q.   Had you known that when you were performing this, would that have made
       a difference in your opinion as filed as opposed to an 8 percent?

Physician Assigns 3 Percent for Pain

A. No, sir. I believe I gave a 3 percent for pain, and therefore, I could not—it's an either/or, and so I gave the 3 percent for pain—I could not have also given it 8 percent.

Range of Motion Method Vastly Increases Impairment

Q. Okay. Now, would you be able to tell us what his impairment would be under the range of motion model?
A. I can try. I believe I can.
Q. Thank you.
A. It's going to take a few seconds.
Q. That's all right, you don't have to do both.
A. Well, I will, because if you use one, you have to be consistent with whichever method that you use. So I'll have to use for the range of motion also for the cervical in making that determination.

[A brief break was taken.]

Doctor Admits Range of Motion Method Should Have Been Used

A. Okay. It would be a 28 percent permanent partial impairment to the whole man. If we include the 5 percent for the L2, then it's a 32.
Q. Okay. And the reason I was asking is it appears back in Section 15.2 of the *AMA Guides*, pages 379 to 380—where it talks about multilevel involvement of the same region . . . and it talks about fractures at multiple levels, disk herniations, or stenosis, would that get more to the question that you've got—you've got the fracture at the same level along with the herniation at the same level, wouldn't you then refer to the range of motion method?
A. Yes, sir, it would.
Q. And if that's the case, then we're looking at a 28 percent impairment.
A. Yes, sir.
Q. And based on the way this edition of the *AMA Guides* reads, that's what you should do in this case, isn't that correct?
A. That is correct.
Q. Okay.

[Mr. Jones]. Is that all you've got, then?

[Mr. Washington]. I believe that's all the questions I have.

Reexamination

[By Mr. Jones (on behalf of employer)].

Inconsistency of Report with Testimony

Q. Doctor, just a few follow-ups. In your original 107, you did not find the range of motion model appropriate?

A.   I did not.

Q.   And what has caused you to change your mind today?

A.   Well, the question asked was an appropriate question, and my responses were to the question, and the question was: Would this case fall within one of the five exceptions set forth in the *AMA Guides*? And it would, and that is because there would be two different conditions within the same level, and those would be the compression fracture and the degenerative disk disease. And according to the *AMA Guides,* if an individual falls in one of those five exceptions . . . the range of motion model should be used. But you really should use both models, and use the greater of the—whichever one comes out to be the largest.

  I felt when I did this examination that the methodology, the DRE model, would appropriately address the issues. But the questions asked were appropriate and my responses were appropriate; and that is, under the *AMA Guides,* the range of motion model would be appropriate in this case.

Q.   And, now, could you explain how you derive your range of motion scores—especially for the cervical?

A.   Yes, sir. For the cervical spine, I used the impairment unoperated with medically documented injury of minimal six months. . . . I forget the wording, I'm sorry.

Q.   That's all right.

A.   Let me see, where is the range of motion—this would be unoperated on with medically documented injury, pain and rigidity associated with none to minimal degenerative changes and structural tests, which is a 4 percent. And then there was one additional one, which was, I think, C4–C5–C6, and then there was C6–C7, I gave an additional 1 percent for that. And then you go to the actual loss of range of motion. I went through each one, which, for the cervical was—let's see, 2 percent for extension, 1 percent for the lateral bending, both sides, and then 1 percent for rotation, both sides, which gave a [total of] 6 percent.

Q.   Now, these are based on the range of motion scores you obtained on your—?

A.   Measurements. Yes, sir.

Q.   Yours of April 4, 2002?

A.   That is correct.

Q.   Okay.

  [Mr. Jones]. I don't think I have anything else for you, unfortunately.

  [The Witness]. Okay. Thank you both.

  [Mr. Washington]. Thank you, Doctor.

  [Deposition was concluded.]

§ 10.08   CARPAL TUNNEL SYNDROME AND DE QUERVAIN'S TENDINITIS[*]

  At issue in the following deposition is an upper extremity impairment rating. The deposition is of the *claimant's* IME physician. The two treating surgeons rated

---

  [*] The authors wish to acknowledge Gary Goldstein, Esq., of Johnson City, TN, for his assistance in the preparation of this section.

the claimant at zero impairment. The claimant's IME physician was found credible by the fact finder despite the fact that the physician no longer sees patients, has not performed surgery since 1998, and performs hundreds of IMEs each year, and the fact that 95 percent of his referrals come from claimants. It is evident from the deposition that the physician was familiar with the *AMA Guides,* was well prepared to testify, and was very comfortable and articulate when testifying. This example amply demonstrates the importance of choosing a rating physician who has competency in the *Guides* and is well prepared to defend the rating he or she has assigned at a deposition or hearing. See summary of this case, *Reece v. J.T. Walker Industries Inc.,* 2007 WL 4322003 (Tenn. Workers Comp. Panel) in § 11.32 of this volume.

Cross-Examination by Employer's Counsel

Background of IME Requested by Claimant's Attorney

Q. And, Doctor, you were—you were asked to perform an IME with regards to S. Reece, is that correct?
A. Yes. Ms. Reece came into my office on December 20, 2005.
Q. Okay. And you were asked to perform that IME on behalf of Mr. Goldstein, is that correct?
A. Well, Mr. Goldstein requested the independent medical examination, yes.
Q. Okay. And were you paid for your independent medical examination?
A. Yes, I was.
Q. Okay, and how much were you paid?
A. Eight hundred dollars.
Q. Okay. And you were paid that by Mr. Goldstein, is that correct?
A. Yes.

Not a Treating Physician

Q. Doctor, you were not a treating physician in this matter, is that correct?
A. That's correct.

Very Experienced, Plaintiff's Expert Witness

Q. Okay. And you haven't practiced surgery for a number of years, is that correct?
A. That's correct. I have not performed surgery since 1998.
Q. Okay. So you're more of a consultant in this matter, is that correct?
A. Yes.
Q. Okay. Now, Doctor, with regard to the IME that you performed in this matter, how many IMEs do you perform on an annual basis?
A. About four hundred.
Q. Okay. And of those IMEs how many depositions do you provide?
A. About a hundred and fifty.
Q. And of those depositions, IMEs, what percentage of those are performed on behalf of plaintiffs or their attorneys?
A. About 95 percent.

Only Saw Claimant Once, 15-Minute Examination

Q. Okay. You evaluated Ms. Reece on one occasion, is that correct?
A. That's correct.
Q. How long did that examination last?
A. I did not make a record as to how long I spent examining Ms. Reece, but in looking back on the scope of my examination it would have been approximately an hour.
Q. Okay. And of that hour how long did you spend performing actual measurements and tests?
A. The physical examination part of it would have been about 15 minutes.
Q. Now, what records were provided for your review prior to your exam?
A. I had the records of Dr. D. Hardin of April 29, 1996 through August 25, 2004. I also had Dr. Hardin's dictated operative record of May 19, 2004, when he did the surgical release of Ms. Reece's right carpal tunnel. In addition, I had the Appalachian Orthopaedic Associates' records; the records of Dr. J. Holbrook from September 2, 2004, through July 12, 2005. And I had Dr. Holbrook's dictated operative records from Mountain Empire Surgery Center of November 10, 2004, and also of March 2, 2005, when Dr. Holbrook surgically released the first dorsal compartment of the right wrist—the first surgery. And also surgically released the left carpal tunnel, which was the second surgery that he performed.
Q. And so you reviewed these records, is that correct?
A. Yes, I did.

Other Physicians Would Not Assign Impairment Rating

Q. Okay. And you're aware that Dr. Hardin did not assign any impairment to Ms. Reece as a result of her carpal tunnel condition, is that correct?
A. Yes, I am.
Q. Okay, and you're aware that Dr. Holbrook didn't assign any impairment to Ms. Reece as a result of her carpal tunnel condition, is that correct?
A. Yes, I am.
Q. Okay. And are you also aware that Ms. Reece had been returned to work without restrictions, is that correct?
A. Yes. That was my impression from my review of those records.
Q. Okay. And again you saw her on December 20, 2005, correct?
A. Yes.
Q. Okay, and that would have been almost two years after her injury or her alleged injuries, is that correct?
A. Yes.

Records Received After Report Written

Q. Okay. Were there any other records that you were not provided that you would have found useful . . . prior to reaching your conclusions?

A. After completing my report I did receive the record from the Southern Rehabilitation Group, which is the consultation record, and the Electrodiagnostic Study Report done by Dr. James P. Little on April 19, 2004.

Q. So you did not review those prior to your report, is that correct?

A. That's correct.

Q. Are there any other records that you didn't review that you would have found useful to review in providing your opinion?

A. There are not any other records that I have received since completing my report and I was not aware of any additional records that may exist that I would like to have examined.

Work History of Claimant

Q. Okay. Now, Doctor, in Ms. Reece's history to you she provided or she reported that she worked at East Tennessee Garment as a seamstress for about twenty years prior to her employment at Rite Screen, would that be correct?

A. In looking back over my report, I did not see that mentioned. And unless I'm overlooking it in my report, I must not have been aware of it or at least I certainly did not include it in my report and I don't have independent recollection of such.

Probing How Forthcoming the Claimant Was to the Physician

Q. So did you believe that Ms. Reece gave you a full, complete and accurate report of her history, prior conditions?

A. Yes, that it was reasonably accurate and thorough.

Q. Okay. Would the fact that she worked as a seamstress for twenty years prior to her employment at Rite Screen have been relevant?

A. It may have been, depending on when she started working at Rite Screen.

Q. Okay. But nonetheless it would have been something that you would have liked to have known, is that correct?

A. Perhaps, depending on the nature of the previous work as a seamstress and also the timing of that work. The timing of that work, assuming that it was repetitive type work, or production type work, would have been very important.

Q. Okay. Did she—did Ms. Reece provide a history to you that she had worked for Rite Screen for about a year prior to her alleged carpal tunnel injuries?

A. I do not have that specifically set forth in my report.

Q. Okay. Did Ms. Reece report to you that she smoked about a pack of cigarettes a day?

A. Yes.

Q. Okay. And did she report that she had smoked a pack of cigarettes a day for about the past fifteen or sixteen years?

A. Yes. And, in fact, she indicated to me that she had smoked for about twenty years, but I didn't ask her specifically how long she had smoked as much as a pack per day.

Q. Okay. Did Ms. Reece tell you that she had been previously diagnosed as having arthritis prior to her alleged injury?

A. No.

Q. Did Ms. Reece tell you that she had been diagnosed as having stiffness in multiple I joint-IP joints prior to her alleged injury?

A. No.

Q. Okay. In your C32 that's been filed in this matter, to which we objected, under your "patient history," let me take you to that, please.

A. Alright.

Q. It indicates . . . I think the last line, the last paragraph, excuse me, second paragraph, last line. "She took a medical leave in August 2004 and has only been able to work for one week since."

A. Yes, that was my impression.

Q. Okay. Were you aware that she had been released to return to full duty on at least two separate occasions? Or excuse me, by two separate physicians?

A. Yes. Dr. Hardin released her according to his record to return to unrestricted work and so did at a later date, Dr. Holbrook.

Q. Okay. Did you explore any reasons as to why she wasn't back at work or had only worked for one week?

A. It was my impression that she had worked only one week because of the ongoing symptoms in both of her upper extremities.

Q. Okay. So that's based upon her subjective history to you, is that correct?

A. Yes.

Confronted with New Information, Doctor Asked to Change Opinion

Q. Okay. And if that subjective history isn't correct, then your opinion as to or your understanding as to why she was off work following her alleged injuries and carpal tunnel releases would not be accurate, is that correct?

A. Well, you'll notice in my report and also in the C32 form, that—that I simply entered the information that she had been on medical leave in August 2004, and had only been able to work for one week since then by the time of my examination. I did not go into detail as to why she was on medical leave or why she had been able to work only for one week. It was a matter of fact that she had not been working by the time of my examination and, of course, that was the point of greatest interest to me when I examined her.

Q. Okay. So you assumed the reason that she was off work or had only worked for one week since August 2004 was because of her carpal tunnel, is that correct?

A. Yes. And other ongoing symptoms. And she had other symptoms in addition to the carpal tunnel syndrome in both upper extremities.

Impairment Rating

Q. Okay. Now, Dr., you assigned Ms. Reece a 9 percent permanent partial impairment to each upper extremity, is that correct?

A. Yes, that's correct.

Q. Okay. And you did that even though Ms. Reece was able to move both upper extremities in a normal fashion, is that correct?

A. Yes. And, of course, carpal tunnel syndrome does not preclude a person's ability to move both upper extremities in a normal fashion.

Q. Okay. So she was able to actively demonstrate normal range of motion of all joints of both upper extremities, is that correct?

A. Yes, that's correct. And, of course, carpal tunnel syndrome permanent physical impairment is not based on loss of motion.

Q. Okay. Now, Dr. Hardin performed surgery on Ms. Reece's right carpal tunnel, is that correct?

A. Yes.

Q. Okay. And Dr. Hardin assigned a zero percent PPI to the right upper extremity, didn't he?

A. Yes.

Q. Okay. Now, you didn't perform surgery on Ms. Reece's right carpal tunnel, did you?

A. That's correct, I did not.

Q. Okay. Dr. Holbrook performed surgery on Ms. Reece's left carpal tunnel, is that correct?

A. Yes.

Q. Okay. And Dr. Holbrook assigned a zero percentage PPI to the left upper extremity, didn't he?

A. Yes, that's correct.

Q. Okay. And you did not perform surgery on Plaintiff's left carpal tunnel, did you?

A. That's correct, I did not.

Q. Okay. So you didn't treat Ms. Reece?

A. That's correct, I did not.

Q. And you didn't perform surgery on Ms. Reece?

A. That's correct.

Q. Okay. Now, Dr., when you—when you evaluated Ms. Reece, did you evaluate her based upon the condition she was in at the time that you saw her on December 20, 2005?

A. In my examination I took into consideration her history which went back to January, 2004, and also the records compiled by her treating physicians and the records that I have listed earlier here in my—the testimony today and also my physical examination. I also took into consideration her residual persistent complaints that she described that were still present by the time of my examination.

Q. Okay. And those would have been subjective complaints, correct, Doctor?

A. Yes.

Doctor Did Not Request Further Diagnostic Testing

Q. Okay. Now, on page 2 of your—of the C32 that was filed in this matter, and actually it may be page 3—there's a section, page 2 of Section D, "Summary of diagnostic testing," is that correct?

A. Yes.

Q. Okay. And I noticed that nothing is checked as far as diagnostics, would that be accurate?

A. That's correct. I felt that based on the records that I had, I had satisfactory testing in order to be able to reach the conclusions given in my report concerning Ms. Reece's condition of her upper extremities and that no additional tests were needed.

Nerve Testing Was Negative

Q. Okay. So you did not rely on the nerve testing performed in July 2005, is that correct?

A. The nerve testing performed in July 2005 at Dr. Holbrook's office was a nerve pace test, which is a surface electrode test, and that was negative. And that did not preclude the ongoing presence of carpal tunnel syndrome, nor did it rule out permanent changes in the median nerve at either of her wrists.

Q. But the nerve testing performed in July 2005 was normal, correct?

A. Yes.

Work Restrictions

Q. Now, Dr., I believe you assigned or at least provided recommendations as to restrictions, is that correct?

A. Yes, I did.

Q. Okay. Did you actually assign these restrictions?

A. Yes, I recommend that they be adopted as permanent because they were based on my findings which were consistent with permanent injury to the median nerves at both of Ms. Reece's wrists. And those permanent changes of injury make her more vulnerable for additional injuries to the median nerves at both wrists than had she not suffered the cumulative trauma of her work for Rite Screen.

Q. Okay. Now, with regards to those restrictions, when you assign restrictions you assign restrictions that don't necessarily reflect the capabilities of Ms. Reece, is that correct?

A. That's correct. What I'm doing as a physician is that I'm warning Ms. Reece that in my opinion based on the objective findings in her case, if she attempts to go beyond the scope of the recommended restrictions she will be placing herself in excessive risk of further injuring her median nerves at both wrists and making her condition worse.

Q. Okay. And, Dr., you do not know the condition of Ms. Reece's wrists prior to January 2004, do you?

A. Only as I have seen them in the records and there were no records that can—that dealt specifically with carpal tunnel syndrome that I recall prior to January 2004. So my assumption has been that she did not have carpal tunnel syndrome prior to January 2004. The records that I have from Dr. Hardin prior to January 2004 had to do with conditions other than the carpal tunnel syndrome.

Q. Okay. And those conditions would be such as arthritis, is that correct?

A. Well, I don't have independent recollection without looking at Dr. Hardin's records, but I'll be happy to do that. In particular on April 29th, 2006 [sic], he saw her for a ganglion cyst on the dorsum, that is, the top of her left foot. And in glancing over that record I don't find any indication of carpal tunnel syndrome or of any arthritis. The next record that he has is February 12, 2004.

Q. And just for the record, Dr., I think you said, that first note, you said, "2006" and it should be . . .

A. 1996.

Q. April 29, 1996?

A. Yes, April 29, 1996.

Q. Okay.

A. Thank you very much for that correction, that is correct.

Two-Point Discrimination Was Normal

Q. Now, Doctor, the two-point discrimination was normal?

A. Yes, it was.

Q. Is that correct?

A. Yes.

Q. And that was in both hands, is that correct?

A. Yes.

Q. And describe for the Court what two point discrimination is?

A. That is the ability of an individual to detect two points as two points instead of one point, that are a measured distance from each other. And in this case, four millimeters, which is—which is normal.

Q. Okay. And when you're testing for that, what are you measuring? Or what do the measurements test for?

A. I'm measuring the individual's ability to interpret two points as two points instead of one point, when the two points are close—as close as four millimeters from each other.

Q. And so when you say the ability to distinguish between two points, that's sensory in nature, correct?

A. Yes, that's right.

Q. Okay.

A. That meant that she had normal sensation in all of the fingertips of all of the digits in both hands.

Q. Okay. And you also, I think you indicated in your report, you paid particular attention to the median innervated muscles of both hands . . .

A. Yes.

Q. . . . and found no localized atrophy or apparent weakness, is that correct?

A. That is correct. The manifestations of her carpal tunnel syndrome were sensory in nature and they were also intermittent as described in my report, which meant that they were off and on. And even though they occurred frequently many times each day, multiple times each day, they nonetheless were off and on. And in a case like that I would expect the sensory findings, the sensory testing in the form of the two point discrimination testing, to be normal and indeed it was in her case.

Q. Okay. So, Doctor, when you measured her sensory testing during your evaluation, it was normal?

A. That's correct.

Q. And Ms. Reece gave you a history of her sensory testing or her sensory abilities in her hands, both hands, to not be normal, is that correct?

A. She gave me the history that she has intermittent numbness and tingling in both of her hands that were specifically in the thumbs, index fingers and middle fingers, which, of course, is in the distribution of the median nerve. And she told me that the numbness and tingling recurred several times each day primarily while she was carrying out her normal activities at home. And that ordinarily she had to stop what she was doing and either warm—run warm water over her hands or massage her hands to relieve the numbness and tingling and she further told me that it usually took her five to ten minutes at a time and as frequently as five to ten times per day to relieve the numbness. And, of course, that varied from day to day depending on the activities in which she was engaged requiring the use of her hands.

Q. But you didn't observe any of this . . . any of these problems . . . during your evaluation of Ms. Reece on December 20, 2005, did you?

A. Well, we're not set up here to have the individual I'm examining go through a lot of use of their hands, such as repetitive use. We're not set up, for example, with a kitchen sink and a sink full of dishes for them to wash or that sort of thing, but I did go ahead in my examination, of course, and carried out specific tests for carpal tunnel syndrome and found them to be positive as indicated in my report.

Current Functional Status of Examinee Challenged

Q. Okay. And you don't know what activities Ms. Reece was engaged in prior to your evaluation of her on December 20, 2005, do you?

A. No. Except that, of course, she gave me the history that she was—that she was not working at the time of my examination and therefore, it was my assumption that she was not engaged in any particular activities that required the continuous or repetitive use of her hands or the vigorous physically demanding use of her hands.

Q. So she didn't report that she had been sewing at home?

A. No, that's correct, she did not.

Q. She didn't report that she had been gardening at home?

A. She did not.

Q. You assigned an impairment for sensory—for loss of sensory ability, is that correct?

A. Yes.

Q. Okay. And that opinion was based upon a history provided to you by Ms. Reece, is that correct?

A. It was based on the combination of her description that the numbness and tingling that she experienced intermittently, multiple times per day, was within the distribution of the median nerve. And then it was also more importantly based on the positive specific tests, clinical tests, for carpal tunnel syndrome that I performed as a part of my physical examination. If her descriptions had not been within the median nerve distribution and/or if the tests for carpal tunnel syndrome that I performed had been negative, then, of course, she would not have qualified for any permanent physical impairment because I would not have found any evidence of permanent changes in the median nerves of both wrists. The most important part of all of that was—was quite clearly the positive clinical findings consistent with bilateral carpal tunnel syndrome.

Only Saw Claimant Once

Q. Doctor, you haven't seen Ms. Reece since December 20, 2005, have you?

A.   That's correct, I have not.
Q.   And you have no plans to see Ms. Reece?
A.   That's—
Q.   . . . again, is that correct?
A.   That's correct. I do not have any plans to see her again.
Q.   Okay. Dr., have all your answers to my questions been within a reasonable degree of medical certainty here today?
A.   Yes.
Q.   Thank you.
A.   You're welcome.

Examination by Claimant's Counsel

Doctor Certified by the American Board of Independent Medical Examiners

Q.   Okay, Doctor, we've got your CV. . . . I think it has been furnished to the court reporter and just for proper recording we would ask that it be attached as Exhibit 3.

[CV is marked and filed as Exhibit No. 3.]

Alright. Without going into that curriculum vitae in detail, Dr. Kennedy, I do want to ask you what the significance is of the board certification that you have obtained from the American Board of Independent Medical Examiners and the necessary preparation to obtain that board certification as it relates to examinations for workers?

A.   In order to be eligible to take the examination administered by that Board, I of course, first had to be qualified in my own field of orthopaedic surgery. That Board Examination and Certification is open to physicians from multiple fields of medicine. So in order to further be qualified to take the examination and become a candidate for certification by that Board, I had to take additional training that had to do specifically with properly performing independent medical examinations and that emphasized the use of the *AMA Guides for the Evaluation of Permanent Physical Impairment.* Then the examination itself was a written examination that lasted about a half day. That Board requires for a renewal of its certification that we go through the cycle of additional training and taking the examination again every five years. So I first took the examination and also passed it the first time that I took it in 1996. And I went through the cycle again, again taking the examination after going through the additional training and also passing the examination in 2001. And then last in the fall of 2005 I went through the cycle still a third time and renewed my certification by that Board through October 2011.

AMA Guides *Not Part of Standard Medical Training*

Q.   Now, Dr. Kennedy, apart from your training and education using the American Medical Association Guidelines, as a general orthopaedic surgeon or as a general physician, are you aware of any training or education using that particular medical book, those guidelines, during the course of a physician's general training?

A. No. We are not—certainly I was not—exposed in a formal manner to the *AMA Guides to the Evaluation of Permanent Impairment,* nor did I receive training for it outside of . . . for its use, outside of the training in preparation for the American Board of Independent Medical Examiners. Now, there are several different organizations in the country that do offer training in the use of the *AMA Guides,* but—but a physician has to specifically apply for and undergo the training. It is not included, that I know of, as a standard part of the curriculum in medical schools or in any of the specialties that I'm aware of, of medicine.

Q. And, Dr. Kennedy, your training, Board Certification, re-certification twice now, I believe.

A. Yes.

Q. Has that significantly aided you in being able to do independent medical examinations pursuant to the Tennessee Workers Compensation Act and its direction to use the AMA's. Guidelines?

A. Yes. And I've also been aided in that regard by the fact that I no longer treat patients and no longer perform surgery and I'm therefore able to focus my attention in a more thorough manner on the skills involved and the knowledge involved in properly performing independent medical examinations and more particularly in using the *AMA Guides to the Evaluation of Permanent Impairment.*

Witness Also Certified by State in Use of AMA Guides

Q. I also noticed on your Curriculum Vitae that—that you are a member of the Medical Impairment Registry of the Tennessee Department of Labor and Work Force Development. Is that correct?

A. Yes, I am.

Q. What is required of the physicians in order to comply with the requirements of that membership, Dr. Kennedy?

A. In addition to the qualifications that we—you and I—have just discussed within the past few minutes, I had to demonstrate and have certified that I have been through training specifically in the use of the current *AMA Guides to the Evaluation of Permanent Impairment,* which is the fifth edition.

Q. And do you currently then utilize this latest edition of the guidelines when you give opinions regarding permanent impairment?

A. Yes, I do. And that edition has been available to me and used as a standard part of my practice since January 2001.

Description of Claimant's Injury

Q. Okay. Now, Dr. Kennedy, specifically relating to Ms. Reece, could you give us a brief description of the injury that was supplied to you by her when you examined her in December of '05?

A. Yes. She told me that in about January, 2004 she had onset first of intermittent nocturnal numbness and tingling in both of her hands that regularly interfered with sleep. And that during that same period she also noticed increasing numbness and tingling with associated aching in both of her hands during her shifts of work for Rite Screen of Elizabethton, Tennessee. Those presentations of carpal tunnel syndrome are classic in that most patients do notice some first at nighttime interfering with sleep. And then later beginning to notice the symptoms while carrying out tasks requiring the use of their hands. She went on to tell me that her work for Rite Screen, a manufacturer of window screens, was production work. Her specific job required that she build window screen frames. The work required her to rapidly and continuously use both hands to press L-shaped brackets or keys into pre-drilled slots in the frames. She often had to pound the brackets into place using the palms of her hands. She then used those inserted brackets to assemble each four-sided frame. She built about 200 window screen frames per hour in this work. And certainly I concluded after my examination of her that the type of work that she did was indeed the type of work, assuming her description to be reasonably accurate and thorough, that is well known to lead to cumulative trauma to the upper extremities and through that cumulative trauma then to cause the changes in the median nerves at both wrists that we have come to call by two commonly used names, the one name, the most common name, of course, is carpal tunnel syndrome, but the other very frequently used name is median neuropathy at the wrist. And neuropathy simply means an abnormality or a pathology of a nerve, in this case, the median nerve.

Q.   Okay, now, Dr. Kennedy, was the history that she gave you consistent with the diagnostic reports that were generated by the treating physicians?

A.   Yes.

Claimant's Complaints

Q.   And if you would, Dr. Kennedy, briefly discuss what her complaints and symptoms were when you saw her?

A.   By the time I saw her she told me that even though she had not been working for some period of months she still had intermittent activity-related and positional numbness and tingling in her thumbs, index fingers and middle fingers. Those symptoms were worse in the right hand than in the left hand. She did not mention her ring finger or her little finger on either hand. She further told me that the numbness and tingling recurred several times each day, primarily while she was carrying out her normal activities at home. She usually was not able to forget about the numbness and tingling even when she was busy. Ordinarily she had to stop what she was doing and run warm water over her hands or massage her hands to relieve the numbness in order to continue any tasks requiring the use of her hands. It usually took her five or ten minutes at a time and as frequently as five to ten minutes to, correction, five to ten times per day to relieve that numbness. And, of course, the frequency of the numbness and tingling varied depending on her uses of both hands.

Verification of Complaints

Q.   Okay. Dr. Kennedy, were you able to verify whether these complaints were valid and if so, how was that done?

A. Well, they were completely consistent with the types of complaints that we expect patients with median neuropathy at the wrist to voice. They were consistent with the findings of carpal tunnel syndrome in the record. And they were also consistent with my own physical findings.

Description of Physical Examination

Q. And what physical examination then did you perform, Dr. Kennedy, for purposes of rating Ms. Reece?

A. I particularly looked at three tests that we commonly use for the presence of carpal tunnel syndrome. The Tinel's sign, which is done by tapping the median nerve at the wrist, was positive on the right involving the thumb, index finger and middle finger. Now, what we expect is that the tapping would lead to changes in the sensation within the distribution of the—of the median nerve, which it did in this case on both hands, not only on the right, but also on the left. Now, the left, the tingling from tapping on the median nerve at the wrist did not include the thumb, it only included the middle finger and the ring finger. But still within distribution of the median nerve. Now, the median nerve compression test was also positive on the right in ten seconds involving the thumb, index finger and the middle finger. And the median nerve compression test was additionally positive on the left after fifteen to twenty seconds involving the index, middle and ring fingers. Now, that is a test that we perform by applying digital pressure, that is, with my examining fingers I apply a gentle pressure to the median nerve itself at the wrist. The Phalen's test was also positive bilaterally involving the entire distribution of each median nerve after about thirty seconds. Now, in the Phalen's test we have the patient simply hold both of their hands with the wrists in maximum flexion to crowd and relatively kink the median nerve at both wrists, which is another form of applying pressure to the median nerve at each of the wrists, and we have them hold that position for a total of a minute. And there we're looking for changes in the sensation in the hand again within the distribution of the median nerve. So all three of the tests that I used for specifically diagnosing carpal tunnel syndrome were positive in each of Ms. Reece's hands.

Q. Okay. Now, this was after both Dr. Hardin's surgery and Dr. Holbrook's surgery?

A. Yes.

Q. Correct?

A. That is correct. And in the situation following each of those operative procedures it was also more than six months following those surgical procedures. And six months has been generally accepted as the minimum time to allow for complete settling of any post-surgical inflammatory changes at the median nerves in the wrists. So that, in other words, by waiting six months we are intentionally attempting not to be misled by any possible or conceivable post-surgical changes in our testing.

Objective Findings

Q. These three tests that you spoke of—the Tinel's, the median nerve compression test, and the Phalen's test—are they objective findings?

A. Yes, they are.

Q. Okay. And what's the significance, Dr. Kennedy, of the distinction between objective findings and subjective findings?

A. An objective finding is something that I can detect independent of what the patient tells me; whereas, the subjective complaint is what the patient perceives and the way the patient describes the symptoms that they perceive.

Q. Okay. Now, Mr. Baker discussed these two doctors that did these surgeries, Dr. Hardin and Dr. Holbrook, and I guess the best thing to do is let's start with Dr. Hardin. In relation to these three clinical tests that you used to determine this median neuropathy or carpal tunnel, as you say, from your review of Dr. Hardin's records can you determine if he even—if he did these tests in order to—to follow up on the right wrist that he did the surgery for to see if she still had persistent positive findings?

A. Well, Dr. Hardin does mention the symptoms in his record that were consistent with ongoing carpal tunnel syndrome after the surgery that he performed for Ms. Reece on May 19, 2004. In particular on July 22, 2004, he mentions tingling in the finger tips of the index and middle fingers. And then he makes the same reference again on August 5, 2004, indicating that she by that time still had numbness in the tops of her index and middle fingers. But I did not find in any of Dr. Hardin's records where he applied the specific tests for carpal tunnel syndrome that are generally relied upon to make the diagnosis of carpal tunnel syndrome. In other words, it appeared to me in the record that he did not, simply he did not address those tests either to say that they were negative or positive. To say that he did or did not perform those tests I just didn't find any mention of those tests in his records.

Q. Okay. But as you just stated, your review of those notes and after the surgery of May 2004, that is, in July and again on August 5, 2004, he does note in the records that there are objective findings of persistent median neuropathy on the right side for Ms. Reece?

A. No, not objective findings. He doesn't address the objective findings beyond simply saying that she still had tingling in the tips of the index and middle fingers. Of course, those symptoms are consistent with median neuropathy because the tingling was in the distribution of the median nerve.

Q. Okay. When you were practicing and doing surgery, if you were presented with these subjective complaints after a surgical procedure, would you take the next step then and do the objective testing?

A. I would not within the first few months after surgery, but certainly prior to signing off on a patient so to speak and particularly prior to determining whether there was evidence of permanent physical impairment, then it was my custom to go through these tests at that time.

Other Ratings Not Done at Maximum Medical Improvement

Q. Okay. Assuming then that Dr. Hardin did this surgery on May 19, 2004, what's the significance of rating Ms. Reece, in relation to these ongoing symptoms, rating her for a percentage of impairment on August 25, 2004?

A. She would not have been at maximum medical improvement by August 25, 2004. It takes at least six months after the surgery for carpal tunnel release to be at maximum medical improvement. And in addition to that when he did voice his conclusion that she had no permanent physical impairment as given in paragraph one of his record of August 25, 2004, he did not indicate in that record or in any other post-operative record that I found whether those specific tests that I had mentioned or any other specific test for carpal tunnel syndrome were positive or not. He simply didn't address them.

Commenting on Rating by Treating Physician

Q.   Okay. The—Mr. Baker has filed a C32 signed by Dr. Hardin where he states that he specifically under the impairment F, abbreviated F, impairment section of that C32, where he gives zero percent scheduled member and zero percent whole-body impairment. The question asked in this form is "What tables did you use in arriving at this percentage?" And his answer is—his answer is, "Page 494-Fifth Edition." Now, Dr. Kennedy, and I'll show you that, based on your testimony and your review of these records, can you reconcile under the *American Medical Association Guidelines* how he arrived at zero percent impairment on August the 25th, 2004, in view of the fact that he just did the surgery in May of that year?

A.   No. I really cannot.

Q.   Alright. Can you reconcile that percentage of impairment outside of the *American Medical Association Guidelines?*

A.   No, not on—not on any criteria that I can think of or that I know of that would be generally accepted as a basis for concluding a rating of permanent physical impairment.

Left Extremity

Q.   Alright. Then, let's go to the left extremity. And again, referring back to the positive clinical findings from your examination in December of 2005 with a positive Tinel's sign, the positive median nerve compression test and a positive Phalen's test. From your review of Dr. Holbrook's notes, can you determine if— if he conducted these tests after he performed the surgery on the left extremity?

A.   I did not find in his record where he performed the three clinical tests that I found to be specifically positive for carpal tunnel syndrome. In particular, I have looked at Dr. Holbrook's records of March 11th, 2005, April 11th, 2005 and July 12th, 2005, and found no mention of the specific clinical examination tests or physical examination tests that I found to be positive. I found no mention of those in any of the three records that I have in front of me compiled by Dr. Holbrook. Again, it's a matter of not addressing them. Whether he did them or did not do them, whether they were negative or positive, there's just no mention of them in the record that I see.

Q.   Okay, now, I see that Dr. Holbrook did the surgical procedure in—on March 2005 on the left.

A.   Yes.

Q.   And his impairment rating as elicited by Mr. Baker, occurred on July 12, 2005.

A.   Yes.

Q. Is that sufficient time in order to give an opinion as to impairment?

A. No.

Disagreement with Impairment Rating of Other Treating Physician

Q. And again, absent any mention of these—these tests that are generally and accepted within the medical community to determine median neuropathy or carpal tunnel as it were, can you reconcile the percentage impairment that Dr. Holbrook found of zero percent in July of 2005 of any—within the American Medical Association Guidelines?

A. No.

Q. Again, outside of the A.M.A. Guidelines, based upon your—your education and being a treating physician for many years as you were, can you reconcile this impairment rating outside of the Guidelines?

A. No.

Q. Now, Dr. Holbrook has in his report of July 12, 2005, he says, "Based on the Fifth Edition of the A.M.A. Guidelines, and having a normal nerve testing, this would ascribe a zero percent PPI regarding the carpal tunnel." Is that a reasonable interpretation of the—of the Guidelines in order to ascribe as he uses the word, a percentage impairment?

A. No.

Q. And could you—you tell us what your justification of that is?

A. The—the basis for diagnosing carpal tunnel syndrome and in fact, the basis for taking a person to surgery and performing surgery for carpal tunnel syndrome, is primarily the clinical findings of the distribution of numbness and tingling and the positive specific tests that I have mentioned. And there are a few other tests which I do not customarily do that are also available and that many physicians customarily use. If a person has clear unequivocal clinical findings consistent with carpal tunnel syndrome, then that is generally accepted as an appropriate basis for surgery assuming, of course, that the person has not responded to attempts of treatment without surgery. And that is true even in the absence of electrodiagnostic studies or in the event that electrodiagnostic studies have been done, even in the presence of negative electrodiagnostic studies that show no abnormalities in the median nerve. There are some very good physiological reasons for that. If you keep in mind that a nerve is made up of many, many fibers that are microscopic that are tiny in size. You can compare a nerve such as a median nerve with a telephone cable. Many, many wires, many many fibers that conduct the function of the nerve through the nerve. When we're sampling those by placing needles into the nerves in electrodiagnostic study, we are specifically getting into the nerve itself and therefore, increasing the chance that we will be sampling in our testing abnormal fibers within the nerve, but we can't sample every fiber within the nerve. And we can't always necessarily sample the particular fibers that are abnormal. And furthermore, we know consistent even with—in Ms. Reece's case, that from time to time, depending on the temperature of the nerve and depending on the amount of inflammation around the nerve, that the nerve can vary in its mainifestation of abnormality. So all of those reasons combine to let us know that there is such a thing as a false negative as we refer to it, electrodiagnostic testing. And therefore, we have not come to rely on electrodiagnostic testing for carpal tunnel syndrome as the gold standard. The gold standard in diagnosing carpal tunnel syndrome, even to the extent of offering a person surgery and performing surgery, is still the clinical diagnosis. And therefore, the clinical diagnosis based on the distribution of the numbness and tingling and these specific tests that I've been discussing earlier, should be the gold standard in my opinion. And I believe most orthopaedic surgeons would agree with this for determining whether there's permanent physical impairment in a case of median neuropathy at the wrist or carpal tunnel syndrome. The same would be true, by the way, for other less commonly encountered peripheral nerve entrapments, such as cubital tunnel entrapment of the ulnar nerve at the elbow, also entrapment of the ulnar nerve at the hand. Also entrapment of the posterior interosseous nerve in the forearm, a branch of the radial nerve. Also for tarsal tunnel syndrome, entrapment of the tibial nerve, sensor branches of the tibial nerve in the—in the lower leg.

Q. Okay. So I take it, Dr. Kennedy, the fact that this statement that "nerve pace has returned to normal limits at 3.7," that statement from Dr. Holbrook, you cannot take that statement and correlate that without doing these clinical tests with a zero percent impairment, can you?

A. That's correct, I cannot. Now, what the nerve pace test indicated in Dr. Holbrook's records, at least by my interpretation, was that she improved after the surgery. And it was my impression when I examined Ms. Reece that the surgery had been of benefit, that she had indeed improved. But that didn't mean that she didn't have permanent injury to the nerves. And, of course, we hope following surgery such as Ms. Reece has undergone, that the surgery would lead to some improvement.

Q. Is that consistent then with Dr. Holbrook saying on July 12, 2005, that there's— there's quite a bit less numbness and tingling?

A. Yes. Even in that same record Dr. Holbrook in his first paragraph on July 12, 2005, seems to indicate that she still has numbness and tingling. He simply says that it's less. And that would mean to me that even at that time she still had or would have had findings consistent with carpal tunnel syndrome had Dr. Holbrook gone ahead and examined her for carpal tunnel syndrome. And such examination does not appear in his record. He does talk about the fact that her surgical wound is well healed and, of course, after surgery we're always concerned with that. He says that she does not have significant tenderness in the palm of her hand. We also—any of us—would be concerned with that following surgery because we wouldn't want to be overlooking the possibility of ongoing inflammatory changes that may represent a—a mild infection in the palm of her hand at the surgical site. He does go on to say that there may be a little swelling over the flexor carpi radialis sheath. That's one of the tendons that is adjacent to, right next to and slightly overlies the median nerve. Again any of us would be concerned about that, that there not be swelling in or around that tendon. And then he gives his attention to the thumb when he says that her basilar grind remains active with some tenderness there consistent with osteoarthritis. That specifically has to do with the base of the thumb. But that's the extent of this physical examination on July 12, 2005. And there's nothing concerning an examination specifically for carpal tunnel syndrome or residuals of median neuropathy at the wrist with regard to physical examination in that paragraph or in any other paragraph of that record.

Q. Okay. And I do note that on this July 12, 2005 office visit, he notes that this is a recheck of the left wrist?

A. Yes. That's given in the first line to the right of the date.

Q. And his previous examination from July 12 again is—is April 11, 2005, about a month after the surgery, and he notes that that office visit again was a recheck of the left wrist, is that correct?

A. That's correct.

Q. Alright. And again, previous to that is March 11, 2005, which is approximately nine days after the surgery. And that's also a recheck of the left wrist, is that correct?

A. That's correct.

Q. Alright. And going backwards then, we have the release on March 2, and his previous office notation is January 11, 2005. And what does the—what is that office visit for, Dr. Kennedy, if you can tell?

A. That is a recheck of the right wrist.

Q. And this recheck of the right wrist does, at least from my reading, show us some—well, it speaks of the Phalen's test and a Tinel's test, doesn't it?

A. Yes, it does.

Q. Okay.

A. And both of those are specific tests for carpal tunnel syndrome. And he indicates that both of those are positive although the Tinel's was only mildly positive. His term for that is, quote, "Not very active," end quote. Which, of course, would mean to me that it was active, just not—not very active.

Q. Okay. Now, this is on the right wrist, which Dr. Hardin had previously done surgery back in 2004, is that correct?

A. That's correct.

Q. And Dr. Hardin's surgery was on May 19th of 2004?

A. Yes, that's correct.

Q. So that's about eight months after his surgery that Dr. Holbrook, according to his notes, found persistent carpal tunnel or neuropathy on the right wrist, is that correct?

A. Yes.

Q. And is that consistent then with your earlier statement that you generally test for this persistent neuropathy after six months?

A. Yes. That would be after the six months, so I believe that Ms. Reece would have by January 11th, 2005, when Dr. Holbrook reported findings consistent with ongoing carpal tunnel syndrome on the right, I believe she would have reached maximum medical improvement from the surgery Dr. Hardin did for her on the right by that time.

Q. And—and as well, Dr. Holbrook's impression was, of course, persistent carpal tunnel syndrome, is that correct?

A. Yes. And that is in the context of the right wrist. This being a recheck of the right wrist as clearly indicated at the heading of this record of January 11th, 2005.

Did Not Assign Impairment Percentage for deQuervain's Disease

Q. Okay. Alright, just briefly, Dr. Kennedy, aside from the causation considerations and the necessity of the surgical procedure caused by the work related cumulative trauma, this deQuervain's surgical treatment that was done by Dr. Holbrook, was that—was that attributed to the—the work related cumulative trauma that Ms. Reece gave you as a history?

A. Yes, deQuervain's is well known to be caused by cumulative trauma. And I concluded that that surgery was both reasonable and necessary arising from the cumulative trauma of the repetitive work that she did for Rite Screen, but I did not find any objective evidence of permanent physical impairment as a result of her deQuervain's disease, which is tenosynovitis of the first dorsal compartment of the wrist.

Q. Okay. So, yeah, I wanted to make that clear. You have not in—in your opinions here today have attributed any permanent impairment to that deQuervain's disease and subsequent treatment, have you?

A. That's correct.

Q. Alright.

A. I have not.

Q. However, have you been able to determine in your review of Dr. Hardin's records whether he attributed that to her work related cumulative trauma?

A. Yes. In Dr. Hardin's records, I believe I recall a statement that he did not attribute that. Let me see if I can find it. Did not attribute that to her work.

Q. Yes, specifically, Dr. Kennedy, in Dr. Hardin's notes of August 5, 2004, or I'm sorry, August 25, 2004, the very last date that he actually saw her?

A. Yes, I just spotted it in the . . .

Q. Yeah.

A. . . . middle of the second paragraph.

Q. What did he explain to Ms. Reece regarding this—this particular problem?

A. Perhaps it's best just to read his entire second paragraph.

Q. Yes sir. Okay.

A. Quote, "I explained to Ms. Reece that I do believe that she has right first dorsal compartment tendonitis. This has been something that she complained of and that she demonstrates clinically. She also has some right elbow lateral epicondylitis, tennis elbow. I do not consider either of these problems to be related to her employment. She does have left carpal tunnel syndrome that I believe is associated with her employment. Should she desire that any of these be treated in the future, I'll be glad to address those as needed. No scheduled follow up." End of quote.

Q. Okay. Now, Dr. Kennedy, as well as Mr. Baker pointed out on October or August 25, 2004, Dr. Hardin released Ms. Reece to return to her production work with n restrictions whatsoever. Is that reasonable under the circumstance that he has just said, that she's got a left carpal tunnel syndrome.

A. No.

Q. And looking at—switching a little bit to Dr. Holbrook's note of September 28, 2004, Dr. Holbrook told Ms. Reece that the deQuervain's release may help her considerably with her pain. He also goes on the state that, "The causation of that often can be associated with repetitive flexion extension and forceful gripping with the hand, which I suspect would be implicated with an assembly type occupation." Is that consistent with your testimony that the deQuervain's release was associated with her work related injuries?

A. Yes.

Q. Alright. Now, I'm aware that the C32 and your Independent Medical Examination have been attached as exhibits, but I think it's at least important to go through some of that here while you're testifying. So let me back up to—to your examination and your findings associated with Ms. Reece's condition and start with whether she has reached maximum medical improvement?

A. Yes. By the time of my examination she had.

Q. Okay. And speaking of maximum medical improvement, is it your testimony, and I think it is, is that it's generally reached about six months after a surgical procedure?

A. For carpal tunnel release.

Q. For carpal tunnel syndrome, is that correct?

A. Yes.

Rating Under the AMA Guides

Q. Alright, now, considering the history that she gave to you, your review of the diagnostic testing and the procedures that the other physicians did as well as your personal examination and the tests, do you have an opinion utilizing the *AMA Guides* within a reasonable degree of medical certainty whether Ms. Reece has a permanent impairment?

A. Yes.

Q. Now, Dr. Kennedy, utilizing the *Guides* then, what is the percentage of impairment that she has?

A. She has 9 percent permanent physical impairment to each upper extremity.

Q. Okay. Now, please explain specifically how you arrived at that percentage of impairment, including the chapters and tables that you used under the *AMA Guides*?

Walkthrough of How Exactly Impairment Rating Was Determined

A. First I would refer you to page 495 in the *AMA Guides,* fifth edition where in the bottom of the left-hand column we're given three scenarios.

Q. Okay.

A. The distinction between the first scenario and the second scenario is positive clinical findings. The beginning of the description of scenario 1. And under scenario 1, we're told in the *Guides* that we should refer to table 1610 on page 482 to grade the sensory abnormalities in the distribution of the particular nerve entrapment, in this case, of course, the median nerve.

Q. Okay.

A. And so referring to that table on page 482 I concluded that Ms. Reece's symptoms in both of her upper extremities and the losses of physical function resulting from her sensory symptoms were consistent with a high grade four finding, namely that she had abnormal sensations, which, of course, as I previously mentioned were in the distribution of the median nerve, but those abnormal sensations were intermittent. When they occurred she could not forget them, even when she was busy. And also when they occurred they temporarily interfered with the use of her hands in ordinary activities of daily living. But, of course, that interference did not constitute actual prevention of any of the normal activities of daily living.

Q. Alright.

A. And then that gave me twenty-five percent of the value, the maximum value of the median nerve, in the involved part of the hand. Then we're told to consult table 1615 on page 492 where the maximum sensory—the maximum value of the sensory function of the median nerve to the upper extremity is given at 39 percent. You may recall a few minutes ago that I told you that she did not have symptoms in the ring finger.

Q. Yes.

A. And so the breakdown of the various digital nerves supplied by the median nerve in table 1615 rates the supply to the ring finger at 3 percent. So I subtracted that from the maximum sensory value of the median nerve of 39 percent to the upper extremity and that gave me the 36 percent shown in table—the table on page 5 of my report.

Q. Okay.

A. So then one quarter of 36 percent or 25 percent of 36 percent is 9 percent. And that's how I arrived at the 9 percent to each upper extremity. Her symptoms and findings on my specific tests for carpal tunnel syndrome were very similar in both of her upper extremities by the time of my examination.

Doctor Thoroughly Familiar with the AMA Guides

Q. Okay. And I note there's a, under that direction of the Guidelines there are three possible scenarios that can be present. And without going into all of those at this time, what do the Guides instruct physicians to do when more than one approach to a rating—to rating an individual can be well justified?

A. That we use and adopt the approach to the rating that would yield the highest percent of permanent physical impairment.

Q. And it has been, of course, your testimony that scenario one is very well justified in this particular case, is that correct?

A. Yes.

Q. Okay.

A. Primarily on the basis that the distinction between scenario [one] and scenario two is the positive physical—positive clinical findings that is given in scenario one.

Causation

A. And that is that her employment through cumulative trauma did cause the median neuropathies at both of her wrists.

Q. Alright. Now, these limitations that you've got in your Functional Capacity Assessment on the C32 as well as in your impairment rating report, are these limitations more likely than not causally related to Ms. Reece's work related injury as given to you?

A. Yes.

Functional Limitations

Q. Alright. What then are the limitations that you have discussed and, I think with Mr. Baker, but again what are these limitations that you recommend for Ms. Reece in her condition?

A. I recommend that her activities of daily living and her employment permanently not require rapid, repeated or continuous motions with either of her hands. She should not attempt any hammering or jerking motions with either of her hands. She cannot be expected to grip with maximum tightness or to hold objects with either hand longer than a few minutes at a time. Her hands should not be subjected to vibrations. She should not attempt to work at heights or under conditions in which her safety and stability would depend on the normal function of her hands. Lifting and carrying or pushing and pulling should not exceed twenty pounds occasionally or ten pounds frequently, assuming the use of both hands together. Lifting and carrying or pushing and pulling using either hand alone should not exceed five pounds occasionally.

Q. Are there any limitations regarding vibrations and such?

A. Yes. Her hands should not be subjected to vibrations.

Q. Now, Dr. Kennedy, looking again at the description that she gave regarding what she did at her production job, where she states that she often had to pound these brackets, making these screens into place using the palms of her hands. Again, would it be reasonable to allow her to go back into that type of production work some three or four months after having a carpal tunnel release?

A. No.

Q. And again, Dr., Dr. Hardin then released her to do that type of work, of course. Again, would it be reasonable under any circumstances to—to release her to return to that type of work with a diagnosis of carpal tunnel untreated in her left extremity?

A. No.

Q. And again, with regard to Dr. Holbrook's treatment of the left extremity when he released her to return to unlimited duty, would it be reasonable to release her to do this type of work in view of the fact that she would have to do two hundred window screen frames per hour?

A. No.

Damage Control

Q. If Ms. Reece were to testify, and I think Mr. Baker insinuated this, that she still does some sewing at home. And if she also testified that, quote, "I sew once in awhile, just a hole up or whatever, but if I was making something I would have to stop and rest if I had to cut it and use my hands." Is that reasonable for her to do that due to the fact that she's had these symptoms and complaints?

A. Yes.

Q. Okay. If she also said, quote, "I live on a farm and I, like I said, I planted my garden. I planted some beans, but I had to stop during that time, you know, because I couldn't—my hands—I couldn't keep digging like I did before. And like I planted flowers in my yard, but like I can't do all the things I used to do. I have to stop at times and give it a rest." Is that consistent with your examination evaluation of this lady?

A. Yes.

Prognosis

Q. Now, in regards to any future rehabilitative treatment, what would you prescribe or recommend for Ms. Reece regarding the condition you had found?

A. Well, I need to introduce my answer by indicating to you that the permanent changes that I found in her median nerves at both wrists make her more vulnerable for additional injuries to those nerves at the wrists than had she not suffered the cumulative trauma of the work for Rite Screen. And with that in mind I believe that a wide range of options for future testing and treatment should remain available to her indefinitely. Such testing should include, but not necessarily be limited to additional electrodiagnostic studies of both upper extremities. And such treatment should include, but not necessarily be limited to prescription medicines, splints for both wrists, therapeutic injections and therapy or physical therapy and additional surgery depending on the findings and recommendations of her treating physicians.

Q. Okay. Are there any long term anatomic changes that are reasonably foreseeable considering the nature of her injury and resulting condition?

A. That would depend on the occurrence or lack of occurrence of any additional injuries to those median nerves in the wrists and I have recommended the restrictions that you and I just went over and that I just read into my testimony in an effort to minimize that risk.

Q. Okay, I think that's all I have, Dr. Kennedy. Answer any questions that Mr. Baker may have, if any.

Recross-Examination by Employer's Counsel

Questioning on Guides Rating

Q. Just have one, Dr. Kennedy. With regards to page 495 of the *AMA Guides*, under "Carpal Tunnel Syndrome," I believe you indicated that there were three possible scenarios that could—that could be present. With regards to scenario one, I believe you testified it's the one that you used to arrive at your impairment here today. What positive clinical findings or median nerve dysfunction did you find?

A. There were none.

Q. Okay.

A. Only the one surface electrode nerve pace test was performed, at least that I found in the record.

Q. Okay.

A. The tests that had been done prior to the surgery, the needle electrode test, was not performed after her surgery.

Q. Okay. And so, Doctor, where it says, "Scenario 1, positive clinical findings of median nerve dysfunction and electrical conduction delays," that's not an "or" is it?

A. No, it is not. And unfortunately in that regard it's indistinguishable from Scenario 2. Again, in my opinion these two scenarios are difficult to distinguish one from the other except for the reference to positive clinical findings in Scenario 1.

Q. Okay. And with regard to Scenario 2, Scenario 2 states, "Normal sensibility and opposition strength with abnormal sensory and/or motor latencies or abnormal EMG testing of the thenar muscles," is that correct?

A. That's correct. In that case a—a positive post-operative electrodiagnostic study would qualify the person under Scenario 2, even if there were no clinical findings consistent with carpal tunnel syndrome. Even if they had no residual numbness or tingling and even if the Tinel's sign were negative and the Phalen's test were negative and the median nerve compression test were negative.

Q. Or if you had a positive Phalen's, a positive Tinel and a positive median, and no electrodiagnostic electrical conduction delay clinical finding, that would also qualify in your Scenario 2, wouldn't it?

A. No, because Scenario No. 2 does not mention those specific positive clinical findings.

Q. Doesn't it say, "Normal sensibility and opposition strength with/or abnormal"?

A. Yes. But the normal sensibility is not required for the diagnosis of, excuse me, reverse that, the abnormal sensibility is not required for the diagnosis of carpal tunnel syndrome as we discussed earlier in my testimony. And muscle weakness such as loss of opposition strength is also not required for the diagnosis of carpal tunnel syndrome. So those are the only two conceivable clinical findings that are mentioned under Scenario 2. And the distribution of the numbness and tingling and the positive tests, the three tests that we've been discussing here today in detail that I found to be positive in each of Ms. Reece's hands, are also not mentioned under Scenario 2. So it's been my interpretation that positive electrodiagnostic studies after MMI at least six months after surgery, even in the absence of any clinical findings such as those three tests, and even in the absence of symptoms of numbness and tingling, would nonetheless qualify the person under Scenario 2 for up to 5 percent physical impairment to the upper extremity.

Q. Okay. And the fact that there was not both positive clinical findings and electrical conduction delays, that means it doesn't qualify under Scenario 1, does it?

A. That is not correct.

Q. Okay.

A. That—that is the unartful part of the wording, particularly of Scenario 1.

Q. Let me ask it a different way, Doctor.

A. In that not every case, and in fact, most of the cases that I encounter of carpal tunnel syndrome after surgery, the electrodiagnostic studies are not repeated as in this case. They were not repeated in the sense that the needle tests were not repeated. And it was the needle tests that were—that were positive before her surgery. So if electrodiagnostically we're comparing apples with apples, we'd want to repeat after the surgery and after MMI the needle test, not the surface electrode test.

Q. Okay, and in this case she didn't have that, correct?

A. That's correct, she didn't have it. But that—

Q. So . . .

A. But that doesn't mean, the fact that she didn't have the test doesn't mean that she didn't have findings consistent with permanent carpal tunnel syndrome as I've testified earlier.

Q. Yes, Doctor, but she did not have positive clinical findings of electrical conduction delays, is that correct?

A. We don't know whether she did or not, because the needle test that was done prior to the surgery was not done after the surgery. We only know that the surface electrode test, the nerve pace test, was normal and reflected improvement. And, of course, that was consistent with her history and her description of symptoms that the surgery had led to improvement, but that didn't mean that the surgery led to effective complete relief or resolution of her symptoms, and more important, resolution of the changes in her median nerves at the wrists, which had become permanent by the time of my examination.

Q. Try one more time, Doctor, The tests that Ms. Reece had in July of 2005, which indicated that she had return of nerve pace?

A. Yes.

Q. Would that be an indication, a clinical finding of electrical conduction delay?

A. No. And it was an indication of improvement.

Criticism of AMA Guides

Q. Okay. So, if Ms. Reece did not have positive clinical findings of median nerve dysfunction and positive clinical findings of electrical conduction delays after her surgery at the time of your evaluation in December 2005, then she should not qualify for Scenario 1 under the *AMA Guides*, page 495?

A. No. And the reason for my answer is, as I've indicated previously, simply that Scenario 1 is unartfully written because it does not make sense from a clinical point of view. And I think I have indicated earlier in my testimony that for the diagnosis of carpal tunnel syndrome, the gold standard remains the clinical findings; that is, the abnormal physical findings in the distribution of the numbness and tingling in the hand. And the gold standard is not yet adopted, as being one of the electrodiagnostic studies, whether through the insertion of needles or with the use of surface electrodes on the skin.

Q. Okay. So, Doctor, if an employee of Ms. Reece's does not fit within Scenario 1, what scenario would she fit within?

A. Well, she doesn't fit in Scenario 2, and she certainly doesn't fit in Scenario 3. She simply fits in Scenario 1, in my opinion, with reasonable medical certainty.

CHAPTER 11

JUDICIAL INTERPRETATION OF THE *AMA GUIDES*

§11.01   ALASKA

Rydwell v. Anchorage Sch., 864 P.2d 526 (Alaska 1993)

The Alaska Supreme Court dealt with the claimant, a building plant operator who developed chest pains. The claimant was initially diagnosed as having left costochondritis with bicipital tendinitis. She was later diagnosed as having mild degenerative disk disease. As the conditions did not translate into a permanent impairment under the American Medical Association's *Guides to the Evaluation of Permanent Impairment* (hereinafter *AMA Guides*), she was given a 0 percent disability rating. The lower court then denied reemployment benefits based on the fact that there was no "permanent impairment."

The Supreme Court affirmed the decision, stating:

> In this case, no impairment was found under the AMA ratings, yet the employee's doctors concluded that she could not meet the physical demands of her job. To find for the employee would create a gray area of "permanent impairment" for purposes of AS 23.30.041(f)(3), which could be satisfied by an impairment registering zero on the *AMA Guides* scale. Such a holding would greatly reduce the predictability, objectivity, and cost-reduction which the legislature imbedded within AS 23.30.190 by incorporating the *AMA Guides* test for impairment, and thus seems counter to legislative intent.
>
> To summarize, under the most appropriate reading of AS 23.30.041, an employee must satisfy two tests in order to be eligible for reemployment benefits. First, before the employee has reached medical stability, a physician must predict that the employee's physical capacities will not be sufficient for the physical demands of her original job. AS 23.30.041(e). This test allows an employee to start vocational rehabilitation before she reaches medical stability, and serves the legislature's goal of encouraging early rehabilitation intervention. Second, once the employee has reached medical stability, she must have a permanent impairment, calculated pursuant to AS 23.30.190(b)'s provisions for use of the *AMA Guides*.

Id. at 530.

Municipality of Anchorage v. Leigh, 823 P.2d 1241 (Alaska 1992)

The Alaska Supreme Court dealt with the claimant, who is a paramedic with the Anchorage Fire Department. He injured his back on October 28, 1988. His employer accepted his claim and paid him temporary total disability (TTD) compensation until January 25, 1989. Prior to termination of the claimant's benefits, the insurance adjuster wrote to the claimant's treating physician, asking if he was "medically stable" as defined by Alaska Stat. § 23.30.265(21). The treating physician responded by letter on January 25, 1989, stating "[a]ccording to the definition of medical stability posed in your letter, the employee falls into your parameters of being medically stable." At a later deposition, the treating physician testified that he would prefer to use the definition of "medical stability" taken from the *AMA Guides* under which he thought the claimant would not be stable for a period of six months to a year.

The court found the statute constitutional and failed to require the use of the *AMA Guides'* definition of medical stability. The court reasoned that the statute's presumption was rational and could easily be overcome by the testimony of the treating physician that medical stability had not been reached. The court stated:

> We hold that [claimant]'s substantive due process attack on the definition of medical stability articulated by AS 23.30.265(21), the presumption provided for in this statute, and the burden placed upon the employee to rebut this presumption should be rejected. [Claimant] has failed to meet his heavy burden of demonstrating that no rational basis exists for these three questioned components of AS 23.30.265(21). Given the legislature's explicit goal of insuring "the quick, efficient, fair and predictable delivery of indemnity and medical benefits to injured workers at a reasonable cost to the employers" who are subject to the Act, we conclude that AS 23.30.265(21) is not arbitrary since it bears a reasonable relationship to a legitimate, rational, governmental policy.

823 P.2d at 1247.

Morrison v. Afognak Logging, Inc., **768 P.2d 1139** (Alaska 1989)

In this case, the claimant filed an application for the adjustment of his claim for an occupational wrist injury, and the Alaska Workers' Compensation Board found that the claimant was entitled to disability benefits based on a 25 percent partial permanent disability. The superior court upheld the award. The Alaska Supreme Court reversed, but it agreed that substantial evidence supported the board's 25 percent permanent partial disability rating. The treating physician rated the impairment at 30 percent using the *AMA Guides* but only after arbitrarily adding 12 percentage points to account both for joint roughness and the fact that the injury was to the claimant's dominant hand. The court held that the board's conclusion of a 25 percent impairment was supported by substantial evidence. First, the board noted that the *AMA Guides* already take into account the fact that the injury is to the dominant hand. Next, the board noted that to the extent the added points were for potential impairment as opposed to existing impairment, the rating departs from the *AMA Guides.* Accordingly, the board deducted the 12 percentage points added by the treating physician, leaving a rating of 18 percent. (The board then added a 7 percent impairment for the injury to the claimant's wrist in reaching its final figure of a 25 percent impairment.)

Ratliff v. Alaska Workers' Compensation Bd., **721 P.2d 1138** (Alaska 1986)

The claimant was a pipefitter/welder when he injured his right knee in January of 1983. The claimant's physician rated the impairment to his lower extremity at 19 percent based on the *AMA Guides.* The claimant received permanent partial disability benefits and sought an additional award. The Alaska Supreme Court held that the claimant was not entitled to a concurrent award of both scheduled and unscheduled benefits.

Yader v. State of Alaska, No. 4FA-84-1315 (Super. Ct. Jan. 30, 1985)

The claimant was injured when a coworker threw a bomb into an outhouse, causing the aggravation of a preexisting hearing disability. The claimant suffered an increased hearing loss and a loss of speech discrimination. The testimony of the claimant's physician regarding the speech discrimination was not considered by the board on the grounds that because speech discrimination was not covered by the *AMA Guides* any testimony concerning such a disability could not be considered.

The court stated that such a strict administrative interpretation was too limited for the intent of the statute. The effect of the board's interpretation of the statute would therefore limit recovery only to medical problems covered by the *AMA Guides.* The court opined that this was not the purpose or intent of the statute, and concluded:

> The facts of this case present a clearly measurable medical impairment. Evidence of impairment and its effect on earning capacity constitute the basis of Workers' compensation legislation. The purpose of this legislation is to provide employees with a remedy for injury sustained in an employment relationship. The Board's interpretation of its regulation clearly precludes recovery in cases of impairment which are not AMA rated. This interpretation overly restricts the legislative intent reflected in AS 23.30.095(j).
>
> The more reasonable application of the Board's regulation would be to apply it strictly when the impairment or disability is, in fact, rated by AMA. Where no such rating is available but acceptable medical testing can support the existence of a disability, that testing should be acceptable evidence for determining an effect on earning capacity.
>
> If AMA guidelines exist for neurosensory loss, then the Board's inferences from Dr. [R.]'s letter were error and AMA guidelines must be used. Because no AMA guidelines for speech discrimination exist, it is appropriate for the board to consider Dr. [R.]'s test results.

Id. at 3–4.

§ 11.02   ARIZONA

Simpson v. Industrial Comm'n, 942 P.2d 1172 (Ariz. Ct. App. 1997)

The Arizona court dealt with a claimant who claimed to be permanently impaired due to chronic pain. The court held that the *AMA Guides* (4th ed. 1993) did not provide the exclusive means for evaluating permanent impairment attributable to persistent residual pain. The court further held that disabling pain resulting from an industrial injury is compensable, even though the degree of impairment may not be ratable pursuant to the *AMA Guides*. The court stated:

> This does not conclude our inquiry; the ALJ provided an alternative basis for his award, concluding that, even if [claimant's] pain complaints are attributable to his industrial injury, they are not compensable because they "do not constitute a ratable impairment under *applicable* AMA Guidelines."
>
> [Claimant] argued at the hearing that he was not obliged to establish a permanent impairment pursuant to the *Guides*, and that he had done so instead on the basis of undisputed medical testimony that his symptoms of pain, though unratable under the *Guides*, preclude him from returning to his date-of-injury employment. In support of this assertion, [claimant] cited *Cassey v. Industrial Comm'n*, 152 Ariz. 280, 283, 731 P.2d 645, 648 (Ct. App. 1987), in which this court concluded that a claimant may establish, independent of the *Guides*, that disabling pain constitutes a permanent impairment by showing (1) a causal relationship between residual pain and an industrial injury and (2) a resulting permanent inability to return to former work.
>
> The ALJ dismissed *Cassey* as applicable only to a prior edition of the *Guides* that provided no basis for rating impairing pain. The ALJ stated:
>
> The *Cassey* holding is . . . inapplicable in this matter since the current edition of the AMA Guidelines (unlike the edition at issue in *Cassey*) does [provide] for the rating of chronic pain complaints. *See Guides to the Evaluation of Permanent Impairment*, Chapt. 15 (4th Ed.). When, as in this case, the AMA Guidelines do provide a "fair, accurate measure of the degree of impairment," there is no need to resort to other factors such as work restrictions to resolve the impairment issue.
>
> . . . Because the medical evidence establishes that [claimant]'s current chronic pain complaints do not constitute a ratable impairment under *applicable* AMA Guidelines, . . . [Claimant] is not entitled to permanent benefits.

(Citations omitted.) In drawing this conclusion, the ALJ misread both pertinent case law and the *Guides*.

Our discussion begins with Industrial Commission Rule R20-5-113(D):

> Upon discharge from treatment the physician shall report any rating of any impairment of function as the result of the injury. Any rating of the . . . functional impairment should be in accordance with the standards for the evaluation of permanent impairment as published by the American Medical Association in "Guides to the Evaluation of Permanent Impairment," if applicable.

Arizona Administrative Code (AAC), R20-5-113(D) (Supp. 96-4).

Pursuant to this rule, impairments "should" be rated under the *Guides*, "if applicable." *Id.* Arizona courts, however, have repeatedly held that "[t]he AMA Guides are not to be blindly applied regardless of a claimant's actual physical condition." *W.A. Krueger Co. v. Industrial Comm'n*, 150 Ariz. 66, 68, 722 P.2d

234, 236 (1986). When the *Guides* do not cover, or do not permit accurate assessment of, a claimant's impairment, that does not mean that the impairment is not compensable. It means rather that the impairment may be established by other means. *See id.* at 68, 722 P.2d at 236; *accord Gomez v. Industrial Comm'n*, 148 Ariz. 565, 569, 716 P.2d 22, 26 (1986); *Smith v. Industrial Comm'n*, 113 Ariz. 304, 306–07, 552 P.2d 1198, 1200–01 (1976); *Adams v. Industrial Comm'n*, 113 Ariz. 294, 295–96, 552 P.2d 764, 765–66 (1976).

Smith and *Cassey* illustrate this general proposition in cases involving the evaluation of disabling pain. In *Smith*, a partially recovered claimant was limited by permanent residual pain from returning to heavy work. 113 Ariz. at 305, 552 P.2d at 1199. The treating physician testified that he could rate the claimant's impairment, but had not done so because the *Guides* provided no methodology for rating subjective pain. *Id.* at 305–06, 552 P.2d at 1199–1200. The Industrial Commission found that the claimant had failed to establish a permanent impairment, but the supreme court set the award aside. The court held the inapplicability of the *Guides* did not preclude evaluating claimant's impairment; it simply necessitated doing so by other criteria. *Id.* at 307, 552 P.2d at 1201.

In *Cassey*, as in *Smith*, a partially recovered claimant suffered from residual impairment pain, and the *Guides* provided no basis for measuring the degree of impairment. 152 Ariz. at 280, 731 P.2d at 645. In *Cassey*, however, no physician suggested, as the treating physician had in *Smith*, that the *degree* of impairment could be evaluated by some other methodology. The Industrial Commission denied compensation, finding that some rating of degree of impairment was necessary. This court set the award aside. We distinguished cases of disabling pain from other cases of permanent impairment. Ordinarily, we explained, the Industrial Commission engages in a bifurcated assessment, first determining "the existence and degree of a permanent impairment," and then determining the disability—the diminution of earning capacity—attributable to the impairment. *Id.* at 283, 731 P.2d at 648. We then explained why different treatment is accorded to cases of residual pain:

> In some cases, however, the claimant must establish the disabling effect of the industrial injury in order to establish a permanent impairment. This is true when residual pain is the permanent injury because pain is compensable as an impairment only when it is disabling . . . . Because of the intertwined issues when pain is the only residual permanent injury, the claimant must be allowed to introduce evidence of disability in order to show impairment. During the first stage, the claimant meets his burden of proof in showing the existence of a permanent impairment if he shows that the pain is caused by his industrial injury and results in his permanent inability to return to his former work. Once this initial burden has been met, claimant is then entitled to go through the second stage, during which he must show that the pain resulted in lost earning capacity. The claimant cannot be barred from proceeding to this second stage by his failure to provide a rating of impairment when none is applicable.

Id. (citations omitted).

In this case, the ALJ acknowledged *Cassey* but found it inapplicable because "the current edition of the AMA Guidelines (unlike the edition at issue in *Cassey*) [provides] for the rating of chronic pain complaints." The ALJ erred in treating the revised *Guides* as providing a comprehensive methodology for evaluating pain. He likewise erred in treating the revised *Guides* as mooting *Cassey* as guiding authority in cases of permanently impairing pain.

Although the current *Guides* indeed provide a methodology for rating "chronic pain complaints" that was absent when *Cassey* was decided, the Guides do not purport to do so for the entire spectrum of disabling pain. To the contrary, the fourth edition of the *Guides* narrowly defines "chronic pain" and distinguishes it from other forms of pain, including "persistent pain." Neither Dr. [S.] nor Dr. [K.] testified that Simpson had "chronic pain" as defined by the *Guides;* nor did either testify that the *Guides'* methodology for evaluating "chronic pain" would permit a fair and accurate measure of Simpson's form of pain; nor did either testify that Simpson had any other condition to which the *Guides'* methodology might apply. Dr. [K.] did not address the point, and Dr. Stojic merely testified that "pain itself" is "not sufficient . . . to make a decision whether the patient incurred any permanency or not" under the *Guides*. This evidence does not support ALJ's conclusion that the *Guides* provided a "fair, accurate measure of the degree of [S's] impairment." Rather, it establishes the contrary to be true.

The claimant has the burden of proving the existence of an industrially-related permanent impairment. *See Brooks v. Industrial Comm'n*, 24 Ariz. App. 395, 399, 539 P.2d 199, 203 (1975). Because the *Guides* were inapplicable in this case, [claimant] was entitled to introduce other evidence to meet this burden. *See Smith*, 113 Ariz. at 306–07, 552 P.2d at 1200–01; *Cassey*, 152 Ariz. at 282, 731 P.2d at 647. Testimony from both medical experts established that [Claimant]'s condition is medically stationary, that he suffers from industrially-related residual pain, and that his pain precludes his return to heavy farm labor. This evidence sufficed to establish impairment under *Cassey*.

942 P.2d at 1176–78.

Vargas v. Industrial Comm'n, 926 P.2d 533 (Ariz. Ct. App. 1996)

The Arizona court dealt with a claimant who suffered a work-related impairment of the right knee. The claimant also had a preexisting non-work-related impairment to his right knee. At issue was the proper way to rate the impairment, taking into account the preexisting condition. The court held that the preexisting impairment should be subtracted from the work-related impairment. The court stated:

We have already observed that the amount of an award for a scheduled disability is governed by A.R.S. section 23-1044(B). When there is a partial loss of use to a scheduled body part, the award is based on expert medical testimony which quantifies the degree of impairment caused by the injury. Typically, the expert medical testimony tracks the *Guides to the Evaluation of Permanent*

Impairment published by the American Medical Association. *See* Ariz. Admin. Code R20-5-113 (1995). The guides are not to be applied rigidly, however, and should be followed only when they truly reflect a claimant's loss. *W.A. Krueger Co. v. Industrial Comm'n*, 150 Ariz. 66, 722 P.2d 234 (1986). We acknowledge that the *Krueger* line of cases did not address multiple impairments to a scheduled body part. However, these cases support the general principle that the guides are a tool for reaching an accurate assessment of a claimant's impairment caused by an industrial injury, and while the rating based on the guides may be accurate for each isolated impairment, it is the overall impairment caused by the industrial injury that is important.

Following this approach, a claimant's total post-industrial injury impairment should be determined first. The preexisting nonindustrial impairment should then be determined and deducted. The remaining impairment, measured as a percentage of the whole impairment, is attributable to the industrial injury and should be the basis for the award. [V.], however, has not shown that the administrative law judge did not follow this approach, or assuming the judge did not, that the outcome would be different if the right method had been applied. Dr. [C.] was able to assign impairment percentages to both the preexisting and the industrial injuries, twenty-nine and ten percent respectively. Yet, there was some indication that the knee was impaired by as much as fifty percent before the industrial injury. There is some indication that the additional impairment may have been due to degenerative arthritis but the evidence on this point was confusing and inconclusive. The burden was on [V.] to clarify the point, and this he failed to do. We cannot say that the ten percent impairment that the administrative law judge attributed to the industrial accident was an inaccurate assessment of the impairment caused by the industrial injury.

926 P.2d at 537–38.

Department of Corrections v. Industrial Comm'n, 894 P.2d 726 (Ariz. Ct. App. 1995)

The Arizona court dealt with a worker who had cardiac arrhythmia. The claimant's impairment was rated at 15 percent by two physicians under the *AMA Guides* (4th ed. 1993). *See AMA Guides* (4th ed. 1993) at 194–96. The court noted that, under Arizona law, a medical opinion can supersede the *AMA Guides* when rating industrial impairment. This case, however, dealt with the interpretation of the apportionment statute. The statute states, in relevant part, that "the impairment [giving rise to apportionment] equals or exceeds a ten percent permanent impairment evaluated in accordance with the American Medical Association guides to the evaluation of permanent impairment." Ariz. Rev. Stat. Ann. § 23-1065(C). The court held that this language mandates that when apportionment is the issue under Ariz. Rev. Stat. § 23-1065(C), the administrative law judge (ALJ) cannot accept a medical expert's opinion disregarding the rating for the purpose of defining a listed condition under subpart (3). The court noted that the question of whether paroxysmal tachycardia is a type of arrhythmia ratable under the *AMA*

Guides is a purely medical question and that the court would express no opinion regarding this question.

The claimant was injured when he fell from scaffolding at work, fracturing the tibial condyle of his right knee. The industrial commission found that the claimant had a 70 percent disability. The court of appeals vacated the award. *Slover Masonry, Inc. v. Industrial Comm'n*, 155 Ariz. 211, 745 P.2d 958 (Ct. App. 1987). The Supreme Court of Arizona reinstated the Industrial Commission's award, holding that where a medical expert, a labor consultant, and the claimant all agreed that the impact of the claimant's disability on his ability to perform his job was greater than 50 percent, but the *AMA Guides* gave only a 50 percent disability rating, the ALJ's 70 percent disability rating was supported by evidence.

The claimant testified that his work as a hod carrier involved seven distinct tasks, but that he could now complete only two of the tasks. The five tasks that he was unable to perform amounted to approximately 70 percent of his job when the tasks were measured in terms of the time allotted for each task. A labor market consultant confirmed that the injury disabled the claimant from performing 65 percent of a hod carrier's job.

The Supreme Court of Arizona was faced with two interrelated issues. First, when may an ALJ reject the *AMA Guides* in determining a claimant's percentage of permanent impairment? Second, did the ALJ in this case abuse his discretion in concluding that the *AMA Guides* did not accurately reflect the true percentage of impairment?

The court noted that normally the commission determines the percentage of the leg's loss based on the treating physician's rating of the impairment resulting from the injury. The physician rates the percentage of functional impairment in accordance with the *AMA Guides* if they apply, with a clinical report to support the rating. *See* Ariz. Comp. Admin. R. & Regs. R4-13-113(D). The *AMA Guides* measure the clinical or physiological percentage of impairment without regard to how the injury may affect a person's ability to perform his job. *See Adams v. Industrial Commission*, 113 Ariz. 294, 295, 552 P.2d 764, 765 (Ariz. 1976). An ALJ may consider a wide range of evidence to ensure "substantial justice." Ariz. Rev. Stat. Ann. § 23-941(F). Even though the *AMA Guides* are important, they are not the philosopher's stone. When they are applicable and when they "truly reflect the claimant's loss," they may be used as the sole indicator or factor to be considered in fixing the percentage of impaired function. *Adams*, 113 Ariz. at 295, 552 P.2d at 765. However, when the ALJ finds that the *AMA Guides* do not provide a fair, accurate measure of the degree of impairment, the ALJ must turn to other factors. Any relevant factor, including the effect on job performance, may be considered, as long as it is not prohibited by statute. Indeed, nonmedical factors may be vital when assessing a disability, despite the *AMA Guides*.

> The administrative law judge is responsible for determining the percentage of disability, not simply the percentage of physiological impairment in the functioning of limbs and organs. The *AMA Guides* measure only clinical, physical

impairment expressed in percentage of loss of motion. The administrative law judge, however, must determine the degree of functional loss or impairment, and thus may consider claimant's inability to pursue the specific craft, job or profession he or she practiced at the time of the incapacitating industrial injury.

The *AMA Guides* are only a tool adopted by administrative regulation to assist in ascertaining an injured worker's percentage of disability. Thus, when the *AMA Guides* do not truly reflect a claimant's loss, the administrative law judge must use his or her discretion to hear additional evidence and, from the whole record, establish a rating independent of the AMA recommendations. *WA. Krueger Co.*, 150 Ariz. at 68, 722 P.2d at 236. That is why A.C.R.R. R4-13-113(D) states that the *AMA Guides* "should" be used to establish a rating of functional impairment "if applicable." If an injury has resulted in a functional impairment not adequately reflected by clinical measurement under the *AMA Guides*, then an administrative law judge must consider impact on job performance.

745 P.2d at 1040.

In this case, it is important to note that the dissenting opinion points out that the majority is in effect adopting a one-to-one translation of impairment to disability that never was intended by the *AMA Guides*.

Salt River Project v. Industrial Comm'n, 877 P.2d 1336 (Ariz. Ct. App. 1994)

The Arizona court dealt with a claimant who had injured both knees. The workers' compensation statute required a 40 percent or greater "general functional disablement" before the second injury fund became liable. The court held that the phrase "general physical functional disablement" is equivalent to a whole-person impairment using the *AMA Guides*. The court stated:

We conclude that the phrase "general physical functional disablement," as it appears in section 23-1065(A)(4), has a technical meaning equivalent to whole-person impairment. The latest edition of the *AMA Guides* defines impairment of the "whole person" to mean impairment of the general physiologic functioning of the person, *AMA Guides* 3 (3d ed. rev. 1990). Because the statutory requirement of a combined impairment of 40 percent or greater must apply to every possible combination of impairments, a common measure of impairment is necessary. The only such universal measure is that of the whole person.

Id. at 1338.

Salt River Project v. Industrial Comm'n, 837 P.2d 1212 (Ariz. Ct. App. 1992)

The Arizona court dealt with the claimant, who injured his neck while working as a welder. He underwent neck surgery during which a previously undiagnosed meningioma was found. The claimant was left with at least a 10 percent permanent impairment and was awarded permanent partial disability.

The employer then pursued a claim for apportionment. The court operated under Ariz. Rev. Stat. Ann. § 23-1065(C), which provides the following:

> In claims involving an employee who has a preexisting physical impairment which is not industrially-related and, whether congenital or due to injury or disease, is of such seriousness as to constitute a hindrance or obstacle to employment or to obtaining reemployment if the employee becomes unemployed, and the impairment equals or exceeds a ten percent permanent impairment evaluated in accordance with the American Medical Association guides to the evaluation of permanent impairment, and the employee thereafter suffers an additional permanent impairment not of the type specified in Sec. 23-1044, subsection B, the claim involving the subsequent impairment is eligible for reimbursement.

In this case, the court found that because a meningioma was not a cerebral vascular accident, it was not listed, and apportionment would not apply. The manner in which the *AMA Guides* is used is significant—that is, needing a 10 percent preexisting physical impairment before apportionment is to apply. This is an improper use of the *AMA Guides* and in light of the changes in the *AMA Guides* (4th ed. 1993), legislative action is recommended.

Conner Mfg. v. Industrial Comm'n, 836 P.2d 464 (Ariz. Ct. App. 1992)

The Arizona court dealt with the claimant, who fractured her ankle, resulting in multiple surgeries and an amputation of the leg. The claimant developed a permanent psychiatric impairment, which was diagnosed as a major affective disorder or a dysthymic disorder.

The court rejected the opinion of dysthymic disorder, which would not be disabling and not ratable under the *AMA Guides*. The court, however, found that the amputation resulted in depression and permanent psychiatric impairment supporting an unscheduled disability award. The court stated:

> [Insurance company] asserts that Dr. [T.]'s testimony that Claimant's affective disorder is impairing is legally insufficient to support the award for an unscheduled disability. [Insurance company] argues that to unschedule the left leg disability, Claimant had to prove that her psychiatric impairment is disabling. To satisfy this burden, the argument continues, Claimant had to prove that the psychiatric impairment increased the disability otherwise resulting from the left leg impairment alone. Because Dr. [T.] agreed with Dr. [A.] that Claimant's psychiatric condition did not increase her disability, [insurance company] contends that Claimant failed to sustain her burden of proof.
>
> * * *
>
> In the present case, [insurance company] has properly conceded medical causation. Given this causal connection between Claimant's amputation and her depression, we see no principled justification for distinguishing Dye.

The Administrative Law Judge therefore correctly concluded that Dr. [T.]'s testimony that Claimant suffered a permanent psychiatric impairment supported an unscheduled disability. We accordingly affirm the award.

Id. at 465, 467. *See also Dye v. Industrial Comm'n*, 153 Ariz. 292, 736 P.2d 376 (Ariz. 1987).

Reno v. Industrial Comm'n, 750 P.2d 852 (Ariz. 1988)

The claimant sustained a fractured wrist and possible shoulder injury during the course of her employment. Her request for a hearing was denied by the Industrial Commission as untimely. The court of appeals affirmed, but the Supreme Court of Arizona reversed, holding that the request for a hearing was indeed timely and that the finding that the disability was "scheduled" was not supported by the evidence.

The claimant's treating physician testified that she had an 11 percent impairment of the upper extremity as a result of her limited shoulder movement. The court noted that if the disability was to the arm, it was a scheduled injury; however, if the injury was to the shoulder, it was an unscheduled injury. The physician testified that the *AMA Guides* do not rate an impairment to the shoulder itself, but rather allow a percentage of impairment to the upper extremity. The court found that the doctor's testimony was unambiguous in that the doctor unequivocally stated that the claimant suffered a disability of not only the arm and upper extremity, but also the shoulder. Thus the finding that the disability was "scheduled" was not reasonably supported by the evidence. *See Dye v. Industrial Comm'n*, 153 Ariz. 292, 736 P.2d 376 (Ariz. 1987).

Tucson Steel Division v. Industrial Comm'n, 744 P.2d 462 (Ariz. Ct. App. 1987)

The employee suffered a lower back strain in the course of employment and was rated as suffering a 15 percent permanent impairment. The court noted that, under *Kucko v. Industrial Comm'n*, 116 Ariz. 530, 570 P.2d 217 (Ct. App. 1977), once a notice of claim status closes a claim based upon permanent impairment from a particular physical condition, and if the notice is unprotested and becomes final, a claimant cannot later attempt to establish causation of some other physical or mental condition.

The source of the problem is the ambiguous term "disability." It may signify functional disability, i.e. impairment, or it may signify earning capacity disability. *See generally Smith v. Industrial Comm'n*, 113 Ariz. 304, 552 P.2d 1198 (1976) (adopting definitions of "permanent impairment" and "permanent disability" in *AMA Guides*). In order to eliminate or at least minimize this ambiguity and sufficiency of notice problem, we recommend that the industrial commission consider modifying the standard closing notice form by using the term "impairment" and by requiring specification of the medical basis for the determination.

744 P.2d at 467 n.2.

Pacific Fruit Express v. Industrial Comm'n, 735 P.2d 820 (Ariz. 1987)

The claimant developed a loss of hearing after he was exposed to high levels of noise during his employment with the fruit company from 1948 to 1957 and from 1960 to 1983. The claimant became aware of his hearing loss in the late 1970s but never missed any time from work nor received any medical treatment for the hearing problem. The claimant filed a claim for Workers' compensation in November 1983. In February 1984, the claimant was diagnosed as suffering from a permanent bilateral high-frequency hearing loss of a type commonly associated with the exposure to loud noise. Several physicians testified that the hearing loss resulted from his working at the fruit company. Even though hearing loss was not ratable under the *AMA Guides*, the physicians recommended that the claimant receive protection, rehabilitation, and periodic audiometric testing in the future. The court concluded that the inability to prove a disability that was ratable under the *AMA Guides*, though precluding a scheduled award, did not preclude a finding that the employee had suffered a compensable injury when the medical testimony established that the employee would incur future expenses and require rehabilitation and periodic audiometric testing.

Cassey v. Industrial Comm'n, 731 P.2d 645 (Ariz. Ct. App. 1987)

The claimant was a delivery truck driver who injured his back while lifting a truck ramp. His workers' compensation claim was closed, and his condition was found to be stationary and without permanent impairment by order of the Industrial Commission. The court of appeals, however, found that the claimant's inability to return to work because of industrial-related pain established permanent impairment, despite the inability of the testifying physicians to rate the impairment either under the *AMA Guides* or under any alternative method.

The claimant's injury was diagnosed by his orthopedic surgeon as a chronic thoracolumbar sprain. The physician stated that because of the chronic muscular pain from the injury, the claimant could not return to regular work. The physician also testified that no further treatment would be helpful. However, the physician was unable to rate the degree of impairment under the *AMA Guides* because the *AMA Guides* do not cover chronic sprains. Because the claimant showed no evidence of neurological impairment and had full range of motion, the physician testified that the *AMA Guides* are inapplicable, as these are the only two criteria the *AMA Guides* use to determine impairment.

A second medical expert testified that the claimant's injury was stationary but that the claimant could return to regular work. The judge found that the claimant could not return to his former position because of the pain, but held that the claimant was not permanently impaired because neither of the two experts had rated the impairment.

The claimant argued that *Desert Insulations, Inc. v. Industrial Comm'n,* 134 Ariz. 148, 654 P.2d 296 (Ct. App. 1982), was inapplicable to this case and that his inability to return to work because of industrial-related pain established permanent impairment. The court agreed. Recent Arizona cases dealing with this issue have established that the *AMA Guides* are not to be blindly applied regardless of a claimant's actual physical condition. Instead, the *AMA Guides* are only a valid guideline where the stated percentage of impairment truly reflects the claimant's loss. *See W.A. Krueger Co. v. Industrial Comm'n,* 150 Ariz. 66, 68, 722 P.2d 234, 236 (Ariz. 1986). In *Gomez v. Industrial Comm'n,* 148 Ariz. 565, 716 P.2d 22, 26 (Ariz. 1986), the Arizona Supreme Court noted that when the *AMA Guides* are inapplicable, the judge must use other factors to determine the degree of permanent impairment. In *Smith v. Industrial Comm'n,* 113 Ariz. 304, 552 P.2d 1198 (Ariz. 1976), the Arizona Supreme Court held that where there is only subjective evidence of pain and where the medical testimony established that the pain is a permanent impairment, the *AMA Guides* need not be used to rate a condition to which they do not apply. The issue that was addressed neither in *Smith,* nor in the other cases, was whether the inability of the testifying physicians to rate the claimant's impairment under the *AMA Guides* or any alternative method precludes a finding of permanent impairment as a matter of law.

In this case the judge relied on *Desert Insulation, Inc. v. Industrial Comm'n,* 134 Ariz. 148, 654 P.2d 296 (Ct. App. 1982), for the proposition that some rating is necessary in order to find a permanent impairment. This reliance, however, was misplaced because *Desert Insulations* is factually distinguishable. In *Desert Insulations,* the medical testimony established that the injury was ratable under the *AMA Guides,* but that the medical expert had not looked it up in the *AMA Guides.* The court in *Desert Insulations* held that because the impairment was ratable under the *AMA Guides,* the claimant's permanent impairment needed to be rated in order to establish a permanent impairment. The court clearly stated that Ariz. Comp. Admin. R. & Regs. R4-13-1 13(D) does not require a rating of impairment, but it does require that any such rating, if made, must be made under the *AMA Guides. Id.* 134 Ariz. at 151, 654 P.2d at 299. In *Cassey,* both medical witnesses testified that the claimant's injury was not ratable under the *AMA Guides.*

Assessing the effects of a permanent impairment is accomplished through a bifurcated procedure. First, the claimant must establish the existence and degree of a permanent impairment. Then the claimant must establish that the impairment diminishes the claimant's earning capacity. *Hunter v. Industrial Comm'n,* 130 Ariz. 59, 633 P.2d 1052 (Ct. App. 1981). Usually the degree of impairment can be assessed independently of its resulting loss of earning capacity. The impairment is generally a question of medical fact while the loss of earning capacity is a question of law. *Alsbrooks v. Industrial Comm'n*, 118 Ariz. 480, 578 P.2d 159 (Ariz. 1978). However, as the *Cassey* court noted:

> In some cases . . . the claimant must establish the disabling effect of the industrial injury in order to establish a permanent impairment. This is true when residual pain is the permanent injury because pain is compensable only when it is disabling. *Smith, supra*, at 304, 552 P.2d 1198 (1976). Thus, in pain cases, the line between the medical question and the legal question is blurred. Because of the intertwined issues when pain is the only residual injury, the claimant must be allowed to introduce evidence of disability in order to show impairment. . . .
>
> Once this initial burden has been met, claimant is then entitled to go through the second stage, during which he must show that the pain resulted in lost earning capacity. The claimant cannot be barred from proceeding to this second stage by his failure to provide a rating of impairment when none is applicable.
>
> The judge found that the claimant had a permanent industrial related condition that prevented him from returning to work. Having found the foregoing to be true, it was error for the judge to conclude that claimant suffered no permanent impairment.

731 P.2d at 648.

W.A. Krueger v. Industrial Comm'n, 722 P.2d 234 (Ariz. 1986)

The Industrial Commission ordered a workers' compensation award based on a 5 percent permanent impairment as a result of a herniated cervical disk. The court of appeals affirmed the award, 150 Ariz. 169, 722 P.2d 337 (Ct. App. 1985), but the supreme court vacated, holding that the original ALJ properly rejected the 5 percent permanent impairment recommended by the *AMA Guides.*

The claimant's compensation claim was accepted and he was seen by several physicians. He underwent a diskectomy to decompress the left C7 nerve. The neurosurgeon who performed the surgery testified that the surgery was successful despite some complaints of continued pain from the claimant. Shortly after the physician informed the claimant that he could return to normal work within two months, the claimant began to report severe and disabling neck pain, the cause of which remained unclear despite a battery of tests. After viewing surveillance films of the claimant performing a variety of physical activities, apparently without difficulty and in a normal manner, the doctor discharged the claimant without permanent disability. Both the operating physician and another physician testified that, although the *AMA Guides* provided for a 5 percent permanent impairment for the surgical removal of a disk (without residual effects), the *AMA Guides* were simply that—guides. It was their opinion that the 5 percent permanent impairment rating was too liberal. The ALJ issued an award closing the claim without permanent impairment. However, after this judge resigned, the claimant's request for administrative review was assigned to another ALJ, who concluded that despite the evidence, the *AMA Guides* must be followed when applicable, and this ALJ issued an award based on a 5 percent permanent impairment. The court of appeals affirmed, but the supreme court reversed, holding that the *AMA Guides* are not to be blindly applied despite a claimant's actual physical condition. Rather, their purpose is to serve as a guideline in rating impairment, and they are valid when the stated percentage truly reflects the claimant's loss. Where the evidence establishes that the *AMA Guides* do not truly reflect a claimant's loss or medical evidence is in conflict, an ALJ may use discretion and make findings independent of the *AMA Guides'* recommendations. *See Gomez v. Industrial Comm'n*, 148 Ariz. 565, 716 P.2d 22 (1986).

Gomez v. Industrial Comm'n, 716 P.2d 32 (Ariz. Ct. App. 1985)

The claimant was issued a scheduled award for a 30 percent loss of the use of his left leg. The claimant sought to increase the award based on the ruling in *Dutra v. Industrial Comm'n*, 659 P.2d 18 (Ariz. 1983). The claimant argued that the 30 percent impairment of the leg should be translated into the 100 percent loss of the use of the leg because of the effects on his ability to return to his former employment. In applying *Dutra* to the facts in this case, no error was made by the court in concluding that the evidence did not justify an award in excess of the percentage established by the *AMA Guides*.

The court held that, regardless of whether the *AMA Guides* furnish a fair measurement of the extent of the functional impairment, the judge must consider the effect of the scheduled impairment upon the claimant's ability to perform his former occupation. Concerning the *AMA Guides*, the court stated:

> Our legislature . . . in an attempt to standardize to some extent the compensation to be awarded for substantially identical injuries, has enacted A.R.S. section 23-1044(g) as a part of our workers' compensation act authorizing the Industrial Commission to adopt a schedule for the rating of disabilities. Accordingly, the commission has enacted a procedural rule, A.C.C.R. R4-13-1 13(D), which adopted the American Medical Association's *Guides to the Evaluation of Permanent Impairment* for determining the percentage rating of functional impairment.
>
> The percentages established in these guides are to be considered conclusive for rating specific impairments which fall within their provisions, but are not conclusive when there is medical evidence that the guides do not adequately cover the specific impairment.

716 P.2d at 36.

Mountain Shadows Resort Hotel v. Industrial Comm'n, 710 P.2d 1066 (Ariz. Ct. App. 1985)

The Arizona Court of Appeals held that the Industrial Commission bases impairment rating on the *AMA Guides*, while compensation is based on the claimant's job and the claimant's ability to perform the job that the claimant was performing at the time of the injury. This is especially important where the *AMA Guides* do not measure the extent of impairment. For an ALJ to make an award which varies from the scheduled percentage, evidence must be presented in sufficient detail to make "an informed comparative evaluation." The question of whether the *AMA Guides* represented a true measure of impairment is not clear, and the ALJ made no finding in this regard. The court stated:

> Considering next, whether the American Medical Association Guides represented a true measure of the impairment, the evidence is unclear and the administrative law judge made no findings in this regard. There was a finding that there was evidence that claimant's right leg had only 46% the strength of his left, but there is evidence that some of the medical witnesses who found a 10% impairment under the American Medical Association Guides took into consideration claimant's loss of strength in his right leg due to muscle atrophy.

Id. at 1070.

Dark v. Industrial Comm'n, 705 P.2d 957 (Ariz. Ct. App. 1985)

The claimant, a heavy-duty diesel mechanic, injured his right arm and was found to have suffered a 15 percent permanent partial disability to his upper right extremity. The award of benefits was set aside for reconsideration in light of judicial decisions changing the law with regard to the increased percentage of disability beyond the actual physical impairment and scheduled benefits. *See Gomez v. Industrial Comm'n*, 716 P.2d 32 (Ariz. Ct. App. 1985), *Norton v. Industrial Comm'n*, 1CA-IC 3138 (Aug. 22, 1985); *Dutra v. Industrial Comm'n*, 135 Ariz. 59, 659 P.2d 18 (Ariz. 1983). The court cited three guiding principles:

> (1) To apply *Dutra* and increase the percentage to over the scheduled award, the claimant must show that as a result of the industrial injury he or she has had an actual loss of earning capacity in excess of the scheduled statutory presumption.
> (2) In any event the claimant is entitled at a minimum to the scheduled statutory presumptive loss of earning capacity based upon loss or physical impairment (as the term has been developed by the prior case law).
> (3) The percentage of impairment may be increased by giving consideration to the various physical requirements of the former occupation which claimant can no longer perform as compared to those physical tasks in which claimant's ability to perform is unaffected.

705 P.2d at 959.

The court concluded:

> One thing we feel comfortable with under *Dutra* is that the administrative law judge is not limited to considerations of medical testimony in applying *Dutra's*

increased percentage as this does not deal with physical impairment, a medical determination. Rather, as noted in *Gomez*, this increase is left to the "considerable discretion" of the administrative law judge, based on a "comparative evaluation" of pre-injury job physical tasks with post-injury job physical tasks. In our opinion, such comparative evidence may consist of lay as well as expert occupational testimony.

Id. at 960.

Perez v. Industrial Comm'n, 685 P.2d 154 (Ariz. Ct. App. 1984)

The claimant was rated as having suffered a 10 percent permanent impairment for injury to the right wrist as a result of a work-related accident. The court concluded:

IT IS FURTHER ORDERED that applicant is entitled to scheduled permanent partial disability compensation benefits . . . for a ten degree loss of supination and pronation of the right wrist, such amount of benefits to be left for administrative determination by carrier pursuant to the *AMA Guides.*

Id. at 155.

After the *Dutra* ruling, the claimant's request for a new hearing was denied. *See Dutra v. Industrial Comm'n*, 659 P.2d 18 (Ariz. 1983). The court held that the prior disability ruling was a final judgment and could not be relitigated. The award correctly applied the law prior to *Dutra*. A retroactive determination of the degree of partial disability would not have been proper.

Low v. Industrial Comm'n, 680 P.2d 188 (Ariz. Ct. App. 1984)

The claimant's physician testified that a dislocated left shoulder resulted in a 24 percent permanent impairment under the *AMA Guides*. The physician stated that because the shoulder controls arm functions, the impairment caused the loss of arm motion in various planes. The physician also stated that the injury caused scarring to the anterior aspect of the shoulder and that the claimant's complaints of numbness were consistent with, and related to, the injury. The ALJ issued an award for scheduled permanent partial disability.

On appeal the award was set aside. In applying *Safeway Stores, Inc. v. Industrial Comm'n*, 27 Ariz. App. 776, 558 P.2d 971 (1976), the court held that a shoulder injury was not a scheduled injury. The permanent shoulder impairment, which was based solely on restricted arm motion, was an unscheduled disability. The location of the residual impairment, not the location of the original injury, determines whether a disability is scheduled or unscheduled. If the residual impairment affects only a scheduled part, the disability is scheduled.

Dutra v. Industrial Comm'n, 659 P.2d 18 (Ariz. 1983)

The claimant was a weight-lifting instructor who injured his left arm resulting in the loss of strength but little loss of motion. The ALJ found a 5 percent impairment rating based on the *AMA Guides* and an additional 5 percent impairment for the loss of strength in the arm. The court of appeals found that loss of strength was a "loss of use" under Ariz. Rev. Stat. Ann. § 23-1044(B)(21) for which compensation must be paid.

An impairment that is not ratable under the *AMA Guides* need not be based on published guides, but it must be based on competent medical evidence. The Arizona Supreme Court held: (1) that there is no compensation for unscheduled injuries unless a loss of earning power is shown; and (2) that, for scheduled injuries, compensation must be based not only upon the job the claimant was performing at the time of the injury but also an inability to perform the claimant's particular job at the time of his injury must be considered in determining the extent of the disability. This decision overruled *Egbert v. Industrial Comm'n*, 93 Ariz. 38, 378 P.2d 482 (1963), and *Weiss v. Industrial Comm'n*, 87 Ariz. 21, 347 P.2d 578 (1959).

The *Dutra* court stated.

> We disagree with the Court of Appeals that loss of use in scheduled injuries must be determined in the abstract without consideration of the job at the time of the injury.
>
> ... And no compensation for unscheduled injuries is allowed unless a loss of earning power is shown.
>
> We hold, however, that as to scheduled injuries, compensation is based upon the job the claimant was performing at the time of the injury. Inability to perform the claimant's particular job at the time of his injury must be considered in determining the extent of the workman's disability.

659 P.2d at 20.

Desert Insulations, Inc. v. Industrial Comm'n, 134 Ariz. App. 148, 654 P.2d 296 (1982)

The claimant's award for permanent impairment resulting from cervical neck sprain was set aside. The percentage of the claimant's impairment was not rated under the *AMA Guides*. When the injury is ratable under the *AMA Guides*, they must be used. The opinion of a physician who rates impairment without referring to *AMA Guides* is insufficient when timely challenged. The court stated the following with regard to the *AMA Guides:*

> A.C.R.R. R4-13-113(D) does not require a rating of impairment, but requires that any such rating, if made, must be made under the AMA guidelines. In *Adams* and *Smith*, our Supreme Court held that this rule will not be interpreted to deprive a claimant of compensation simply because his particular

impairment is not ratable under the AMA guidelines. Thus, the court held that the guidelines were not exclusive, and where they do not apply, other criteria can be used to rate the Impairment. That is not, however, the situation here. There is no dispute here over the applicability of the *AMA Guides* to respondent's impairment. Therefore, his impairment must be rated, if at all, under the AMA guidelines.

Id. at 300. *See also Adams v. Industrial Comm'n*, 552 P.2d 764 (Ariz. 1976); *Smith v. Industrial Comm'n*, 113 Ariz. 304, 552 P.2d 1198 (Ct. App. 1976).

Hunter v. Industrial Comm'n, 130 Ariz. 59, 633 P.2d 1052 (Ct. App. 1981)

The claimant developed a bronchial hypersensitivity ("meat wrapper's asthma") as a result of exposure to fumes from polyvinyl chloride. The ALJ gave no award for permanent impairment and found no disability. On review, the court found that the claimant suffered a permanent functional impairment and was entitled to a loss-of-earning-capacity determination. Although the condition was not ratable under the *AMA Guides*, the *AMA Guides* apply only to the extent that they cover the specific impairment and the impairment percentage thereof. The court stated:

> The uncontroverted testimony of both medical witnesses . . . was that petitioner had developed a bronchial hypersensitivity known as meat wrapper's asthma and caused by her industrial exposure to fumes from polyvinyl chloride, which is contained in the material used to wrap meat for sale in markets. Further, both doctors agreed that petitioner's industrially caused physical condition permanently precludes her from functioning in any employment which would expose her to polyvinyl chloride or other lung irritants. The industrial commission may not arbitrarily disregard testimony. We find that the only reasonable inference here is that petitioner has a permanent industrially caused functional impairment.
>
> Neither doctor was able to rate petitioner's condition under the *AMA Guides*. However, the *AMA Guides* apply only to the extent that they cover the specific impairment and the percentage thereof. Since both doctors testified that petitioner's industrially-caused hypersensitivity permanently precludes her from returning to work as a meat wrapper, we find that petitioner has met her burden of proving a permanent functional impairment causally related to her employment. Accordingly, she is entitled to proceed to a hearing to determine whether her impairment has caused a loss of earning capacity.
>
> Because the uncontroverted medical testimony in this case is that petitioner's industrially-caused condition has permanently restricted her functional ability to return to work as a meat wrapper, the award finding no permanent impairment was in error.

Id. at 1054–55.

Cavco Industries v. Industrial Comm'n, 129 Ariz. App. 429, 631 P.2d 1087 (1981)

The claimant injured her left thumb and left knee, thus entitling her to unscheduled benefits. The award was upheld on appeal. The court held that where the *AMA Guides* do not cover the specific impairment, they do not apply and the physician may use other means to rate the impairment.

> *AMA Guides* apply where they cover a specific impairment and where the percentage truly reflects claimant's loss.
>
> * * *
>
> Since the *AMA Guides* did not cover the specific impairment involved here, the *Guides* did not apply. Dr. [M.] could utilize means other than the *AMA Guides* to determine and rate the thumb impairment.
>
> In the instant case, sufficient guidance is given to the Industrial Commission by the definition of permanent impairment . . . to guard against arbitrary and irrational findings of impairment.

Id. at 1090, 1092.

Alsbrooks v. Industrial Comm'n, 578 P.2d 159 (Ariz. 1978)

The Arizona court dealt with the issue of prior injuries that are not industrially caused, and subsequent industrial injuries. The court recognized the difference between a permanent impairment and a permanent disability and adopted the following definitions of these terms as found in the preface to the *AMA Guides*:

> (1) Permanent Impairment. This is a purely medical condition. Permanent impairment is any anatomic or functional abnormality or loss after maximal medical rehabilitation has been achieved, which abnormality or loss the physician considers stable or non-progressive at the time evaluation is made. It is always a basic consideration in the evaluation of permanent disability. (2) Permanent Disability. This is not a purely medical condition. A patient is "permanently disabled" or "under permanent disability" when his actual or presumed ability to engage in gainful activity is reduced or absent because of "impairment" which in turn, may or may not be combined with other factors. Determination of permanent impairment is a medical question while evaluation of a permanent disability is a law question.

Id. at 161.

Chavez v. Industrial Comm'n, 118 Ariz. 141, 575 P.2d 340 (Ct. App. 1977)

The claimant injured his back at the same anatomical level of a previous injury. A partial laminectomy was performed in 1966 and again in 1971. There was medical testimony that the claimant suffered no permanent impairment as a result of the second injury, but rather only an aggravation of a prior condition. The medical witnesses agreed that the *AMA Guides* were not useful in this situation where the surgery involved reentry into the same surgical level as was involved in a previous injury.

The use of the *AMA Guides* was not required where there was unanimity among the physicians that the *AMA Guides* did not apply. The *Chavez* court stated:

> None of the physicians who testified felt that *AMA Guides* were useful in a situation such as this where there has been a re-entry into the same surgical level as was involved in petitioner's 1966 industrial injury. We agree and decline to require medical practitioners to follow the guides where there is unanimity that they are inapplicable to the problem in question.

Id. at 343.

Smith v. Industrial Comm'n, 113 Ariz. 304, 552 P.2d 1198 (1976)

The claimant suffered a low back injury but was denied an award for permanent disability because the Industrial Commission found no evidence of impairment under the *AMA Guides.* There was no objective finding of pain, only subjective complaints of pain. The court, however, stated that the rule of the Industrial Commission requiring the use of the *AMA Guides* may not be interpreted in such a way as to deprive the claimant of just compensation. Subjective pain may constitute a permanent impairment and thus compensation can be awarded. The court stated:

> Chapter II of the *AMA Guides* entitled "The Peripheral Spinal Nerves" substantiates this position, wherein it stated: "subjective complaints of pain which cannot be substantiated along these lines are not considered within the scope of this guide." We read the plain import of this language to mean not that such a physical condition is not compensable, but simply that the guide does not cover this situation.
>
> We hold that petitioner must be given the opportunity to be rated by other criteria.
>
> In a case where subjective pain is determined to constitute a permanent impairment, compensation should be awarded according to the terms of A.R.S 23-1044.

Id. at 1201.

§ 11.03 ARKANSAS

Jones v. Wal-Mart Stores, Inc., 2007 WL 2713381 (Ark. Ct. App.)

The Arkansas Court of Appeals dealt with the claimant, Jones, who injured her back at work and was subsequently terminated. She had an MRI which showed a bulging disk. The ALJ denied permanent disability benefits due to lack of a physician's report assigning a permanent impairment rating.

The court found the *AMA Guides* should have been used to determine an impairment rating, even in the absence of a physician's report. Quoting from *Polk County v. Jones*, 74 Ark. App.—, 47 S.W.3d— (2001). The court stated:

> "The Commission can, and indeed, should, consult the *AMA Guides* when determining the existence and extent of permanent impairment, whether or not the relevant portions of the *Guides* have been offered into evidence by either party.
>
>   *Polk County* also contends that the Commission exceeded the scope of its authority when it assessed its own impairment rating rather than relying solely on its determination of the validity of ratings assigned by physicians. We disagree. It is the duty of the Commission to translate evidence into findings of fact. Johnson v. General Dynamics, 46 Ark. App. 188, 878 S.W.2d 411 (1994). In the instant case, the Commission was authorized to decide which portions of the medical evidence to credit, and translate this medical evidence into a finding of permanent impairment using the *AMA Guides.*

Polk County, 74 Ark. App. at 164–65, 47 S.W.3d at 907–08.

    In this case, as in *Johnson* and *Polk County*, the Commission was authorized to decide which portions of the medical evidence to credit and translate the medical evidence into a finding using the *AMA Guides*, as to whether the claimant met her burden of proof. Because the Commission denied appellant benefits solely because there was no impairment rating assigned by a physician, we reverse and remand for the Commission to determine whether appellant proved the existence and extent of a permanent impairment.

2007 WL 2713381, at *6–*7.

Excelsior Hotel v. Squires, 2005 WL 2375225 (Ark. Ct. App. Sept. 28, 2005)

    The Arkansas court dealt with a worker who fell at work, fractured his ribs, and claimed a lung injury. His physician rated him at 30 percent whole-person impairment under the *Guides* for the lung impairment. At issue on appeal was whether there was substantial evidence to support the 30 percent rating. The appellate court ruled that there was, because the employee's physician based the rating on pulmonary function testing and testified that he had used AMA criteria. The court stated:

> On May 12, 1999, Dr. Griebel opined that appellee had "[r]eactive airway disease syndrome, asthma secondary to pulmonary contusion syndrome as suffered from fall with multiple rib fractures." In a letter dated January 8, 2001, Dr. Griebel noted that appellee had developed a left pleural effusion that was drained and had suffered extensive left-chest fractures. He further

noted that appellee "has continued to manifest significant shortness of breath and had a reactive airway, almost asthma-like, condition since his fall." He opined that appellee "has significant obstructive airway defect abnormalities on his pulmonary function testing, as documented on the values of November 18, 1999, with an FEVI of 2.13, 53% of predicted." He also thought appellee "has some limitation of his lung capacity secondary to pleural thickening and scarring from the severe rib fractures." He further noted that appellee was asymptomatic prior to the injury and symptomatic after the injury, that appellee had shown no evidence of reversal, and that appellee would have "some problem requiring medication and treatment of this for a prolonged period of time." Based on the pulmonary-function test, Dr. Griebel concluded that, by American Medical Association criteria, the appellee had a permanent impairment of thirty percent to the body as a whole. In his deposition testimony, Dr. Griebel stated that appellee's reactive airway disease was secondary to the injury he received and that he was "primarily looking at the reactive airway disease." He agreed that the impairment rating was the result of the injury appellee sustained.

In challenging the Commission's findings, appellants contend that there was not substantial evidence that appellee had developed a permanent lung condition as a result of a work-related incident. To summarize their multiple assertions, they argue that there was no evidence of an injury to the lung caused by the accident; that there was no evidence that appellee's injury was the major cause of his disability; that Dr. Griebel's rating did not comply with the *AMA Guides*; and that the findings used to obtain that rating were not objective.

On appeal, we view the evidence in a light most favorable to the Commission's decision, and we uphold that decision if it is supported by substantial evidence. *White v. Georgia-Pacific Corp.*, 339 Ark. 474, 6 S.W.3d 98 (1999). Further, we will not reverse the Commission's decision unless we are convinced that fair-minded persons with the same facts before them could not have reached the conclusions arrived at by the Commission. *Id.*

We conclude that there was substantial evidence to support the Commission's finding that appellee sustained a permanent anatomical impairment of thirty percent to the body as a whole. There was substantial evidence that appellee's lung condition was a compensable injury and that this injury was the major cause of his permanent disability, as Dr. Griebel stated that the reactive airway disease was secondary to the accident, that he was "primarily" looking at reactive airway disease, that appellee was asymptomatic prior to his injury and symptomatic after his injury, and that appellee had shown no reversal and would require medication and treatment for a prolonged period. Also, substantial evidence supported the Commission's decision that his permanent impairment rating was established by medical evidence supported by objective findings, including the results of appellee's pulmonary-function testing, which, as found by the Commission, was objective. *See Emerson Elec. v. Gaston*, 75 Ark. App. 232, 58 S.W.3d 848 (2001). While appellants assert that the tests did not comply with *AMA Guides*, Dr. Griebel stated that he used AMA criteria in assessing appellee's permanent impairment. Consequently, we affirm the Commission's decision.

2005 WL 2375225 at *1–*2.

Excelsior Hotel v. Squires, 115 S.W.3d 823 (Ark. Ct. App., Div. IV 2003)

The Arkansas court dealt with a worker who fell from a ladder and claimed a pulmonary impairment. At issue was whether the pulmonary function tests used under the *AMA Guides* to evaluate the claimant's impairment were "objective" as required by statute. The court remanded this case back to the Workers' Compensation Commission to make specific findings on this issue. The court stated:

> [A] compensable injury must be established by medical evidence supported by objective findings. [Ark. Code Ann. § 11-9-102(4)(D) (Repl. 2002)] "Objective findings" are "those findings which cannot come under the voluntary control of the patient." [Ark. Code Ann. § 11-9-102(16)(A)(i) (Repl. 2002); *see Emerson Elec. v. Gaston*, 75 Ark. App. 232, 58 S.W.3d 848 (2001).] Any determination of the existence or extent of physical impairment must be supported by objective and measurable physical findings. [Ark. Code Ann. § 11-9-704(c)(1)(B) (Repl. 2002)] Here, the ALJ concluded that the tests were objective; he did not make specific findings of fact to support that conclusion.
>
> While there may be evidence in the record sufficient to support an award of benefits, neither the ALJ nor the Commission made the specific findings of fact necessary for this court to carry out a meaningful review. The failure of the Commission to make these specific findings of fact requires reversal and remand of this case.

115 S.W.3d at 828.

Mays v. Alumnitec, 64 S.W.3d 772 (Ark. Ct. App. 2001)

The Arkansas court dealt with a worker who injured her lower back while lifting long pieces of aluminum onto a table. She was taken to the emergency room and then seen by her family physician, Dr. Tilley. Tilley's various medical reports found muscle spasms, positive pain with straight leg raising, and decreased range of motion secondary to pain. The court affirmed the denial of benefits as the claimant failed to satisfy her burden of proving objective findings that were not within the claimant's voluntary control. The court reasoned:

> Appellant claims that the Commission erred in determining that straight-leg-raising tests and range-of-motion tests were not objective findings for the purpose of determining compensability. We disagree. This court addressed this very issue in *Cox v. CFSI Temp. Employment*, 57 Ark. App. 310, 944 S.W.2d 856 (1997). In *Cox*, appellant argued that a range-of-motion test should be considered an objective finding when determining compensability. *Id.* This court disagreed with appellant and held that pursuant to the applicable statutes a range-of-motion test was not an objective finding when determining compensability. *Id.* Arkansas Code Annotated Section 11-9-102(4)(D) (Supp. 2001) states that "[a] compensable injury must be established by medical

evidence, supported by 'objective findings.' " Section 11-9-102(16) (Supp. 2001) provides in relevant part that:

> (A)(i) "Objective findings" are those findings which cannot come under the voluntary control of the patient.
>
> (ii) When determining physical or anatomical impairment, neither a physician, any other medical provider, an administrative law judge, the Workers' Compensation Commission, nor the courts may consider complaints of pain; for the purpose of making physical or anatomical impairment ratings to the spine, straight-leg-raising tests or range-of-motion tests shall not be considered objective findings.

However, *Cox* does not fully articulate why straight-leg-raising tests and range-of-motion tests cannot be a basis for objective findings. We take this opportunity to clarify our holding that neither test is objective for purposes of determining compensability. The *American Medical Association Guides* must give way to the statutory definition of objective findings as defined by the General Assembly. Although subjective criteria may be included in the *AMA Guides* when determining a permanent physical impairment rating, clearly the portions of the impairment rating guide that are based upon subjective criteria cannot supersede the statutory definition provided by the General Assembly. Thus, to the extent that there is a conflict, the General Assembly's statutory definition takes precedence over any subjective criteria included in the *AMA Guides*.

Furthermore, the legislature has plainly stated through Arkansas Code Annotated Section 11-9-704(c)(3) (Repl. 1996), that the ALJs, the Commission, and this court shall strictly and literally construe the provisions of the Workers' Compensation Act. *See Duke v. Regis Hairstylists*, 55 Ark. App. 327, 935 S.W.2d 600 (1996). Appellant bears the burden of proving a compensable injury by a preponderance of the evidence. Ark. Code Ann. § 11-9-102(4)(E)(i) (Supp. 2001). We find that appellant failed to do so because the abstract is devoid of any objective findings which are not under the voluntary control of appellant. It is clear that muscle spasms, even those detected by someone other than a physician, can constitute objective medical findings to support compensability. *See Estridge v. Waste Management*, 343 Ark. 276, 33 S.W.3d 167 (2000). Here, the only evidence of muscle spasms was the documentation in Dr. Tilley's June 14, 2000, report, which indicated only a complaint by appellant of muscle spasms in her right leg. Thus, it was only a subjective complaint by appellant, rather than an objective observation by a physician, therapist, or nurse. Although it has been held that passive range-of-motion tests may be proven to be objective findings where the testing was described in the record by the treating physician, at least for the limited purpose of assessing permanent impairment caused by a shoulder injury, *see Hayes v. Wal-Mart Stores Inc.*, 71 Ark. App. 207, 29 S.W.3d 751 (2000), the only evidence found in this case regarding a range-of-motion test or a straight-leg-raise test came from Dr. Tilley's various reports. The record is devoid of testimony that either test was not under appellant's voluntary control.

Therefore, we hold that the evidence is insufficient to demonstrate an objective finding. Failure to establish a compensable injury, supported by objective findings, is fatal to appellant's claim.

Id. at 774–75.

Polk County v. Jones, 74 Ark. App. 159, 47 S.W.3d 904 (Ark. Ct. App. June 13, 2001)

The claimant injured his head and neck when he fell forward into a large piece of timber while working for the employer. The employer accepted his injuries as compensable, and paid all reasonable medical expenses as well as temporary total disability benefits. However, the employer controverted the claimant's claim that he was entitled to benefits for a permanent partial impairment. A hearing was held, and the only permanent partial impairment rating introduced into evidence was a 10 percent rating assigned by Dr. F. The Workers' Compensation Commission refused to consider the rating assigned by Dr. F. because it was not supported by objective findings as required by the Arkansas Workers' Compensation Act, and further because, in arriving at the rating, Dr. F. considered complaints of pain, which violated another provision of the Workers' Compensation Act. However, the commission then consulted the *AMA Guides* and determined that, based primarily on objective findings of disk herniations, the claimant was entitled to compensation for an 8 percent permanent impairment rating. The employer now appealed from this award.

The employer argued on appeal that the commission committed reversible error in independently assessing a permanent impairment rating based on a document that was not in the record.

A CT scan and myelogram had been performed. One physician noted mild disk bulging at several levels that was not of any pathological significance. A second physician noted small central disk herniations. The trial court considered this objective finding of herniations, consulted the *AMA Guides*, and awarded an 8 percent rating. The appellate court found that the trial court was within the scope of its authority when it consulted a section of the *AMA Guides* that was not in the record. The appellate court also overruled *Hope Livestock Auction Co. v. Knighton*, *supra*, to the extent that it prohibited the commission from referring to a manual that is not in the record when by law the manual must be consulted to decide an issue in dispute.

The court held that the commission "can, and indeed, should, consult the AMA *Guides* when determining the existence and extent of permanent impairment, whether or not the relevant portions of the *Guides* have been offered into evidence by either party." The appellate court also noted that the commission was authorized to decide which portions of the medical evidence to credit, and translate this medical evidence into a finding of permanent impairment using the *AMA Guides.*

***Hapney v. Rheem Mfg. Co.*, 342 Ark. 11, 26 S.W.3d 777 (Ark. Sept. 14, 2000)**

This case involved workers' compensation benefits related to a ruptured cervical disk. The supreme court, in *Hapney v. Rheem Mfg. Co.*, 341 Ark. 548, 26 S.W.3d 771 (Ark., Jun 8, 2000), held that the gradual onset for back injuries specified in Ark. Code Ann. § 11-9-102(4)(A)(ii)(b) (Supp. 1999) applies to injuries to the neck or cervical spine. The employer petitioned the supreme court to rehear that decision.

In the June 8 decision, the court relied on *Newberg v. Thomas Industries*, 852 S.W.2d 339 (Ky. Ct. App. 1993), where the Kentucky Court of Appeals held that the cervical vertebrae are part of the worker's back. The Kentucky court based its decision on the *AMA Guides* (1st ed. 1971), which provided, "The back is a unit of the whole man, [and] may be divided into three sections: the cervical, dorsal, and lumbar regions."

At the rehearing, the employer argued that the definition of back in the *AMA Guides* (2nd ed. 1984), *AMA Guides* (3d ed. 1983), *AMA Guides* (4th ed. 1993) had changed. The court noted:

> In fact, the *Guides*, 4th edition, at page 13, in discussing the musculoskeletal system, describes that system as being comprised of the upper extremity, the lower extremity, the spine, and the pelvis, each to be considered a unit of the whole person. While the term "spine" is used, "neck" or "back" is not. Moreover, a discussion of the spine in the fourth edition, at page 94, states that symptoms related to the back *and* spine are among the most common of adults' everyday complaints, thus demonstrating that the two are not the same thing. The *Guides*, 4th edition, at pages 116–17, further recognizes the "neck" as a distinct unit in connection with measuring range of motion.

26 S.W.3d at 778.

Based on this, the court found that the claimant's gradual onset injury was not a "back" injury and held that the Workers' Compensation Commission was correct in rejecting the claimant's argument that she sustained a compensable back injury under Ark. Code Ann. § 11-9-102(4)(A)(ii)(b).

***Wal-Mart Stores, Inc. v. Williams*, 2000 WL 528252 (Ark. Ct. App. May 3, 2000)**

The claimant injured her back when working for appellant in October 1997. She saw Dr. L. At the time, the claimant suffered from pain in her back and left leg. Despite conservative treatment, the claimant's suffering continued to worsen. In Dr. L.'s notes, he stated that the claimant had unusual symptoms that did not necessarily relate to her injury or his findings. The claimant was then referred to Dr. W., an orthopedic surgeon. Conservative treatment failed and an IME by a neurosurgeon was performed. After a myelogram and post-myelogram CT scan, which, according to Dr. W.'s notes, showed "nerve root cut off on the L5 root on the left as well as a CT scan which showed disc material at that level," Dr. W. decided surgical treatment was reasonable. Despite the claimant's lack of authorization, Dr. W. performed the surgery. According to the surgical notes, "a large chunk of disc material was removed as a single piece which had been pinning the nerve root." Thereafter, appellee's condition improved, and she returned to work. Later, Dr. W. stated the claimant had reached maximum medical improvement and was entitled to a 10 percent anatomical impairment rating based on the objective finding that there was a "surgical excision of disc."

The ALJ awarded benefits commensurate with its findings, and its ruling was affirmed and its conclusions were adopted by the full commission.

The employer, on appeal, argued inter alia that the commission erred by awarding permanent impairment benefits to the claimant because Dr. W.'s objective findings for purposes of permanent impairment were insufficient. The appellate court considered the ALJ's findings (which were adopted by the commission) that stated in part:

> While Dr. [W.] did not specifically refer to the A.M.A. Guides or use the words "AMA Guides," the preponderance of the evidence shows he relied on the AMA Guides in making the impairment rating. [. . .] It is clear that Dr. [W.] relied on the AMA Guides as required by statute. There is no suggestion that any other Guide was used, and the claimant has demonstrated by a preponderance of the evidence the accuracy of the 10% rating using the AMA Guides. . . .

2000 WL 528252, at *4.

> The appellate court found:
>
> Dr. [W.]'s rating did not specifically mention the A.M.A. *Guides;* however, the evidence presented by appellee demonstrated the accuracy of the rating pursuant to the A.M.A. *Guides.* Further, the Commission found that there was sufficient objective medical findings to warrant the award of permanent impairment benefits. Appellant conceded that appellee suffered a compensable injury, and appellee testified that she continued to suffer from problems since her surgery. Moreover, in Dr. [W.]'s reply to appellant's claims manager stated that the basis of his rating was the "surgical excision of disc." Thus, the statutory requirement that the award be based on objective physical findings is clearly met. Our review leads us to the conclusion that the Commission's decision was supported by substantial evidence and we, therefore, affirm.

Id.

Swift-Eckrich, Inc. v. Brock, **975 S.W.2d 857 (Ark. Ct. App. 1998)**

The Arkansas court dealt with a claimant who was struck by an automobile in her employer's parking lot. She was knocked unconscious and has no memory of that event. CT scans taken during her hospitalization revealed cerebral edema and interhemispheric hemorrhage. Neuropsychological testing by Dr. I. was done in February 1995 and March 1996. The testing was interpreted by Dr. I., who concluded that the claimant sustained residual defects in verbal memory and higher level balance, and that she sustained loss of smell and taste secondary to cranial nerve damage. Based on those factors, Dr. I. concluded that the claimant had sustained permanent physical impairment of 5 percent to the body as a whole. The claimant returned to her preinjury job and wage. The employer accepted her injury and treatment as compensable but controverted the permanent impairment rating.

The court held that the claimant's permanent impairment rating was supported by substantial evidence. As such, the commission did not err in relying on Chapter 4 of the *AMA Guides* to determine what constitutes objective findings of impairment. The employer had argued that the commission should have relied on Chapter 14 of the *AMA Guides*. The court stated:

> Appellant argues that [claimant]'s problems stem from underlying psychiatric problems, and that the injuries are not permanent impairments "supported by objective and measurable physical or mental findings" as required by Arkansas Code Annotated section 11-9-704(c) (Repl. 1996). Objective findings are defined as "those which cannot come under the voluntary control of the patient." Ark. Code Ann. § 11-9-102(16) (Supp. 1997); *see University of Ark. Med. Sciences v. Hart*, 60 Ark. App. 13, 958 S.W.2d 546 (1997); *see also Keller v. L.A. Darling Fixtures*, 40 Ark. App. 94, 845 S.W.2d 15 (1992) (holding that objective findings are based upon observable criteria perceived by someone other than claimant). Thus, the claimant's pain and other verbal responses to clinical tests may not be considered. *Duke v. Regis Hairstylists*, 55 Ark. App. 327, 935 S.W.2d 600 (1996). Appellant argues that because [claimant]'s problems are psychiatric, Chapter 14 of the AMA *[Guides] to the Evaluation of Permanent Impairment*, 4th ed., determines what will constitute sufficient objective findings. Appellant contends that the medical testimony used the incorrect standards of an earlier edition, and, therefore, is insufficient.
>
> On the other hand, [claimant] argues that because her injury involved a physical trauma to the brain, Chapter 4 of the Guidelines determines what will constitute sufficient objective findings, and that Chapter 4 was properly used in this case.
>
> The Commission is to determine the credibility of the medical evidence and may review the basis for the opinion. *See Foxx* and *Reeder, supra*. The Commission found that [claimant]'s cognitive dysfunction and impairments were caused by actual physical trauma to the brain, and looked to Chapter 4 of the Guidelines in finding impairment. Its opinion emphasized the CT scans, which showed cerebral edema and interhemispheric hemorrhaging. In reviewing the basis for the medical opinion, the Commission found that the evidence was sufficiently objective to support a finding of impairment under Chapter 4 of the Guidelines, and it cannot be said that the Commission erred in making that determination.

Appellant claims that this evidence demonstrates a compensable injury, but does not constitute objective findings of impairment. Appellant seems to argue that [appellee]'s compensable injury is not the major cause of any permanent impairment, which prevents awarding of permanent benefits. *See Smith v. Gerber Prods.*, 54 Ark. App. 57, 922 S.W.2d 365 (1996). Arkansas Code Annotated section 11-9-102(5)(F)(ii)(a) (Repl. 1997) provides that "permanent benefits shall be awarded only upon a determination that the compensable injury was the major cause of the disability or impairment." "Major cause" is that which is more than half of the cause. Ark. Code Ann. § 11-9-102(14).

Although [claimant]'s complaints of pain and headaches are indications over which she has voluntary control, and are not to be considered as objective findings, her intracranial bleeding, cranial nerve damage with loss of smell and taste, and the results of her [CT] scan are objective findings according to *Duke, supra*. Conflicting evidence as to whether something is a major cause is a question of fact accorded the Commission, *Blytheville v. McCormick*, 56 Ark. App. 149, 939 S.W.2d 855 (1997). Here, the Commission found that [claimant]'s injuries were a result of head trauma, not underlying mental problems. It cannot be said that the Commission's decision was not based on substantial evidence.

975 S.W.2d at 858–60.

Department of Parks & Tourism v. Helms, 959 S.W.2d 749 (Ark. Ct. App. 1998)

The Arkansas court dealt with a claimant who was injured when she slipped and fell on the job. The claimant's treating physician gave her a 4 percent whole-person impairment based on range-of-motion testing under the *AMA Guides*. The court held that this rating was invalid because the claimant did not prove that the result of her range-of-motion testing was not within her voluntary control. The court stated:

Lastly, appellant argues that the four-percent impairment rating assessed by Dr. [M.] on March 8, 1996, is invalid because Dr. [M.] used active range-of-motion tests that do not qualify as "objective and measurable" under the Workers' Compensation Act. Appellant asserts that any impairment rating attributable to appellee's right shoulder injury cannot be predicted on active range-of-motion tests. Dr. [M.] gave appellee a seven-percent shoulder impairment pursuant to the American Medical Association Guidelines, which correlates to a four-percent impairment to the body as a whole. Arkansas Code Annotated § 11-9-102(16)(A)(ii) (Repl. 1996) states:

When determining physical or anatomical impairment, neither a physician, any other medical provider, an administrative law judge, the Workers' Compensation Commission, nor the courts may consider complaints of pain; for the purpose of making physical or anatomical impairment ratings to the spine, straight-leg-raising tests or range-of-motion tests shall not be considered objective findings.

This was not an evaluation of spine impairment. However, appellee did bear the burden to prove physical or anatomical impairment by objective and measurable physical findings. Ark. Code Ann. § 11-9-704(c)(1)(B) (Repl.

1996). "Objective findings" are those findings that cannot come under the voluntary control of the patient. Ark. Code Ann. § 11-9-102(16)(A)(i) (Repl. 1996). Dr. [M.] stated that he based the impairment rating on active range-of-motion tests. The legislature has eliminated range-of-motion tests as a basis for physical or anatomical impairment ratings to the spine *by definition*. It was incumbent upon appellee to present evidence that active range-of-motion tests are objective tests. In other words, it was incumbent upon her to present proof that those tests do not come under the voluntary control of the patient. She did not do so. In fact, there is authority to suggest that active range-of-motion tests are based almost entirely on the patient's cooperation and effort. *See* American Medical Association, *Guidelines to the Evaluation of Permanent Impairment* (3d ed. 1988). "The full range possible of active motion should be carried out by the subject and measured by the examiner. If a joint cannot be moved actively by the subject or passively by the examiner, the position of ankylosis should be recorded." *Id.* at 14. Because appellee did not present any objective physical findings to support the percentage of impairment to the body as a whole, we cannot uphold the Commission's decision on this point since it does not provide a substantial basis for its award.

959 S.W.2d at 752–53.

Foxx v. American Transp., 924 S.W.2d 814 (Ark. Ct. App. 1996)

The Arkansas court dealt with a claimant who presented evidence that he suffered a 5 percent whole-person impairment. The Workers' Compensation Commission denied the permanent impairment based on the fact that the claimant could still work. The court reversed the commission and held that the commission should have been concerned only with anatomical impairment, not disability. The court stated:

> In finding that [claimant] failed to prove a 5% permanent anatomical or functional impairment, the Commission weighed the medical evidence along with other evidence of [claimant] physical capabilities. Although Dr. [M.] assigned a 5% impairment rating, Dr. [J.] failed to assign a rating and Dr. [P.] opined that [claimant]'s healing period had ended and that he suffered no permanent functional impairment. The resolution of conflicting medical evidence is a question of fact to be determined by the Commission. *Brantley v. Tyson Foods, Inc.*, 48 Ark. App. 27, 887 S.W.2d 543 (1994). In addition to the conflicting medical evidence, the Commission relied on the fact that [claimant] was capable of engaging in relatively heavy labor activities. However, as [claimant] points out, the issue presented to the Commission was whether [claimant] had suffered an anatomical impairment, not whether he had suffered a wage-loss disability. We held in *Second Injury Fund v. Fraser-Owens*, 17 Ark. App. 58, 702 S.W.2d 828 (1986), that " 'anatomical impairment' means the anatomical loss as reflected by the common usage of medical impairment ratings." *See Second Injury Fund v. Yarbrough*, 19 Ark. App. 354, 721 S.W.2d 686 (1986). The bases for these medical impairment ratings are found generally in *Guides to the Evaluation of Permanent Impairment*

(3d ed. 1988) published by the American Medical Association. In the introduction to chapter one of this publication, the following definition is found:

> The accurate and proper use of medical information to assess impairment depends on the recognition that, whereas impairment is a medical matter, disability arises out of the interaction between impairment and external demands, especially those of an individual's occupation. As used in the *Guides*, "impairment" means an alteration of an individual's health status that is *assessed by medical means*, "disability," *which is assessed by nonmedical means*, is an alteration of an individual's capacity to meet personal, social, or occupational demands or statutory or regulatory requirements, [emphasis in original]

Clearly, the Commission considered [claimant]'s capacity to perform strenuous occupational demands in deciding whether he suffered an anatomical impairment. Its opinion included the following:

> Despite all claimant's continued complaints of pain and unknown to his healthcare providers, claimant was working for respondent and ran a cleaning business and lawn care business. Claimant did the cleaning and the yard work himself. He had apparently begun these operations while he was off work for the carpal tunnel syndrome. He continued to work after the knee and back difficulties. In fact, claimant's tax return[s] indicate that his cleaning service grossed over $30,000 in 1993.
>
> The evidence shows that claimant was working on lawns with a lawn mower that weighs between 200 and 300 pounds. A videotape illustrates that claimant was quite mobile. He was able to move the lawn mower in and out of a trailer without significant difficulties. There were many other activities on the videotape which indicate that claimant was able to run, jump and actively work.
>
> The preponderance of the evidence does not establish that claimant is entitled to any benefits, even the contingent 5% disability benefits. The Administrative Law Judge apparently relied primarily upon medical reports. However, the videotape indicates that claimant was able to participate in gainful employment at 100% capacity.
>
> Claimant was able to lift mowers and perform many other activities. Therefore, claimant has failed to prove by a preponderance of the credible evidence that he has any impairment. Therefore, we find that respondent should not be liable for a 5% disability rating. When the medical reports, specifically Dr. [M.]'s assessment, [are] weighed against the preponderance of the credible evidence, it is clear that claimant has not sustained a 5% disability rating.

While these evidentiary findings would be highly relevant and appropriate in determining wage-loss disability, wage-loss disability was not an issue. However, the Commission held that, because [claimant] "was able to participate in gainful employment at 100%" he was not entitled to *any* benefits.

We agree with [claimant] that the Commission has blurred the distinction between anatomical impairment and wage-loss. The landmark case of *Glass v. Edens*, 233 Ark. 786, 346 S.W.2d 685 (1961), involved a decision of the Commission which held that evidence other than clinical findings could not be considered to arrive at a rating for permanent partial disability. The supreme court reversed and remanded because disability in excess of anatomical impairment was sought. *See also Ray v. Shelnutt Nursing Home*, 246 Ark. 575, 439 S.W.2d 41 (1969). Here, disability (wage-loss) in excess of anatomical impairment has never been sought by [claimant].

924 S.W.2d at 815.

Reeder v. Rheem Mfg. Co., 832 S.W.2d 505 (Ark. Ct. App. 1992)

The Arkansas court dealt with a claimant who developed carpal tunnel syndrome and underwent a surgical release. The impairment ratings of 6 percent and 15 percent were questioned as to whether they complied with the "objective and measurable physical findings" of the statute. As to using the *AMA Guides*, the court stated:

While the claimant contends that subjective complaints are acceptable criteria in the American Medical Association's *Guides to the Evaluation of Permanent Impairment*, we note as respondent points out that those guides had been published prior to the legislative enactment of Sec. 11-9-704(c)(4). Had the General Assembly desired to make those guides the basis for an award of permanent impairment they could have done so. However, the General Assembly chose not to make the guides the basis for an award of permanent impairment.

Id. at 506.

The court went on to find that the test grip strength tests were sufficiently objective to satisfy the statute.

Milburn v. Concrete Fabricators, 709 S.W.2d 822 (Ark. Ct. App. 1986)

The claimant suffered a broken right femur and possible hip injury. He appealed a decision of the Workers' Compensation Commission limiting his recovery to a scheduled injury. The court of appeals held that claimant's hip injury was not a scheduled injury and thus should have been apportioned to the body as a whole.

The claimant's treating physician testified that he had previously rated the claimant at 30 percent partial impairment to the lower extremity, which would translate into 12 percent permanent partial impairment under the *AMA Guides*. The court concluded that the appellant clearly sustained a hip injury attributable to his broken leg.

Although a scheduled injury cannot be apportioned to the body as a whole absent total disability, *Anchor Construction Co. v. Rice*, 252 Ark. 460,479 S.W.2d 573 (1972), the Arkansas Supreme Court held in *Clark v. Shiloh*

Tank & Erection Co., 259 Ark. 521, 534 S.W.2d 240 (1976), that a claimant who had received a scheduled injury could receive additional compensation for an injury which was found to be attributable to the scheduled injury . . . Arkansas Statutes Annotated Section 81-1313(c)(3) (Repl. 1976), provides scheduled injury payments for a "leg amputated at the knee, or between the knee and the hip." It is clear that the appellant's problem is not between the hip and the knee. While *medically* speaking, a hip may be considered a part of the leg, from a *legal* point of view, a hip injury is an injury to the body as a whole under the Workers' Compensation Law.

Id. at 823.

Ouachita Marine & Industrial Corp. v. Morrison, 428 S.W.2d 216 (Ark. 1969)

The claimant refused to undergo surgery to treat a ruptured lumbar disk. The court allowed a Workers' Compensation Commission award of 60 percent permanent partial disability. Several physicians estimated that with surgery the claimant would be 15 percent to 20 percent impaired. The court left discretion in fixing the award to the commission, and pointed out the distinction in the *AMA Guides* between *permanent impairment* and *permanent disability*. The physician's role is evaluating permanent impairment, not permanent disability. Limiting an award would confuse the terms *permanent impairment* and *permanent disability* and confuse the medical role.

With regard to the *AMA Guides*, the court stated:

The American Medical Association in its "Guides to the Evaluation of Permanent Impairments to the Extremities and Back" points out in the preface the important distinction between permanent impairment on the one hand and permanent disability on the other hand. It is there stated that the physician's role in the evaluation of permanent disability is limited in its scope to the evaluation of permanent impairment or an appraisal of the nature and extent of the patient's illness or injury. It is further pointed out that the evaluation of permanent disability, which is an appraisal of the patient's present and probable future ability to engage in gainful activity, is an administrative and not a medical responsibility and function.

Id. at 220.

§ 11.04   COLORADO

Dillard v. Industrial Claim Appeals Office of State of Colo., 134 P.3d 407 (Colo. 2006)

Claimant in this case slipped on ice in front of her workplace and hit her head on the sidewalk. The division-sponsored medical examination physician rated the claimant's mental impairment at 5 percent, which, when combined with the physical impairments ratings and converted to a whole-person rating, produced a DIME rating of 29 percent, thus pushing the claimant's impairment rating above the 25 percent threshold and doubling the statutory cap on benefits. The State Supreme Court held that the mental impairment rating could not be combined with the physical impairment rating to exceed the statutory cap, as Colorado statute calls for mental distress to be compensated under a separate section of the act. The court stated:

> In regard to mental impairment claims, the *AMA Guides* support the legislature's intent to prevent the combination of mental impairment with physical impairment in assigning a whole-person rating. According to the *AMA Guides*, an "impairment rating" roughly represents in percentage form the extent to which a person's health status is altered by injury. Generally, physicians combine all types of injuries into a "whole person" assessment. The *AMA Guides* even contain charts for the combination of different types of injuries.
>
> However, mental impairments are not included in these charts. The *AMA Guides* clearly state in regard to mental impairments that "there is no available empirical evidence to support any method for assigning percentage of impairment of the whole person. . . ." The *AMA Guides* explain:
> "Eventually research may support the direct link between medical findings and percentage of mental impairment. Until that time the medical profession must refine its concepts of mental impairment, improve its ability to measure limitations, and continue to make clinical judgments."
>
> The claimant's assertion of her entitlement to the higher cap contained in section 8-42-107.5 rests on the assertion that the General Assembly intended for mental impairments to be combined with physical impairments in calculating a whole person rating. We conclude that the General Assembly clearly intended otherwise. It prevented combining mental impairment injuries with scheduled and nonscheduled injuries to reach a whole person rating. The DIME physician in Dillard's case contravened the legislature's intent in calculating a 29% whole person rating for her.

134 P.3d at 18–20.

Wilson v. Industrial Claim Appeals Office of State of Colo., 81 P.3d 1117 (Colo. Ct. App. 2003)

The Colorado court dealt with an employee who suffered a back injury. The employee and the employer each chose a physician to perform an IME. The claimant's IME physician rated the impairment at 38 percent of the whole person, which included 5 percent for the lumbar spine and 13 percent for reduced range of motion of the lumbar spine. The employer's IME physician rated the impairment at 25 percent of the whole person, which did not include a rating for the lumbar spine impairment because the physician concluded it was not work related.

The DIME physician issued a 29 percent whole-person rating, which included 5 percent for the lumbar spine and 2 percent for reduced range of lumbar motion. After the employer admitted liability for the 29 percent rating, the claimant requested a hearing to overcome the DIME physician's impairment rating as it pertained to lumbar range of motion.

At the hearing, the claimant's IME physician testified that the DIME physician did not properly complete the ratings worksheet for lumbar range of motion because the DIME physician failed to record certain measurements, and that he also failed to use the dual inclinometer method of measurement prescribed by the *AMA Guides* (3d ed. 1990). Accordingly, the claimant's IME physician concluded that the DIME physician's lumbar impairment rating was invalid.

The ALJ found that the testimony of claimant's IME physician was speculative and unpersuasive with respect to the DIME physician's failure to use dual inclinometers. Instead, the ALJ found that the DIME physician properly measured claimant's lumbar range of motion and that the DIME physician was able to verify the validity of these measurements by comparing them to claimant's straight-leg-raising measurements. The ALJ concluded that the DIME physician's failure to record some of the measurements on the worksheet did not prove the rating itself was incorrect and that because the DIME physician's measurements for cervical and thoracic range of motion were "very similar" to those of the IME physician's, the DIME physician used the correct methodology when measuring lumbar range of motion.

The court ruled that whether the IME physician correctly applied the *AMA Guides* was a question of fact and not of law and affirmed. It stated:

> Claimant correctly states that a DIME physician must rate medical impairment in accordance with the provisions of the AMA Guides, Sections 8-42-101(3.7), 8-42-107(8)(c), C.R.S.2002. The DIME physician's finding concerning a claimant's impairment rating is binding on the parties unless overcome by clear and convincing evidence. [Section 8-42-107(8)(c); *Whiteside v. Smith*, 67 P.3d 1240, 1246–47 (Colo. 2003). Whether the DIME physician correctly applied the AMA Guides, and whether the rating itself has been overcome, are questions of fact for determination by the ALJ, and not, as claimant asserts, questions of law. [*See Wackenhut Corp. v. Industrial Claim Appeals Office of State of Colo.*, 17 P.3d 202, 204 (Colo. Ct. App. 2000).]
>
> Here, the evidence supports the ALJ's rejection of the testimony of claimant's IME physician that the DIME physician must have used the single, rather than the required dual, inclinometer method. Indeed, claimant's IME physician admitted that he was "speculating" concerning the DIME physician's methodology and that the DIME physician's measurements for lumbar flexion could be interpreted as the result of either type of measurement.
>
> Further, the fact that the DIME physician failed to record certain measurements on the ratings worksheet did not require the ALJ to conclude that the required measurements were not done or done improperly. As the ALJ found, the DIME physician's measurements of cervical and thoracic impairment

were nearly identical to those of claimant's IME physician, and the DIME physician compared the lumbar range of motion measurements to claimant's straight leg raising measurements. Thus, the ALJ could reasonably infer that the DIME physician recognized and applied the correct rating methods and criteria, but simply failed to record all the data on the worksheet.

Claimant's assertion that the evidence equally supports the contrary inference, namely, that the DIME physician did not recognize and apply the correct rating methods, is unavailing. [*See Metro Moving & Storage Co. v. Gussert*, 914 P.2d 411, 415 (Colo. Ct. App. 1995) ("If two equally plausible inferences may be drawn from the evidence, we may not substitute our judgment for that of the ALJ."); *see also Pacesetter Corp. v. Collett*, 33 P.3d 1230, 1234 (Colo. Ct. App. 2001) ("We are bound by the ALJ's factual determinations, even when the evidence is conflicting and would have supported a contrary result.")].

81 P.3d at 1117.

Wackenhut Corp. v. Industrial Claim Appeals Office of State of Colo., 17 P.3d 202, 2000 CJ C.A.R. 5916 (Colo. Ct. App. 2000)

The claimant's treating physician determined that claimant suffered a 5 percent whole-person impairment for his lumbosacral injury, but apportioned the entire rating to a preexisting 1993 back injury. However, the division-sponsored IME physician gave the claimant a 14 percent whole-person rating. He testified that he relied upon a medical note from a chiropractor that the treatment for the claimant's prior back injury was for a left thoracocostal sprain injury, involving the left sacroiliac and left cervical area, and stated that, in contrast, the claimant's current injury involved the right sacroiliac area. The IME physician therefore determined that apportionment was not appropriate for the injury to the claimant's lumbar spine and opined that the claimant was entitled to a whole-person rating of 14 percent. The ALJ awarded benefits based on the 14 percent figure.

On appeal, the employer asserted that because the *AMA Guides* (3d ed. 1988) do not distinguish between right and left sacroiliac injuries, the ALJ erred determining that the IME physician correctly applied the *AMA Guides* when he did not apportion disability to the claimant's back.

The court considered whether apportionment was required in this case. Here, the IME physician testified that while the range-of-motion measurements, as used in Table 53 of the *AMA Guides*, do not distinguish between left and right sacroiliac injuries, the *AMA Guides* are applied only after an area of objective dysfunction is found after clinical examination. On the basis of many factors, the IME physician concluded that the current injury to the right sacroiliac area was "quite different" and "separate" from the prior injury. The court noted that the physician properly considered numerous factors (including history) in his clinical evaluation, and that he properly (and consistently with the *AMA Guides*) concluded that the injury affected only one side of the back. "Therefore, we find no error in the ALJ's conclusion that the IME physician's rating was performed consistently with the requirements of the AMA Guides."

    17 P.3d at 204.

McLane Western, Inc. v. Industrial Claim Appeals Office, **996 P.2d 263 (Colo. Ct. App. 1999)**

    The Colorado court dealt with a claimant who injured her back. Her treating physician placed her at maximum medical improvement (MMI) on September 11, 1997, and found no ratable impairment.

    The claimant then underwent a division-sponsored IME. The IME physician agreed with the date of MMI, but assessed a permanent whole-person impairment rating of 9 percent. The IME physician based the impairment rating partially on Table 53(II)(B) of the *AMA Guides* (3d ed. rev. 1990), which assign a 5 percent rating when the claimant has suffered an "intervertebral disc or other soft tissue lesion" in the lumbar spine that is unoperated, "with medically documented injury and a minimum of six months of medically documented pain and rigidity with or without muscle spasm."

    The employer contested the results of the IME, asserting that the claimant had failed to show a minimum of six months of medically documented pain. The court rejected this argument. It stated:

> Employer contends that because claimant did not suffer medically documented pain for the six months after her injury, and prior to MMI, no impairment rating could be assessed under Table 53 as a matter of law. In other words, employer maintains that the MMI date is determinative of whether a claimant has shown six months of documented pain for the purposes of applying Table 53. We disagree.
>
> Section 8-40-201(11.5), C.R.S. 1999, defines MMI as the date when any medically determinable physical or mental impairment caused by the injury becomes stable and no further treatment is reasonably expected to improve the condition. Thus, MMI serves as the point of demarcation between temporary and permanent disability. *See Singleton v. Kenya Corp.*, 961 P.2d 571 (Colo. App. 1998).
>
> Once a disability has become permanent, the resulting physical impairment must be determined in accordance with the *AMA Guides*. *See* § 8-42-101(3.7), C.R.S. 1999. But, contrary to employer's contention, the *AMA Guides* do not require that the documented pain occur prior to MMI.
>
> As the Panel observed, an injury could produce some determinable and stable medical impairment at a certain point, yet remain unratable under the *AMA Guides* because insufficient time had passed. The Panel further noted that to hold as employer urges would create an anomalous situation in which a group of claimants suffering the identical injury, but reaching MMI at different times, could become subject to different medical impairment ratings and different levels of disability compensation.

Nor does *Golden Animal Hospital v. Horton*, 897 P.2d 833 (Colo. 1995), require a different result as employer asserts. There, the supreme court interpreted the compensation scheme for permanently disabled minors. The court concluded that the phrase, "at the time of the determination of such permanency," contained in what is now § 8-42-102(4), C.R.S. 1999, referred to the date on which permanency was determinable, which was when an employee has reached MMI. The court rejected the contention that permanency was determinable on the date of the hearing.

However, the court did not consider the language in the *AMA Guides* which is at issue here. Thus, the general holding in *Golden Animal Hospital v. Horton, supra*, is inapposite in determining how a "medically documented injury and a minimum of six months of medically documented pain" may be shown.

We therefore reject employer's contention that, as a matter of law, permanent impairment must be determined at the time of MMI, and cannot be assessed under Table 53 unless claimant shows that six months of documented pain occurred prior to MMI.

996 P.2d at 265.

Judge B., in a special concurrence, commented on the current Colorado statute's shortcomings. Included was a discussion on how basing benefits strictly on impairment, and not on earning capacity, can be problematic. He stated:

I concur in the majority's analysis and conclusion. I write separately only to note yet another difficulty created when the new system of calculating certain permanent disability benefits was superimposed onto, but did not entirely replace, the earlier system. The difficulty this case illustrates is a potential gap between the end of eligibility for temporary benefits and the beginning of eligibility for permanent benefits.

Under the previous workers' compensation system, permanent partial disability (PPD) awards for most injuries were calculated based upon a rating of industrial disability, which measured the worker's loss of earning capacity in the labor market. The calculations took into consideration the injured worker's general physical condition and mental training, ability, former employment, and education. *Duran v. Industrial Claim Appeals Office*, 883 P.2d 477 (Colo. 1994); *Colorado AFL-CIO v. Donlon*, 914 P.2d 396 (Colo. App. 1995).

The system was both fair and logical. For example, a physical worker with limited abilities and no high school education might suffer a back injury identical to that suffered by a clerical worker with excellent abilities and a college degree. The resulting physical impairments might be identical. However, aside from any difference in the average weekly wage used to calculate benefits, the impact on the earning capacity of the physical worker might be substantially greater because of more limited employment alternatives with the impairment. The former system reflected that reality.

More importantly here, eligibility for temporary and permanent benefits was based on the same concept and the occurrence of a single event, maximum medical improvement (MMI). At that point, entitlement to temporary benefits ceased and permanent benefits were to be determined. *See Eastman Kodak Co. v. Industrial Commission*, 725 P.2d 107 (Colo. App. 1986).

After amendments to the Workers' Compensation Act in 1991 and 1992, a new system of calculating permanent benefits was superimposed onto the existing system. The Act now requires that benefits for most permanent injuries be calculated based solely on medical impairment, pursuant to the American Medical Association Guides to the Evaluation of Permanent Impairment (3d ed. 1991) (AMA Guides). *See* § 8-42-107(c), C.R.S. 1999; *Askew v. Industrial Claim Appeals Office*, 927 P.2d 1333 (Colo. 1996).

The calculation of permanent benefits no longer takes into consideration the individual worker's abilities, education, and experience. It therefore does not measure the actual impact on earning capacity. However, as just discussed, identical medical impairments to two workers will generally have a greater impact on the earning capacity of the worker with the more limited ability, education, and experience.

The result is that detrimental financial impact of the new system falls most greatly on those whose earning capacities are most compromised—those most in need of permanent disability benefits. In addition, under the new system even substantially similar injuries can result in substantially different awards, depending on whether the injury is rated under a remaining part of the old system or under the new system. *See Duran v. Industrial Claim Appeals Office, supra; Colorado AFL-CIO v. Donlon, supra.*

Aside from any concern with the logic or fairness of such a system, difficulties are created by superimposing it upon, but not entirely replacing, the existing system. For example, confusion can result from still basing apportionment of liability for two separate injuries on industrial disability, while basing benefits on medical impairment. *See Askew v. Industrial Claim Appeals Office, supra; Waddell v. Industrial Claim Appeals Office*, 964 P.2d 552 (Colo. App. 1998) (Briggs, J. concurring).

This case illustrates a different difficulty. It arises from the relationship between the system for awarding temporary benefits and the new system of awarding permanent benefits.

Temporary benefits are still based on industrial disability, and eligibility still supposedly ceases when the worker reaches MMI, even if the worker is unable to return to employment with the employer. *See* § 8-42-105, C.R.S. 1999; *see also* § 8-42-106, C.R.S. 1999 (pertaining to temporary partial disability). The new system also still uses MMI to trigger the requirement for the treating physician to make the medical rating upon which permanent benefits, now termed medical impairment benefits, are to be based. *See* § 8-42-107(c), C.R.S. 1999.

However, the treating physician is to make the calculation pursuant to the *AMA Guides. See* § 8-42-107(c). As this case illustrates, those guides may not permit the calculation of medical impairment benefits for some months after the injured worker has reached MMI.

The result is that there can be a gap in the time between MMI and the calculation of medical impairment benefits. The current statutory scheme does not address this time gap.

It is therefore unclear whether, for example, the employer must continue paying temporary benefits, even though the worker has reached MMI. If not, the injured worker will be deprived of temporary benefits during the hiatus between MMI and the determination of medical impairment benefits. For a worker who has reached MMI but, because of the injury, cannot return to the old employment or quickly find alternative employment, deprivation of any benefits during the hiatus can be devastating.

Force a square peg into a round hole and gaps will surely appear. Hopefully, the General Assembly will fill this critical gap in our current Workers' compensation system.

Id. at 266–67.

Lambert & Sons, Inc. v. Industrial Claim Appeals Office, 1998 Colo. App. LEXIS 168 (Colo. Ct. App. July 9, 1998)

The Colorado court dealt with a claimant who sustained an admitted industrial injury to his back in 1995 and reached maximum medical improvement that same year. After performing a division-sponsored IME, the physician assigned the claimant a 12 percent whole-person physical impairment rating. Because the claimant had sustained a prior industrial back injury, however, the physician noted that apportionment was probably warranted, but could not be calculated until the medical records and impairment rating for the first injury were reviewed.

Later, the physician examined the records and discovered that the claimant had received a 12 percent impairment rating from the first injury. In a subsequent deposition, the physician stated that all the claimant's impairment was preexisting. He also stated, however, that he was unsure whether the impairment resulted from the first or second injury and that the second injury may have permanently exacerbated the claimant's preexisting condition.

At the hearing, the claimant testified that before the second injury he was asymptomatic from the first injury and was able to perform heavy construction work. Furthermore, he testified that since the second injury he had been unable to perform heavy work. The ALJ found this testimony credible and persuasive.

The ALJ denied the Colorado insurance authority's request to apportion the claimant's impairment between the first and second injuries, finding that the insurance authority had failed to overcome by clear and convincing evidence the 12 percent impairment rating issued by the IME physician. The court held that it was proper not to apportion out the preexisting impairment where that impairment was asymptomatic at the time of the later injury. The court stated:

Accordingly, we hold that apportionment is not appropriate when a claimant is issued a medical impairment rating for a previous injury, and prior to the second injury the claimant's condition improves to the point that he or she is asymptomatic. Thus, while there might be an actual impairment rating for the first injury, it is not conclusive and may be rebutted, as here, by credible evidence of an improvement of condition.

1998 Colo. App. LEXIS 168, at *7.

Walker v. Jim Fuoco Motor Co., 942 P.2d 1390 (Colo. Ct. App. 1997)

The Colorado court dealt with a claimant who sustained a shoulder and arm injury while working. Because no physician had rated the claimant's impairment as to being to the neck, back, or head, the ALJ ruled that the claimant had suffered a scheduled impairment for "loss of an arm at the shoulder." The claimant argued that he should have received a whole-person rating because, under the *AMA Guides*, the shoulder is considered to be part of the trunk and the body and because the claimant testified that the pain runs into his neck. The court upheld the ALJ's finding that the claimant had suffered a scheduled injury. The court stated:

> Claimant contends that his injury must be rated as a whole person injury and that benefits must therefore be awarded under § 8-42-107(8). He argues that he is entitled to benefits based on a whole person rating because under the American Medical Association *Guides to the Evaluation of Permanent Impairment (AMA Guides)*, the shoulder is considered to be a part of the trunk of the body, and because he testified that the pain runs up into his neck. We perceive no error in the award of benefits.
>
> When a claimant's injury is listed on the schedule of disabilities, the award for that injury is limited to a scheduled disability award. Section 8-42-107(1)(a), C.R.S. (1996 Cum. Supp.). In this context, "injury" refers to the situs of the functional impairment, meaning the part of the body that sustained the ultimate loss, and not necessarily the situs of the injury itself. *Strauch v. PSL Swedish Healthcare Sys.*, 917 P.2d 366 (Colo. Ct. App. 1996). Whether a claimant suffered an impairment that can be fully compensated under the schedule of disabilities is a factual question for the ALJ, the determination of which must be upheld if supported by substantial evidence. *Langton v. Rocky Mountain Health Care Corp.*, 937 P.2d 883 (Colo. Ct. App. 1996).
>
> Section 8-42-107(2)(a) provides the period of compensation for "the loss of an arm at the shoulder." Claimant argues that, under either a dictionary definition or the *AMA Guides*, a 100% loss of the arm would be measured well below the shoulder joint. However, on at least two prior occasions other divisions of this court have rejected the argument that the *AMA Guides* are controlling on the issue of the situs of the functional impairment. *Langton v. Rocky Mountain Health Care Corp., supra; Strauch v. PSL Swedish Healthcare System, supra.*
>
> While the *AMA Guides* are being used by physicians in calculating the nature and extent of the medical impairment, *see* § 8-42-101(3.7), C.R.S. (1996 Cum. Supp.), the Guides do not determine the situs of the functional impairment. That question is to be resolved by applying the statutory impairment

standards to the facts of the case. *See Langton v. Rocky Mountain Health Care Corp., supra.*

Here, the ALJ applied the proper legal standard in determining that claimant's impairment was within the scheduled impairment category for "the loss of an arm at the shoulder." Section 8-42-107(2), C.R.S. (1996 Cum. Supp.). The treating physicians found no impairment beyond the shoulder, and also were of the view that the impairment principally affects claimant's arm movements. There thus is substantial evidence to support the ALJ's finding that claimant sustained a functional impairment listed on the schedule of disabilities.

942 P.2d at 1391–92.

Askew v. Industrial Claim Appeals Office, 927 P.2d 1333 (Colo. 1996)

The Colorado court dealt with a claimant who had a preexisting asymptomatic back condition and then injured his back at work. The court held that his medical impairment benefits should not be apportioned and reduced to account for the preexisting condition. The court reasoned:

Here, [claimant]'s degenerative back condition was not known to him prior to a physical examination for his industrial injury. Dr. [A.] nevertheless determined that 7% of [claimant]'s 14% whole person impairment was due to a preexisting, yet dormant, back condition. However, there was no medical basis for Dr. [A.] to establish the level of impairment prior to the industrial accident. Indeed, the record reveals that [claimant] had no pain in his back, was not treated for any back condition, and worked without hindrance prior to the injury at Sears. As Dr. [H.] stated in his December 1993 letter:

With regard to these degenerative changes, it is my opinion that these changes very well may have pre-existed his injury. We have here a man who is 50 years old who has lived with these changes for many years and had no symptoms what so ever [sic] until his injury occurred. It is clear to me that the injury is the cause for his problems. Had this injury not occurred, there is no reason to think that the patient would have developed back pain problems. Furthermore, we have no reason to think that if he did not have these degenerative changes, that the same accident would not have caused him ongoing back pain.

Thus, based on our review of the record, apportionment cannot be justified other than on an arbitrary basis and was therefore inappropriate under these circumstances.

III.

We conclude that the orders of the Panel and of the ALJ allowing apportionment, and the court of appeals' opinion affirming those orders, were incorrect as a matter of law and that [claimant] was entitled to full compensation based on an impairment rating not diminished by apportionment. Upon review of the Workers' Compensation Act, the case law interpreting a previous disability as used in section 8-43-104(2), and the *AMA Guides*, it is clear that those provisions contemplate apportionment only when a prior disability, as defined by the *AMA Guides*, is a contributing factor to a subsequent industrial injury. Here, because [claimant] had an asymptomatic, degenerative back condition, there was no prior disability as contemplated by the statutes and the *AMA Guides*, and apportionment was therefore inappropriate. Thus, we reverse the judgment of the court of appeals and remand for further proceedings consistent with this opinion.

927 P.2d at 1339.

Mountain City Meat v. Oqueda, 919 P.2d 246 (Colo. 1996)

The Colorado court dealt with five separate cases in which the claimants had suffered both scheduled and nonscheduled injuries. Under the Colorado statute, nonscheduled injuries are to be rated under the *AMA Guides*. The court held that the scheduled injury should first be converted to a whole-person impairment and then combined with the nonscheduled impairment. The court reasoned:

> The CCIA and the employers argue that nothing in the statute explicitly provides for the conversion of the extremity impairment rating to a whole person rating. However, we must construe the statute as a whole "so as to give consistent, harmonious, and sensible effect to all its parts." *People v. Andrews*, 871 P.2d at 1201. The *AMA Guides* are incorporated by the statute, and they explicitly contain a table for converting extremity injuries to a whole person rating. Section 8-42-101(3.7), requires that after July 1, 1991, "all physical impairment ratings used under articles 40 to 47 of this title [the Workers' Compensation Act] shall be based on the revised third edition of the 'American Medical Association Guides to the Evaluation of Permanent Impairment', in effect as of July 1, 1991." The director of the division of Workers' compensation was required by section 8-42-101(3.5)(a)(II), 3B C.R.S. (1995 Supp.), to promulgate rules establishing a system for the determination of medical impairment rating guidelines for impairment ratings based on the *AMA Guides*. These rules mandate that "all permanent impairment ratings shall be based upon the [*AMA Guides*]," and that when determining permanent physical impairment ratings, the physician shall "[u]se the instructions and forms contained in the *AMA Guides*." Rule XIX(A), (D), 7 C.C.R. 1101–3 (1995).
>
> Not only do the *AMA Guides* espouse the principle "that all impairments affect the individual as a whole," they also state that "[p]ractically all impairment values involving several organ systems . . . should be combined using the Combined Values Chart unless the text gives other instructions." *AMA Guides* at xviii. To fully and correctly characterize the impairment, the *AMA Guides* provide that the evaluation should be carried out according to the directions in the *Guides* utilizing the tables contained therein. In particular, the Combined Values Chart applies whenever it is necessary to express the impairment in a percentage of the whole person. *AMA Guides* 3. Thus, the

statute contains a methodology for the conversion of an extremity rating to a whole person rating, and the addition of this rating with the head, neck, or torso rating, in ascertaining the whole person impairment award.

IV.

Accordingly, we hold that, when an employee is involved in a work-related accident that results in both a scheduled injury and a non-scheduled injury, the scheduled injury must be converted to a whole person impairment rating and combined with the non-scheduled injury's whole person impairment rating in calculating permanent disability benefits.

919 P.2d at 254.

Advanced Component Sys. v. Gonzales, 935 P.2d 24 (Colo. Ct. App. 1996)

The Colorado court dealt with a claimant who injured his eye, resulting in functional loss and disfigurement. His physician rated his functional loss and then combined, pursuant to the *AMA Guides*, a 5 percent whole-person impairment for his disfigurement. The court reversed the award of a 5 percent impairment for disfigurement because this was not a "permanent medical impairment" under the statute. The court stated:

> Finally, the fact that a disfigurement may be considered to be an "impairment" under the *AMA Guides* is of little moment. It is only if a "permanent medical impairment" under § 8-42-107 is present that the *AMA Guides* apply. Referring to the *AMA Guides*, rather than to the statutes, to determine whether the *AMA Guides* should be referred to, results in illogical, circular reasoning.
>
> We conclude, then, that a non-dysfunctional disfigurement under § 8-42-108 is not a medical impairment under § 8-42-107 and that such disfigurement cannot increase the amount of compensation to be awarded under § 8-42-107. Likewise, such a disfigurement cannot be considered to be an additional impairment for purposes of a single award under *Mountain City Meat Co. v. Industrial Claim Appeals Office, supra.*
>
> Here, the treating physician made clear that he rated claimant's functional loss, *i.e.*, his partial loss of vision, separately from the rating he attributed to claimant's disfigurement. Further, neither the treating physician nor the *AMA Guides* suggest that the impairment rating given for disfigurement is to be based upon any resulting functional impairment; it is to be based solely upon disfigurement, not functional loss.
>
> Under these circumstances, therefore, because the employee had only a single impairment, *i.e.*, his functional loss of use of sight, the analysis adopted by *Mountain City Meat Co. v. Industrial Claim Appeals Office, supra*, is inapposite, and claimant is entitled only to an award under the schedule.

935 P.2d at 27.

Strauch v. PSL Swedish Healthcare Sys., 917 P.2d 366 (Colo. Ct. App. 1996)

The Colorado court dealt with a claimant who suffered a work-related rotator cuff tear. At issue was whether this was a scheduled or nonscheduled injury. The court held that the *AMA Guides* could not be relied upon in this case to show that the shoulder was part of the torso. The court reasoned:

> Because it is the situs of the functional impairment that is at issue, and not the place on the body that the initial harm is inflicted, the *AMA Guides'* demarcation of where the torso stops and the extremity begins is of no consequence here. Thus, we are not persuaded by the foreign authorities relied upon to establish as a matter of law that the shoulder is not part of the arm.
>
> Claimant also argues that "loss of the arm at the shoulder" must be considered synonymous with "amputation of the upper extremity" because an illustration from the *AMA Guides* provides that amputation of the upper extremity occurs when the arm is lost midway between the elbow joint and the shoulder joint. Therefore, she reasons, because her injury occurred on a portion of her anatomy proximal to the point that the *AMA Guides* define an upper extremity amputation, she did not sustain a loss of an arm and, therefore, she must be compensated on a whole person basis rather than based on the statutory schedule. We are not persuaded.
>
> As noted above, it is the situs of the functional impairment, not the situs of the initial harm, that is the relevant inquiry. Thus, because the ALJ determined that the only functional impairment occurred to the arm, the situs of the initial harm, here, the shoulder joint, is of no consequence. Correspondingly, the exhibit is not probative.
>
> Furthermore, a review of the record reveals that the exhibit relied upon by claimant to equate loss of the arm at the shoulder with amputation was used by the physician merely to establish a record concerning the anatomical locations that the physician pointed to during his testimony.
>
> Accordingly, we conclude that it is not improper to base an award that includes disability to the shoulder on the proportionate loss to the use of the arm when, as here, the functional impairment occurs only in the arm. Because the ALJ determined that the claimant's injury affected only the use of her arm, and because that determination is supported by substantial evidence, we may not disturb the ruling of the ALJ.

917 P.2d at 368–69.

Askew v. Sears, Roebuck & Co., 914 P.2d 416 (Colo. Ct. App. 1995)

The Colorado court dealt with a claimant who injured his back at work. A court-appointed IME physician rated the claimant's impairment at 14 percent under the *AMA Guides* (3d ed. rev. 1990). Six percent of the rating was apportioned to a preexisting asymptomatic osteoarthritic degeneration. The claimant challenged that apportionment. The court rejected the claimant's argument that apportionment was a legal question and not a medical question. The court noted, however, that the instructions as to apportionment in the main body and glossary of the *AMA Guides* arguably conflict with the applicable statute mandating that the IME physician determine apportionment. The court also rejected the claimant's argument that because the preexisting condition was asymptomatic, no apportionment should apply. The court reasoned that in this case, the apportionment determination was properly based upon the *AMA Guides.*

Metro Moving & Storage Co. v. Gussert, **914 P.2d 411 (Colo. Ct. App. 1995)**

The Colorado court dealt with a claimant who injured his back and was rated by a court-appointed physician at a 0 percent permanent impairment under the *AMA Guides* (3d ed. rev. 1990). The claimant challenged that impairment rating, and the ALJ found a 9 percent permanent impairment based upon the testimony of the claimant's physician. The issue before the court was whether there was clear and convincing evidence that justified the ALJ's decision not to adopt the court-appointed physician's 0 percent rating. The court held that whether there was clear and convincing evidence was a question of fact and that substantial evidence existed to uphold the ALJ's decision to disregard the court-appointed physician's 0 percent rating. The court stated:

> In challenging the ALJ's findings, the respondents advance three arguments. They contend that even if Dr. R. did change the numerical measurements of claimant's lumbar flexion, it does not establish, clearly and convincingly, that his impairment rating was invalid. They also argue that the mere omission from Dr. R.'s report of an affirmative statement that he used an inclinometer does not establish, by clear and convincing proof, that he did not use the instrument. Finally, they argue there was no basis in the evidence for the ALJ's finding that Dr. R. should have used table 53 of the *AMA Guides.* We reject these contentions.
>
> Dr. R.'s lumbar flexion measurements are found in the record; the original readings are heavily crossed over with ink, rendering the original figures illegible. Dr. H. stated that these markings could be interpreted as alterations of previously recorded measurements, and he testified that the substituted measurements are in the normal range. Dr. R. did not testify. On these facts the ALJ could reasonably infer that Dr. R. altered the original measurements in order to arrive at "normal" readings.
>
> The ALJ also found there was no "credible evidence" that Dr. R. has used an inclinometer as recommended by the *AMA Guides.* The ALJ found that when Dr. H. used an inclinometer to measure the claimant's lumbar flexion, he found a measurable impairment. Conversely, Dr. R.'s report does not state whether he had used an inclinometer, and his findings indicate no measurable loss or impairment. Under these circumstances, the ALJ could reasonably infer that, if Dr. R. had used an inclinometer, his rating also would have shown some degree of measurable impairment.

> We reject the argument that Dr. H.'s opinions were "conjectural." Dr. H. examined the claimant on two separate occasions, and had taken into account the report and supporting documentation submitted by Dr. R. Dr. H. cited those portions of the *AMA Guides* which he considered appropriate and pointed to specific evidence justifying application of those sections in measuring claimant's impairment. Thus, Dr. H.'s opinions were fully grounded in the evidence or plausible inferences drawn therefrom.
>
> The ALJ found the foregoing evidence to be of "clear and convincing" quality, and we are bound by his assessment of its weight. Like the panel, we conclude that the evidence is substantial and sufficient to support the ALJ's order.

914 P.2d at 415.

Duran v. Industrial Claim Appeals Office, 883 P.2d 477 (Colo. 1994)

The claimant challenged the constitutionality of two sections of Colorado's Workers' Compensation Act. Section 8-42-107(2) of the Colorado Revised Statutes provides a schedule of compensation for the partial loss of a hand, an arm, a foot, a leg, sight, or hearing; Colo. Rev. Stat. § 8-42-107(8) provides a schedule of compensation for the total loss of a hand, an arm, a foot, sight, or hearing calculated from whole-person impairment under the *AMA Guides*. Under Colo. Rev. Stat. § 8-42-107, a worker with a 100 percent impairment of an arm could receive 300 percent more benefits than a worker with a 95 percent impairment of an arm. The court held that Colorado's act passed constitutional muster under the equal protection clause. The court reasoned that, although the legislative classification between partial and total injuries is imperfect, the classification is rationally related to a legitimate governmental interest.

City of Aurora v. Vaughn, 824 P.2d 825 (Colo. Ct. App. 1991)

The Colorado court dealt with the claimant, who suffered an industrial hearing loss. The tests performed on the claimant were an audiogram, air conduction, bone conduction, SVTs, compliance testing, discrimination testing, tympanograms, stapedial reflexes, and an electronystagmography. The court affirmed the award of a 47 percent scheduled loss, finding that the *AMA Guides* were not appropriate. The court stated:

> Employer argues that the ALJ erred in failing to compute claimant's impairment pursuant to the AMA Guidelines, as testified to and explained by, its experts. We reject this argument.
>
> Dr. [J.]'s opinion that the American Medical Association *Guidelines* were inapplicable to claimant's circumstances and that his impairment determination, based on the formula proposed by the Committee for Hearing Bioacoustics and Biomechanics of the National Academy of Sciences and Natural Resources Council which relied upon factors more appropriate to claimant's situation, was given more credence by the ALJ as the trier of fact. And, even

one of employer's experts agreed that the formula used by Dr. [J.] more accurately measured claimant's hearing loss than the AMA formula.

We agree with the panel that the ALJ reasonably could infer from Dr. [J.]'s testimony that claimant had lost essentially 47 percent of his ability to perceive, distinguish, and comprehend sounds across the frequencies of human hearing. We also agree with the panel that this inference, implicitly drawn by the ALJ, supports the award.

824 P.2d at 826.

Jefferson County Sch. v. Headrick, 734 P.2d 659 (Colo. Ct. App. 1986)

The claimant worked as a wood-shop instructor for 14 years and was exposed to excessive noise five to six hours per day in the shop. He experienced some difficulty in hearing during 1982. His physician performed several tests and recommended that the claimant wear protective earpieces when working. The claimant continued to work, using the protective earpieces, when possible. However, he became eligible for, and elected to take, voluntary retirement in 1984, primarily because of a continued hearing loss from excessive loud noise from circumstances with no hope of controlling the noise factor. His hearing loss was such that a hearing aid would not be effective.

The claimant's physician diagnosed a noise-induced hearing loss in 1985. A second doctor diagnosed bilateral sensorineural hearing loss, most likely caused by excessive noise exposure. This doctor testified, however, that, pursuant to the *AMA Guides*, the claimant's percentage of hearing loss was zero. Nonetheless, the *AMA Guides* were explained by the claimant's treating physician as being inaccurate in the claimant's case because the *AMA Guides* failed to consider the excessive noise that the claimant was exposed to in the work environment. The Industrial Commission concluded that the claimant's hearing loss was a compensable occupational disease and that the claimant's last injurious exposure occurred while the claimant was in the petitioner's employ.

On review, the petitioner argued that the commission erred in concluding that the claimant sustained a compensable hearing loss because the *AMA Guides* indicated that the claimant had no impairment. However, the doctor's opinion that the *AMA Guides* was inapplicable to the claimant's circumstances was given credence by the commission, even though there was some evidence to the contrary.

§11.05 CONNECTICUT

Misenti v. International Silver Co., 729 CRD-6-88-9 (Conn. Workers' Comp. Comm'n Oct. 1989)

The claimant was awarded permanent partial disability benefits based on a 50 percent loss of use of both hands resulting from chronic contact dermatitis. The respondents argued that because there was no orthopedic or neurologic permanent impairment, there could be no disability found under Conn. Gen. Stat. § 31-308(b). The court concluded, however, that the commissioner could reasonably infer that the chronic dermatitis suffered by the claimant reached sufficient levels to impair the motion and use of his hands.

> No less an authority than the *AMA Guides to the Evaluation of Permanent Impairment* has stated "Impairments of other body systems, such as behavioral problems, restriction of motion or ankylosis of joints, and respiratory, cardio-vascular, endocrine, and gastrointestinal disorders, may be associated with a skin impairment. When there is permanent impairment in more than one body system, the degree of impairment for each system should be evaluated separately and combined, using the combined value chart, to determine the impairment of the whole person." The AMA's suggested evaluation methods as to skin impairments lends credence to a finding of permanent disability of claimant's hands due to the skin disorder. Respondents have cited no precedents holding that Sec. 31-308(b) permanent disability can only be based on ortho-pedic or neurologic impairment.

729 CRD-6-88-9, at 3–4.

Piscitelli v. Connecticut Coke/Eastern Gas & Fuel Assocs., 575 CRD-3-87 (Jan. 1989)

The claimant was exposed to coal dust during the course of his employment between 1942 and 1969. The commissioner originally awarded the claimant a 10 percent respiratory impairment, or a 5 percent impairment of each lung. In amended findings, the commissioner awarded a 10 percent permanent partial disability of the respiratory system. The claimant appealed, seeking instead a 20 percent impairment of the respiratory system, which is equivalent to a 10 percent permanent partial impairment of the whole person based on the *AMA Guides*. Losses to organs or organ systems that are not scheduled in Conn. Gen. Stat. § 31-308(b) are controlled by Conn. Gen. Stat. § 31-308(d), which provides that

> [i]n addition to compensation for total or partial incapacity for a specific loss of a member or loss of use of the function of a member of the body or for disfigurement or scarring, the commissioner may award such compensation as he deems just for the loss or loss of use of the function of any organ or part of the body not otherwise provided for herein, taking into account the age and sex of the claimant, the disabling effect of the loss of or loss of function of the organ involved and the necessity of the organ or complete functioning of the organ with respect to the entire body, but in no case more than the sum equivalent to compensation for seven hundred and eight weeks.

The court noted that actual practice and custom within the commission has assigned various values in terms of weeks of payments for unscheduled organ losses. In the current case, a lung was assigned a 175-week value.

The establishment of various values for unscheduled losses is permissible under Conn. Gen. Stat. § 31-308(d). The court stated:

> As to the whole person disability ratings used by the AMA publication, this tribunal held in *Repasi v. Jenkins Bros.*, 4 Conn. Workers' Comp. Rev. op. 82, 227 CRD-4-83 (1987) our "Workers' Compensation Act does not provide for an award of benefits on the basis of whole-man rating." *Id.* at 85. However, the consideration of such ratings in reaching a decision as to the percentage loss of or loss of use of function is permitted under the broad discretionary powers granted to a commissioner in making such assessments. *See id.* at 85. We find the award for a 10% impairment of the respiratory system in the present matter was well within the Commissioner's discretion.

575 CRD-3-87 at 4.

§ 11.06   DELAWARE

Pekala v. E.I. DuPont De Nemours & Co., 2007 WL 1653496 (Del. Super.)

The Superior Court of Delaware dealt with the employee, Pekala, who developed hypersensitivity to mold during his 27-year career with DuPont. His claim was accepted and his medical treatment was covered until he was fired in 2001. He then filed and lost a wrongful termination suit. His subsequent workers' compensation claim for permanent respiratory impairment benefits was denied.

The fifth edition of the *AMA Guides* was utilized in this case.

Dr. Greenberg testified the claimant had no permanent impairment. Dr. Johanning testified that Mr. Pekala had a 20 percent permanent respiratory impairment, despite normal pulmonary function test (PFT) results. He based the 20 percent on the claimant's performance on the Methacholine Challenge Test. The board found no evidence of permanent impairment. The board emphasized the fact that Dr. Johanning did not articulate the detailed effects on Mr. Pekala's daily living, a requirement pursuant to the *AMA Guides*.

The court found substantial evidence to support the board's denial of benefits.

Wykpisz v. Steel, 2001 WL 755376 (Del. 2001)

The claimant, *Wykpisz*, injured his back and right shoulder in February of 1998 while carrying a steel beam for the employer, a steel company. The claimant was initially awarded total disability. The Industrial Accident Board subsequently granted the employer's petition to terminate benefits, and the claimant appealed that decision to the board, who denied the appeal. The appeals court affirmed that decision.

The claimant's treating physician and medical expert, a specialist in pain management, found the claimant "temporarily totally disabled from all work." The physician diagnosed a right trapezius strain, right posterior shoulder sprain, cervical thoracic lumbosacral strain, and fibromyalgia. The physician placed the claimant on a schedule of physical therapy and prescribed drug therapy. The claimant continued to complain of significant pain. The physician opined that the appellant sustained a 5 percent permanent impairment to his right upper extremity and a 3 percent impairment to his cervical spine resulting from the February 1998 work accident (the claimant also suffered another work injury after that at issue and prior to trial).

An orthopedic surgeon and expert for the employer diagnosed the claimant (a few days after the injury) with a soft-tissue injury to the right girdle region and opined that the claimant should have recovered completely within a few weeks. He agreed that the claimant was likely suffering from posterior shoulder and right trapezius strain but disagreed with the claimant's physician's diagnosis of cervical thoracic, lumbar strain, and fibromyalgia. The orthopedic surgeon found no objective findings to support these diagnoses and noted that fibromyalgia requires widespread pain in 11 of 18 possible tender areas "on both sides of the body, above and below the right waist" for over a three-month time span and could not be diagnosed several days after an injury. The orthopedic surgeon noted that the appellant demonstrated "positive signs of functional overlay whether it's malingering, or exaggeration, or some other psychiatric diagnosis." *See* 2001 WL 755376 at 1. The orthopedic surgeon was unable to locate any *AMA Guides* that would give impairment ratings based on the *claimant's* subjective pain complaints. The orthopedic surgeon testified that all four of his examinations were essentially normal in terms of objective findings. However, based solely on the claimant's subjective complaints, the surgeon gave a 3 percent permanent impairment to the right upper extremity resulting from the February 1998 work accident, as well as a 3 percent permanent impairment to the cervical spine as a result of an unrelated January 1999 work accident.

The board accepted the orthopedic surgeon's diagnosis and held that the appellant sustained soft-tissue injuries from the February 1998 work accident that should have been resolved in several weeks. The board also found that the appellant did not sustain 3 percent impairment to the right shoulder because both doctors based their ratings on the appellant's subjective complaints, which the board found were not reliable and not on objective findings supported by the *AMA Guides.* On review, the appellate court found substantial evidence in the record to support the board's decision. It noted that because the board found the claimant's subjective complaints to be unreliable, it was appropriate for it to discount the permanency ratings provided by the doctors because they were solely based upon these unreliable complaints.

2001 WL 755376, at *2.

Turbitt v. Blue Hen Lines, Inc., 711 A.2d 1214 (Del. 1998)

The Delaware court dealt with a case in which the claimant's permanent partial disability rating had been based on the *AMA Guides* (3d ed. 1988).

A long-haul trucker employed by the appellee, a trucking company, injured his lower back in a work accident in September 1995. Following surgery in April 1996, the claimant was unable to continue his preinjury duties as a truck driver. At the Industrial Accident Board hearing, the physician, testifying through deposition on behalf of the claimant, provided the only medical testimony concerning the claimant's disability. He opined that the claimant had a 34 percent permanent partial disability of the spine. The physician arrived at his 34 percent conclusion based on his own clinical experience, the *Manual for Orthopedic Surgeons*, and the *AMA Guides*. He acknowledged that the *Manual for Orthopedic Surgeons* is no longer being published. The physician further acknowledged that he did not use either of the two models recommended in the *AMA Guides* for guidance in determining the permanent partial disability and that he used the *AMA Guides* (3d ed. 1988) rather than the *AMA Guides* (4th ed. 1993). The trucking company tendered no medical evidence in support of its position.

The board, "relying primarily on its own experience in these matters," concluded that the claimant had a lower back permanent partial impairment of 15 percent. It found the physician opinion not to be credible as a result of his reliance on the outdated *Manual for Orthopedic Surgeons* and *AMA Guides* and his failure to use either of the models in the *AMA Guides* (4th ed. 1993). The board also relied on a previous case in which it awarded 23 percent permanent partial impairment to a claimant with a spinal injury that it considered more severe than the claimant's. On appeal, the superior court upheld the board's determination, finding "no error in the Board's use of its precedent as a gauge for appropriate awards for particular categories of injuries. . . ."

The Delaware Supreme Court reversed the board's finding of a 15 percent disability. The court stated:

> In workers' compensation cases, it is necessary that all findings and evidence be in the record. Arthur Larson & Lex K. Larson, Larson's Workers' Compensation Law § 80.23 (1997). The Board operates in a quasi-judicial capacity and is, therefore, bound to observe fundamental principles of justice, such as due process. *See General Chem. Div. Allied Chem. & Dye Corp. v. Fasano*, Del. Super., 47 Del. 546, 94 A.2d 600 (195[3]). As a general rule, an award of compensation cannot be supported by facts ascertained by the Board, but not put in evidence so as to permit scrutiny and contest. *Id.*
>
> Whatever "institutional experience" or administrative expertise the Board possesses may be used as a tool for evaluating evidence but not as a source for creating evidence. Nor may the Board compare the claim under consideration to other cases decided by it, without affording the parties notice and opportunity to dispute the applicability of such cases. *See Larson, supra*, § 79.62. Unlike judicial bodies, which may rely upon, and take instruction from, previous rulings for legal standards, the Board should refrain from using cases from its own experience for factual comparison, unless invited by the parties to do so.

The Board rejected Dr. [F.]'s evaluation on the basis that he used what it considered to be outdated guidelines but did not articulate the specific effect the use of such material had upon Dr. [F.]'s evaluation. Rejection of evidence on the basis of credibility must be supported by specific references to the evidence of record which prompts disbelief. *Lemmon*, 690 A.2d at 913–14. General observations concerning outdated material will not suffice to provide an independent basis for fixing a different percentage of disability. In sum, we conclude that the Board's finding of a 15% disability, to the extent it is based on the Board's institutional experience and the partial rejection of Dr. [F.]'s testimony on grounds of "credibility," is not supported by substantial evidence and must be reversed.

711 A.2d at 1216.

Butler v. Ryder M.L.S., 1999 Del. Super. LEXIS 29 (Del. Super. Ct. Feb. 1, 1999)

The Delaware court dealt with a claimant who slipped and fell and injured her lower right extremity. The worker claimed that the Industrial Accident Board lacked sufficient evidence to support its findings of a 14 percent impairment. Specifically, she argued that the board erred by failing to assign an impairment rating for the chondromalacia condition, simply because the condition is not listed in the *AMA Guides* (4th ed. 1993). Additionally, she argued that the board should not have simply deferred to the *AMA Guides*, especially when both doctors agreed that she suffered from the condition. The court agreed and remanded for specific findings for an award based on chondromalacia. It stated:

> In the present case, the Board decided it would "not assign any additional impairment on the basis of Claimant's chondromalacia, which, as Dr. [R.] noted, is no longer specifically mentioned in the *AMA Guides*." This Court finds that this is an insufficient explanation as to why the Board chose to disregard the percentage attributed to the chondromalacia condition. Similar to *Turbitt*, the Board rejected Dr. [R.]'s evaluation because he relied on an older edition of the *AMA Guides*, without stating the effect the use of the materials had on his evaluation.

1999 Del. Super. LEXIS 29, at *8.

Simmons v. Delaware State Hosp., 660 A.2d 384 (Del. 1995)

The Delaware court dealt with a claimant who injured her neck while working as a hospital activity aide. The claimant's treating physician testified that the claimant has a 25 percent to 30 percent permanent impairment of her neck. Her employer's doctor testified that the claimant has a 5 percent impairment of the neck under the *AMA Guides*. The claimant's treating physician did not rely on any guides. The board indicated that it did not find the testimony of the claimant's treating physician persuasive because the doctor did not rely on any guides. The court affirmed the board's decision to accept the testimony of one expert witness over another.

§11.07 DISTRICT OF COLUMBIA

Negussie v. District of Columbia Dep't of Employment Servs., 915 A.2d 391 (D.C. 2007)

The District of Columbia Court of Appeals dealt with the claimant, Negussie, who suffered a left upper arm fracture in a head-on collision. Negussie's treating physician used the *AMA Guides* and arrived at a 28 percent impairment of the left upper extremity, taking into account pain, weakness, loss of function, and endurance. Dr. Farber used the fourth edition of the *Guides* and the same factors to arrive at a 6 percent permanent impairment of the upper extremity.

The ALJ commented extensively on his lack of discretion to deviate from the disability percentages presented by the medical doctors and then awarded 6 percent using Dr. Farber's evaluation. The court rejected the nondiscretionary standard and stated:

> Hence, we hold that ALJs have discretion in determining disability percentage ratings and disability awards because, as used in the Act, "disability" is an economic and legal concept which should not be confounded with a medical condition, and that in this case the ALJ erred by following decisions of the Director of DOES that require ALJs to choose a disability percentage rating provided either by the claimant's or the employer's medical examiner.

915 A.2d at 398.

§11.08 FLORIDA

Bishop v. Baldwin Acoustical & Drywall, 696 So. 2d 507 (Fla. Dist. Ct. App. 1997)

The Florida court dealt with a claimant whose work-related injury resulted in a two-level spinal fusion. The claimant sought permanent total disability benefits. The judge of compensation claims (JCC) denied this claim. Because the JCC found that the claimant had not proven permanent total disability by medical testimony of physical restrictions combined with vocational evidence, or by proof of a lengthy, but unavailing job search, he denied the claim. The court upheld his denial. The court held that the JCC did not commit an error by refusing to consider the employer's attorney's suggestion that the claimant's impairment would be rated at 12 percent under the *AMA Guides*. The court reasoned:

> The dissent asserts that the Judge of Compensation Claims committed an error of law because he refused to credit the employer's attorney's suggestion that the *AMA Guides* would rate claimant's impairment at 12 percent. The attorney's attempt to suggest what the impairment rating would be under the *AMA Guides* does not, however, constitute competent substantial evidence as a matter of law. Obviously, the attorney's questions are not evidence in this case, and moreover, Dr. [D.] never agreed with the attorney's suggestion as to an appropriate impairment rating. The exchange between the employer's lawyer and Dr. [D.] went as follows:

> **Q.** (By counsel for the Employer/Carrier) In Florida we've got, uh, unlike probably, Alabama, we use the, uh, some guides that are specific on impairment ratings. And I want to show you the guide that was effective at the time, *AMA Guide* Third Edition. Using this guide, it would appear to me that, un, his impairment rating . . . you get 12 percent.
> **A.** (By Dr. [D.]) You see the name of this book? Says "Guides to the Evaluation." The way I was taught to do evaluations for disabilities at Duke University . . . I use that as a guide. . . . This is a guide. Two-level back fusion. Good, bad, indifferent, is 40 percent disability, anatomic rating in my book.
>
> * * *
> I mean, a disability rating is like an oil painting. I mean, I did it. That's mine. If y'all don't like it, they've got plenty of guys that will paint you a picture.
> **Q.** I know. I'm not arguing with you and I understand. But if there was somebody that used the *AMA Guides* and looked at the *AMA Guides*, he would have a 12 percent. But you say it's 40.
> **A.** Based on what I have already said and how I arrive at that, I'd say it's 40.
> **Q.** But if you look strictly to the book, which I know you don't do, it would be a 12?
> **A.** That's a guide.
> **Q.** That's right.
> **A.** It's not a rating book.
> **Q.** But if you look at the guide?
> **A.** You could use that as a guide and then you've got to say what you know about the patient, includes in there too.
> **Q.** So what you do in the patient is, the 12 percent the guide. But what you look at is his age, his education, his past industrial history.
> **A.** I try to do all that, and that culminates in that.
> **Q.** And that's what you come up with, the 40?
> **A.** It seems to be a little easier in Alabama.

Appellant contends that the JCC overlooked case law holding that a physician's failure to apply the *AMA Guides* renders the evaluation incompetent only as to the amount of impairment, and not to the fact that some impairment exists. This argument, however, is beside the point. The JCC in this case in fact found a "serious injury . . . traumatic enough to aggravate any pre-existing back condition the claimant might have had thereby necessitating two surgical fusions." Even were we to assume some degree of permanent impairment, however, the result here would not change because the claimant failed to meet his burden of proof on other elements of the claim.

The case primarily relied upon by the dissent, *Cabrera v. Universal Trusses, Inc.*, 429 So. 2d 768 (Fla. Dist. Ct. App. 1983), is not instructive on the issue before the court. In *Cabrera*, the treating physician did in fact assign a permanent impairment rating. The physician's mistake in that case was to rely upon the guidelines of the American Academy of Orthopedic Surgeons, rather than upon the *AMA Guides*. 429 So. 2d at 769. Here, the doctors persisted in providing a disability rating rather than an anatomic impairment rating as required by the *AMA Guides*. *See Photo Electronics Corp. v. Glick*, 398 So. 2d 900 (Fla. Dist. Ct. App. 1981) (doctor is qualified to testify only as to anatomic or functional impairment within his medical expertise; JCC alone must make determination of disability). Moreover, *Cabrera* was a wage loss case, in which the proof of some degree of permanent impairment would have presumably led to an entitlement to wage loss under the then-existing workers' compensation law. The present case is a permanent total disability case in which the claimant bears the burden of demonstrating medical or vocational inability to perform even light work on an uninterrupted basis. § 440.15(1)(b), Fla. Stat. (1987). The remand suggested by the dissent would of necessity be for the purpose of allowing claimant to completely retry his case, and not merely for "further findings."

In summary, this case is not simply about a JCC's insistence that a doctor's testimony as to permanent impairment comport with the *AMA Guides*. Instead, this case involves a failure of proof on the part of the claimant, the party in this case with the burden of proof. Indeed, given the extremely thorough treatment of the issues by the JCC, we are unable to see what the difference would be in this case, even were we to assume a 12 percent impairment rating.

696 So. 2d at 511–12.

Torres v. Smithkline Beecham Co., 659 So. 2d 327 (Fla. Dist. Ct. App. 1995)

The Florida court dealt with a worker hurt in 1989. The court held that the impairment was properly rated for this injury under the *AMA Guides* rather than the Minnesota schedule used for rating, as the *AMA Guides* were required under the workers' compensation statute in effect in 1989.

Injured Workers Ass'n v. Department of Labor, 630 So. 2d 1189 (Fla. Dist. Ct. App. 1994)

The Florida court dealt with a suit, brought by the Injured Workers Association of Florida and the AFL-CIO, challenging the validity of a workers' compensation rule regarding the rating of permanent impairment. A Florida workers' compensation impairment rating guide was adopted for injuries after November 1,

1992. This guide is to be "more comprehensive than the *AMA Guides*" and was to include the *AMA Guides* (3d ed. 1988), Sneller charts, and the Minnesota D/O/U disability schedules.

The court found the workers' compensation rule constitutional despite some question about its implementation. The court stated:

> Employees also argue that the rule is invalid because the guide rates mental impairments differently than they formerly were rated—mental impairments used to be rated on a numerical scale. The evidence, however, included the opinion that mental impairments cannot be reduced to meaningful numbers, a fact reflected in the elimination of numerical scales for mental impairments in the third edition of the *AMA Guides.* Employees thus failed to show that the guide [rule] is ill-founded. The hearing officer's determination that the rule is a valid exercise of legislative authority must be sustained because it is supported by competent, substantial evidence.
>
> Employees yet argue that because the guide purports to be exclusive and because the *AMA Guides* recognize loss of range of spinal motion as a permanent impairment but the instant guide does not, therefore the courts are closed to this impairment, in violation of the Florida and federal constitutions. Employees particularly argue a denial of access to courts, guaranteed by section 21 of the Florida Constitution, a denial of due process, guaranteed by section 9 of the Florida Constitution, and a denial of equal protection, guaranteed by section 2 of the Florida Constitution. We disagree, because the instant rule presents no facial unconstitutionality. Whether the rule is unconstitutional as applied must await an appropriate case. Employees thus failed to overcome the rule's presumption of facial constitutionality.

630 So. 2d at 1192.

Glisson v. State Dep't of Management Servs., 621 So. 2d 543 (Fla. Dist. Ct. App. 1993)

The Florida court dealt with the claimant, who sought in-the-line-of-duty disability retirement benefits. He had two back operations and was rated at a 10 percent permanent impairment of the whole body. He was rejected for retirement benefits because of the reasoning that if the claimant had only a 10 percent impairment of the back, he could not be totally disabled.

The court pointed out the mistaken use of the *AMA Guides* and the terms *impairment* and *disability* by the Retirement Commission and stated:

> The accurate and proper use of medical information to assess impairment depends on the recognition that, whereas impairment is a medical matter, disability arises out of the interaction between impairment and external demands, especially those of an individual's occupation. As used in the *Guides*, "impairment" means an alteration of an individual's health status that is assessed by medical means; "disability," which is assessed by

nonmedical means, is an alteration of an individual's capacity to meet personal, social, or occupational demands or statutory or regulatory requirements. Stated another way, "impairment" is what is wrong with a body part or organ system and its functioning; "disability" is the gap between what the individual can do and what the individual needs or wants to do.

Considered in light of this explanation of the different meanings of the terms "impairment" and "disability," it becomes apparent that there is no necessary inconsistency in this case between Dr. [B.]'s opinion that appellant had sustained a 10 percent permanent impairment of the whole body as a result of the back injury; and his opinion that, as a result of the back injury, appellant was incapable of performing any employment for which he might otherwise be qualified and was, therefore, permanently and totally disabled.

621 So. 2d at 545, 546.

Kessler v. Community Blood Bank, 621 So. 2d 539 (Fla. Dist. Ct. App. 1993)

The Florida court dealt with the claimant, who injured his back while working as a phlebotomist (drawing blood). A physician, who was authorized by the employer, did an examination and wrote a two-and-one-half-page report finding the claimant was at MMI and had no residual "permanent disability."

The court found that taking the physician's statement as to the existence of no permanent disability and concluding that this was the same as no permanent impairment were part of a reversible error. The court stated:

First, the record lacks competent substantial evidence to support the finding of "no residual permanent impairment." Having carefully reviewed the record, including the doctors' depositions and medical reports and the JCC's order, and having considered the live testimony presented at hearing, we are convinced that Dr. [H.]'s report is the key evidentiary source on which the JCC relied to find a date of MMI and an absence of permanent impairment. However, the JCC erred in accepting as pivotal Dr. [H.]'s finding of "no residual permanent disability," and concluding from Dr. [H.]'s report that claimant has "no residual permanent impairment." *Photo Electronics Corp. v. Glick*, 398 So. 2d 900, 901 (Fla. 1st DCA 1981). Dr. [H.]'s report does not comply with section 440.15(3)(a)(3), Florida Statutes (1989), which deals with impairment benefits and requires a permanent impairment rating pursuant to a schedule "based on generally accepted medical standards" such as the American Medical Association Guidelines. As we noted in *Photo Electronics*, a medical doctor "is qualified to testify only as to anatomic or functional impairment" within the doctor's medical expertise, whereas a JCC's function is to consider that testimony and, along with any evidence of loss of wage-earning capacity, translate it into a disability rating. In *Photo Electronics*, we held that a treating physician's opinion about a claimant's *disability* constituted testimony "beyond his competence as a medical expert." *Id.* (Emphasis added.) The E/C's argument notwithstanding, the difference between "disability" and "impairment" in this particular statutory context is not mere semantics, nor does the intermingling of the terms constitute mere harmless error. Because the record fails to support the JCC's determination on the impairment issue, we are compelled to reverse and remand for further proceedings.

621 So. 2d at 541, 542.

Gainesville Coca-Cola v. Young, **596 So. 2d 1278 (Fla. Dist. Ct. App. 1992)**

The Florida court dealt with the claimant, who was a route salesperson and had a freight elevator door slam on his right hand. He was initially rated with a 0 percent impairment and later rated at 1 percent due to subjective pain and a decreased grip strength, that is, a rating of 110 percent for the left hand and 85 percent for the injured right hand. The court remanded the case on the issue of the impairment rating, as the judge failed to say why he accepted the 1 percent rating and not the 0 percent rating. The court stated:

> Generally, no explanation need be given when some medical testimony is accepted and other testimony rejected. The Amended Order is deficient, however, in that the JCC's reason for accepting [physician]'s 1% impairment rating, in the face of other medical testimony of a 0% rating, is not apparent from the record.

596 So. 2d at 1279.

Shaw v. Publix Supermarkets, Inc., **609 So. 2d 683 (Fla. Dist. Ct. App. 1992)**

The Florida court dealt with the claimant, who sustained serious injuries to her upper extremity and dominant right hand. Her treating physician sent her for 54 occupational therapy treatments with little progress. The treating physician found that she had a 40 percent impairment to the whole person.

The claimant was examined on one occasion by a physician specializing in reconstructive surgery, who found a 10 percent impairment to the whole person under the *AMA Guides*. The surgeon opined that the claimant could work three and one-half hours per day.

The court reversed the denial of benefits, finding that the claimant was permanently and totally disabled. The court stated:

> Claimant is a widow in her late 50's, with an eighth-grade education and limited ability to read and write. She had seasonal employment as a sectionizer at a citrus company from 1957 until 1971, when the company closed down. She commenced employment at Publix in 1977. Dr. [M.], a psychologist, evaluated claimant in March 1991 and described her as a woman of "low average intelligence." Evidence of other marketable vocational skills is lacking. Claimant

cannot return to her former level of employment at Publix, and no job other than in labeling was offered.

609 So. 2d at 686.

Wilson v. Harris Corp., 557 So. 2d 50 (Fla. Dist. Ct. App. 1989)

The claimant, who had suffered a lower back injury as a result of a fall at work, appealed the denial of temporary partial disability benefits. The district court of appeals reversed the deputy commissioner's decision, holding that the deputy commissioner improperly rejected an osteopathic physician's expert opinion that the claimant had suffered a permanent physical impairment (not specified by the court), even though the physician did not use the *AMA Guides*. The physician's testimony indicated that his opinion was based on testing, his own training and experience, and the severity of the claimant's complaints, and he further testified that he treated the claimant for back problems approximately 53 times.
The court stated:

> A deputy is not precluded from awarding benefits just because the *AMA Guides* are not used to determine the degree of impairment caused by a particular injury. *Dayron Corporation v. Morehead*, 509 So. 2d 930 (Fla. 1987). A deputy may rely on medical testimony utilizing other generally accepted medical standards. These include qualified expert testimony by a physician with training, expertise, and experience in treating a claimant or similarly injured patients. *Rodriguez v. Dade County School Board*, 511 So. 2d 712 (Fla. Dist. Ct. App. 1987); *Patterson v. Wellcraft Marine*, 509 So. 2d 1195 (Fla. Dist. Ct. App. 1987).

557 So. 2d at 51.

Christian v. Greater Miami Academy, 541 So. 2d 701 (Fla. Dist. Ct. App. 1989)

The personal representative of a deceased worker who had suffered a ruptured disk was denied claims for past due total disability benefits, medical care, and wage loss benefits for permanent total disability benefits. The decedent's physician testified that the industrial accident resulted in a permanent impairment of between 5 percent and 6 percent. The deputy rejected this testimony on the grounds that the doctor did not make proper use of the *AMA Guides*. The court of appeals disagreed, finding that the doctor clearly testified that his rating was based on the *AMA Guides*.

> The deputy rejected [physician]'s permanency rating because [physician] had "extrapolated" a bit of it from his own experience, rather than relying on the *AMA Guides*. In so doing, the deputy apparently overlooked [physician]'s testimony that he based 5 percent of his impairment rating on the *AMA Guides* for a patient who had a ruptured disc and was totally asymptomatic. [Physician] then indicated that claimant's syndrome was a little worse than someone

who has had a ruptured disc and is somewhat symptomatic. He indicated that her arthritic changes made her disability somewhat greater than 5 percent. It was only this 1 percent, making the total permanency rating 6 percent, that [physician] extrapolated from his own experience in treating patients with ruptured discs and pre-existing arthritic conditions. Clearly, at least 5 percent of claimant's permanency rating was squarely based on the *AMA Guides* and was not attributable to her pre-existing arthritic condition.

541 So. 2d at 704 n.3.

Philpot v. City of Miami, 541 So. 2d 680 (Fla. Dist. Ct. App. 1989)

The claimant appealed the denial of a claim for medical treatment and compensation benefits resulting from a head injury and postconcussion syndrome. The district court of appeal reversed, holding that, insofar as the injury at issue is covered by the *AMA Guides*, an impairment rating should be based on them.

However, where the *AMA Guides* do not adequately address the subject impairment (post-traumatic neurosis), the deputy may rely on a physician's qualified expert opinion, which utilizes experience in treating the claimant, and such an opinion will suffice without reliance on a medical manual or the *Guides*. *Wilson v. Harris Corporation*, 14 EL.W 434, 435 (Fla. 1st Dist. Ct. App., Feb. 15, 1989); *Shop & Go, Inc. v. Hart*, 537 So. 2d 667 (Fla. 1st Dist. Ct. App. 1989), quoting *Patterson v. Wellcraft Marine*, 509 So. 2d 1195, 1197 (Fla. 1st Dist. Ct. App. 1987).

Id. at 683–84.

Shop & Go, Inc. v. Hart, 537 So. 2d 667 (Fla. Dist. Ct. App. 1989)

The employer appealed from an order of the deputy commissioner finding that the claimant had suffered a permanent impairment. The claimant was examined by three different physicians, including her treating physician and two general surgeons to whom she had been referred by her treating physician. Only the treating physician was of the opinion that the claimant had suffered a permanent impairment. The treating physician, however, testified that the *AMA Guides* did not cover the claimant's particular medical problem and based his opinion on experience and on his treatment of the claimant. The district court of appeals concluded that the treating physician's testimony constituted competent substantial evidence to support the finding of permanency.

This court has repeatedly held that where the *AMA Guides* do not adequately address impairment, as in the instant case, the Deputy Commissioner may properly rely on "a physician's qualified expert opinion which utilizes experience in treating a claimant, and that such an opinion will suffice without reliance on a medical manual or guide." *Patterson v. Wellcraft Marine*, 509

So. 2d 1195 at 1197 (Fla. Dist. Ct. App. 1987); *United General Construction v. Cason*, 479 So. 2d 833 (Fla. Dist. Ct. App. 1985); *Martin County School Board v. McDaniel*, 465 So. 2d 1235 (Fla. Dist. Ct. App. 1984). *Cf. Maggard v. Simpson Motors*, 451 So. 2d 529 (Fla. Dist. Ct. App. 1984). In *Martin County School Board v. McDaniel, supra*, the treating physician in the instant case monitored the claimant's complaints for an extended period of time (two and one half years) and his records indicate an evaluation of the pattern of claimant's subjective symptoms, a program of medication, and testing as a foundation for his opinion of permanent impairment. In *Maggard supra* (in which the deputy commissioner's finding of no permanent impairment was affirmed), the claimant's treating physician's opinion of permanency was based solely on the claimant's complaints of chronic pain, from which the physician assumed that the claimant had aggravated a pre-existing back condition.

537 So. 2d at 668.

Morris v. C.A. Meyer Paving & Constr., 516 So. 2d 302 (Fla. Dist. Ct. App. 1987)

The claimant's left testicle was surgically removed after an industrial accident. The claimant's urologist testified that the claimant had suffered a 10 percent permanent impairment attributable to the loss of one testicle based on the *AMA Guides*. The district court of appeals reversed the denial of the claim, holding that the surgical removal of the employee's testicle constituted an "amputation" within the meaning of the workers' compensation statutes.

Rodriguez v. Dade County Sch. Bd., 511 So. 2d 712 (Fla. Dist. Ct. App. 1987)

The claimant appealed from orders of the deputy commissioner reserving jurisdiction for the determination as to whether the claimant was entitled to wage loss benefits for her back injury. The district court of appeals held that the deputy commissioner erred in concluding that, because a physician's opinion was not based on the *AMA Guides*, it did not constitute competent, substantial evidence. The court reiterated what it felt "should now be well established."

> If the *AMA Guides* do not cover a particular injury, a doctor's opinion regarding permanent impairment need not be referenced to the Guidelines, if it is supported by other generally accepted medical standards, including the doctor's prior experience in treating similar injuries. *See Trindade v. Abbey Road Beef 'n' Booze*, 443 So. 2d 1007 (Fla. Dist. Ct. App. 1983); *Rhaney v. Dobbs House, Inc.*, 415 So. 2d 1277 (Fla. Dist. Ct. App. 1982). As this court emphasized in *Rhaney*, certain conditions and injuries that result in permanent impairment are not always covered by the *AMA Guides*.

Id. at 713.

McCabe v. Bechtel Power Corp., 510 So. 2d 1056 (Fla. Dist. Ct. App. 1987)

The claimant appealed a finding of the deputy commissioner denying a claim for wage loss benefits, rehabilitation, and future medical care due to an injury to his knee. The district court of appeals reversed in part, holding that the deputy commissioner's finding that the worker suffered no permanent impairment to the knee was not supported by substantial evidence. The court concluded that the deputy commissioner's rejection of an orthopedic surgeon's testimony, primarily because the surgeon "changed" his testimony, was not supported by the record where the *AMA Guides* in effect at the time of the surgeon's original medical report did not allow him to give the worker's injury any degree of permanent impairment. A later version of the *AMA Guides*, however, changed the rating for knee injuries, and the surgeon then rated the worker's injury, indicating some permanency attributable to the accident in question.

> This explanation does not constitute a "change" in testimony, but is clearly consistent with his prior reports, which discussed claimant's pain and loss of stability in his knee. The deputy's expressed rationale for rejecting [physician]'s testimony is not supported by the record.

Id. at 1059.

Patterson v. Wellcraft Marine, 509 So. 2d 1195 (Fla. Dist. Ct. App. 1987)

The claimant suffered a fall while at work in September 1984, which resulted in an injury to her lower back. The claimant's injury was initially diagnosed as a lumbar strain, and rest was prescribed. Upon returning to work, she continued to suffer muscle spasms, soreness, and pain in her lower back. In 1985 she was admitted to the hospital, where a diagnostic myelogram and CT (computed tomography) scan were performed, both of which were negative. She returned to light duty work but continued to experience pain. She was eventually terminated because of absences on the job. She revisited one of her treating physicians, who recommended that she not continue work until she had received a second opinion. That second opinion came from a neurosurgeon, who not only concurred with the previous treating physician's assessment but also concluded that the claimant had suffered a permanent anatomical impairment of 5 percent, pursuant to the *AMA Guides*. The neurosurgeon explained that his disability rating was actually a subjective assessment based on watching the patient move from side to side and forward and back. The neurosurgeon stated that his opinion was based primarily on his experience and evaluation of the claimant.

In denying the claim for wage loss, the deputy commissioner rejected this second opinion because it was based on subjective complaints only. Instead, the deputy commissioner relied on testimony from a third physician, who determined that the claimant had suffered no permanent impairment because the claimant appeared to have full range of motion. The district court of appeals reversed.

> Dr. [K.]'s determination that claimant suffered no permanent impairment was based exclusively upon the *AMA Guides*, which have no applicability to the type of injury suffered by claimant: lumbar back strain. In *Florida Sheriffs Youth Fund v. Harrell*, 438 So. 2d 450 (Fla. Dist. Ct. App. 1983), this court observed that soft tissue injury is not covered by the *Guides*, because they do not measure impairment to the back or pelvis in the absence of limitation of motion. Quoting with approval from the attending physician's testimony, we observed that as to soft tissue injuries, the *Guides* do not truly address such injuries, because they refer to either disk lesions or fractures. The *AMA Guides'* failure to take into consideration the type of soft tissue injury described by Dr. [M.] was also discussed by this court in *Martin County School Board v. McDaniel*, 465 So. 2d 1235 (Fla. Dist. Ct. App. [1984]) (*on rehearing en banc*), *appeal and cross-appeal dismissed*, 478 So. 2d 54 (Fla. 1985), in which we observed the basic similarities between the facts in *Harrell* and those in *McDaniel*, wherein both patients suffered soft tissue injuries, and medication was prescribed for the specific purpose of preventing acute muscle spasms.

Id. at 1197.

Dayron Corp. v. Morehead, 509 So. 2d 930 (Fla. 1987)

The claimant was seeking an award for wage-loss benefits due to a permanent impairment from contact dermatitis, resulting from the exposure to cutting oils in the workplace. The Florida Supreme Court affirmed the deputy commissioner's award of benefits and held that the *AMA Guides* did not apply to preclude a finding of permanent impairment where the claimant suffered a disability due to occupational disease that permanently impaired his ability to work but did not affect his activities of daily living.

The claimant contended that Fla. Stat. chs. 440.01 to 440.60 (1985), dealing with permanent impairment, require the evaluation of the claim under the *AMA Guides* (2d ed. 1984). The *AMA Guides* give a range of 0 percent to 5 percent impairment rating of the whole person under the category pertaining to permanent skin impairment. An example in the *AMA Guides*, which, the claimant contended, was analogous to this case, provided a 0 percent disability rating. The court noted, however, that a comment to the cited example anticipated the possible confusion over the terms *disability* and *impairment*, stating that a worker may indeed have a 0 percent impairment under the *AMA Guides*, but the worker may nonetheless be "disabled" under workers' compensation law.

> When an injury is not covered by the *AMA Guides*, it is permissible to rely upon medical testimony of permanent impairment based upon other generally accepted medical standards. *Deseret Ranches v. Crosby*, 461 So. 2d 295 (Fla. Dist. Ct. App. 1985). Here Morehead's condition is addressed in the *AMA*

Guides, but it is evaluated only in terms of medical impairment without regard to the wage loss which may result from disability. The statute on occupational diseases provides that Workers' compensation shall be paid for disablement. Section 440.151, Fla. Stat. (1985). Section 440.151(3) reads: (3) Except as hereinafter otherwise provided in this section, "disablement" means the event of an employee's becoming actually incapacitated, partially or totally, because of an occupational disease, from performing his work in the last occupation in which injuriously exposed to the hazards of such disease; and "disability" means the state of being so incapacitated. Thus, it appears that a claimant who suffers a permanent disability from an occupational disease is entitled to compensation even though he is not affected if he does not return to work under the conditions which cause his disability. *See Conner v. Riner Plastering Co.*, 131 So. 2d 465 (Fla. 1961).

509 So. 2d at 932.

Coq v. Fuchs Baking Co., **507 So. 2d 138 (Fla. Dist. Ct. App. 1987)**

On appeal from the commissioner's denial of workers' compensation benefits for bakers' asthma, the district court of appeals reversed, finding that the deputy commissioner erred in considering the testimony of a physician who concluded, based on the *AMA Guides* (which were inapplicable), that the claimant suffered a permanent impairment.

The claimant worked as a commercial baker for six years. He began to suffer acute asthma attacks, including one that required hospitalization. In finding no permanent impairment, the deputy commissioner relied on testimony that applied the *AMA Guides* to the claimant. However, the court noted that the *AMA Guides* do not cover an occupational allergy that prevents the claimant from working in his chosen profession. The *AMA Guides* (2d ed. 1984) establish permanent impairment for a respiratory condition only if the claimant suffers from dyspnea or impaired ventilatory capacity. The court cited *Dayron Corp. & Claims Ctr. v. Morehead*, 480 So. 2d 235 (Fla. Dist. Ct. App. 1985), which sustained a finding that a machinist was permanently impaired from contact dermatitis associated with exposure to cutting fluids.

> An asthmatic is rated as severely impaired under the AMA Guidelines if a person, despite optimum medical therapy, has had six or more attacks yearly, requiring emergency room or hospital care. *AMA Guides* at 86, 98. While the claimant was found to have asthma, his condition was regarded as controllable if he stayed away from aerosol flour.

507 So. 2d at 140 n.1.

Kenney v. Juno Fire Control Dist., **506 So. 2d 449 (Fla. Dist. Ct. App. 1987)**

The claimant appealed the deputy commissioner's denial of temporary total disability benefits for an injury to a cervical disk. The district court of appeals reversed, holding that the claimant was entitled to temporary total disability benefits between the time the claimant was released by a second doctor as having reached MMI with a 0 percent disability rating under the *AMA Guides* and the time the claimant returned to the first doctor. The first doctor's opinion that the claimant was temporarily totally disabled was objectively confirmed by disk surgery.

Consoweld Distribs. v. Slaughter, 502 So. 2d 503 (Fla. Dist. Ct. App. 1987)

Although the deputy commissioner erred in considering testimony regarding permanent impairment that was based on the *AMA Guides*, the error was harmless when there was competent medical testimony establishing both that the claimant suffered a permanent impairment and that the *AMA Guides* did not apply to the claimant's condition. When a permanent impairment cannot reasonably be determined under the *AMA Guides*, other generally accepted medical criteria may be used to establish impairment. *See Trindade v. Abbey Road Beef 'n' Booze*, 443 So. 2d 1007, 1012 (Fla. Dist. Ct. App. 1983).

Cuccarollo v. Gulf Coast Bldg. Contractors, 500 So. 2d 547 (Fla. Dist. Ct. App. 1986)

The claimant appealed a denial of benefits. The district court of appeals found that substantial evidence supported the finding that no permanent impairment was shown. The claimant's doctor testified that the claimant had reached MMI with a 5 percent permanent partial impairment, but he admitted that this rating was based on subjective complaints and that it was doubtful that the claimant met the threshold requirements established for permanent impairment under Florida law. The physician also testified that, although he did not agree with the *AMA Guides*, the type of injury sustained by the claimant was covered by the *AMA Guides* and called for a 0 percent impairment rating.

OBS Co. v. Freeney, 475 So. 2d 947 (Fla. Dist. Ct. App. 1985)

The claimant suffered contact dermatitis as a result of exposure to wet cement while working as a journeyman plasterer. The skin condition did not affect his daily living as long as he did not work as a plasterer. If he continued to work as a plasterer, he would be "totally incapacitated." Under old law, the claimant was entitled to benefits, either partial or total, for an occupational disease. Under the present law, a permanent impairment must be established under the *AMA Guides* or under other generally accepted medical criteria. The court held that the degree of impairment in this case could not be determined by the *AMA Guides*. In dealing with the chapter "The Skin," the *AMA Guides* refer to how the skin impairment affects the person's "ability to perform the activities of daily living." *AMA Guides* (2d ed. 1984) at 203. The court pointed out the absence of a reference to how a condition affects the ability to perform a specific job. The court accepted the expert opinion of the treating physician that the claimant suffered a permanent impairment, and found a permanent impairment due to the claimant's inability to work in his chosen profession. The *AMA Guides* were not controlling because they did not address the claimant's economic loss. The court stated:

> Claimant clearly suffers from permanent impairment which has resulted in his "incapacity because of the injury to earn in the same or any other employment the wages which the employee was receiving at the time of the injury." Section 440.02(9) Florida Statutes. Due to his skin condition, claimant cannot work in his chosen occupation, where he earned a relatively high salary, and, in all likelihood, is unable to earn an equal wage in other employment without further training. Although not presented as an issue, we note that neither the employer nor its servicing agent has provided claimant any rehabilitation services as required by section 440.49(a), Florida Statutes. In the situation before us, claimant's condition is directly related to his occupation. Under the terms of the *AMA Guides*, there is no impairment if the injury does not affect the employee's daily living. In the case sub judice, claimant's skin condition does not affect his daily living as long as he does not work in his job. Essentially, as long as claimant does nothing, there is no impairment.
>
> Although the *AMA Guides* do not award the permanent impairment to claimant's skin condition, we affirm and agree with the deputy that, under the particular factual circumstances at bar, the *AMA Guides* are not exclusively controlling because the *AMA Guides* do not address claimant's evident economic loss, which is the basis of the wage-loss concept.

Id. at 950–51.

Martin County Sch. Bd. v. McDaniel, 465 So. 2d 1235 (Fla. Dist. Ct. App. 1984)

The claimant's low back injury was not covered by the *AMA Guides*, but permanent impairment was found based on the opinion of a physician. The court found that expert medical opinion will suffice in some circumstances without the reliance on a manual or guide. The use of a prescribed guide is "obligatory to the extent feasible." *Id.* at 1241. Florida Stat. ch. 440.15(3)(a)3 requires that, with or without a guide, "impairment shall be based on medically demonstrable medical standards." In this case, the physician's opinion and the complaints of the claimant were deemed sufficient to support a finding of permanent impairment.

Walker v. Gulf & W. Food Prods., 461 So. 2d 993 (Fla. Dist. Ct. App. 1984)

The deputy commissioner accepted the testimony of two out of three physicians that the claimant suffered no permanent impairment. One physician found a 5 percent impairment rating for a shoulder and neck injury under the *AMA Guides*. The findings of this physician were rejected by the deputy commissioner, and the court agreed. The court noted that, when presented with several medical opinions, the deputy commissioner may pick and choose which opinions to accept or reject.

Deseret Ranches v. Crosby, 461 So. 2d 295 (Fla. Dist. Ct. App. 1985)

The claimant worked as a cowboy. In 1981 he injured his lower back but continued to work while undergoing medical treatment. In 1982 the claimant injured his neck and shoulder. The claimant's injuries did not constitute impairment under the *AMA Guides*, but permanent impairment was found after referring to the guidelines prepared by the American Academy of Orthopedic Surgeons (AAOS), the *AAOS Manual* (1965) (*AAOS Manual*). When an injury is not covered by the *AMA Guides*, "the deputy may rely on medical testimony of permanent impairment based upon other generally accepted medical standards." *See Trindade v. Abbey Road Beef 'n' Booze*, 443 So. 2d 1007 (Fla. Dist. Ct. App. 1983).

Hunt-Wilde Corp. v. Kitchen, 452 So. 2d 2 (Fla. Dist. Ct. App. 1984)

The claimant's low back injury had a 0 percent impairment rating under the *AMA Guides*. However, an orthopedic surgeon found a disability of 5 percent of the whole man based on the *AAOS Manual*. The court held that appellate courts must apply the law in existence at the time of appeal. Therefore, the issue of permanent impairment was remanded for consideration in light of *Trindade v. Abbey Road Beef 'n' Booze*, 443 So. 2d 1007 (Fla. Dist. Ct. App. 1983). The prerequisite that wage-loss benefits must be based on the *AMA Guides* was modified to incorporate the proposition that generally accepted medical criteria are sufficient as the basis for an award.

Coca-Cola Co. Foods Div. v. Hawk, 451 So. 2d 1025 (Fla. Dist. Ct. App. 1984)

The claimant suffered a bulging disk as a result of an occupational accident. The claimant's physician attempted to apply the *AMA Guides* to find permanent impairment but testified that the *AMA Guides* did not take into account the claimant's condition. Therefore, the physician relied on his training and expertise in rating the impairment. The court found no error in the award of permanent impairment.

> The doctor testified that although he applied the *AMA Guides* to claimant's injury, the *Guides* did not take into consideration claimant's physical condition consisting of a bulging disc that was definitely connected with the accident and injury. He therefore relied on his training, experience and expertise in assigning claimant a permanent impairment rating. Dr. [M.]'s testimony was competent to establish the requisite permanent impairment for wage loss.

Id. at 1026.

Maggard v. Simpson Motors, 451 So. 2d 529 (Fla. Dist. Ct. App. 1984)

The Florida appellate court found that the existence and degree of permanent impairment must be proved based on the *AMA Guides*, the *AAOS*

Manual, or other generally accepted medical criteria. An impairment rating based on the claimant's subjective complaints of chronic pain is, therefore, not allowed. The court stated:

> Although we have held that medical testimony on the issue of permanent impairment need not necessarily be based on the *AMA Guides* . . . we have not gone so far as to approve a permanent impairment rating based on the claimant's subjective complaints of chronic pain.

Id. at 530.

Brandon v. Hillsborough County Sch. Bd., 447 So. 2d 982 (Fla. Dist. Ct. App. 1984)

The claimant suffered a lumbar strain as a result of a work-related accident. Under the *AMA Guides*, the claimant was found to have no permanent impairment. Even if other generally accepted medical criteria were used, the record indicated that the claimant had no permanent physical impairment.

> The present case is not one in which "permanent impairment" can not reasonably be determined under the criteria utilized in the guides, in which event such permanent impairments may be established under other generally accepted medical criteria. And even were this a proper instance for utilization of other medical evidence, the record in the present case provides competent, substantial evidence, independent of the *Guides*, to support the deputy's explicit finding that claimant has sustained a permanent physical impairment cognizable under section 440.15(3), Florida Statutes.

Id. at 983.

Spaugh v. Munyan Painting Contractors, 444 So. 2d 1100 (Fla. Dist. Ct. App. 1984)

The claimant's physicians did not express an impairment rating in terms of the *AMA Guides*. The impairment ratings for injuries before August 1, 1979, need not be based on the *AMA Guides*. The case was remanded for determination not based on the *AMA Guides*.

Frank's Fine Meats v. Sherman, 443 So. 2d 1055 (Fla. Dist. Ct. App. 1984)

For accidents occurring on or after August 1, 1979, permanent impairment must be proved by "medically or scientifically demonstrable findings and cannot be based on the claimant's complaints or the deputy's evaluation of those complaints and mere observation of the claimant."

Id. at 1056.

Trindade v. Abbey Road Beef 'n' Booze, 443 So. 2d 1007 (Fla. Dist. Ct. App. 1983)

The claimant suffered torn cartilage and a torn anterior cruciate ligament, causing excessive loss of range of motion. Although the injury was covered by the *AMA Guides*, because there was no loss of range of motion, no impairment rating could be given. In interpreting Fla. Stat. ch. 440.15(13)(a) and 440.15(13)(b), the court held that permanent impairment shall be

> determined pursuant to the *AMA Guides* unless such permanent impairment cannot be reasonably determined under the criteria utilized in the *Guides*, in which case permanent impairment may be established under other generally accepted medical criteria for determining impairment.

443 So. 2d at 1012.

The 10 percent permanent impairment rating based on the *AAOS Manual*, as determined by the treating physician, was upheld. The *AMA Guides*, where applicable, are to be used as the primary rating schedule but shall not be used to deny benefits simply because they do not make provisions for the conditions causing the impairment. The court stated:

> First, as a practical matter, over four years of experience have shown the futility of attempting to view the *AMA Guides* as a comprehensive, all inclusive schedule of permanent impairments. This valuable treatise, viewed by the Division as the "best available," is nevertheless—according to much credible medical testimony reflected in the cases coming before us— incomplete and unsuited to the determination of permanent impairment resulting from certain types of injuries.
>
> We therefore hold that for purposes of determining wage loss benefits in accordance with Section 440.15(3)(a) and (b), the existence and degree of permanent impairment cannot be reasonably determined under the criteria utilized in the *Guides*, in which event such permanent impairment may be established under other generally accepted medical criteria for determining impairment.

Id. at 1011–12.

Florida Mining & Materials v. Moore, 443 So. 2d 328 (Fla. Dist. Ct. App. 1983)

A physician testified that the claimant had a permanent impairment under the *AMA Guides*, but permanent impairment benefits were nonetheless denied. The court stated:

> The issue of whether the claimant had a permanent physical impairment was not only ripe for determination, but was clearly litigated at the hearing on the

claimant's first claim for wage-loss benefits. As is apparent from the deputy's first order, the claimant simply failed in his proof of a permanent impairment.

Id. at 329.

Peck v. Palm Beach County Bd. of County Comm'rs, 442 So. 2d 1050 (Fla. Dist. Ct. App. 1983)

The claimant police officer sustained a permanent hearing loss due to noise on the firing range on November 1, 1978. At that time, no hearing protection was required. The claimant suffered hearing loss for the frequencies 2,300 to 8,000 Hz, but the *AMA Guides* did not cover hearing loss beyond 2,000 Hz. The court stated that the *AMA Guides* are to be used to gauge the degree of permanent impairment for claims arising out of accidents occurring only on or after August 1, 1979. Injuries occurring before that time, but which were decided using the *AMA Guides*, must be redetermined in accordance with the law existing at the time.

Rich v. Commercial Carrier Corp., 442 So. 2d 1011 (Fla. Dist. Ct. App. 1982)

A physician's testimony that he considered other factors in addition to the *AMA Guides* did not render his testimony invalid as to the existence of permanent impairment. Thus, the deputy commissioner erred when he found that the claimant had no permanent physical impairment.

Revenswood-Griffin Volunteer Fire Dep't v. Newman, 442 So. 2d 321 (Fla. Dist. Ct. App. 1982)

The issue of the need to use *AMA Guides* for the evaluation of permanent impairment was not raised before the deputy commissioner at the hearing. As a result, the issue was not preserved for appellate review.

United States Sugar Corp. v. Whitton, 440 So. 2d 427 (Fla. Dist. Ct. App. 1983)

The claimant was found by the deputy commissioner to have suffered a 10 percent permanent partial disability. The court of appeals upheld the finding despite the absence of an impairment rating based on the *AMA Guides*. The court concluded that, despite such absence, a loss of wage earning capacity was supported by the record.

> The evidence was sufficient from which the deputy could find causal relationship and conclude that claimant suffered some permanent impairment, on which a finding of loss of wage earning capacity is initially contingent, despite there being no impairment rating based on the American Medical Association *Guides*.

Id. at 428.

Recon Paving, Inc. v. Cook, 439 So. 2d 1019 (Fla. Dist. Ct. App. 1983)

The *AMA Guides* were used in this case to translate an 80 percent loss of vision in the left eye to a 32 percent loss of total vision and a 30 percent impairment of the body as a whole. Concerning the *AMA Guides*, the court stated:

> [Claimant] lost virtually all vision in his left eye in January 1981, when it was pierced by a broken chisel fragment. Appropriate medical testimony and the deputy's findings, employing the *AMA Guides to the Evaluation of Permanent Impairment*, translated [claimant]'s impairment as a 32 percent loss of total vision and a 30 percent impairment of the body as a whole.

Id. at 1020.

Florida Sheriffs Youth Fund v. Harrell, 438 So. 2d 450 (Fla. Dist. Ct. App. 1983)

The claimant suffered a chronic fibromyositis or sprain in the sacroiliac area. She was found to have a 5 to 10 percent impairment of the body as a whole, based on the physician's experience and on the manual issued by the AAOS. The injury was not covered by the *AMA Guides*, and the deputy commissioner was not in error in relying on the competent medical testimony about permanent impairment. The award was thus upheld. Concerning the *AMA Guides*, the court stated:

> The evidence is undisputed that the impairment resulting from the soft tissue injury described by Dr. [E.] is not covered in the *AMA Guides*. Under virtually indistinguishable circumstances, this court in *Quality Petroleum Corp. v. Mihm, supra*, recognized that the circumstances warranted an exception to the required use of the *AMA Guides*. We do so as well in case *sub judice* and hold that it was not error for the deputy to rely upon competent medical testimony of permanent impairment based upon other generally accepted medical standards, particularly where it was contemplated over four years ago that the *AMA Guides* were to be used only on a temporary basis pending the adoption of a permanent schedule by the Division of Workers' Compensation. No such schedule has been adopted.

Id. at 452.

Tampa Bay Moving Sys. v. Frederick, 433 So. 2d 628 (Fla. Dist. Ct. App. 1983)

The claimant suffered a broken wrist and a lumbar spine sprain. The physician's finding of 6 percent permanent impairment was upheld by the deputy commissioner despite the fact that the physician did not specifically state that his opinion was based on the *AMA Guides*. Though the court did not wish to encourage or condone ambiguous medical evidence, absent a showing of a specific error by the deputy commissioner, the award was upheld. There is a lighter burden on the deputy commissioner and the court when an express reference to the *AMA Guides* is made. The court stated:

> [I]t is the deputy who has the responsibility and authority to determine whether an impairment falls within the prescribed regulatory standards. That the evidence supporting the determination does not contain the words "based on the *AMA Guides*" does not render it incompetent, and no such objection was ever stated before the deputy in this case.

Id. at 630.

Cabrera v. Universal Trusses, Inc., 429 So. 2d 769 (Fla. Dist. Ct. App. 1983)

The deputy commissioner's denial of wage-loss benefits because the physician did not base the impairment rating on the *AMA Guides* was reversed and remanded for reconsideration. The use of the *AMA Guides* is mandatory with certain exceptions, such as when the impairment is clearly visible or when the injury is not covered in the *AMA Guides.* The failure to use the phrase "based on the *AMA Guides*" will not work to deny compensation benefits for permanent impairment.

Jefferson Stores, Inc. v. Cromes, 429 So. 2d 368 (Fla. Dist. Ct. App. 1983)

The claimant suffered a knee injury, but his physician did not use the *AMA Guides* to arrive at an impairment rating. The court stated, "Although the award in this case was not dependent on a specific degree of impairment . . . in order to establish uniformity in the assessment of some permanent impairment, it was incumbent on the deputy commissioner to base his finding on medical testimony in line with the *AMA Guides.*" *Id.* at 369.

Refrigerated Transp. Co. v. Edmond, 428 So. 2d 338 (Fla. Dist. Ct. App. 1983)

Wage-loss benefits are not awardable unless the injured employee has suffered a permanent impairment that is scientifically demonstrable to the deputy commissioner, is visible by his own observations, or is based on the *AMA Guides.* In this case, there was no medical testimony that the claimant had a permanent impairment based either on the *AMA Guides* or on objective observations. The court found that the claimant's subjective complaints alone would not support an award for permanent impairment. The award of wage-loss benefits was reversed.

> Although two physicians, including claimant's initial treating physician, testified that claimant had sustained a permanent impairment, none of this testimony was based on the *AMA Guides* or objective observations . . . based on the absence of any competent medical testimony to indicate that claimant had sustained a permanent impairment based on the *AMA Guides* or other

scientifically demonstrable findings, we must reverse the award for wage loss benefits.

Id. at 340.

Acosta v. Kraco, Inc., 426 So. 2d 1120 (Fla. 1983)

The claimant contended that Fla. Stat. ch. 440.15(3)(b) 3.d. (1979), requiring the termination of wage-loss benefits when a claimant reaches age 65, is unconstitutional. The claimant, who suffered a back injury after age 65, was found to have a 6 percent permanent impairment based on the *AMA Guides.* The deputy commissioner found that the claimant had reached the threshold age and could not receive benefits. The court found that the claimant had no standing to raise the constitutional issue because the claimant failed to prove that but for the statute he would be entitled to wage-loss benefits.

Paradise Fruit Co. v. Floyd, 425 So. 2d 9 (Fla. Dist. Ct. App. 1982)

The Florida court held that the *AMA Guides* provide a mandatory schedule unless either the permanent impairment is obviously visible and demonstrable to the deputy or the particular impairment is not covered by the *AMA Guides.* The injury in this case fell under the *AMA Guides*, but the claimant suffered no loss of range of motion as required by the *AMA Guides.* Therefore, the claimant did not have a permanent impairment under the *AMA Guides.*

Quality Petroleum Corp. v. Mihm, 424 So. 2d 112 (Fla. Dist. Ct. App. 1982)

The claimant suffered a leg injury described as a hematoma with partial infection. A physician testified that this injury was not addressed by the *AMA Guides.* Accordingly, there was no error by the deputy commissioner in relying on the medical testimony based on other generally accepted medical standards. The court stated:

> Where the uncontradicted sworn testimony establishes that an injured employee has suffered permanent impairment, but that impairment is not addressed by the American Medical Association's *Guides*, it is not error for the deputy to rely on medical testimony of permanent impairment based upon other generally accepted medical standards.

Id. at 113, 114.

Morrison & Knudsen/Am., Bridge Div. v. Scott, 423 So. 2d 463 (Fla. Dist. Ct. App. 1982)

The claimant suffered a low back injury that was compensable and covered by the *AMA Guides.* The award for pain and suffering was an error because pain and suffering are not factors in assessing an impairment from low back injuries. Where specific tables for assessing impairment are set out in the *AMA Guides,* they may not be combined with other tables or subjective factors to produce awards in excess of those set out in the *AMA Guides. See Jamar Sportswear, Inc. v. Miller,* 413 So. 2d 811 (Fla. Dist. Ct. App. 1982).

Peter Butts Painting v. Golden, **421 So. 2d 774 (Fla. Dist. Ct. App. 1982)**

The claimant's back, neck, and shoulder injury was not ratable under the *AMA Guides.* Thus, the finding of permanent impairment was erroneous.

Jones Mahoney Corp. v. Hutto, **421 So. 2d 703 (Fla. Dist. Ct. App. 1982)**

The claimant suffered a fractured humerus but had no limitation in the range of motion. The court of appeals overturned the deputy commissioner's award of wage-loss benefits because the claimant did not have a permanent impairment under the *AMA Guides* and because the impairment was not obviously visible and demonstrable to the deputy commissioner.

Clay Hyder Trucking v. Persinger, **419 So. 2d 900 (Fla. Dist. Ct. App. 1982)**

The issue of whether the deputy commissioner erred by predicating the wage-loss award on a disability rating that was not explicitly stated to be in accordance with the *AMA Guides* could not be reached because the employer did not present this issue to the deputy commissioner, either before, during, or after the hearing.

Vannice Constr. Co. v. Silverman, **419 So. 2d 369 (Fla. Dist. Ct. App. 1982)**

The employer/carrier contested the deputy commissioner's acceptance of a medical rating that was not based on the *AMA Guides.* The court found that even though the reliance on the rating was a "technical error," the issue was closed because the employer failed to bring the issue to the deputy commissioner's attention during the 30-day period before the order became final.

E.C. Goldman Roofing v. Rogers, **418 So. 2d 426 (Fla. Dist. Ct. App. 1982)**

The claimant's employer appealed from a decision of the deputy commissioner awarding wage loss benefits for permanent impairment. The appellant contended that the rating assigned to the claimant was not a sufficient basis for the award of wage-loss benefits because the rating was not based on the *AMA Guides to the Evaluation of Permanent Impairment.* However, the "contention was not raised before the deputy commissioner, thus any error was not preserved for this court's review." *Id.* at 427.

Racz v. Chennault, 418 So. 2d 413 (Fla. Dist. Ct. App. 1982)

The claimant suffered low back strain and a psychogenic pain disorder or hysterical conversion neurosis. The court stated that the denial of his claim for physical and psychiatric impairments because his treating psychiatrist's testimony was not based on the *AMA Guides* was an error.

Mathis v. Kelly Constr. Co., 417 So. 2d 740 (Fla. Dist. Ct. App. 1982)

The claimant's knee injury was covered by the *AMA Guides*. There was no detectable loss of range of motion, but the claimant's physician testified that the claimant had a 30 percent permanent partial impairment. The court held that there would be no finding of permanent impairment and called for the exclusivity of using the *AMA Guides*.

Dade Am. Host Supply v. Perez, 417 So. 2d 296 (Fla. Dist. Ct. App. 1982)

The claimant's back injury was rated at a 15 percent permanent impairment by a physician who did not use the *AMA Guides*. The deputy commissioner's acceptance of this rating was an error, but the court would not reverse the award. The error was readily correctable; however, the cross-examination of the physician did not constitute "substantially raising" the issue before the deputy commissioner.

Rhaney v. Dobbs House, Inc., 415 So. 2d 1277 (Fla. Dist. Ct. App. 1982)

The claimant suffered an occupational injury to his hand. The workers' compensation statute requiring the use of the *AMA Guides* to determine permanent impairment, pending the adoption of a permanent impairment schedule, was held to be constitutional, if it was applied in such a way as to permit permanent impairment to be proved by qualified expert testimony or other accepted medical guides.

Sunland Hosp. v. Garrett, 415 So. 2d 783 (Fla. Dist. Ct. App. 1982)

In workers' compensation appeals, the court will not reverse for readily correctable errors that the deputy commissioner was not asked to correct within the time available for correction. In this case, the error was the absence of an impairment rating using the *AMA Guides* or some other rating formula. The employer could have raised the issue during the hearing or within the time available for correction.

Spring Air Mattress Co. v. Cox, 413 So. 2d 1265 (Fla. Dist. Ct. App. 1982)

The claimant was diagnosed as suffering from carpal tunnel syndrome. The treating physician rated the claimant at a 5 percent permanent partial disability. Although the deputy commissioner did not use words "based on the *AMA Guides*" in making the award, the rating was found to be in substantial compliance with the *AMA Guides*. Specifically, the physician's finding of permanent impairment based on the claimant's subjective complaints of pain fell within the parameters of the *AMA Guides*. The physician found the loss of function due to (1) sensory deficit, pain, or discomfort; (2) loss of muscle strength; and (3) the pain's interference with the claimant's daily life. The physician also noted that the claimant's symptoms followed the dermatome distribution and appeared to be caused by some form of impairment to the peripheral spinal nerves.

Jamar Sportswear, Inc. v. Miller, 413 So. 2d 811 (Fla. Dist. Ct. App. 1982)

The claimant suffered a compensable heart attack. A physician rated the impairment at 50 percent, but did not use the *AMA Guides* as required by the Florida workers' compensation statute.

According to the statute, once a diagnosis is made, the applicable table in the *AMA Guides* must be used, and it may not be combined with any other table or subjective factor to produce a rating in excess of that permitted.

Bill Watson's Int'l Inn v. Clairborne, 409 So. 2d 1208 (Fla. Dist. Ct. App. 1982)

The deputy commissioner's finding that the claimant's impairment rating was based on the *AMA Guides* was upheld in this case.

Cumberland Farm Food Stores v. Meier, 408 So. 2d 700 (Fla. Dist. Ct. App. 1982)

The Florida court found that the claimant failed to show that she had suffered a permanent impairment from her back injury or psychiatric condition. Her physician did not base his opinion of permanent impairment on the *AMA Guides*, and the claimant's psychiatric condition, upon which benefits were based, was deemed to be temporary.

Taylor v. International Paper Co., 404 So. 2d 808 (Fla. Dist. Ct. App. 1981)

The claimant suffered thrombophlebitis of the leg and was granted permanent partial disability for the lower extremity. The claimant's attempt to have a rating based on the whole-man concept was rejected by the court. The deputy commissioner found that the claimant's injury was confined to the leg and did not involve the circulatory system as the claimant maintained.

Decor Painting & Iowa Mut. Ins. Co. v. Rohn, 401 So. 2d 899 (Fla. Dist. Ct. App. 1981)

An impairment rating of the claimant's broken ankle that was not based exclusively on the *AMA Guides* was invalid. The court noted the exclusivity of the *AMA Guides* under Fla. Stat. ch. 440.15(3)(a) (1979). Other subjective factors, such as pain and suffering, could not be used to produce a rating in excess of that permitted by the *AMA Guides.*

Tallahassee Memorial Regional Medical Ctr. v. Snead, **400 So. 2d 1016 (Fla. Dist. Ct. App. 1981)**

The claimant's award of a 10 percent permanent partial disability was increased to 15 percent by the deputy commissioner after evidence was offered that the claimant's condition had worsened. Even though the deputy commissioner did not use the *AMA Guides*, his modification of the award was sustained by the court: "Although we find the *Guides* should apply, the deputy's failure to apply the *Guides* does not constitute reversible error because the evidence is sufficient to support modification based on loss of wage earning capacity." *Id.* at 1017.

Flanigan's Enters., Inc. v. Pont, **395 So. 2d 1217 (Fla. Dist. Ct. App. 1981)**

Without evidence of permanent impairment based on the *AMA Guides*, the claimant failed to prove he was entitled to wage-loss benefits. Such failure of proof did not bar the claimant from submitting proof in the future.

Buro v. Dino's Southland Meats, **354 So. 2d 874 (Fla. Dist. Ct. App. 1978)**

The claimant slipped and fell on a greasy floor while working as a cashier at a meat market. The claimant's injuries affected her lower back, neck, shoulders, and legs. She was found to have a 10 percent permanent partial impairment of the body as a whole by a physician using the *AMA Guides.*

§11.09 GEORGIA

Sutton v. Quality Furniture Co., **381 S.E.2d 389 (Ga. Ct. App. 1989)**

The claimant sustained a compensable injury to both elbows. Upon returning to work, he filed a claim to recover permanent partial disability benefits based on residual pain. The court of appeals held that the statute requiring disability or bodily loss ratings to be based on the *AMA Guides* did not preclude an award for permanent partial disability benefits for pain alone, despite the failure of the *AMA Guides* to provide a method for evaluating an impairment based on pain. The claimant submitted a letter from the director of the AMA explaining that: "The AMA and other guides' near silence on pain . . . is not due to failure to recognize pain as a potentially chronically impairing condition, but due to our inability to agree upon methods of evaluation or measuring pain." *Id.* at 390.

The court noted that, prior to the enactment of the statute requiring impairment ratings to be based on the *AMA Guides*, there was no question that permanent partial benefits could be awarded based on a physical impairment resulting solely from pain. *See, e.g., Durden v. Liberty Mut. Ins. Co.*, 151 Ga. App. 399, 259 S.E.2d 656 (1979). It also seems clear that benefits for total disability due to pain alone may still be awarded. *See State v. Graul*, 181 Ga. App. 573, 353 S.E.2d 70 (1987). Georgia Code Ann. § 34-6-1(15) does not mandate reliance on the *AMA Guides*, but rather requires use of the *AMA Guides* or "any other recognized medical books or guides." Finally, it appears that the *AMA Guides* do not prohibit the assessment of disability due to pain, but instead the *AMA Guides* simply do not address the issue.

General Motors Corp. v. Summerous, 317 S.E.2d 318 (Ga. Ct. App. 1984)

The claimant suffered a head injury while on the job and developed paranoid schizophrenia. The injury was found to be compensable, as it resulted from a physical injury. The claimant was found to have a 20 percent psychiatric impairment. The physician's rating was not based on the *AMA Guides*, but it was found to be within the range of rating in the *AMA Guides*. The physician's "rating of appellee's impairment, based upon his professional experience, certainly falls within the range of criteria in Class 2 [of the *AMA Guides'* Criteria for Evaluating Permanent Impairment Due to Psychoses] and is not otherwise invalidated based upon his lack of reliance on the publication." *Id.* at 321, 322.

§ 11.10   HAWAII

Duque v. Hilton Hawaiian Village, 98 P.3d 640 (Haw. 2004)

This case dealt with a worker who suffered a work-related lower back injury in 1991 and was at that time given a 2 percent impairment rating under the third edition of the *AMA Guides*. In 1997 the worker suffered a subsequent work-related back injury. He was then evaluated under the fourth edition and the revised third edition. The evaluating physician evaluated the claimant's impairment as 18 percent under the revised third edition, but only 5 percent under the fourth edition. At issue on appeal was which edition of the *Guides* must be used. The court held that the claimant's rating was *not* required to be made under the latest edition of the *Guides*. The court's reasoning is reproduced below. Note that the court cites extensively from the *Guides* themselves to support its holding that the latest edition of the *Guides* need not be used.

> We conclude, as to Claimant's first contention, that the LIRAB erred when it ruled as a matter of law that Claimant's PPD rating must be determined by use of the most current edition at that time, the Fourth Edition. In our view, exclusive use of the most current edition of the applicable medical guide available at the time of evaluation is not mandated by either HRS § 386-33 or Hawai'i Administrative Rule (HAR) § 12-10-21 or § 12-10-28 for determining an injured employee's PPD rating.

HRS § 386-33(a) is silent on the issue of whether the most recent edition of the Guides should be used to calculate an employee's PPD rating where the employee's prior injury was evaluated under a different edition of the Guides. However, HRS § 386-33(a) does contemplate that comparisons must be made between prior and subsequent injuries that would result in increased disability ratings.

Specifically, HRS § 386-33(a) states in relevant part as follows:

(a) *Where prior to any injury an employee suffers from a previous permanent partial disability already existing prior to the injury for which compensation is claimed*, and *the disability* resulting from the injury combines with the previous disability, whether the previous permanent partial disability was incurred during past or present periods of employment, *to result in a greater permanent partial disability* or in permanent total disability or in death, then weekly benefits shall be paid[.] (Emphases added.)

HAR § 12-10-28(a) further requires that "[t]he extent of medical impairment preexisting the work injury, *shall be assessed by a physician* pursuant to Section 12-10-21(a)." (Emphasis added.) To measure impairment, Section 12-10-21(a) permits the use of "[i]mpairment guides issued by the American Medical Association, Academy of Orthopedic Surgeons, and any other such guides which the director deems appropriate and proper." HAR § 12-10-21(a). The use of the Guides and other guides was affirmed by this court in Cabatbat v. County of Hawaii, Dep't of Water Supply, 103 Hawai'i 1, 78 P.3d 756 (2003). We determined that "HAR § 12-10-21, which states that the AMA Guides *may* be used as a reference, permits reliance on the AMA Guides, but does not mandate their use to the exclusion of other appropriate guides." Id. at 6, 78 P.3d at 761 (emphasis in original).

In this case, the Guides were used exclusively to determine Appellant's PPD rating. See Fifth Edition at iii (stating that the Guides have "become the most commonly used source for assessing and rating an individual's permanent impairment in the United States, and, increasingly abroad"). In effect, Claimant argues that the Third Edition should be utilized to evaluate the PPD rating for his subsequent 1997 work injury, while Employer urges that the then current edition of the Guides should be used.

The Fourth Edition recommended use of the most current Guides edition. See Fourth Edition at 5. ("The American Medical Association strongly discourages the use of any but the most recent edition of the Guides, because the information in [earlier editions] would not be based on the most recent up-to-date material.") The rationale for this position is that "the pace of progress and advance in medicine continues to be rapid, and that a new look at the impairment criteria for all organ systems is advisable[.]" Id., Foreword at v. The Fifth Edition, which is the most current edition, continues the Fourth Edition approach of incorporating the latest scientific knowledge by "*updat[ing]* the diagnostic criteria and evaluation process used in impairment assessment, incorporating available scientific evidence and prevailing medical opinion." Fifth Edition at 1 (emphasis added). Thus, the Fifth Edition declares that "[t]he most recent edition of the Guides is . . . the latest blend of science and medical consensus." Id. at 12, 78 P.3d 756.

But, the AMA also recognizes that the Guides are only "a tool for evaluation of permanent impairment" used by the physician, id. at 13, 78 P.3d 756, and "may be used as a *component in disability assessment*[,]" id. at 12, 78 P.3d 756 (emphasis added). It is cautioned that "the Guides is not to be used for direct financial awards nor as the sole measure of disability." Id. Rather, "[t]he impairment evaluation . . . is only one aspect of disability determination. A disability determination also includes information about the individual's skills, education, job history, adaptability, age, and environment requirements and modifications." Id. at 8, 78 P.3d 756. Accordingly, the AMA recognizes that "[a]ssessing these factors can provide *a more realistic picture of the effects of the impairment* on the ability to perform complex work and social activities." *Id.* (Emphasis added). Hence, in applying the Guides the impairment rating is one factor in a sum of considerations employed in arriving at a disability decision. As emphasized by the Fifth Edition, "[i]mpairment percentages derived from the Guides criteria should not be used as direct estimates of disability." Id. at 13, 78 P.3d 756.

Pertinent to this case, the Fifth Edition posits that "[a]lthough a previous evaluator may have considered a medical impairment to be permanent, unanticipated changes may occur: the condition may have become worse as a result of aggravation or clinical progression, or it may have improved." Id. at 21, 78 P.3d 756. In these circumstances, the AMA states that the person evaluated should be assessed using the current edition of the Guides: The physician should assess the current state of the impairment according to the criteria in the Guides. If an individual received an impairment rating from an earlier edition and needs to be reevaluated because of a change in the medical condition, the individual is evaluated according to the latest information pertaining to the condition in the current edition of the Guides. Id. But "[i]f apportionment is needed, the analysis must consider the nature of the impairment and its relationship to each alleged causative factor, providing an explanation of the medical basis for all conclusions and opinions." Id. In this case, an apportionment between the earlier 1991 injury and the subsequent 1997 injury is required. Under such circumstances, the Fifth Edition vests in the physician the ultimate determination of the appropriate Guides to use. For example, in apportioning a spine impairment, first the current spine impairment rating is calculated, and then an impairment rating from any preexisting spine problem is calculated. The value for the preexisting impairment rating can be subtracted from the present impairment rating to account for the effects of the intervening injury or disease. Using this approach to apportionment requires accurate information and data to determine both impairment ratings. If different editions of the Guides are used, the physician needs to assess their similarity. If the basis of the ratings is similar, a subtraction [between the value for the preexisting impairment rating from the present impairment rating to account for the effects of the intervening injury or disease] is appropriate. If they differ markedly, the *physician needs to evaluate the circumstances and determine if conversion to the earlier or the latest edition of the Guides for both ratings is possible. The determination* should follow any state guidelines and *should consider whichever edition best describes the individual's impairment.*

Id. (Emphases added). Thus, the Fifth Edition instructs physicians to consider and evaluate which edition is most appropriate to use in making an impairment rating in any particular case.

It follows then that a physician may use the most current edition of the Guides when evaluating an employee's PPD rating. However, a physician is not limited to reliance on the most current edition. The Guides themselves instruct that, in light of his or her education and training, a physician should draw on medical expertise and judgment to select the most appropriate guide to utilize in assessing an individual's impairment.

In the case at bar, Dr. Langworthy used both the Third Edition and the Fourth Edition to evaluate Claimant's 1997 subsequent work injury and arrived at two separate and different ratings. As previously mentioned in the January 22, 1999, report, Dr. Langworthy reported a 10% PPD rating of the whole person (5% preexisting from the prior work injury) using the Fourth Edition's DRE criteria.

In a supplemental report six months later on July 27, 1999, Dr. Langworthy reported that Claimant's condition would be rated at 18% PPD of the whole person if the Third Edition were used. The record is devoid, however, of any indication by Dr. Langworthy of which edition best describes Claimant's impairment. In the hearing before the Director to determine the appropriate PPD award for Claimant, Director relied on the Third Edition rating because "it seem[ed] reasonable to use the Third Edition, Revised as the claimant's prior award of 5% PPD of the whole person was premised on the Third Edition, Revised." In its hearing the LIRAB concluded that the Director erred because "[t]he Fourth Edition of the AMA Guides should have been utilized" it being the most current edition published at the time of the evaluation. Because, under the Guides, an impairment rating is one that must be determined by a person qualified to render an opinion in that regard, the record was insufficient for the Director or the LIRAB to conclude whether one or the other rating was the most appropriate to describe Claimant's impairment. The AMA explains that "[p]hysicians have the education and training to evaluate a person's health status and determine the presence or absence of an impairment." See Fifth Edition at 8. See also HAR § 12-10-28(a) (stating that "medical impairment . . . shall be assessed by a physician"). The LIRAB's decision mandating the use of the Fourth Edition in this case would preclude a physician from drawing upon his or her medical judgment and expertise in determining the most appropriate edition to apply.[1] Accordingly, this case must be remanded to permit such judgment and expertise to be exercised by appropriate qualified persons.

98 P.3d at 645–47.

---

[1] Claimant's contention (3) that the LIRAB erred when it failed to include in its findings of fact that Dr. Langworthy did not review Dr. Burke's November 10, 1992, rating report based on the Third Edition for Claimant's 1991 injury when he performed his rating on January 22, 1999, using the Fourth Edition, is subsumed in this discussion, in light of our disposition.

Cabatbat v. County of Hawaii, Dep't of Water Supply, 78 P.3d 756 (Haw. 2003)

The Hawaii court dealt with a van driver who was involved in a motor vehicle accident and suffered a temperomandibular joint (TMJ) injury. The court held that the Labor and Industrial Relations Appeals Board erred in relying exclusively on a part of the *AMA Guides* (4th ed. 1993) in affirming a Hawaii Department of Labor and Industrial Relations Disability Compensation Division (DCD) decision determining that claimant-appellant Clarence Cabatbat (Cabatbat) suffered a permanent partial disability (PPD) of 8 percent as a result of a work-related injury to his TMJ. The court further held that Hawaii Administrative Rule (HAR) § 12-10-21 permitted the use of other guides, and the board's decision was against the reliable, probative, and substantial evidence on the record. The court reasoned:

> In connection with Cabatbat's first point, HAR Title 12, Subtitle 3, Chapter 10, Subchapter 2, § 12-10-21, entitled "Disabilities," states, in relevant part that "[i]mpairment rating guides issued by the American Medical Association, American Academy of Orthopedic Surgeons, and any other such guides which the director deems appropriate and proper *may be used as a reference or guide* in measuring a disability." (Emphasis added.) "The general principles of construction which apply to statutes also apply to administrative rules. As in statutory construction, courts look first at an administrative rule's language." *International Bhd. of Elec. Workers, Local 1357 v. Hawaiian Tel. Co.*, 68 Haw. 316, 323, 713 P.2d 943, 950 (1986) (citing 1A *Sutherland Statutory Construction* § 31.06 at 532 (4th ed. 1985 Rev.); *Kaiama v. Aguilar*, 67 Haw. 549, 553, 696 P.2d 839, 842 (1985)); *see also Brown v. Thompson*, 91 Haw. 1, 9, 979 P.2d 586, 594 (1999). Thus, because an "interpretation of a statute is . . . a question of law reviewable de novo, under the right/wrong standard," *Bank of Hawai'i v. DeYoung*, 92 Haw. 347, 351, 992 P.2d 42, 46 (2000), the interpretation of a rule presents a question of law. We review the Board's interpretation of HAR § 1 2-10- 21, then, under the right/wrong standard.
>
> HAR § 12-10-21, by its terms, provides that the *AMA Guides may* be used to determine impairment ratings. HAR § 12-10-21 goes on to state that "an employee *shall* be deemed totally disabled" if the employee is unable to complete a regular daily shift due to an injury. (Emphasis added.) In this context, this court has subscribed to the proposition that *where the verbs "shall" and "may" are used in the same statute*, especially where they are used in close juxtaposition, we should infer that *the legislature realized the difference in meaning and intended that the verbs used should carry with them their ordinary meanings. Gray v. Administrative Dir. of the Court, State of Hawai'i*, 84 Hawai'i 138, 149, 931 P.2d 580, 591 (1997) (citation, internal quotation marks, and brackets omitted) (emphases added); *see also Krystoff v. Kalama Land Co.*, 88 Hawai'i 209, 214, 965 P.2d 142, 147 (1998). Thus, "the close proximity of the contrasting verbs 'may' and 'shall' requires a *non-mandatory*, i.e. a discretionary, construction of the term 'may,' " *Gray*, 84 Hawai'i at 149, 931 P.2d at 591. Therefore, HAR § 12-10-21, which states that the AMA Guides *may* be used as a reference, permits reliance on the AMA Guides, but does not mandate their use to the exclusion of other appropriate guides.

The Board, however, construed HAR § 12-10-21 to require the use of the AMA Guides only. In rejecting the ratings determined pursuant to the Recommended Guide, the Board gave weight only to the AMA Guides, to the exclusion of all other guides. *See* discussion *supra* Part I. But, correctly construed, HAR § 12-10-21 does not preclude the use of guides other than the AMA Guides. Thus, the Board's construction of HAR § 12-10-21 was wrong.

Moreover, a restrictive interpretation of HAR § 12-10-21 runs afoul of the liberal construction to be afforded the provisions of HRS chapter 386 (1993 & Supp. 2002). . . . In *Respicio v. Waialua Sugar Co.*, 67 Haw. 16, 675 P.2d 770 (1984), this court observed that "Hawai'i's workers' compensation statute is to be accorded beneficent and liberal construction in favor of the employee, to fulfill the humanitarian purposes for which it was enacted." *Id.* at 18, 675 P.2d at 772. Such a policy has been in effect since the early twentieth century. See *Davenport v. City & County of Honolulu*, 100 Hawai'i 481, 491, 60 P.3d 882, 892 (2002) ("It is well-established in Hawai'i that chapter 386 is social legislation that is to be interpreted broadly."); *Shipley v. Ala Moana Hotel*, 83 Hawai'i 361, 365, 926 P.2d 1284, 1288 (1996) ("[W]orkers' compensation laws should be liberally construed in order to accomplish the intended beneficial purposes of the statute."); *Silva v. Kaiwiki Milling Co.*, 24 Haw. 324, 329 (Terr. 1918) ("Compensation acts being highly remedial in character, though in derogation of the common law, should generally be liberally and broadly construed to effectuate their beneficent purposes.").

HAR § 12-10-21 is promulgated pursuant to HRS § 386-72 (1993). HRS § 386-72 authorizes the director of the department of labor and industrial relations (director) to adopt rules and provides that, "[i]n conformity with and subject to chapter 91, the [director] shall make rules, *not inconsistent with this chapter*, which the director deems necessary for or conducive to its proper application and enforcement." (Emphasis added.) Hence, HAR § 12-10-21 may not conflict with the provisions of HRS chapter 386.

In that regard, HRS § 386-3 (1993 & Supp. 2002) provides that, "[i]f an employee suffers personal injury . . . in the course of the employment, . . . the employee's employer . . . *shall pay compensation* to the employee[.]" (Emphasis added.) Pursuant to HRS § 386-32 (1993 & Supp. 2002), "[w]here a work injury causes permanent partial disability, the employer *shall pay* the injured worker *compensation* in an amount" computed under HRS § 386-32. (Emphasis added.) Under HRS § 386-71 (1993), the director must "take all measures necessary for[] the prompt and *proper payment of compensation.*" (Emphasis added.)

Under the foregoing provisions, payment of benefits which fails to properly compensate an injured worker would be antithetical to a liberal and broad construction result in inadequate compensation and render HAR § 12-10-21 inconsistent with HRS chapter 386.

Given a proper reading of HAR § 12-10-21, the Board's decision to rely solely upon a part of the AMA Guides for the disability rating was clearly erroneous in view of the reliable, probative, and substantial evidence on the record. *See* HRS § 91-14(g)(5).

The Board made the following relevant findings of fact (findings):

6. The record contains two undated TMJ impairment ratings by Dr. Nakashima. Both of these ratings placed [Cabatbat's] permanent

impairment for his TMJ condition at twenty-three percent of the whole person. Dr. Nakashima used two guides, the Recommended Guide to the Evaluation of Permanent Impairment of the Temporomandibular Joint ("Recommended Guide") and the American Academy of Head, Facial, Neck Pain and TMJ Orthopedics, to rate [Cabatbat's] permanent impairment.

7. [Cabatbat] was also rated by Dr. Todd Tasaki, a dentist, on June 1, 1998. Dr. Tasaki rated [Cabatbat's] permanent impairment for his TMJ disorder at eighteen percent of the whole person. Dr. Tasaki based his June 1 rating on range of motion restriction, as well as, diet restricted to avoidance of hard foods.

8. When asked by [the] Employer in September 1998, to rate [Cabatbat's] permanent impairment using the AMA Guides, Dr. Tasaki rated [Cabatbat's] impairment at six to eight percent of the whole person based on dietary restrictions. This section of the AMA Guides allows a range of five percent to nineteen percent impairment of the whole person when diet is limited to semisolid or soft foods. Under the AMA Guides, dietary restrictions are considered to be the most objective criteria by which to evaluate permanent impairment. The AMA Guides further allow other effects of the TMJ condition to be considered in conjunction with parts of the AMA Guides that deal with the nervous system or pain. *We credit Dr. Tasaki's rating done under the AMA Guides.* (Emphasis added.)

Initially, we note that Drs. Nakashima and Tasaki did consider the AMA Guides in their evaluation of Cabatbat's impairment. In contrast to the Board's findings, the evidence on the record demonstrates that Dr. Nakashima did rely in part on the AMA Guides in evaluating Cabatbat's impairment. Dr. Nakashima related that his rating of Cabatbat's TMJ injury was determined using the "guide for permanent impairment established by the American Academy of Head Neck Facial Pain and Orthopedics. *It also takes into consideration the AMA Guide[s] for permanent impairment.*" (Emphasis added.)

Dr. Tasaki asserted that the AMA Guides do not rate TMJ disorders in the same manner that other joint disorders are rated. Dr. Tasaki reasoned that TMJ disorders could be rated by applying the same criteria used within the AMA Guides to rate other joint disorders. Thus, Dr. Tasaki also relied in part upon the AMA Guides' standards for rating impairments caused by joint disorders. *See supra* note 7.

Additionally, Dr. Chong concluded that Cabatbat's impairment rating was "determined by using the guide for permanent impairment established by the American Academy of Head Neck Facial Pain and Orthopedics[.] . . . *The [AMA] Guides for Permanent Impairment were also taken into consideration.*" (Emphasis added.)

The Board also erred in relying solely on the AMA Guides because the AMA Guides themselves instruct that they should not be the only factor considered in assessing impairments. The AMA Guides state that

> [i]t should be understood that the Guides do[] not and cannot provide answers about every type and degree of impairment. . . . *The physician's judgment and his or her experience, training, skill, and thoroughness in examining the patient* and applying the findings *to Guides' criteria will be factors* in estimating the degree of the patient's impairment.

AMA Guides at 3 (emphases added).

Thus, the AMA Guides direct that the physician's judgment is a factor to be considered when determining an impairment rating. The DCD's County's independent expert, Dr. Tasaki, specifically declared that the AMA Guides inadequately addressed impairments that resulted from TMJ disorders. *See* discussion *supra* Part I. Dr. Chong pointed out the limiting language in the AMA Guides. *See* discussion *supra* Part I. All three dentists judged the AMA Guides to be inadequate in evaluating TMJ impairments; yet, the Board failed to consider their judgments as factors in determining Cabatbat's PPD rating.

The AMA Guides further emphasizes that "impairment percentages derived according to *Guides* criteria should not be used to make direct financial awards or direct estimates of disabilities." [AMA Guides at 5.] The AMA Guides cautions that disability determinations should not be based solely on the Guides; however, the Board relied exclusively upon an impairment rating "derived according to the Guides criteria," despite this limiting language. *Id.*

In *In re Wal-Mart Stores*, 145 N.H. 635, 765 A.2d 168 (2000), the Supreme Court of New Hampshire held that the compensation appeals board properly deviated from the AMA Guides to accurately evaluate the respondent's impairment. [AMA Guides at 172.] In that case, the court observed that New Hampshire's Workers' compensation statute specified that the AMA Guides were to be used in determining permanent impairment. *Id.* However, the court explained that "[t]he *AMA Guides* expressly allows a physician to deviate from the guidelines if the physician finds it necessary to produce an impairment rating more accurate than the recommended formula can achieve." *Id.* (quoting *Appeal of Rainville*, 143 N.H. 624, 732 A.2d 406, 412 (1999) ("[the AMA Guides] does not and cannot provide answers about every type and degree of impairment because of the infinite variety of human disease, and the constantly evolving field of medicine, and the complex process of human functioning" (quoting the AMA Guides, 4th ed. (1993), at 3)).

Similarly, in *Slover Masonry, Inc. v. Industrial Comm'n of Arizona*, 158 Ariz. 131, 761 P.2d 1035 (1988), the Arizona Supreme Court held that an administrative law judge (ALJ) is not bound to follow the AMA Guides as the sole measure of impairment. *Id.* at 1036. The court reasoned that the "ALJ must consider *all competent and relevant evidence* in establishing an accurate rating of functional impairment, even if a medical expert asserts that the AMA Guides are perfectly adequate to measure loss of motion." *Id.* at 1040 (emphasis added). The court acknowledged that

> [t]he AMA Guides are only a tool adopted by administrative regulation to assist in ascertaining an injured worker's percentage of disability. Thus, *where the AMA Guides do not truly reflect a claimant's loss, the ALJ must use his discretion to hear additional evidence and, from the whole record, establish a rating independent of the AMA recommendations. Id.* (Emphasis added.)

According to the AMA Guides and Drs. Nakashima, Tasaki, and Chong, the Board should not have relied solely upon the AMA Guides to evaluate Cabatbat's TMJ injury. Under the circumstances, the AMA Guides would "not truly reflect" Cabatbat's TMJ impairment. *Id.*

The Board stated in its findings that "[t]he authors [of the Recommended Guide] sought to have the Recommended Guide endorsed by the AMA and to have it included in the Fourth Edition of the AMA Guides. It was not included as the most objective criteria to evaluate permanent impairment." The Board cites no source or authority for this statement, and none is evident in the record. Hence there is no reliable, probative, or substantial evidence in the record to support this statement.

The Board also found that "[t]he AMA Guides further allow other effects of the TMJ condition to be considered in conjunction with parts of the AMA Guides that deal with the nervous system or pain." In the same vein, the County argues that Drs. Nakashima, Tasaki, and Chong failed to consider "the effects of the TMJ condition with parts of the AMA Guides that deal with the nervous system or pain." However, the DCD restricted Dr. Tasaki's analysis to § 9.3, Table 6 of the AMA Guides. *See supra* page 5. As previously mentioned, this table allows for an impairment rating of TMJ disorders based only on dietary restrictions. Thus, it is incongruous for the Board to suggest or the County to argue that the dentists could have provided ratings that took into consideration the nervous system or pain, when the DCD specifically limited the impairment rating analysis to § 9.3, Table 6 of the AMA Guides.

On the other hand, all three dentists believed that Cabatbat's TMJ injury should have been assessed according to criteria such as those found in the Recommended Guide. As Drs. Nakashima and Chong noted, the Recommended Guide is "the most widely used method in dentistry for determining jaw joint permanent impairment." The Board therefore erred when it disregarded the reports applying the criteria found in the Recommended Guide.

In conclusion, neither HAR § 12-10-21, nor the AMA Guides mandate that impairment ratings be determined solely based upon the AMA Guides. The Board's interpretation of HAR § 12-10-21 was wrong. The requirement to use a part of the AMA Guides, to the exclusion of the Recommended Guide, under the circumstances of this case, would violate HRS chapter 386. Finally, there is reliable, probative, and substantial evidence on the record that the Recommended Guide appropriately addressed Cabatbat's TMJ impairment. For the foregoing reasons, the October 4, 2000, decision and order of the Board is vacated, and the case remanded for a redetermination of Cabatbat's PPD rating.

78 P.3d at 760–765.

§ 11.11   IDAHO

Nelson v. David L. Hill Logging, 865 P.2d 946 (Idaho 1993)

The Idaho court dealt with an employee who claimed he should have been given a higher rating for permanent partial disability. The report on the claimant's rating stated that the rating was made in accordance with the tables in the "Second Edition of the Journal of the American Medical Association." The claimant asserted that because the panel had misnamed the *AMA Guides*, their evaluation was a misuse of the *AMA Guides* and hence invalid. The court would not consider this argument, as the court did not have a copy of the disputed *AMA Guides* in the record of appeal.

Pomerinke v. Excel Trucking Transp., 859 P.2d 337 (Idaho 1993)

The Idaho Supreme Court dealt with the claimant, who injured his back and neck while working as a truck driver. He underwent the removal of a cervical disk and surgery for thoracic outlet syndrome. The claimant challenged the ratings based on the Industrial Commission's use of the *AMA Guides* without reference to the *AMA Guides'* being included in the record and without advance notice to the parties. The court held against the claimant, and stated:

> While the above cases make it somewhat unclear as to whether the Commission may use the *AMA Guides* on its own motion and without expert testimony to support them, the Commission in the present case cited the *AMA Guides* merely in support of its supposition that the medical panels included pain in their impairment ratings. There is nothing in the Commission's findings or order which indicate it relied on the *AMA Guides* in assessing [claimant]'s condition or formulating its own impairment rating. Instead, the Commission adopted the rating of the independent medical panels and indicated that "[o]n the medical record presented, the Referee concludes that the independent medical panels took pain into account, and considered real limitations imposed by pain upon the Claimant's activities." Given the limited purpose for which the Commission consulted with the *AMA Guides*, we find no error.

Id. at 343.

Poss v. Meeker Mach. Shop, 712 P.2d 621 (Idaho 1985)

The claimant suffered injuries to the back, neck, and shoulder when a piece of sheet metal fell on him. The *AMA Guides* were used by the treating physician and by the insurance company's rating panel. The claimant maintained that the rating panel did not take into account his subjective complaints of pain and his unique living condition and lifestyle in arriving at its impairment rating. The court disagreed.

> It is also clear from the record that Dr. [L.] and his fellow doctors on the panel relied on the same American Medical Association guidelines that an Idaho doctor would have relied on in arriving at an impairment evaluation. Those guidelines include consideration of subjective factors such as complaints of pain.

Id. at 624.

Johnson v. Amalgamated Sugar Co., **702 P.2d 803 (Idaho 1985)**

The *AMA Guides*, mentioned only in the dissenting opinion, were used by the treating physician to rate the claimant's permanent impairment due to a heart condition.

Hite v. Kulhenak Bldg. Contractor, **524 P.2d 531 (Idaho 1974)**

The claimant suffered a partial loss of his right arm and a complete loss of his right kidney. The physician rated the claimant as suffering a 10 percent permanent impairment of a whole man for the loss of the kidney. The claimant appealed, arguing that the *AMA Guides* or other medical treatises should not be admitted as substantive proof because they constituted hearsay. The court held that the Industrial Commission is not bound by the same rules of evidence as a court of law, and that the findings of the commission as to the extent of a disability are binding, if supported by competent evidence. The court stressed that Industrial Commission proceedings should be as expeditious as possible while still being fair. To that end, the commission may recognize treatises or works dealing with topics in which the commission possesses no expertise. Thus, the *AMA Guides* were held to be competent evidence.

> Since the guides were properly admitted into evidence by the commission, there is substantial, competent evidence in the record supporting their determination that the loss of one kidney is equivalent to the loss of ten percent of the whole man and that decision is therefore affirmed.

Id. at 533.

§ 11.12   IOWA

Coffman v. Kind & Knox Gelatine, Inc., **2006 Iowa App. LEXIS 784 (Ct. App. July 26, 2006)**

The Iowa court dealt with a by-products supervisor, Coffman, who sustained injuries to his eyes when a valve on a tank of hydrochloric acid burst. Coffman contended that the injury was not simply to his eyes (which would be a scheduled injury) but extended to his "body as a whole" (which would be an unscheduled injury resulting in greater compensation). Coffman alleged that the injury to his visual system included chronic headache, dizziness, and halo effect, and that these "spill over" effects went beyond the simple loss of use of his eyes and extended his injury to the body as a whole. The commissioner's order was unclear as to whether the claimant's injury should be treated as a scheduled or an unscheduled injury. The appellate court remanded the case back to the commissioner to determine whether the claimant's injuries supported a scheduled or an unscheduled loss.

Christensen v. Snap-On Tools Corp., 602 N.W.2d 199 (Iowa Ct. App. 1999)

The Iowa court dealt with a claimant who injured her arm. At issue was whether the hearing commissioner should have considered lay testimony regarding loss of use of the right arm. The court stated:

> The commissioner is required to consider all the evidence, both medical and non-medical. *Christensen v. Snap-On Tools Corp.*, 554 N.W.2d 254, 257 (Iowa 1996);
> *Terwilliger v. Snap-On Tools Corp.*, 529 N.W.2d 267, 273 (Iowa 1995); *Miller v. Lauridsen Foods, Inc.*, 525 N.W.2d 417, 421 (Iowa 1994). Lay witness testimony is both relevant and material upon the cause and extent of injury. *Christensen*, 554 N.W.2d at 257; *Miller*, 525 N.W.2d at 421.
> Assessing the weight of the testimony is within the agency's exclusive domain. *Robbennolt*, 555 N.W.2d at 234; *Burns v. Board of Nursing*, 495 N.W.2d 698, 699 (Iowa 1993). Courts must not reassess the weight of the evidence on judicial review. *Id.*
> The industrial commissioner on remand correctly outlined the proper considerations in assessing lay testimony. However, the commissioner then stated in the decision:
>
>> There is no indication that any of the lay witnesses called by claimant *have any medical training*. Their opinions on claimant's overall fatigue and loss of energy are based on firsthand observation and are accepted as accurate. However, their conclusions as to claimant's actual loss of use of her right arm *are not supported by any medical evaluation methods or techniques*. The lay witnesses called by claimant *are not trained in evaluating* loss of functional impairment, or in the use of the *AMA Guides*.
>
> The commissioner is not required to accept lay testimony at face value. *Kiesecker v. Webster City Meats, Inc.*, 528 N.W.2d 109, 111 (Iowa 1995). However, assessing the lay testimony on the basis that it is not medical testimony defeats the purpose of requiring the commissioner to consider both medical and lay testimony. Given the importance of this consideration, *Christensen*, 554 N.W.2d at 258, *Terwilliger*, 529 N.W.2d at 273, we hold the commissioner cannot dismiss lay testimony solely for the reason it is not medical testimony.
> The decision of the industrial commissioner and the district court is reversed and remanded for a proper consideration and weighing of the lay testimony.

602 N.W.2d at 201.

Robbennolt v. Snap-On Tools Corp., 555 N.W.2d 229 (Iowa 1996)

The court dealt with a claimant who severely cut his third finger, which later had to be amputated. At issue was the appropriateness of the claimant's

20 percent impairment of his right hand. The court upheld this impairment rating and stated:

> [Claimant] claims error in the commissioner's decision in not assigning more than a disability of twenty percent scheduled member impairment of his right hand. He asserts he has at least an uncontroverted forty percent hand loss and forty percent arm loss. He argues that the decision is not sufficiently detailed to show the path taken through conflicting evidence. He believes the commissioner "secretly adopted the AMA *Guides* to evaluation of permanent impairment rating without considering other evidence." The other evidence is [claimant]'s testimony of pain and numbness in the thumb, web, palm, graft site, and forearm.
>
> He states that the guides also offer no measurement of loss of hand grip and pinch strength or of arm-lifting strength. In the absence of countering evidence to negate, he believes a higher disability rating than twenty percent is mandated. He says this is because otherwise uncontroverted law and subjective evidence of functional impairment [are] disregarded.
>
> [Employer] argues that there is a great deal of evidence that [claimant] has sustained very little impairment of his activities either at work or elsewhere. [Employer] points to the recitation by the commissioner of [claimant]'s problems both as recited by the examining doctor, by [claimant] himself, and by a counselor who helped him on unresolved grief of the loss of his finger.
>
> We note that the deputy detailed the loss of pinch strength, pain, functional use of his hand, and other decreased use experienced by [claimant]. The deputy then stated:
>
> > It is expressly found that claimant has a decreased ability to lift with the right upper extremity as well as decreased grip and pinch strength in the right hand. These factors are sufficient to demonstrate that claimant's overall impairment is an impairment to the hand and not an impairment to the right third finger only.
>
> Regarding the emotional trauma the deputy said:
>
> > It is expressly found that claimant's emotional concerns and reactions as presented in this record were part of the normal sequelae of recovery from the significant injury. It is further expressly found that these conditions did not rise to the level of an independent debilitating psychological condition such that claimant's impairment is to the body as a whole and not to the hand.
>
> [Claimant] complains that there is virtually no rationale for how the commissioner deduced that he had sustained only a twenty percent loss of permanent function in the right hand. He says the commissioner noted, but did not analyze, the findings of functional capacity evaluations. He says the commissioner also noted, but did not analyze, the medical knowledge that a ray resection significantly lessened the grip strength in the hand. He questioned that the twenty percent disability just happened to be the same percentage as the only medical rating percentage in evidence.

[Employer] points out accurately that there is no medical opinion in this case that [claimant] has a permanent functional impairment beyond the twenty percent. The AMA *Guides*, relied on by the examining doctor, have been specifically adopted as a guideline for determining PPD. [Employer] also argues that there is no rule of law that requires an award greater than the impairment rating determined by the AMA guidelines where a claimant makes complaints of pain or fatigue.

We believe that [employer]'s argument on this point is sound. Where the commissioner has recognized and written about [claimant]'s condition and deficiencies, as was done here, the evidence is sufficient to support a reasonable conclusion reached. Here, the conclusion of the deputy, commissioner, district court, and court of appeals was that a twenty percent award was appropriate, viewing the record as a whole. *See ALCOA v. Employment Appeal Bd.*, 449 N.W.2d 391, 394 (Iowa 1989). [Claimant]'s argument is actually that the commissioner did not properly assess the evidence. On judicial review of agency action, the court's review is not *de novo*. The court must not reassess the weight of the evidence because the weight of the evidence remains within the agency's exclusive domain. *Burns v. Board of Nursing*, 495 N.W.2d 698, 699 (Iowa 1993).

[Claimant] insists that the commissioner should be directed to consider and weigh any impairment beyond that which is measurable under the AMA guidelines, and if rejected, "to detail the reasons for rejecting each of the various facts and evidence advanced by [claimant] in favor of the advanced percentages." He quotes the examining doctor's opinion that the AMA guidelines do not attempt to measure the medically immeasurable. Pain is not a feature that is utilized in determining impairment because medical impairment is only dealing with the medically measurable loss of function. For this reason, Robbennolt insists that the medically immeasurable must be quantified by the commissioner in much the same way a jury quantifies pain and suffering and other intangible losses.

There is no requirement in the statutes or our case law commanding the commissioner to validate the agency's decisions with precise detail and specificity. If this was required, the agency's efficiency and capacity to expedite decisions for the benefit of the injured worker would collapse under the dead weight of detail. [Claimant]'s argument ignores our well-recognized rule that the agency's decision is final if supported by substantial evidence and if correct in its conclusions of law. *Heatherly*, 397 N.W.2d at 670. It is also contra to the purpose of our review as set out by the legislature in section 17A.19(8). We affirm the district court decision on this issue.

555 N.W.2d at 233–34.

Second Injury Fund v. Bergeson, 526 N.W.2d 543 (Iowa 1995)

The Iowa court dealt with a claimant who injured his knee at work. The claimant was evaluated, pursuant to Iowa Admin. Code r. 343-2.4(85) (1993), under the *AMA Guides*. The claimant was awarded a 10 percent impairment of his right knee. The plaintiff argued that because the claimant's right knee did not affect his ability to work or to do the things he did before the injury, the claimant suffered no loss of use of his leg. The court disagreed and found that the 10 percent rating was supported by the *AMA Guides.* (Under the *AMA Guides,* impairment does not mean disability.) The court also noted that no medical evidence or testimony rebutted the 10 percent rating.

Lauhoff Grain Co. v. McIntosh, 395 N.W.2d 834 (Iowa 1986)

The claimant fell from a railroad car and fractured his femur at the point just below the hip joint. The surgery to repair the fracture was successful, and the claimant was able to return to work; however, complications developed in the hip joint because of damage to the head of the femur. The key issue was whether the claimant was entitled to benefits for a "scheduled" injury to the leg, or to industrial disability benefits under Iowa Code § 85.34(2)(u) on the basis that the hip surgery had extended his disability to the body as a whole.

Both sides appealed the commissioner's award of benefits. The district court affirmed. The Iowa Supreme Court held that the statutory definition of *leg* did not include the hip, and that the commissioner was not required to apply the leg schedule to the hip impairment.

The court noted that several other jurisdictions had addressed the question of whether injuries to hips and shoulders are considered to be injuries to the leg or arm, respectively, or disabilities to the body as a whole. Most jurisdictions find in favor of the whole-body compensation under statutes similar to the Iowa statutes. *See* 395 N.W.2d at 838 for these citations. Furthermore, Iowa Admin. Code r. 500-2.4(85) provides that the *AMA Guides* are adopted as "guides" that "may" be used to establish an impairment rating, and further provides that nothing in the rule shall be construed to prevent the use of medical opinions, other guides, and so forth, for the purpose of establishing an impairment rating. Finally, the *AMA Guides* relied on by the appellant were a doubtful authority in this case because they included the hip as part of the "lower extremity," a term not present in the statutory schedule.

Caylor v. Employers Mut. Casualty Co., 337 N.W.2d 890 (Iowa Ct. App. 1983)

The *AMA Guides* were used to rate the impairment to the claimant's leg. Iowa Admin. Code r. 500-2.4 provides for the use of the *AMA Guides* as follows:

> The *Guides to the Evaluation of Permanent Impairment* published by the American Medical Association are adopted as a guide for determining permanent partial disabilities under section 85.34(2) a-r of the Code. The extent of loss or percentage of permanent impairment may be determined by the use of this guide and payment of weekly compensation for permanent partial scheduled injuries made accordingly. Payment so made shall be recognized by the industrial commissioner as a prima facie showing of compliance by the employer or insurance carrier with the foregoing sections of the Iowa Workers' Compensation Act. Nothing in this rule shall be construed to prevent the

presentations of other medical opinion or guides for the purpose of establishing that the degree of permanent impairment to which the claimant would be entitled would be more or less than the entitlement indicated in the *AMA Guides*.

337 N.W.2d at 895.

Graves v. Eagle Iron Works, 331 N.W.2d 116 (Iowa 1983)

Iowa Admin. Code r.500-2.4 adopts the *AMA Guides* for determining permanent partial disabilities under the Iowa workers' compensation statute. In this case, the Industrial Commission did not apply the distinction between impairment and disability as urged by the *AMA Guides*. The court stated:

> The medical testimony in this case went only to physical impairment and did not purport in any way to measure petitioner's industrial disability. Iowa Administrative Code 500-2.4 adopts the *AMA Guides* for determining permanent partial disabilities under the statute. It seems that these guides urge physicians to note the difference between impairment and disability, a distinction petitioner urges in support of his position. The distinction was nevertheless not applied by the commissioner because of our cases which hold to the contrary. They do not allow an employee with a scheduled injury to present evidence of industrial disability; such admissible only when the employee suffered a total or nonscheduled disability.

331 N.W.2d at 118.

§ 11.13   KANSAS

Thompson v. U.S.D., No. 512, 2007 WL 2580530 (Kan. Ct. App. 2007)

The Kansas Court dealt with the claimant, Thompson, who alleged reflex sympathetic dystrophy (RSD) as a result of an injury at work. Dr. Rosenthal, the treating surgeon, rated her impairment under the fourth edition of the *Guides* as was required under the applicable statute. On February 1, 2005, Thompson's physician, Dr. Poppa, D.O., evaluated Thompson regarding the extent of her injury. Poppa opined that Thompson had reached maximum medical improvement regarding her right scapulothoracic and anterior chest wall chronic myofascitis at that time. He believed Thompson had sustained a 20 percent impairment of her right upper extremity. In his report, Poppa stated:

> [I]t is my opinion she has a 20% impairment of her right upper extremity. The Fourth Edition Guides were consulted but do not adequately address her present condition. Then utilizing Table 3 on page 20, Ms. Thompson's 20% upper extremity impairment converts to a 12% whole person impairment.

In assessing Thompson's RSD, Poppa concluded that Thompson had a 20 percent impairment of the whole body pursuant to a physician paper from the American Association of Disability Evaluating Physicians (AADEP). Poppa did not solely rely on the method indicated by the *AMA Guides* because he felt the AADEP physician paper more adequately considered a patient's functional capabilities in assessing their activities of daily living. While Kansas only recognizes the fourth edition, Poppa relied on the fifth and sixth editions of the *AMA Guides*, which address the deficiencies in the fourth edition regarding assessment of impairment for RSD.

Based on the combined values derived from the *AMA Guides* and the AADEP physician paper, Poppa ultimately concluded that Thompson suffered an overall 30 percent impairment of the whole person. 2007 WL 2580530, at *3.

The court held that Dr. Poppa was required to use the mandated fourth edition since RSD was rateable under that edition and not subsequent editions. It stated:

> As indicated by the administrative law judge, the fourth edition of the *AMA Guides* specifically indicates the manner in which a physician may derive an impairment rating for RSD. Moreover, Poppa concedes RSD is contained within the fourth *AMA Guides*, but that the impairment rating is not to his liking. While it is unfortunate that a physician may be bound by an outdated version of the *AMA Guides* this court is obligated to read the statute as written. Allowing a physician to rely on more recent editions of the *AMA Guides* and other publications would open the door to what the proper guide is and should be. No doubt evaluating physicians would seek a reference providing the most favorable rating for their patient or client. The statute was clearly enacted to avoid just that and provide clear standards for calculating consistent impairment ratings.
>
> Furthermore, it is nonsensical to conclude that the legislature intended "if the impairment is contained therein" to include impairments expressly mentioned in the fourth edition of the *AMA Guides*, but modified in the fifth and sixth editions.
>
> This is simply not a logical or legitimate reading of the statute. The statute is clear and unambiguous. If this court reads the statute as Thompson suggests, it would effectively be determining what the law should be. Had the legislature intended the statute to be interpreted in this manner, it would have directed the evaluating physician to utilize the most current edition of the *AMA Guides* or other widely accepted method, but it did not.
>
> Finally, when legislative intent is in question, the court must presume that the legislature, by expressly including specific terms, intends to exclude any items not expressly included in the specific list. Kansas Industrial Consumers Group, Inc. v. Kansas Corporation Comm'n, 36 Kan.App.2d 83, 96, 138 P.3d 338, rev. denied, 282 Kan. 790 (2006). As such, specifically referencing the fourth edition necessarily excludes subsequent editions of the *AMA Guides*. Therefore, the Board did not err in excluding Poppa's impairment rating for failure to rely on the fourth edition of the *AMA Guides* as required by K.S.A. 44-510d(a)(23) and K.S.A. 44-510e(a).

Id. at *6–*7.

Carrizales v. Winsteads Rests., 82 P.3d 875 (Kan. Ct. App. 2004)

The Kansas court dealt with a worker who suffered a low back injury. He was rated under the fourth edition of the *Guides* as a DRE category II, based on radiculopathy detected by a positive straight leg raise test. The rating doctor, however, found no evidence of loss of reflexes or atrophy and did not administer any electrodiagnostic tests. At issue was whether or not this rating was supported under the *AMA Guides* by having sufficient evidence of radiculopathy. The court held that it was. It stated:

> Winsteads argues it is not attacking the credibility of Dr. Egea's diagnosis but rather questions whether the diagnosis fits the criteria of category III of the *AMA Guides* upon which the diagnosis was based. Specifically, the description and verification section of DRE Lumbosacral Category III: Radiculopathy states: "The patient has significant signs of radiculopathy, *such as* loss of relevant reflex(es), or measured unilateral atrophy of greater than 2 cm. above or below the knee, compared to measurements on the contralateral side at the same location. The impairment *may* be verified by electrodiagnostic findings. See Table 71, p. 109, differentiators 2, 3, and 4." (Emphasis added.) AMA Guides to the Evaluation of Permanent Injuries § 3/102 (4th ed. 1995).
>
> Winsteads argues that because Dr. Egea testified he did not find Carrizales had a loss of relevant reflexes, atrophy, and made no electrodiagnostic findings, his diagnosis was not supported by the AMA Guides. The plain language of the AMA Guides for category III only requires that "the patient has significant signs of radiculopathy." The items described above are only examples of findings which may support such a diagnosis. Electrodiagnostic findings are clearly optional.
>
> Dr. Egea specifically found significant signs of radiculopathy. His testimony of Carrizales' straight leg raise test positive result was deemed "a prominent sign for lumbar radiculitis or radiculopathy." Dr. Prostic admitted the positive straight leg raise test is a physical finding consistent with a diagnosis of radiculopathy. Dr. Egea also relied on all of Carrizales' symptoms in making his diagnosis. Dr. Prostic's testimony indicated that certain of Carrizales' symptoms could indicate radiculopathy.
>
> The Board's findings that Dr. Egea's impairment rating was based on the AMA Guides is supported by substantial competent evidence. At 2–3.

Martinez v. Excel Corp., 79 P.2d 230 (Kan. App. 2003)

The Kansas court dealt with a trimmer who developed severe bilateral carpal tunnel syndrome and bilateral Guyon's syndrome. The worker's physician recommended a surgical carpal tunnel release, but the claimant refused. After hearing testimony from Martinez and reviewing deposition testimony from several expert witnesses, the ALJ awarded compensation based on a 25.5 percent disability rating. The award represented an average of two impairment ratings—one rating was an estimate of Martinez's injuries if he would have undergone the carpal tunnel surgery, and the other rating was based upon his present condition without the surgery. The judge reasoned that Martinez could later request the surgery and possibly reduce his disability substantially and, therefore, should not receive compensation based upon the highest impairment rating.

Both Martinez and Excel appealed this decision to the Workers' Compensation Board. The board increased the award based upon a 39.5 percent impairment rating. This award was an average of the impairment ratings of the twoexpert witnesses, Dr. Villanueva and Dr. Pedro Murati, for Martinez's present condition. These impairment ratings were determined according to the American Medical Association's *Guides to the Evaluation of Permanent Impairment (AMA Guides)*, as required by K.S.A. 44-510e. The board noted that according to the *AMA Guides*, a patient's decision to not undergo surgery should neither increase nor decrease his or her impairment rating. The Board concluded that Martinez's "present functional impairment rating should be based upon his actual present physical condition rather than based upon speculation of what it might be in the event he underwent multiple surgeries and achieved successful results." The employer appealed. The court upheld the board's rating and stated:

> Finally, Excel alleges that statements in the AMA Guides that a patient's refusal to undergo surgery should not decrease the impairment rating are inapplicable to this case. He argues that the applicable law is K.A.R. 51-9-5 and not comments in the AMA Guides.
>
> K.A.R. 51-9-5 and comments found in the AMA Guides apply to two different concepts. K.A.R. 51-9-5 applies to termination of compensation benefits, while comments in the AMA Guides refer to adjustment of the impairment rating. The Board correctly noted that K.S.A. 44-510e specifically requires the impairment rating to be based on the AMA Guides. As a result, it was not error for the Board to consider these comments and conclude that Martinez' impairment rating should not be based upon speculation about his results after a successful surgery.
>
> Because the Board went on to find that Martinez' refusal of surgery was reasonable under K.A.R. 51-9-5 and because we have affirmed that ruling, we find it unnecessary to address this argument any further.

79 P.2d at 235.

Durham v. Cessna Aircraft Co., **945 P.2d 8 (Kan. Ct. App. 1997),** *review* *denied*, **No. 96-77514-AS (Kan. Dec. 23, 1997)**

The Kansas court dealt with a worker who suffered a repetitive use injury to his shoulder. The employee was awarded a 30 percent whole-person impairment by the ALJ. The Workers' Compensation Board reduced the award to 29.67 percent impairment to the left extremity only. The claimant appealed and cited the *AMA*

Guides in his brief. The court rejected the appeal based on the *AMA Guides*, as they were never submitted into evidence. The court stated:

> Claimant bases part of his argument on what the AMA Guidelines say about the finding of an impairment for pain. He attaches a copy of the applicable Guidelines to his brief. The problem is that these Guidelines were never introduced into evidence and are not part of the record on appeal. Claimant cannot cure this deficiency by attaching the Guidelines to his brief as an appendix. "An appellant has the burden to designate a record sufficient to establish the claimed error. Without an adequate record, an appellant's claim of alleged error fails." *McCubbin v. Walker*, 256 Kan. 276, 295, 886 P.2d 790 (1994). Further: "Assertions in an appellate brief are not sufficient to satisfy inadequacies in the record on appeal." *Smith v. Printup*, 254 Kan. 315, 353, 866 P.2d 985 (1993). The record contains no support for claimant's argument concerning the AMA standards.

945 P.2d at 9.

Adamson v. Davis Moore Datsun, Inc., 868 P.2d 546 (Kan. Ct. App. 1994)

The Kansas court dealt with an employee who was awarded a 20 percent psychological impairment. The court was forced to decide whether the award was supported by proper evidence when the rating physician had not used the *AMA Guides*. The court held the award was proper and stated:

> Dr. [W]'s failure to use the AMA Guidelines when rating the extent of [claimant]'s psychological impairment does not invalidate his opinion. *See Racz v. Chennault, Inc.*, 418 So.2d 413, 415 (Fla. Dist. App. 1982). We have previously recognized the subjective nature of any psychological injury. *Ruse v. State*, 10 Kan. App. 2d 508, 511, 708 P.2d 216 (1984). Although legislative changes effective July 1, 1993, require that functional impairment be established by both competent medical evidence and by utilizing "the third edition revised, of the American Medical Association Guidelines for the Evaluation of Physical Impairment, if the impairment is contained therein," L. 1993, ch, 286, § 34, the 1993 amendments are not applicable here. The provisions of K.S.A. 44-510e(a) in effect at the time of the 1983 injury would not require usage of the AMA Guidelines.

Id. at 552.

§11.14 KENTUCKY

Leaseway Motor Co. Transp. v. Cline, 2007 WL 858834 (Ky.)

The Supreme Court of Kentucky dealt with the claimant, Cline, who suffered a series of work-related injuries in 1985, 1988, 1992 or 1993, and 2001. Dr. Kriss, using the fifth edition of the *AMA Guides*, found a 16 percent combined impairment rating and apportioned it 4 percent for each injury. Dr. Rapier found a 21 percent whole-body impairment and apportioned equally among the 1988, 1992, and 2001 injuries.

The ALJ awarded 16 percent but refused to exclude any of the impairment when calculating the award, reasoning that there were pre-existing symptoms but no evidence of pre-existing impairment. The ALJ also noted that Ky. Rev. Stat. § 342.730(1)(e) excluded impairment for non-work-related disabilities and previously compensated disabilities but did not exclude impairment from prior work-related but uncompensated injuries.

The court affirmed the 16 percent award without finding that the employer failed to prove pre-existing impairment. The court stated:

> Chapter 342 requires a worker's disability rating to be based on a permanent impairment rating that is determined under the *Guides*. As noted by the Board, *the Guides* contain a method to separate pre-existing impairment from ultimate impairment. It requires the impairments to be calculated separately and requires the pre-injury impairment to be subtracted from the post-injury impairment. Although Drs. Kriss and Rapier referred to specific provisions in the *Guides* when assigning the ultimate impairment, neither did so when estimating the claimant's pre-existing impairment. Under the circumstances, it was both reasonable and within the ALJ's authority to conclude that their estimates were not credible evidence of the impairment that existed immediately before the injury and to conclude that the employer failed to meet its burden of proof. No medical evidence compelled a different finding.
>
> The decision of the Court of Appeals is affirmed.

2007 WL 858834, at *5.

Knott Floyd Land Co. v. Fugate, 2007 WL 4462301 (Ky.)

The Supreme Court of Kentucky dealt with the claimant, Fugate, who worked as a mechanic, a coal truck driver, and later as a mechanic in a strip mine. His work exposed him to loud noises. The claimant had significant hearing loss, underwent surgery, and had complete hearing loss in his right ear. He applied for permanent impairment benefits.

Dr. Windmill assigned a 17 percent permanent impairment rating in both ears, assuming an equal hearing loss in both ears. He attributed a 14 percent permanent impairment rating to noise-induced hearing loss. Dr. Woods assigned a 16 percent permanent impairment rating and, factoring out the right ear deafness after surgery, attributed a 12 percent rating due to occupational noise exposure.

The court found that the *AMA Guides* do not address the situation presented in this claim and that physicians are permitted to use their clinical judgment.

The court affirmed the award for the work-related binaural hearing loss, stating:

> No medical evidence refuted the physicians' assumption that the claimant's work-related hearing loss probably was bilateral and symmetrical. Nor did any medical evidence indicate that the *Guides* failed to authorize the method that they used to assign a permanent impairment rating based on noise-induced hearing loss. Under the circumstances, no reasonable basis supported a conclusion that the percentages they assigned were merely speculative. On remand, the ALJ must award benefits based on the evidence of work-related binaural hearing loss.
>
> The decision of the Court of Appeals is affirmed.

2007 WL 4462301, at *4.

Finley v. DBM Techs., 217 S.W.3d 261 (Ky. App. Ct. 2007)

The Kentucky Court of Appeals dealt with the claimant, Finley, who sought benefits for the arousal of her congenital scoliosis. A January 30, 2002 back injury at work aroused the dormant scoliosis (for which there had been no prior treatment) into a disabling injury. Finley underwent a diskectomy and fusion. Dr. Clendenin opined that the claimant had a 23 percent impairment and apportioned 13 percent to the congenital scoliosis, under the most recent edition of the *AMA Guides*.

The ALJ adopted the apportionment.

The court found that to be characterized as active, an underlying pre-existing condition must be symptomatic and impairment rateable pursuant to the *AMA Guides* immediately prior to the occurrence of the work-related injury, and the burden of proving the existence of a pre-existing condition falls upon the employer. The court vacated the decision and remanded it, stating that:

> The ALJ specifically found that "the scoliosis was a pre-existing Condition which was exacerbated by the January 30, 2002, work injury." The ALJ, however, failed to make specific findings of fact upon whether the congenital scoliosis was a dormant condition and whether the scoliosis was temporarily or permanently aroused by the work-related injury. Given that the medical evidence was undisputed, we believe the ALJ was compelled to find that the scoliosis constituted a pre-existing dormant condition. See Powell v. Winchester Garment Co., 312 Ky. 38, 226 S.W.2d 341 (1950); Melcher v. Drummond Mfg. Co., 312 Ky. 588, 229 S.W.2d 52 (1950).
>
> As to whether the scoliosis was temporarily or permanently aroused, a review of the record reveals that the medical evidence overwhelmingly demonstrated that Finley's scoliosis was permanently aroused and resulted in permanent impairment. However, one medical expert, Dr. Michael Best, opined that Finley's scoliosis was only temporarily aroused but then inexplicably assigned a five percent permanent impairment rating due to the scoliosis.

In any event, we conclude that the ALJ erroneously failed to make an essential finding of fact upon whether Finley's pre-existing dormant scoliosis was temporarily or permanently aroused by the work-related back injury. As a reviewing body, neither we nor the Board should attempt to supplant such a finding of fact. See Bright v. American Greetings Corp., 62 S.W.3d 381 (Ky. 2001); Aden Min. Co. v. Hall, 252 Ky. 168, 66 S.W.2d 41 (1933); Rudd v. Ky. Mfg. Co., 574 S.W.2d 928 (Ky. App. 1978). We would also caution the ALJ that the scoliosis must have completely reverted to a dormant state to support a finding of temporary arousal.

217 S.W.3d at 265–66.

Colwell v. Dresser Instrument Div., 2006 Ky. LEXIS 297 (2006)

The Kentucky court dealt with a worker who sought to reopen her settled disability claim, alleging that her injury had become permanently and totally disabling. An administrative law judge relied on a physician's testimony that the 12 percent impairment rating to which the parties had agreed during settlement was still appropriate and had not changed. The issue on appeal was whether the *AMA Guides'* impairment rating was the only objective measure under which to gauge a patient's worsening condition. The appellate court stated:

> Chapter 1 of the 5th Edition explains that the purpose of the *Guides* is to establish a standardized, objective approach to evaluating medical impairments. It defines impairment as being "a loss, loss of use, or derangement of any body part, organ system, or organ function." Impairment is considered to be permanent "when it has reached maximum medical improvement (MMI), meaning it is well stabilized and unlikely to change substantially in the next year with or without medical treatment." Impairment may be manifested objectively or subjectively, and "[a]lthough the Guides emphasizes objective assessment, subjective symptoms are included within the diagnostic criteria." Whole person impairment ratings established in the *Guides* "estimate the impact of the impairment on the individual's overall ability to perform activities of daily living, *excluding work.*" (Emphasis in original.) Confronted with that statement in *Adkins v. R & S Body Co.*, 58 S.W.3d 428 (Ky. 2001), the court noted that although the purpose of an income benefit is to compensate an injured worker for a loss of earning capacity (occupational disability) and although the 1996 Act bases a worker's disability from an injury on the resulting AMA impairment rating, the rating is but one consideration in determining the amount of the worker's benefit. Therefore, although the formula found in KRS 342.730(1)(b) and (c) may imperfectly measure an individual worker's loss, it is not arbitrary and unconstitutional.
>
> *Ira A. Watson Department Store v. Hamilton, supra,* and *McNutt Construction/First General Services v. Scott,* 40 S.W.3d 854 (Ky. 2001), explain that a permanent impairment rating is prerequisite to a finding of permanent total disability under KRS 342.0011(11)(c) but that other factors also are relevant.

Among them are a worker's post-injury physical, emotional, intellectual, and vocational status; how those factors interact; and the likelihood that the worker will be able to find work consistently under normal employment conditions.

KRS 342.125(1)(d) requires a change of disability to be shown by "objective medical evidence of a worsening . . . of impairment." The statute does not refer to the *Guides*, to permanent impairment rating, or to permanent disability rating. We conclude, therefore, that although a greater permanent impairment rating is objective medical evidence of a worsening of impairment, it is not the only evidence by which the statute permits a worsening of impairment to be shown. Chapter 342 does not define the term "objective medical evidence"; however, KRS 342.0011(33) does define "objective medical findings" as being "information gained through direct observation and testing of the patient applying objective or standardized methods." Mindful that KRS 342.0011(1) requires a harmful change in the human organism to be evidenced by objective medical findings in order to be compensable, we are convinced that KRS 342.125(1)(d) and KRS 342.730(1) require no less at reopening. If such findings demonstrate that an injured worker suffers a greater loss, loss of use, or derangement of a body part, organ system, or organ function due to a condition caused by the injury, they demonstrate a worsening of impairment. A worsening of impairment may or may not warrant increasing the worker's permanent impairment rating under the Guides.

2006 Ky. LEXIS 297, at *11–*14.

Williams v. FEI Installation, 2005 WL 3488386 (Ky. Ct. App. Dec. 22, 2005)

The Kentucky court dealt with a 56-year-old factory worker who fell at work, injured his elbow, and was diagnosed with an ulnar nerve contusion. The claimant experienced numbness in the outer three fingers of his hand. His physician rated his impairment at 7 percent whole person under the fifth edition of the *Guides*. This rating was based on 4 percent for the body as a whole and 3 percent for pain. The employer's physician rated the claimant at 0 percent impairment, referenced the *Guides* in general, but did not expressly state how he arrived at the 0 percent rating. The ALJ found for the employer and denied benefits. The Appeals Court affirmed, holding that where there was conflicting evidence, the ALJ was free to accept the 0 percent finding of the employer's physician. The court reasoned:

> Williams claims that the ALJ erred by not awarding him PPD benefits. Williams argues that the ALJ was required to determine his permanent impairment based on a valid impairment rating given by the independent medical examiners. Williams argues that Dr. Auerbach's rating was substantiated and met valid criteria, but Dr. Moskal's was not, and, thus, the ALJ, and ultimately the Board, failed to rely upon valid impairment ratings based on the AMA *Guides*. We are mindful that an ALJ may not disregard uncontradicted medical evidence "when the question is one properly within the province of medical experts[.]" However, the medical evidence in this case is not uncontradicted. We conclude

that the ALJ properly exercised his discretion in giving more weight to the evidence presented by Dr. Moskal as to Williams's impairment rating.

Dr. Auerbach assigned Williams a 7% permanent partial impairment rating based on the AMA *Guides*, while Dr. Moskal assigned a 0% rating based on the AMA *Guides*. Relying on the report of Dr. Moskal, the ALJ determined that Williams had sustained a work-related injury; however, there was no permanent impairment, and a 0% impairment rating was assigned based on the AMA *Guides*. The ALJ found that there was insufficient evidence to award PPD benefits under KRS 342.730(1)(b).

Since the 1996 amendments, KRS 342.730 has required a recipient of permanent income benefits to have an AMA impairment rating. Although the 2000 amendments changed the methods by which a partial disability award is calculated, the statute retained the use of an AMA impairment as the basis for calculating a partial disability award. Dr. Auerbach set forth the calculations he used in arriving at the 7% impairment rating; however, during his deposition, Dr. Auerbach admitted that he did not follow "the directives of the AMA *Guides*" in assessing the rating. On the other hand, Dr. Moskal referenced the AMA *Guides*, but did not expressly state how he reached the 0% impairment rating.

A physician's AMA rating can be challenged by taking his deposition; however, there is no evidence that Williams deposed Dr. Moskal. In Dr. Auerbach's deposition, he opined that his rating was "more reliable because it has a normal bell curve," but testified that he respects Dr. Moskal's opinions. The ALJ could have used Dr. Auerbach's contradictory opinion to discount Dr. Moskal's credibility, but chose not to. When the evidence is in conflict, the ALJ is at liberty "to believe part of the evidence and disbelieve other parts even if it comes from the same witness or the same adversary party's total proof[,]" and matters of credibility and the weight to be assigned to, and inferences drawn from, various testimony are solely for the ALJ. A party challenging the ALJ's factual findings must do more than present evidence supporting a contrary conclusion to justify reversal.

Williams had the burden of proof on the issue, and the ALJ resolved the issue against him. Where the party with the burden of proof was unsuccessful before the ALJ, the issue on appeal is "whether the evidence was so overwhelming, upon consideration of the entire record, as to have compelled a finding in his favor. . . . [T]o be compelling, the evidence produced in [his] favor [] must be so overwhelming that no reasonable person could reach the conclusion of the [ALJ]." The determinative question to be answered is whether the ALJ's finding is "so unreasonable under the evidence that it must be viewed as erroneous as a matter of law" [citations omitted]. The Board found that the ALJ relied on the substantial evidence of Dr. Moskal's opinion and provided a sufficient explanation for rejecting the impairment rating assessed by Dr. Auerbach, and we conclude that in doing so, the Board did not "overlook [] or misconstrue [] controlling statutes or precedent, or commit[] an error in assessing the evidence so flagrant as to cause gross injustice. Thus, we affirm the denial of permanent partial disability benefits."

2005 WL 3488386 at *3–*4.

Note: In footnote 16, the court noted the deposition testimony where the claimant's physician attempted to justify his 7 percent rating. This testimony shows that the physician admitted to not following the *Guides*.

The Board's opinion reveals the following regarding Dr. Auerbach's assessment of Williams's permanent impairment:

> On deposition, Dr. Auerbach explained that he utilized Table 16-15 of the AMA *Guides* to assess a 7% upper extremity impairment due to sensory deficit or pain, which converts to a whole-body rating of 4%. He conceded on cross-examination that the proper use of Table 16-15 requires the evaluator to grade the percentage of sensory deficit according to Table 16-10 and then multiply that percentage by 7%, which is the maximum rating provided under Table 16-15 for sensory loss. Dr. Auerbach confirmed that he did not follow that protocol. Though he acknowledged that Williams does not have a total sensory loss, Dr. Auerbach assessed the maximum rating allowed under Table 16-15, anyway, because he felt anything less failed to take into account the seriousness of the injury and surgery. Dr. Auerbach explained that this was the same rationale for his assessment of the maximum 3% allowed under the Pain Chapter. Here, too, Dr. Auerbach conceded that he did not follow the protocol set out in the AMA *Guides*. He testified, "It has a—a formula which is very complicated, and the—and I tried using the—the scoring system and using—I just used my own judgement [sic]." When asked whether he was "kinda just throwing the 3 percent impairment rating for pain in to get to where you think you should be," Dr. Auerbach responded, "Probably."

2005 WL 3488386, at *3.

Adams v. Coastal Coal Company, 2005 WL 2674978 (Ky. Oct. 20, 2005)

Adams, a coal miner, injured his back at work. Adams was rated by both his doctor and the employer's doctor using the DRE method under the fifth edition of the *Guides*. At the deposition, however, the claimant's doctor stated that he should have used the range-of-motion (ROM) method, which would have resulted in almost doubling the claimant's impairment rating. The court upheld the ALJ's choice to believe the employer's doctor. The court reasoned that the facts and evidence did not compel the ALJ to accept the ROM impairment rating. It stated:

> Contrary to the claimant's assertion, we are not convinced that these facts compelled the ALJ to rely on an impairment that was assigned under the ROM Model. Addressing impairment to the spine, page 379 of the Fifth Edition of the *Guides*. Section 15.2, states that "[t]he DRE method is the principal methodology used to evaluate an individual who has had a distinct injury." *[See also id.* at 374.] Pages 379–80 [of the *Guides]* list five types of situations

in which the ROM method is used. Of these, the claimant focuses on items 2 and 4, which state as follows:

2. When there is multilevel involvement in the same spinal region (eg [sic], fractures at multiple levels, disk herniations, or stenosis with radiculopathy at multiple level[s] or bilaterally).

4. Where there is recurrent radiculopathy caused by a new (recurrent) disk herniation or a recurrent injury in the same spinal region.

He also focuses on page 380, Section 15.2a, which summarizes the procedure for determining whether an individual has multi-level involvement that warrants use of the ROM Model as follows:

4. Determine whether the individual has multi-level involvement or multiple recurrences/occasions within the same region of the spine. Use the ROM method if:

a. there are fractures at more than one level in a spinal region,
b. there is radiculopathy bilaterally or at multiple levels in the same spinal region,
c. there is multi-level motion segment alteration (such as multi-level fusion) in the same spinal region, or
d. there is recurrent disk herniation or stenosis with radiculopathy at the same or a different level in the same spinal region; in this case, combine the ratings using the ROM method.

Dr. Templin assigned a DRE impairment when completing his report. When deposed, he stated that the presence of a compression fracture and degenerative disk disease within the same level would warrant the use of the ROM Model in this case and that the claimant's ROM impairment would be 28%, or it would be 32% if the compression fracture were considered. In contrast, Dr. Bean was convinced that there was no compression fracture. He also stated that there was no disc herniation, radiculopathy, or unstable motion segment and no multi-level involvement of the lumbar spine such as multiple fractures, herniations, or bulges; therefore, he thought it was inappropriate to use the ROM Model to assess the claimant's impairment.

Although medical evidence is required to establish the amount of AMA impairment that an injury causes, it is for the ALJ to determine which medical evidence is most persuasive. KRS 342.285; *Kentucky River Enterprises v. Elkins*, J07 S.W.3d 206, 210 (Ky. 2003). In doing so, the ALJ is free to consult the *Guides*. Confronted with what amounted to a difference of medical opinions regarding the nature of the claimant's condition and the proper application of the *Guides*, the ALJ found Dr. Bean's testimony to be more persuasive than Dr. Templin's. When preparing their written reports, Drs. Bean, Templin, and Travis all assigned a 5% lumbar impairment using the DRE Method. Although Dr. Templin testified subsequently that the ROM method was more appropriate, testimony from Drs. Bean and Travis that there were no compression fractures negated the basis for the opinion. Although Dr. Bean stated that it was not his practice to use the ROM Method and that the claimant had problems at multiple levels of his lumbar spine, it is clear from his testimony that he found none of the conditions that Section 15.a specifies for use of the ROM Method. Furthermore, there was no evidence that the *Guides* require the use of the ROM Method where there are multi-level degenerative changes such as he found. Substantial evidence supported the finding that Dr. Bean's use of the DRE Model was justified and the decision to rely upon it. *Special Fund v. Francis*, 708 S.W.2d 641, 643 (Ky. 1986).

2005 WL 2674978, at *4–*5.

Lanter v. Kentucky State Police, 171 S.W.3d 45 (Ky. 2005)

The Kentucky Supreme Court dealt with a law enforcement officer who received a head injury during a training exercise at the police academy. The ALJ found that the physical brain injury the officer suffered properly resulted in a rating under Chapter 13 of the *Guides* only (Chapter 13 addresses disorders of the nervous system). The claimant appealed and claimed that the ALJ should have in addition awarded benefits under Chapter 14 (addressing mental and behavioral disorders). The Kentucky Supreme Court held that the evidence supported the ALJ's finding that the *Guides*, as properly applied in this case where there was a physical brain injury, required a rating under Chapter 13 only. The court stated:

> At issue presently is whether the medical evidence compelled a finding that harmful changes resulting from the head trauma warranted a disability rating based upon impairments under both Chapter 13 and 14 of the *Guides*.
> After summarizing the lay and medical evidence, the ALJ stated as follows: From a psychological perspective, four physicians have rendered opinions regarding Lanter's impairment. Dr. Shearer assigned Lanter a 30% impairment, Dr. Granacher and Dr. Pagani assigned Lanter a 14% impairment, and Dr. Borack assigned Lanter a 47.5% impairment. Having reviewed the evidence and the appropriate portions of the *AMA Guides*, the [ALJ] notes that Dr. Shearer's impairment would require Lanter to suffer from severe episodic loss of consciousness or awareness to the point that Lanter's activities would need to be supervised, protected, or restricted. While it is clear that Lanter does have some occasional loss of awareness, it is not to the extent necessary to support Dr. Shearer's impairment rating. Dr. Borack's impairment is based on mental and behavioral disorders. To qualify for the high end of a Class 3 impairment, Lanter must have impairment levels compatible with some but not all useful functioning rising nearly to the level of significant difficulties with useful functioning. Furthermore, the *Guides* state on page 364 that, "a moderate impairment does not imply a 50% limitation in useful functioning, and an estimate of moderate impairment in all four categories does not imply a 50% impairment of the whole person." On the other hand, the impairment ratings of Dr. Pagani and Dr. Granacher more nearly indicate Lanter's ability to perform activities of daily living and the need for some direction. Therefore,

the [ALJ] finds that Lanter has a 14% impairment from a psychological standpoint.

Taking into account the claimant's difficulty performing classwork due to his mental and physical restrictions but also his age (25), education (two years of college), history of sedentary to medium work, and his ability to drive, to research his condition on the Internet, and to perform the majority of his activities of daily living, the ALJ determined that he was capable of some type of work.

The claimant maintains that his head injury caused both brain damage and a psychological condition. Pointing to the ALJ's references to a psychological injury while relying on a neurological impairment, he maintains that the ALJ "overlapped and misinterpreted" Chapters 13 and 14 of the *Guides*, considered only the first condition, and disregarded the second. He asserts that only Drs. Borack and D'Souza testified regarding a psychological condition and that only Dr. Borack analyzed the impairment the condition caused. Therefore, the ALJ was required to accept Dr. Borack's uncontradicted testimony that the condition caused a 47.5% impairment. We disagree.

Chapter 13 of the *Guides* provides criteria for evaluating brain dysfunction, emphasizing the deficits or impairments that may be identified during a neurologic evaluation. *Id.* at 305. It acknowledges, however, that "[b]ecause neurologic impairments are intimately related to mental and emotional processes and their functioning, the examiner should also understand Chapters 14, Mental and Behavioral Disorders, and 18, Pain" and that "[a]dditional impairments based on those chapters *may* need to be considered." (emphasis added). *Id.* at 306; *see also id.* at 321–22. Section 13.3f (Emotional and Behavioral Impairments) of Chapter 13 contains Table 13-8, which sets forth the criteria for rating such impairment. Furthermore, Section 13.3f states that "[e]motional, mood, and behavioral disturbances illustrate the relationship between neurology and psychiatry. *Emotional disturbances originating in verifiable neurologic impairments (e.g., stroke, head injury) are assessed using the criteria in this chapter*" (emphasis added). *Id.* at 325. Some of the psychiatric features listed as examples include irritability, outbursts of rage or panic, aggression, withdrawal, depression, mania, and emotional fluctuations. Section 13.3f also states that "[n]eurologic impairments producing psychiatric conditions are assessed using the neurologic examination, with an expanded neuropsychiatric history and the necessary ancillary tests." *Id.*

The introduction to Chapter 14 of the *Guides*, states, in part, as follows: This chapter discusses impairments due to mental disorders and considers behavioral impairment of function that may complicate any condition. As did Chapter 13 (The Central and Peripheral Nervous System), this chapter assesses the brain; however, here the emphasis is on evaluating brain function and its effect on behavior for mental disorders. Unlike the other chapters in the *Guides*, this chapter focuses more on the *process* of performing mental and behavioral impairment assessment. Numerical impairment ratings are not included; however, instructions are given for how to assess an individual's abilities to perform activities of daily living. (Emphasis original.) *Id.* at 357–58. The introduction also notes that the Fifth Edition stresses the importance of the DSM-IV [fourth edition of *Diagnostic and Statistical Manual of Mental Disorders*] criteria for determining a mental impairment and includes more case examples to exemplify the relationship between diagnosis, symptoms, and impact on the ability to perform activities of daily living. Current research finds little relationship between psychiatric signs and symptoms and the ability to perform competitive work. *Id.* at 361–62. Evaluating impairment is based on the extent of function in four main categories: (1) ability to perform activities of daily living; (2) social functioning; (3) concentration, persistence, and pace, which relate to the ability to sustain focused attention long enough to permit the timely completion of necessary tasks; and (4) ability to adapt to stressful circumstances without deterioration or decompensation. Chapter 14 describes a Class 2 impairment as being mild, which "implies that any discerned impairment is compatible with most useful social functioning." *Id.* at 363. It describes a Class 3 impairment as being moderate, which "means that the identified impairments are compatible with some, but not all useful functioning." *Id.* Chapter 14 does not assign percentages to impairments, but as the ALJ noted when analyzing the evidence, it does state that "a moderate impairment does not imply a 50% limitation in useful functioning, and an estimate of moderate impairment in all four categories does not imply a 50% impairment of the whole person." *Id.* at 364.

Depending on the evidence, a claim of psychological harm from a traumatic brain injury could be raised under either of two theories: (1) that the emotional effects of having sustained such an injury resulted in behavioral symptoms; or (2) that the brain damage caused by the injury resulted in both neurological and behavioral symptoms. No medical expert attributed the claimant's behavioral symptoms to the emotional effects of the training incident or of living with the harm that it caused. At issue, therefore, is whether the evidence compelled the ALJ to award benefits for the effects of the claimant's brain damage based not only on his impairment under Chapter 13 but also on an impairment under Chapter 14.

The proper interpretation of the *Guides* and the proper assessment of impairment are medical questions. *See Kentucky River Enterprises, Inc. v. Elkins*, 107 S.W.3d 206, 210 (Ky. 2003). In the present case, no physician testified regarding the proper application of the *Guides* when evaluating impairment from a traumatic brain injury that causes both neurological and behavioral symptoms. Faced with impairment ratings that were assigned under Chapters 13 and 14 and the task of selecting an impairment rating that was a reasonable estimation of the claimant's condition, the ALJ appropriately consulted the *Guides* when considering the medical evidence and deciding upon which experts to rely. Chapter 13 clearly indicates that an additional impairment may be warranted in certain instances based on behavioral factors that originate in the brain due to organic damage from a head injury, but it does not indicate that behavioral symptoms always warrant an additional impairment. Furthermore, it appears to indicate that any additional impairment for emotional or behavioral disorders is to be determined under the criteria found in Section 13.3f of Chapter 13 rather than under Chapter 14. *Id.* at 325.

We find nothing in the ALJ's reference to the impairment "from a psychological standpoint" or "psychological perspective" together with a discussion of impairments that were assigned under Chapters 13 and 14 of the *Guides* that evinces a misunderstanding of the medical evidence or a confusion regarding Chapters 13 and 14. In summarizing the evidence, the ALJ specifically noted that the claimant was no longer taking any medication for the neurological or behavioral effects of his injury and had no scheduled medical appointments. It is apparent from the analysis that followed that the ALJ found the impairments assigned by Drs. Shearer and Borack to be excessive in light of the claimant's restrictions and found the impairments assigned by Drs. Pagani and Granacher to "more nearly indicate [the claimant's] ability to perform activities of daily living and the need for some direction." The decision was reasonable under the evidence that was available and was properly affirmed on appeal. *Special Fund v. Francis*, 708 S.W. 2d 641, 643 (Ky. 1986).

171 S.W.3d at 46–52.

Thornton v. Volt Services Group, 2005 WL 1412530 (Ky. June 16, 2005)

The Kentucky Supreme Court dealt with a trash collector who injured his back while lifting a heavy object. The claimant's doctor testified that the claimant suffered impairment from a bulging disk at L4–L5 on the left and a herniated disk on the right at L5–S1. The employer's doctor did not address the herniated disk, and the ALJ did not award benefits for the herniated disk, but did award benefits for the bulging disk. The Supreme Court reversed and remanded with instructions to award additional benefits for the herniated disk. The court reasoned that where the ALJ is presented with conflicting evidence on an impairment rating, he is free to choose between the evidence. However, the ALJ must not disregard uncontradicted medical evidence on the *Guides*. The court noted that proper interpretation of the *Guides* "is a complex matter that requires medical expertise." The court stated:

> KRS 342.730(1)(b) bases the amount of an income benefit for partial disability on the injured worker's impairment as determined under the standards set forth in the AMA *Guides*. Thus, the claimant bore the burden of proving that the injury caused both an L5–S1 herniation and L4–5 disc bulge and of proving the amount of impairment that the *Guides* would authorize. The proper interpretation of the *Guides* with regard to orthopedic injuries is a complex matter that requires medical expertise. This is particularly true when the experts assign impairments using different models or more than one model. *See Thomas v. United Parcel Service*, 58 S.W.3d 455 (Ky. 2001). When medical experts differ concerning the proper application of the *Guides* and an injured worker's impairment rating, it is the ALJ's function to weigh the conflicting evidence and to decide which is more persuasive. *Paramount Foods, Inc. v. Burkhardt*,

695 S.W.2d 418 (Ky. 1985). When medical evidence is uncontradicted, the ALJ may not disregard it. *See Mengel v. Hawaiian-Tropic Northwest & Central Distributors, Inc.* [618 S.W.2d 184 (Ky. App. 1981)] If an ALJ finds against the party with the burden of proof, their burden on appeal is to show that the finding was unreasonable because the favorable evidence was so overwhelming that it compelled a favorable finding. *Special Fund v. Francis*, 708 S.W.2d 641, 643 (1986). We are convinced that the claimant met that burden.

The claimant asserted that the injury caused a bulging disc at L4–5 on the left and a herniated disc at L5–S1 on the right. Dr. Lach testified that both conditions were due to the work-related accident and that the claimant continued to experience some radiculopathy. When addressing impairment, he explained that the Range of Motion model accounted for lesions on opposite sides that caused opposite problems. Using the Range of Motion model, he assigned a 7% impairment for the herniated disc and a 5% impairment for the bulging disc, for a combined impairment of 12%. Dr. Lach also stated that the DRE model permitted a 10–13% impairment for a herniated disc and associated radiculopathy under lumbar Category III. He explained that the claimant apparently did not have the associated radicular complaints when he saw Dr. Guarnaschelli, so Dr. Guarnaschelli placed him in Category II. Dr. Lach did not assign an impairment for the bulging disc under the DRE model or state that the model would permit an impairment rating for a bulging disc. Nor did he state that the *Guides* preferred the use of one model over the other in the present situation.

The questions to which Dr. Guarnaschelli responded were not made part of the record. It may well be that he considered the claimant's entire condition. Nonetheless, it is impossible to determine from his report whether he did so or whether the questions to which he was responding concerned only the left-sided symptoms and their cause. His report refers to radiographic and MRI evidence, but it does so solely in the context of addressing the central and left paracentral disc bulge and the low back, left hip, and left leg pain. It makes no reference whatsoever to an L5-S1 herniation or to any right-sided symptoms. Although Dr. Lach thought that Dr. Guarnaschelli assigned the 5% Category II impairment based upon the herniated disc, the ALJ determined that he assigned it based upon the bulging disc. Neither party has asserted that the finding was erroneous under the *Guides*. Furthermore, although Dr. Lach did not assign a DRE impairment to the condition, he did assign a 5% impairment under the Range of Motion model. Under the circumstances, the conclusion that Dr. Guarnaschelli assigned the impairment based upon the bulging disc was reasonable under the evidence. It may not be disturbed on appeal. *Special Fund v. Francis, supra.*

Dr. Lach testified affirmatively that in addition to the bulging disc, the claimant had a herniated disc at L5–S1 on the right side with associated radiculopathy. His report stated that it was caused by the work-related accident and that it warranted a DRE Category III impairment because there was associated radiculopathy or warranted a 7% Range of Motion impairment. His report also indicated that a herniated disc warranted a DRE Category II impairment if radiculopathy had been present but later resolved. Absent the questions to which Dr. Guarnaschelli was responding, absent any reference in his report to the herniated disc or right-sided symptoms, and absent any other indication that he directed his report to the claimant's entire condition, the impairment Dr. Guarnaschelli assigned could not reasonably be viewed as being the product of a difference of opinion regarding the existence of the herniated disc, its cause, or any resulting impairment.

Although the claimant testified that he continued to experience symptoms in both legs, the ALJ was persuaded by the evidence that his right leg problems had resolved to the point that surgery was no longer necessary. Therefore, the ALJ was compelled to rely on Dr. Lach's uncontradicted testimony that a herniated disc with radiculopathy that later resolved would come within DRE Category II, which warranted a 5–8% impairment, or his uncontradicted testimony that the herniated disc warranted a 7% Range of Motion impairment. There was no evidence that the use of either model was preferred or required by the *Guides* under the circumstances. On remand, the ALJ must determine the impairment the herniated disc caused and award income benefits based on the claimant's entire condition.

The decision of the Court of Appeals is reversed, and the claim is remanded to the ALJ for further consideration.

2005 WL 1412530, at 5–6.

Brasch-Barry General Contractors v. Jones, 175 S.W.3d 81 (Ky. 2005)

In this case, the Kentucky Supreme Court dealt with a worker who injured his back. At hearing, the employer's experts testified that the worker suffered a category II DRE disability and assigned a 10 percent impairment. The worker's doctor, Dr. Reasor, testified that the worker received a category IV, 26 percent impairment. On cross-examination, Dr. Reasor admitted that he had not followed the "textbook definition" of the *Guides* in assigning this impairment. The ALJ awarded 26 percent impairment, and the employer appealed, without first requesting a rehearing. At issue in the case was whether the ALJ's acceptance of the 26 percent rating, which deviated from the *Guides*, was a question of law, which allows for direct appeals to the Workers' Compensation Board, or a question of fact, which prohibits appeals unless a motion for rehearing is made. The Supreme Court held that the ALJ's acceptance of a rating that deviated from the *Guides* was a question of law, not of fact. Therefore, the court affirmed the board's throwing out of the 26 percent impairment rating. The court stated:

> On April 14, 2000, Jeff Jones suffered a back injury in the course of his employment with Appellant. Soon thereafter, Jones sought medical attention and filed for workers' compensation benefits. During a hearing to determine the extent of these benefits, medical evidence was introduced before Bonnie Kittinger, an administrative law judge (ALJ). The medical evidence consisted of testimony and/or reports from three doctors regarding the extent of Jones'

workplace injury. Two of the doctors determined that Jones' condition qualified as a "DRE lumbar Category III" disability under the American Medical Association's Guides to the Evaluation of Permanent Impairment, Fifth Edition ("AMA Guides"). As a "Category III" disability, Jones' impairment rating could range between ten and sixteen percent (10–16%). These doctors assessed Jones at ten percent (10%) permanent impairment. One of the doctors, Dr. Gary Reasor, determined that Jones' condition qualified as a "DRE lumbar Category IV" disability under the AMA Guides. A "Category IV" disability would allow an impairment rating for Jones between twenty and twenty-six percent (20–26%). Dr. Reasor assessed Jones at twenty-six percent (26%) permanent impairment.

During cross-examination. Dr. Reasor conceded that Jones did not meet the textbook definition for a "Category IV" disability under the AMA Guides, but rather, his condition fell within the parameters of a "Category III" disability. However, Dr. Reasor maintained his conclusion of twenty-six percent (26%) total impairment for Jones, explaining that the category definitions in the AMA Guides are meant to be used solely as the name of the text implies, as a guide. He further surmised that the category definitions were perhaps flawed or incomplete in this instance. From this testimony, the ALJ made the following finding:

> Despite persistent and skillful cross-examination by the Defendant, Dr. Reasor steadfastly maintained that Plaintiff's permanent impairment was 26%. He insisted that the AMA *Guides* are only that, guidelines, not final authority. The ALJ, as a finder of facts, must depend on interpretation of the *Guides* by a medical professional. Based on Dr. Reasor's medical reports and deposition testimony, Plaintiff is found to have a 26% permanent impairment as the result of his work injury on April 14, 2000.

Without filing a petition for rehearing, Appellant appealed directly to the Board pursuant to KRS 342.285. The Board ruled that in order to comply with KRS 342.730(1)(b), impairment ratings must be determined in accordance with the category definitions contained in the AMA Guides. Since Dr. Reasor failed to base his impairment rating on the category definitions contained in the AMA Guides, the Board held that his finding of twenty-six percent (26%) permanent impairment was not, as a matter of statutory law, supported by substantial evidence. Based on this analysis, the ALJ's finding of twenty-six percent (26%) impairment was reversed and the case was remanded back to the ALJ for a determination which was consistent with the Board's opinion.

Pursuant to KRS 342.290, Jones appealed the Board's decision to the Court of Appeals. Finding "the issue on appeal in this case [to be] of a completely factual nature," the Court of Appeals reversed the Board's decision because it determined that the issue was ultimately unpreserved for review. It ruled that pursuant to *Eaton Axle Corporation v. Nally*, 688 S.W.2d 334 (Ky. 1985), the Board could not address the issue unless Appellant timely filed a petition for reconsideration in accordance with KRS 342.281. Because we find the Board's ruling to pertain to a question of law and not fact, we reverse the Court of Appeals' decision and remand for further proceedings.

The statute which directs the procedure for review in this case is KRS 342.285. KRS 342.285 grants parties the right to appeal ALJ decisions directly to the Workers' Compensation Board under the following conditions:

> An award or order of the administrative law judge as provided in KRS 342.275, *if petition for reconsideration is not filed* as provided for in KRS 342.281, *shall be conclusive and binding as to all questions of fact,* but either party may in accordance with administrative regulations promulgated by the commissioner appeal to the Workers' Compensation Board for the review of the order or award. *Id.* (Emphasis added.)

KRS 342.285 goes on to define the Board's duties on review, which have been summarized by this Court as follows:

> No new evidence may be introduced before the Board and *the Board may not substitute its judgment for that of the ALJ concerning the weight of evidence on questions of fact.* The scope of review of the Board is limited to determining whether the ALJ's decision was: authorized, not procured by fraud, in conformity with Chapter 342, supported by the evidence, and not arbitrary or capricious. (Emphasis added.) *Smith v. Dixie Fuel Co.,* 900 S.W.2d 609, 612 (Ky. 1995).

Pursuant to our interpretation of KRS 342.285 and the plain language contained therein, issues regarding questions of law need not be preserved pursuant to a petition for reconsideration, but rather, may be appealed directly to the Board. The decision in *Eaton Axle, supra,* is completely consistent with the review procedures set forth in KRS 342.285 since it merely requires that a petition for reconsideration be filed in accordance with KRS 342.281 whenever the complaining party wishes to preserve a question of fact for appellate review. *Id.* at 338. ("The purpose of this rule is to require that all justiciable issues are disposed of before the appellate process begins.")

In this case, the Court of Appeals classified the Board's ruling as being "of a completely factual nature." However, in *Whittaker v. Reeder,* 30 S.W.3d 138 (Ky. 2000), we reiterated that it is the Board's province on appeal to ensure that ALJ decisions are in conformity with Chapter 342 (the Workers' Compensation Act) and that such determinations constitute questions of law, and not fact. *Id.* at 144.

The Board's decision squarely and appropriately construed the intent of KRS 342.730 and was not based on any factual considerations (such as credibility or weight to be attributed to the evidence) determined by the ALJ. Accordingly, the issue was one of law and did not require Appellant to first file a petition for reconsideration pursuant to KRS 342.281 in order to preserve it for review before the Board. Since the issue was appropriately preserved, the Board did not err in addressing its merit. At 82.

AK Steel Corp. v. Johnston, 153 S.W.3d 837 (Ky. 2005)

This case dealt with two steel workers, Johnston and Allen, who claimed permanent impairments from occupational hearing loss. Johnston worked for 40 years in the defendant's steel mill and was age 59 when his hearing impairment was rated. Allen worked in the steel mill for 35 years and was age 60 when his hearing loss was evaluated for permanent impairment. The Supreme Court of Kentucky held that statistical evidence estimating age-related hearing loss does not rebut the statutory presumption that a binaural hearing impairment that converts to 8 percent or more under the *AMA Guides* is entirely work related. Each claimant was evaluated by a Dr. Windmill.

Regarding Mr. Johnston:

> Dr. Windmill evaluated the claimant and completed a Form 108-HL. He reported a 9% AMA impairment that within a reasonable medical probability was work-related. In response to a question whether any part of the impairment was due to the natural aging process, he replied, "Approximately 20% of Mr. Johnston's hearing loss can be explained based on the natural aging process."
>
> When deposed, Dr. Windmill explained that when completing the Form 108-HL, he had estimated the effect of age-related factors by consulting tables that were appended to the hearing conservation amendment to the Federal Noise Control Act. He testified that the hearing loss chapter of the *American Medical Association's Guides to the Evaluation of Permanent Impairment* (Guides) does not account for age, and that there is no specific test or method to separate various causes of hearing impairment in an individual. He stated that the tables were based on statistical averages and might or might not apply to Mr. Johnston because not all people have a hearing loss due to age. He explained that although the tables are not part of the Guides, the only way to estimate what portion of an impairment is due to aging is to use them. Using the tables, he had estimated that 20% of Johnston's hearing loss was age-related, but he explained that that was not to say that 20% of Johnston's impairment was due to his age.

153 S.W.3d at 1.

As for Mr. Allen:

> As in the Johnston case, Dr. Windmill evaluated the claimant and completed a Form 108-HL. He reported an 8% AMA impairment that, within a reasonable medical probability, was work related. In response to a question whether any part of the impairment was due to the natural aging process, he replied, "Approximately 25 to 30% of Mr. Allen's hearing loss can be explained based on the natural aging process."
>
> When deposed concerning the method for estimating age-related impairment, Dr. Windmill explained that the tables that were appended to the hearing conservation amendment to the Federal Noise Control Act showed average

hearing levels by age and that he had used the tables as a basis for his estimate of Mr. Allen's age-related hearing loss. Addressing the effect of age on hearing, Dr. Windmill explained that many factors cause ear damage over time such as noise, medications, chemicals, diet, and artery disease. The effects of such damage are generally measurable between the ages of 45–50 and increase progressively. Some age-related effects would be expected at age 60. Dr. Windmill stated, however, that an estimate that age accounted for 25% of Mr. Allen's hearing loss did not mean that it accounted for 25% of his 8% AMA impairment because AMA impairment considers only hearing loss at the middle frequencies involved in speech. In his opinion, using the tables to apportion part of an AMA impairment to age is akin to comparing apples and oranges. Although it is not difficult to do, "[i]t's definitely speculative." Asked whether he could state with reasonable medical probability that some portion of Mr. Allen's impairment was not due to occupational noise exposure, he stated, "No."

153 S.W.3d at 1–2.

The court explained its holding as follows:

Appellees Johnston and Allen sought income benefits based upon evidence of an AMA impairment due to hearing loss. Each produced evidence warranting a presumption that his impairment was a compensable injury. Although the university evaluator testified that tables have been compiled regarding the average hearing loss at particular ages and although he estimated that a portion of these Workers' hearing impairments was age-related, he also testified that not all individuals suffer from age-related hearing loss, that the only way to apportion the cause of hearing loss in an individual with occupational noise exposure is to use the tables, and that he could not state with certainty that an individual with such exposure actually had an age-related hearing loss. At issue is whether KRS § 342.7305 permits a consideration of the entire AMA impairment due to hearing loss, without regard to age-related changes, or whether it requires part of the impairment to be excluded based upon evidence that part of the underlying hearing loss is age-related. The question then becomes whether statistical evidence estimating age-related hearing loss partially rebuts KRS § 342.7305(4)'s presumption that a worker's entire impairment is work-related and requires an apportionment of causation. KRS § 342.7305(1) requires the amount of binaural hearing impairment to be determined under the Guides. KRS § 342.7305 makes no reference to age-related changes, which are included in AMA impairment under the Guides; whereas, KRS § 342.7305(2) creates an exception to the Guides by excluding impairment from tinnitus. Furthermore, it permits an income benefit only in those instances where the AMA impairment due to hearing loss equals or exceeds 8%. Table 11-3, found on page 251 of the Fifth Edition of the Guides, indicates that a 98.9–100% binaural hearing impairment converts to a 35% AMA impairment and that a 21.5–24.5% binaural hearing impairment converts to an 8% AMA impairment. It is apparent, therefore, that the 8% threshold found in KRS § 342.7305(2) represents a substantial binaural hearing impairment.

When responding to the Form 108HL, Dr. Windmill estimated that 20% of Johnston's hearing impairment and approximately 25–30% of Allen's hearing impairment was age-related. Hence, even if one were to assume that they were among those individuals who suffer from age-related hearing loss as well as occupational hearing loss, the overwhelming majority of their hearing impairment was occupational. It appears, therefore, that the threshold limits income benefits to instances where the impairment is substantial and workplace trauma is likely to be a substantial cause. In view of KRS § 342.7305's explicit reliance on the Guides and KRS § 342.7305(2)'s explicit provision to exclude tinnitus from an AMA impairment when calculating an income benefit, we are convinced that the legislature would have been equally explicit if it had intended for there to be another exclusion based upon age. Likewise, in view of Dr. Windmill's testimony, we are not convinced that an AMA impairment based upon hearing loss must be apportioned between age-related and work-related causes absent an explicit provision in KRS § 342.7305(4). Each of these workers proved an AMA impairment that equaled or exceeded 8%; therefore, each was entitled to partial disability benefits that were based upon his AMA impairment. Mr. Allen was properly awarded a partial disability benefit that was based on his 8% impairment. Mr. Johnston's claim was dismissed, however, and must be remanded for the ALJ to award an income benefit that is based upon his full 9% impairment.

The decision of the Court of Appeals in each of these appeals is affirmed. All concur.

153 S.W.3d at 4–5.

Jewish Hosp. v. Ray, 131 S.W.3d 760 (Ky. Ct. App. 2004)

This case involved a nurse who slipped and fell on July 1, 2000, injuring her left hand, neck, and lower back. At issue was which edition of the *AMA Guides* must be used to evaluate the claimant's condition. The applicable statute in Kentucky requires use of the "latest edition available." On March 1, 2001, the workers' compensation commissioner proclaimed through certification that the fifth edition of the *Guides* is the latest edition available. The court held that under these circumstances, the fifth edition was the proper edition to use, even though the fourth edition was the latest edition available at the time of the injury. The court reasoned:

> As previously discussed, Ray filed her claim for benefits on December 30, 2002. Thus, the "latest edition available" at that time was the Fifth Edition. Jewish Hospital asserts that a change in the latest edition of the AMA Guides is the legal equivalent of a statutory amendment by the Legislature. The argument follows that the ALJ's decision to utilize the Fifth Edition of the AMA Guides in determining Ray's impairment rating constituted a retrospective application of KRS § 342.730(1)(b) in violation of KRS § 446.080(3), which provides that "[n]o statute shall be construed to be retroactive, unless expressly

so declared." Jewish Hospital cites Spurlin v. Adkins, in support of its argument. Therein, the Supreme Court of Kentucky stated that "in instances where the amendment at issue has affected the level of income benefits payable for a worker's occupational disability, the Court has consistently determined that . . . the law on the date of injury or last injurious exposure controls."

First and foremost, we are unpersuaded that a change in the latest edition of the AMA Guides is the legal equivalent of a statutory amendment. Jewish Hospital cites no case law in support of this contention and we are of the opinion that the language "latest edition available" contained in KRS § 342.730(1)(b) reflects nothing more than a conscious regard on the part of the Legislature of the ever-evolving medical standards applicable to work-related injuries.

Moreover, even if we were to assume that the adoption of each subsequent version of the AMA Guides represents a statutory amendment, Jewish Hospital's argument still fails. It is well-established that Workers' compensation statutes are to be interpreted in a manner consistent with their munificent and beneficent purpose. As previously discussed, KRS § 342.730(1)(b) requires that income benefits for permanent partial disability be based on a permanent impairment rating as determined by the "latest edition available" of the AMA Guides. In order to accept Jewish Hospital's argument, we would have to read the statute as meaning that an injured worker's permanent impairment rating is to be determined by the "latest edition available [*at the time of the injury*]" [emphasis added]. Had the Legislature intended such a result, surely it would have included the phrase "at the time of the injury." To hold otherwise would contravene the very purpose of the Workers' Compensation Act, which is to aid injured or deceased workers or their dependents.

Based on the foregoing reasons, the opinion of the Workers' Compensation Board is affirmed. All concur.

131 S.W.3d at 763–64.

George Humfleet Mobile Homes v. Christman, 125 S.W.3d 288 (Ky. 2004)

The Kentucky court dealt with a worker who injured his back when falling from a ladder. At issue was under which edition of the *AMA Guides* should evaluation be made when a claimant is injured during the period of currency of an earlier edition of the *Guides*, but the claim is adjudicated during the period of currency of a later edition of the *Guides*. The court held that Kentucky's statute mandating the use of the "latest edition available" of the *Guides* must be interpreted to mean that the ALJ must use the latest edition that has been certified as being available on the date proof closes. The court justified its decision to a large part on the belief that later editions of the *Guides* are more accurate and complete than the earlier editions. The court stated:

A partial disability benefit is the product of three factors: 662/3 of the worker's average weekly wage, an AMA impairment that is assigned under the "latest edition available" of the *Guides*, and a statutory factor that increases with impairment. It is undisputed that the impairment for a particular condition may be different using different editions of the Guides. Yet, although the amount of a worker's impairment has a two-fold effect on the amount of his income benefit, neither KRS § 342.730(1)(b) nor the regulations specify at what point in the history of a claim the latest edition available is to be determined. Among the possibilities are: the date of the injury, the date that the particular impairment is assigned, the date that the worker reaches maximum medical improvement (MMI), the date that proof time expires, and the date of the ALJ's decision.

The employer maintains that it would be most reasonable to interpret KRS § 342.730(1)(b) as permitting an ALJ to rely on a physician who used the latest edition available at the time the impairment rating was assigned.

Although the version of KRS § 342.730(1)(b) that was effective on the date of the claimant's injury governs the calculation of his income benefit, neither party has asserted that the phrase "latest edition available" refers to the latest edition that was available on the date of injury. An impairment rating is assigned when an injured worker recovers to the point that his condition is stable, in other words, to the point that he is at MMI. It is apparent from the frequency with which the Guides have been updated and from the increasing size of successive volumes that the art and science of evaluating impairment are continuously evolving. For that reason, we are convinced that the methods prescribed in the most recent edition are likely to be the most accurate and may be used without regard to the date of injury, just as the most recent life expectancy table may be used. See Stovall v. Great Flame Coal Co., 684 S.W.2d 3 (Ky. App., 1984). We conclude, therefore, that the use of a Fourth-Edition impairment was not required when calculating the claimant's benefit simply because it was the latest edition available on the date of his injury. We also conclude that because the methods prescribed in the most recent edition are likely to be the most accurate, the impairment from which a benefit is calculated must be based on those methods, regardless of the date of the underlying medical evaluation or the date of MMI.

Despite the foregoing conclusions, we are convinced that the legislature did not intend for the applicable edition of the Guides to be determined by the date of the ALJ's decision. Under such an interpretation of KRS § 342.730(1)(b), proof time would end, the hearing would be held, and the claim would be briefed, all before the parties knew for certain what edition of the Guides governed the claim. We conclude, therefore, that the phrase "latest edition available" refers to the latest edition that has been certified as being generally available as of the date that proof time closes. We have observed many times that one of the purposes of the 1996 amendments was to incorporate more objective standards for awarding income benefits. For that reason, we are convinced that although an ALJ is free to choose among impairments that were assigned under the latest edition available at the closing of proof, an ALJ is not free to rely upon an impairment that was assigned under an earlier edition. Two options are available in instances where proof time spans the date on which a new edition of the Guides is certified as being generally available.

The ALJ may extend proof time and permit proof to be re-taken under the latest edition where fairness dictates, or the parties may agree to have the claim decided under the previous edition.

125 S.W.3d at 293–94.

Napier v. Middlesboro Appalachian Reg'l Hosp., **2004 WL 538123 (Ky. Mar. 18, 2004)**

The Supreme Court of Kentucky dealt with this case involving a worker who injured her right shoulder and back. The court held that the claimant failed to satisfy her burden of proof regarding permanent impairment when her physician did not specifically mention the *AMA Guides* in assigning a 10 percent impairment to "the whole body." The claimant had agued that the ALJ should have taken judicial notice of the fact that the rating physician's practice in performing ratings is to use the *Guides*. The court reasoned:

> Since December 12, 1996, KRS § 342.730 has required a recipient of permanent income benefits to have an AMA impairment rating. In fact, the formula for calculating permanent partial disability awards takes into account the extent of the worker's AMA impairment. KRS § 342.730(1)(b). The claimant maintains that because Dr. Muffly regularly testifies in workers' compensation claims, the ALJ should have taken judicial notice that he would have reported an impairment using the most current rating required by law. As support for the argument, the claimant notes that neither the statutes nor administrative regulation explicitly require a physician to state that an impairment rating was made under the most current edition of the Guides. She maintains that the reason they do not is that all parties, including physicians who perform IME exams, understand that any impairment rating must be stated under the most current edition of the Guides.
>
> The burden was on the claimant to prove every element of her claim, including the extent of her AMA impairment. Contrary to her assertion, physicians who assign impairment ratings do not necessarily do so under the latest available edition of the Guides. See George Humfleet Mobile Homes v. Christman, 2003-SC-0047-WC, rendered January 22, 2004. Furthermore, because Dr. Muffly's practice with respect to assigning impairment ratings is not an adjudicative fact in this claim, it would have been inappropriate for the ALJ to take judicial notice concerning his practice even if the other requirements of KRE § 201 were met. It may well be that Dr. Muffly assigned the 10% impairment under the Fifth Edition of the Guides as the claimant asserts. The fact remains, however, that his report made no reference to the Guides or even to a chapter, section, page, chart, or table from which the ALJ could have reasonably inferred that it was. Under the circumstances, his report was not substantial evidence to support a partial disability award.

2004 WL 538123, at *1.

Appalachian Racing, Inc. v. Blair, 2003 WL 21355872 (Ky. June 12, 2003)

The Kentucky court dealt with a waitress who slipped, fell, and injured her back. The treating doctor diagnosed lumbar disk disease and a chronic lumbar sprain. He reported an impairment rating of 12 to 15 percent. The report did not specify the pages or tables in the *AMA Guides to the Evaluation of Permanent Impairment* (*AMA Guides*) upon which the rating was based.

When deposed on February 27, 2001, the treating doctor testified that the claimant sustained a herniated disk at L4–L5 with permanent peripheral neuritis and impending peripheral neuropathy, a bulging disk at L5–S1 with degenerative disk disease, and a chronic lumbar sprain as a result of her fall. He supported his diagnosis with a radiology report from Dr. Amin concerning the June 3, 2000, MRI. He explained that he preferred to rely upon Dr. Amin's report because, as a radiologist, he had specialized training in interpreting diagnostic films. Dr. Amin noted a disk herniation at L4–L5 with slight nerve encroachment and a bulging disk at L5–S1. Asked whether the claimant's problems with her neck had pretty well resolved, the doctor testified, "Yes, I think they have." Asked what the claimant's AMA impairment would be under the fourth edition of the *AMA Guides*, the doctor testified that it would be 12 to 15 percent, based on abnormal neurological findings and a herniated disk. Asked whether he used the DRE tables when assigning that percentage, he testified, "Yes." Dr. Bryson then testified that under the third edition of the *AMA Guides*, the claimant fell into DRE category III for the lumbosacral spine and category II for the cervical spine. The ALJ determined that the doctor had misapplied the *Guides* and adjusted the impairment rating to 10 percent based on his reading of the fourth edition of the *Guides*. The court affirmed and stated:

> Although Dr. Bryson testified that he used the Third Edition of the *Guides* when assigning a category III impairment to the lumbar spine and a category II impairment to the cervical spine, the DRE method was not available until the Fourth Edition. The employer concedes that the category II and III ratings were actually based upon the Fourth Edition, which was the latest available edition. It maintains, however, that the 12–15% impairment was improper because the Fourth Edition does not provide for ranges of impairments and concludes that the ALJ was compelled to rely upon Dr. Amin's testimony of a 10% impairment. Furthermore, the employer asserts that no physician specifically testified to a 10% impairment and maintains, therefore, that it was an abuse of discretion for the ALJ to interpret the *Guides*, to determine that the neck impairment was 2–5%, and to find that the claimant's lumbar impairment was 10%. We disagree.
>
> The employer correctly asserts that Dr. Bryson assigned a combined impairment of 12–15% and did not specifically state that the claimant's lumbosacral impairment was 10% or that her cervical impairment was 5%. Nonetheless, it is undisputed that under the Fourth Edition of the *Guides*, a DRE category III lumbosacral impairment is 10%, and a category II cervical

impairment is 5%. After determining that Dr. Bryson's assessment of the claimant's back condition was more credible, the ALJ simply relied upon his testimony that the condition fell into category III of the DRE table, read the table, and determined that a lumbosacral category III warranted a 10 % AMA impairment. Having reviewed the table in question, it is apparent to the Court that no medical expertise is required to equate DRE categories I–V to AMA impairments. Thus, it was not an abuse of discretion for the ALJ to do so.

2003 WL 21355872, at *2.

Kentucky River Enterprises, Inc. v. Elkins, No. 2001-CA-002776-WC (Ky. Ct. App. June 28, 2002), *rev'd in part and remanded, aff'd in part*, 107 S.W.3d 206 (Ky. 2003)

The Kentucky appellate court dealt with a mechanic and heavy equipment operator who injured his back while lifting a five-gallon can of oil on September 8, 2000. He had suffered a previous work-related back injury in 1989. The Workers' Compensation Board summarized the lay and medical testimony in the case as follows:

> In support of his claim, Elkins submitted testimony from Dr. Mukut Sharma, his treating orthopedic surgeon. Dr. Sharma began treating Elkins on September 14, 2000. In his records from the initial visit, Dr. Sharma indicated Elkins reported having low back pain for approximately five weeks and denied any recent injury. The doctor stated that after a conversation with Elkins on November 7, 2000, he amended his report to reflect that Elkins indicated a history of five days of low back pain on the initial visit. Dr. Sharma diagnosed a herniated disc at L5–S1 with degenerative changes at L4-L5. He performed a discectomy on Elkins on October 25, 2000. He stated that Elkins had a good result from that surgery. Dr. Sharma reviewed records from Dr. Kennedy, the orthopedic surgeon that performed Elkins'[s] low back surgery in 1990. Dr. Sharma stated that Dr. Kennedy performed essentially the same type of procedure at the L4–L5 level in 1990 as he had performed in 2000 at the L5–S1 level.
>
>   Dr. Sharma stated that Elkins'[s] functional impairment following the 2000 injury would be something less than 10%, perhaps 7% or 8%. He stated this impairment was made using the Range of Motion Model. When asked about the DRE Model, he stated that radiculopathy would indicate a 10% impairment, but still estimated Elkins'[s] impairment would be less than 10%. Dr. Sharma acknowledged that the *AMA Guides* indicate that a preexisting impairment to the same anatomic system should be subtracted from the current impairment to determine the impairment related to the most recent injury. When asked whether the impairment related to his 1990 injury should be subtracted from the 2000 injury, Dr. Sharma stated "the answer is yes or no." He stated Elkins might have improved to the point he had no impairment following his 1990 surgery. He stated, however, that he had no reason to disagree with Dr. Kennedy's

assessment of a 14% impairment in 1990. Dr. Sharma was uncertain how to apply the language from the *Guides* indicating that a preexisting impairment should be subtracted from the current impairment when the injuries are to two different disc levels in the low back.

Elkins also submitted testimony from Dr. James Templin, a specialist in pain management and occupational medicine. Dr. Templin diagnosed an L5–S1 disc herniation with subsequent laminectomy and discectomy at L5–S1; chronic low back pain syndrome; and left leg radiculopathy. He noted Elkins'[s] history of a prior L4–L5 disc herniation with surgery. Dr. Templin assessed a 10% impairment for Elkins'[s] low back problems using the DRE model in the *AMA Guides*, Fourth Edition. He noted the presence of scar tissue from the previous surgery and some degenerative disc changes; the arousal of which he felt contributed to Elkins'[s] current condition. Dr. Templin stated Elkins felt that 5% of his left leg radiculopathy problems were due to his previous injury, while the remaining 95% were due to his current condition. On that basis, Dr. Templin apportioned 5% of his 10% impairment (i.e., .5%) to a preexisting active condition, and the remaining 9.5% to the 2000 injury.

Kentucky River submitted records from the Whitesburg ARH, which included records from Dr. Tidal and Dr. Sharma. Dr. Tidal saw Elkins on September 11, 2000, just after the alleged injury. There was no mention of a work-related injury at that time, only a mention of long-standing low back pain. The initial record of Dr. Sharma, dated September 14, 2000, as noted above, indicated Elkins gave a history of a recurrence of low back pain about five weeks prior with no history of recent injury.

Kentucky River also submitted testimony from Dr. Leon Ensalada, a specialist in occupational medicine. Dr. Ensalada reviewed Elkins'[s] medical records. He concluded that Elkins had not suffered an injury on September 8, 2000. He based this conclusion on the Whitesburg ARH records and Dr. Sharma's records indicating a history of five weeks of low back pain. Dr. Ensalada also concluded that Elkins suffered a 10% impairment under the *AMA Guides* prior to September 2000 and this was due to the 1989 injury. Dr. Ensalada also concluded that Elkins had no impairment as the result of any September 2000 injury and has suffered no occupational consequences as a result of such an injury. Dr. Ensalada stated Elkins should have had permanent restrictions of lifting no more than fifty pounds occasionally or twenty-five pounds frequently and avoiding repetitive bending, stooping, and twisting. He believed these restrictions would also be appropriate subsequent to the 2000 discectomy surgery.

Kentucky River also submitted testimony from Dr. Richard Sheridan, an orthopedic surgeon. Dr. Sheridan also believed Elkins had not suffered an injury on September 8, 2000. He stated the L5–S1 herniation was due to increased stresses at that disc space occurring over a ten year period subsequent to the prior low back injury at L4–L5. He assessed a 10% impairment under the *AMA Guides* using the DRE Model and believed Elkins also would have had a 10% preexisting active impairment due to the L4–L5 disc injury. He believed there was no need to place any restrictions on Elkins'[s] physical activities.

Lay testimony was submitted from Benny Bentley, a co-worker of Elkins'[s]. Bentley testified he was working with Elkins on September 8, 2000.

He stated Elkins carried a five-gallon can of oil to the truck they were working on, and he indicated he had hurt his back and could not lift the oil. Bentley stated he performed all the lifting and completed servicing the truck. He stated Elkins returned to work in [a] supervisory capacity following his surgery and did no heavy work.

Id. at 2.

The employer argued that the 9.5 percent impairment rating was invalid as it did not conform with the *Guides.* The Court affirmed the 9.5 percent impairment rating based upon a 10 percent impairment for the 2000 injury and an apportionment subtraction under the *Guides* of .5 percent for the 1989 injury. The court reasoned:

> Next, Kentucky River contends that the ALJ erred in awarding benefits to Elkins for a permanent partial disability based upon the 9.5% functional impairment rating assessed by Dr. Templin since it was not calculated pursuant to the *AMA Guides.* In support of its argument, Kentucky River emphasizes that, under the DRE model (use of which is required unless specified conditions are met), impairment ratings are only assessed in 5% increments and, as such, Dr. Templin's 9.5% rating necessarily fails to comply with the *Guides.* As the Board has effectively addressed this argument, we reproduce that portion of its opinion below:

>> We would direct Kentucky River's attention to the fact that Dr. Templin actually assessed a 10% impairment rating, but excluded .5% as being due to preexisting active conditions. The 10% rating is explicitly based on the *AMA Guides* using the DRE Model. Since Dr. Templin's impairment [rating] is in fact based upon the *Guides*, we find no error with the ALJ's use of that rating.

>> Kentucky River also argues it was error for the ALJ to utilize an impairment rating that did not take into account the impairment attributable to Elkins'[s] 1989 injury. It relies on that portion of the Fourth Edition *AMA Guides* at Section 3.3f, p. 101, which provides:

>>> 9. From historical information and previously compiled medical data, determine if there was a preexisting impairment. If the previously compiled data can be verified as being accurate, they may be used in apportionment (see Glossary). The percent based on the previous findings would be subtracted from the percent based on the current findings.

>>> Kentucky River argues Dr. Kennedy assessed a 14% impairment in 1990 and that Dr. Sheridan and Dr. Ensalada both believed Elkins had a 10% preexisting impairment. Kentucky River therefore contends Elkins cannot receive income benefits since the only evidence of impairment indicates that his current impairment rating is no higher than the preexisting impairment.

> We must disagree with this argument also. We note that Dr. Sharma stated it is quite possible that Elkins may have ultimately recovered from the 1990 injury and surgery to the point he would not warrant an impairment rating. Furthermore, Dr. Templin assessed a 10% impairment, but excluded .5% as being due to a preexisting impairment. While it could be argued that Dr. Templin's method for assessing the preexisting impairment is not in keeping with the directives of the *Guides*, Kentucky River has not so argued. Since Dr. Templin did assess Elkins'[s] current impairment and then excluded the portion due to the preexisting impairment, we believe his methods, to that extent, comport with the *Guides*.

The Board's reasoning is sound; we agree that the ALJ did not err in opting not to exclude any additional impairment as being attributable to the 1989 injury. *Id.* at 6.

Shaffer v. Lourdes Hosp., 2000 WL 1763242 (Ky. Ct. App. Dec. 1, 2000)

In this appeal, the claimant was denied income benefits for permanent disability because she did not submit an impairment rating based on the *AMA Guides*, as was required under the statute in effect at the time of the injury (the timing was also an issue).

The claimant, who was employed as a hospital cook, sustained a series of injuries to her back in the course of her employment with the employer. She sustained her first two injuries in November 1991 and in February 1992. Although she received medical treatment after these injuries, and she was off work after the first incident, the claimant did not file a claim at that time. She asserts that she suffered another injury to her back on November 13, 1995, while she and a co-worker were lifting a pot of soup. Finally, the claimant testified that she sustained an additional injury to her back on August 1, 1996, when a large coworker slipped and fell on the claimant, elbowing her in the back. She stated that an incident report was filled out, but she did not seek medical treatment at that time, and she continued to work until May 23, 1997. The claimant has not worked since that time.

After a series of hearings, in which the claimant was awarded and denied income benefits several times, the Workers' Compensation Board affirmed the ALJ's denial of benefits, based on the failure to provide an impairment rating.

Originally, the claimant relied on medical records and the deposition testimony from her treating physician, Dr. [D.]. Dr. [D.] stated that the claimant's condition was a progression of the degenerative condition which first became symptomatic after the 1991 injury. While he agreed that the 1991 and 1992 injuries contributed to her condition, Dr. [D.] stated that the 1995 and 1996 injuries acted in a cumulative fashion resulting in the claimant's current low back condition. However, Dr. [D.] did not state the disability as a percentage of impairment under the *AMA Guides*.

The appeals court agreed with the board that a finding of either permanent partial disability or permanent total disability requires proof that the employee has a permanent disability rating. A permanent disability rating requires a permanent impairment rating, which in turn requires evidence of a rating of whole body impairment as determined by the *AMA Guides*. Thus, the claimant was required to present proof of an AMA rating to be eligible to receive income benefits.

The appeals court agreed with the board that the result was harsh considering the other evidence supporting the ALJ's finding that the claimant is totally occupationally disabled. It nonetheless refused to ignore the plain language of the statute that required the disability rating to be based upon an impairment rating and affirmed the denial of income benefits.

Knott County Nursing Home v. Wallen, 2001 WL 629401 (Ky. Ct. App. June 8, 2001)

The claimant, while working, fell and injured her lower back. As a consequence of these physical injuries, the claimant claimed psychiatric impairment. She was evaluated by Dr. [M.], a licensed clinical psychologist, and Dr. [C.], a psychiatrist.

Dr. [M.] diagnosed the claimant with major depression, pain disorder, borderline intellectual functioning, dependent traits, status post back injury with chronic intractable pain, and psychological and environmental problems. Using the *AMA Guides* (4th ed. 1993), Dr. [M.] assessed a Class 3 impairment. Dr. [M.] translated the claimant injuries into a 25 percent impairment rating. Dr. [C.] diagnosed the claimant with, inter alia, chronic dysthymia, personality disorder, and psychosocial stressors of financial compromise. Dr. [C.] opined that the claimant has a 0 percent whole-body psychiatric impairment due to her work-related accident.

The ALJ relied on Dr. [M]'s ratings and found the claimant to have a 35 percent whole-person impairment rating, 25 percent of which was attributable to her psychological impairment and 10 percent of which was attributed to her low back injury. The board affirmed the ALJ's ruling, and the appellate court in turn affirmed the board's ruling. The court noted that Dr. [M] assessed the mental impairment according to the *AMA Guides* (4th ed. 1993) as Class 3, then turned to the *AMA Guides* (2d ed. 1984) to assign a percentage. Dr. [M] reasoned that because a Class 3 impairment corresponds to moderate impairment, and because the *AMA Guides* (2d ed. 1984), when dealing with a moderate impairment, provides for estimating whole-body impairment in a range of 25 percent to 50 percent, the claimant's impairment could be estimated at 25 percent. The appeals court then adopted the board's reasoning:

> We believe that the argument raised by counsel in this case highlights the fact that often the legal community and the medical community are simply not operating on the same page. In order for there to be an award of permanent partial disability, the ALJ is bound to the formula contained in KRS 342. In order

to accomplish this, the ALJ must have in hand a functional impairment rating. The current edition of the *AMA Guides* on the other hand, state [sic] that there is no empiric evidence to support any method for assigning a percentage of impairment of the whole person. It seems to us it would border on absurdity to allow an ALJ to award permanent total disability in an injury case where there is also a psychiatric/psychological component wherein the medical expert testifies as to classification of impairment as opposed to percentages of impairment, and to deny another claimant a permanent partial disability award because there is a classification of impairment but no corresponding finding of a percentage of impairment. What remains is that we are left with clinical judgments which may not be based on empirical evidence but made of necessity. As Dr. [M.]'s Class 3 moderate impairment rating corresponds on the low end to the moderate impairment of 25% to 50% contained in the 1983 *Guides*, we can find no fault with, or any error in, the ALJ's reliance on that evidence.

2001 WL 629401, at *2.

Ball v. Big Elk Creek Coal Co., 1999 WL 1086306 (Ky. Ct. App. Nov. 19, 1999)

The Kentucky court dealt with a claimant who injured his low back. The ALJ found a 10 percent impairment based on DRE category III. The ALJ made the following findings of fact:

2. I am presented with three separate findings as to the functional impairment under the AM [sic] Guidelines. Dr. [T.] found a 17% impairment using the Range of Motion Model. Dr. [S.] found no impairment under the AMA Guidelines. Dr. [R.] assessed a 10% DRE Category 3 and/or in the alternative, a 20% under the Range of Motion Model.

3. The Defendant-Employer argues that Dr. [T.]'s assessment of impairment was incorrect in that the guidelines require that the DRE Model be used unless the diagnosis does not fall within the Diagnostic Related Estimates and a specific reason for not using the DRE model is set forth. I conclude after reading Dr. [T.]'s report that there is no basis for not using the DRE model. The "disagreement" plaintiff seeks to rely upon in using the Range of Motion Model is not a disagreement between two evaluating physicians, but the inability of one evaluating physician to "fit" the case into the DRE Model. This is not the case here.

Of the two remaining physicians, I am more convinced by the evidence given by Dr. [R.]. I find that plaintiff has sustained a 10% impairment to the body as a whole based upon DRE Category 3. Dr. [R.] specifically finds evidence of some radiculopathy. I, therefore, conclude that plaintiff's disability rating under the AMA Guidelines is 10%.

1999 WL 1086306, at *1–*2.

The claimant appealed on the basis that the ALJ should have been free to choose any impairment rating assigned by a doctor as long as the doctor used the

AMA Guides as a "guide" only, as opposed to a strict formula, in arriving at a functional impairment rating. The court affirmed the ALJ's decision. It reasoned:

> The Legislature, in its amendment to KRS 342.730, and since 1987, has required impairment ratings to be determined under the Guides to the Evaluation of Permanent Impairment, American Medical Association, latest edition available. The latest edition available currently is the 4th edition of the *Guides*. The *Guides*, 4th Edition, at chapter 3, § 3.3, p. 94, (AMA Guidelines) states: "The evaluator assessing the spine should use the Injury Model, if the patient's condition is one of those listed in Table 70 (p. 108). . . . If none of the eight categories of the Injury Model is applicable, then the evaluator should use the Range of Motion Model." Additionally, in § 3.3 at p. 94, (AMA Guidelines), the contributors to the *Guides* state:

>> For evaluating spine impairments, past *Guides* editions have used a system based on assessing the degree of spine motion and assigning impairment percents according to limitations of motion. Impairment percents related to the range of motion were to be combined with percents based on diagnoses or therapeutic approaches and neurologic impairments.

> The contributors to the *Guides*, as further stated in § 3.3, p. 94, (AMA Guidelines), state:
> In this edition of the *Guides*, the contributors have elected to use two approaches. One component, which applies especially to patients' traumatic injuries, is called the "Injury Model." This part involves assigning a patient to one of eight categories, such as minor injury, radiculopathy, loss of spine structure integrity, or paraplegia, on the basis of objective clinic findings. The other component is the "Range of Motion Model," described above and recommended in previous *Guides* editions.
> The AMA Guidelines further provide in this section:

>> All persons evaluating impairments according to *Guides* criteria are cautioned that either one or the other approach should be used in making the final impairment estimate. If one component were used according to *Guides* recommendations, then a final impairment estimate using the other component usually would not be pertinent or germane. However, if disagreement exists about the category of the Injury Model in which a patient's impairment belongs, then the Range of Motion Model may be applied to provide evidence on the question.

> The newer injury model has been designated under the AMA Guidelines as the "Diagnosis-Related Estimates (DRE) Model."
> In the specific procedures and directions for physicians performing evaluations in § 3.3f, p. 101 (AMA Guidelines), it is provided that:

>> 6. If the physician cannot place the patient into an impairment category, or if disagreement exists about which of two or three categories to use for

the patient, the physician should use the Range of Motion Model as a differientiator, as explained in section 3.3b (p. 95, "Differientiators").

Moreover, under § 3.3b, p. 99, the AMA Guidelines provide:

If the physician cannot decide into which DRE category the patient belongs, the physician may refer to and use the Range of Motion Model. . . . Using the procedures of that model, the physician combines an impairment percent based on the patient's diagnosis with a percent based on the patient's spine motion impairment and a percent based on neurologic impairment, if it is present. The physician uses the estimate determined with the Range of Motion Model to decide placement within one of the DRE categories. The proper DRE category is the one having the impairment percent that is closest to the impairment percent determined with the Range of Motion Model.

We agree with the interpretation given by the ALJ that the "disagreement" referred to in § 3.3 is not a disagreement among the evaluating physicians, but the inability of the evaluating physician himself to decide into which DRE category a patient belongs. Here, Dr. [R.] was able to decide that Ball was DRE Category III, or 10%. Dr. [R.] gave the 20% impairment rating based on the Range of Motion Model only at Ball's subsequent request. Further, Dr. [R.] did not use the 20% impairment rating to decide placement within any DRE Category.

The ALJ relied on the 10% impairment rating offered by Dr. [R.] since Dr. [R.] had specifically found evidence of radiculopathy or symptoms in [claimant]'s legs as a result of his low back injury. In reviewing the medical reports from each of the evaluating physicians, we note that [claimant] complained to each physician of occasional numbness, tingling or pain in his lower extremities since his low back injury. These are symptoms of radiculopathy.

Within the AMA Guidelines, DRE Lumbosacral Category III: Radiculopathy, under which Dr. [R.] determined that [claimant] had a 10% permanent impairment rating, the *Guides* state that: "The patient has significant signs of radiculopathy, such as loss of relevant reflex(es), or measured unilateral atrophy of greater than 2 cm. above or below the knee, compared to measurements on the contralateral side at the same location . . . ." Thus, we conclude that contrary to the assertion that ALJ's interpretation of what is required of an Administrative Law Judge in determination of a claimant's permanent impairment rating, the ALJ is not simply free to choose any functional impairment rating assigned by physicians unless the specific procedures and directions as contained in the Guidelines are undertaken. As the ALJ correctly noted, Dr. [T.], in his report, though he had identified one of [claimant]'s complaints as radiculopathy in the lower extremities, made no effort to offer an impairment rating utilizing the DRE Model as directed by the AMA Guidelines.

Id. at *2–*3.

Whittaker v. Johnson, 987 S.W.2d 320 (Ky. 1999)

The Kentucky court dealt with a claimant who injured his back and returned to light-duty work at full wages. He was rated at 5 percent functional impairment pursuant to the *AMA Guides*. After the injury, he returned to light-duty work at full wages. The ALJ who considered this workers' compensation claim determined that the claimant's injury had not resulted in any appreciable degree of permanent occupational disability, that half of the 5 percent functional impairment was active before the injury, and that the claimant was entitled to income benefits based on a 2.5 percent functional impairment.

At issue was whether an award of income benefits for permanent impairment was allowable without any showing of occupational disability. The court held that the worker needs to sustain at least some occupational disability in order to be entitled to an award. It reasoned that the statute's use of the word *impairment* rather than *disability* was a distinction without a practical difference. The court stated:

> It is undisputed that the legislative purpose of the 1994 amendment was to limit the amount of compensation which was paid to those workers with no present loss of income. Under those circumstances, we regard it as unlikely that the legislature intended to permit awards to workers who suffered no occupational disability whatsoever when it was unnecessary to do so in order to accomplish that goal. This is particularly true in view of the fact that such awards were not permitted before the amendment and in view of the fact that a finding of occupational disability is permitted by KRS 342.0011(11), even where the worker has suffered no present wage loss. Considering the premise underlying the decision in *Cook*, considering the fact that the word "impairment" is not used in describing the purpose of the award but in the formula for computing the amount of the award, and considering the apparent purpose of the 1994 amendment, we conclude that the legislature's choice of the word "impairment" rather than "disability" in the formula for computing an award pursuant to KRS 342.730(1)(b), although a more precise choice of language, was a distinction without a practical difference.
>
> Just as KRS 342.730(1)(c) [formerly KRS 342.730(1)(b)] requires the worker to have sustained at least some occupational disability as a threshold requirement for becoming entitled to an award of income benefits for permanent, partial disability, the amended version of KRS 342.730(1)(b) requires the worker to have sustained at least some occupational disability before becoming entitled to such an award. The formula for computing the minimum amount of an award pursuant to both subsections utilizes the figure for functional impairment which is determined by the *Guides*. The difference between subsections (1)(b) and (1)(c) is that in those instances where a worker can demonstrate a greater occupational disability but has suffered no present wage loss, the maximum award is limited to two times the worker's functional impairment.
>
> The decision of the Court of Appeals is hereby reversed. The ALJ's conclusion that the evidence in this case did not support a finding of

occupational disability is undisputed; therefore, the claim is remanded for further proceedings which are consistent with that finding.

987 S.W.2d at 324.

Newberg v. Price, 868 S.W.2d 92 (Ky. 1994)

The Kentucky Supreme Court dealt with a claimant who sought benefits for coal workers' pneumonoconiosis. Four different physicians measured the height of the claimant at 67, 68, 69¼, and 70 inches, respectively. The ALJ then determined that the claimant was 70 inches tall and recalculated the percent of normal represented by each of the reported spirometric values. He also determined that all the recalculated forced expiratory volume measurement (FEV_1) values were less than 80 percent of the predicted normal.

The court found that an ALJ cannot pick and choose among various height measurements, then recalculate the percent of normal by substituting a chosen height for that report. The court stated:

> There was no evidence whatever that the height measurement chosen by the ALJ was any more accurate than the others, and there was no stipulation as to height. Unlike *Newberg v. Wright*, this was not a case in which, even when using the most unfavorable height measurement, the claimant qualified for the greater benefit. Under the circumstances present herein and regardless of differences in the worker's reported height, the ALJ must rely on the height measurement and the percentages of normal represented by the worker's spirometric values as reported by each of the physicians. The evidence, as reported, supported the award of a retraining incentive benefit only. . . . We also remind litigants that the American Medical Association's *Guides to the Evaluation of Permanent Impairment* indicate that the worker's height should be measured in centimeters, not in inches as is commonly done and was done in the instant case. Because there are approximately 2.54 centimeters per inch, the use of a measuring device calibrated in centimeters should enhance the accuracy of measurement. Furthermore, measurement of the worker's height in centimeters would prevent computational errors which arise in converting inches to centimeters in order to use the tables containing predicted normal values. We also note that the *Guides* indicate that the worker's height should be measured with the worker standing in stocking feet.

Id. at 94. *See Newbert v. Wright*, 824 S.W.2d 843 (Ky. 1992).

Varney v. Newberg, 860 S.W.2d 752 (Ky. 1993)

The Kentucky Supreme Court dealt with the claimant, who developed coal workers' pneumoconiosis and filed a workers' compensation claim.

Dr. M. had examined the claimant on February 8, 1989, two days before the claimant's 60th birthday. Dr. M. reported that the claimant was 71 inches tall, that he had category 1 disease, that his forced vital capacity (FVC) value was 77 percent of the predicted normal, and that his FEV_1 value was 82 percent of the predicted normal. Dr. A. had examined the claimant a few weeks later, on March 13, 1989. He reported that the claimant was 72 inches tall, that he had category 1 disease, that his FVC value was 96 percent of the predicted normal, and that his FEV_1 value was 88 percent of the predicted normal. On deposition, however, it was discovered that Dr. A. had used an earlier edition of the *AMA Guides.* At the claimant's request, he recalculated his FEV_1 figure as being less than 80 percent of the predicted normal value, using the latest edition of the *AMA Guides.*

The court found that it was important that the physicians accurately measure the claimant's height in centimeters:

> We have observed that discrepancies in the various physicians' height measurements appear to occur relatively frequently in pneumoconiosis claims. We would remind litigants that the AMA guidelines indicate that a worker's height should be measured, not in inches but in centimeters, with the worker standing in his stocking feet.

Id. at 754. The court affirmed the award of a retraining incentive benefit and stated:

> When KRS 342.732(2) is applied to the facts of this case, it is clear this appeal must fail. Dr. [W.] reported an FVC value that was 89 percent of the predicted normal. Therefore, it is not necessary to consider Dr. [A.]'s 96 percent of normal value that was based on an earlier edition of the AMA guidelines. Dr. [M.] reported a FEV_1 value of 82 percent. Under these circumstances, a retraining incentive benefit is the maximum benefit to which claimant is entitled by law. KRS 342.732(1)(a).

Id. at 755.

Newberg v. Garrett, **858 S.W.2d 181 (Ky. 1993)**

The Kentucky Supreme Court dealt with the claimant who sought total disability benefits due to a combination of a back injury and coal workers' pneumoconiosis.

The Workers' Compensation Board was divided on the issue of whether the ALJ properly limited the claimant to a retraining incentive benefit rather than awarding a 75 percent permanent, partial occupational disability. The majority emphasized that there was no competent medical testimony and that the physicians' spirometric tests were invalid. The board ruled that the ALJ was required in this case (1) to rely on the two studies reported as valid and (2) to rely on the lower of the two statutorily required spirometric values, in this case the FVC value. Because the claimant's FVC values in the two valid studies were less than 80 percent of the predicted normal, the ALJ was required to award a 75 percent disability.

The court affirmed the award of a 75 percent disability based on coal workers' pneumoconiosis despite the fact that the two physicians testifying for the employer said the results were invalid due to poor patient effort. The court reasoned that no physician reviewed all the test results and came to the conclusion that the overall test results were invalid.

The court stated:

> Applying the foregoing to the instant case, we note that, although the ALJ explained in great detail why he had concluded that all the spirometric results in evidence were invalid, there was no medical testimony regarding precisely what relationship between a worker's FEV_1 value and MVV value indicates that the overall test results are invalid. Based on a comment, not by Dr. [B.], as stated by the ALJ, but by Dr. [M.], the ALJ determined that the large discrepancy between the FEV_1 and MVV values reported by Doctors [M.] and [B.] indicated invalid test results. However, no physician reviewed all of the reported test results and determined that to be the case. Furthermore, a review of the record indicates that the discrepancies in the FEV_1 and MVV values reported by Doctors [B.] and [M.] were substantially different. There was no evidence of how large a discrepancy between FEV_1 and MVV is necessary to indicate a poor patient effort or of the degree to which other factors might cause such a discrepancy.

Id. at 184–85.

The evidence of record compelled a finding that the claimant's greatest FVC value was less than 80 percent of the predicted normal and that the impairment resulted from his exposure to coal dust. Accordingly, the claimant was entitled to benefits pursuant to Ky. Rev. Stat. Ann. § 342.732(1)(b) (Baldwin).

Newberg v. Thomas Indus., 852 S.W.2d 339 (Ky. Ct. App. 1993)

The Kentucky court dealt with the claimant, who injured his back and neck at work. He was awarded a 10 percent permanent disability. An apportionment dispute arose, the issue being whether cervical vertebrae (vertebrae in the neck) are part of a worker's back for statutory purposes.

The court held that, based upon the *AMA Guides*, the back includes cervical vertebrae. The court stated:

> We understand the employer's argument concerning the popular and common distinction between "back" and "neck." However, for the purposes of Chapter 342 the Legislature has specifically provided at KRS 342.730(1)(b)2 that the American Medical Association's *Guides to the Evaluation of Permanent Impairment* (1977 edition) (*Guides*) is to be used in evaluating Workers' disabilities. The *Guides* on page one states: "The back is a unit of the whole man. It may be divided into three sections: the cervical, dorsal, and lumbar regions. The cervical region has seven vertebrae (C1–C7). The dorsal region has twelve vertebrae (D1–D12). The lumbar region has five vertebrae (L1–L5)." From

this definition it is clear that the "back" for the purposes of our Kentucky Workers' compensation law is to include the cervical vertebrae.

Id. at 340, 341.

Blue Diamond Coal/Scotia Coal v. Beale, 847 S.W.2d 61 (Ky. Ct. App. 1993)

The Kentucky court dealt with the claimant, whose work history reflected 20 years of coal dust exposure during his employment by Scotia. Additionally, the claimant had smoked since he was 14 years of age or younger.

The claimant was examined by seven physicians, all of whom testified that he had a forced expiratory volume measurement (FEV_1) of less than 55 percent of the expected normal.

Three physicians found positive evidence of coal workers' pneumoconiosis by x-ray. Three other physicians found no such evidence and attributed the claimant's respiratory impairment to cigarette smoking. The seventh physician found category 1/1 pneumoconiosis by x-ray, but was of the opinion that the claimant's respiratory impairment resulted from pulmonary emphysema induced by cigarette smoking.

The court affirmed the award of benefits finding that an irrebuttable presumption was created under the *AMA Guides* if either forced vital capacity (FVC) or FEV_1 fell below a certain percentage of predicted value.

The court stated:

> Table 8 of Chapter 5 of the latest (1988) AMA guidelines discussing classes of respiratory impairment "makes it clear that if either the FVC or the FEV_1 . . . is below a certain percentage of predicted value there is some impairment." Dr. [A.], one of the examining physicians, offered his interpretation of the AMA guidelines and concluded, solely on the basis of his FEV_1 value, that [claimant] suffered Class 4 impairment. We are satisfied that the AMA guidelines as interpreted by Dr. [A.] sufficiently support the ALJ's award. This Court may not reverse a decision of the Workers' Compensation Board unless the evidence compels a decision in the appellant's favor. That is not the situation here. Furthermore, a contrary interpretation of KRS 342.732(2) would undermine the statute's reliance on the AMA guidelines.

Id. at 62.

Beale v. Highwire, Inc., 843 S.W.2d 898 (Ky. Ct. App. 1993)

The Kentucky court dealt with the claimant, who was suffering from coal workers' pneumoconiosis, category 1. The ALJ took the testimony of six physicians but had to recalculate the claimant's spirometric performance because the physicians utilized inappropriate norms for the claimant's age and height.

The court found the recalculations by the judge proper and stated:

> The Special Fund first argues that the ALJ erred in recalculating [claimant]'s spirometric performance. We conclude that his action was proper. The statute specifically requires that the spirometric results be based on the values contained in the latest AMA guidelines. The guidelines provide for a consistent objective standard for evaluating test results. The ALJ did not conduct his own medical evaluation of [claimant], nor did he modify the volume measurements obtained by the physicians. He used the predicted normal values, together with [claimant]'s stipulated height of 69 inches, and recalculated the actual percent of deviation from the norms. The calculations by the ALJ did not require any medical expertise. It merely calculated [claimant]'s lung functions according to the predicted norms provided for one of his age and height in the guidelines. We conclude that the action by the ALJ was correct, proper, and administratively efficient.

Id. at 900.

The court went on to find that recovery is permitted if the work-caused lung deficiency is based on either his capacity or expiratory volume. The court stated:

> The Board's interpretation is supported by the 1984 edition of the AMA guidelines, and those guidelines were in effect when the statute was enacted. We do not believe the legislature intended to deprive a coal worker of benefits if his work-caused lung deficiency is based on either his capacity or expiratory volume. We conclude that the conjunctive "or" in subsection (2) allows recovery if the largest volume for either FVC or FEV_1 is less than 80 percent.

Id. at 901.

Wright v. Hopwood Mining, 832 S.W.2d 884 (Ky. 1992)

The Kentucky Supreme Court dealt with the claimant, who sought workers' compensation for coal workers' pneumoconiosis. The ALJ ruled that the claimant suffered from category 1 disease and awarded benefits. The issue became whether the ALJ may exercise discretion in choosing from among several of the claimant's spirometric test values. The FEV_1 spirometric test values upon which the ALJ awarded benefits follows in Table 9-1.

TABLE 11-1

The Claimant's Spirometric Test Values

Physician	FEV_1 value
Dr. P.	68.0%
Dr. M.	72.0%
Dr. B.	82.0%
Dr. L.	84.0%
Dr. A.	88.6%
Dr. D.	92.0%

The court ruled that the highest FVC and FEV_1 values must be used. The court stated:

> Considering the plain meaning of the language, the fact that spirometric test values are affected by the subject's effort, and the apparent attempt by the legislature to incorporate more objective standards for the award of benefits, we believe that the legislature clearly intended for none but the highest FVC value and the highest FEV_1 value to be considered in determining the level of benefits to be awarded.

Id. at 885.

Newberg v. Reynolds, 831 S.W.2d 170 (Ky. 1992)

The Kentucky Supreme Court dealt with the 54-year-old claimant who worked in coal mining for 33 years and developed pneumoconiosis. The ALJ reviewed the medical evidence and ruled that the claimant had contracted category 1 coal workers' pneumoconiosis. He noted that the highest FVC value was greater than 80 percent of the predicted normal value; however, the highest FEV_1 value was less than 80 percent but greater than 55 percent of the predicted normal value. Accordingly, the ALJ found that the claimant had sustained a 75 percent permanent, partial disability, and ruled that the claimant was entitled to benefits pursuant to Ky. Rev. Stat. Ann. § 342.732(1)(b) (Baldwin).

The court affirmed the award, finding that, based on the *AMA Guides*, the entire 75 percent permanent partial impairment was compensable. The court stated:

> We note also that both KRS 342.732(1)(b) and KRS 342.732(2) refer to "respiratory impairment resulting from exposure to coal dust." It is apparent when reviewing the American Medical Association's *Guides to the Evaluation of Permanent Impairment,* upon which the legislature relied in drafting these statutes, that depressed spirometric test values may measure respiratory impairment caused by factors other than exposure to coal dust. Therefore, in a claim for benefits pursuant to KRS 342.732(1)(b) the claimant must prove not only that his spirometric test results indicate the requisite degree of respiratory impairment, he must also prove that his exposure to coal dust was a significant factor in causing the impairment.
>
> * * *
>
> It is apparent from reading KRS 342.732 that the legislature sought to create a scheme of benefits for workers who had contracted coal Workers' pneumoconiosis. It is also apparent that they sought to award a higher level of benefits to those workers who demonstrated a respiratory impairment which resulted from exposure to coal dust in addition to demonstrating category 1 pneumoconiosis. Because there is no evidence that the degree of impairment attributable to exposure to coal dust and to smoking can be separated, there is at

present no medical basis to rule that a particular portion of the resulting occupational disability is not compensable because it is due to cigarette smoking. Furthermore, the legislature has provided no statutory formula for apportioning compensability.

831 S.W.2d at 172.

Newberg v. Wright, 824 S.W.2d 843 (Ky. 1992)

The Kentucky Supreme Court dealt with the claimant, who alleged he contracted category 1 coal workers' pneumoconiosis and was found to have sustained a 75 percent permanent partial disability. The judge had to check the calculation and choose the correct *AMA Guides* percentage. At the hearing on this case, counsel for the claimant argued that, although he had no dispute with the FEV_1 value reported by Dr. A., the calculation of that value as a percent of the predicted normal value for a man of the claimant's age and height was erroneous. Dr. A., who testified for the Special Fund, failed to state the claimant's height in his report. However, the spirometric tracing sheet, submitted with the report as required by Ky. Rev. Stat. Ann. § 342.316(2)(b)2.b. (Baldwin), indicated that the claimant's height was 70½ inches.

The ALJ noted that he was without authority to look behind the test values reported by the physicians; however, because Ky. Rev. Stat. Ann. § 342.732(1)(b) (Baldwin) requires the use of the *AMA Guides* to calculate the reported values as a percent of the predicted normal value, he did not have the authority to check the calculated percentage to ascertain that the *AMA Guides* were used and used correctly. According to the tables found in the *AMA Guides*, the predicted normal values are a function of age and height. Because Dr. A. had failed to state the claimant's height in his report, the ALJ used the height reported by Dr. W., the other medical expert, to find the appropriate normal value and to check Dr. A.'s calculation of the percent of predicted normal value represented by his 2.8 test value. When Dr. A.'s 2.8 test value was compared to the normal value for a 69-inch-tall, 61-year-old man, found in the appropriate table in the latest edition of the *AMA Guides*, the resulting percent of the predicted normal value was 78 percent.

The court found no error and stated:

> The Special Fund does not assert that the ALJ's percentage calculation was mathematically incorrect. Its argument is that the ALJ was without authority to check and to correct the erroneous percentage calculation. Under these circumstances, however, we believe that the ALJ did act within his authority when he checked the calculation of the percentage of normal represented by Dr. [A.]'s FEV_1 test value and when he found that the correct percentage represented by that value was 78 percent.

Id. at 844.

Newberg v. Chumley, 824 S.W.2d 413 (Ky. 1992)

The Kentucky Supreme Court dealt with the claimant, who was on total workers' compensation benefits for pneumoconiosis. He settled his workers' compensation case for $22,000 and proceeded against the Special Fund. The ALJ ruled that the claimant's radiographs indicated category 1 pneumoconiosis. The largest FVC was 76 percent, whereas the largest FEV_1 was 47 percent. Because the FVC value was greater than 55 percent, the Special Fund argued that the award of benefits pursuant to Ky. Rev. Stat. Ann. § 342.732(1)(c) (Baldwin) was erroneous.

The court held that the employee was entitled to total disability benefits and that the Special Fund was required to pay 75 percent of the lifetime award. The court found that, because the claimant exhibited spirometric test values of less than 55 percent, he was entitled to benefits. The court stated:

> According to the AMA *Guides to the Evaluation of Permanent Impairment* (*Guides*), upon which the legislature relies in KRS 342.732, spirometry is a forced expiratory maneuver which measures the ventilatory capacity of the lungs and indicates the degree of pulmonary impairment. There are three component parts of the maneuver: forced vital capacity (FVC), forced expiratory volume in the first second (FEV_1), and the ratio of these measurements expressed as a percentage (FEV_1/FVC ratio). The *Guides* indicate that forced vital capacity (FVC) is a valid and reliable index of significant pulmonary impairment due to interstitial, restrictive lung disease, such as coal Workers' pneumoconiosis. An abnormally low forced expiratory volume in the first second (FEV_1) indicates an obstructive pulmonary impairment, some causes of which are chronic bronchitis, emphysema, and asthma. The *Guides* note a high correlation between work status and FEV_1 values. Because the result of either test is affected by the degree of the patient's cooperation, the *Guides* indicate that the greatest result obtained on each test is the most accurate representation of the actual impairment. The *Guides* also indicate that a patient may suffer pulmonary impairment due to either restructive or obstructive disease, or due to both. An abnormally low value on either test indicates a respiratory impairment. KRS 342.316(2)(b)2.b., which governs the admissibility of evidence obtained by the spirometric testing, requires that FVC or FEV_1 values reported by a physician be the largest obtained from at least three acceptable spirometric maneuvers. The highest value reported by a physician for FVC or FEV_1, therefore, represents at least two other values, both of which are less than or equal to the value used in evidence. Where a claimant's highest FEV_1 value in evidence is less than 55 percent, he actually has exhibited at least three FEV_1 values of less than 55 percent to each physician who submitted medical evidence.

824 S.W.2d at 415.

Palmore v. Allgood, 767 S.W.2d 328 (Ky. Ct. App. 1989)

The claimant's neurosurgeon testified that the claimant incurred a 15 percent occupational disability to the body as a whole based on the *AMA Guides*. The neurosurgeon testified that 5 percent of the claimant's disability could be attributed to dormant, degenerative disk changes, and the remaining 10 percent could be attributed to the disk herniation the claimant suffered at work. The Workers' Compensation Board followed the neurosurgeon's conclusions in apportioning liability.

Cook v. Paducah Recapping Serv., 694 S.W.2d 684 (Ky. Ct. App. 1985)

This case raised the question whether the claimant could collect benefits even though his functional impairment was held not to result in an occupational disability. The court stated:

> Based upon the evaluation of the extent of functional impairment by physicians using the guidelines of the American Medical Association, it still remains the prerogative of the Workers' Compensation Board to translate the percentage of functional impairment into occupational disability, if any. If, as in this case, the Board determined that no occupational disability exists, there can be no award of benefits even though there does exist some functional impairment.

Id. at 687.

Vance v. Howell, slip. op. (Ky. Ct. App. Mar. 22, 1985)

This case was remanded for reevaluation in accordance with the *AMA Guides*. The Workers' Compensation Board must make the following two determinations: (1) the percentage of functional disability based on the *AMA Guides* and (2) the percentage of occupational disability. The board must award whichever is greater to the employee.

§11.15   LOUISIANA

Lanoue v. All Star Chevrolet, 867 So. 2d 755 (La. App. 1st Cir. 2003)

The Louisiana court dealt with a car saleswoman who received lacerations to and a fractured left arm as a result of a work-related accident. The case was remanded for an impairment rating under the *AMA Guides* because the claimant's physician had rated her impairment, not under the *AMA Guides*, but the "orthopedic surgeon's manual." The court stated:

> The claimant's treating physician, Dr. Joe A. Morgan, an orthopedist, opined that the claimant had a five-percent, permanent physical impairment to the left upper extremity from a fracture at her left elbow joint. However, in rendering this opinion, he acknowledged that the anatomical rating came from his "orthopedic surgeon's manual." Louisiana Revised Statute 23:1221(4)(q) specifically requires that the percentage of anatomical loss of use as provided in subparagraph (o) must be "as established in the most recent edition of the

American Medical Association's 'Guides to the Evaluation of Permanent Impairment'" in order for benefits to be awarded under La. R.S. 23:1221(4). Since Dr. Morgan indicated that his rating was based simply on his orthopedic surgeon's manual, benefits for permanent partial disability cannot be awarded on the basis of this evidence. We will, therefore, remand this matter to the OWC for the taking of additional evidence as to the extent of the claimant's anatomical loss of use under the American Medical Association's "Guides to the Evaluation of Permanent Impairment." Thereafter, the WCJ should determine whether the claimant is entitled to permanent partial disability benefits under La. R.S. 23:1221(4). *See Durbin v. State Farm Fire & Casualty Company*, 558 So.2d 1257, 1261 (La. App. 1st Cir. 1990).

Wise v. Lapworth, 614 So. 2d 728 (La. Ct. App. 1993)

The Louisiana court dealt with the claimant, who, on September 22, 1988, fell 22 feet off a roof and fractured his elbow. As a result, he developed arthritis and had continuing pain. When the claimant sought permanent partial compensation, his claim was denied because he failed to overcome the 25 percent impairment threshold.

At the trial, the testimony of the physician as to a disability rating was excluded because of discovery agreements among counsel.

The court affirmed the denial and stated:

In order to recover benefits under the workers' compensation statutes, a worker must show that he falls within one of the scheduled provisions in La. R. S. 23:1221. The statute provides for temporary total disability, permanent total disability, supplemental earnings benefits, and permanent partial disability. Wise has not proved any total disability. Therefore, the categories of temporary total disability and permanent total disability are inapplicable.

Under the permanent partial disability provision, Wise must prove a loss of use of physical function greater than 25 percent as established in the American Medical Association "Guides to the Evaluation of Permanent Impairment," copyright 1984. See: La. R.S. 23:1221(4)(q), amendment eff. January 1, 1986. Wise was unable to show any disability rating at trial, due to the exclusion of Dr. [A.]'s testimony and his failure to produce any other evidence in this regard. Therefore, he has not borne his burden of proof for benefits under this provision.

Id. at 733.

Durbin v. State Farm Fire & Casualty Co., 558 So. 2d 1257 (La. Ct. App. 1990)

The claimant, a television repairman, injured his knee on the job and was awarded workers' compensation benefits. The employer and the insurer appealed the finding that the claimant had a 45 percent permanent partial impairment of his left knee. La. Rev. Stat. Ann. § 23:1221(4) (West) provides that no benefits shall be awarded for permanent partial disability unless anatomical loss of use or amputation or loss of function is greater than 50 percent as established in the *AMA Guides.* The claimant's physician testified that the claimant suffered a 45 percent permanent partial disability based on *The Standard Textbook of Orthopedics for Rating Permanent Physical Impairments.*

> Since the trial court relied on Dr. [K.]'s assessment of disability and his assessment was not based on the American Medical Association (AMA) guidelines as required by La. R.S. 23:1221(4)(q), the trial court erred in finding [claimant] permanently partially disabled. *See Sumrall v. Crown Zellerbach Corporation,* 525 So. 2d 272 (La. Ct. App. 1st Cir. 1988). Since the record does not contain any other evidence of the extent of [claimant]'s disability, we think it is appropriate to remand this case to the trial court for the taking of additional evidence as to the extent of [claimant]'s disability under the AMA guidelines.

558 So. 2d at 1261.

Sumrall v. Crown Zellerbach Corp., 525 So. 2d 272 (La. Ct. App. 1988)

The claimant sustained an accidental injury to his right knee in the course and scope of his employment. The employer appealed the trial court's award of permanent partial disability benefits, and the court of appeals vacated the award, finding that the statute (requiring that permanent partial disability be found only when the loss of use is greater than 50 percent as established by the *AMA Guides*) did not permit the use of lay testimony in determining the percentage of disability. The court also stated that a physician's evaluation that did not indicate whether the *AMA Guides* were followed could not be used in determining the extent of the claimant's disability.

Two of the disability evaluations did not indicate whether the *AMA Guides* were used. A third evaluation was based on the *AMA Guides* as well as the *AAOS Manual*, published by the AAOS. Because the statutory provision in question was new and had as yet received little interpretation or application, the court found it appropriate to remand the case for the taking of additional evidence.

Anderson v. Aetna Casualty & Sur. Co., 505 So. 2d 199 (La. Ct. App. 1987)

The claimant slipped and injured his knee for the second time while loading a fertilizer truck. The court found that the claimant did not suffer from a permanent partial disability, which was compensable under La. Rev. Stat. Ann. § 23:1221(4) (West). Under the statute as it existed at the time of the claimant's injury, the claimant would have had to establish that his loss of function or use was greater than 50 percent as established by the *AMA Guides.* (The Louisiana legislature subsequently amended this statute and reduced the required percentage to 25 percent loss of function or use.).

Captain v. Sonnier Timber Co., 503 So. 2d 689 (La. Ct. App. 1987)

The claimant suffered a fracture of the distal third of his left fibula and a severely sprained ankle. The fracture healed without complications, but the sprain continued to cause problems. The claimant sought an award for permanent partial disability. The court pointed out that 1983 amendments to the Workers' Compensation Act changed the provisions covering permanent impairment. The new act provided for what were referred to as "schedule benefits" under the old law, under the heading of "permanent partial disability." However, as the court pointed out, these benefits are limited by La. Rev. Stat. Ann. § 23:1221(4)(q) (West), which, at the time of the accident, stated that no benefits shall be awarded unless the anatomical loss of use or amputation is greater than 50 percent as established in the *AMA Guides*.

> Since the degree of impairment will be determined by medical experts, and since the statute dictates the effect of that determination on the benefits available to a claimant, legal evaluation of disability under this paragraph is foreclosed. Dr. [C.] assigned impairment values of 20 percent of the foot and ankle, or 16 percent of the left leg. Since the statute stated that permanent partial disability benefits shall not be awarded for an impairment of less than 50 percent, [claimant] is not entitled to recover under this paragraph. (We note that the harshness of this provision has been ameliorated by a reduction of this threshold from 50 percent to 25 percent. 1985 La. Acts. No. 926.)

503 So. 2d at 692.

§ 11.16   MAINE

Bourgoin v. J.P. Levesque & Sons, 726 A.2d 201 (Me. 1999)

The Maine court dealt with a client who suffered a 23 percent whole-person permanent impairment resulting from his work-related back injury. The claimant, citing the language of the *AMA Guides*, also sought an impairment award for his preexisting diabetic condition. The court affirmed the denial of benefits for his preexisting nonwork injury. The court stated:

> Bourgoin relies, in part, on the reference to the American Medical Association, *Guides to the Evaluation of Permanent Impairment* (2d ed. 1984). The foreword to the *AMA Guides* discusses the consideration of "all physical and mental impairments" when determining whole body permanent impairment. *Id.* at iii. The *AMA Guides* also discuss, however, the necessity of, and procedure for, apportioning impairment between work and nonwork causes in various legal contexts where apportionment is required. *Id.* at ix. We, therefore, are not persuaded that the reference in the statute to the *AMA Guides* demonstrates a legislative intent to make an employer liable for permanent impairment benefits resulting from a preexisting and wholly nonwork condition.

726 A.2d at 203.

§11.17 MARYLAND

Getson v. WM Babcorp, 694 A.2d 961 (Md. 1997)

The Maryland court dealt with a claimant who suffered a work-related injury to his shoulder. At issue was whether this injury was properly classified as a scheduled injury to the arm or as a catchall "other cases" injury. The court held that the shoulder injury was not a scheduled injury to the arm. The court reasoned that the *AMA Guides* cannot be used to determine which body parts the "arm" includes. The court stated:

> As the legislative history illustrates, the General Assembly initially adopted the *AMA Guides* as an interim method of evaluation for use until the Commission adopted guides for permanent evaluation. The Commission then promulgated COMAR 14.09.04, which incorporates by reference certain provisions of the *AMA Guides*. Section 9-721, the current version of the statute governing evaluation of permanent impairment, mandates that physicians evaluate permanent impairment in accordance with the Commission's regulations and sets out certain types of information that must be included in the evaluation. *See Sears Roebuck v. Ralph*, 340 Md. 304, 313, 666 A.2d 1239, 1243 (1995) (discussing legislative history of § 9-721).
>
> This legislative history does not reveal an intent on the part of the General Assembly to incorporate the terminology of the *AMA Guides*. In fact, the General Assembly adopted the *AMA Guides* solely as interim guides to be used until the Commission promulgated guides of its own. The provision of § 36C that referred to the *AMA Guides* was deleted as obsolete when § 36C was placed in Title 9 of the Labor and Employment Article. Maryland Laws 1991, ch. 8, at 946 (Revisor's Notes). The current version of § 9-721 does not mention the *AMA Guides*, but refers only generally to the Commission's regulations. We agree with the circuit court and Court of Special Appeals that "the plain meaning of the statute is devoid of any such intent to 'enact the AMA' division of body parts."
>
> Furthermore, COMAR 14.09.04.01 incorporates by reference only those provisions of the *AMA Guides* that are specified in COMAR 14.09.04.02; the Commission did not incorporate the entire *AMA Guides*. COMAR 14.09.04.02 does not refer to the *AMA Guides'* terminology, but rather requires that evaluating physicians employ the numerical ratings and the reporting format from the *AMA Guides*. Nowhere does the regulation mandate or suggest that the particular terminology used in the *AMA Guides* substantively changes workers' compensation law.
>
> In summary, nothing in the statutes, regulation, nor in the *AMA Guides* disturbs § 9-627's division of injuries into those specifically listed and those "Other cases" addressed by § 9-627(k). Section 9-627 specifically lists loss of an arm, but it fails to mention loss of a shoulder. Incorporating portions of the *AMA Guides* in an administrative regulation cannot rewrite § 9-627. The circuit court did not err in affirming the Commission's award of permanent partial disability benefits based on § 9-627(k), "Other cases."

694 A.2d at 966–67.

Sears, Roebuck & Co. v. Ralph, **666 A.2d 1239 (Md. 1995)**

The Maryland court dealt with a claimant who injured his lower back at work. The claimant saw his physician on several occasions after the accident and died of unrelated causes nine months after his accident. Four months after the claimant's death, the claimant's physician prepared a report opining that the claimant had suffered a 40 percent permanent impairment according to the *AMA Guides* (3d ed. 1988). The appellants challenged the validity of this posthumous rating. The court dismissed the challenge and noted that the physician had seen and examined the claimant several times before his death. The court stated:

> Where the underlying information and data obtained by the physician during the decedent's lifetime enable the physician to express a permanent impairment evaluation in conformity with the *Guides*, nothing in the statutes, the legislative history, or the regulations excludes that evaluation simply because the underlying information and data had not been expressed in the form of a *Guides*-complying report until after the claimant's death.

Id. at 1243.

The court noted that it did not address the issue of whether the physician's report was in strict accordance with the *AMA Guides* or what the sanction might be if the court found that there had not been strict compliance.

§ 11.18   MINNESOTA

Deschampe v. Arrowhead Tree Serv., **428 N.W.2d 795 (Minn. 1988)**

The claimant sustained a severe closed head injury as a result of a fall from a tree. The workers' compensation judge (WCJ) found that the claimant was 88.1 percent permanently partially disabled. The workers' compensation court of appeals affirmed some of the findings regarding the percentage of whole-body disability for certain impairments and modified others, substituting its own finding that the claimant sustained a 97.9 percent permanent partial disability. The Minnesota Supreme Court held that the court of appeals exceeded its authority in substituting a 70 percent rating for the WCJ's 50 percent rating as to complex integrated cerebral function disturbance. The supreme court held that where the assignment of permanent partial disability ratings under two or more sections of the brain injury subpart of the central nervous system schedule was necessary to represent the employee's disablement, the ratings for two or more categories of impairment may be combined using the statutory formula.

> We recognize that the AMA *Guides to the Evaluation of Permanent Impairment* limits disability ratings for permanent impairment resulting from dysfunction of the brain to one category of impairment even though the brain injury may result in more than one category of impairment. *AMA Guides* 61–66

(2d ed. 1984). The disability schedule for the central nervous system, however, neither references the *AMA Guides*, see Minn. Rule 5223.0010, subp. 4 (1984), nor includes any limiting language.

Id. at 800 n.1.

§ 11.19 MISSISSIPPI

Smith v. Jackson Constr. Co., 607 So. 2d 1119 (Miss. 1992)

The Mississippi Supreme Court dealt with the claimant, who was injured when a jackhammer fell and hit his leg. He was left with chronic osteomyelitis and a venous problem.

The permanent impairment was rated by the physician in the following manner:

> Applying the 1984 American Medical Association Guides to the Evaluation of Permanent Impairment (2d ed. 1984), Dr. [S.] believed that the venous problem caused [claimant] a permanent medical impairment of 15 percent of the body as a whole or a 30 percent permanent partial impairment to his leg. Dr. [S.] not only believed that [claimant] was temporarily totally disabled from the time he first saw [claimant] until he reached a maximum medical recovery, but that [claimant] was also probably temporarily totally disabled from the time of his injury until he saw Dr. [S.]. Dr. [S.] further testified that [claimant]'s condition would cause him work limitations because standing in one position for five or ten minutes would be unhealthy and he would have to be able to sit down and elevate his leg if it began to hurt or swell.

Id. at 1122.

The court went on to find, however, that when a claimant is permanently and totally disabled, the claimant should be entitled to permanent and total workers' compensation and not just a permanent partial disability award.

§ 11.20 MONTANA

S.L.H. v. State Compensation Mut. Ins. Fund, 15 P.3d 948, 2000 MT 362 (Mont. Dec. 28, 2000)

In November 1991, the claimant was kidnapped from her job as a bartender and severely beaten and raped. The claimant's employer was enrolled in a compensation plan and insured by the State Fund. The State Fund accepted liability for the claimant's injuries, though it disputed the claimant's permanent mental impairments. The trial court found that the claimant had a 1 percent mental impairment rating and denied benefits. The claimant appealed the claim.

The claimant's psychiatrist, Dr. E., diagnosed the claimant with post-traumatic stress disorder and major depressive disorder. Dr. E. then evaluated the claimant's impairments using the *AMA Guides*. The claimant was also referred to Dr. G. for a physical impairment rating. Although Dr. G. is neither a psychologist nor a psychiatrist, and was asked to evaluate only the claimant's physical impairment, he provided a mental impairment evaluation as well.

At trial Dr. E. testified that the claimant's mental impairments were mild to moderate, falling between classes 2 and 3 according to the *AMA Guides*. The state statute at issue, § 39-71-711, MCA, which provides the procedure for rating impairments, requires that the rating must not only be "based on the current edition of [the *AMA Guides*]," it "must be expressed as a percentage of the whole person." The trial court read this to require that an impairment rating be expressed by *the evaluator* as a percentage. Thus, the court asked Dr. E. to provide a percentage for the claimant's mental impairments. Abiding by the *AMA Guides'* warning against assigning percentages to mental impairments, Dr. E. refused to translate the claimant's mental impairment evaluation into a percentage. The Workers' Compensation Court did not question the accuracy and validity of Dr. E.'s evaluation, and in fact, the court concluded that the claimant suffered "severe psychological injuries." Nonetheless, the court held it was insufficient to satisfy the percentage requirement in § 39–71-711(1)(c), MCA. Dr. G., on the other hand, in contravention of the *AMA Guides'* admonishment, but in compliance with § 39–71-711(1)(c), MCA, expressed his ratings of the claimant's mental impairments as percentages: 1 percent for her post-traumatic stress disorder and 0 percent for her major depressive disorder. Relying on Dr. G.'s impairment ratings, which were the only percentages provided by an impairment evaluator, the court found that the claimant suffered a 1 percent permanent mental impairment rating.

The appeals court then considered whether the court erred when it held that Dr. E.'s inability to express her evaluation of the claimant's mental impairments as a percentage was fatal to her claim.

The claimant contended that the statute contains an internal inconsistency, because the *AMA Guides* (3d ed. 1988) and *AMA Guides* (4th ed. 1993) specifically advise practitioners against the use of percentages for mental impairments.

The appellate court concluded that the trial court erred in its reading of the statute as requiring *the evaluator* to express her evaluation of impairment as a percentage. Thus, it erred when it required that Dr. E. translate her evaluation into percentages before it would consider the evaluation for impairment rating purposes. In its analysis, the appellate court found that the statute contained no express language stating who must translate the impairment evaluation into a percentage. It stated that the court's interpretation asked Dr. E. to do the impossible—both express mental impairments as a percentage and base her evaluation on the current *AMA Guides*, which proscribes the use of percentages to express mental impairments. The appellate court found that the statute does not specifically require that the evaluator be the one translating the impairment evaluation into a percentage. It concluded that the court could have reached a more reasonable result and furthered the legislative intent by examining the plain language of the statute for a more reasonable alternative. It reversed the court's finding regarding mental impairment and remanded it so that the Workers' Compensation Court can assign a percentage based on the evidence in the record for the claimant's mental impairment.

§11.21 NEBRASKA

Jacob v. Columbia Ins. Group, 511 N.W.2d 211 (Neb. Ct. App. 1994)

The Nebraska court dealt with the claimant, who got his hand caught in a sanding machine while working as a cabinet maker. Before he could be released, most of his hand and the skin and flesh up to the middle of his forearm had been sanded off. The injuries to the claimant's hand and forearm were very extensive. For a time, the doctors considered amputating the left hand, although they were ultimately able to save part of it. The part of the hand that remained was of questionable utility. Between October 23, 1989, and April 1992, the claimant underwent skin-grafting procedures, operations to insert and remove plastic rods that ran from his forearm to his hand, procedures for the reconstruction of the tendons in his arm, fusion of a joint in his little finger, and other procedures.

The physician rated the impairment of the hand at 92 percent. He testified as follows:

Q. You didn't do any analyses or subjective analyses of the ability to use the hand before and after 1989 in arriving at your opinions, did you?

A. No.

Q. It's strictly the math that comes out of the [*AMA Guides*]?

A. That's correct.

Q. So if [claimant]'s testimony was to the effect that his left hand was nothing more than an object that he could use to push and pull other things with, you would disagree with him in that regard?

A. I would still state that he has 92 percent loss of that hand.

Q. Because you perform your calculations and you go back to the book and decide what the extent is and then you reduce it by whatever may have been created, again by the book, in the 1984 accident?

A. That's correct.

The court awarded a 100 percent loss of the hand, finding that the hand was useless. The court stated:

His testimony ignores that part of Sec. 48–121(3) which states, "Permanent total loss of the use of a finger, hand, arm, foot, leg, or eye shall be considered as the equivalent of the loss of such finger, hand, arm, foot, leg, or eye." Dr. [G.] clearly did not consider the evidence on the usefulness of the hand, because the *AMA Guide*[s] did not provide for such a consideration, and therefore, his testimony that [claimant] suffered only a 92 percent impairment of the hand is not properly based on the evidence presented and the applicable statute.

The determination of the usefulness of [claimant]'s left hand is hardly a medical question. It is obvious that [claimant]'s hand is useless for industrial purposes, although he may get some incidental, de minimis benefit from it. We find as a matter of law that the hand is useless and that [claimant] has suffered 100 percent disability to his left hand.

Id. at 219.

§ 11.22   NEVADA

***Rosser v. State ex rel. State Indus. Ins. Sys.*, 113 Nev. 1125, 946 P.2d 185 (1997)**

The Nevada court dealt with a claimant who had a preexisting 36 percent whole-person impairment under the *AMA Guides* due to valvular heart disease and arrhythmias. The claimant was later found to be permanently and totally disabled as a result of post-traumatic stress disorder. The court was asked to decide whether the 36 percent *impairment* rating under the *AMA Guides* should be used to apportion and reduce the claimant's permanent total *disability*. The court stated:

> [Claimant] contends that an apportionment of a permanent total disability is improper if the preexisting condition is non-disabling. He maintains that respondents were not justified in apportioning thirty-six percent of his PTD [permanent total disability] award because he was not disabled by his preexisting heart condition. Thus, [claimant]'s argument turns on whether his heart condition constituted a "disability" for purposes of 616.580(1)(b).
>
> He also contends that the *AMA Guides* should not have been utilized because they are inapplicable to PTD claims.
>
> * * *
>
> Respondents contend that permanent total disability awards under NRS 616.580(1)(b) should be determined in the same manner as permanent *partial* disabilities under NRS 616.605(6), to wit: by utilization of the American Medical Association's *Guides to the Evaluation of Permanent Impairment* ("AMA Guides"). This position is taken despite the fact that NRS 616.580, the PTD apportionment statute, failed to provide its own mechanism or formula for the apportionment of prior existing disabilities.
>
> * * *
>
> First we note that the American Medical Association itself has recognized that the *AMA Guides* are ill equipped to rate such subjective factors as one's age, training or education. Although the legislature has concluded that the guides are appropriate for evaluation of partial disabilities, we believe that the omission of the *AMA Guides* from the PTD provisions was based on legitimate concerns that such apportionments would be arbitrary or that the *AMA Guides* had less validity in the context of PTD awards. Thus, we hold that the *Guides* are but one of a number of resources that can be utilized in assessing the degree to which apportionment is appropriate.
>
> * * *

On remand, the SIIS must support its decision to apportion [claimant]'s PTD award with documentation comprehensively addressing the scope and nature of [claimant]'s preexisting heart condition. SIIS must, per *Bokelman*, establish that [claimant]'s heart problems, separate and apart from the societal factors causing "odd-lot" disability prevented him from returning to the work force in some other reasonably constructive capacity. Thus, the SIIS must provide substantive documentation correlating application of the *AMA Guide[s]*.

13 Nev. Adv. Opinion at 4–8.

Maxwell v. SIIS, 849 P.2d 267 (Nev. 1993)

The Nevada Supreme Court dealt with the claimant, who fell at work. The claimant was offered a 15 percent impairment for her back and disfigurement and a 5 percent impairment for psychological problems.

In Nevada, Nev. Rev. Stat. § 616.605(2) provides that the percentage of disability is to be determined in accordance with the *AMA Guides*. However, Nev. Rev. Stat. § 616.605(3) provides that "no factors other than the degree of physical impairment of the whole man may be considered in calculating the entitlement to compensate for a permanent partial disability."

The court found that Nevada does not permit an award for psychological conditions despite the specific language of the *AMA Guides*. The court stated:

The language of NRS 616.605(3) is too clear and explicit to interpret in any manner other than according to its plain meaning. We hold that the language of NRS 616.605(3) limiting permanent partial disability awards to awards for "physical impairment" precludes the award of compensation for psychological conditions resulting from an industrial accident, including Maxwell's resulting depression. While we realize that psychological impairment can be just as debilitating as any physical malady, NRS 616.605(3) represents a clear legislative mandate restricting permanent partial disability awards to physical injuries. We accept that mandate, and we decline to construe NRS 616.605 in a manner which distorts the legislature's will.

849 P.2d at 267.

Ransier v. State Indus. Ins. Sys., 766 P.2d 274 (Nev. 1988)

The claimant, a carpenter, injured his right knee while working in 1984, the same knee for which the claimant had undergone surgery in 1960. The knee failed to respond to treatment, and the joint was eventually replaced. The Nevada Supreme Court held there was sufficient evidence to support the decision to apportion the worker's medical disability, and that the rating physicians properly used the most recent edition of the *AMA Guides*.

The claimant argued that the rating physicians improperly used the *AMA Guides* (2d ed. 1984) rather than a previous edition that was in effect when the injury occurred. The prior edition would have provided an increased impairment rating. Nev. Rev. Stat. § 616.625 provides that "except as otherwise provided by specific statute, the amount of compensation and benefits . . . must be determined as of the date of the accident or injury to the employee." However, the supreme court notes that Nev. Rev. Stat. § 616.605(2) specifically provides that physicians must use the most recent edition of the *AMA Guides.*

§ 11.23   NEW HAMPSHIRE

Appeal of Fournier, 786 A.2d 854 (N.H. 2001)

The New Hampshire Supreme Court dealt with a claimant who developed carpal tunnel syndrome in her right wrist in May 1992. Both her treating physician and the IME physician rated her at a 10 percent impairment of the right upper extremity under the fourth edition of the *Guides.* Previously, in 1986, the claimant was diagnosed with a work-related thoracic outlet syndrome and was awarded 25 percent permanent partial disability for her right upper extremity. The court held that the proper way to deal with the previous injury to a different area of the upper extremity was to combine the impairment percentages for the two injuries and then subtract off the previous 25 percent impairment. This resulted in an additional 8 percent impairment. The court reasoned:

> The employer contends that nothing in these opinions indicates that the doctors intended the ten percent impairment to be in addition to the twenty-five percent previously awarded. The petitioner argues that the ten percent impairment was intended to be in addition to her prior award because both doctors knew of her prior injury and were asked to opine about the impairment related to her carpal tunnel syndrome only. The petitioner cites a letter from the employer's counsel to Dr. O'Neil forwarding the petitioner's medical records and stating: "Ms. Fournier does seem to have a history of extremity problems dating back over ten years. I am particularly interested only in that permanency which may relate specifically to the injury which she claims to have incurred around May 1992 when she began to develop carpal tunnel like symptoms."
>
> The petitioner also contends that the doctors' opinions could have been clarified by the *AMA Guides to the Evaluation of Permanent Impairment* (4th ed. 1993) (*Guides*), which she claims the CAB refused to consider. The petitioner argues that the *Guides* should have been consulted because their use is required by administrative rule and both doctors referenced them in their opinions. See N.H. Admin. Rules, Lab 508.01(d).
>
> The employer argues that the CAB properly refused to accept the *Guides* because our remand order did not contemplate considering new evidence. In addition, the employer notes that the doctors' opinions reference only a single table from the *Guides* and do not indicate that they used the section relied upon by the petitioner. Finally, the employer argues that the panel could not review the *Guides* on its own, but rather required competent medical expert testimony to explain the *Guides'* use.

We disagree with the employer's characterization of the *Guides* as "evidence," and conclude that the CAB could have properly considered the *Guides* because their use is required by administrative rule, as authorized by statute. *See* N.H. Admin. Rules, Lab 508.01(d); RSA 281-A:32, XIV (Supp. 2000). We therefore examine the *Guides* to evaluate the legal sufficiency of a doctor's permanent impairment assessment. *See Appeal of Rainville*, 143 N.H. 624, 631, 732 A.2d 406 (1999).

The petitioner contends that because the *Guides* instruct doctors evaluating a current impairment to subtract any previous impairment, Doctors Kilgus and O'Neil must have subtracted the prior twenty-five percent impairment in arriving at the ten percent impairment assessment related to the carpal tunnel syndrome. We disagree. The *Guides* do not instruct doctors, as a matter of course, to subtract a previous impairment. They require such a procedure if "apportionment" of an impairment is necessary. *Guides* at 2/10. "Apportionment" is a term of art in the *Guides* which is defined as "an estimate of the degree to which each of various occupational or non-occupational factors may have caused or contributed to a particular impairment." *Id.* at 3/15. Thus, apportionment would be appropriate if, for instance, the petitioner had had a previous carpal tunnel injury caused by something other than her work for the employer.

The petitioner herself, however, insists that the previous twenty-five percent impairment award and the ten percent impairment award she now seeks relate to separate injuries to different portions of her right upper extremity; namely, an injury to her neck and shoulder in 1984 and an injury to her wrist in 1992. Where different portions of the same upper extremity are affected, the *Guides* instruct that "the hand, wrist, elbow, and shoulder impairments are combined using the Combined Values Chart . . . to determine the total upper extremity impairment," which is then "converted to a wholeperson impairment using Table 3." *Id.* at 3/15; *see also id.* at 3/24.

The record before us indicates that both Dr. Kilgus and Dr. O'Neil assessed only the upper extremity impairment due to the petitioner's carpal tunnel syndrome. Specifically, both doctors stated that their assessment was taken from Table 16 on page 3/57 of the *Guides*, which estimates upper extremity impairment due to entrapment neuropathy. *See id.* at 3/56-3/57. Neither doctor purported to assess an impairment rating for any other condition.

As the foregoing indicates, however, this conclusion does not mean that the petitioner is entitled to an additional ten percent upper extremity impairment award, for a total award of thirty-five percent. Rather, the petitioner's upper extremity impairments would be combined according to the Combined Values Chart in the *Guides*. *See id.* at 2/8. Using the Combined Values Chart, a twenty-five percent shoulder impairment combined with a ten percent entrapment neuropathy impairment would result in a total upper extremity impairment of thirty-three percent. *See id.* at 3/22. Thus, we conclude that the additional upper extremity impairment attributable to the petitioner's carpal tunnel syndrome is thirty-three percent minus twenty-five percent, or eight percent. Since RSA 281-A:32, IX directs the award to be calculated according to the percent of whole person impairment, the petitioner is entitled to a five percent whole person impairment in accordance with Table 3 at page 3/20 of the *Guides*.

Id. at 857.

Appeal of Cote, **781 A.2d 1006 (N.H. 2001)**

The New Hampshire Supreme court dealt with a claimant who injured his back at work. The claimant's physician evaluated the claimant at 20 percent impairment under the range-of-motion model. The employer's physician assigned a 5 percent impairment under the injury model, even though the employer's physician never physically examined the claimant. The Compensation Appeals Board rejected the claimant's expert's testimony, as it was based on the injury model, and accepted the employer's expert's rating even though he never physically examined the claimant. The supreme court upheld the board's decision to give credence to the employer's expert, but vacated and remanded to allow the claimant to present expert evidence based on the injury model.

In re Wal-Mart Stores, **765 A.2d 168 (N.H. Dec. 28, 2000)**

While employed, the claimant injured his left shoulder lifting and separating snow blowers. The neurosurgeon who operated on the respondent determined that he suffered a 28 percent permanent impairment. An independent physician retained by the insurance carrier calculated his impairment at 15 percent. The board awarded compensation based on the 28 percent figure. The employer appealed the decision, contending that there was a conflict of interest on the board, and, *inter alia*, that the 28 percent rating deviated from the applicable *AMA Guides*. The appellate court remanded the case because a member of the Compensation Appeals Board, after hearing the case but before issuing a decision, took up the representation of an injured worker against the employer. The appellate court also considered the neurosurgeon's method of evaluation, because the issue would likely come up in the rehearing.

The court noted that a state statute, RSA 281-A:32 (1999) controls the determination of permanent impairment awards, then stated, "Paragraph IX of that section identifies the *AMA Guides* to be used in making evaluations for such awards." 765 A.2d at 172.

Here, the neurosurgeon used the range-of-motion model to determine permanent impairment. The *AMA Guides*, however, require that the injury model be used whenever possible to assess permanent impairment. *See AMA Guides* § 3.3i at 108, § 3.3j at 112 (4th ed. 1993). The neurosurgeon, however, determined that the preferred model did not apply to the respondent's injury, and, as allowed by the *AMA Guides*, he employed the range-of-motion model. While his initial evaluation did not contain an explicit explanation for his deviation from the preferred model, his subsequent letter, coupled with his initial report, provided a full evaluation and analysis. The court noted:

> The *AMA Guides* expressly allows a physician to deviate from the guidelines
> if the physician finds it necessary to produce an impairment rating more accu-
> rate than the recommended formula can achieve. [Citations omitted] In this

case, there is record evidence to show that deviation from the guidelines was necessary to evaluate accurately the impairment suffered by the respondent.

765 A.2d at 172.

The court affirmed the trial court's award.

Appeal of Rainville, 1999 N.H. LEXIS 6 (N.H. Feb. 8, 1999)

The New Hampshire court dealt with a construction worker who was diagnosed with multifocal myofascial pain syndrome with multiple sympathetic phenomena. His treating physician rated his impairment at 18 percent of the person as a whole. The claimant's claim was rejected because the impairment evaluation deviated from the expressly recommended methodology of the *AMA Guides*. The court reversed and remanded. It stated:

> Since the petitioner does not dispute the board's finding that he did not suffer a compensable spinal injury, we turn to the petitioner's second claim that the board erroneously dismissed Dr. [N.]'s assessment of his permanent impairment. Dr. [N.] found that as a result of his myofascial pain, the petitioner had an approximately twenty percent loss of function of each shoulder, allowing for a twelve percent impairment of each upper extremity, and a diagnosis-specific impairment of five percent secondary to neck pain. Combining these values according to the relevant table in the *AMA Guides*, Dr. [N.] concluded that the petitioner suffered an eighteen percent impairment of the whole person. The employer contends that the board correctly rejected Dr. [N.]'s evaluation because he failed to follow the *AMA Guides* as required by RSA 281-A:32, IX. During the hearing before the board, Dr. [N.] admitted that the *AMA Guides* does not refer to myofascial pain and that the petitioner did not have any of the listed physical conditions. Dr. [N.] testified that the *AMA Guides* "has a couple of sections that allow you to go outside . . . of [its] basic techniques of range of motion [to assess impairment]." The employer argues that Dr. [N.] erred by evaluating the petitioner under an injury not recognized by the *AMA Guides* and by failing to perform the proper tests to assess the petitioner's physical abilities. Whether the statutory requirements of RSA 281-A:32, IX have been satisfied is a legal question, which we review de novo. *See Petition of Blackford*, 138 N.H. 132, 134–35, 635 A.2d 501, 502–03 (1993). RSA 281-A:32, IX mandates that the *AMA Guides* be used to calculate the percent of the whole person impaired as a result of multiple permanent bodily losses. In other words, it is the statute that governs whether a permanent impairment exists; the *AMA Guides* applies only to the determination of appropriate compensation for a permanent impairment. We therefore examine the *AMA Guides* to evaluate the legal sufficiency of Dr. [N.]'s assessment. We note that the *AMA Guides* expressly acknowledges it "does not and cannot provide answers about every type and degree of impairment" because of the "infinite variety of human disease," the constantly evolving field of medicine, and the complex process of human functioning. *See AMA Guides* § 1.3, at 3. Accordingly, the *AMA Guides* advises that a "physician's judgment and his or her experience,

training, skill and thoroughness in examining the patient and applying the findings to *Guides* criteria will be factors in estimating the degree of the patient's impairment." *Id.* While this estimate "should be based on current findings and evidence," *id.* § 2.2, at 8, "if in spite of an observation or test result the medical evidence appears not to be of sufficient weight to verify that an impairment of a certain magnitude exists, the physician should modify the impairment estimate accordingly, describing the modification and explaining the reason for it in writing." *Id.* The *AMA Guides* expressly allows a physician to deviate from the guidelines if the physician finds it necessary to produce an impairment rating more accurate than the recommended formula can achieve. This decision to use alternative methodology must, however, be grounded in adequate clinical information about the patient's medical condition. *See id.* § 1.2, at 3. Additionally, in order to allow a third party to compare reports properly, physicians must use a standard protocol in evaluating and reporting impairment. *See id.* ch. 2 Preface at 7. "A clear, accurate, and complete report is essential to support a rating of permanent impairment." *Id.* § 2.4, at 10. Within the report, an evaluating physician is expected to provide a full medical evaluation, analysis of the medical findings with respect to the patient's life activities, and comparison of the results of analysis with the impairment criteria. *See id.* Hence, in view of the *AMA Guides's* own instructions and our liberal construction of RSA 281-A:32, IX, *see Appeal of Lalime,* 141 N.H. at 537–38, 687 A.2d at 997, we hold that if a physician, exercising competent professional skill and judgment, finds that the recommended procedures in the *AMA Guides* are inapplicable to estimate impairment, the physician may use other methods not otherwise prohibited by the *AMA Guides. Cf. City of Aurora v. Vaughn,* 824 P.2d 825, 827 (Colo. Ct. App. 1991) (where procedures in *AMA Guides* judged inapplicable to claimant's hearing loss, physician could properly rely on alternative reliable tests). The reasons for such a deviation must be fully explained and the alternative methodology set forth in sufficient detail so as to allow a proper evaluation of its soundness and accuracy. We caution that our decision does not permit physicians or claimants to deviate from procedures simply to achieve a more desirable result. To satisfy the statutory requirements of RSA 281-A:32, IX, a deviation must be justified by competent medical evidence and be consistent with the specific dictates and general purpose of the *AMA Guides.* Whether and to what extent an alternative method is proper, credible, or permissible under the *AMA Guides* are questions of fact to be decided by the board. *See Vaughn,* 824 P.2d at 827 (as trier of fact, agency entitled to rely on expert testimony supporting deviation from *AMA Guides*). We hold only that the board may not disregard a physician's impairment evaluation solely because it deviates from the express recommended methodology of the *AMA Guides.* In this case, Dr. [N.] explained in his written report and oral testimony that the nature of the petitioner's medical condition rendered his impairment incapable of measurement by the range of motion test provided by the *AMA Guides.* He consequently resorted to an alternative method in calculating the petitioner's impairment, a decision which by itself does not exceed the statutory mandate of RSA 281-A:32, IX. Because the board did not disclose the facts underlying its decision to deny a permanent impairment award on the basis of multiple bodily losses, *see* RSA 541-A:35 (1997), we are unable to determine whether the board reached its conclusions in accordance with the principles set forth above. *Cf. Foote v. State Personnel Commission*, 116 N.H. 145, 148, 355 A.2d 412, 414 (1976) (reviewing court needs findings of basic facts by the agency to ascertain whether the conclusions it reached were proper). Accordingly, we vacate the board's denial of a permanent impairment award and remand for a new hearing. On remand, the claimant may present evidence substantiating the calculation of his impairment rating and setting forth the reasons for deviating from the *AMA Guides*. In light of this ruling, we need not address the petitioner's remaining arguments. Affirmed in part; reversed in part; vacated in part; remanded. All concurred.

1999 N.H. LEXIS 6, at *16–*21.

Petition of Gilpatric, 639 A.2d 267 (N.H. 1994)

The New Hampshire Supreme Court dealt with a claimant who challenged his award of 8 percent permanent impairment. The claimant argued that the *AMA Guides* had been misapplied and that his medical diagnosis did not constitute competent medical testimony to support the hearing officer's decision. The court disagreed and affirmed the 8 percent rating:

> We hold that Dr. [O.]'s diagnosis and evaluation constitute competent medical testimony that supports the hearing officer's decision. Dr. [O.]'s diagnosis of "bilateral carpal tunnel syndrome with bilateral carpal tunnel releases" matched the diagnoses of other physicians, including that of Gilpatric's treating physician, Dr. [M.], who examined her and submitted reports to the department. Dr. [O.]'s calculation of eight percent permanent impairment, following the "Guides to the Evaluation of Permanent Impairment" published by the American Medical Association, is also found to be reliable. *See* RSA 281-A:32, XIV (Supp. 1993); N.H. Admin. Rules, Lab 514.03. Since the department based its decision on a competent diagnosis, we reject [claimant]'s contention that the American Medical Association guidelines were misapplied.

Id. at 269–70.

Petition of Blackford, 635 A.2d 501 (N.H. 1993)

The New Hampshire Supreme Court dealt with the claimant, who as an 18-year-old sustained a traumatic brain injury in an automobile accident. He was left with partial paralysis of his right arm and leg and epilepsy. A neurologist evaluated the claimant's permanent impairment under the *AMA Guides* as follows:

> Dr. [R.] assessed a 35 percent impairment of complex integrated cerebral functions, a 30 percent impairment for emotional disturbances, and "an episodic

neurological disorder of 20 percent impairment of whole person function."
Dr. [R.] concluded with an assessment of "whole person permanent impairment"
(a scale which measures the degree of permanent impairment) of 35 percent.

Id. at 502.

The court affirmed the 20 percent award for the seizure disorder but denied
the 15 percent for loss of brain function. The reasoning of the court was as follows:

> Dr. [R.] found a total whole person impairment of 35 percent, of this total,
> 20 percent was assessed for the episodic seizure disorder. The balance he
> attributed to emotional disturbance and "impairment of complex integrated
> cerebral functions." As these impairments would apparently result in loss of
> brain function, and as the brain is not a scheduled body part under the statute,
> the department properly denied an award therefor. The seizure disorder,
> however, would result in physically manifested losses of use of all parts of
> the body.
>
> The statute provides for an award based on permanent impairment to the
> "whole person" when injury results in total or partial loss of use of more than
> one scheduled body part. The petitioner sustains such a loss each time he has a
> seizure, and to that extent his doctor concluded that 20 percent of his "whole
> person function" is impaired. We hold that the labor department erred in ruling
> that the petitioner failed to demonstrate a potential compensable loss of use.

Id. at 503.

Petition of Blake, 623 A.2d 741 (N.H. 1993)

The New Hampshire Supreme Court dealt with the claimant, who developed
a repetitive motion injury in her hand. Her physician gave her a 91 percent
permanent impairment rating made up of 60 percent of the right upper extremity
and 31 percent of the left upper extremity. An IME report was done on July 8, 1991.
The physician sent a copy of the work capacity evaluation (IME report) to the
insurance company along with a lengthy cover letter explaining the results and
containing his conclusions and recommendations. On July 19, 1991, the physician
sent the insurance company a one-page "impairment report" that contained his
calculation of a 5 percent impairment of the right upper extremity and a 3 percent
impairment of the left upper extremity, resulting in an 8 percent impairment of the
whole person.

The court upheld the award of 8 percent based upon the IME, despite the fact
that the report did not mention the *AMA Guides.* The court found that the report was
in accordance with the *AMA Guides* as it was generated by an AMA "computer
program." The court stated:

> The petitioner next argues that the hearing officer's decision was illegal,
> unreasonable, arbitrary, and capricious, and an abuse of discretion, because
> it was based solely upon Dr. [O.]'s impairment report. First, the petitioner

contends that the hearings officer should not have considered the impairment report because it did not refer to the "American Medical Association Guides to the Evaluation of Permanent Impairment" (*AMA Guides*), as required by RSA 281-A:32, XIV (Supp. 1992). In a letter received by the labor department of September 13, 1991, however, Dr. [O.] stated that his permanent impairment figure was "generated from a program based exclusively on the third edition of the '*AMA Guides* to the Evaluation of Permanent Impairment.' " Thus, we reject the petitioner's contention.

Id. at 745.

Hailsen v. Seabrook Clam Co., 623 A.2d 225 (N.H. 1993)

The New Hampshire Supreme Court dealt with a claimant who injured his knee at work. The claimant underwent arthroscopic surgery and was left with chondromalacia and tenderness.

The court affirmed a finding of no permanent impairment under the *AMA Guides*, stating:

> Dr. [M.] examined the plaintiff in August 1990. When asked, "So the only thing wrong with his knee was some mild tenderness," he answered affirmatively. Dr. [M.] also testified that the plaintiff was not permanently impaired under the American Medical Association (AMA) guides to the evaluation of permanent impairment. *See* RSA 281-A:32, XIV (Supp. 1992) (labor commissioner has adopted *AMA Guides* to promote uniformity in rating permanent impairment). The doctor continued to be of the opinion that the plaintiff's injury to his right knee was a mild degenerative joint disease and testified that he could not determine whether the degenerative changes were aggravated by the March 8, 1987 injury.

Id. at 226.

§11.24 NEW MEXICO

Yeager v. St. Vincent Hosp., 973 P.2d 850 (N.M. Ct. App. 1998)

The New Mexico court dealt with a claimant who was exposed to a strong chemical odor in a laboratory. This exposure caused tightness in her chest and throat, headache, difficulty breathing, coughing, and wheezing. Before her exposure to chemicals, the claimant had had numerous respiratory problems, including asthma, bronchopulmonary aspergillosis, and allergies, but had been physically active and participated in step aerobics. Since the exposure, she had not been able to participate in these activities and had had to take prednisone, a steroid used to treat certain allergic and inflammatory diseases, much more frequently than before the exposure. In addition, she had been unable to tolerate chemical fumes since the exposure. The claimant underwent an IME, and the evaluating physician refused to assign an impairment rating. After a hearing, the WCJ assigned an impairment rating of 26 percent to the claimant. The court held that, under the facts of this case, it was impermissible for the WCJ to assign an impairment rating on her own. It stated:

> Employer argues that worker was not entitled to workers' compensation benefits because there was no expert medical testimony on the degree of impairment attributable to her workplace injury. Employer argues that the WCJ improperly assigned an impairment rating herself after examining the complicated medical testimony and applying the American Medical Association Guides to the Evaluation of Permanent Impairment (4th ed. 1993) [hereinafter *AMA Guides*]. Whether a WCJ may assign an impairment rating in the absence of expert testimony as to the degree of impairment has not been answered by the courts of New Mexico.
>
> Under our workers' compensation statute, an
>
>> "impairment" means an anatomical or functional abnormality existing after the date of maximum medical improvement as determined by a medically or scientifically demonstrable finding and based upon the most recent edition of the American medical association's guide to the evaluation of permanent impairment or comparable publications of the American medical association.
>
> NMSA 1978, § 52-1-24(A) (1990) (effective January 1, 1991). Thus, our statute requires the use of the *AMA Guides* when determining whether a worker is impaired, and if impaired, the degree of worker's impairment. We recognize that the *AMA Guides* were specifically developed to bring greater objectivity to estimating the degree of a worker's permanent impairment, *see Madrid v. St. Joseph Hosp.*, 1996 NMSC 64, P18, 122 N.M. 524, 928 P.2d 250, but note that the *AMA Guides* do not establish a rigid formula that must be followed. Rather, they provide a guide that will help make the determination of permanent impairment more objective. *See id.* P 19.
>
> Given that the *AMA Guides* are to be applied in a flexible manner, New Mexico courts have recognized that a WCJ has some discretion in applying the *AMA Guides* and determining the appropriate impairment rating. Specifically, our courts have held that a WCJ may choose between experts' conflicting opinions of a worker's impairment rating, *see Madrid*, 1996-NMSC-064, P 19, may assign a rating when the most recent edition of the *AMA Guides* does not address a particular type of injury or ailment, *see Peterson v. Northern Home Care*, 1996 NMCA 30, P18, 121 N.M. 439, 912 P.2d 831, and may discount or lower an expert's impairment rating when evidence casts doubt on the worker's reports of pain. *See id.* P 10. However, these cases do not recognize an unfettered discretion in the WCJ to determine the impairment rating. Rather, they recognize that a WCJ may assign an impairment rating in three limited circumstances.
>
> Despite the limited circumstances in which a WCJ may assign an impairment rating, Worker argues that the WCJ was entitled to do so here, in the absence of medical testimony on the percentage of impairment, because

the *AMA Guides* recognize that "any knowledgeable person can compare the clinical findings with the *Guides* criteria and determine whether or not the impairment estimates reflect those criteria." *AMA Guides*, § 2.1, at 2/8. According to worker, the WCJ is a "knowledgeable person" who may compare the expert's clinical findings to the *AMA Guides* and assign an impairment rating once the expert concludes that a worker has an impairment caused by a workplace accident. Worker's argument is overbroad.

Although the WCJ may be capable of utilizing the *AMA Guides* and assigning an impairment rating in many cases, we disagree that the WCJ was capable of doing so here. The *AMA Guides* themselves recognize that the presence of certain respiratory ailments, including asthma, complicates the quantification of worker's postaccident respiratory impairment. Accordingly, "impairments in persons with [asthma, hypersensitivity pneumonitis, pneumoconiosis, and lung cancers] should be evaluated by physicians with expertise in lung disease, and the impairment [rating] should be left to the physician's judgment." *AMA Guides*, § 5.3, at 5/164.

Here, consistent with the *AMA Guides*, Dr. [D.], who was not a pulmonologist, refused to assign an impairment rating precisely because he felt that only a lung specialist could assess worker's impairment. Given the interplay between worker's preexisting medical conditions and postexposure symptoms, assigning an impairment rating would require more than a mechanical comparison of the objective test results with the *AMA Guides*. Where, as here, both the *AMA Guides* and the medical expert recognize that only a specialist can accurately evaluate this type of impairment, it is unreasonable to think that a layperson would be capable of assigning an appropriate impairment rating. Thus, we hold that the WCJ erred by assigning an impairment rating in this case.

Our holding today does not question the WCJ's right to choose between experts' conflicting impairment ratings, nor the WCJ's right to assign a rating in the absence of an AMA guideline. However, we decline to allow the WCJ to assign a rating in cases where no lung specialist has provided an impairment rating and where the worker has one of the preexisting pulmonary conditions specifically listed in the *AMA Guides* as requiring a lung specialist. *AMA Guides*, § 5.3, at 5/164. We do not hold that the WCJs may never assign an impairment rating because we recognize that there are impairments that can be objectively measured and that do not interact with other medical conditions. In those cases, a WCJ may compare the objective clinical findings to the *AMA Guides* and assign an impairment rating without error. However, in cases that require some medical judgment in order to determine the degree of impairment, the WCJ may not determine the worker's impairment rating without a medical expert opinion. Here, the testimony of a lung specialist is required. Thus, we reverse the WCJ's finding of a 20 percent impairment rating and remand so that the WCJ may enter judgment in favor of employer.

Worker suggests that our remand should allow a pulmonologist to provide an impairment rating. We will not remand for additional testimony because worker did not satisfy her initial burden of providing the medical evidence necessary to prove that she had a compensable claim, *see Tafoya v. Kermac Nuclear Fuels, Corp.*, 71 N.M. 157, 160, 376 P.2d 576,

578 (1962), when she failed to provide a lung specialist's assignment of an impairment rating. *Compare* § 52-1-24(A) (explicitly requiring reliance on the *AMA Guides*) *with AMA Guides*, § 5.3, at 5/164 (requiring a lung specialist to assign a rating when the worker's injury compounds certain preexisting pulmonary conditions).

Worker's burden to provide evidence of her impairment as rated by a lung specialist was clear when she brought her case. Indeed, worker appears to have understood that a specialist was required. During a pretrial hearing on whether to appoint an independent medical examiner (IME), worker's attorney stated that the IME should be "a doctor who has expertise diagnosing RADS [reactive airway disease syndrome] and occupational asthma." Nevertheless, when the WCJ told the parties that she intended to appoint Dr. [D.], who was not a pulmonologist, and that she would give the parties an opportunity to object to Dr. [D.]'s appointment, Worker did not object. Thus, Worker understood that a specialist was necessary to her case, but failed to provide a specialist and failed to object to the appointment of an IME that was not a specialist. Under these circumstances, remanding for the testimony of a specialist would simply give worker a second chance to assert her claim for disability benefits after she initially failed to satisfy her burden at trial. Accordingly, we remand simply to allow the WCJ to enter judgment in employer's favor.

973 P.2d at 853–55.

Chavarria v. Basin Moving & Storage, 127 N.M.67, 976 P.2d 1019 (N.M. Ct. App. 1999)

The New Mexico court dealt with a claimant who suffered a lower back injury. The claimant underwent fusion surgery and had permanent metal instrumentation implanted in his spine. The claimant's physician assigned a 25 percent impairment rating. The WCJ awarded a 5 percent impairment. The court reversed and remanded. It reasoned that the WCJ may have assigned a rating based on postoperative conditions, and this is not consistent with the *AMA Guides*. The court also reasoned that the WCJ failed to properly consider whether the claimant had a separate psychological disorder and chronic pain. It stated:

> According to NMSA [N.M. Stat. Ann.] 1978, § 52-1-24(A) (1990), an impairment is "an anatomical or functional abnormality existing after the date of maximum medical improvement as determined by a medically or scientifically demonstrable finding and based upon the most recent edition" of the *AMA Guides*. The parties do not dispute that in order to assess Worker's impairment rating the Injury Model of the *AMA Guides* should be used. *See AMA Guides* § 3.3, at 3/94. Under the Injury Model, lumbosacral spine (lower spine) impairments as experienced by worker are described in terms of diagnosis-related estimates (DREs), and the DRE level corresponds to a percentage impairment rating. *See id.* § 3.3b, at 3/95. "With the Injury Model, surgery to treat an impairment does not modify the original impairment estimate, which remains

the same in spite of any changes in signs or symptoms that may follow the surgery and irrespective of whether the patient has a favorable or unfavorable response to treatment." *Id.* § 3.3d, at 3/100.

The *AMA Guides* further clarify use of the Injury Model by an illustrative example. *See id.* § 3.3g, at 3/103. In the example, a woman with signs of radiculopathy underwent disk removal and spinal fusion, which caused her symptoms to recede. Nevertheless, the proper impairment rating was 10% despite the resolution of the symptoms because the resolution of symptoms following a surgical procedure does not reduce the impairment rating estimate. We interpret this example to mean that the impairment rating that is applicable prior to surgery does not change as a result of a worker having undergone surgery, regardless of the results.

To the extent that employer argues that this provision of the *AMA Guides* conflicts with our statutory definition for impairment, we disagree. Under our statute, impairment is assessed after the MMI [maximum medical improvement] date by use of the *AMA Guides* and the *AMA Guides* dictate that, in cases involving lower spine impairment, the original impairment estimate rating is not altered by the fact that a claimant has undergone surgery. When the language of the statute is clear, as in this case, we give effect to the language. *See Chavez v. Mountain States Constructors,* 1996 NMSC 70, P23, 122 N.M. 579, 929 P.2d 971. Nor do we believe that we are applying the *AMA Guides* too rigidly. *Cf. Madrid v. St. Joseph Hosp.,* 1996 NMSC 64, P19, 122 N.M. 524, 928 P.2d 250 (noting that *AMA Guides* provide a general framework and not a rigid formula that must be followed). Use of the Injury Model, which both parties agreed applied in this case, provides very specific and clear guidance as to how an impairment rating is assessed.

Under the Injury Model, lower spine-related complaints in DRE Category II involve mild spine function impairment while those in DRE Categories III through V relate to documentable findings that are more serious such as radiculopathy and loss of motion segment integrity. *See AMA Guides* § 3.3g, at 3/102–3/103. For example, DRE Category II involves minor impairment with no objective sign of radiculopathy and no loss of structural integrity; DRE Category III involves the presence of radiculopathy; DRE Category IV involves the loss of motion segment integrity; and DRE Category V involves both radiculopathy and loss of motion segment integrity. *See id.* § 3.3g, at 102 and 3/110, Table 72. The impairment rating assigned for DRE Category II is 5%; DRE Category III is 10%; DRE Category IV is 20%; and DRE Category V is 25%.

From her findings, it appears the WCJ may have relied upon postoperative test results in concluding that there was no physical evidence of radiculopathy. The WCJ made findings that no valid medical testing supports worker's radiculopathy complaints. As discussed above, assigning the rating based upon postoperative conditions is not consistent with the *AMA Guides.*

127 N.M. at 71–72.

The court continues:

Worker claims that the WCJ improperly failed to give separate impairment ratings based on worker's allegations of a psychological disorder and chronic pain. Our reading of the *AMA Guides* indicates that, in particular circumstances, it is possible that certain disorders would rise to such a level that a separate impairment rating would be warranted for psychological disorder or chronic pain. *See AMA Guides* § 14.2, at 293–95; § 15, at 307–313.

In this case, there was evidence that worker did not suffer from either a psychological disorder or chronic pain. For example, the WCJ made certain observations that indicated that worker's complaints of pain were not credible. The WCJ observed worker during the hearing and noted that he had no difficulty moving from one position to another. The WCJ's findings included testimony from Dr. [D.] that worker was "capable of working from a psychological or psychiatric standpoint." Dr. [D.] testified that worker had some loss of function, but not an amount that would disable or impair a person so that he could not function socially or occupationally. According to Dr. [D.], worker was eating well, and his mood and energy were good. Dr. [C.] provided testimony that for this type of lower spine injury, the impairment rating accounted for chronic pain. Dr. [S.] also believed the impairment rating included chronic pain.

While this evidence appears sufficient to support the WCJ's findings, the improper exclusion of Dr. [Sh.]'s relevant testimony requires reversal on this issue. *See State ex rel. State Highway Comm'n v. Bassett*, 81 N.M. 345, 346, 467 P.2d 11, 12 (1970) ("If relevant and admissible, it would be reversible error for the court to refuse to accord [evidence] any weight which, in effect, would amount to its exclusion."). Dr. [Sh.] testified at his deposition that worker suffered from mood disorder and chronic pain. He assigned impairment categories under the *AMA Guides* for mental impairment and chronic pain, which he believed to be causally connected to worker's work injury.

We cannot say that if the WCJ had considered Dr. [Sh.]'s testimony, the WCJ would not have found that worker was entitled to a separate impairment rating for mental impairment or chronic pain or both. Therefore, we remand for reconsideration from the existing record of separate impairment ratings based on psychological disorders and chronic pain, taking into consideration Dr. [Sh.]'s testimony, which the WCJ erroneously excluded.

127 N.M. at 74.

Torres v. Plastech Corp., 947 P.2d 154 (N.M. 1997)

The New Mexico court dealt with a claimant who developed carpal tunnel syndrome. At issue was whether the statute of limitations had run out, thus barring the claimant's claim for a scheduled loss. The court remanded the case for further proceedings. It stated:

In order to demonstrate an impairment under the scheduled injury section, it is not necessary to present evidence conforming to the AMA guidelines under the definition of impairment in Section 52-1-24(A). *Lucero v. Smith's Food & Drug Ctrs., Inc.*, 1994 NMCA 079, 118 N.M. 35, 36–38, 878 P.2d 353, 354–56 (distinguishing between impairment as defined in Section 52-1-24(A) and impairment under the scheduled injury section). Rather, an impairment for scheduled injury purposes "is an infirmity or defect that limits the physical functioning of the worker's body." *Twin Mountain Rock v. Ramirez*, 1994 NMCA 020, 117 N.M. 367, 369, 871 P.2d 1373, 1375 (Ct. App. 1994).

There must be sufficient evidence for a workers' compensation judge to determine a total loss of use or "the degree of such partial loss of use" of the scheduled member. Section 52-1-43(A), (B). In evaluating the loss of use, however, it is not necessary to consider "the occupation of the worker and how the loss of the specific member of the body may affect his or her ability to perform the duties of his or her job." *Hise Constr. v. Candelaria*, 98 N.M. 759, 760, 652 P.2d 1210, 1211 (1982). Thus, in order to trigger the statute of limitations, a worker must know or have reason to know that he or she suffered an injury which limits or makes useless one of the body members listed in Section 52-1-43. *See Romero v. American Furniture Co.*, 86 N.M. 661, 663, 526 P.2d 803, 805 (Ct. App. 1974) ("A workman would be on notice of a compensable scheduled injury when it becomes or should reasonably become apparent to him that he suffered 'a partial loss of use' of the scheduled body member.").

947 P.2d at 161.

Madrid v. St. Joseph Hosp., 928 P.2d 250 (N.M. 1996)

The New Mexico court dealt with a constitutional challenge to the adoption of the *AMA Guides*. The plaintiff alleged that the New Mexico Workers' Compensation Act's adoption of the *AMA Guides* was an unlawful delegation of legislative authority and denied workers equal protection in determining the existence or extent of disability. The court held that the adoption of the *AMA Guides* was not a violation of due process and is not arbitrary when applied to conditions that are not ratable under the *AMA Guides*. The court reasoned:

> All of the aforementioned grounds for incorporating the standards of a private entity without finding a delegation of legislative authority are applicable to Section 24, which references the AMA *Guide*. Section 24 has incorporated the standards of a well-recognized, independent authority, in order to provide guidance to medical professionals and Workers' compensation claims adjudicators on the complex issue of impairment. The AMA *Guide* was specifically developed to "bring greater objectivity to estimating the degree of long-standing or 'permanent impairment'." AMA *Guide, supra*, at v. In compiling the AMA *Guide*, the American Medical Association obtained the assistance of experts in the complex area of permanent impairment, calling on "well-qualified individuals" and "physicians from all the state medical societies and medical specialty societies." *Id.* Many other states use the AMA *Guide*, or a similar rating method, to evaluate impairment for purposes of Workers' compensation benefits.
>
> > Contrary to Appellants' argument, use of the AMA *Guide* as prescribed by Section 24 does allow for an element of discretion as specifically explained by the AMA *Guide:*

[N]o formula is known by which knowledge about a medical condition can be combined with knowledge about other facts to calculate the percentage by which the employee's industrial use of the body is impaired. [Therefore, the Workers' Compensation] Commission also must consider the nature of the injury and the employee's occupation, experience, training, and age [to] award proportional compensation.

AMA *Guide, supra*, § 1.4. The AMA *Guide* is a general framework, requiring flexibility in its application. While the AMA *Guide* was intended to help standardize the evaluation of a worker's impairment, it was not intended to establish a rigid formula to be followed in determining the percentage of a worker's impairment. Where evidence is conflicting, the ultimate decision concerning the degree of a worker's impairment and disability rests with the workers' compensation judge. Furthermore, where the AMA *Guide* is an inadequate reference, the statute explicitly allows for reference to other AMA publications. Section 52-1-24. Section 24 clearly has a discretionary component.

It is impractical to expect our Legislature to establish standards for evaluating physical impairment in workers' claims. The New Mexico Legislature could have concluded that it lacked the resources to develop independent standards, opting instead to utilize the standards established by a highly respected entity that possessed the expertise for such an undertaking. Prohibiting the Legislature from adopting the standards developed by experts within a rapidly changing medical specialty would obstruct the Workers' Compensation Administration's efforts to provide accurate evaluations of impairment.

In addition, new developments in medical science relevant to evaluating impairments demand periodic modifications of the standard adopted by Section 24. The AMA *Guide* is periodically updated to encompass these new developments. AMA *Guide, supra*, at 1. Periodic revisions of the standard will not transform an otherwise constitutional and non-delegatory statutory provision into an unconstitutional delegation of legislative power. Where a standard is periodically updated because of new scientific developments recognized by eminent professionals interested in maintaining high standards in science, the standard may still be adopted by the Legislature. *See, e.g., Wakeen*, 57 N.W.2d at 369.

The AMA *Guide* was developed, and is utilized, for many purposes beyond evaluation of impairment within a workers' compensation claim. While the AMA *Guide* has become an important tool for evaluating impairment for workers' compensation claims, it is also utilized in adjudicating "Social Security Administration cases, and other types of cases." AMA *Guide, supra*, at 1. Furthermore, the AMA *Guide* is "useful anywhere when questions arise about people's physical and mental functioning and capabilities." *Id.* Clearly the AMA has developed a standard which has independent significance beyond adjudication of workers' compensation claims. The New Mexico Constitution does not prohibit the Legislature from availing itself of the independent work of a private organization.

In light of all the relevant considerations—the eminence of the medical professionals who compile the AMA *Guide*, the complexity of the issue of impairment, the number of jurisdictions that have adopted the AMA *Guide* or similar publications, the practical necessity of adopting this mutable standard, the discretionary component of using the AMA *Guide*, and the significance of the AMA *Guide* outside of the statutory reference—we find no delegation of legislative authority in Section 24.

Appellants have failed to establish that use of the AMA *Guide* and predetermined modifiers in evaluating disability is arbitrary and lacks some rational relationship to a legitimate legislative purpose. *Id.* Appellants argue that the Act produces arbitrary disability determinations because, unlike the previous versions of the Act, it does not permit the workers' compensation judge to exercise discretion by applying extenuating factors to determine disability. *See, e.g., Anaya v. New Mexico Steel Erectors, Inc.*, 94 N.M. 370, 373, 610 P.2d 1199, 1202 (1980) (stating that disability determination analyzed percentage claimant was unable to perform previous job, taking into consideration " 'age, education, training, experience and physical condition and previous work experience' " with emphasis on importance of trial judge's discretion). This Court will not address which version of the Act is superior; rather, we consider whether the current version of the Act is arbitrary.

Contrary to Appellants' assertions, the current version of the Act requires the workers' compensation judge to consider the unique facts of each worker's claim and is not arbitrary. As discussed earlier, the AMA *Guide* requires medical professionals to incorporate the unique circumstances of each claim in order to arrive at an impairment rating. Additionally, the Act itself explicitly states that any finding of impairment may be modified by the claimant's age, education, and physical capacity. *See* §§ 52-1-26, 26.4. It is evident that the AMA *Guide* is what it purports to be—a guideline to be used in conjunction with the expertise of the medical professional in order to arrive at a percentage of impairment based on the unique circumstances of each claim. *See* AMA *Guide, supra,* § 1.3. Therefore, the amended version of the Act incorporates discretionary factors to determine disability and does not produce arbitrary disability awards.

Appellants further argue that the Act is arbitrary because some conditions which result in impairment are not contained in the AMA *Guide*. *See, e.g., Sutton v. Quality Furniture Co.*, 191 Ga. App. 279, 381 S.E.2d 389, 389–90 (1989) (illustrating that some impairments, such as chronic pain, are not addressed by the AMA *Guide*), *cert. denied* (May 11, 1989). This argument fails because other comparable AMA publications may be utilized to evaluate impairment when the AMA *Guide* is insufficient. *See* § 52-1-24(A). Similarly, other jurisdictions allow workers' compensation judges to consider generally-accepted standards in awarding Workers' compensation benefits when the injury at issue is not covered by the AMA *Guide*. *See, e.g., Dayron Corp. v. Morehead*, 509 So. 2d 930, 931 (Fla. 1987) ("When an injury is not covered by the AMA *Guides*, it is permissible to rely upon medical testimony of permanent impairment based upon other generally accepted medical standards."); *Slover Masonry, Inc. v. Industrial Comm'n*, 158 Ariz. 131, 135,

761 P.2d 1035, 1039 (1988) (noting that where the AMA *Guide* is inadequate, the administrative law judge may turn to other factors in assessing impairment). Under the Act, application of the AMA *Guide* in evaluating impairment does not preclude use of other AMA publications in evaluating impairment. Further, the AMA *Guide* explicitly provides that it "does not and cannot provide answers about every type and degree of impairment." AMA *Guide, supra,* § 1.3. It is a "guideline to be used in conjunction with the expertise of the medical profession." *Id.* While the Legislature intended to preclude arbitrary determinations, it did not intend to exclude determinations by medical professionals in situations not covered by the *Guide.* Thus, the Act does not produce an arbitrary determination of disability.

928 P.2d at 258–60.

Peterson v. Northern Health Care, 912 P.2d 831 (N.M. Ct. App. 1996)

The New Mexico court dealt with a claimant who was evaluated as having a "mild to moderate" psychological impairment under the *AMA Guides* (3d ed. 1988) or the *AMA Guides* (4th ed. 1993). No numerical rating was assigned by the evaluating physician, as he had testified that the AMA discourages, if not prohibits, the assignment of percentages for rating mental impairment. The rating physician further testified that, under the *AMA Guides*, a mild impairment is an impairment that is compatible with most useful functioning, while a moderate impairment is compatible with some, but not all, useful functioning. The court remanded the case and held that the trial judge should have assigned a numerical rating based upon the testimony of the physician regarding the meaning of mild to moderate impairment.

Toynbee v. Mimbres Memorial Nursing Home, 833 P.2d 1204 (N.M. Ct. App. 1992)

The New Mexico court dealt with the claimant who was employed as a nurse's aide and who injured her back and knee on July 2, 1986. The claimant was awarded a 15 percent permanent partial disability of her whole body.

The court rejected the appeal requesting a higher award by the claimant. The decision was based on the fact that there was a lack of evidence in the record establishing more than a 15 percent impairment. The court stated:

Our examination of the record indicates that the medical experts called by worker to testify concerning causation and the percentage of worker's disability resulting from her work-related accident did not testify that she suffered a permanent physical impairment to her body as a whole, in excess of 15 percent under the existing American Medical Association's (AMA) guides to the evaluation of permanent impairment, or under a comparable AMA publication. Absent such testimony, worker's argument on appeal that she is entitled to a percentage of permanent partial disability greater than 15 percent is flawed because of a lack of expert medical testimony indicating that worker suffered a higher percentage of disability under AMA guidelines. In *Barela* we interpreted the Interim Act to necessitate proof by specific "reference to AMA guidelines [or comparable publications by the American Medical Association] to prove permanent physical impairment in order to establish partial disability." *Id.* at 363, 785 P.2d at 274; sec. 52-1-25. In light of the absence of the requisite testimony as required by Section 52-1-25 of the Interim Act, we affirm the WCJ's findings with respect to worker's percentage of overall permanent partial disability.

Id. at 1209. *See Barela v. Midcon of N.M., Inc.*, 785 P.2d 271 (N.M. Ct. App. 1989).

Barela v. Midcon of N.M., Inc., **785 P.2d 271 (N.M. Ct. App. 1989)**

The employer and its insurer appealed a decision of the New Mexico Workers' Compensation Division of the Department of Labor, which held that the claimant was disabled as a result of a work-related accident. The court of appeals reversed, holding that the claimant was improperly awarded permanent total disability benefits where the claimant failed to present any expert medical evidence that his disability, resulting from injuries to his feet and back, was medically or scientifically demonstrable as shown in the *AMA Guides* or publications pertaining to the evaluation of permanent impairment.

The claimant was employed as a construction laborer when, in June 1986, he began to experience pain in his left foot. He quit work on July 31, 1986, because of continued problems involving his foot. The claimant began to experience pain in his right foot during August and September 1986, as well as pain in his lower back in November 1986. His employer paid workers' compensation benefits to the claimant from August 2, 1986, to December 24, 1986, and from April 5, 1987, to November 1, 1987. After the termination of the payment of benefits, the claimant filed a claim seeking an award of permanent disability. A Workers' Compensation Division hearing officer determined that the claimant had been temporarily totally disabled from December 24, 1986, through April 5, 1987, and permanently totally disabled beginning November 2, 1987. The hearing officer concluded that the claimant sustained accidental injuries to his feet in June 1986 that resulted in plantar fasciitis, primarily in the left foot, and an aggravation of a preexisting condition of spinal stenosis in his lower back.

The claimant's orthopedic surgeon stated that the claimant suffered from plantar fasciitis, which affected his feet to some extent, but the physician could not quantify such condition or assign a percentage of impairment to the disability as recognized by the *AMA Guides*. The physician also testified that he had not determined the claimant's impairment rating or functional capacity evaluation and had not filled out the impairment rating form as provided by the Workers' Compensation Division for determining medical impairment. He stated that without such an assessment, it would be "like taking a number out of the blue, unless you have AMA guidelines that [apply] to the problem." The claimant did not elicit any testimony concerning permanent physical impairment ratings as recognized by *AMA Guides* or other scientific sources that would relate to his back condition.

The respondents contended on appeal that the claimant failed to present any expert evidence that his disability resulting from injuries to his feet and back was medically or scientifically demonstrable as shown in the *AMA Guides* or comparable publications pertaining to the evaluation of permanent impairment. The claimant conceded that the physician did not testify concerning the disability according to the *AMA Guides*, but argued nevertheless that the legislature did not intend such evidence to constitute an essential element of proof for claims of permanent total disability. The claimant reasoned that because the Interim Act, N.M. Stat. Ann. § 52-1-24 (Michie), defining permanent disability, did not contain language similar to that in § 52-1-25, relating to partial disability (requiring proof of disability as shown by a medically or scientifically demonstrable finding in the *AMA Guides* or comparable publications), the legislature did not intend such a requirement for claims of total disability.

The court of appeals agreed that § 52-1-24 does not explicitly require reference to AMA publications in order to establish total disability, while § 52-1-25 specifically requires reference to AMA guidelines. Nevertheless, the court found it appropriate to read § 52-1-24 as incorporating the § 52-1-25 requirement of the reference to the *AMA Guides* to prove "permanent physical impairment." The court stated:

> First, this court's experience with the Interim Act convinces us that the legislature that enacted the Act was not concerned with the detailed interrelationships among the provisions of the Act and how the Act would be applied to various recurring, although unusual circumstances. The apparent legislative intent was to establish certain benchmarks and to leave to the courts the task of "rationalizing" the provisions of the statute. Thus, in interpreting the Interim Act one should not necessarily infer that a requirement imposed explicitly in section 52-1-25 and omitted from section 52-1-24 was therefore intended not to apply to section 52-1-24.
>
> Second, we know of no logical reason to require reference to AMA guidelines in proving permanent physical impairment when one is attempting to establish partial disability but not when one is attempting to establish total disability. Third, because of the statutory interrelationship between findings of partial and total disability, interpreting Section 52-1-24 as not requiring reference to AMA guidelines could lead to results that we doubt were intended by the legislature.

785 P.2d at 275.

The court noted that once the causal connection between a worker's injury and impairment has been established by expert medical testimony, under the former Workers' Compensation Act, the extent of the plaintiff's disability could be established by nonmedical witnesses. *Smith v. City of Albuquerque*, 105 N.M. 125, 720 P.2d 1379 (Ct. App. 1986). However, under the Interim Act, where a worker is claiming either permanent total disability or permanent partial disability, in addition to other proofs required, "We conclude that the worker must also establish a permanent physical impairment as required under Section 52-1-25." *See Strickland v. Coca-Cola Bottling Co.*, 760 P.2d 793 (N.M. Ct. App. 1988), (holding that in order to establish permanent partial disability, a worker must prove the existence of an anatomic or functional abnormality "as determined by a medically or scientifically demonstrable finding as presented in the American Medical Association's guides or comparable publications"). 785 P.2d at 275. The proof of such disability, the court concluded, is a prerequisite to the recovery of partial or total disability under the Interim Act.

Montez v. J&B Radiator, 779 P.2d 129 (N.M. Ct. App. 1989)

The claimant injured her back while at work. She underwent surgery and was subsequently released to her previous employment. Claimant argued that N.M. Stat. Ann. § 52-1-25 (Michie) of the Interim Act violated equal protection in that the act creates a distinct class of injured claimants, namely those injured during the effective dates of the Interim Act, who are entitled to fewer disability benefits because partial disability under the Interim Act had to be based on the *AMA Guides*. The claimant argued that these classifications do not survive either equal protection or heightened scrutiny.

The court of appeals found it unnecessary to decide either which standard applied or whether the Interim Act survived scrutiny, because the court held that the act did not create two separate classifications subject to different treatment. All workers injured during the effective period of the Interim Act were subject to the same statutory provisions on partial disability. "To hold that the legislature unconstitutionally violates equal protection when a change in a statutory scheme creates groups of people subject to different treatment would mean that the legislature could never change the laws." 779 P.2d at 132.

The claimant also contended that the Interim Act provides only a threshold of factors that must be reached before a finding of partial disability can be made, and that, once met, the hearing officer may then make a discretionary determination of the percentage of disability. The court disagreed:

> We believe the meaning of section 52-1-25 is clear. The legislature intended that partial disability be determined in accordance with the AMA guidelines for permanent impairment. This is what the hearing officer did, and we will not disturb his finding.

Id. at 133.

Strickland v. Coca-Cola Bottling Co., 760 P.2d 793 (N.M. Ct. App. 1988)

The claimant appealed the final disposition of the Department of Labor denying compensation and related benefits. The court of appeals found that the

Interim Act applied and the claimant did not prove permanent partial disability under the interim provisions, which require that disability due to anatomic or functional abnormality be determined using the *AMA Guides* or other comparable publications. The claimant conceded that there was no evidence introduced as to any guidebook or comparable publication.

The court also found that the term *injuries* in the statute (indicating that provisions defining total and partial disability shall apply to injuries occurring on or after the effective date of the section) means compensable injuries rather than accidents. Thus, a claimant who suffered an accident before the effective date, but whose injury became compensable after the effective date of the Interim Act, was subject to the interim provisions of the act. In this case, the accident occurred on May 15, 1986. The claimant concedes he did not suffer a compensable injury until June 2, 1986. The court cited *Romero v. General Elec. Corp.*, 104 N.M. 652, 725 P.2d 1220 (Ct. App. 1986), which held that the significant date for the purpose of determining when the statute of limitations begins to run is the date when a worker knew or should have known he suffered a compensable injury. The court also noted that the right to compensation should be measured at the time the cause of action becomes effective. *Cf. Noffsker v. Barnett & Sons*, 72 N.M. 471, 384 P.2d 1022 (1963).

§ 11.25   NORTH CAROLINA

Parrish v. Burlington Indus., Inc., 321 S.E.2d 492 (N.C. Ct. App. 1984)

The Workers' Compensation Commission found that the claimant had a 40 percent physical impairment of her lungs. The *AMA Guides* were used to arrive at this rating. In cases of occupational disease, the percentage of impairment and percentage of disability are not necessarily the same. The case was remanded to allow the commission to recalculate its findings because it found a disability rating equal to the impairment rating. On remand, the commission must consider that a high (40 percent to 50 percent) rating for impairment for an occupational disease probably will result in a 100 percent disability for work. The court noted:

> The Commission found as a fact that plaintiff is permanently partially disabled in the same degree as her physical impairment. The opinion and award recites parenthetically that the Commission used "AMA classifications" in reaching its findings. The reference apparently is to the [*AMA Guides*] 66–77 (1977). The guidelines in that publication establish 50%–70% impairment as the most severe class of respiratory disease. *Id.* at 75–76. The publication's description of symptoms indicates that a person in this classification would be totally disabled for most types of employment. *Id.* Obviously, the loss of respiratory capacity in a living compensation claimant cannot be total—as can, for

instance, the loss of sight or mobility—because some percentage of respiratory capacity is essential to sustain life. It thus would seem that the percentage of respiratory impairment and the percentage of disability are not necessarily identical . . . indeed, for claimants in the highest classification they are unlikely to be so.

Id. at 494–95.

§11.26   NORTH DAKOTA

Saari v. North Dakota Workers Compensation Bureau, **598 N.W.2d 174 (N.D. 1999)**

The North Dakota court dealt with a claimant who injured his neck and shoulder in 1987. He was evaluated for permanent impairment in 1997 using the *AMA Guides* (4th ed. 1993). The claimant argued that the wrong edition of the *AMA Guides* was used. The court disagreed. It stated:

> Saari contends the Bureau should have used the Third Edition of the AMA *Guides,* rather than the Fourth Edition of the AMA *Guides,* in determining his PPI. Under the circumstances, we disagree.
>
> The new PPI law, which became effective on July 10, 1996, provides in part:
>
> > Unless otherwise provided by this section, a doctor evaluating the impairment of an injured employee shall use the edition of the American medical association's "Guides to the Evaluation of Permanent Impairment" in effect on the date of the employee's evaluation to establish a rating for impairment of function.
>
> N.D.C.C. § 65-05-12.2(6). In *McCabe,* 1997 ND 145, ¶ 16, 567 N.W.2d 201, this Court, in order to avoid a constitutional conflict, construed former N.D.C.C. § 65-05-12 and N.D.C.C. § 65-01-02(26), as adopting the "most recent" and "most current" edition of the AMA *Guides* in effect at the time of those statutory enactments. *See also Feist,* 1997 ND 177, ¶ 13, 569 N.W.2d 1; *Coleman v. North Dakota Workers Compensation Bureau,* 1997 ND 168, ¶ 5, 567 N.W.2d 853; *McCollum v. North Dakota Workers Compensation Bureau,* 1997 ND 163, ¶ 8, 567 N.W.2d 811. In this case, the Fourth Edition of the AMA *Guides* was published in June 1993, was the most recent edition of the AMA *Guides* when N.D.C.C. § 65-05-12.2 became effective on July 10, 1996, and was in effect on the date of [Dr. S.]'s December 1997 evaluation. Under *McCabe* and its progeny, we conclude the Bureau did not err in determining [Dr. S.]'s PPI under the Fourth Edition of the AMA *Guides.* [Dr. S.] has not argued that the language used in N.D.C.C. § 65-05-12.2(6) constitutes an unconstitutional delegation of power by the Legislature to the American Medical Association, so we do not address the question. [Citations omitted]

In 1999, the Legislature enacted House Bill 1422 which amended N.D.C.C. § 65-01-02(26) to delete any reference to the AMA *Guides* and amended N.D.C.C. § 65-05-12.2(6) to read:

> A doctor evaluating permanent impairment shall include a clinical report in sufficient detail to support the percentage ratings assigned. The bureau shall adopt administrative rules governing the evaluation of permanent impairment. These rules must incorporate principles and practices of the American medical association's "Guides to the Evaluation of Permanent Impairment" modified to be consistent with North Dakota law, to resolve issues of practice and interpretation, and to address areas not sufficiently covered by the guides. Until rules adopted under this subsection become effective, impairments must be evaluated under the fourth edition, third printing, of the guides.

> 1999 N.D. Sess. Laws ch. 551, §§ 1 and 2. These amendments "apply to all impairment evaluations performed after July 31, 1999, regardless of the date of injury or date of claim filing." 1999 N.D. Sess. Laws ch. 551, § 4.

598 N.W.2d at 181–82.

Hoyem v. North Dakota Workers Compensation Bureau, 578 N.W.2d 117 (N.D. 1998)

The North Dakota court dealt with a claimant who injured his back in 1990. In 1993 he was evaluated for permanent impairment and rated at 22 percent using the range-of-motion model of the *AMA Guides* (3d ed. rev., 1988). In 1994 his treating physician was informed that the Workers' Compensation Bureau was now using the *AMA Guides* (4th ed. 1993) and the DRE model.

The claimant's impairment was recalculated under the *AMA Guides* (4th ed. 1993) and found to be 5 percent (DRE Category II). At issue on appeal were which edition of the *AMA Guides* to use and whether the claimant is entitled to an evaluation and rating for pain under the *AMA Guides*. The parties later agreed that the *AMA Guides* (3d ed. rev., 1988) should have been used. The court held that the bureau's order denying him a rating and evaluation for pain was proper. It stated:

> [Claimant] argues the Bureau's order denying him an evaluation and rating for pain must be reversed and remanded, because the Bureau improperly evaluated his pain under Chapter 15 of the Fourth Edition instead of under Appendix B. The Bureau responds Chapter 15 of the Fourth Edition is "nearly identical" to Appendix B, and Hoyem is not entitled to an evaluation for chronic pain, because his claim involves a chronic pain issue similar to the one we reviewed and rejected in *Feist v. North Dakota Workers Comp. Bur.*, 1997 ND 177, 569 N.W.2d 1. The Bureau argues a reasoning mind could have reasonably determined [claimant] was not entitled to a separate chronic pain evaluation under the AMA *Guides*.

In *Feist*, 1997 ND 177, P16, 569 N.W.2d 1, the claimant argued he was entitled to an evaluation for an additional impairment based on chronic pain under Chapter 15 of the Fourth Edition. The Bureau argued the claimant was not entitled to an additional permanent impairment for pain because his pain was included in his impairment rating under the DRE Model of the Fourth Edition.

We decided the Third Edition of the AMA *Guides* applied to the claimant's demand for a chronic pain evaluation, and we described the requirements for a "chronic pain" rating under that edition:

> The AMA Guides recognize pain as being either "acute" or "chronic." AMA *Guides* (3rd ed.), p. 240. The Stedman's Medical Dictionary (5th Lawyers' Edition 1982) p. 20, defines "acute" as "short and sharp course, not chronic"; and, at p. 278, Stedman's defines "chronic" as "of long duration; denoting a disease of slow progress and long continuance." According to the AMA *Guides*, chronic pain may "contribute to the evolution of the chronic pain syndrome. Within the framework of this definition, chronic pain may exist in the absence of chronic pain syndrome, but chronic pain syndrome always presumes the presence of chronic pain." Chronic pain syndrome "represents a biopsycho-social phenomenon of maladaptive behavior with far reaching medical, social, and economic consequences." AMA *Guides* (3rd ed.), p. 241. The AMA has outlined "characteristics (the six D's) [that] should be considered as establishing the diagnosis of a chronic pain syndrome." *Id.* The six characteristics are: duration, dramatization, drugs, despair, disuse, and dysfunction.

Feist, 1997 ND 177, P17, 569 N.W.2d 1.

We held although the claimant presented evidence he suffered from pain, he did not present medical evidence he suffered from chronic pain or had been diagnosed with chronic pain syndrome as those terms were used in the Third Edition. *Feist*, 1997 ND 177, P18, 569 N.W.2d 1. We therefore affirmed the Bureau's decision the claimant was not entitled to an evaluation for chronic pain.

Here, the Bureau adopted the ALJ's recommendation about [claimant]'s claim for a chronic pain evaluation:

> 6. (Conclusion of law) Under Chapter 15 of the *American Medical Association's Guides to the Evaluation of Permanent Impairment*, Fourth Edition, "chronic pain" is synonymous with "chronic pain syndrome"; describes a biopsychosocial behavior in which the original physiologic cause usually no longer serves as an underlying pain generator; is maladaptive and grossly disproportional to any underlying noxious stimulus; and is distinguishable from persistent somatic pain causally related to a physiologic source such as a tissue injury or pathologic state.
>
> 7. (Findings of fact) [Claimant] continues to experience persistent low-back pain. That pain is somatic and derives from a physiologic

condition, variously diagnosed as "degenerative disk disease with radio-graphic evidence of spinal stenosis" and "chronic [low back] strain and underlying spondylosis." It increases or diminishes in intensity relative to the extent of exertional activities involving his low back. He has continued to work despite his pain, and any diminishment in his level of participation in family and social activities is pursuant to a rational attempt to avoid exacerbating the spinal point source of his pain. His pain-related behavior is rational, is not maladaptive, and is not grossly disproportional to his identified condition.

8. (Conclusion of law) The greater weight of the evidence establishes that the persistent somatic low-back pain that [claimant] experiences derives from an identified physiologic source, and is not chronic pain within the scope and intent of Chapter 15 of the *American Medical Association's Guides to the Evaluation of Permanent Impairment*, Fourth Edition. As such, his referral for a chronic pain evaluation is not warranted.

The ALJ's recommendation effectively follows our *Feist* analysis of chronic pain under the Third Edition. [Claimant], like the claimant in *Feist*, presented evidence he suffered from pain, but the Bureau adopted the ALJ recommendation finding [claimant] had not established he suffered from "chronic pain," and he had not been diagnosed with "chronic pain syndrome" as those terms are used in the AMA *Guides*. Based on this record and the requirements for a chronic pain rating in Appendix B, a reasoning mind reasonably could conclude the Bureau's finding [claimant] did not suffer from chronic pain and had not been diagnosed with chronic pain syndrome was proven by the weight of the evidence. We conclude the Bureau's finding is supported by a preponderance of the evidence. [Claimant] has therefore failed to establish he was entitled to an evaluation for chronic pain under Appendix B.

[Claimant] also claims Appendix B differentiates between "acute pain" and "acute recurrent pain" and contends he was entitled to an impairment rating for "acute recurrent pain" under the emphasized language for evaluating pain as an impairment in Appendix B:

> Acute pain: Impairment and any resulting disability are primarily a function of the underlying pathological process, giving rise to physical tissue damage and nociceptive pain. In most instances, impairment and disability will be partial and temporary.
>
> Acute recurrent pain: The considerations of impairment and any resulting disability are the same as in acute pain. However, given the chronic nature of the underlying pathological process, impairment and disability could well be total and permanent.

[Claimant] argues "it is clear from a comparison of 'Appendix B: Pain and Impairment' and 'Chapter 15: Pain' that the concept of 'acute recurrent pain' is emphasized in the former and deemphasized in the latter." [Claimant] thus asserts he was entitled to an impairment evaluation and rating for "acute recurrent pain" under Appendix B.

[Claimant] did not raise this distinction as an issue to the Bureau and to the district court within the framework of his argument that Appendix B applied to his claim for a pain evaluation and rating. We have often said issues not raised before an administrative agency will not be considered for the first time on appeal. *E.g. Symington v. North Dakota Workers Comp. Bur.*, 545 N.W.2d 806, 810 (N.D. 1996). We therefore decline to address [claimant]'s argument about acute recurrent pain.

We affirm the Bureau's decision [claimant] was not entitled to an evaluation for chronic pain and chronic pain syndrome.

578 N.W.2d at 119–21.

McCabe v. North Dakota Workers Compensation Bureau, 567 N.W.2d 201 (N.D. 1997)

The North Dakota court dealt with a claimant who injured his neck and back. The claimant reached maximum medical improvement in 1994. At issue was which edition of the *AMA Guides* to use to measure the claimant's permanent partial impairment benefits. The relevant statutory language required use of the "most current" or "most recent" edition of the *AMA Guides*. The claimant argued that to interpret this language to incorporate future versions of the *AMA Guides* automatically into the statute would allow an unconstitutional delegation of legislative power to the American Medical Association. The court held that the language must be construed to mean the most recent edition at the time of the statute's enactment. The court stated:

> The answer to a question of law disposes of this appeal. The question is, under our statutory scheme, which version of the *Guides* should have been used to evaluate [claimant]'s impairment? When [claimant] was evaluated in 1994, the relevant statutes were NDCC 65-05-12 and 65-01-02(26). NDCC 65-05-12 authorized payment for permanent impairment after the claimant had attained maximum medical improvement, and directed use of the *Guides* to evaluate impairment:
>
>> Any rating of the percentage of functional impairment should be in accordance with the standards for the evaluation of permanent impairment as published in the *most recent edition* of the American medical association's "Guides to the Evaluation of Permanent Impairment" unless proven otherwise by clear and convincing medical evidence. [Emphasis added.]
>
> That relevant language had been enacted in 1989, *see* 1989 N.D. Sess. Laws ch. 765, § 4, and had not been amended or reenacted before [claimant]'s PPI evaluations in 1994.

The relevant language in NDCC 65-01-02(26), defining permanent impairment, had also been enacted in 1989:

> Permanent impairment means the loss of or loss of use of a member of the body existing after the date of maximum medical improvement or recovery, and includes disfigurement resulting from an injury if such disfigurement diminishes the ability of the employee to obtain employment. The loss must be determined in accordance with and based upon the *most current edition* of the American medical association's "Guides to the Evaluation of Permanent Impairment." Any impairment award, not expressly contemplated within the American medical association's "Guides to the Evaluation of Permanent Impairment", must be determined by clear and convincing medical evidence.

See 1989 N.D. Sess. Laws ch. 765 § 1 [emphasis added]. The entire section was amended and reenacted in 1991. *See* 1991 N.D. Sess. Laws ch. 714, § 23. Each section directed use of "the most current (recent) edition of the *Guides*" for rating the percentage of permanent impairment.

The chronologies of enactment of the relevant statutes and of publication of the various versions of the *Guides* shape the question of law to be answered in this case. When the statutory language designating the *Guides* as the standards for evaluation of permanent impairment was adopted in 1989, the Third Edition of the *Guides*, which designated only the ROM Model for evaluating spinal injuries, was in effect. The Third Edition Revised of the *Guides*, which retained the ROM Model, was published in December 1990 and was in effect when NDCC 65-01-02(26) was amended and reenacted in 1991. The Fourth Edition of the *Guides* was published in June 1993. The Fourth Edition designated the DRE Model as the preferred method for evaluating spinal injuries, but retained the ROM Model to be used to assist in determining what DRE category applied if there was uncertainty.

The Bureau argues that the Fourth Edition was the "most recent" and "most current" edition of the *Guides* when [claimant] was evaluated in 1994, so use of the DRE Model was designated. [Claimant] argues that the interpretation urged by the Bureau, automatically incorporating future versions of the *Guides* into the statute, would allow an unconstitutional delegation of legislative power to the American Medical Association. He therefore asserts we must instead read the statutes as incorporating the "most recent" and "most current" version of the *Guides* in existence when the statutes were enacted. Accordingly, [claimant] asserts, because the Fourth Edition with the DRE Model had not been published when the relevant statutes were enacted in 1989 and when NDCC 65-01-01(26) was reenacted in 1991, only the ROM Model could be used to evaluate his degree of permanent impairment.

We must construe statutes to avoid constitutional conflicts. *E.g., Shaver v. Kopp*, 545 N.W.2d 170, 173 (N.D. 1996); *Basin Elec. Power Coop. v. North Dakota Workers Compensation Bureau*, 541 N.W.2d 685, 689 (N.D. 1996). As *Peterson v. Peterson*, 1997 ND 14, ¶ 26, 559 N.W.2d 826, illustrates, if a statute is capable of two constructions, one that would render it of doubtful constitutionality and one that would not, the constitutional interpretation must be selected.

The interpretation of the relevant statutes urged by the Bureau in this case would raise significant constitutional conflicts. This case presents ambiguous statutes capable of two different constructions, one of doubtful constitutional validity. Accordingly, we adopt the construction that does not raise constitutional conflicts. Peterson, 1997 N.D. 14, ¶ 26, 559 N.W.2d 826. We therefore construe NDCC 65-05-12 and 65-01-02(26) to adopt the "most recent" and "most current" edition of the Guides in existence at the time of their enactment. As a matter of law, that interpretation directed use of the ROM Model to evaluate [claimant]'s percentage of impairment when the PPI evaluations were done in 1994.

567 N.W.2d at 203–05.

Coleman v. North Dakota Workers Compensation Bureau, 567 N.W.2d 853 (N.D. 1997)

The North Dakota court dealt with a claimant who injured his back and was evaluated for permanent partial impairment benefits under the *AMA Guides* (4th ed. 1993). The relevant statutory language required use of the "most current" or "most recent" edition of the *AMA Guides.* The claimant argued that to interpret this language to incorporate future versions of the *AMA Guides* automatically into the statute would allow an unconstitutional delegation of legislative power to the American Medical Association. The court held that the language must be construed to mean the most recent edition at the time of the statute's enactment.

McCollum v. Workers Compensation Bureau, 567 N.W.2d 811 (N.D. 1997)

The North Dakota court dealt with a claimant who injured his neck and back. At issue was which edition of the *AMA Guides* to use to measure the claimant's permanent partial impairment benefits. The relevant statutory language required use of the "most current" or "most recent" edition of the *AMA Guides.* The court held that the language must be construed to mean the most recent edition at the time of the statute's enactment.

Feist v. North Dakota Workers Compensation Bureau, 569 N.W.2d 1 (N.D. 1997)

The North Dakota court dealt with a claimant who had injured his back at work. The claimant claimed that he was entitled to a chronic pain evaluation under Chapter 15 of the *AMA Guides* (4th ed. 1993). The court held that he was not entitled to such an evaluation, as that edition of the *AMA Guides* was not in use at the time and the claimant had not presented medical evidence that he was suffering from chronic pain syndrome. The court stated:

> [Claimant] contends he is entitled to a chronic pain syndrome evaluation under Chapter 15 of the *AMA Guides* Fourth Edition in order to assess an additional impairment based on chronic pain. According to [claimant], the record supports that he has established a "presumptive diagnosis of chronic pain warranting an evaluation under Chapter 15." The Bureau argues [claimant] is not entitled to an additional permanent impairment for pain because the DRE Category III rating contemplated [claimant]'s pain.
>
> The *AMA Guides* recognize pain as being either "acute" or "chronic." *AMA Guides* (3rd ed.), p. 240. The *Stedman's Medical Dictionary* (5th Lawyers' Edition 1982), p. 20, defines "acute" as "[o]f short and sharp course, *not chronic;*" and, at p. 278, Stedman's defines "chronic" as "[o]f long duration; denoting a disease of slow progress and long continuance." (Emphasis added.) According to the *AMA Guides*, chronic pain may "contribute to the evolution of the chronic pain syndrome. Within the framework of this definition, chronic pain may exist in the absence of chronic pain syndrome, but chronic pain syndrome always presumes the presence of chronic pain." Chronic pain syndrome "represents a biopsychosocial phenomenon of maladaptive behavior with far-reaching medical, social, and economic consequences." *AMA Guides* (3rd ed.), p. 241. The AMA has outlined "characteristics (the six D's) [that] should be considered as establishing the diagnosis of a chronic pain syndrome." *Id.* The six characteristics are: duration, dramatization, drugs, despair, disuse, and dysfunction.
>
> Feist completed a chronic pain management program in February 1993. On February 19, 1993, the coordinator of the program reported [claimant] "demonstrate[d] no chronic pain behavior." At the hearing, [claimant] presented evidence establishing he suffers from pain; however, he did not present medical evidence establishing [that] he was suffering from "chronic pain," nor that he was diagnosed with "chronic pain syndrome." [Claimant] has not established he suffers "chronic pain," nor that he has been diagnosed with "chronic pain syndrome."
>
> Because the *AMA Guides* Third Edition was applicable when [claimant]'s impairment was evaluated in 1994, and because [claimant] has not shown he was diagnosed with "chronic pain syndrome," we need not address the issues [claimant] has raised with regard to interpreting provisions of the *AMA Guides* Fourth Edition for a "chronic pain syndrome" evaluation or impairment assessment.

569 N.W.2d at 6.

Kroeplin v. North Dakota Workmen's Compensation Bureau, 415 N.W.2d 807 (N.D. 1987)

An employee injured her right knee in a fall in the employer's parking lot and sought a permanent partial impairment award. The Workmen's Compensation Bureau denied the claim and the district court affirmed. The North Dakota

Supreme Court reversed, holding that the employee was entitled to the award despite the fact that the impairment was not substantiated by objective medical evidence under the *AMA Guides*.

The North Dakota Workmen's Compensation Bureau Directive 51C requires that the existence and degree of permanent impairment be based on medically and/or scientifically demonstrable findings, and adopts the *AMA Guides* as the primary standard for determining permanent impairment when it is not inconsistent with the North Dakota Workmen's Compensation Act. The directive also provides that "[n]othing in this directive shall be construed to prevent the presentation of demonstrable medical and/or scientific findings which are not contemplated by the American Medical Association 'Guides' in determining permanent impairment."

As interpreted by the bureau, the *AMA Guides* require an objective demonstration of impairment by loss in range of motion, strength loss, or sensory deficits. The bureau in Directive 51C held that "The claimant has not substantiated loss of range of motion to her knee, strength loss, or motion or sensory deficit to a degree which entitles to her [sic] a permanent partial impairment award pursuant to the *AMA Guides*."

> In *Lyson v. N.D. Workmen's Compensation Bureau*, 129 N.W.2d 351 (N.D. 1964), this court rejected the Bureau's contentions that it was "liable for compensation to a claimant, . . . , only to the extent that his disability may be demonstrated by objective physical findings." We see no reason to treat impairment differently than disability in this respect. It has been judicially recognized that "where pain is sufficiently severe to prevent a normal function of the member a partial loss of use of that member results." *Williamson v. Aetna Cas. & Sur. Co.*, 101 Ga. App. 220, 113 S.E.2d 208, 211 (1960). *See also Smith v. Industrial Comm'n*, 113 Ariz. 304, 552 P.2d 1198 (1976). . . . We conclude that the Workmen's Compensation Act authorized a permanent impairment award to an injured worker whose impairment was not objectively demonstrable. . . .
>
> Both physicians discerned pain and its effect. They identified objective evidence (chondromalacia and calcification) indicative of impairment, although not ratable under the *AMA Guides*. Both physicians found that [claimant] had an impairment, but they differed as to the degree. Accordingly we remand for further proceedings by the Bureau to determine the extent of impairment.

415 N.W.2d at 810.

Kavonius v. North Dakota Workmen's Compensation Bureau, 306 N.W.2d 209 (N.D. 1981)

The *AMA Guides* were mentioned in a footnote to a discussion of the claimant's eye injury.

> Prior to the injury, the visual acuity of [claimant]'s left eye was 20/30, which, according to the [*AMA Guides*] equates to a loss of approximately 10 percent of

central vision. Following the injury, the visual acuity of his left eye was 20/800, which equates to a loss of 95 percent of central vision. Thus, the injury caused an 85 percent loss of central vision in his left eye.

Id. at 210.

§ 11.27   OHIO

Dunn v. Eaton Corp., **1999 Ohio App. LEXIS 1758 (Ohio Ct. App. Mar. 1, 1999)**

The Ohio court dealt with a claimant who injured his eye when an eight-inch heated steel "billet" ejected from a furnace and struck him in the forehead. The claimant's claim for permanent partial disability was rejected. The hearing officer stated that the claimant "has not sustained a 40 percent loss of vision of the left eye. Claimant derives the 40% figure from the percentage loss of the visual field." The hearing officer went on to observe that the *AMA Guides* describe "vision" as being made up of three facets, visual field being only one of the three, and concluded that "there is no case law, statute, or rule that supports the claimant's contention that a loss of visual field directly correlates to loss of vision." The claimant appealed. The court found that although the hearing officer appeared to be incorrect in applying the *AMA Guides*, the claimant's appeal must fail for procedural reasons. It stated:

> The initial hearing officer stated that "there is no case law, statute or rule that supports claimant's contention that a loss of visual field directly correlates to loss of vision," and the reviewing officer determined that appellant had failed to present precise evidence of his loss of uncorrected vision. However, our review of the AMA guidelines reveals that impairment of an individual eye is determined by combining "loss of central vision" with "loss of visual field" and "loss of ocular motility." While the evidence is uncontroverted that appellant suffered a 40% loss of visual field to the left eye, there is no evidence that appellant has suffered loss to his "central vision" or ocular motility.
>
> Although the "combined values chart" that governs single eye impairment does not contemplate cases like appellant's, where there is substantial loss of visual field but no other loss, the formula by which the chart is generated indicates that appellant has suffered at least a 40% impairment in his left eye. Moreover, the Industrial Commission Medical Examination Manual has apparently incorporated the AMA guidelines as the basis for evaluating vision loss. It therefore appears to this Court that both hearing officers were incorrect.
>
> However, we agree with appellee that the orders did not deny appellant the right to participate in the Worker's Compensation Fund, but rather incorrectly calculated the extent of appellant's disability. In *Zavatsky v. Stringer* (1978), 56 Ohio St. 2d 386, 384 N.E.2d 693, the Supreme Court held:
>
>> A determination of "extent of disability" under R.C. 4123.519 presupposes that claimant has been allowed the "right to participate" in the Workers' Compensation Fund for injury to a specific part or parts of the

body involving the loss or impairment of bodily functions. The decision of the Industrial Commission as to "extent of disability" constitutes a determination of the basis for the computation of the compensation or benefits payable under the provisions of the Workers' compensation law for those losses or impairments of bodily functions allowed as compensable injuries.

Id. at paragraph two of the syllabus. Under the foregoing standard, the decision to deny appellant's motion for compensation for his visual loss clearly resulted from the hearing officer's misapplication of the appropriate guidelines. It was not a denial of appellant's right to participate in the system, but rather a determination that his visual field loss was not so severe as to be separately compensable. Appellant's argument that the hearing officer misapplied the AMA Guidelines is essentially a claim of abuse of discretion, which is properly brought by mandamus action. *See, e.g., State ex rel. Kroger Co. v. Stover* (1987), 31 Ohio St. 3d 229, 232–33, 510 N.E.2d 356.

We therefore believe that the trial court correctly concluded that the administrative decision at issue in this case affected only the extent of appellant's participation in the worker's compensation system for his ocular injury, rather than his right to participate in the system. For the foregoing reasons, appellant's sole assignment of error is overruled and the judgment of the Common Pleas Court of Marion County is affirmed.

1999 Ohio App. LEXIS 1758, at 9–10.

State ex rel. Dresser v. Industrial Comm'n, 652 N.E.2d 1020 (Ohio 1995)

The Ohio court dealt with a claimant who asserted a total permanent disability due to post-traumatic stress disorder. In awarding benefits to the claimant, the board relied on a physician's report, even though that physician did not examine the patient personally. The board accepted that physician's conclusions, even though these conclusions differed from those of the physicians who had personally examined the claimant. The court held that, although that physician was legally required to accept the factual findings of the physicians who had actually examined the claimant, he was not encumbered by their conclusions predicated on these findings.

State ex rel. McLean v. Industrial Comm'n, 25 Ohio St. 3d, 90 495 N.E.2d 370 (1986)

The claimant suffered a crushed right foot, which required the amputation of the foot approximately two and a half inches above the ankle. The claimant was granted compensation for the loss of his foot. His application for additional compensation was denied by the Industrial Commission. The claimant appealed to the regional board of review, alleging that the commission abused its discretion by failing to award compensation for the loss of his leg. The court held that the commission did not abuse its discretion in denying additional compensation.

The court referred to the *AMA Guides* as supporting the finding that the injury should not get a higher rating than the loss of a foot. The court stated:

> [P]ublication No. FA-480 instructs examining physicians that they may use among other publications, the American Medical Association's *Guides to the Evaluation of Permanent Impairment* as a guide for determining impairment. The AMA publication, while not identical to the bureau's Claims Examiner's Manual, in that it is based on a gradation of impairment, does not result in a greater impairment to the lower extremity than would the amputation of the foot at the ankle.

495 N.E.2d at 372.

State ex rel. Ferris v. Comm'n, Franklin App. No. 85AP-599 (May 20, 1986)

The claimant was awarded temporary total benefits for a herniated disk. Later the award was increased to include an award for a 50 percent permanent partial disability. In 1982 his claim for dysthymic disorder was allowed. The hearing officer granted a 25 percent increase, from a 50 percent to a 75 percent permanent partial impairment. The hearing officer used the combined values chart from the *AMA Guides* for a 50 percent psychiatric impairment to arrive at the 75 percent rating. The claimant then filed a writ of mandamus asking for a 100 percent rating, claiming that the Industrial Commission abused its discretion by using the combined effects chart because there was no medical evidence on the chart's effects. The referee concluded that the combined effects chart is merely a reference device to be used by physicians. The referee then recommended a limited writ of mandamus ordering the commission to consider properly the combined effects of the allowed conditions because the referee found no medical evidence on the combined effects. The court of appeals granted a limited writ of mandamus, saying that the combined effect is a matter of medical expertise.

§ 11.28   OKLAHOMA

Conaghan v. Riverfield Country Day Sch., 163 P.3d 557 (Okla. 2007)

The Oklahoma Supreme Court dealt with the claimant, Conaghan, who injured her right knee at work. The independent medical examiner and the treating physician rated the knee at 12 percent permanent partial disability. A physician, selected by the claimant, rated her impairment at 45 percent under the *AMA Guides*. The court dealt with the interpretation of the two statutory provisions.

The rebuttable presumption in favor of the treating physician's opinion was upheld as it may be rebutted by another physician's objective medical evidence.

The court did find, however, the language in the statute restricting the workers' compensation court's determination of impairment and disability within the range of opinions of the treating physician and the independent medical examiners was constitutionally infirm, and it was stricken. The court stated:

> We conclude that the rebuttable presumption in favor of the treating physician's opinions, codified at 85 O.S. Supp. 2005, § 17(A)(2)(a), is facially consistent with our extant jurisprudence governing presumptions. Under this conclusion, when the workers' compensation court admits the treating physician's report into the record as competent, probative evidence, the report is prima facie evidence of causation, disability, and/or medical and rehabilitation needs as set out in the report and the burden of proof is shifted to the opposing party to offer evidence to the contrary; when the opponent, here the claimant, offers objective medical evidence to the contrary and the court admits that evidence into the record as competent, probative evidence, the presumption disappears; and the judge then proceeds to weigh all evidence and adjudicate the issues presented.
>
> We also conclude that the language "within the range of opinions of the treating physician and the Independent Medical Examiner" in subparagraph 17(A)(2)(b) violates our constitutional separation of powers provision and it should be severed from the statute. The language "within the range of opinions of the treating physician and the Independent Medical Examiner" is severed from the remainder of the provisions in 85 O.S. Supp. 2005, § 17(A)(2)(b). Accordingly, we reverse the paragraphs in the order of the workers' compensation court that are inconsistent with this opinion and leave the remainder of the order in effect.

163 P.3d at 565–66.

Moore v. Uniroyal Goodrich, 935 P.2d 1193 (Okla. Ct. App. 1997)

The Oklahoma court dealt with a man who claimed he had suffered a work-related cumulative trauma injury. The Workers' Compensation Court found that the claimant suffered from non-work-related rheumatoid arthritis. This finding was based on a medical report from Dr. A. The Oklahoma Court of Appeals held that Dr. A.'s report was proper evidence despite its not being in compliance with the *AMA Guides*. The court stated:

> Respondent's medical expert found Claimant's symptoms to be the result of rheumatoid arthritis. It was his unequivocal opinion that rheumatoid arthritis was not job-related, nor was it aggravated by Claimant's work. He found no work-related disability.
>
> On appeal, Claimant argues that the report of Respondent's medical expert, Dr. A., is incompetent and thus could not be a proper evidentiary basis for the denial of the claim. Specifically, it is claimed the report is not in compliance with the AMA *Guides*. We find this contention to be insufficient to overturn the decision of the three judge panel.

Rule 21 of the Workers' Compensation Rules, 85 O.S. 1991 Ch. 4, App. requires [that a] physician's evaluation of the extent of permanent impairment shall be prepared in substantial compliance with the AMA *Guides to the Evaluation of Permanent Impairment.* This presumes that such impairment is work-related. It seems obvious that when a physician is of the opinion that any disability is *not work-related,* compliance or noncompliance with the *Guides* as to the extent of impairment is immaterial. That there be a *work-related* injury, one that arises out of and in the course of employment, is a requirement for compensability under the Workers' Compensation Act. The finding that there was no such injury moots any dispute over the disability rating.

935 P.2d at 1194.

Green v. Glass, 920 P.2d 1081 (Okla. Ct. App. 1996)

The Oklahoma court dealt with a worker who suffered from tinnitus due to exposure to loud noise over a period of time. It held that the claimant was not denied equal protection under the law through the Oklahoma Workers' Compensation Act's mandated use of the *AMA Guides.* The court stated:

Claimant first argues that the exclusive use of the American Medical Association *Guides to the Evaluation of Permanent Impairment (Guides),* as mandated by Workers' Compensation Court Rule 32, 85 O.S. 1991, Ch. 4, App. and 85 O.S. 1991 § 22(3), denies her equal protection of the law under the Fourteenth Amendment to the U.S. Constitution, and under Article 2, § 2 of the Oklahoma Constitution. Claimant's argument is premised on the assertion that evaluation of hearing loss must be based on the *Guides,* but in evaluating other injuries, according to Claimant, a physician may deviate from the *Guides* if an adequate explanation is given.

The authorities cited by Claimant do not demonstrate any disparate treatment. Section 3(11) of Title 85, Oklahoma Statutes (1991), the version in effect on Claimant's conceded "date of injury," required all evaluations on non-scheduled members to follow the *Guides.* Rule 20, Workers' Compensation Court Rules, 85 O.S. 1991, Ch. 4, App., makes a similar requirement as does Rule 32. We can find no basis for Claimant's argument that hearing loss claims are treated any differently than injuries to other non-scheduled members. In the absence of "unequal" treatment, Claimant cannot demonstrate any denial of equal protection, and the trial court's decision will not be disturbed on the basis of Claimant's constitutional argument.

920 P.2d at 1082.

Farm Fresh, Inc. v. Bucek, 895 P.2d 719 (Okla. 1995)

The Oklahoma court dealt with a worker who was awarded permanent total disability benefits. The claimant was awarded permanent total disability benefits even though two physicians had rated his impairment under the *AMA Guides* at

16 percent and 11 percent. The key legal issue the court had to deal with was the definition of the terms *impairment* and *disability*. In defining these terms, the court quoted favorably from and relied heavily on the *AMA Guides* (3d ed. 1988). The court stated:

> The American Medical Association *Guides to the Evaluation of Permanent Impairment [AMA Guides]* provides helpful insight into the impairment-disability dichotomy. An impairment is viewed as a "medical matter;" whereas disability is deemed to "arise out of the interaction between impairment and external demands." ... In short, permanent partial disability, as distinguished from other payout classes, contemplates recompense for lost physical fitness. .... The issue of permanent total disability turns on the evaluation of the worker's present capacity "to earn any wages in any employment for which he is presently suited or fitted by education training or experience." The determination of a claimant's disability-based benefits is a fact question for the trial tribunal.

Id. at 723–24. The award of benefits was affirmed.

Mercury Marine v. Lumpkin, 887 P.2d 1388 (Okla. Ct. App. 1994)

The Oklahoma court dealt with a claimant who was rated under the *AMA Guides* at a 14 percent whole-body impairment by a physician appointed by the Workers' Compensation Court. The Workers' Compensation Court rated the claimant's whole-body impairment at 27 percent. The court held that the Workers' Compensation Court had deviated from the court-appointed rating physician's impairment rating by more than 10 percent without specifically indicating the reason for the deviation, as required by the statute. The court ordered the matter remanded, with instructions to modify the award to no more than a 24 percent impairment or to explain specifically the basis for exceeding the 24 percent rating.

Special Indem. Fund v. Choate, 847 P.2d 796 (Okla. 1993)

The Oklahoma Supreme Court dealt with a claimant who filed claims for a respiratory injury and a hearing loss. The two matters were heard together and resulted in separate awards against the employer of a 15 percent permanent partial disability to the body as a whole because of injury to the respiratory system and a 15 percent binaural hearing loss.

The court of appeals determined that the claimant's medical evidence was incompetent because it did not conform to the Combined Values Chart of the *AMA Guides* and that the claimant had a 28 percent impairment as a result of combining the two injuries using said chart.

The court found that objection to the fund's medical evidence was incorrectly sustained and that the Combined Values Chart was not intended to be used in cases involving a material increase in impairment.

The court stated:

> [Claimant] argues on appeal the trial tribunal action in excluding the evidence was proper because Dr. L.Y. stated in his report he used the *AMA Guides* in his examination and opinion and when a doctor so states his report must completely adhere to the *AMA Guides*. We can conceive of no rationale requiring complete exclusion of medical evidence on this ground. At most it would go to the credibility of the doctor. Such an apparent inconsistent statement as that contained in the report might merely exhibit some type of oversight in drafting the report.

* * *

> It is our opinion the Legislature, when it exempted evaluation of hearing loss from the *AMA Guides*, by treating such a loss separately, controlled by its own schedule of compensation, intended such a loss would be exempted for all purposes, including combining such loss with another impairment to a different portion of the body in evaluation of whether a material increase is warranted against the Fund.
>
> A second reason we do not believe the Legislature intended the Combined Values Chart of the *AMA Guides* to be used in evaluation of a material increase in a proceeding against the Fund is the Chart does not measure a material increase in the combination of two or more impairments. Although the purpose of the Chart is a method to combine two or more impairments into one impairment rating to the body as a whole, as the explanation provided in the preface quoted above makes clear, use of the Chart would inevitably lead to no situation (or very few) where a material increase could be awarded because combination of two whole person impairment ratings would equal less than the sum of the two added together. We find such a result absurd and we will not presume the Legislature intended it.

Id. at 807, 809.

Lacy v. Schlumberger Well Serv., 839 P.2d 157 (Okla. 1992)

The Oklahoma Supreme Court dealt with the claimant who alleged a work-related respiratory injury. The employer offered the testimony of a physician, a board-certified internal medicine specialist, who concluded that the condition was asthma and not work related. This physician used computer equipment to perform his exam.

The court found that because a proper objection was not made in a timely fashion, the reliance by the physician on computerized equipment for performing spirometric evaluations was in conformity with the *AMA Guides*. The court stated:

> The Court of Appeals found a deviation from the Guides because Dr. [S.] stated that he did not know whether the predicted values used by his computerized equipment for performing spirometric evaluations were identical to those taken from the *AMA Guides* and acknowledged that he had taken the predicted

values from the computer. Dr. [S.] stated in his deposition that he was "sure they must be in conformance with AMA guidelines" but that he did not know if the values were identical. The statement that the predicted values used by the computer were in conformity with the *AMA Guides* was not questioned by claimant. More importantly, no actual deviation from the *Guides* was ever claimed by claimant or is shown by the record. Therefore, the statement that the predicted values used by the computer are in conformity with the *Guides* stands uncontroverted, and there is no basis for finding a deviation from the *Guides.*

Id. at 163.

Weyerhaeuser Co. v. Washington, **838 P.2d 539 (Okla. Ct. App. 1992)**

The Oklahoma court dealt with the claimant, who was employed for one year in 1972 and again from August 1988 until February 1990. Her duties as a crew person included operating various saws, vacuuming paint from boards, and working on the S.I. line. The claimant testified that during her last term of employment she was exposed to various chemicals and airborne particulates, including formaldehyde, paint, sawdust, and asbestos. She used only a paper mask in the area where rejected boards were recycled. As a full-time employee, she was exposed to these substances on almost a daily basis, with February 1990 as the approximate date of the last exposure.

The claimant also smoked. She developed a permanent impairment rated at 25 percent of the lungs and 5 percent of the upper respiratory system.

The court affirmed the award, finding that the employer failed to prove that the smoking contributed to the impairment. The court stated:

> The *Guides* provide that data on environmental exposures and use of tobacco are important factors when an examining physician is asked to give an opinion on apportionment between causes of a lung disorder. American Medical Association, *Guides to the Evaluation of Permanent Impairment,* 108 (3rd ed. 1988). The *Guides* define "apportionment" as:
>
>> [T]he determination of the degree to which each of various occupational or nonoccupational factors has contributed to a particular impairment. For each alleged factor, two criteria must be met: (a) The alleged factor could have caused the impairment, which is a *medical* decision, and (b) in the particular case, the factor did cause the impairment, which is a *nonmedical* determination.

Id. at 540.

The claimant denied any respiratory impairment before returning to work in 1988. Under those circumstances, the employer had the burden of proving not only a preexisting impairment, but also its extent. The employer presented no evidence, either through its expert or by cross-examination of the claimant's physician, that the claimant's voluntary use of cigarettes may have been a contributing factor in the impairment to her lungs and upper respiratory system.

See id. at 541.

Parks v. Blue Circle, Inc., 832 P.2d 11 (Okla. 1992)

The Oklahoma Supreme Court dealt with a claimant who testified that he had smoked a pack of cigarettes a day intermittently for 10 to 15 years. The claimant further testified that he had been exposed to dust and chemicals for 18 years while working for the respondent. In his Form 3, the claimant maintained he had suffered injury to his lungs and upper respiratory system. The claimant testified that he bowled once a week and played golf three or four times a week. He carried his clubs and walked the 18 holes 75 percent to 80 percent of the time that he played golf.

Two doctors who examined the claimant found no impairment. Neither doctor performed a D_{co} test. The court found that a 0 percent respiratory rating could be done without performing a D_{co} test. The court stated:

> In the present case, neither doctor specifically stated that the complaints were consistent with the ventilatory function tests. We do not find this to be a fatal flaw in that both doctors stated that their reports complied with the American Medical Association's *Guides to the Evaluation of Permanent Impairment.* In order for the report to be in compliance with the *Guides*, it was necessary that the doctor tendering the report find that the complaints were not of greater severity than the ventilatory function tests would indicate. Neither of the reports was incompetent for failure to give the D_{co} test.

Id. at 11.

Kropp v. Goodrich, 829 P.2d 33 (Okla. 1992)

The Oklahoma Supreme Court dealt with a respiratory impairment case. The employer introduced the medical report of a physician, who found that there was no impairment. The spirometry tests on which the physician based his report were within the 95 percent confidence interval. The claimant gave the physician a history, stating that the claimant could climb two flights of stairs before slowing down and that there was no limit to the distance he could walk on a level surface. The claimant stated that he could keep up with people his own age but noted that he did not play backyard football because of shortness of breath. The physician stated that the claimant's history of being able to keep up with people his own age and walking as far as he wanted was consistent with this exam.

The court affirmed the denial of benefits, finding that whether complaints are of greater severity than the spirometry results are an area of medical discretion and that a D_{co} test is not always required before a claimant may be rated at 0 percent impairment. The court stated, "In the present case, the spirometry tests were within the 95% confidence interval. The result of the spirometry test allowed for a rating of zero impairment." *Id.* at 34.

TRW/REDA Pump v. Brewington, 829 P.2d 15 (Okla. 1992)

The Oklahoma Supreme Court dealt with permanent partial disability awards to six workers' compensation claimants. The court found that in three of the cases, the appeal from the workers' compensation court was patently frivolous and awarded attorney fees. With regard to the *AMA Guides*, the court found:

1. The statute does not require use of the *AMA Guides* when an injury is to a scheduled member,
2. The loss of range of motion is an appropriate method to evaluate impairment, and
3. The upper respiratory impairment is controlled by Table 5 (air passage defects).

The court stated:

> The American Medical Association *Guides to the Evaluation of Permanent Impairment* (3rd ed. 1988) require range of motion tests [to] be repeated at least three times and which must fall within +/−10% or 5 degrees (whichever is greater) of each other to be considered consistent. 1988 *AMA Guides*, pg. 71. The 1984 *Guides* do not require such repetition.
>
> We note from a review of the American Medical Association *Guides to the Evaluation of Impairment* (2d ed. 1984), upper respiratory system impairment appears to be controlled by and is to be evaluated in accordance with Table 5. . . .

829 P.2d at 31.

Oklahoma Tax Comm'n v. Evans, 827 P.2d 183 (Okla. Ct. App. 1992)

The Oklahoma court dealt with an award that combined the permanent partial impairment to both of the claimant's hands with a permanent partial impairment to the body as a whole. The State Fund argued that although the Oklahoma statute provides an exception for using the *AMA Guides* in evaluating permanent impairment of scheduled members, the exception for evaluating impairment to the scheduled members themselves does not extend to combining impairment to scheduled members for purposes of evaluating impairment to the body as a whole. The State Fund argued that permanent impairment to the body as a whole can be evaluated only pursuant to the *AMA Guides* and that the *AMA Guides* do not provide for combining impairment to scheduled members for that purpose.

The court held that combining the rating into an impairment of the body as a whole was not incorrect. The court stated:

> Claimant's doctor, the State Fund's doctor, and the independent, court-appointed doctor *all* combined the impairment to claimant's hands into impairment to the body as a whole and the evaluation and opinion of those doctors is ample competent evidence to support the order of the three-judge panel. The modification of the trial court's award of benefits by combining the permanent partial impairment to both of claimant's hands into permanent partial impairment to the body as a whole was neither erroneous as a matter of law nor unsupported by competent evidence.

Id. at 184.

Davis v. B.F. Goodrich, 826 P.2d 587 (Okla. 1992)

The Oklahoma Supreme Court dealt with the claimant, who filed a workers' compensation claim alleging injury to his lungs and upper respiratory system caused by continuous exposure to hazardous chemicals, including industrial talc and fumes, while employed. The claimant began working for the employer on March 15, 1971, and worked there for 15 years.

The employer submitted a medical report that did not include a VO_2 or a D_{co} test. The issue was whether this was permitted under the *AMA Guides.* The court reviewed the requirements under the *AMA Guides* for rating a respiratory Impairment and found that the testing was not required before reaching a 0 percent impairment. The court stated:

> The test schema for physiologic testing clearly indicates that when the FEV_1 [forced expiratory volume], the PVC, and the ratio of the two are within the normal limits (the predicated value minus the 95 percent confidence interval) and the patient's respiratory complaints are consistent with those measurements, the physician is not required under the 1984 *Guide*, to administer a D_{co} test or a VO_2 test. As stated earlier, if the results of the FEV_1, the PVC, and the ratio of the two are within the normal range and consistent with the claimant's complaints, then the physician can give a classification of zero impairment, and it would be unnecessary to administer either of the other two tests. The 1984 *Guide* simply does not require a physician to always give the D_{co} or the VO_2 test before giving a Class 1 zero impairment rating.

Id. at 591. Justice K., dissenting, stated:

> Section 3(11) vests in a purely private organization, the American Medical Association, the unbridled authority to set standards for permanent impairment which govern an employee's right to collect compensation for on-the-job injuries. This delegation is made *without guides, restrictions, or standards.* It has resulted in the requiring of often unnecessary but expensive tests which

increase the cost of the system, the cost of workers' compensation insurance, the cost of doing business, and the cost of products to the ultimate consumers. The Legislature may not delegate the legislative power to a privately controlled national organization. Section 3(11) is unconstitutional because it vests the American Medical Association with the authority to determine the standards for the evaluation of permanent impairment—a power reserved to the Legislature acting in its law-making capacity.

Id. at 599.

Houston v. Zebco, 821 P.2d 367 (Okla. 1991)

The Oklahoma Supreme Court dealt with a claim for cumulative trauma hearing loss due to noise exposure at work. At the hearing, the medical testimony of the claimant was found to be incompetent and without probative value, as the doctor did not present a detailed history as required by the *AMA Guides.* The issue became whether the claimant would be given an opportunity to present new or additional medical evidence. The supreme court found that the claimant should be given this opportunity and stated.

> The trial judge never specifically explained his reasons for determining petitioner's medical evidence was incompetent and wholly without probative value. On appeal, respondents put forward two central rationales for the trial judge's ruling in such regard. First, Dr. G.C.M. based his opinion as to causation on mere speculation because he had a complete lack of knowledge of petitioner's noise exposure at work. Second, as to the extent of impairment, Dr. G.C.M. deviated from the American Medical Association *Guides to the Evaluation of Permanent Impairment* (2d ed. 1984) by adding into the impairment rating a percentage for tinnitus (a sensation of noise or ringing in the ears), when such a percentage may only be added when a unilateral hearing loss is found, rather than a bilateral one.
>
> Thus, before the instant claim was denied, petitioner should have been given an opportunity to either substitute another medical evaluation or to stand on her medical evidence, something not afforded by the trial judge.

Id. at 369.

Hollytex Carpet Mills, Inc. v. Hinkle, 819 P.2d 289 (Okla. Ct. App. 1991)

The Oklahoma court dealt with a claimant who alleged that she developed asthma as a result of exposure to "fly away" carpet fibers at work. The medical report offered as evidence for the employee found a 22 percent impairment but used the *AMA Guides* (2d ed. 1984) instead of the *AMA Guides* (3d ed. 1988). The workers' compensation statute required that the examining physician use the latest edition of the *AMA Guides* in effect at the time of the incident for which workers' compensation was sought. However, the court found the report incompetent and remanded the case because, in addition to using the incorrect edition, the report did not contain the required raw data. The court stated:

> That is to say that Rule 20(C) requires a physician to set forth in his report "the physician's findings on examination, including a description of the examination and any diagnostic tests," while the *AMA Guides* themselves require a physician's opinion as to degree of respiratory impairment/disability to be based on the results of two spirometric maneuvers and the ratio thereof, i.e., forced vital capacity (FVC), forced expiratory volume in the first second (FEV$_1$), and the ratio of these results (FVC/FEV$_1$). In the present case, Dr. L.'s report contains none of the raw data from claimant's spirometric maneuvers as required by Rule 20(C), and Dr. L.'s opinion shows on its face to be based on below-lower-limit-of-normal findings on only two of the tests, FVC and FEV$_1$, without a finding as to the result of the ratio of FVC and FEV, as required by the *AMA Guides*, Second Edition.
>
> This being the case, we find Dr. L.'s report incompetent under the *AMA Guides*, Second Edition, and the lower court's finding to the contrary in error.

Id. at 291.

Huffman v. General Motors Corp., 811 P.2d 106 (Okla. Ct. App. 1991)

The Oklahoma court dealt with a claimant who developed a respiratory condition as a result of exposure to silicon bronze spray at work. The claimant offered a medical report from a physician in support of his claim at trial. The physician's report concluded that the claimant's spirometric test results were normal, but he nevertheless rated him for permanent partial disability based upon dyspnea. The employer objected to this report, arguing it was not in substantial compliance with the *AMA Guides* (2d ed. 1984). The trial judge admitted the physician's report and found the claimant 55 percent permanently partially disabled. The court found that the medical report was admissible based on dyspnea, as the report was in substantial compliance with the *AMA Guides* (2d ed. 1984), which permitted the physician to consider other personal and psychological factors.

Oklahoma State Penitentiary v. Weaver, 809 P.2d 1324 (Okla. Ct. App. 1991)

The claimant injured her arm in a prison riot. She later developed a psychological overlay. After the hearing, the trial court found the claimant had sustained no compensable injury to her neck and had suffered no permanent partial disability to her right arm. However, the trial court determined the claimant to be 15 percent permanently partially disabled due to post-traumatic stress syndrome. The employer attacked the medical report as not being in compliance with the *AMA Guides*, as the physician did not observe the patient's activities of daily living, social function, concentration persistence, or adaptive functioning. The court affirmed the decision, finding that the physician need not make the observations personally. The court stated:

> We find that Section 14.3 of the *Guides* does not require the examining physician to observe the patient in the areas above-described; rather, the *Guides* require severity of psychological impairment be assessed in terms of functional limitations on activities in the specified four areas. Further, Section 14.2 of the *Guides* states that information from both medical and non-medical sources may be used to obtain detailed descriptions of the patient's activities in the four areas, and such information may be provided by anyone having knowledge of the patient's functional limitations.
>
> Under the *Guides*, the presence and severity of psychological impairment should be documented primarily on the basis of information and reports from other physicians and care-givers, as well as information regarding the patient's functional limitations. *See Guides* Section 14.2, Section 14.3 The medical narrative report in the instant case not only contains a detailed description of claimant's functional limitations in the four areas above-noted, but also notes test results and the fact that claimant's examining physician had reviewed the reports of three other physicians who had examined claimant. Further, the record reflects that claimant proffered a supplemental report in which the examining physician notes that the *Guides* require a physician's judgment in rating psychological impairment to be based on clinical impression rather than empirical evidence. *See, Guides* Section 14.5. We thus hold the admission of claimant's examining physician's reports, which were in substantial compliance with 85 O.S. Section 3(11) and Rule 20, was not error.

Id. at 1327.

Branstetter v. TRW/Reda Pump, 809 P.2d 1305 (Okla. 1991)

The claimant worked with chemicals and developed obstructive lung disease. At the hearing, the employer introduced a report from a physician, who stated that, in his opinion, the claimant was not disabled. The pulmonary function testing performed under this physician's direction was, in his judgment, inconclusive. The computer-generated report of the FEV_1 test indicated severe obstructive lung defect but contained a handwritten note by the pulmonary specialist who interpreted the tests, saying, "Inconsistent data suggests suboptimal performance." The physician's lengthy report concluded that the test results were invalid because the claimant did not cooperate with the testing and that, as a result, the *AMA Guides* could not be applied.

The Oklahoma Supreme Court found that the doctor could not just say the claimant was not trying on the spirometry test and deny benefits without first following up with the VO_2 estimated exercise capacity test required by the *AMA Guides* when the "individual has not performed maximally or correctly in the spirometry." The court stated, "We must here also find that the Employer's medical report is insufficient under the *AMA Guides*." *Id.* at 1308.

Collins v. Halliburton Servs., 804 P.2d 440 (Okla. 1990)

The claimant began operating a turret lathe in 1973. Her employment as a machinist continued until March 21, 1984, when a back injury and a heart condition allegedly forced her to stop working. This action was filed March 25, 1986. The claimant testified that she was exposed to various chemicals and fumes at work, including smoke produced by the lathe, machine coolant, propane exhaust, cigarette smoke, and oil. She stated, and one physician agreed, that she acquired an upper respiratory condition as a result of long-term exposure to these chemicals and fumes.

The court denied the claim, finding that the claimant had had asthma for many years. The court stated:

> A year-and-a-half after [claimant] left [employer], an industrial hygienist performed air quality tests at the facility where she had worked. He determined from these tests that the fumes and smoke present were well within OSHA limits and rendered an expert opinion that the facility was safe for workers. The trial court admitted these test results and conclusions, but refused to consider a medical report offered by [employer] because the report did not comply with the *AMA Guides to the Evaluation of Permanent Impairment* pursuant to Workers' Compensation Rule 20. The trial court, however, did admit medical records indicating that [claimant] had visited an asthma specialist and had been a "known adult onset asthmatic" for 20 years. These records further showed that [claimant] had been taking medication for the asthma for many years. [Claimant] denied having had asthma.

Id. at 441–42.

York v. Burgess-Norton Mfg. Co., 803 P.2d 697 (Okla. 1990)

The claimant sustained an employment-related injury to his lungs and upper respiratory system. He was rated under the *AMA Guides*. The employer's physician found that, despite a forced vital capacity (FVC) of only 44 percent of the predicted value, the claimant had no lung disease. The physician "took exception to the *Guides*" and gave the claimant a 0 percent impairment rating.

The court found that because the physician did not perform an estimated VO_2 test, the report was an unauthorized departure from the *AMA Guides*, and thus could not support a denial of benefits.

In addition, the court found that the claimant's physician's report complied with the *AMA Guides* despite the fact that the report lacked the precise amount of toxic exposure sustained by the claimant. The court found that the evidence supported the presence and extent of permanent impairment.

Zebco v. Houston, 800 P.2d 245 (Okla. 1990)

The claimant sought disability compensation for a respiratory impairment from the inhalation of air pollutants. The court of appeals vacated the workers' compensation court award, but the supreme court remanded with instructions. The supreme court held that, although the physician's opinion presented by the claimant had no probative value due to the physician's lack of any knowledge about frequency, duration, and source of lung-irritating exposure, the claimant was entitled to another opportunity to prove her claim. The evidence of the extent of the exposure and the nature of the spray indicated that the claimant could have secured a favorable opinion based on a complete history.

The employer argued that the claimant's medical opinion lacked probative value because the physician failed to comply with the *AMA Guides*, formed his opinion from an incomplete history, and could not describe the nature, concentration, or source of the air pollutants to which the claimant had been exposed. The *AMA Guides* state that the examiner should question the employee about exposures to dusts, gases, vapors, and fumes, including the year of first exposure, the extent of the exposure, the total number of years of exposure, an estimate of the hazard that the agent posed, and the number of years since the exposure ceased. Absent such specific information, the claimant's history must be considered deficient and devoid of probative force. However, the physician need not have known the chemical content or the names of the contaminants, the size of the building, or the results of any environmental studies, as the court of appeals would have required.

The claimant's history indicated that for six or seven years she had worked on a machine drilling holes into plastic parts. During the performance of this task, claimant was exposed to a "red lubricant spray" that the machine injected onto the drill. The court felt that this description amply indicated that the employee inhaled some chemical ingredient that could have been pathogenic. The court concluded:

> For evaluation of respiratory impairment from inhalation exposure to "dusts, gases, vapors and fumes" the *AMA Guides* require that the examining physician ask the claimant about, and hence consider, the "extent of exposure." (*AMA Guides*, 2d ed. at 86.) Although the claimant's doctor admitted he did not know the frequency of the claimant's exposure to the spray which came from the machine at work, the claimant testified that she had inhaled the lubricant for at least half of each working day. In light of these facts, coupled with those revealed in the employer's medical report about the nature of the spray, it appears that the claimant may on remand secure a favorable opinion based on her complete history.

Id. at 248.

The court also noted that it *did not* intimate that the *AMA Guides* require the physician to know with precision the extent of exposure. In this case, the cross-examination of the claimant's doctor revealed a lack of any knowledge about the frequency, duration, or even the source of lung-irritating exposure. *See id.* at 248 n.11.

Williams v. Vickers, Inc., 799 P.2d 621 (Okla. 1990)

The claimant machinist sought an award of disability compensation for a hearing loss attributable to his employment. The trial judge denied the claim, and the court of appeals affirmed. The supreme court vacated the opinion of the court of appeals but sustained the order denying the claim, holding that the denial was supported by the evidence, including the employer's audiogram showing no considerable difference in test patterns before and after the alleged injury.

The employer offered its own physician's medical report in which the claimant's hearing was evaluated in accordance with the standards prescribed by not only Rule 37, but also by those of Rule 32, which replaced Rule 37 as of June 1, 1987. Rule 32 was hence in effect at the time this claim was filed. Rule 32 requires strict adherence to the criteria set out in the *AMA Guides* "in all claims filed on or after the effective date of this rule." In the *AMA Guides* (2d ed. 1984), the maximum sound frequency to be used in hearing tests is 3,000 Hz, while the provisions of Rule 37 made 4,000 Hz the highest test frequency. Applying Rule 37's criteria, the employer's medical expert found hearing impairment at sound levels above 3,000 Hz, but under Rule 32 (or the current edition of the *AMA Guides*) standards no hearing loss was found. The claimant conceded that if Rule 32's evaluation standard were applicable, his hearing loss would not be compensable.

The court of appeals sustained the claim's denial, holding that Rule 37 was inconsistent with Okla. Stat. tit. 85, § 3(11) (supp. 1985), which required use of the latest (then 1984) edition of the *AMA Guides*, and the statute must control. The court also concluded that the change from Rule 37 to Rule 32, which took place after the injury was alleged to have occurred, had no substantial effect on the claimant's rights. The supreme court granted certiorari because the dispositive question was not which rule applied, but rather whether the trial court's denial of the claim was supported by the record. The court believed that it was.

> Nothing in the record supports the assumption that the Workers' Compensation Court both chose to apply Rule 32 and found that the claimant incurred no permanent hearing loss. The very terms of the order show that the claim was denied solely for lack of work-related injury. Only if a compensable injury is found to have occurred could the claimant be compensated for permanent impairment resulting from his harm. The trial judge's finding that no on-the-job injury had occurred obviated any need for choosing between Rules 37 and 32.

799 P.2d at 624.

Gaines v. Sun Refinery & Mktg., **790 P.2d 1073 (Okla. 1990)**

The Oklahoma Workers' Compensation Court ruled that the claimant had not suffered an accidental injury arising out of and in the course of his employment. The court of appeals reversed, holding that the physician's report offered by the respondent was not in compliance with the *AMA Guides*, and therefore no competent evidence supported the order of the workers' compensation court.

The court first examined the question of whether the employer's physician's report failed to follow the *AMA Guides* as required by Rule 20, which requires a statement that the evaluation is in substantial compliance with the *AMA Guides.* Any deviation from the *AMA Guides* must be explained by the doctor in his report. Okla. Stat. tit. 85 § 3(11) (supp. 1987). The test to determine the question of substantial compliance is "whether, from a medical report's four corners, an unexplained, facially apparent and substantial deviation from the *Guides* can be detected by mere reference to their text." *Whitener v. South Cent. Solid Waste Auth.*, 773 P.2d 1248 (Okla. 1989).

The *AMA Guides* require that three preliminary evaluations be performed in order to determine the condition of an individual's respiratory system. Because the physician in question conducted only two of the three evaluations, and did not explain the deviation, the court found that his report did not substantially comply with the *AMA Guides*, and thus did not constitute competent evidence.

The employer argued that the claimant's physician's report did not comply with the *AMA Guides* because it was based on inaccurate or incomplete history. The court agreed:

> Our analysis is that the history relied on by Dr. A. does not show an unexplained, facially apparent and substantial deviation from the *Guides.* It does, however, show a significant departure from the Guidelines when evaluated in light of other uncontroverted evidence. For example, it is clear that the Doctor failed to make a specific and detailed history with regard to past "exposures to dust, gases, vapors and fumes." The *Guides* require that "each job" be so covered. Dr. A. made mention of [claimant]'s prior employment but apparently made no inquiry into the "specific activities" which would have revealed eleven years of contact with toxic chemicals and fumes. He did not question the claimant regarding the period or extent of exposure nor did he estimate the hazard posed by the toxic chemicals and fumes. We realize that in many instances, the omission of an historical fact may not invalidate a doctor's report. *Refrigerated Transp. Inc. v. Creek*, 590 P.2d 197, 200 (Okla. 1979). Nevertheless, in the present case, the specific details required by the *Guides* seem critical to Dr. A.'s report.
>
> We thus find that the history was not in substantial compliance with the *AMA Guides*, was further flawed for lack of accuracy in a material way, and that the employer's objection based on lack of probative value should properly have been sustained.
>
> [Employer] also contends that Dr. M.'s report failed to meet the standards of Rule 20. [Employer] had objected to the probative value of the report at trial, thus preserving the error for appellate review. Dr. M.'s report makes no mention of [claimant]'s prior history of heavy smoking or his prior exposure to toxic chemicals and fumes. Again, these facts are critical, and their omission is an unexplained, substantial deviation from the *Guides.* The report also lacks details as to the tests performed and their results. Application of the rule of *Perlinger* and *LaBarge* requires that the report not be considered as competent evidence, as it does not substantially comply with Rules 20(a), (c), and (h).

790 P.2d at 1079. *See LaBarge v. Zebco*, 769 P.2d 125 (Okla. 1988); *Perlinger v. J.C. Rogers Constr. Co.*, 753 P.2d 905 (Okla. 1988).

The court then went on to discuss the state of appellate review with respect to the issue of compliance with the *AMA Guides*. The court noted that other courts have been generous with objecting parties concerning the specificity of the objection required to preserve an issue for appellate review.

> In this case, as with most other recently reviewed by us, the grounds given at trial for objections have been general, not specific. As a practical matter, the appellate courts are being employed to be courts of first review as to whether the *AMA Guides* are met. Such is not the function of appellate courts. Trial courts are not traditionally reversed for error unless the error was called to their attention at a time when they themselves could reasonably be expected to correct it. *Middlebrook v. Imler, Tenny & Kugler*, 713 P.2d 572 (Okla. 1985).
>
> Henceforth the appellate courts of this state will not reverse for failure to follow Rule 20 or the *AMA Guides* unless the objection is made in compliance with Rule 21 that also states the specific grounds under section 2104. The objection may be either for lack of competency or lack of probative value, but an objection with a mere reference to lack of *AMA Guides* will not suffice for specificity. . . . Absent objections to medical reports made with such specificity the appellate courts hereafter will rely on a reporting physician's Rule 20-required assertion that his report substantially complies with *AMA Guides*, and appealing parties in Compensation Court cases will not be heard to advance arguments-thereon at this level that were not expressed at the trial of the case. Because arguably this decision overrules "clear past precedent," its application will be prospective only.

Id. at 1080.

Finally, the court announced its modification of the *Perlinger* rule. *See Perlinger v. J.C. Rogers Constr Co.*, 753 P.2d 905 (Okla. 1988). Until now, if both parties' medical reports were found to be incompetent, the cause was remanded for proceedings to allow competent evidence to be presented. However, if only one party's reports were found to be incompetent, the party opposing the admission of the report received benefits of the rule announced in *Perlinger*.

> In *Perlinger*, the doctor's report of the prevailing respondent was held on appeal to be not in compliance with the *AMA Guides*. The report submitted by the losing claimant was the only competent evidence which could be considered. This Court reasoned that because the claimant's report was the only competent evidence, judgment must be entered in favor of the claimant, awarding the disability percentage stated in the claimant's report. This type of ruling has been considered by some to legitimize recovery by windfall in such cases.
>
> Such a rule favored a party who remained mostly silent at trial with regard to errors in the Opponent's medical report. A reward for such silence is inconsistent with the norm now set forth by this Court which encourages parties to specifically object to errors in the doctor's report at the first

opportunity. Rather than making a perfunctory objection at trial and raising specific objections for the first time on appeal, we seek to facilitate the trial court's review of the medical reports by encouraging meaningful objections which allow the trial court an opportunity to review and correct such errors before they reach the appellate stage.

There are many cases now pending on appeal which were tried without the benefit of our pronouncements in Part II. We determine that in light of today's ruling it would be inconsistent in such cases to continue to reward litigants who successfully nullify the victorious opposition's only medical evidence on appeal. We now declare the better practice to be as herein provided, and thus modify *Perlinger* and *LaBarge*, to the extent that they would necessitate total victory for any party obtaining a reversal on appeal under Rule 20. Henceforth, and until such time as 4 cases shall come before us tried after the mandate herein, when a medical report which is the sole basis of an award or denial of award is held to be incompetent or non-probative as evidence under Rule 20 of the Rules of the Workers' Compensation Court, this Court will reverse the judgment on which it is based and remand for further proceedings, following the example of *Stockton*, 653 P.2d at 200–01.

790 P.2d at 1081. *See LaBarge v. Zebco*, 769 P.2d 125 (Okla. 1988); *Perlinger v. J.C. Rogers Constr. Co.*, 753 P.2d 905 (Okla. 1988); *see also Special Indent. Fund v. Stockton*, 653 P.2d 194 (Okla. 1982).

Orrell v. B.F. Goodrich, 787 P.2d 848 (Okla. 1990)

The workers' compensation court denied a former employee's claim for permanent partial disability relating to lung damage. The court of appeals reversed and remanded with instructions to enter an award for a 20 percent permanent partial disability. The Oklahoma Supreme Court held that (1) the trial court erred by refusing to consider evidence of the former employee's doctor in support of the conclusion that the former employee was 20 percent permanently partial disabled, on the grounds that the evidence did not comply with the *AMA Guides*; and (2) the appeals court erred in not considering evidence of the former employer's doctor that the former employee had suffered a 0 percent impairment, on grounds that the evidence did not comply with the *AMA Guides*.

The claimant worked at a tire manufacturing plant for 31 years. After he retired in 1986, he filed a claim for compensation with the Oklahoma Workers' Compensation Court, alleging that the exposure to certain chemicals had caused reduced breathing capacity and injury to his lungs and upper respiratory system. The claimant's doctor opined that the claimant had a Class 2 impairment due to injury to his lungs and rated that impairment at 20 percent permanent partial impairment. The employer's doctor found no such impairment and alternatively stated that even if the claimant had a respiratory impairment, it would not be expected to result from his work.

The trial judge denied the claim after sustaining the employer's objection to the competence of the deposition of the claimant's doctor as being in conflict with the *AMA Guides*. The court of appeals reversed, holding that it was the employer's medical evidence that was not in compliance with the *AMA Guides*, and remanded the case with directions to enter an award for a 20 percent permanent partial disability based on the claimant's doctor's deposition, the only evidence it deemed competent.

The supreme court held that the medical evidence of both parties was in substantial compliance with the *AMA Guides* and was therefore of sufficient probative value to be relied on by the trial judge. Accordingly, the case was remanded. The court noted that certain pulmonary function tests, generally known as spirometric tests, consisting of ventilatory function measurements, were performed by both doctors. The record was clear that the correct application of the formulas called for by the *AMA Guides* in relation to these physiologic tests would result in the claimant being classified as having a 0 percent impairment Although the claimant's doctor agreed with this, he also took into consideration the claimant's dyspnea and any pertinent personal factors in reaching his conclusion that the claimant did suffer a permanent impairment.

The *AMA Guides* (2d ed. 1984) were in effect at the time of both evaluations. Under Table 1, "Classes of Respiratory Impairment," an impairment rating of 10 percent to 25 percent may be given if a claimant experiences dyspnea when walking fast on level ground or when walking on a hill or if the patient can keep pace with persons of the same age and body build on level ground but not on hills or stairs, even if the spirometry results produce values within the lower limit of normal utilizing the formulas called for by the *AMA Guides*. Table 1 specifically indicates that such a range of impairment may be given when such dyspnea is experienced or when one of the ventilatory function tests involved is abnormal to the degree required. The employer pointed to a footnote to Table 1 and the textual discussion contained in the *AMA Guides* for the use and interpretation of the spirometry results as mandating that one of the test results be abnormal for an impairment rating to be made. The court, however, did not read the material relied on to stand for the proposition the employer posited. Rather, the court held that the language merely means that if a medical practitioner is going to use these ventilatory function test results as the sole function of an impairment rating, at least one of the test results must be abnormal to the degree indicated in Table 1. It did not mean that no impairment rating may be given under the applicable *AMA Guides* in the absence of such an abnormal result if other criteria in Table [1] do indicate impairment. "Although the [1984] *Guides* indicate dyspnea may not be the sole criterion for evaluation of impairment, both Table 1 and the text preceding it indicate dyspnea, when taken into account along with other physiologic and personal factors may give rise to an impairment rating." *Id.* at 852.

The court's decision was further buttressed by its review of the then recently enacted *AMA Guides* (3d ed. 1988), which specifically provide that the severity of dyspnea "[d]oes not constitute a criterion upon which impairment of lung function is based." *AMA Guides* (3d ed. 1988) at 108. Table 8, "Classes of Respiratory Impairment," the counterpart to Table 1 in the *AMA Guides* (2d ed. 1984), also does not include dyspnea as a criterion. *Id.* at 117.

> Although the obvious import of this change was an attempt to utilize more objective criteria in rating respiratory impairment, it does not impact our decision concerning the 1984 *Guides*, applicable at the time of the evaluations in question, which specifically did include dyspnea as a criterion as long as the physiologic and personal factors specified in the *Guides* were considered.

787 P.2d at 852 n.8.

The employer's doctor was of the opinion that the claimant suffered from no permanent partial impairment. He also stated that even if a respiratory impairment did exist, "One would not expect it to be from his work at B.F. Goodrich." The court of appeals determined the quoted statement as to causation was speculative and was insufficient to support a valid medical assessment concerning the cause and effect of the claimant's condition. The supreme court concluded that this was an error because, if the employer's opinion of no impairment was properly made under the *AMA Guides*, even assuming the alternative "speculative" opinion as to causation was couched in impermissible equivocal terminology, this would not necessarily undercut the validity of the "no impairment" assessment.

Wheat v. Heritage Manor, 784 P.2d 74 (Okla. 1989)

The claimant, a licensed nurse, sustained injuries to her head, neck, and eyes when she suddenly turned away from a combative patient and struck a door. A hearing took place to determine the issue of permanent partial disability. The workers' compensation court affirmed the findings of the judge that the claimant failed to adduce any probative medical evidence upon which an award for permanent partial disability could have been based. The Oklahoma Supreme Court found that the claimant should have been allowed to substitute another evaluation, but agreed that the medical expert's evaluation did not give legally sufficient reasons for deviating from the *AMA Guides* "standards."

The claimant's medical expert testified that she suffered a 45 percent permanent impairment due to her concussion, medication-induced liver ailment, mental depression, and economic disability. The employer urged that the evaluation was not probative because it was based at least in part on future impairment and because the physician impermissibly and unexplainably deviated from the *AMA Guides*. The expert stated that this was a very unusual case and that he did not find references to help break down any of the percentages. Therefore, "in a manner that I'm used to," the physician somehow arrived at the 45 percent permanency, which included some percent for the liver. The supreme court rejected the testimony.

> An evaluation of permanent impairment for workers' compensation purposes must be made by applying the standards prescribed in the *AMA Guides*. (*See* 85

O.S. Supp. 1985 section 3(11); Rule 20(i), Workers' Compensation Court Rules, 85 O.S. 1981, Ch. 4, App.). Deviations from the statutorily-mandated regime are not permissible without an adequate medical explanation. Id. (*See also LaBarge v. Zebco, Ok.*, 769 P.2d 125, 129 [1988]; *Special Indem. Fund v. Stockton, [Old.]*, 653 P.2d 194, 200 [1982]; *Norwood v. Lee Way Motor Freight, Inc.*, Okl. App., 646 P.2d 2, 6 [1982]. Here, the expert's admission that he deviated from the *Guides* poses the question whether his explicit reasons for so doing are legally sufficient. In light of the quoted portions of his deposition testimony, we hold they are not. The claimant's medical witness never explained what was so "unusual" about claimant's condition that he could not apply the mandatory AMA standards for evaluating permanent impairment. Although he had stated that the *Guides'* chapter on mental and behavioral disorders was inapplicable to this case, he gave no medical grounds for his conclusion.

Id. at 78.

Spangler v. Lease-Way Automotive Transp., 780 P.2d 209 (Okla. Ct. App. 1989)

The claimant appealed a decision of the workers' compensation court that rated his permanent partial disability due to an occupational back injury at 10 percent. The court of appeals held both that the employer's medical evidence was incompetent and could not be considered by the trial court and that the employee's evidence supported a finding of a 23 percent permanent partial disability.

The employer's medical experts submitted three letters of various dates. Only the last two letters were verified, and these two were not complete reports, only brief updates. The court of appeals agreed with the claimant that the instant case was controlled by *LaBarge v. Zebco*, 769 P.2d 125 (Okla. 1988). In *LaBarge*, the Oklahoma Supreme Court found:

> The unverified discharge summary, and the three letters cannot be welded into a medical report which is in compliance with Rule 20. Only one of the letters can be considered as the medical report, because Rule 20 requires a report to be signed by the physician and contain a verification statement. The signed letter is facially flawed and fails to comply with Rule 20.

780 P.2d at 210.

The court in the instant case concluded that the *LaBarge* case was directly analogous, and that the employer's medical evidence could not be considered by the trial court. The only competent evidence found a 23 percent disability rating. Thus the order of the workers' compensation court was vacated with instructions to enter an award for a 23 percent permanent partial disability to the body. Both the concurring and dissenting opinions discussed application of Rule 20 and the *AMA Guides.*

Edwards v. Amoco, 776 P.2d 566 (Okla. Ct. App. 1989)

The claimant sought an award for compensation benefits, alleging a reduced breathing capacity as a result of exposure to pulmonary irritants while employed by the defendant. The court of appeals sustained the trial court's denial of the claim, holding that the fact that both physicians failed to state that they followed the *AMA Guides* was not significant to the reports' admissibility where the *AMA Guides* were in fact substantially followed.

> We find that in view of the two complete examinations of Petitioner by Drs. F. and M. as well as their detailed reports, the fact that the doctors failed to state that they followed the *AMA Guides* is not significant; the *AMA Guides* were substantially followed, as well as Workers' Compensation Rule 20, 85 O.S. 1981 Ch. 4, App. *See LaBarge v. Zebco*, 769 P.2d 125 (Okla. 1988); *Perlinger v. J.C. Rogers Construction Co.*, 753 P.2d 905 (Okla. 1988), and, *Special Indemnity Fund v. Stockton*, 653 P.2d 194 (Okla. 1982). Although the test results conducted by Dr. F. were invalid and could not be considered by the trial court as competent medical evidence for that reason, Dr. M.'s spirometry test and accompanied report was competent evidence supporting the trial court's finding.
>
> To sustain Petitioner's contention would be to give precedence to pure technicality rather than to substance. The Court declines to do so.

Id. at 569.

Whitener v. South Cent. Solid Waste Auth., 773 P.2d 1248 (Okla. 1989)

The claimant sought a review of the workers' compensation court's denial of benefits for permanent partial disability due to a respiratory impairment. The court of appeals vacated the decision, but the supreme court affirmed the denial of benefits, holding that the employer's medical report conformed to the standards prescribed in the *AMA Guides*. The report indicated that the claimant's lungs were not permanently impaired, even though the data from two of the three tests indicated permanent impairment. The *AMA Guides* permit impairment rating to rest on results of but one of three breathing measurements. Okla. Stat. tit. 85, § 3(11) (1987).

The claimant also argued that the employer's medical expert's opinion was defective because some of its numerical data deviated from the data the *AMA Guides* called for, and that, regardless of whether the numbers affected his impairment classification, the report had no probative value because it contained inaccurate or erroneous data. The supreme court disagreed, finding that the data analysis substantially conformed to the *AMA Guides*.

> A medical expert's permanent impairment evaluation must substantially comply with the methods and standards prescribed by the *Guides*. Noncompliance

may be apparent from mere reference to the *Guides*. That was the case in *LaBarge v. Zebco, Ok.*, 769 P.2d 125 (1988). There, a specific impairment percentage for each of two ruptured discs that required surgery was plainly mandated by the AMA manual and ignored by the rating physician. The *LaBarge* test for determining whether the standards are followed when clearly applicable is whether, from a medical report's four corners, an unexplained, facially apparent and substantial deviation from the *Guides* can be detected by mere reference to their text. The claimant's attack on the employer's letter-report calls for a different analysis of its probative force.

Here, the *Guides* contain tables from which "normal" values are obtained according to raw data, i.e. height and age. A constant, called the "95 percent confidence interval," must be subtracted from the table-derived number. Percentages must then be calculated to compare "normal" values with actual values. Evaluating respiratory impairment by the use of mechanical ventilatory tests requires at least one calculation: subtracting the given constant from each value derived from a table. In short, mere reference to the *Guides* does not facially reveal here that their commands went unheeded when the employer's physician evaluated the claimant's compensable impairment to the lungs. . . .

[T]he only noteworthy inaccuracy to be found is in the numbers which *the claimant* tenders as correct. Using the employer's raw data, he failed to subtract the appropriate constant from the values which were derived from the *Guides'* tables. This error doubtless has led the claimant to believe that the employer's medical expert fatally deviated from the mandatory norms for evaluating respiratory impairment. The employer's medical evidence is clearly not flawed for lack of probative value. We hold it free of legally vitiating deficiency.

773 P.2d at 1252.

Case v. Mack Trucks, 773 P.2d 765 (Okla. Ct. App. 1989)

The Oklahoma Workers' Compensation Court denied the petitioner's claim for compensation based on permanent impairment to the respiratory system. The court of appeals affirmed the denial, holding that the examining physician's reports complied with the requirements of applicable statutes and rules. The physician's narrative reports, which concluded that the claimant sustained no permanent impairment, met with statutory requirements despite the fact that they did not specifically state that the evaluations were in substantial compliance with the *AMA Guides*. The medical reports contained detailed information regarding the injury, complaints, test results, and medical reports that substantially complied with the areas required to be addressed by the rules. Okla. Stat. tit. 85 § 3(13) (Supp. 1985); Workers' Compensation Court Rules 20, 20(3)(i); Okla. Stat. Ann. tit. 85, ch. 4, app.

The claimant cited *Special Indemnity Fund v. Stockton*, 653 P.2d 194 (Okla. 1982), for the proposition that examining physicians must state that their evaluations were in substantial compliance with the *AMA Guides*. The court found reliance on *Stockton* misplaced; in *Stockton*, the medical reports were found to be grossly deficient and in substantial disaccord with the applicable statutes. In the current case, the medical reports to which the claimant objected contained the relevant history, descriptions of injury and complaints, descriptions of examinations and tests, evaluations of the extent of permanent impairment, and notarized declarations regarding the truth of all statements. Although Rule 20(3)(i) requires a statement that the valuation was in substantial compliance with the *AMA Guides*, the court found that the failure to provide such a statement did not render the medical reports insufficient in this case. The court stated:

> First, Rule 20 mandates that the *Guides* be the basis for testimony and conclusions concerning permanent impairment. *Goodrich v. Hilton*, 634 P.2d 1308, 1310 (Okl. 1981.) This insures a reasonable degree of accuracy and uniformity among medical reports and provides the court with enough scientific information upon which to make an intelligent decision. *Stockton*, 653 P.2d at 200. This mandate is satisfied if the medical report tendered is in substantial compliance with the applicable statutes. *Stockton*, 653 P.2d at 200; *Perlinger v. J.C. Rogers Construction Co.*, 753 P.2d 905 (Old. 1988); *LaBarge v. Zebco*, 769 P.2d 125 (Okl. 1988).
>
> Our review of the record in the instant case reveals that of the ten areas required by Rule 20 to be addressed, the medical reports in question substantially complied with nine and one-half, including the examinations and diagnostic procedures used and the findings based thereon. The exception to strict compliance with Rule 20(3)(i) was the failure to include a statement of compliance. As the necessity for compliance is to provide the court with an accurate and scientific report, we hold that such omission does not render these medical reports incompetent for failure to substantially comply with Rule 20.
>
> Second, Rule 20(3)(i) specifically requires the statement of substantial compliance with the *Guides* to be in reference to those and other detailed factors upon which an evaluation of permanent impairment is based. In the instant case, both medical reports in question reached medically documented conclusions that no permanent impairment existed. Thus, it is reasonable to infer that the directive to state "detailed factors upon which the physician's evaluation of permanent impairment" was based was thought irrelevant. It is not inconceivable to conclude that as no permanent impairment was found to be evaluated, a statement of factors supporting an evaluation of such impairment—which included a statement of compliance with the *Guides*—was unnecessary.

Id. at 766.

Dry v. Pauls Valley Health Care Facility, 771 P.2d 238 (Okla. Ct. App. 1989)

The claimant was denied benefits for injury to her respiratory system. The court of appeals sustained the denial, finding evidence to support the determination that the claimant sustained an accidental personal injury to the respiratory system, but that the claimant lost no compensable time due to the injury. The claimant argued on appeal that the employer's medical evidence was not based on the *AMA Guides*, but the court rejected this contention because the claimant failed to object timely to the admission of the evidence when offered. Although *LaBarge v. Zebco*, 769 P.2d 125 (Okla. 1988), requires that impairment ratings be based on the *AMA Guides* and that any substantial deviations from the *AMA Guides* be explained, in the *LaBarge* case, the employee objected to the competency of the doctor's report, whereas the claimant in the current case failed to object to the reports in question.

LaBarge v. Zebco, 769 P.2d 125 (Okla. 1988)

The employee suffered ruptured disks while operating a forklift for her employer. After receiving temporary total disability payments, the claimant sought benefits for medical treatment and for permanent disability. The workers' compensation court affirmed a trial judge's finding that the claimant was 12 percent permanently impaired. The Oklahoma Supreme Court vacated that decision, finding that the medical evidence presented by the employer failed to comply with the statutory requirements, and therefore it was not competent evidence, nor could it be considered in determining a percentage of permanent disability.

The physicians' reports to which the employee objected consisted of four letters and a discharge report. Three of the letters were neither signed nor verified. One letter was signed but contained an unsigned verification statement rubber stamped at the bottom. The discharge report was signed but did not contain a verification statement. The court noted that the unverified discharge statement and the three unsigned letters could not be melded into a medical report in substantial compliance with workers' compensation court Rule 20, which requires that medical reports comply with the *AMA Guides*. Only the signed and verified letter could be considered as the medical report, but that letter also failed to comply with Rule 20 because it did not contain (1) the relevant history, (2) any description or findings of diagnostic tests, (3) the date of injury, (4) a discussion of physical rehabilitation procedures, (5) a statement of the period of temporary and total disability or the date of termination, or (6) a basis for the physician's determination that the employee was only 5 percent disabled. Even though the letter stated that it was in substantial compliance with the *AMA Guides*, the *AMA Guides* provide that each operated disk constitutes a 5 percent disability to the body as a whole. Because the doctor operated on two disks, the *AMA Guides* call for a 10 percent permanent partial disability rating. The court found it apparent from this factor alone that the doctor did not use the percentages required by the *AMA Guides*.

On the other hand, the employee's medical evidence, with the exception of the date of termination of the temporary total disability benefits, was a "textbook" example of a competent medical report in compliance with Rule 20. Because that evidence was competent and uncontroverted, the court found it unnecessary to remand for a finding of permanent impairment, and instead relied on the employee's physician's evidence for a finding of 40 percent permanent impairment.

The court noted that medical evidence that is not in substantial compliance with Rule 20 is not competent evidence upon which the trial court can base its conclusions:

> When, as here, a party essentially offers no evidence to establish a defense, there is a failure of proof. The legislature in Rule 20, has made an accommodation to doctors to provide a medical report rather than appear at trial to avoid professional inconvenience. Even though the proceedings are informal, these unsigned letters do not pass muster. Precious judicial resources must not be frittered away in a "game of overs" by either the employer or the employee. The employer has had its day in court to establish its defense on a time and materials basis. It is elementary that where there is a failure of proof there can be no judgment in that party's favor.

Id. at 128.

King v. Razien Oil Co., 768 P.2d 385 (Okla. Ct. App. 1989)

The claimant filed for workers' compensation benefits, alleging an injury to his lungs and upper respiratory tract due to the exposure to raw gas, diesel fumes, welding fumes, chemicals, hydrogen sulfide gas, and dust. The trial court found that the claimant had not sustained any impairment to his respiratory system, but the court of appeals vacated and remanded. The court held that the employer's medical evidence was not competent where the employer's physician admitted that his opinion was based on test values that were unreliable and inaccurate because the worker would not cooperate during the examination.

> Instead of advising the court of an inability to carry out a proper examination, the physician simply assumed that had the claimant cooperated, the test results would have reflected no abnormality, and based on such assumption opined that there was indeed no impairment.
>
> This was inappropriate. The lack of a valid diagnostic premise to support the respondent's doctor's opinion made it incompetent.
>
> The Preface to the *Guides* touches on this general subject and makes it quite clear that, with regard to rating permanent impairment, a physician's conclusions about an individual's clinical status should be based on or justified by the "history, the physical examination, and the laboratory tests and other diagnostic procedures." A valid determination of injury or quantification of impairment must depend on valid information regarding pre-injury status and accurate testing and diagnostic tests. "If the rater does not have sufficient information to measure change accurately, the rater should not attempt to do so." says the *Guides* Preface. The "opinion of physicians about nonmedical issues [should not] influence the outcome" that is, the rating, and the Preface concludes with this relevant admonition:

"While medical information is of little value in predicting functional ability or the lack of it, an appropriate use of the knowledge about an individual's health may be of help in explaining an observed performance failure. However, in such a case, the analysis should consider whether or not the specific medical condition can cause the type of observed failure, which is a medical decision, and whether or not in the particular case it did cause the failure, which is not a medical decision." (*AMA Guides.* 2d ed. at x.)

The rationale underlying these guidelines is applicably helpful in resolving the issues in this case. By basing his opinion on the claimant's alleged failure to cooperate, the doctor departed from appropriate *Guides* procedures, made a nonmedical decision and executed an impermissible invasion of the court's province. By reason thereof the respondent's medical report is not competent medical evidence on the vital issue of job-related impairment.

Id. at 387.

Perlinger v. J.C. Rogers Constr. Co., 753 P.2d 905 (Okla. 1988)

The claimant injured his back while shoveling sand for his employer. The court of appeals affirmed the workers' compensation court's award of an 8 percent permanent partial disability to the body as a whole. The supreme court vacated and remanded, holding that a chiropractor's report which stated that the claimant was not disabled did not constitute competent evidence upon which the award could be based. Instead, the claimant was entitled to a finding of a 25 percent permanent disability based upon the only competent evidence presented at the hearing.

The employer's expert's report did not mention application of the *AMA Guides*, which violated workers' compensation court Rules 20 and 23 and the rule of *Special Indem. Fund v. Stockton*, 653 P.2d 194, 200 (Okla. 1982). In addition, the Form 4 contained neither a complete history of the petitioner nor the physician's findings on examination, including a description of any diagnostic tests and x-rays. The report described only the treatment rendered and the general types of tests as required by Rule 20.

> Because the report offered by respondent lacked any probative force and failed to substantially comply with Rule 20, the report was not competent evidence for which the trial court could base its conclusion. *Henry v. Smith*, 742 P.2d 35 (Okla. Ct. App. 1987).

Tulsa County v. Roberts, 738 P.2d 969 (Okla. Ct. App. 1987)

The claimant sustained an injury to his right hip while operating a large commercial floor buffer for his employer. The workers' compensation court entered judgment for the claimant. The court of appeals held that the workers' compensation court erred in awarding the claimant compensation for a 25 percent permanent partial disability to the right hip instead of determining a percentage of disability to the body as a whole. However, the physician's use of an edition of the *AMA Guides* later than the 1977 edition specified in workers' compensation court Rule 20 did not alone render that physician's opinion invalid where the earlier edition provided no help and the physician explained his reliance on the later edition.

The employer complained that the impairment percentage given by the employee's expert was invalid because it was based on an edition of the *AMA Guides* more current than the 1977 edition specified by workers' compensation court Rules 20 and 23. This argument, the court stated, appeared to be "an over-indulgence in legalistic surrealism."

> If, as we think, it is the intent and purpose of the rules to require an expert to use the *AMA Guides* where possible in evaluating consequences of work-related injuries and an expert draws on the latest edition because an earlier edition offers no help, to deny him the right to do so would manifest ultimate contempt for common sense. Moreover, Rule 20(i) provides that adherence to the First Edition of the *AMA Guides* is not required if the reason for deviating is stated, which the expert did in this case. The employer's third contention—that claimant's expert erred in calculating the amount of claimant's impairment—does have merit. The percentage of lost hip motion should have been translated by the physician into a whole man percentage of disability. But as we will see his testimony contains sufficient data to enable one to correctly interpret his report and convert the figures into the proper *Guides*-based impairment figures.

Id. at 971.

General Tool & Supply v. Somers, 737 P.2d 581 (Okla. Ct. App. 1987)

The claimant was eight months pregnant when she slipped on an oily substance and fell while at work, twisting her right ankle and causing her to fall to one knee. That evening the claimant began to experience pain and contractions. She immediately sought medical attention, and the next day a cesarean section was performed, but the child was stillborn. The trial court entered an award both for the injury to the claimant's reproductive system and for the resulting psychological overlay.

The court of appeals sustained the award of benefits for permanent partial impairment, holding that the claimant's physician adequately explained his disability rating under the *AMA Guides*, and that such medical evidence was in substantial compliance with the workers' compensation rules.

The employer contended that the claimant's medical evidence on the issue of psychological overlay did not properly use the *AMA Guides* and thus was of no probative value. The court disagreed:

> Petitioner complains that because Respondent's doctor based her rate of impairment on mild to moderate emotional disturbance under ordinary stress and belonging in "class 2 page 63 of the *Guides*" and that section deals with emotional disturbance resulting from organic brain damage, the doctor

improperly classified the injury. Further, that by failing to use the proper applicable section of the *Guides* his impairment rating is not in compliance with Title 85 O.S. 1981, Ch. 4 App. Rule 20, and does not present the trial court with any competent medical evidence upon which to base its disability award. Rule 20 requires the evaluation of permanent impairment be in accord with the *Guides to Evaluation of Permanent Impairment* as published by the American Medical Association. Compliance with Rule 20 is mandatory when medical evidence is supplied by a writ medical report. Competent evaluation of permanent impairment requires an adequate and complete medical examination, and substantial compliance with the *Guides*. Where deviation from the *Guides* occurs, the physician is required to explain such deviation. *Special Indemnity Fund v. Stockton*, 653 P.2d 194 (Okl. 1982). The record reflects that Respondent's doctor, in his deposition testimony introduced at trial, adequately explained his disability rating under Ch. 2, p. 63 of the *Guides*, and we find that Respondent's medical evidence is in substantial compliance with Rule 20.

Id. at 582.

Special Indem. Fund v. Stockton, 653 P.2d 194 (Okla. 1982)

The claimant was an oil field worker with a history of injuries. The worker's compensation court found the claimant to be 100 percent permanently disabled. The examining physicians did not comply with the *AMA Guides*, nor did they state their reasons for deviating from the *AMA Guides* as required by statute. The physicians did not take into account the fact that the claimant was still working. An evaluation of a permanent impairment must be supported by competent evidence, including substantial compliance with the *AMA Guides*, and if there is deviation from the *AMA Guides*, a physician must state the basis for the deviation with a full medical explanation. The claimant's award was vacated and remanded for further proceedings.

Texas Okla. Express v. Sorenson, 652 P.2d 285 (Okla. 1982)

Workers' compensation court Rule 20 requires that the *AMA Guides* be used for evaluating permanent impairment. When a physician deviates from the *AMA Guides*, the physician's basis for deviation shall be given with full medical explanation. Rule 20 states: "Expert medical or rehabilitation testimony may be offered by (1) a verified or declared report, (2) deposition, or (3) oral examination in open court." The court, taking into consideration that it is costly and time-consuming to have physicians actually appear at the time of trial for the purpose of giving live testimony, encourages the production of medical evidence by verified or declared report which shall contain the following:

(i) Any other detailed factors upon which the physician's evaluation of permanent impairment is based, including the fact that the evaluation is in substantial accordance with the *"Guides to the Evaluation of Permanent Impairment"* as published by the American Medical Association in 1977. Whenever the physician deviates from the *"Guides"* the basis for his deviation shall be stated together with full medical explanation. (If the injury occurred before July 1, 1978, the physician's testimony need not be based on or in accordance with the *"AMA Guides"* but must include such detailed factors upon which his evaluation of permanent disability is based.)

Id. at 288.

Altus House Nursing v. Roberts, 646 P.2d 9 (Okla. Ct. App. 1982)

The claimant suffered a fractured left femur near the hip joint. The femoral neck and head were replaced with a metal prosthesis. The *AMA Guides* were purportedly used to evaluate this impairment, but the *AMA Guides* do not address how hip joints should be evaluated. The court's findings did not deviate impermissibly from the *AMA Guides*, and the award was upheld.

Norwood v. Lee Way Motor Freight, Inc., 646 P.2d 2 (Okla. Ct. App. 1982)

The claimant injured his shoulder and cervical spine. The insurer's physician rated permanent partial impairment at 0 percent; the claimant's physician rated it at 35 percent; the court-appointed physician gave an impairment rating of 21 percent. The trial judge awarded 29 percent permanent partial disability. These discrepancies resulted from the differing uses of the *AMA Guides* and the confusion about rating separate injuries, adding injury ratings and using the combined rating tables. The court stated: "These labyrinthine calculations and the attendant arguments ably demonstrate the need for further clarification of the workers' compensation rules relative to the *AMA Guides*." *Id.* at 4.

The shoulder injury was rated at a 15 percent impairment of the whole body and the cervical spine injury at a 14 percent impairment of the whole body. Before the adoption of the *AMA Guides*, these values would have been added to arrive at the total disability rating. Under the *AMA Guides*, the combined values chart is to be used, which yields a rating of 27 percent—less than adding the rates and less than if the injuries were incurred in separate accidents. The court called this an "illogical result." *Id.* at 4.

The court stated, "We find the objective standards of measuring functional impairment to be a major step toward achieving uniformity and fairness in rating workers' disabilities." However, the court went on to say that separate ratings should be added rather than combined using the tables and that in no case should the final rating be less than the sum of its parts. *Id.* at 5.

The award of 29 percent permanent partial disability was found to be within the range of competent testimony, and thus was upheld. The *AMA Guides* can be deviated from when "scientifically sound" reasons are proved. Okla. Stat. tit. 85,

§ 3(11) (Supp. 1977). These reasons also should be liberally construed in favor of injured workers.

Montgomery Ward & Co. v. Johnson, 645 P.2d 1051 (Okla. Ct. App. 1982)

The claimant received a workers' compensation award for physical and mental injuries after being struck in the face by a falling display board. The employer argued that the claimant's family physician's testimony as to the claimant's psychiatric condition should be ignored because the physician did not frame his diagnosis in current diagnostic terms, and because he did not do a psychiatric evaluation of the claimant. The court rejected these arguments and stated that there was no evidence that the diagnostic term *depressive neurosis* was outdated. The court cited the use of the term in a "work that has lately received widespread acclaim among defending employers, the American Medical Association *Guides to the Evaluation of Permanent Impairment.*" *Id.* at 1053.

Peabody Gallon Corp. v. Workman, 643 P.2d 312 (Okla. 1982)

The claimant suffered a noise-induced hearing loss. The evaluation of a noise-induced hearing loss was exempted from the statutory requirement that the rating physician assess the permanent impairment by substantially complying with the *AMA Guides.* Both the claimant's physician and the employer's physician testified that the *AMA Guides* did not adequately cover the claimant's hearing loss. The court stated that the award was supported by competent medical evidence.

B.F. Goodrich v. Hilton, 634 P.2d 1308 (Okla. 1981)

The claimant was awarded a 20 percent permanent partial disability for an injury to the knee. The claimant's physician found a 40 percent impairment of the leg as a result of the injury but did not use the *AMA Guides.* The employer's physician found no impairment based on the *AMA Guides.* The court-appointed physician found a 10 percent permanent partial disability. The relevant statute calls for the use of the *AMA Guides* for evaluating permanent impairment with the exception of total loss of use or amputation of a member listed in Okla. Stat. tit. 85, § 22(3) (Supp. 1978). The claimant's injury was found to fall within the exception. Thus, the court upheld the award of a 20 percent permanent partial disability.

§ 11.29   OREGON

In re Compensation of Clemons, 169 Or. Ct. App. 231, 9 P.3d 123 (Or. Ct. App. July 26, 2000)

In May 1996, the claimant experienced pain and numbness along the left posterior lateral thigh, calf, and foot while driving a forklift at work. That fall the employer accepted a claim for "left-sided sciatica," and also closed the claim with an award for temporary total disability but without an award of permanent disability. The claimant sought reconsideration, and Dr. S., a medical arbiter, was asked to describe objective findings of permanent impairment that resulted from the accepted sciatica, including ranges of motion and muscle strength. In his report, the arbiter noted "slight loss of strength of inversion and eversion of the left ankle and foot estimated at 4+/5. The nerve root involved is L5." The arbiter also noted that range-of-motion measurements did not meet the AMA validity requirements but concluded that "the measurements themselves are accurate and could be used to determine impairment." 169 Or. App. at 233–34. Based on the arbiter's report, the Department of Consumer and Business Services awarded scheduled disability for the claimant's loss of foot strength and unscheduled disability for his loss of range of motion. An ALJ affirmed the award of scheduled and unscheduled disability. In affirming the award of unscheduled disability, the ALJ relied on the opinion of the medical arbiter as to loss of range of motion. The board affirmed the ALJ.

The employer appealed the board's ruling, contending, inter alia, that the board was not allowed to use range-of-motion findings that did not meet AMA validity criteria. The arbiter, Dr. S., stated that the relationship between total sacral motion and straight leg raising does not meet the AMA validity requirements. He also stated, "Despite this, I believe that the measurements themselves are accurate and could be used to determine impairment." 169 Or. App. at 234. The ALJ ruled that Dr. S.'s measurements could be used even though they did not comply with the AMA validity requirements. The ALJ interpreted the applicable statute (OAR 436-035-0007(27)) and decided that the findings were valid unless the physician opined that they were not. The board adopted the ALJ's reasoning. On appeal, the employer argued that the statute does not permit the board to rate findings of impairment that are not valid under the AMA criteria. The claimant's interpretation (adopted by the board) was that the fact that a finding of impairment is not valid under the AMA criteria is immaterial to the question whether it is ratable.

The appellate court found that the claimant's interpretation—that a finding of impairment that is not valid under the AMA criteria is presumed to be ratable unless the physician provides a written opinion explaining why the finding is invalid—was incorrect. The court instead held, "under OAR 436-035-0007(27) (1996), if a finding of impairment does not comply with the AMA criteria, it may not be used to rate a claimant's impairment." *Id.*

The court reversed and remanded the board's ruling.

Tinh Xuan Pham Auto v. Bourgo, 922 P.2d 1255 (Or. Ct. App. 1996)

The Oregon court dealt with an employer who appealed from a ruling excluding from evidence a copy of the *AMA Guides*. The ALJ denied admission of the *AMA Guides* on the ground that there was no evidence identifying where the *AMA Guides* came from and no evidence demonstrating that it was any different from information already admitted. The court affirmed the ALJ's exclusion of the *AMA Guides.*

In re Compensation of Bohnke, 640 P.2d 685 (Or. Ct. App. 1982)

The claimant developed serum hepatitis in the course of her employment. She later developed a psychological condition as a result of her illness. The *AMA Guides* were used to rate the claimant's psychological condition. The impairment of her psychological condition contrasted with her loss of earning capacity.

§ 11.30   PENNSYLVANIA

Richcreek v. W.C.A.B. (York International Corp.), 786 A.2d 1054 (Pa. Commw. 2001)

The Pennsylvania court dealt with a worker who claimed work-related hearing loss. At issue was the impairment rating of a Dr. Zemo. Dr. Zemo opined that the claimant had a precipitous high-tone sensorineural hearing loss in both ears. In addition, at lower frequencies, the claimant had a bilateral conductive loss, which Dr. Zemo clinically diagnosed as otosclerosis. Using the AMA guidelines, Dr. Zemo opined that the claimant had a binaural impairment of 20.6 percent. However, Dr. Zemo further indicated that it was necessary to use bone conduction studies to assess the claimant's sensineural function because the conductive component or otosclerosis is not caused by noise. Using the bone conduction scores, Dr. Zemo calculated that the claimant had a binaural disability of 7.5 percent. The worker claimed that the WCJ erred in relying on Dr. Zemo's method of using the worker's bone conduction scores to calculate his hearing impairment. The court disagreed and affirmed the WCJ's reliance on Dr. Zemo's rating. The court stated:

> As previously stated Dr. Zemo did calculate Claimant's hearing loss in accordance with the *AMA Guides*, which requires a pure tone, air conduction test. An employer nonetheless may introduce evidence that the hearing loss is not work-related. "Just because [the doctor] utilized the *AMA Guides* does not mean that any percentage of hearing loss found under that standard was work related. The *AMA Guides* only provide the standards against which any hearing loss is measured; it is for the medical expert to determine what percent of that is attributable to the workplace." *Washington Steel Corporation v. Workers' Compensation Appeal Board (Waugh)*, 734 A.2d 81, 84 (Pa. Commw. 1999).
> Subsequent to *Mozena*, this court decided *Bethlehem Steel Corp. v. Workers' Compensation Appeal Board (Graaf)*, 768 A.2d 1237 (Pa. Commw. 2001), which involved the results of both an air conduction and bone conduction test. In that case, the WCJ credited the testimony of the employer's doctor that based on an audiogram, the claimant suffered a 17.1 percent hearing loss. The employer argued, however, that the WCJ erred

in not also considering the doctor's testimony that the claimant suffered from non-occupational hearing loss, which when measured by a bone conduction test, resulted in an impairment of 13.4 percent. In addressing the employer's argument, this court observed that the WCJ is the ultimate finder of fact and the arbiter of credibility and weight and can accept or reject the testimony of any witness. *Graaf* at 1240 (citing *Jordan v. Workmen's Compensation Appeal Board (Consolidated Electrical Distributors)*, 550 Pa. 232, 704 A.2d 1063 (1997)). In *Graaf*, we stated that "the Employer failed to prove that a non-occupational cause impaired Claimant's hearing to an extent that required a deduction. Therefore, the WCJ [was] free to accept the portion of Dr. Brennan's testimony, which calculated Claimant's binaural hearing loss at 17.2 percent." *Graaf* at 1240.

In accordance with *Graaf*, it is for the WCJ to determine whether a non-occupational cause has impaired a claimant's hearing such that a deduction is required. Here, the WCJ credited the testimony of Employer's doctor that a non-occupational cause, otosclerosis, impaired Claimant's hearing to an extent that required a deduction. As observed by the Supreme Court in *Mozena*, a bone conduction test, along with an air conduction test, constitutes a complete audiogram and a comparison of the two is useful in determining whether the hearing loss is conductive or sensorineural. Here, Dr. Zemo quantified the Claimant's hearing loss through the use of bone conduction and air conduction tests and we find no error in the WCJ's reliance upon Dr. Zemo's testimony.

Claimant also argues that in accordance with *The Budd Company v. Workers' Compensation Appeal Board (Curran)*, 762 A.2d 419 (Pa. Commw. 2000), because Claimant's initial audiogram in 1970 revealed a zero percent impairment and his most recent audiogram in 1996, according to Dr. Zemo, revealed a 24.4 percent impairment, Claimants' impairment, when properly calculated, is 24.4 percent (24.4 percent minus 0 percent). *Budd* is distinguishable, however, in that the WCJ credited the testimony of the doctor that "the entire . . . impairment was the result of Claimant's exposure to hazardous occupational noise." *Id.* at 421. Here, the WCJ credited the testimony of Dr. Zemo that Claimant's impairment was not entirely due to occupational noise. In fact, Dr. Zemo stated that Claimant's initial audiogram in 1970 evidenced a high tone loss related to occupational noise, but using the *AMA Guides*, he had a zero percent hearing loss. "As you follow his audiograms the impairment starts to develop in low-tone loss beginning in 1992 and he appeared to have a 12.2 percent binaural change. As you follow this through my audiogram today, this was developing otosclerosis. . . ." (R.R. at 64A.) Thus, the WCJ attributed Claimant's hearing loss to otosclerosis, not occupational noise.

In this case, Dr. Zemo concluded that the majority of Claimant's loss of hearing is a result of otosclerosis, which is not a result of noise exposure. The WCJ credited Dr. Zemo's diagnosis, and because it is supported by substantial evidence, we may not overturn the WCJ's decision.

Id. at 1057–58.

LTV Steel Co., Inc. v. W.C.A.B. (Mozena), **562 Pa. 205, 754 A.2d 666 (Pa. July 19, 2000)**

In this consolidated case, the court considered whether section 306(c)(8)(i) of the Workers' Compensation Act allows a reduction in liability for hearing loss for any portion that is attributable to nonoccupational causes, including presbycusis.

The employee suffered a bilateral hearing loss from his long-term exposure to occupational noise at the employer's plant. He testified to his hearing loss, and presented the deposition testimony of Dr. B., board certified in otolaryngology, who opined that the claimant had suffered a binaural hearing loss of 26.56 percent from work-related causes. Dr. B. based his finding on the *AMA Guides*, as required by the Act. The employer, LTV, introduced testimony of its own otolaryngologist, Dr. Bu., who also conducted an audiogram on the claimant and concluded that he suffered a binaural hearing loss of 23.4 percent. However, Dr. Bu. ascribed 8.11 percent of the claimant's hearing loss to the aging process (presbycusis). Dr. Bu. determined that he could attribute only 15.31 percent of the hearing loss to other causes, such as work-related factors. To obtain the percentage that he claimed was caused by presbycusis, Dr. Bu. relied on the 1999 standard of the International Organization for Standardization (ISO 1999).

The WCJ relied on the claimant's expert, Dr. B., and found that the claimant suffered a 26.56 percent hearing loss caused by long-term exposure to hazardous occupational noise. LTV received no credit for any age-related hearing loss. LTV appealed this finding, but the commonwealth court affirmed the board and held that the *AMA Guides* did not allow a reduction in benefits for hearing loss caused by the aging process.

The employee of USX worked as a crane operator at the employer's blast furnace. He claimed that as a result of his long-term exposure to occupational noise at the steel mill, he suffered a bilateral hearing loss. He acknowledges that his nonoccupational activities and pre-USX employment in the U.S. Army exposed him to loud noises. The WCJ concluded that the claimant's military service did not adversely affect his hearing. The claimant's expert, Dr. D., an otolaryngologist, testified for the claimant and opined that he had suffered a 30 percent binaural hearing loss according to the *AMA Guides.* Dr. D. attributed the entire hearing loss to the claimant's long-term exposure to noise at USX. However, USX's expert, Dr. C., testified that an examination of the claimant revealed a 20.5 percent hearing loss, pursuant to the *AMA Guides.* Dr. C. attributed 6.8 percent of the claimant's hearing loss to presbycusis and 13.7 percent of the hearing loss to occupational noise. While recognizing that the *AMA Guides* make no provision for age-related hearing loss, Dr. C. relied on ISO 1999 to reach his conclusion.

The WCJ relied on USX's expert and concluded that the claimant suffered a 20.5 percent loss of hearing from long-term exposure to hazardous, occupational noise. However, the WCJ rejected Dr. C.'s assertion that there should be any reduction for the natural aging process. The WCJ awarded a benefit to the claimant.

The board affirmed, and USX then appealed to the commonwealth court, which held that, although an employer is generally free to introduce evidence of nonoccupational causes of hearing loss, natural aging based on the ISO 1999 is not a permissible factor for reducing an employer's liability.

The supreme court consolidated the appeals from the commonwealth court and considered whether the Act permits deduction from a claimant's total binaural hearing impairment that portion of the impairment caused by presbycusis.

> The only standard provided by the legislature in Act 1 is the *AMA Guides.* There is no mention of ISO 1999 in Act 1. We find it useful in interpreting the intent of the legislature that it considered age as a factor but, ultimately, provided no method for assessing its effect. We also recognize that presbycusis is distinguishable from other nonoccupational factors. There is no reliable scientific (controlled) means of quantifying how aging impairs the hearing of a given individual. Whereas, the effect of many other nonoccupational factors is quantifiable. Courts have reduced an employer's responsibility for benefits where it established that a nonwork-related cause was the substantial contributing factor of hearing impairment. [Citation ommitted] We find no merit to the contention by LTV that the decision by the Commonwealth Court precludes employers from presenting evidence of *all* nonoccupational causes. Where the nonoccupational causes of a specific individual's hearing impairment is quantifiable using the *AMA Guides,* either side may present evidence of the percentage of loss.

754 A.2d at 675–76.

The court concluded:

> Because there is no way to distinguish, scientifically or mathematically, the amount of hearing loss caused by acoustic trauma from that caused by the aging process, and [the Act] provides for no standard to measure presbycusis, we find that [the Act] does not permit a deduction from a claimant's total binaural hearing impairment for that portion of the impairment caused by presbycusis.

Washington Steel Corp. v. WCAB (Waugh), 734 A.2d 81 (Pa. Commw. Ct. 1999)

The Pennsylvania court dealt with a claimant who claimed work-related hearing loss. The Workers' Compensation Appeal Board determined that the claimant suffered a 12.2 percent hearing loss under the *AMA Guides.* It assumed that this hearing loss was work related. The court held that this was an incorrect assumption. It stated:

> Employer argues that the Board erred in reversing the WCJ's decision because the WCJ discredited both Claimant's testimony and that of his medical expert and, as such, he failed to produce any evidence that he suffered a binaural

hearing loss of at least 10%. We agree. The WCJ only found Dr. [B.]'s testimony credible, and Dr. [B.] testified that Claimant's hearing loss was due to his hunting activities over 40 years. Specifically, when asked if he had formed an opinion as to the cause of any of Claimant's hearing loss, he responded:

A. Yes. I believe he has noise-induced hearing loss primarily due to gunfire shooting from the right shoulder. (Notes of Testimony at p. 18.)

Additionally, when asked if he attributed any of Claimant's hearing loss to his exposure to noise at work, he responded:

A. What I believe is that he could have had some occupational noise-induced hearing loss in early years of employment. As I mentioned, if he had, he would have reached a maximum level by the early '80s. And, also, I said and I believe it's questionable whether he was exposed to enough noise on a time-weighted average basis all together because he wore hearing protection and he said for ten years he worked in almost ten years he worked in a booth which he said was much quieter. (Notes of Testimony at pp. 24–25.)

When further asked if he attempted to quantify the extent to which there was any hearing loss using any accepted formula, Dr. [B.] stated:

A. Yes. We used the American Medical Association Guides to the Evaluation of Permanent Impairment; and based on those guides, [claimant] had an 11.2 percent hearing impairment on the right, a 16.9 percent hearing impairment on the left, and a binaural hearing impairment of 12.2 percent. (Notes of Testimony at p. 20.)

While the Board determined that Dr. [B.] found that Claimant suffered a binaural hearing loss of 12.2% utilizing the *AMA Guides* and assumed that figure was attributed to his exposure to noise at work, Dr. [B.] specifically testified to the contrary. Just because Dr. [B.] utilized the *AMA Guides* does not mean that any percentage of hearing loss found under that standard was work related. The *AMA Guides* only provide the standards against which *any* hearing loss is measured; it is for the medical expert to determine what percent of that loss is attributable to the workplace.

Because the WCJ is the ultimate fact finder and determiner of credibility, *Buczynski v. Workmen's Compensation Appeal Board (Richardson-Vicks, Inc.)*, 133 Pa. Cmwlth. 532, 576 A.2d 421 (1990), and he found Dr. [B.] credible, the Board erred by determining that Claimant had proven he suffered a 12.2% hearing loss for which he was entitled to Workers' compensation benefits. Accordingly, the decision of the Board is reversed.

734 A.2d at 84 (citation omitted).

Rockwell International v. WCAB (Meyer), 741 A.2d 835 (Pa. Commw. Ct. 1999)

The Pennsylvania court dealt with a claimant who claimed work-related hearing loss. The employer's physician concluded that he suffered 14.7 percent binaural hearing impairment according to the *AMA Guides*, 4.9 percent of which was caused by aging. The employer's physician, Dr. B., explained that because the *AMA Guides* did not take into account the effects of aging, he consulted the International Standard for 1999 of the International Organization for Standardization (ISO 1999), which had been adopted by the American National Standards Institute (ANSI), to arrive at the percentage of the claimant's hearing loss attributable to aging. Dr. B. admitted, however, that the claimant's audiometric curve was consistent with noise-induced hearing loss.

The WCJ found Dr. B. more credible than Dr. Be. and concluded that of the claimant's 14.7 percent total binaural hearing loss 4.9 percent was due to aging. The WCJ, however, credited the claimant's testimony that he experienced hearing loss during the course of his employment, with a greater amount of loss during the earlier years of his employment, and found that Dr. B.'s opinion supported the claimant's testimony in this regard. Nevertheless, the WCJ denied the claimant's claim petition because the claimant's percentage of work-related hearing loss was below the 10 percent threshold required by Section 306(c)(8)(iii) of the Workers' Compensation Act before hearing loss was compensable because of the 4.9 percent deduction for aging.

The claimant appealed to the Workers' Compensation Appeal Board, which reversed, holding that the WCJ erred as a matter of law in allowing an age-related deduction based on ISO 1999 under *USX Corp. v. Workers' Compensation Appeal Board (Rich)*, 727 A.2d 165 (Pa. Commw. Ct. 1999). It then awarded benefits to the claimant based on the 14.7 percent level of binaural hearing impairment testified to by Dr. B. before he took the age-related deduction. The court affirmed the board's reversal of the WCJ's denial of benefits.

Philadelphia Fed'n of Teachers v. Ridge, 150 F.3d 319 (3d Cir. 1998)

The plaintiffs in the case challenged the constitutionality of Pennsylvania's 1996 workers' compensation reform law. The U.S. Court of Appeals for the Third Circuit rejected this claim by holding that the issue was not yet ripe for adjudication. The court reasoned:

> Section 4 of Act 57 amended Section 306 of the WCA [Workers' Compensation Act] to add section 306(a.2), 77 P.S. § 511.2 (West Supp. 1997), permitting employers to require an employee to submit to an impairment rating evaluation after the employee receives total disability benefits for 104 weeks. *See* 77 P.S. § 511.2(1). Pursuant to section 511.2, an impairment rating evaluation is performed by a licensed physician chosen by the parties or appointed by the Department of Labor and Industry (the "Department"). *See id.* The purpose of the evaluation is to determine the level of the employee's impairment rating. If the employee's impairment rating is fifty percent or greater under the American Medical Association's Guide to the Evaluation of

Permanent Impairment, he or she remains classified as "totally disabled." *See* § 511.2(2). If, however, the examination results in an impairment rating that is less than fifty percent, the employee is reclassified as "partially disabled." *See id.*

The change in status from "totally disabled" to "partially disabled" does not automatically affect the amount of compensation that the insurer must pay the employee. Rather, the Act provides that "unless otherwise adjudicated or agreed to based upon a determination of earning power under [§ 512.2(2)], the amount of compensation shall not be affected as a result of the change in disability status and shall remain the same." *See* § 511.2(3). The change in status does, however, affect the length of time that a claimant may receive workers' compensation benefits. An employee who is classified as "totally disabled" is entitled to collect benefits for as long as he or she remains classified as such. An employee with a partial disability, however, is eligible to receive benefits only for a period of 500 weeks, or approximately ten years. *See* § 511.2(7).

Before changing an employee's disability status, an employer must provide the employee with sixty days notice that his or her impairment rating evaluation showed that the employee was less than fifty percent impaired. *See* § 511.2(2). The Act also provides that "an employee may appeal the change to partial disability at any time during the five hundred-week period of disability; Provided, That there is a determination that the employee meets the threshold impairment rating that is equal to or greater than fifty percentum impairment. . . ." § 511.2(4).

Plaintiffs seek a declaration that, on its face, WCA § 306(a.2), 77 P.S. § 511.2, violates the due process clauses of the United States and Pennsylvania constitutions, U.S. Const. amend. XIV; Pa. Const., art. 1, § 1. Although the Act provides employees whose status is changed to partially disabled the right to appeal their change in status, *see* 77 P.S. § 511.2(4), plaintiffs maintain that the procedures that will ultimately be employed by the Department during this "appeal process" will deprive their members of the right to procedural due process of law. Plaintiffs rest this claim on the fact that the term "appeal" is not defined in the statute and that, typically, an appeal to the Worker's Compensation Board, as opposed to a hearing, does not involve a fact-finding procedure and de novo adjudication. Plaintiffs further allege that the Act is rendered facially unconstitutional by the fact that the appeal process contained in § 511.2(4) is only available following a determination that the employee is equal to or greater than fifty percent impaired. 77 P.S. § 511.2(4). Plaintiffs also seek to enjoin enforcement of the statute.

We are inclined to disagree with the district court that there is uncertainty regarding whether the statute will ever operate against any of the plaintiffs' members; rather, we find persuasive plaintiffs' argument that such an eventuality is almost certain. There is, however, a great deal of uncertainty regarding how the statute will operate against plaintiffs' members. It is this uncertainty that renders the claim unfit for judicial review. Plaintiffs ask the court to declare constitutionally deficient procedures that have yet to be applied. Such a judgment would be premature. Rather, we believe that review of plaintiffs' procedural due process claim must be done in the context of a specific factual setting.

We might still review plaintiffs' procedural due process claim despite our conclusion that it is best considered in the context of a specific factual setting if denial of pre-enforcement review would work a significant hardship to the plaintiffs. In this case, however, we discern no hardship that will result from withholding review of the constitutionality of WCA § 304(a.2) until a court is able to review the procedures actually employed by the Department. Even assuming that an employee is deprived of his or her due process rights in the future by those procedures, the change in disability status will not affect the level of benefits provided to the employee for five hundred weeks. *See* 77 P.S. § 512.2(7). The employee will, therefore, have ample time to challenge the constitutionality of the procedures employed before being deprived of any benefits.

150 F.3d at 321–24.

§11.31   SOUTH DAKOTA

Cantalope v. Veterans of Foreign War Club of Eureka, 4 SD 4, 674 N.W.2d 329 (S.D. 2004)

The South Dakota court dealt with a bartender who suffered an asthmatic episode at work, resulting in injury to her lungs. The incident occurred when the bar was filled with a heavy concentration of cigarette and cigar smoke. The claimant was taken to the hospital and diagnosed with subcutaneous pneumomediastinum, which is air rupturing into body tissues. She was ordered to undergo eight weeks of bed rest and never returned to her employment with the VFW.

The claimant was awarded permanent partial disability benefits, and the employer appealed on the grounds that the *AMA Guides* does not contain specific instructions on how to rate the claimant's specific condition. The court affirmed the awarding of permanent partial disability benefits. It stated:

> Jennifer claimed permanent partial disability under SDCL 62-4-6(24) which allows compensation for permanent partial disability. In order to compute the statutory compensation allowed, a claimant must be evaluated and given an impairment rating. Such rating shall be expressed as a percentage to the affected body part, using the Guides to the Evaluation of Permanent Impairment established by the American Medical Association, fourth edition, June 1993 (Guides). SDCL 62-1-1.2. There is a disclaimer in the Guides explaining that not all questions can be directly answered because of the variables involved in medical practice. Guides at 3. Furthermore, the AMA Guides are not intended to establish a rigid formula, though where use of the AMA Guides is required by statute, a deviation must be justified by competent

medical evidence and be consistent with the specific dictates and general purpose of the Guides. AMJUR Workers 406. Here, Jennifer's physician admitted the Guides do not address her specific injury. However, the Guides offer a means to assess impairment.

Whether the statutory requirements of SDCL 62-1-1.2 have been satisfied is a legal question, which we review de novo. SDCL 62-1-1.2 mandates that the AMA Guides be used to calculate the percent of the impairment to the whole person. Other states also statutorily specify the use of the AMA Guides for impairment assessment. . . . As this court has not reviewed this statute under the circumstances presented here, we will consider how other states have dealt with the Guides. In New Hampshire, the court held that if a physician, exercising competent professional skill and judgment, finds that the recommended procedures in the AMA Guides are inapplicable to estimate impairment, the physician may use other methods not otherwise prohibited by the AMA Guides. . . . *In re* Rainville, 732 A.2d 406, 413, 143 N.H. 624, 632 (1999). Similarly, in New Mexico, the court noted, "[t]he AMA Guide is a general framework, requiring flexibility in its application." *Madrid v. St. Joseph Hosp.*, 928 P.2d 250, 258, 122 N.M. 524, 532, (1996). While the AMA Guides was intended to help standardize the evaluation of a worker's impairment, it was not intended to establish a rigid formula to be followed in determining the percentage of a worker's impairment. *Id.*

Here, the physician used the Guides, Jennifer's medical history, and his professional experience to determine Jennifer had a 10 to 15% impairment rating. And while the Guides do not contain ratings on Jennifer's specific injury, they do contain methods for evaluating respiratory injuries. The physician further explained that while under one of the Guides' rating tests Jennifer would show no impairment, she nevertheless has a permanent injury to her lung, greatly increasing her risk to redevelop the condition and increasing her susceptibility to pneumomediastinum or pneumothorax. Consequently, at trial, the physician testified that Jennifer had a 10 to 15 percent whole person impairment under that portion of the Guides that allow independent physician assessment when the specific injury is not covered. Although we acknowledge that the physician's methodology was subjected to substantial critical review in his deposition, that deposition was incorporated into the trial record, and the trial court ultimately found that a 10 to 15 percent impairment did exist. Whether and to what extent an alternative method is proper, credible, or permissible under the AMA Guides are questions of fact to be decided by the board. *In re* Rainville, 732 A.2d at 413, 143 N.H. at 632 (citing *City of Aurora v. Vaughn*, 824 P.2d 825, 827 (Colo. Ct. App. 1991) (as trier of fact, agency entitled to rely on expert testimony supporting deviation from AMA Guides)). Here, this matter was tried before the circuit court, and that trier of fact found the physician's alternative methodology credible. Considering the totality of the evidence, we do not conclude that the trial court's finding was clearly erroneous.

Where the legislature has expressly incorporated a private organization's standards into our statutes and where those standards expressly allow for professional discretion in reaching a determination, such discretion, if supported by competent medical evidence and if consistent with the general purpose of the AMA Guides, satisfies the statutory requirements of SDCL 62-1-1.2.

674 N.W.2d at 336–37.

Caldwell v. John Morrell & Co., 489 N.W.2d 353 (S.D. 1992)

The South Dakota Supreme Court dealt with the claimant, who ruptured a disk at work and underwent surgery. He was later given a permanent partial disability based on a 40 percent rating. The department determined that the claimant was entitled to a 40 percent permanent partial disability rating based on the "loss of use" analysis. Although the physician gave the claimant a 15 percent medical impairment, the department also considered evidence of the claimant's extensive loss of time necessary each day for the treatment of his injury (40 percent), the fact that he spent his free time engaged in sedentary activities, his lost earning capacity of 35 percent as measured by the fact that he was no longer able to work and his loss of strength (90 percent, measured by a functional capacity assessment).

Other than the testimony of that physician, no other medical doctor or any vocational expert testified on the claimant's loss of employability or loss of use.

The court found that the testimony of a vocational expert was required. The court also found that how the employee spent his free time and the amount of time he spent in treatment was not to be considered in arriving at a permanent partial disability rating. The court stated:

> In speaking of the limited nature of a medical impairment rating we went on to quote from the American Medical Association, *Guide[s] to the Evaluation of Permanent Impairment*, x (2d ed. 1984):
>
>> The physician who makes a determination about impairment must keep in mind that a permanent impairment rating is not the same as a disability rating. Permanent medical impairment is related directly to the health status of the individual, *whereas disability can be determined only within the context of the personal, social, or occupation demands*, or statutory or regulatory requirements *that the individual is unable to meet as a result of the impairment.*
>
>> When we quoted the above emphasized language, we did so for illustration only and did not intend to say that an employee should be compensated under our act for any impairment of his personal/social life.
>
> * * *
>
> In our opinion the analysis required in all but a rare possible case is of sufficient complexity and is of such nature that the trier of fact must be enlightened by an expert before a rational decision can be made.

Id. at 361, 362, 364.

§ 11.32   TENNESSEE

Pesce v. Aerostructures/Vought Aircraft Indus., **2007 WL 906707**
(Tenn. Spec. Workers' Comp. App. Panel)

The Tennessee Supreme Court dealt with the claimant, Pesce, an aircraft worker who suffered an acute injury to her left knee. Pesce had a large osteochondral fragment surgically removed, and this left her with a loss of joint space in the patellofemoral joint. The fifth edition of the *Guides* does not cover this injury.

Dr. Byrd rated her at 15 percent impairment of the lower extremity—6 percent of the whole person. Dr. Bacon rated her at 15 percent as well. Dr. Dyer found that her injury fell between a partial and full meniscectomy.

The court affirmed the lower court's decision, finding that the trial court acted within its discretion in relying on the testimony of the treating physician over non-treating physician in determining that the workers' compensation claimant suffered a 15 percent impairment as a result of her work-related knee injury, even though the treating physician's opinion was based on medical guidelines for arthritis rather than for the knee condition. The court stated:

> In this case, the trial court chose to accept the testimony of the treating physician who personally observed the loss of joint space in the patellofemoral joint of Ms. Pesce's knee and equated that loss to a table in the A.M.A. Guides that specifically deals with loss of joint space in the patellofemoral joint of arthritis patients. This compared to the testimony of a physician who did not observe the injury and equated the injury to surgery on the meniscus which is located in another joint of the knee. In our opinion, under these circumstances, it was appropriate for the trial court to have relied on the testimony of the treating physician, Dr. Byrd, in determining the degree of Ms. Pesce's impairment.

2007 WL 906707, at *5.

Reece v. J.T. Walker Indus., Inc., **2007 WL 4322003**
(Tenn. Spec. Workers' Comp. App. Panel)

The Supreme Court of Tennessee dealt with a production worker, Reece, who was diagnosed with bilateral carpal tunnel syndrome, and later, deQuervain's tendinitis on the right side.

The fifth edition of the *AMA Guides* was used to determine permanent impairment. Drs. Hardin and Holbrook found no permanent impairment, but Dr. Kennedy assigned 9 percent impairment to each upper extremity.

The court ratified the trial court's acceptance of Dr. Kennedy's opinion as he was a board certified orthopedic surgeon and independent medical examiner. The court stated:

> Based on the depositions, Dr. Kennedy was clearly the most qualified to testify about the application of the "A.M.A. Guides." The other two doctors

performed cursory examinations of Ms. Reece even before she reached her maximum medical improvement and opined she had no permanent partial disability. The information gleaned by Dr. Kennedy could have been found by Dr. Hardin and Dr. Holbrook had they performed the tests of anatomical impairment required by the "A.M.A. Guides." Hence, like the trial judge, we find that Dr. Kennedy was clearly the most credible and his testimony deserved the most weight. We therefore conclude that the trial court correctly accredited Dr. Kennedy's testimony.

2007 WL 4322003, at *5.

Note: The court modified the award of permanent partial disability from both hands to both arms. This did not affect the amount of compensation due to the claimant.

Blanton v. CVS Tenn. Distrib., Inc., 2006 Tenn. LEXIS 197 (2006)

The Tennessee court dealt with a worker injured on an assembly line. The employee was seen by a number of doctors for her physical and psychiatric injuries. A psychiatrist testified that she suffered from post-traumatic stress syndrome. The psychiatrist used the second edition's numbers, in conjunction with the fifth edition's. The employer challenged the admission and consideration of the psychiatrist's impairment rating because he used an outdated edition of the *AMA Guides.* The general rule is that a physician testifying in a workers' compensation case is required to use the most recent edition of the *AMA Guides* in rendering an opinion as to impairment of an employee. Tenn. Code Ann. § 50-6-204(d)(3). However, the statute also states "or in cases not covered by the AMA Guides an impairment rating by any appropriate method used and accepted by the medical community." Because the appeal dealt with vocational disability and not anatomical impairment, the court never ruled on the issue of the use of the second edition's numbers for a psychiatric impairment. The court stated:

> [Dr. Workman] went on to further testify that he was of the opinion Ms. Blanton had a Class 2 impairment under the AMA Guidelines, Fifth Edition, which is stated to be a mild impairment rating. When he was questioned as to how he reached the 11 percent rating, he said the Fifth Edition of the guidelines do not give numerical numbers for impairment and that since the legal system requires a numerical rating doctors have no guide and that this has resulted in great controversy in his profession without any official solution. He said he and other members of his profession look back to the Second Edition of the guidelines to get some idea about a numerical rating and this edition gave a 10 to 20 percent impairment for a Class 2 rating and he settled on 11 percent in Ms. Blanton's case.
>
> The employer cites the case of *Humphrey v. David Witherspoon, Inc.*, 734 S.W.2d 315 (Tenn. 1987), where the Supreme Court reversed the trial court for permitting a young chiropractor to base his testimony on an old edition of the *AMA Guides* and held it was an error to admit the chiropractor's testimony. However, we take note of the ruling of the Supreme Court in

Davenport v. Taylor Feed Mill, 784 S.W.2d 923 (Tenn. 1990), where it was held [that] the rule announced in *Humphrey* was subsequently qualified and that a rating that conforms to the statutory requirements is unnecessary when causation and permanency are already established. [However], in the *Lyle* case, the court held that the use of the guides was unnecessary, although preferable, where causation and permanency have been established by expert testimony because the issue then becomes the extent of vocational disability and not anatomical disability.

In the present case, causation and permanency were not issues as the trial court was informed at the beginning of the trial that the sole question was the extent of permanent disability. Therefore, we do not find the reference to the Second Edition by Dr. Workman to be significant in this appeal.

2006 Tenn. LEXIS 197, at *5–*6.

Brown v. Nissan N. Am., Inc., 2006 Tenn. LEXIS 1138 (Tenn. Spec. Workers' Comp. App. Panel at Nashville, July 24, 2006)

The Tennessee court dealt with a factory worker, Brown, who injured his right knee when working on an Altima chassis line. The issue presented at trial was the extent of the worker's vocational disability caused by the knee injury. Dr. Rogers, the treating physician, testified that a 2 percent impairment for the meniscus tear was appropriate. Dr. Walter W. Wheelhouse, an independent medical examiner, testified that his interpretation of the *AMA Guides* allowed a 2 percent impairment for the tear as well as a 5 percent impairment for chondromalacia (cartilage degeneration). After reviewing the deposition evidence de novo, the appellate court concluded that more weight should have been given to the IME's higher rating based implicitly upon the IME physician's training in use of the *AMA Guides*. The appellate court stated:

> In his deposition, Dr. Rogers testified that Brown had a permanent partial impairment of 2% of the right lower extremity, based on AMA Guidelines. Dr. Wheelhouse had a different opinion. In his deposition testimony, he explained that he had recently attended an AMA Guides training session that dealt with assigning impairment ratings for chondromalacia, and he was instructed to use a 5 to 7% impairment rating of the lower extremity. In this case, the trial judge gave more weight to the testimony of Dr. Wheelhouse, along with considerations for the factors used to determine an employee's vocation disability. The trial court found the occasional swelling and restrictions in his activities, during both his work activities and his off-work activities, to indicate that Brown suffered a vocational disability of 10% to the leg. We conclude, based on a de novo review of the record, that the trial court did not err in assigning a 10% permanent partial disability to Brown.

2006 Tenn. LEXIS 1138, at *2.

Note: The court further strongly implies that it felt that the IME physician's training in the use of the *Guides* was a decisive factor when it notes in footnote 2 that "Dr. Wheelhouse is certified in the evaluation of disability and impairment ratings by the American Academy of Disability Evaluating Physicians. In order to gain this certification, Dr. Wheelhouse had to take several classes and pass a certification test on the *AMA Guidelines*, Fifth Edition."

Earls v. Sompo Japan Ins. Co. of Am., 2006 Tenn. LEXIS 295 (Tenn. Spec. Workers' Comp. App. Panel at Nashville, Apr. 11, 2006)

The Tennessee court dealt with a factory worker, Ms. Earls, who injured her back while picking up welded parts from an assembly line. Two physicians performed independent medical examinations on Earls, both finding that a disk bulge like that observed in Earl's MRI could be caused by acute injury. The doctors, however, could not agree on the correct DRE impairment rating, as one doctor did not consider the claimant to have objective findings and one doctor did. The court accepted the doctor who rated the claimant in category II DRE based upon the "objective" evidence of decreased range of motion and guarding during the examination. The court stated:

> There was a dispute between Drs. Landsberg and Haynes as to whether Ms. Earls sustained a permanent impairment as a result of the condition of her back. Our review of the record indicates this dispute centers on which of the DRE Categories established by the *AMA Guides to the Evaluation of Permanent Impairment* (5th Edition) applies to Ms. Earls. According to the testimony of these physicians, Category I describes an individual with subjective complaints of back pain with no objective or substantial clinical findings. Category II relates to an individual who has subjective complaints with objective findings confirming those complaints but no radiculopathy or alteration of structural integrity. Category III requires a finding of radiculopathy. Dr. Haynes stated that in his opinion Ms. Earls' complaints were subjective, without objective confirmation placing her in DRE Category I, precluding the finding of an impairment. Dr. Haynes admitted, however, that the MRI revealing a disc bulge at L4–5 abutting the L4 nerve root was an objective finding that correlated with the complaints made by Ms. Earls. He also agreed that the reduced range of motion he found in Ms. Earls' back was a significant clinical finding
>
> According to Dr. Landsberg, the disc bulge revealed on the MRI confirmed the complaints of Ms. Earls and placed her in Category II, indicating an impairment rating of 5 to 8 percent. Dr. Landsberg assigned a 6 percent impairment because of the intermittent radiculopathy and her other symptoms. Similarly, because of the injury and the clinical finding of a loss of range of motion and guarding during the range of motion examination, Dr. Landsberg found objective evidence of injury to Ms. Earls' thoracic spine and assigned a 5 percent impairment. According to the *AMA Guides* these two impairments combine for an eleven impairment of the body as a whole. While the trial

court made no specific finding as to impairment, we again infer that it found a permanent impairment.

2006 Tenn. LEXIS 295, at *21–*23.

Long v. Mid-Tennessee Ford Truck Sales, Inc., 160 S.W.3d 504 (Tenn. 2005)

The Tennessee court dealt with a worker who injured his foot at work. He claimed that this injury in turn caused back pain, leg pain, sleep apnea, and weight gain. The trial court disagreed. The court stated that a whole-person impairment is available under Tennessee law only if injury to a scheduled member (such as the worker's foot, in this case) caused a *permanent* injury to an unscheduled portion of the body. On appeal, the Supreme Court of Tennessee held that the claimant did not present sufficient evidence that his back and leg pain were caused by the foot injury. The court also held that the evidentiary record did not provide evidence that his weight gain and sleep apnea were permanent. The court reasoned that "the mere fact that the AMA Guides provides a method for converting a scheduled member impairment to a whole-body impairment does not permit an award for whole-body disability. Rather, we must find a whole-body impairment under Tennessee law."

Morrow v. International Mill Serv., Inc., 2004 WL 1064299 (Tenn. Spec. Workers' Comp. App. Panel 2004)

The Tennessee court dealt with a claimant who fell 12 feet and injured his back and who was found to be 8 percent impaired. The employer appealed this finding, claiming that the rating doctor used the wrong chart in the *AMA Guides*. The court upheld the 8 percent rating and noted that the rating doctor testified to the specific portion of the *Guides* he used to support his 8 percent rating.

Chapman v. Bekaert Steel Wire Corp., 2003 Tenn. LEXIS 982 (Tenn. Spec. Workers' Comp. App. Panel Oct. 16, 2003)

The Tennessee court dealt with an operations technician, Chapman, who experienced pain in his neck and shoulders. Chapman eventually had surgery on two levels of cervical disks. Dr. Brophy, one of the participating physicians in the surgery performed, testified that Chapman suffered a 10 percent permanent partial disability according to the *AMA Guides* (5th ed.). Dr. Brophy based his impairment rating on the ROM method of measuring impairment. Dr. Boals, the only other physician to give an impairment rating, testified that according to the surgery performed on Chapman and the two-level fusion, Chapman would suffer 34 percent permanent partial disability to the whole body. Dr. Boals based his impairment rating on the DRE method. In their depositions, Dr. Brophy and a Dr. Lochemes testified that under the *AMA Guides*, Dr. Boals should have used the ROM method to evaluate Chapman. The trial court excluded Dr. Boals's testimony "because of his failure to comply with the AMA Guidelines in evaluating Chapman." The appeals court reversed the decision. It stated:

> This Court concludes, however, that Dr. Boals' testimony should not have been excluded. Even if Dr. Boals' evaluation deviated from the AMA Guidelines, the record still shows that he relied on the Manual for Orthopedic Surgeons in Evaluating Permanent Physical Impairment. Since both resources are named in the Workers' Compensation Statute, Dr. Boals was entitled to rely on either one of them in arriving at his impairment rating. Therefore, the deposition should not have been excluded on the basis of Dr. Boals' failure to comply with the AMA Guidelines in evaluating Chapman.
>
> Furthermore, the deposition should not have been excluded under Tennessee's standard for determining the admissibility of expert evidence. Under this standard, "[t]he trial court is not required to determine that the principles and methodology employed are generally accepted by the scientific community. The court needs only to determine that the principles and methodology are scientifically valid and reliable." *McDaniel v. CSX Transp., Inc.*, 955 S.W.2d 257, 257 (Tenn. 1997). "[T]he court need not weigh or choose between two legitimate but conflicting scientific views. The court instead must assure itself that the opinions are based on relevant scientific methods, processes, and data, and not upon an expert's mere speculation." *Id.* at 265.
>
> In this case, Dr. Boals did not merely speculate. In his deposition, Dr. Boals explained the scientific procedures used to arrive at his results. While these scientific procedures may deviate from the normal method of evaluating an injury such as Chapman's, the reasons for the deviations are explained by the expert.
>
> The proper course for the trial court, at this point, would have been to admit the testimony. Dr. Boals is entitled to be listened to, but he does not have to be agreed with. The trial court then, should have decided the weight to give to the two legally admissible competing scientific views. 2003 WL 22446716 at 2.

Thomas v. Magna Seating Sys. of Am., Inc., 2003 Tenn. LEXIS 711 (Tenn. Spec. Workers' Comp. App. Panel Aug. 15, 2003)

The Tennessee court dealt with a sewing machine operator who developed an overuse syndrome, left upper extremity, with chronic epicondylitis. At issue was whether the trial court was within its discretion when it accepted the testimony of the IME physician. The court held that the trial court was within its discretion in accepting the IME physician's testimony and noted that the IME physician was board certified in the use of the *AMA Guides*. It stated:

> Dr. Boals' qualifications include board certification in the use of the AMA Guidelines. He testified as follows:
>
> > Historically we must look at the history of the Guides. In the third and fourth editions, which were used over the last twenty-five years, there

was a general suggestion that when there was an unlisted impairment that the physician examiner should use his experience in arriving at impairment rating. Now, in the fifth edition of the Guides new language has been inserted that's never been there before. In chapter one, page eleven, the authors are very—make a very strong statement that if there is an unlisted impairment it can be compared to conditions in the same area that have the same functional results.

In this case Dr. Stonecipher's testimony is essentially negative in that he was unable to ascertain her specific problem, whereas Dr. Boals' testimony is more positive in that he identified her problem and was of the opinion her impairment based on the AMA Guidelines was 10% to the left upper extremity, and was work related.

Where there is a conflict between medical experts, a trial court has the discretion to accept the opinion of one medical expert over that of another unless evidence preponderates against that medical opinion. *Kellerman v. Ford Lion, Inc.*, 920 S.W.2d 333, 335 (Tenn. 1996); *Johnson v. Midwesco*, 801 S.W.2d 804, 806 (Tenn. 1990). The trial court was well within its discretion in accepting the testimony of Dr. Boals in this case. 2003 WL 21957145 at 1–2.

Cain v. Whirlpool Corp., 2001 WL 873459 (Tenn. Spec. Workers' Comp. App. Panel 2001)

In this Workers' compensation case, the claimant injured his left shoulder while working for the employer. Dr. W. surgically repaired the injured shoulder, then—because the pain persisted—Dr. K. performed a second surgery (a distal clavicle resection). Dr. K. estimated the claimant's permanent medical impairment at 6 percent to the whole body, using the *AMA Guides.* The claimant's attorney then referred him to Dr. E., a chiropractor, for an examination and evaluation. By the use of range-of-motion tests, Dr. E. estimated the claimant's permanent impairment at 16 percent to the shoulder or 10 percent to the body as a whole. The claimant then returned to work (with 10-pound weight-lifting restriction) at a wage equal to or greater than what he was earning before the accidental injury, was laid off along with other workers, then refused to return following the layoff, though invited to do so.

The trial court gave equal weight to the two estimates of permanent medical impairment and awarded permanent disability benefits based on 2½ times the average of the 16 percent and 6 percent, or 27.5 percent, to the body as a whole. On appeal the employer claimed, among other things, that the award of permanent partial disability benefits was excessive. The employer contended the award was excessive because the maximum award should have been 2½ times the medical doctor's 6 percent impairment rating, rather than 2½ times the average of the medical doctor's and chiropractor's rating. The claimant conceded that the court should have used the chiropractor's 10 percent whole-body rating rather than the 16 percent shoulder rating, but that the doctor's and surgeon's ratings were correctly given equal weight. The appellate court agreed, found that both the doctor's and surgeon's opinions were correctly given equal weight, and adjusted the award:

> [The trial judge] should have averaged 10 percent (Dr. [E.]'s impairment rating to the body as a whole) and six percent, which would result in an award of two and one-half times 8 percent, or 20 percent to the body as a whole. The judgment is modified accordingly.

2001 WL 873459, at *3.

Rowland v. Northbrook Health Care Center, 2001 WL 873475 (Tenn. Spec. Workers' Comp. App. Panel July 30, 2001)

In this workers' compensation appeal, the employer argued that the award of permanent partial disability benefits based on 70 percent to the body as a whole was excessive. The claimant was a 49-year-old nurse's assistant who injured her lower back while lifting a patient at work. She continued working with pain for two weeks, then sought medical attention. She was referred to Dr. N., who diagnosed a herniated disk and performed corrective surgery. While recuperating, the claimant developed a staph infection. The doctor released her to return to work with permanent lifting restrictions. She tried to return to work but was unable to work because of residual pain. She returned to Dr. N., who ordered a second MRI. The test showed postoperative scarring and recurring disk herniation. After rehabilitation, the employer attempted to return the claimant to light-duty work, but the claimant resigned because of disabling pain, although the employer was willing to make accommodations for her.

Dr. N. assigned a permanent impairment rating, based on the *AMA Guides*, of 12 percent to the whole body. The claimant testified she could not work. Accordingly, the trial court found that the claimant's refusal to return to work was reasonable and awarded permanent partial disability benefits based on 70 percent to the body as a whole.

On appeal, the employer argues that the permanent partial disability award should not exceed 2½ times the medical impairment rating because the claimant failed to make a reasonable attempt to return to work. The appellate court noted, "An injured employee is competent to testify as to her own assessment of her physical condition and such testimony should not be disregarded. *Walker* at 208 (Tenn. 1998)." The trial judge based his award, in part, on the claimant's testimony that she was unable to perform her assigned duties because of her injuries. The appellate court declined to disturb the trial judge's finding and affirmed his judgment.

Key v. Savage Zinc, Inc., No. M200000306WCR3CV, 2001 WL 758736 (Tenn. Spec. Workers' Comp. App. Panel July 6, 2001)

The claimant was a 58-year-old male with a fourth-grade education. He had worked for the defendant for 18 years. Previously, in 1994, he suffered a left shoulder rotator cuff injury while working for the defendant. This required surgery performed by Dr. K., who after surgery rated the claimant at 15 percent permanent partial disability to the body as a whole. In June 1996, the claimant injured his right shoulder while pulling and hammering railroad spikes. In July 1996, Dr. K. performed an open rotator cuff repair and acromioplasty on the right shoulder. In his operative report, he noted that the glenohumeral ligaments were intact. Dr. K. assigned restrictions on lifting and upon reaching above shoulder level. After recovery and physical therapy, the claimant returned to work for the defendant in a less physically demanding job.

Dr. K. assigned a 15 percent anatomical impairment rating to the claimant's right shoulder or upper extremity, equivalent to 9 percent to the body as a whole based only on loss of range of motion. Dr. K. did not include grip strength as a factor in his impairment rating. Dr. G. then evaluated the claimant and assigned a 17 percent anatomical impairment rating to the upper extremity, equivalent to 10 percent to the body as a whole. He based this rating upon loss of motion *and* excisional arthroplasty of the acromioclavicular (AC) joint. Dr. G. found significant weakness and loss of movement of the right shoulder and noted that the claimant would be unable to use this arm to any degree in an overhead or outstretched position for pushing, pulling, or lifting. The claimant was not satisfied with these impairment ratings because his workers' compensation claim arising from the 1994 similar injury to the left shoulder settled based on a 15 percent medical impairment rating to the body as a whole assigned by Dr. K. The claimant testified that Dr. K. had told him that the rating to the right shoulder would be the same. Also, the claimant believed that his right shoulder injury was worse than his left shoulder injury because he was right handed and used that hand more often. The claimant then saw an orthopedic surgeon, Dr. L., for an independent medical evaluation. She assigned the claimant a 24 percent anatomical impairment rating to the upper extremity, equivalent to 14 percent to the body as a whole using the *AMA Guides*. Dr. L. based her rating on loss of function of the shoulder joint (both AC and glenohumeral), and pain and loss of grip strength as a result of loss of muscle mass.

The trial court then found the claimant to have a 35 percent vocational disability, which was 2½ times the 14 percent anatomical impairment rating to the body as a whole.

One of the issues on appeal was whether the trial court committed prejudicial error by giving more weight to the testimony of Dr. L., an evaluating physician, than to Dr. K., the claimant's treating physician, as well as Dr. G., another evaluating physician. The appellate court noted that the trial court had the discretion to accept the opinion of one medical expert over another medical expert and thus found no error on the part of the trial court.

Another issue on appeal was whether the trial court committed prejudicial error by giving weight to Dr. L.'s opinion that the claimant's loss of grip strength should be considered in evaluating his impairment. The court noted that the medical testimony differed with regard to whether grip strength should be included as a factor in the claimant's impairment rating. Neither Dr. K. nor Dr. G. used grip strength in determining the rating—Dr. K., in fact, stated that he believed that, although the claimant had not gotten all of his grip strength back, grip strength would not affect his rating. Dr. L. did use a grip strength test in rating the claimant, and opined that loss of grip strength can be significant enough to warrant being a factor in an impairment rating, especially in a manual laborer such as the claimant. The appellate court found no error on the part of the trial court regarding the grip strength issue and proceeded to affirm the judgment of the trial court.

Gates v. Jackson Appliance Co., 2001 WL 720624 (Tenn. Spec. Workers' Comp. App. Panel June 27, 2001)

The plaintiff was 50 years old at trial. In April 1995, the plaintiff strained a muscle in the groin area of his left leg while moving a basket of parts. Dr. C. told him in June 1995 that he "tore the muscle and it would be a nagging and reoccurring thing" and that he had a problem he was going "to have from that point forward." Since then, the plaintiff has seen various doctors and others for various treatments—none of which, the plaintiff testified, has provided him any lasting relief from pain.

Dr. N., an orthopedic surgeon, saw the plaintiff in the fall of 1997. Dr. N. agreed with the original diagnoses and reported left adductor flexor strain, chronic at this point. Dr. N. placed permanent work restrictions, and believed the plaintiff had reached his maximum medical improvement on November 3, 1997. He assigned no permanent impairment because the *AMA Guides* do not assign an impairment for chronic muscle strain. Dr. N. did state "he could still have a permanent injury."

The plaintiff testified he began to have emotional problems in July or August 1997. In the summer of 1998, he first complained to Dr. N. of emotional problems, who recommended a psychiatric consultation. On January 29, 1998, Dr. K., Ph. D., examined the plaintiff for a psychological and vocational evaluation. Dr. K. described the plaintiff as "significantly depressed" in the moderate range caused by the chronic pain from his work injury. Dr. K. stated the claimant's prognosis of his condition was very likely to be permanent. Dr. K. opined the claimant was excluded from 10 percent of jobs in the national open labor market by Dr. N.'s restrictions. Dr. K. did not assign any jobs excluded due to the claimant's depression. Dr. K. explained the *AMA Guides* (4th ed. 1993) do not provide a numerical rating for mental impairment but classifies disorders as mild, moderate, or severe. Under the *AMA Guides* (2d ed. 1984), moderate impairment would be 25 percent to 50 percent impairment to the body.

The trial court awarded the claimant 25 percent permanent partial disability to the body as a whole, which included the mental injury. On appeal, the defendant contended, inter alia, that (1) the testimony of Dr. N. was insufficient to prove the permanency of the claimant's depression, (2) the testimony of Dr. N. was insufficient to prove the permanency of the claimant's disability due to his leg injury, and (3) the claimant's recovery exceeded the maximum amount allowed pursuant to Tenn. Code Ann. § 50-6-241(a)(1).

The only medical proof of permanent injury, either mental or to the leg, came from Dr. N., an orthopedic surgeon. He testified, "As long as he has continued pain and it interferes with his lifestyle, [he] will continue to have depression, usually requiring some type of treatment, whether it be medications or counseling." Similarly, Dr. N.'s testimony was the only medical evidence to consider concerning permanency of a leg injury. Dr. N. did not assign a permanent impairment rating because the *AMA Guides* do not rate a chronic muscle strain. When asked, "Does the fact that you were unable to assign a numerical impairment rating under the *AMA Guides* mean that this gentleman has not suffered a permanent injury?" Dr. N. answered, "No, he could still have a permanent injury." The appellate court found that these statements supported the trial court's finding of permanency.

The state workers' compensation statute requires that the award be based upon a multiple of the medical impairment rating. Because Dr. N. did not assign a numerical anatomical impairment rating for the claimant's leg injury or his depression, the defendant claimed that the claimant was not entitled to receive any award of permanent partial disability. The trial court stated that an anatomical impairment rating was not mandatory when the evidence supported an award of benefits. The appeals court agreed. The court went on to reason that the defendant's position

> is further without support in the present case due to [the psychologist's] finding that [claimant]'s moderate depression would be rated at twenty-five (25) to fifty (50) percent to the body under the 2nd Edition of the *AMA Guidelines*. The difficulty in rating mental injuries was discussed in Ivey v. Trans Global Gas & Oil, 3 S.W.3d 441, 445 (Tenn. 1999), where the rating doctors acknowledged the current 4th Edition of the *AMA Guidelines* does not assign a numerical percentage of impairment for mental injuries, and, therefore, the rating doctors relied on the earlier 2nd Edition of the *AMA Guidelines* to support a fifty (50) percent impairment to the body as a whole.
>
> This panel is mindful of the decisions which require expert medical evidence and not that of a psychologist to establish causation and permanency of a mental injury. [Citations omitted] However, once causation and permanency of a mental injury have been established by medical testimony, vocational experts such as Dr. [K.] may express an opinion as to the extent of vocational disability.

2001 WL 720624, at *3.

The appellate court affirmed the award.

Russell v. Bill Heard Enterprises, Inc., 2001 WL 721062 (Tenn. Spec. Workers' Comp. App. Panel June 26, 2001)

The claimant was performing mechanical work on a motor home while at work. He fell and was injured. The employer provided medical care primarily by

Dr. W. The claimant suffered a complete rotator cuff tear, which was surgically repaired. The employee developed a mild infection at the surgical site and tendinitis of the right wrist. He returned to light duty three or four weeks after surgery and to full duty several months later. Dr. W. assigned a permanent impairment rating of 10 percent to the right upper extremity, which he equated to 6 percent to the whole person, using appropriate guidelines.

The doctor testified that the *AMA Guides* provide a rating for the removal of the distal clavicle, but not for a rotator cuff repair or acromioplasty. It was his opinion that only a loss of range of motion in the shoulder would allow for an impairment rating over and above the rating for the distal clavicle. He conceded that the acromioplasty, which became necessary because of the accidental injury, creates an anatomical change in the shoulder, but gave no impairment rating for it because the guidelines do not assign a rating for that procedure.

The claimant was then evaluated by Dr. B., an orthopedic surgeon. Dr. B. estimated the claimant's permanent impairment at 10 percent for the resection of the distal clavicle, then referred to a section of the guidelines that encourages physicians to express their belief that there is additional impairment, provided they explain their reasons for holding such opinions. Explaining his reasons, Dr. B. opined, over the objection of the defendant and based upon his own guidelines developed over the years, that the acromioplasty should result in an impairment rating of 10 percent, but less than that when combined with the distal clavicular resection, and opined further that a tear of the rotator cuff will result in an impairment rating of between 5 percent and 20 percent, depending on the severity.

The trial court awarded benefits based on "impairment and disability" of 20 percent to the body as a whole. On appeal, the employer contended that it was error for the trial court to consider Dr. B.'s opinion because it was not based on statutorily acceptable guidelines. The court noted that a physician's testimony as to the extent of a claimant's permanent medical impairment must be based on the most recent edition of the *AMA Guides* or the *Manual for Orthopedic Surgeons in Evaluating Permanent Physical Impairment*. Therefore, the court held that it was error for the trial court to consider Dr. B.'s estimate of 20 percent permanent medical impairment.

The court then reduced the award, because the only proper rating was Dr. W.'s 6 percent. Thus, the award should have been based upon that rating.

Short v. Dietz Mobile Home Transport, 2001 WL 370317 (Tenn. Spec. Workers' Comp. App. Panel Apr. 16, 2001)

The claimant was injured when the mobile home on which he was working was accidentally lowered onto him. He suffered a compression or crush-type injury to his mid-back area. Four neurosurgeons saw the claimant, and three testified. Dr. J. rated the claimant as retaining a 5 percent permanent impairment to the body as a whole based upon the elements of DRE Category II for the thoracolumbar spine. He employed the "Injury Model" portions of the *AMA Guides* in assessing the medical impairment, and his rating of 5 percent was for less than a 25 percent compression of one vertebral body. Dr. W. agreed with the diagnosis and with his measurement of the T12–L1 compression as being less than 25 percent. Dr. W. agreed that the claimant was neurologically intact, that a compression of this degree ordinarily would resolve itself satisfactorily, and that there was no evidence of radiculopathy. However, Dr. W. employed Table 75 on the *AMA Guides* and rated the claimant as retaining a 7 percent anatomical impairment. Dr. H. found decreased range of motion in the back. He rated the claimant's fracture, disk rupture, and radiculopathy at the T12–L1 area as a "thoracolumbar, Category 3 impairment under the diagnostic related estimates of the *AMA Guides* at 15 percent. In addition, Dr. H. rated the thoracic strain under a "diagnostic related estimate, Category 2" under the *AMA Guides* at 5 percent, for a total anatomical impairment rating of 20 percent to the body as a whole.

The trial judge found that the claimant suffered a 15 percent anatomical impairment and awarded permanent partial disability benefits in the amount of 60 percent to the body as a whole. The employer appealed from the amount of the award on the grounds that the trial judge could not determine an anatomical impairment rating that did not match exactly the assessment of at least one doctor who testified and that the impairment rating was excessive.

> The trial judge evaluated the relative credibility of the three doctors who testified, carefully explained his reasons for choosing to rely most heavily on one of them, and modified slightly the impairment rating given by that doctor, for reasons that the trial judge examined.

2001 WL 370317, at *4.

The appellate court affirmed the trial judge's right to determine an impairment rating somewhere between the highest and the lowest rating but not exactly the rating of any one doctor.

Jackson v. Goodyear Tire & Rubber Co., 2001 WL 303508 (Tenn. Spec. Workers' Comp. App. Panel Mar. 29, 2001)

The claimant was a 51-year-old female who, while working for the employer, performed a variety of jobs. In April 1997, the plaintiff developed problems with both her arms. Dr. C. diagnosed the claimant as suffering from bilateral carpal tunnel syndrome predominantly on the right side. An open carpal tunnel release was performed on the claimant's right arm on September 19, 1997. This was followed by the same procedure for the left arm two years later.

Dr. C. used the Jamar Dynamometer to test the plaintiff's grip strength in her right arm and determined that she had suffered no anatomical impairment. He stated that the plaintiff did have a grip strength loss to her right arm. Because it was less than 10 percent, he declined to award impairment and released the plaintiff to return to work without restriction. In rating the plaintiff's grip strength loss, he used the tables contained in the *AMA Guides* as opposed to the tables accompanying the Jamar Dynamometer. He did not test the plaintiff's left arm with the Jamar Dynamometer but instead used opposition strength and two-point discrimination tests.

Dr. B. conducted IMEs on the claimant after the second surgery. Dr. B. used the Jamar Dynamometer in testing the plaintiff's grip strength as well as the accompanying tables rather than the tables contained in the *AMA Guides*. Dr. B. opined that the plaintiff had suffered a 10 percent impairment to her right arm and a 20 percent impairment to her left arm. On cross-examination, he testified that if he had used the *AMA Guides*, the plaintiff would have had normal grip strength in both arms. Dr. B. also testified that he did not use the AMA tables because they were outdated and flawed and that the Jamar Dynamometer tables were more accurate.

The trial court determined that the plaintiff had suffered a 20 percent permanent partial disability to her right arm and a 30 percent permanent partial disability to her left arm as the result of bilateral carpal tunnel syndrome. The employer appealed the award, contending that the medical impairment rating provided by Dr. B. was invalid because he did not use the *AMA Guides* when evaluating the plaintiff's grip strength.

The appeals court noted that the applicable statute (T.C.A. § 50-6-204(d)(3)) clearly provided the guidelines physicians were required to use in determining anatomical impairments. It then disallowed the grip strength testing performed by Dr. B. because it was not performed using the *AMA Guides*. However, the court upheld the award, stating that the trial judge correctly relied on numerous factors to determine vocation disability. The court quoted precedent that stated, "An employee should not be denied compensation solely because she is unable to present a witness who will testify to the exact percentage of her medical impairment. [Citation omitted]" 2001 WL 303508, at *4.

Phillips v. Marvin Windows, 2000 WL 987312 (Tenn. Spec. Workers' Comp. App. Panel July 18, 2000)

The claimant was 42 years of age at trial. In September 1996, she was lifting a bundle of door panels when she felt a pop in her lower back, with pain in her back and left leg. She was referred to Dr. P. An MRI revealed a very mild degenerative joint disease in her lower facet joints. Dr. K. saw the claimant for a second opinion in November 1996. Dr. K. also found a full range of motion in her back and stated that her examination and symptoms suggested lumbar radioculopathy. Because her symptoms continued, the claimant asked to see another doctor. She was seen by Dr. J. in October 1997. He diagnosed mild fascial pain. Dr. B. examined the claimant for an independent medical evaluation in August 1997. On examination, he found a full range of motion, and x-rays showed moderate joint arthritis. Dr. B. diagnosed her condition as facet joint arthritis of the lumbar spine, which was either caused by or aggravated by her work. He assigned a 7 percent permanent impairment to the body as a whole. Drs. P., K., and J. did not place any restrictions on the claimant or find she had any permanent impairment.

The employer appeals the award that was based on the 7 percent impairment rating. On appeal, the employer contended, inter alia, that Dr. B.'s finding of permanent impairment should be disregarded because his impairment rating of 7 percent permanent impairment was based on Table 75, Section IIC, page 133, of the *AMA Guides* (4th ed. 1993). Table 75, Section IIC assigns a 7 percent impairment of the whole person when the following is present in an intervertebral or other soft-tissue lesion of the lumbar spine, "unoperated on, stable, with medically documented injury, pain and rigidity associated with moderate to severe degenerative changes on structural tests; includes unoperated on herniated nucleus pulposes with or without radiculopathy." The employer pointed out that Dr. B.'s diagnosis was facet joint arthritis of the lumbar spine and submitted that this diagnosis did not fall within the parameters of Table 75. Thus, the impairment rating was not valid. The employer argues that without any "valid" impairment rating, it was error for the trial court to award any vocational disability.

At trial on cross-examination, Dr. P. stated it was possible to assign a 7 percent impairment rating for moderate to severe degenerative changes or a 5 percent impairment rating for none to minimal degenerative changes to an intervertebral disk or other soft-tissue lesion where there is an injury, pain, and rigidity, although he chose not to assign any impairment to the claimant.

The court rejected the employer's argument regarding the validity of Dr. B.'s rating:

> This panel is unable to determine whether Dr. [B.] relied on the appropriate table in the *AMA Guides* or not. Even if he did not use the proper table, as [employer] contends, we do not believe Dr. [B.]'s opinion of permanent impairment should be totally rejected as "invalid." Numerous awards have been affirmed on appeal even though reliance on the *AMA Guides* was imprecise, once causation and permanency are established by expert testimony. [Citations omitted.]

2000 WL 987312, at *2.

The court then affirmed the award.

Thurman v. Maytag Cooking Products, Inc., 2000 WL 502844 (Tenn. Spec. Workers' Comp. App. Panel Apr. 27, 2000)

The plaintiff was injured in February 1996 during the course and scope of his employment with the defendant when he struck his right elbow on a steel box. The plaintiff continues to have trouble using his right arm. The only issue at trial was whether and to what extent the plaintiff suffered permanent vocational disability as a result of the elbow injury.

Dr. J., an orthopedic doctor, treated the plaintiff for epicondylitis as a consequence of the work-related injury. The records show Dr. J.'s treatment included a tennis elbow strap and anti-inflammatory medication. He also suggested elective surgery might improve the plaintiff's condition. The plaintiff reached maximum medical improvement; however, he still had pain and decreased grip strength but not enough to have a 10 percent impairment under the guidelines, according to Dr. J.'s records. He released the plaintiff to work "as tolerated." Dr. J. told the plaintiff he would always experience trouble with the injured arm.

Dr. H., an orthopedic surgeon, also treated the plaintiff. He diagnosed lateral and medial epicondylitis of the right elbow and treated the plaintiff with injections of Depo-Medrol. He restricted the plaintiff from lifting over 20 pounds with his right arm and restricted repetitive motion of the right elbow, hand, and wrist. Dr. H. found the plaintiff sustained a 5 percent permanent impairment to the upper extremity and based the calculation mainly on Table 34 of the *AMA Guides*.

The trial court found a 25 percent partial permanent disability.

On appeal, the defendant argued that the medical impairment rating of Dr. H. predicated on Table 34 on page 65 of the *AMA Guides* was not competent or credible because the doctor failed to perform or review any tests that would establish the underlying factual basis for application of the referenced table. The court responded to this argument:

> The medical records of Dr. [H.] do not reflect he did any tests to determine the extent of disability suffered by the plaintiff. On the other hand, the records do not show he did not. We may not assume an insufficiency of Dr. [H.]'s report on the record before us.
>
> Beyond this, when the record indicates from all the medical evidence and the testimony of the plaintiff show he has suffered a permanent injury, an award may be made even when there is no medical attribution of a percentage of disability. [Citation omitted].

2000 WL 502844, at *2.

The appellate court then affirmed the trial court's ruling.

Scruggs v. Wal-Mart Stores, Inc., 2000 WL 371198 (Tenn. Spec. Workers' Comp. App. Panel Apr. 4, 2000)

The plaintiff, 44, was employed since 1991, primarily as a cashier. Her right hand began to swell in 1992 while on the job; she was prescribed medication to eliminate the swelling. In July 1995, while scanning a five-pound bag of nectarines, the plaintiff lost control of her right hand and dropped the bag. Results of a nerve test were normal, the pain eventually went away, and her medical bills were paid by the employer. In July 1997, she advised the company that she was again having problems with her right hand. She saw Dr. J. in August 1997 and advised him that she was having problems with both wrists, but her right was worse than her left. She moved to light work. When she returned to work as a cashier, her pain returned, and did not disappear after she was moved to another job.

The employer sent the plaintiff to Dr. J., a board-certified orthopedic surgeon. At trial, Dr. J. opined that the plaintiff did not sustain any permanent partial impairment or any tendinitis. Dr. B., an orthopedic surgeon, saw the plaintiff in November 1997. The plaintiff gave Dr. B. her history and told him of her pain. Dr. B. opined that the plaintiff suffered from tendinitis of the forearm, or overuse syndrome. As a result, Dr. B. opined that the plaintiff had a 5 percent permanent physical impairment to each arm as a result of her tendinitis.

On appeal, the employer asserted, inter alia, that the trial court erred in holding that the plaintiff incurred a permanent impairment. The appeals court found that the trial court properly found a permanent partial disability, based on the depositional testimony of Dr. B. The employer further contended that Dr. B.'s rating was not based upon either the *AMA Guides* or the orthopedic manual, as required by statute. The appellate court noted Dr. B.'s testimony on the matter:

Q. On that report [C-32] you indicated that the five percent impairment rating to both arms that you had given [the plaintiff] was based upon Table 34, page 65 of the *AMA Guides*, Fourth Edition; is that correct?

A. True.

Q. Now under that section, Doctor, there's formula that's used to derive percentage of loss of grip strength; is that correct?

A. You can use that, yes sir.

Q. Did you use that?

A. The formula or—You might get larger ratings if I use that formula. I just thought some diminished grip.

Q. So you didn't use the formula there to rate her loss of grip strength; is that correct?

A. No. And as you say, there is some subjectivity to it. Sometimes if you use those formulas you get rather a high disability ratings, up to 30 percent of the arm sometimes. That's the reason I think you ought to use your judgment rather than just the chart.

Q. Well the table you reference, Doctor, does it not instruct you that you're to use that formula and the rating under that table? This is Table 34, page 65 of the guides.

A. If you want me to I'll use that table. It would be a lot more than 5 percent—if you want me to use that table.

Q. How did you arrive at that five percent under Table 34 without using the formula provided under that table.

A. I just used my own judgment. There are other factors such as pain, swelling.

Q. Well where did you get the five percent from?

A. Out of my head. I can use that formula. The normal grip strength for a female is— 23.4 times 2.2. It would be 20 percent loss—it would be 10 percent loss of extremities if you went strictly by this table. That's the reason I thought it was just five percent.

2000 WL 371198, at *4–*5.

The appellate court found "no reason to disagree with the trial court's determination" and affirmed the trial court's ruling. *Id.* at 5.

Brown v. Campbell County Bd. of Educ., 915 S.W.2d 407 (Tenn. 1995)

Two claimants with mental impairments challenged the constitutionality of the *AMA Guides.* In each situation, the claimant was not assigned a percentage of impairment under the *AMA Guides*, as the *AMA Guides* do not supply percentages regarding mental impairment. The trial court found the adoption of the *AMA Guides* unconstitutional. The supreme court reversed. Under the statute in question, the disability awards must be made under the *AMA Guides*, or if the impairment is not covered by the *AMA Guides*, then "by any appropriate method used and accepted by the medical community." The court held that the appropriate standard for assessing the constitutionality of the *AMA Guides* is the reduced scrutiny standard employing the rational basis test. The court stated:

> Plaintiffs argue that the use of the *Guides* as contemplated by Tennessee Code Annotated Section 50-6-241 violates equal protection because (1) numerical percentage ratings are not provided for certain medical conditions, such as mental impairment or chronic pain, (2) factors other than a physician's interpretation of anatomical impairment are not considered in determining vocational disability and, (3) the *AMA Guides* themselves caution against their exclusive use in fashioning awards of vocational disability.
>
> Plaintiff's assertions about the *Guides* are largely accurate. The *Guides* do not provide percentages ratings for some physical and mental impairments. *See e.g., AMA Guides* at § 14.7 (behavioral and mental disorders) & 15.8 (pain conditions). Additionally, the *Guides* caution against their exclusive use in determining vocational disability. . . .
>
> Our recognition that the system is imperfect does not mean that it is unconstitutional. The reasonable and legitimate state interests applicable to the multipliers—uniformity, fairness and predictability, are equally applicable to the use of the *Guides*. . . . The *Guides* themselves acknowledge that their use "increases objectivity and enables physicians to evaluate and report medical impairment in a standardized manner, so that reports from different observers are more likely to be comparable in content and completeness." Thus, the legislation is reasonably related to and accomplishes significant state interests.
>
> If the *Guides* were not used, medical opinions would be more subjective, and perhaps, arbitrary. It is no surprise that most states either mandate, recommend, or frequently use the *Guides* in workers' compensation cases. . . . Plaintiffs argue that workers whose injuries are not covered by the *Guides* receive no benefits. This is simply not true. . . . Our legislature has recognized that the *Guides* do not cover all types of injuries. When the injury in question is not covered by the *Guides*, the rating is to be based on "any appropriate method used and accepted by the medical community." Thus, a medical expert can still provide an impairment rating based upon the expert's training and experience consistent with methods used and accepted by the medical

profession. . . . Because the legislature has provided a reasonable rating alternative for medical conditions not included in the *Guides*, plaintiffs' arguments that those whose conditions [are] not covered by the *Guides* are discriminated against is without merit.

Id. at 415–16.

The court remanded the case and asked the evaluating physician to provide a percentage of impairment apart from the *AMA Guides* based upon the physician's training and experience.

Harless v. Huntsville Manor Nursing Home, C.A. No. 7258 (Ch. Ct. Scott County, Tenn. Aug. 31, 1994)

The Tennessee court dealt with the claimant, who was employed as a nurse's aide and injured her back at work on January 16, 1993. The claimant came under the care of Dr. F. for neurosurgical consultation on March 5, 1993. Dr. F. treated the claimant conservatively.

The claimant continued to complain of continuous pain in her back with a radiation of pain into her left thigh. She has also complained of intermittent left leg pain and tingling in her left foot.

Although the primary care was given by Dr. F., the claimant sought an independent medical evaluation with Dr. K. According to Dr. K., the claimant suffered from a central and painful left herniation of the L4 disk. According to Dr. K., the claimant was totally unable to return to her employment as a nurse's aide from the date of her injury of January 16, 1993, through the date of his evaluation on April 1, 1994. According to Dr. K., the claimant needs surgical intervention for her back problems.

The claimant questioned the constitutionality of the portion of the state Workers' Compensation Reform Act of 1992, which uses the *AMA Guides* to set permanent partial disability benefits. The Workers' Compensation Reform Act of 1992, more particularly Tenn. Code Ann. § 50-6-241(a), applies to injuries arising on or after August 1, 1992, to cases in which an injured employee is eligible to receive permanent partial disability benefits for unscheduled injuries, and in which an employee returns to employment at a wage equal to or greater than the wage the employee was receiving at the time of the injury. The maximum permanent partial disability award that the employee may receive is 2½ times the medical impairment rating, determined pursuant to the provision of the *AMA Guides, The Manual for Orthopedic Surgeons in Evaluating Permanent Physical Impairment* by the AAOS (*AAOS Manual*), or, in cases not covered by either of these, an impairment rating by any appropriate method used and accepted by the medical community. Additionally, pursuant to Tenn. Code Ann. § 50-6-241(b), when an employee is eligible to receive permanent partial disability benefits for unscheduled injuries and the preinjury employer does not return the employee to employment at a wage equal to or greater than the wage the employee was receiving at the time of the injury, then the maximum permanent partial disability award the employee may receive is six times the medical impairment rating determined pursuant to the provision of the *AMA Guides*, the *AAOS Manual*, or, in cases not covered by either of these, an impairment rating by an appropriate method used and accepted by the medical community. In making such a determination, the court must consider all pertinent factors, including lay and expert testimony; the employee's age, education, skills, and training; local job opportunities; and the employee's capacity to work at types of employment available in the claimant's disabled condition.

Under Tenn. Code Ann. § 50-6-241(c), the multipliers established by the previously described subsections are intended to be maximum limits. If the court awards a multiplier of five or greater, then the court shall make specific findings of fact detailing the reasons for awarding the maximum impairment.

This court made several significant findings with regard to the portion of the Workers' Compensation Reform Act of 1992 using the *AMA Guides*. The court found:

1. Low back syndrome or chronic back pain syndrome is not a condition adequately addressed by the *AMA Guides*. Civil Action No. 7258 at 2.

2. There is no appropriate method used and accepted by the medical community for granting the plaintiff an appropriate impairment rating outside of use of the *AMA Guides*. *Id.* at 2.

3. Tenn. Code Ann. § 50-6-241(a)(1) is arbitrary, capricious, illegal, and unconstitutional because it violates the equal protection clause of the Fourteenth Amendment of the United States Constitution and unfairly discriminates between workers whose medical problems are recognized by the *AMA Guides* and those whose problems are not, such as workers with mental trauma and chronic pain syndrome. *Id.*

4. Tenn. Code Ann. § 50-6-241(a)(1) is illegal and unconstitutional because the statute also violates the equal protection clause of the Fourteenth Amendment of the United States Constitution, in that it provides workers who return to the same employment with less disability than those workers who do not return to the same employment. *Id.* at 3.

5. Tenn. Code Ann. § 50-6-241(c) is arbitrary, irrational, illegal, and unconstitutional and in violation of the equal protection clause of the Fourteenth Amendment of the United States Constitution because the statute requires that the multipliers established by Tenn. Code Ann. §§ 50-6-241(a) and 50-6-241(b) are maximum limits. The court further found that the ratings in the *AMA Guides* have nothing whatever to do with the inability to work. In the real world of an actual work injury, a worker with a slight impairment might be (given the nature of the worker's occupation) completely unable to continue in that trade, whereas another worker might suffer a

more serious injury and yet (because of the nature of the worker's occupation) be able to continue working. The incorporation of the *AMA Guides* into the statutory scheme of the Tennessee Workers' Compensation Act in spite of these truths is therefore arbitrary, capricious, and irrational. *Id.*

The court further found and declared Tenn. Code Ann. §§ 50-6-241(a)(1) and 50-6-241(c) to be arbitrary, irrational, illegal, and unconstitutional because these statutes unreasonably classify injured workers whose injuries are recognized by the *AMA Guides* and those whose injuries are not so recognized. *Id.* at 4. The court went on to award $30,808.64, which represented disability benefits in the amount of an 86 percent permanent partial disability to the body as a whole.

Henson v. City of Lawrenceburg, 851 S.W.2d 809 (Tenn. 1993)

The Tennessee Supreme Court dealt with the claimant, who injured his back on August 18, 1989. He underwent disk surgery in March 1990 and was left with residual pain. As a result of the pain, he was assigned a 5 percent impairment rating and released to return to work with a 25-pound lifting restriction.

The parties stipulated that the claimant had been involved in two prior workers' compensation claims that resulted in settlement awards of a 20 percent disability to the left knee and a 50 percent disability to the left leg. The parties also stipulated that the two prior injuries to the left lower extremity "related" to 28 percent to the body as a whole under the *AMA Guides.*

Based on the foregoing evidence, the trial judge found the claimant to be 100 percent totally and permanently disabled. The City of Lawrenceburg was ordered to pay 45 percent of the award, and the Second Injury Fund of the Department of Labor was ordered to pay 55 percent.

The court found that a prior award should be equated to a percentage of the body as a whole under the *AMA Guides.* The court stated:

> Here, the employee has received two prior workers' compensation awards, both involving a scheduled member—the left lower extremity. The parties stipulated that the prior awards of 20 percent to the left knee and 50 percent to the left leg equate to a 28 percent disability to the body as a whole under the AMA guidelines. If the prior awards are combined with the award of 75 percent to the body as a whole announced by our holding today, the total disability exceeds 100 percent of the body as a whole, and the Second Injury Fund is liable for the excess of 3 percent. Despite the stipulation, the Second Injury Fund argues that the prior scheduled-member awards may not be treated as an award to the body as a whole for subsection (b) purposes.
>
> * * *
>
> We are, therefore, persuaded that in the limited context of determining the liability of the Second Injury Fund, the statute's purpose is accomplished by equating a prior scheduled-member award to a percentage of the body as a whole by reference to the AMA guidelines, and that the legislature must have

so intended. To conclude otherwise would thwart the statute's purpose. Accordingly, we have determined that the Second Injury Fund is liable for 3 percent of the award, which is the amount that exceeds 100 percent after combining the prior awards of 28 percent and the present award of 75 percent.

Id. at 813.

Elmore v. Travelers Ins. Co., 824 S.W.2d 541 (Tenn. 1992)

The Tennessee Supreme Court dealt with the claimant, who injured her back at work. The claimant was examined by a physician, who found no permanent partial impairment. The claimant argued that the testimony of this physician should not be permitted because he did not use the *AMA Guides.* The court stated that, as the doctor found no permanent impairment, he did not have to use the *AMA Guides*:

> The plaintiff argues the trial judge erred in admitting the medical proof of Dr. [M.], because he did not follow the AMA Guidelines in assessing permanent impairment, or use an inclinometer to measure range of motion. We disagree.
>
> The decision of whether to admit expert testimony into evidence rests within the sound discretion of the trial judge. Dr. [M.] examined the plaintiff for the purpose of determining whether she suffered a permanent disability as a result of her work-related fall. Because he did not find any permanent disability, Dr. [M.] was not required to go further and utilize the AMA Guidelines to assign the plaintiff a permanent disability rating to make his testimony competent. The trial judge did not abuse her discretion in admitting Dr. [M.]'s testimony on the issues of permanency and causation.

Id. at 543. It is also important to note that this court also held that a physical therapist is not qualified to rate permanent impairment.

Bolton v. CNA Ins. Co., 821 S.W.2d 932 (Tenn. 1991)

The Tennessee Supreme Court dealt with the claimant, who fell off a catwalk and injured his neck. On December 7, 1989, the claimant was referred by his attorney to a licensed physical therapist for evaluation. After a variety of tests, the physical therapist determined that he had limitations in cervical motion and lumbar motion. Based on this evaluation, the physical therapist later testified, over objection, that she used the *AMA Guides* to give him an impairment rating. She said that he had a 6 percent impairment based on the limited range of cervical motion and a 13 percent impairment based on the limited range of lower back motion, for a total whole-body impairment rating of 18 percent. The court found that the physical therapist was not competent to assess permanent disability or impairment using the *AMA Guides*, stating:

> Accordingly, under these statutes, we hold that a physical therapist is not qualified to form and express an expert opinion as to the permanent

impairment or permanent physical restrictions of an injured person. Additionally, given the limitations inherent in the workers' compensation statutes allowing only physicians to use AMA Guidelines to assess permanent impairment, limitations imposed by the licensing statutes restricting the physical therapist's scope of practice, limitations implied by analogy through case law restricting the testimony of other health care specialists, and the legislative history of the 1988 amendment allowing physical therapists to conduct an initial evaluation without a physician's referral, we hold that a physical therapist's testimony must be limited to objective findings and cannot encompass an opinion on ultimate disability. As a result, that part of the vocational expert's opinion which was solely based on the opinions of the physical therapist as to permanency and physical restrictions was inadmissible evidence.

Id. at 938.

Harness v. CNA Ins. Co., 814 S.W.2d 733 (Tenn. 1991)

The Tennessee Supreme Court dealt with the claimant, a 36-year-old man with a third-grade education. He injured his back at work on June 26, 1989. The orthopedic surgeon assessed a permanent disability of 5 percent to the upper extremity, or 3 percent impairment of the body as a whole, based on the *AMA Guides* (3d ed. 1988). The orthopedic surgeon placed no restrictions upon the claimant's work activities, but testified that the claimant might continue to suffer pain and discomfort from hard manual labor. The internist assessed a permanent impairment rating of 5 percent to 10 percent to the body as a whole, based upon the *AMA Guides* (2d ed. 1984). The insurer sought to disqualify the testimony of the internist based upon his use of an out-of-date version of the *AMA Guides*. The court rejected the defense and stated:

> In this case, Dr. [P.]'s use of an outdated edition of the *AMA Guides* is not dispositive, since permanency was already established through the testimony of Dr. [J]. CNA's argument ignores that testimony entirely. Under the rule announced in *Davenport*, Dr. [P.]'s testimony was competent and admissible as proof of the extent of [the claimant]'s *vocational* disability.
> While CNA does not contest the sufficiency of the nonmedical proof, we note that a vocational expert testified that [claimant] was precluded from "at least 50 percent of the jobs that he could have done prior to the injury." We find that both the expert and nonexpert proof preponderate in favor of the trial court's award of benefits based upon a 25 percent permanent vocational disability.

Id. at 735. *See Davenport v. Taylor Feed Mill*, 784 S.W.2d 923 (Tenn. 1990).

Davenport v. Taylor Feed Mill, 784 S.W.2d 923 (Tenn. 1990)

The claimant sustained a ruptured lumbar disk while lifting a 100-pound feed bag. The Tennessee Supreme Court held that permitting a physician to rate the claimant's anatomical impairment based on an old edition of the *AMA Guides* was not an error where vocational, not anatomical, disability was at issue.

The claimant's orthopedic surgeon concluded that the claimant had a 12 percent disability rating based on the *AMA Guides* (2d ed. 1984). Tenn. Code Ann. § 506-204(d)(3) requires that any medical report prepared by a physician furnishing medical treatment shall be based on the *AMA Guides* or the *AAOS Manual.* In addition, Tenn. Code Ann. § 50-6-204 (d)(3) states that a physician shall use the most recent edition of either publication. The defendant's appeal rested on the wording of this section and on *Humphrey v. David Witherspoon, Inc.*, 734 S.W.2d 315 (Tenn. 1987), which held that a chiropractor's testimony based on an older edition of the *AMA Guides* was inadmissible. That rule of law was, however, subsequently qualified. A rating that conforms to the statutory requirements is unnecessary when causation and permanency are already established. *See Lyle v. Exxon Corp.*, 746 S.W.2d 694, 699 (Tenn. 1988); *Corcoran v. Foster Auto GMC, Inc.*, 746 S.W.2d 452, 457 (Tenn. 1988). The *Davenport* court held:

> In *Lyle* we held that "use of one of the two guides named in the statute was unnecessary, although preferable, where causation and permanency have been established by expert testimony, because the issue then becomes the extent of vocational disability, not anatomical disability." 746 S.W.2d at 699. In the present case, Defendants specifically admitted that Plaintiff had a "permanent impairment," and they never questioned the causation element. In fact, the Chancellor found that the central issue for him to decide was the amount of permanent partial disability. Thus, vocational, and not anatomical, disability was the issue at trial, and the admission of [doctor's] rating was not error.

784 S.W.2d at 925–26.

Vanatta v. Tomlinson, 774 S.W.2d 921 (Tenn. 1989)

The claimant, who sustained injuries to her right elbow, right hip, and lower back, was awarded temporary total disability benefits and benefits for permanent partial disability of 85 percent of the body as a whole. The claimant's physician testified that, as a result of a nerve injury and surgery, the claimant had lost 8 percent of the function of the right arm, which translated into a 2 percent permanent partial impairment to the body as a whole. The Tennessee Supreme Court found that the evidence supported the determination that the worker suffered a permanent partial disability of 85 percent to the body as a whole, notwithstanding the fact that the disability award was 14 times the anatomical disability rating given by treating physicians. A vocational expert testified that the worker, who was unable to read or do mathematical computations at a fifth-grade level, was essentially unemployable for most jobs that required any kind of manual labor.

Reagan v. Tennessee Man. League, 751 S.W.2d 842 (Tenn. 1988)

The claimant was employed as a patrolman with a police department when he was involved in an automobile accident, causing severe fractures in his right leg.

He was awarded a permanent partial disability to the body as a whole. The Tennessee Supreme Court reversed, holding that the injury to a scheduled member did not authorize an award of permanent partial disability to the body as a whole. The court stated:

> The mere fact that a medical impairment rating to a particular member may translate, for purposes of the [*AMA Guides*] into a disability rating to the body as a whole does not alter the rule that if an injury is to a scheduled member only, the statutory schedules must control the disability award.
>
> * * *
>
> We recognize of course, that the trial judge is not confined to the medical rating in making the ultimate award. The fact that Dr. [J.] estimated that appellee would retain 35 percent permanent partial disability to the leg does not confine the trial judge to that percentage if other testimony justifies a different award. There is no material evidence in the record, however, to justify an award based upon unscheduled injury to the body as a whole.

Id. at 844.

Jaske v. Murray Ohio Mfg. Co., 750 S.W.2d 150 (Tenn. 1988)

The claimant developed carpal tunnel syndrome as a result of her employment as a production worker. The Tennessee Supreme Court affirmed the trial court's conclusion that the claimant sustained a 20 percent permanent partial disability of both hands. The orthopedic surgeon who performed the first surgery testified that the claimant had suffered a 5 percent permanent impairment to each hand. The orthopedic surgeon who performed the second surgery testified that the claimant suffered a 10 percent permanent partial disability to each hand. Both of these ratings were based on the *AMA Guides.*

Lyle v. Exxon Corp., 746 S.W.2d 694 (Tenn. 1988)

The claimant injured his back while performing his job as a filling station attendant and was eventually awarded benefits for a 60 percent permanent partial impairment to the body as a whole. The defendant argued on appeal that the claimant failed to prove the permanency of his disability by expert testimony because the claimant's physician's testimony on permanency was not based on the *AMA Guides* or the *AAOS Manual.* The supreme court disagreed:

> This Court recently held in *Corcoran v. Foster Auto GMC, Inc.*, 746 S.W.2d 452 (Tenn. 1988) that use of one of the two guides named in the statute was unnecessary, although preferable, where causation and permanency have been established by expert testimony, because the issue then becomes the extent of vocational disability, not anatomical disability.

Id. at 699.

Corcoran v. Foster Auto GMC, Inc., 746 S.W.2d 452 (Tenn. 1988)

The claimant, a mechanic, suffered a hernia during the course of his employment. The law court granted the defendant's motion for summary judgment, dismissing the claimant's request for permanent partial disability, but the Tennessee Supreme Court reversed, holding that when medical evidence established permanency, the failure of a medical expert to attribute a percentage of anatomical disability does not justify a denial of compensation if other evidence demonstrates that the award is appropriate.

The only medical testimony was introduced through the deposition of a peripheral vascular surgeon whose services had been approved and accepted by the defendants. This physician stated that the claimant should not do any heavy lifting because there would be a tendency to reinjure his abdominal area. When asked to attribute a disability impairment rating, the physician stated:

> I don't have any idea how to do a disability rating. I wrote this insurance company and I told them I felt like he should not do any heavy lifting or straining in the future. . . . I've never seen a disability rating form and I have no experience in filling out one . . . and have never used one.

Id. at 455.

Nevertheless, the physician stated that the claimant was not 100 percent disabled and that he could perform sedentary work. He felt that the claimant could safely lift up to 30 pounds, but any more than that would dramatically increase the risk of recurrence. After the claimant suffered one such recurrence, the physician wrote that it would be in the best interest of the claimant to do no more heavy lifting in a work capacity. The physician reiterated that "I have no information as to a disability rating on this man."

The trial court reasoned that because the physician failed to attribute an anatomical disability rating to the claimant, it was without guidance to determine the extent of the vocational disability and thus would be speculating if it assessed the extent of permanent partial disability. The court determined that the testimony that a mechanic is required to lift heavy objects was not credible, and noted that the record contained no expert testimony that the claimant suffered a permanent disability.

The supreme court noted that the accident occurred on July 1, 1985, and thus the standard of review in this case was de novo pursuant to Tenn. Code Ann. § 50-6-225(e) (Supp. 1987). This standard of review differs from that previously provided and requires this court to examine in more depth factual findings and conclusions of law in workers' compensation cases. *See Humphrey v. Witherspoon, Inc.*, 734 S.W.2d 315 (Tenn. 1987). The supreme court is no longer bound by the findings of the trial court in these cases, and instead determines where the preponderance of the evidence lies.

> The trial court denied compensation to Plaintiff because the doctor to whom he was taken by Defendants would not or could not rate the degree of Plaintiff's

permanent anatomical disability. In the recent case of *Humphrey v. Witherspoon, Inc.*, 734 S.W.2d 315 (Tenn. 1987), we briefly discussed the provisions of Tenn. Code Ann. section 50-6-204(d)(3) (Supp. 1987). In *Humphrey* the medical expert failed to use the most recent edition of the *Guides to the Evaluation of Permanent Impairment*, contrary to the express requirements of the statute. 734 S.W.2d at 317. For this and other reasons, the Court reversed the judgment of the trial court in awarding the plaintiff compensation for permanent partial disability and remanded the case for a new trial in which the extent of impairment could be properly determined. *Id.* at 318. We did not, however, construe the statutory language providing that "[a] practitioner shall be required to give an impairment rating based on one (1) of the two (2) publications noted above." Originally, Chapter 393, section 3, 1985 Public Acts, which was effective July 1, 1985, provided that "[a] practitioner shall be required to give an impairment rating based on the *AMA Guides.* Given that the express purpose of the statute is "[t]o provide uniformity and fairness for all parties," the statutory language, taken as a whole, clearly evidences a legislative intent to standardize the methods of rating percentages of anatomical disability to minimize arbitrariness and encourage predictability in such assessments by medical experts. The statute does no more than require that medical experts use one of two statutorily approved guides whenever rating an injured employee's anatomical impairment and does not affect in any way the employee's burden of proof as previously established by the statute and the case law. We do not think that, when medical evidence establishes permanency, the failure of a medical expert to attribute a percentage of anatomical disability can justify a denial of compensation if the other evidence demonstrates that an award of benefits is appropriate. Otherwise the remedial purpose of the Workers' Compensation Act could easily be frustrated. In *Martinez v. Meharry Medical College*, 673 S.W.2d 141 (Tenn. 1984), this Court refused to permit denial of compensation because a doctor to whom the employee was sent by the employer failed to submit the statutorily required medical report. "The failure of [the physician] to furnish the requested medical report cannot in any way be blamed on the plaintiff. She was in no way responsible for his conduct; he was an employee of the defendant-employer. . . ." *Id.* at 144. Similarly, an employee cannot control the medical expert's compliance with this statutory requirement.

746 S.W.2d at 457.

White v. United Indus. Syndicate, 742 S.W.2d 635 (Tenn. 1987)

The claimant developed carpal tunnel syndrome as a result of her job, which required that she fold between 700 and 800 cardboard boxes each day. The Tennessee Supreme Court affirmed the trial court's finding that the claimant suffered a 60 percent permanent partial disability in both arms as a result of the carpal tunnel syndrome. The court held that the statute requiring medical reports to be prepared in accordance with the *AMA Guides* applied prospectively only, not retrospectively.

The defendant employer argued that the claimant's expert's testimony did not comply with Tenn. Code Ann. § 50-6-204(d)(3). Before its amendment in 1986, that section provided that physicians furnishing medical treatment to a claimant shall use the *AMA Guides* (3d ed. 1977), or the most recent subsequent edition, in determining the degree of anatomical impairment. However, the trial court found that the claimant's cause of action arose almost two months before the effective date of the statute. Thus, unless Tenn. Code Ann. § 50-6-204(d)(3) was to be applied retrospectively, it did not control the current case.

Section 50-6-204(d)(3) was added to the Tennessee Workers' Compensation Act by 1985 Tenn. Pub. Acts ch. 393, § 3. The Tennessee Supreme Court addressed the retrospective application of a different section of chapter 393 in *Alley v. Consolidation Coal Co.*, 699 S.W.2d 147 (Tenn. 1985). Alley found that nothing in chapter 393 indicated whether § 14 was to be applied prospectively or retrospectively, although the Act specifically provided for the prospective application of chapter 393, § 1. *Alley v. Consolidated Coal Co.*, 699 S.W.2d 147 at 148. The *Alley* court continued by saying:

> This court has previously held that "[i]t is ... entirely possible for some portions of a public act to be prospective in operation and others to be retrospective. We are of the opinion, however, that the intention of the General Assembly to achieve that result should be clearly and unequivocally expressed." *Woods v. TRW Inc.*, 557 S.W.2d 274, 276 (Tenn. 1977). In the *Woods* case it was also noted that "[o]rdinarily, ... statutes enacted by the General Assembly are given prospective operation and will be so construed unless a clear intention to the contrary is found in their provisions." As heretofore noted, there is nothing in the Act itself which indicates any intention on the part of the legislature that Section 14, though it pertains to procedural matters, is to be applied retrospectively. Neither does the legislative history of the Act or tapes of legislative debates help in deciding the intent of the legislature. In fact, the debates show that the question of retrospective versus prospective application was never discussed. This leaves us in the position of having to follow basic rules of law in determining the intent of the legislature.

Id.

The court then determined that the intent of the legislature was for 1985 Tenn. Pub. Acts ch. 393, § 14 to be applied only prospectively. The court found that the reasons given in *Alley* for applying § 14 prospectively were equally applicable to chapter 393, § 3. Thus, Tenn. Code Ann. § 50-6-204(d)(3) applies only to causes of action that arose on or after July 1, 1985. Because the cause of action in this case arose before July 1, 1985, the admission of the medical testimony on permanent disability was not clearly erroneous.

Humphrey v. David Witherspoon, Inc., 734 S.W.2d 315 (Tenn. 1987)

The claimant, a truck driver, sought workers' compensation benefits for a work-related back injury. The Tennessee Supreme Court held that Tenn. Code

Ann. § 50-6-204(a)(4), which authorized the use of the *AMA Guides* (or the *AAOS Manual*), did not disqualify chiropractors from testifying as to the claimant's disability when the testimony is both in accordance with the *AMA Guides* and within the chiropractor's area of expertise.

> Chiropractors have long been held competent to testify as experts in this state within the limited scope of their licensure.
>
> * * *
>
> We do not believe that the legislature intended in enacting the statute above quoted to modify these decisions or to exclude chiropractic testimony provided that the witness used the appropriate guide in making an evaluation and provided that the testimony was within the scope of his expertise and licensure.

734 S.W.2d at 318.

In this case, the court notes that Tenn. Code Ann. § 50-6-204(a)(4) expressly permits the inclusion of doctors of chiropractic in the list of "physicians or surgeons" to be designated by the employer and utilized by the employee. *See* 734 S.W.2d at 318 n.3. This statute was in effect at the time of the claimant's injury.

§ 11.33   TEXAS

Fireman's Fund Ins. Co. v. Weeks, 2007 WL 4460608 (Tex. App.—El Paso)

The Texas Court of Appeals dealt with the claimant, Weeks, who injured his back at work and underwent a spinal fusion. Dr. Mauldin rated the claimant's impairment at 20 percent. Dr. Singleton, the designated doctor, rated the impairment at 10 percent. Dr. Chapman rated the impairment at 25 percent. The hearing officer accepted the 10 percent rating, but the district court went with the 25 percent rating.

The court used the fourth edition of the *Guides*. The court found that surgery is not to be considered in the rating under the injury model and that doctors may not use their medical judgment or experience to take surgery or the effect of surgery into account when assigning impairment ratings.

The court found evidence as to Doctor Chapman's impairment rating legally insufficient and stated:

> Finally, in his deposition testimony, which was read into evidence at trial, Dr. Chapman answered affirmatively when asked whether he found loss of motion segment integrity based upon the fact that Weeks had undergone surgery. In addition, Dr. Chapman answered affirmatively when asked whether the reason that he had put Weeks into DRE category V, rather than DRE category III, rested on the fact that Weeks had a spinal fusion. Accordingly,

Dr. Chapman's impairment rating was based upon a factor not permitted by the Guides. The evidence as to Dr. Chapman's impairment rating was therefore legally insufficient to support the judgment. We sustain Issue One.

2007 WL 4460608, at *5.

Barrigan v. MHMR Servs. for Concho Valley, 2007 WL 27732 (Tex. App.—Austin)

The Texas Court of Appeals dealt with the claimant, Barrigan, who injured her back at work and underwent a two-level spinal fusion. Dr. Sanders, using the fourth edition of the *Guides*, performed range of motion testing and issued a 20 percent impairment rating. Dr. Foxcroft performed a "required medical examination" and rated the impairment at 10 percent. The court found that Dr. Foxcroft was qualified to render an opinion despite the fact that he is not board certified in orthopedic surgery by the American Board of Medical Examiners and despite the fact that his orthopedic training is only recognized in Canada.

The court affirmed the 10 percent award and the disregarding of the Workers' Compensation Commission Advisories, which state that a multilevel fusion is equivalent to "multilevel spine segment structural compromise" per DRE IV. The court stated:

> Dr. Foxcroft examined Barrigan and applied the fourth edition of the *Guides* to determine that Barrigan's impairment rating was 10%. Dr. Foxcroft testified that the impairment rating was based on his physical examination of Barrigan and the history related to him by Barrigan. The primary methodology for determining impairment ratings is the injury model set forth in the fourth edition of the *Guides*. Under this model, a doctor uses objectively verifiable evidence to place patients into one of eight diagnosis-related estimate (DRE) categories. The assigned DRE category then determines the patient's impairment rating. Dr. Foxcroft testified that he did not use the Commission advisories in his determination of Barrigan's impairment rating because the advisories are discretionary. That is, the Commission does not require doctors to use the advisories when determining an impairment rating. When asked why he chose not to use the advisories, Dr. Foxcroft testified that he understood the law to require him to follow the *Guides*, but that use of the Commission advisories was discretionary. Dr. Foxcroft's testimony is consistent with the labor code which expressly requires the use of the *Guides* when determining an impairment rating for the purpose of awarding impairment benefits. [Tex. Lab. Code Ann. § 408.124 (West 2006).].

2007 WL 27732, at *6.

Note: See Lumbermans Mutual Casualty Co. case at 212 S.W.3d 870 (2006), for additional information on the advisories.

Texas Dep't of Ins. v. Lumbermen's Mut. Ins. Co., 212 S.W.3d 870 (Tex. App.—Austin 2006)

The Texas court dealt with an injured employee who had sued his insurance carrier. Prior to this case, a Texas state division that administered the Texas Workers' Compensation Act published two advisories that contradicted sections in the *AMA Guides*. The employee's physicians based their impairment ratings on the *AMA Guides*, whereas the defendant insurance company's physicians relied on the advisories. The court interpreted the relevant Texas statute and determined that the state legislature required physicians to use only the *AMA Guides*, and not the advisories, for making their impairment ratings. The court held that the advisories were ultra vires and invalid ad hoc rules. The court stated:

> The Workers' Compensation Division is required to use the *Guides to the Evaluation of Permanent Impairment*, published by the American Medical Association (AMA), in determining the existence and degree of an injured worker's permanent impairment. The legislature granted the Division discretion to adopt the fourth edition of the *Guides*, which it did on June 7, 2000, after public notice and comment. The fourth edition of the Guides must be used for impairment ratings issued on or after October 15, 2001.
>
> While it is doubtless correct that medical judgment and experience are necessary to assign impairment ratings to injured workers, the *Guides* unambiguously states that "[w]ith the Injury Model, surgery to treat an impairment does not modify the original impairment estimate, which remains the same in spite of any changes in signs or symptoms that may follow the surgery and irrespective of whether the patient has a favorable or unfavorable response to treatment." Thus, under the injury model of the *Guides*, doctors may not use their medical judgment or experience to take surgery or the effect of surgery into account when assigning impairment ratings. By issuing and applying advisories that allow doctors to do just that, the Division has acted outside its statutory authority because the fourth edition of the *Guides* is the only permissible source for determining impairment ratings within the Texas workers' compensation system.
>
> Although the current statutory scheme may warrant revision or amendment, the Division is not authorized to suggest any alternative criteria for determining impairment ratings.

2006 Tex. App. LEXIS 9326, at *15–*16.

Lara v. Pacific Employers Ins. Co., 2003 WL 21517857 (Tex. App.—El Paso July 3, 2003)

The Texas court dealt with a Levi Strauss employee who suffered a back injury while pulling a cart that weighed approximately 30 pounds. The sole issue on appeal was the employee's impairment rating. The court held that the rating physician was justified in invalidating the claimant's range of motion measurements because of his findings of symptom magnification. The court reasoned:

> Lara generally asserts that Dr. Simonsen had no authority to invalidate the range of motion findings based upon his conclusion that she was magnifying her symptoms. In her view, Dr. Simonsen was restricted to performing the measurements required by the AMA Guide (Third Edition) and could not invalidate them even if he concluded that Lara had intentionally restricted her ROM. As already noted in this opinion, the Workers' Compensation Commission Appeals Panel has repeatedly held that an evaluating physician is permitted to invalidate ROM findings based upon the doctor's observation and clinical experience. Nothing in the AMA Guide (Third Edition) requires the type of mechanistic approach advocated by Lara and we decline to read it into the AMA Guide (Third Edition).
>
> Lara also takes issue with Dr. Simonsen's utilization of the McKenzie evaluation and Waddel testing during his examination. She maintains that only the AMA Guides may be considered in making an impairment rating. Dr. Simonsen explained that with the McKenzie evaluation, he asks the patient to perform repeated movements in order to assess what effect the different movements have on the patient's pain level and other symptoms. Once he determines which movements aggravate the symptoms, he prescribes different movements and exercises designed to eliminate the symptoms. For example, a patient with a herniated disc in the lumbar spine frequently feels increased pain if she repeatedly bends forward. If she bends backward, however, the pain will often centralize in the lumbar spine or disappear completely. Dr. Simonsen explained that because people bend forward some 200 to 400 times every day, and often never bend backward, constant pressure on the front of the disc can eventually cause it to bulge. Performing the opposite movement may relieve the patient's pain. Dr. Simonsen believed the McKenzie system is more sensitive than motor and sensory testing. Although Dr. Simonsen determined that Lara's pain was made significantly worse during flexion movements, and he criticized her prior therapy for including flexion movements, there is no evidence that he used the McKenzie system rather than the tests prescribed by the AMA Guides in determining her impairment rating. Further, the AMA Guides contemplate that the evaluating physician will assess the patient's condition, course of treatment and response to treatment.
>
> Dr. Simonsen explained that Waddel testing is named after an English orthopedic surgeon, Gordon Waddel. It is one method of determining whether a patient is giving truthful responses. The examining physician uses light touch and then asks the patient for a reaction. For example, the examiner might place the weight of his hands on the patient's shoulders. If the patient were to state that it caused terrible pain, the examiner might suspect that the patient was not being honest. With respect to Lara, light touch caused severe pain in the neck and lower back. When Dr. Simonsen merely placed his hands on Lara's shoulders, she complained of severe pain in the lower back. Additionally,

he placed his hands on Lara's hips and rotated her a few degrees to the right and then the left. The movement should not cause any pain in the spine because the examiner is rotating the upper body as a unit and there is no rotation of the spine. When Lara complained of horrible pain in the spine, he formed the opinion that she was not being truthful. Because it is appropriate for an examining physician to invalidate range of motion measurements if he concludes that a patient is magnifying her symptoms, Dr. Simonsen's use of Waddel testing to assist him in assessing the truthfulness of Lara's responses is proper.

The record before us reflects that the 9 percent impairment rating is supported by some evidence. Consequently, Lara's sufficiency challenge fails. Her sole issue on appeal is overruled and the judgment of the trial court is affirmed.

2003 WL 21517857, at *5–*6.

Insurance Co. of State of Pennsylvania v. Martinez, 18 S.W.3d 844 (Tex. App.—El Paso Apr. 27, 2000)

The claimant was injured while working in April 1995 and filed for workers' compensation benefits. In accordance with Texas Labor Code § 408.123(a), which requires the treating physician to assign an impairment rating (IR) after the injured worker reaches a state of maximum medical improvement, the claimant's physician assigned him a 10 percent whole body impairment rating. Although the Texas Labor Code requires that an impairment rating be assessed using the *AMA Guides* (3d ed. 1988), it is undisputed that the claimant's physician used the *AMA Guides* (4th ed. 1993).

Under Texas law, the first impairment rating assigned to an employee is considered final if it is not disputed within 90 days after it has been assigned. However, more than two years after the doctor assigned the initial IR, the claimant contested it, asserting that because the physician used the wrong edition of the *AMA Guides*, his impairment rating had never been properly certified and had not become final despite his failure to dispute it within 90 days. The trial court hearing officer agreed. The employer's carrier appealed this decision, and the Workers' Compensation Appeals Panel found that the claimant should have disputed the IR within 90 days. The claimant then appealed the decision of the panel to the trial court. There, he filed a motion for summary judgment in which he again argued that the 90-day deadline for disputing his impairment rating had never been triggered. The trial court entered summary judgment in favor of the claimant, affirmed the hearing officer's decision, and remanded the cause to the Texas Workers' Compensation Commission (TWCC) for further proceedings. Texas Labor Code § 410.258(a) requires that the TWCC be given notice of the trial court's intent to enter judgment and be provided with a copy of the proposed judgment. The employer's insurance company asserted on appeal that summary judgment here was void because the parties failed to comply with the notice provision. The statute specifically states that a judgment entered without complying with the notice requirements is void. The appellate court found that, before the trial court entered summary judgment, no notification was filed with the commission as mandated by Texas Labor Code § 410.258. The trial court was therefore without jurisdiction to render judgment. The appellate court declared the judgment void, set it aside, and dismissed the appeal.

Brookshire Bros., Inc. v. Lewis, **997 S.W.2d 908** (Tex. App.—Beaumont 1999)

The Texas court dealt with a plaintiff who injured his back. The employer was a nonsubscriber to the Texas workers' compensation law. The claimant therefore sued in tort. At issue was the legal sufficiency of the plaintiff's impairment ratings. The court held that the evidence in the record was legally and factually sufficient to support past and future impairment. The court stated:

> In its eighth and ninth points of error, [employer] attacks the legal and factual sufficiency of the evidence to support the jury's damage award for past and future physical impairment.
>
> Dr. [E.] testified regarding [claimant]'s surgeries and resulting impairment. [Claimant]'s first surgery, performed in August 1990, was for a partial laminectomy of a large disc herniation at the L4–5 segment on the right side. In August of 1991, following the second injury, an MRI revealed a new herniation at the same segment level, this time on the left side, along with a new small disc herniation at the L5-S1 segment on the left side. By September 1991, [claimant] was experiencing pain in both legs and a second surgery was performed. In March 1993, [claimant] was diagnosed with nerve root compression on the left side. He was found to have a recurrent extrusion of a disc fragment on the left side at the L5-S1 level which was the same disc herniation operated on in the second surgery. He also had new abnormalities at segments L2–3 and L3–4. A third surgery was performed to remove the extruded disc fragment.
>
> At the request of [employer], Dr. [F.] examined [claimant] to determine limitations related to his back injuries. Dr. [F.]'s description of [claimant]'s back condition contained the following comments:
>
>> Prior to his third surgery, I saw the patient and we established he had multiple-level degenerative lumbar disc disease. It was thought because of this a fusion was not indicated because of disease above and below the area where he had his herniated discs. . . . The patient has persisted in having a lot of pain. He describes this as being constant pain which is worse with movements, such as standing, stooping, bending, or lifting. Even sitting after a period of time causes him to have increased pain. The pain is mainly in the back and into the left leg. It is really very severe when he first gets up in the morning. He has trouble mobilizing, but once he starts to move around he seems to have less discomfort. The patient currently is using [pain medication] which helps alleviate the pain but certainly does not take it away completely. . . . On occasion, his legs give out, and, on one of these occasions, he actually fell. . . .

Dr. [F.]'s notes also indicated that [claimant] had a 14% lumbar range of motion impairment. Based upon the American Medical Association's *Guides to the Evaluation of Permanent Impairment,* Dr. [F.] concluded that [claimant] had a "27% impairment of the whole person." Dr. [F.] also advised a weight lifting restriction of 20 pounds.

Dr. [E.] offered the following addition to Dr. [F.]'s impairment rating:

[T]his patient has multilevel degenerative disc pathology on the lumbar spine which has been minimally improved with two lumbar operations. He is not a candidate for lumbar fusion because of the number of levels involved. He tried to go back to work after his first surgery, but developed progressive problems and was unable to continue. He further developed an additional disc herniation which required additional surgery. This patient will have continued problems with his back. He has undergone an Impairment Rating evaluation through Dr. [F.]. His data on his range of motion indicates that he has significant impairment of range of motion of his back. This is, in part, what accounts for his relatively high impairment rating. I understand that Dr. [F.], the orthopedist on the case, had indicated that the patient could function in an employment position where he was not required to lift anything heavier than 20 pounds. I am in agreement with this with the following addition. This patient has limited range of motion of the low back and any effort to stress his back with regard to range of motion will only increase his symptoms.

Dr. [E.] acknowledged that [claimant]'s back will never be the same as before, and further stated that there was nothing further that could be done to improve [claimant]'s condition.

Using the sufficiency standards of review as set forth earlier in this opinion, we find the evidence was legally and factually sufficient to support past and future physical impairment. Viewing the evidence in the light most favorable to [claimant], the testimony of Drs. [E.] and [F.] adequately establishes past and future physical impairment. In addition, considering and weighing all the evidence, the damage award is not so contrary to the overwhelming weight of the evidence as to be clearly wrong and unjust. Points of error eight and nine are overruled.

997 S.W.2d at 922–23.

Old Republic Ins. Co. v. Rodriguez, **966 S.W.2d 208 (Tex. App. 1998)**

The Texas court dealt with an employee who injured his low back and left knee. His workers' compensation case was tried before a jury, and the jury awarded him a 30 percent impairment. The employer appealed on the basis that the claimant's expert had made a clerical error in calculating the permanent impairment. The court held that a minor clerical error was not grounds to keep evidence of the impairment rating from the jury. The court stated:

Old Republic maintains that Dr. [P.]'s 31 percent impairment rating should not have been submitted to the jury because his clerical mistake rendered it invalid under the American Medical Association guidelines. We find no cases on point. We cannot, however, accept Old Republic's contention. In this case, the substance of Dr. [P.]'s examination and the resulting impairment rating were not shown to be invalid pursuant to AMA guidelines. Rather, it was shown that Dr. [P.] made a clerical error in using the AMA tables to combine impairment ratings. The jury believed the substance of Dr. [P.]'s impairment findings and appropriately corrected his clerical mistake by finding a 30 percent, rather than a 31 percent, impairment. We do not believe that the statute should be construed to deprive a litigant, whether that litigant be an injured employee or a workers' compensation insurance carrier, of the right to present its impairment evidence to the jury simply because the doctor committed a minor clerical error such as the one in this case. Accordingly, we overrule Old Republic's third, fourth and fifth points of error.

966 S.W.2d at 210–11.

Rogers v. Morales, 975 F. Supp. 856 (N.D. Tex. 1997)

The U.S. district court dealt with a plaintiff who was alleged to have been suffering from fibromyalgia. Fibromyalgia is not listed in the *AMA Guides*, and thus the plaintiff's workers' compensation claim was denied. The plaintiff sued in federal court in an attempt to have the Texas workers' compensation statute declared unconstitutional. The court held that the plaintiff's claim should be decided by a Texas state court. The court reasoned:

> The Plaintiff is in effect asking this Court in part to overrule the decision in *Texas Workers' Compensation Commission v. Garcia*, 893 S.W.2d 504 (Tex. 1995). Plaintiff alleges she suffers from a condition known as fibromyalgia. For determining disability under the Workers' Compensation Act, Texas uses a *Guide to Evaluation of Permanent Impairment* as published by medical authorities. Fibromyalgia is not listed in the *Guide*, therefore, Plaintiff's claim for Workers' compensation was denied. In *Garcia, id.* at 526, the Court withheld expressing any opinion as to whether or not the Workers' Compensation Act might violate the due process of law as applied to a claimant who was suffering from a known and diagnosed permanent physical ailment, not included under the *Guides*. Thus, the Texas Supreme Court has never been presented with the opportunity to rule on the question of whether or not the Workers' Compensation Act is unconstitutional wherein it fails to list a medically recognized diagnosis. In such a circumstance, abstention is appropriate, thus giving the Texas Courts the opportunity to construe their own statutes.
>
> It is, therefore, Ordered the claim with regard to the constitutionality of the Texas Workers' Compensation Act of 1991 be dismissed without prejudice as this Court invokes the Abstention Doctrine.

975 F. Supp. at 857–58.

Texas Workers' Compensation Comm'n v. Garcia, 893 S.W.2d 504 (Tex. 1995)

The Texas court dealt with a facial constitutional challenge to several provisions of the Texas Workers' Compensation Act. Under this facial challenge, the challenging party had the burden of proving that the Act, by its terms, always operates unconstitutionally. The trial court had made several findings of fact regarding the *AMA Guides.* These included:

> (1) the Act adopts an improper use of the *Guides.* . . . and that such use of the *Guides* as the determining factor to compensate injured workers for losses occasioned by their injuries is unreasonable and arbitrary and is not reasonably related to any individual or societal interest of the State of Texas.
>
> (2) the impairment ratings generated from use of the *Guides* have no adequate scientific base; [and] have no reasonable relationship to true impairment;
>
> (3) the 15% threshold as a qualification for supplemental income benefits is arbitrary in and of itself, and further that it is based upon an impermissible and arbitrary use of the *AMA Guides*, [and]
>
> (4) a significant number of workers . . . who sustain disabling injuries will have less than 15% impairment based on the *Guides*, [and thus will be] totally denied access to supplemental income benefits under the Act.

Id. at 519–20.

The plaintiffs challenged, under the equal protection clause, a provision of the Act whereby supplemental income benefits were allowed only to persons rating at least 15 percent impairment under the *AMA Guides.* The court rejected this challenge, reasoning that

> [t]he Joint Select Committee criticized the subjectivity and inconsistency of long-term benefit awards under the former act, recommending a more objective system utilizing impairment along with traditional disability factors. The Legislature accordingly based supplemental benefits on actual lost wages, but with a threshold requirement that the claimant suffer at least a 15 percent impairment. It was not irrational for the Legislature to distinguish between moderately severe impairment likely to interfere with long term employment from less severe impairment. Setting the threshold at 15 percent is a rational means of accomplishing this purpose. [P.B.], an economist specializing in compensation issues and former executive director of the National Commission on State Workers' Compensation Laws, testified that the 15% threshold "culls out those impairments that are not very serious . . . [leaving] supplemental income benefits for workers with more serious impairments." That a 15 percent impairment does not perfectly correspond to occupational impairment does not render the threshold invalid under the equal protection clause.

Id. at 524.

The plaintiffs also challenged, under the equal protection clause, the Act's provision which states that a claimant reaches "maximum medical improvement" no later than two years after benefits begin to accrue, regardless of whether the claimant's condition has actually stabilized. The court rejected this challenge as well and reasoned:

> First, it is not apparent that the Act's definition of "maximum medical improvement" creates any classification, as it merely establishes what is in essence a two year cap on temporary income benefits for all claimants. Second, even if it could be viewed as creating a cognizable class, it is not irrational. The Legislature could have concluded that some absolute limit on temporary income benefits—which constitute a major benefit under the Act—was a necessary component of an efficient compensation system. Two years is not an arbitrary place to draw the line, as there was medical testimony at trial that most injured workers will actually reach maximum medical recovery within that time period.
>
> Moreover, in those rare situations where the claimant's condition has not stabilized after two years, the presumption will almost always benefit the claimant by inflating the impairment rating. If the claimant is still recovering after two years, the impairment rating, which is determined at maximum medical improvement, will be higher than the actual degree of permanent impairment.
>
> For the foregoing reasons, we conclude that the Act's definition of "maximum medical improvement" does not violate the Texas Constitution's guarantee of equal protection.

Id. at 525.

The plaintiffs finally challenged the accuracy of the *AMA Guides* in measuring impairment. The court upheld the constitutionality of the Texas Workers' Compensation Act's use of the *AMA Guides* and reasoned:

> [J.G.], an orthopedic surgeon, testified that the sections dealing with injuries to lower extremities have not been updated to reflect new diagnostic techniques. The *Guides* editor testified that, although they are not complete in terms of organ systems, they do not rate mental trauma or chronic pain. Dr. [S.], a contributing author to the *Guides*, testified that the rating numbers lack "scientific validity" because they are not based on broad epidemiological studies. The trial court found that "[the *Guides* do not permit impairment ratings for many disabling injuries including mental trauma injuries and chronic pain syndrome," and that "impairment ratings generated from use of the *Guides* have no adequate scientific base."
>
> The *Guides* editor further testified, however, that the *Guides* are the most reliable method of measuring physical impairment currently available. Dr. [S.] also testified that the rating tables are based on "thorough state of the art analysis" and that there is currently no better method for evaluating physical impairment. [T.M.], author of the spine section, confirmed the *Guides* are the "reference of choice" for evaluating impairment. As noted earlier, numerous states use the *Guides* to measure impairment. On this record, we conclude that

the Legislature's adoption of the *Guides* as the basis for determining impairment does not violate substantive due process of law.

Id. at 525–26.

The court also noted, in dicta, two possible areas of challenge that were not raised by the plaintiffs:

> Not all impairments, however, are rated under the *Guides*. Accordingly, several states using impairment as a basis for benefits do not require strict reliance on the *Guides*. Our Act, however, does not allow such flexibility, as it specifically requires all determinations of impairment to be made under the *Guides*. We express no opinion as to whether the Act might violate due process of law as applied to a claimant suffering from a permanent physical impairment that is not rated under the *Guides*.
>
> * * *
>
> The act specifically requires the Commission to use the " 'Guides to the Evaluation of Permanent Impairment,' third edition, second printing, dated February 1989." Tex. Lab. Cod § 408.124(b). At the time of trial that particular printing was out of print, having been superseded by a more recent edition. Dr. [E.], the editor of the *Guides*, testified that although the newer edition may alter some rating numbers it contained "no major changes." Dr. [E.] had not studied the newer version in detail at the time of his testimony. Although the Legislature's specification of a particular edition of the *Guides*, now out of print, creates a potential administrative problem, plaintiffs do not contend that it rises yet to the level of a constitutional violation.

Id. at 526, n.24.

Texas Workers' Compensation Comm'n v. Garcia, 862 S.W.2d 61 (Tex. Ct. App. 1993)

The Texas court dealt with a constitutional challenge to the Texas Workers' Compensation Act's use of the *AMA Guides*. The Act required use of the second printing of the *AMA Guides* (3d ed. 1988). The court found the Act's use of the *AMA Guides* unconstitutional. The court stated:

> The Act's application of the *Guides* suffer[s] from the same shortcomings. There is no opportunity for workers who cannot qualify as impaired under the *Guides* to show that they in fact have lost wage earning capacity; workers with unlisted impairments, no matter how severe or disabling, are ineligible for any benefits; workers with injuries not quite severe enough to rise to the presumptively severe level of a 15 percent rating might, due to individual factors, actually be more severely disabled. Most significantly, the Act does not allow any adjustment for individualized factors relating to loss of wage earning capacity. (Page 88.)
>
> * * *

The 15 percent threshold is not rationally related to the statute's purpose to increase compensation for injured workers. Its effect is just the opposite. Further, the classification is arbitrary in that there was absolutely no justification offered for the decision to make those with ratings of 15 percent or more eligible for supplemental income benefits—the only long-term benefits provided by the Act—and those with 14 percent ratings or less ineligible for those benefits. The arbitrariness of this classification is demonstrated by evidence establishing that only a relative handful of the workers who suffer serious injuries that curtail, perhaps significantly, their earning capacities will be eligible for supplemental benefits. It is underscored, too, by the examples of severely disabled workers with ratings below 15 percent, and workers with relatively minor injuries—those that do not affect earning ability—who receive ratings of 15 percent or more.

The effect of the arbitrary 15 percent cutoff is to create an irrebuttable presumption that an injured worker who has received an impairment rating below 15 percent does not need and is not entitled to supplemental income benefits. It also created an unreasonable classification between those workers who receive a 15 percent or more impairment rating and those who do not.

For these reasons, the 15 percent threshold violates the equal protection and due course provisions of our constitution.

Id. at 88, 89–90.

Garcia v. Eagle Pass Auto Elec., Inc., No. 90-11-10301-CV (Dist. Ct., Maverick County, Tex. Dec. 31, 1990)

Finding that the plaintiffs will probably prevail at trial, the Maverick County District Court issued a temporary injunction. The injunction enjoined the Texas Workers' Compensation Commission from issuing any final decision regarding the amount of impairment income benefits or supplemental income benefits a worker is to receive for injuries occurring on or after January 1, 1991, until judgment in this cause of action is entered by this court.

The plaintiffs argued that the Texas Workers' Compensation Act (1989 Tex. Sess. Law Serv. 2d C.S. 1 ch. 1 (Vernon) (hereinafter the Act), is unconstitutional because it violates the following several provisions of the Texas Constitution: Article I, §§ 13 and 19 (the due course and open courts provisions); Article I, § 15 and Article V, § 10 (right to jury trial); Article I, §§ 3 and 3a (equal rights); and Article II, § 1 (separation of powers). Also, to recover supplemental income benefits, the Act requires that a worker must have a rating of 15 percent or greater impairment based on the *AMA Guides.* The court agreed that the Act adopts a mechanical application of the *AMA Guides* in awarding impairment income benefits.

The court also found as facts:

1. The Act makes no provision for the distribution of the *AMA Guides*, despite the fact that the *AMA Guides* are not easily available either to the general public or to injured workers

2. The *AMA Guides* do not permit percentage impairment ratings for certain compensable injuries such as mental trauma and chronic pain syndrome

3. A significant numbers of workers who sustain disabling injuries will have less than a 15 percent impairment based on the *AMA Guides*

4. The Act adopts an improper use of the *AMA Guides;* the use of the *AMA Guides* as the determining factor to compensate injured workers for losses occasioned by their injuries is unreasonable and arbitrary and is not reasonably related to any individual or societal interest of the State of Texas

5. The Act provides for judicial review of certain issues by an aggrieved party who has exhausted the administrative remedies, but the factfinder must adopt one of the impairment ratings made in accordance with the *AMA Guides;* with regard to certain medical determinations, the findings of a designated doctor must be presumed to be correct

6. The Act treats workers and employers in significantly different manners: employers are not required to be covered by the Act and may drop coverage after January 1, 1991; workers who are currently covered have no such option if their employer elects to retain coverage after January 1, 1991. Such workers are given no opportunity to withdraw and opt for their common-law rights.

The court concluded that the replacement of the plaintiff's rights at common law and under the former workers' compensation law by the new workers' compensation law is not a fair or reasonable replacement of the plaintiff's rights, and violates Article I, §§ 3, 3a, 13, 15, and 19 of the Texas Constitution. The court found determination of eligibility for impairment income benefits and supplemental income benefits based exclusively upon the *AMA Guides* is arbitrary and unreasonable, and § 4.24 of the Act is in violation of Article I, §§ 3, 3a, 13, 15, and 19, and Article V, § 10, of the Texas Constitution.

§ 11.34   UTAH

Kaiser Steel Corp. v. Industrial Comm'n, **709 P.2d 1168 (Utah 1985)**

The claimant was 33 percent permanently impaired due to arthritis and a pulmonary condition before his accident. In 1977 the claimant injured his knee and was found to have a 5 percent impairment of his lower extremity and a 2 percent impairment of the whole man, according to a special medical panel. The claimant challenged the panel's findings and claimed that the *AMA Guides* suggested a higher impairment rating than found by the panel. The chairman of the panel explained that the difference between the panel's determination and the *AMA Guides* was "due to the age of the guides and the recognition that they are based on more disabling, progressive congestive diseases (such as emphysema) than claimant's nonprogressive restricted lung capacity." *Id.* at 1170. The court accepted the panel's findings, because the claimant offered no testimony to contradict the chairman's testimony.

Gardner v. Edward Gardner Plumbing & Heating, 693 P.2d 678 (Utah 1984)

The claimant, a plumber, was injured in an auto accident. The standard of the *AMA Guides* was adopted to distinguish the extent of the impairment resulting from the claimant's subjective complaints of pain. Subjective complaints of pain are required to be substantiated by independent evidence. However, the testimony that was intended to show objective indicators of pain, such as the extent to which the claimant's pain interfered with his daily life, was excluded by the ALJ. On appeal, the court stated:

> The testimony sought and the evidence proffered plainly were relevant to the issues before Commission. The question was whether the claimant was entitled to disability benefits based on his complaints of pain. Both parties cited and relied upon the section of the *AMA Guides* dealing with pain from peripheral spinal nerve damage, the type of injury most likely to have caused plaintiff's pain. Dr. [H.] contended that none of the independent evidence of pain, i.e., the extent to which the claimant's pain interfered with the performance of his daily activities was present. The direct testimony of plaintiff's doctor, and the cross-examination of Dr. [H.] were all intended to show that plaintiff's pain interfered with his functioning as a plumber. By his actions, the administrative law judge precluded plaintiff from undermining one of Dr. [H.]'s premises—that plaintiff was not impaired in his functioning—and, therefore, effectively precluded plaintiff from meeting the evidence against him. In addition, plaintiff's doctor should have been allowed to comment on his specific points of disagreement with the medical panel's report. That was the reason for his testifying at the hearing. He was familiar with plaintiff's condition, and he could have focused the attention of the administrative law judge on the precise points of the report concerning which he had different information or conclusions.

Id. at 682.

Jacobson Constr. v. Hair, 667 P.2d 25 (Utah 1983)

The conversion tables from the *AMA Guides* for combined partial-man ratings were used to rate the claimant's injuries. An impairment from an industrial accident is to be measured by the standard of a previously injured man.

Northwest Carriers v. Industrial Comm'n, 639 P.2d 138 (Utah 1981)

The court differentiated an evaluation of permanent impairment from an evaluation of permanent disability. Impairment is a medical evaluation, whereas disability is an administrative evaluation.

§ 11.35   VERMONT

Stamper v. University Apartments, Inc., 522 A.2d 227 (Vt. 1986)

The claimant sustained a back injury during the course of his employment. The Commissioner of the Department of Labor and Industry awarded the claimant a 25 percent permanent partial disability and vocational rehabilitation benefits. The employer appealed, arguing that the commissioner erred in relying on commission Rule 10(b) to reject the *AMA Guides* for computing the degree of impairment and instead relying on expert testimony. (Rule 10(b) provides that the *AMA Guides* will serve as the authority in resolving disputes over the degree of impairment unless they are inconsistent with these rules or the provisions of Vt. Stat. Ann. tit. 21 § 648.) Specifically, the employer argued that the *AMA Guides'* schedules were determinative of the claimant's disability, and that the commissioner's alternative method of computing disability was an exercise of unbridled discretion. The supreme court disagreed.

> In *Bishop v. Town of Barre*, 140 Vt. 564, 577–78, 442 A.2d 50, 56 (1982), we held that under 21 V.S.A. section 648, the amount of compensation for back injuries must be assessed based on the percentage of loss of the back's function rather than on the degree of impairment to the whole person. Because the [AMA] *Guides* are premised on a whole person standard, their use in assessing back injuries is inconsistent with section 648, as interpreted in Bishop, making the Commissioner's rejection of them in his calculation of disability appropriate.

552 A.2d at 229.

§ 11.36   VIRGINIA

Bader v. Norfolk Redevelopment & Hous. Auth., 396 S.E.2d 141
(Va. Ct. App. 1990)

The claimant sought permanent impairment benefits for a hearing loss sustained while he was employed by the defendant. The Industrial Commission awarded compensation according to the American National Standards Institute (ANSI) standard on practitioners.

The claimant's contended that the ANSI standards used by the commission were outdated, that they were substantially lower than the AMA measurements, and that use of the ANSI standard deprived the claimant of just compensation and was thus contrary to the letter and spirit of the Workers' Compensation Act. The claimant's physician testified that recent medical studies advocate the use of a 3,000 Hz measurement for determining a hearing loss, because that frequency is critical to predicting the degree of difficulty a person will have in speech discrimination with a background noise. The ANSI standard does not measure hearing loss above 2,000 Hz. The physician stated that the ANSI standard is the standard to which an audiometer must be calibrated in order to use the hearing determination chart, but that the AMA standards are much newer and more widely used in measuring hearing loss.

The court could not reach an informed decision as to the merits of the challenge to the continued validity of the hearing-loss determination chart, and therefore remanded, stating:

> There is no expert medical opinion in the record regarding hearing loss standards other than the testimony of [claimant]'s physician, Dr. [B.]. The commission's opinion notes that "the Commission on Review is not willing to change its approved guideline for determining hearing loss as it recognizes there are arguments in both directions in this respect." Although we recognize that the commission adopted the Hearing Determination Chart in the light of its informed experience, without an adequate statement of the findings of fact, rulings of law and other matters pertinent to the issue of the current weight of medical opinion favoring the ANSI standard among practitioners we are unable to reach an informed decision as to the merits of Bader's challenge to its continued validity. We therefore remand the case with directions that the commission make the appropriate findings concerning the commission's decision to use the ANSI guidelines rather than the AMA guidelines in this case.

Id. at 145.

§11.37   WEST VIRGINIA

Repass v. Workers' Compensation Division, 569 S.E.2d 162 (W. Va. 2002)

This was a consolidated appeal of two different workers' compensation cases. At issue was the validity of the *AMA Guides'* (4th ed. 1993) DRE Model. A divided West Virginia Supreme Court of Appeals held that the use of the DRE (as opposed to ROM) model conflicted with West Virginia's workers' compensation statute, and is thus invalid. This decision is one of the most significant *Guides* cases in a number of years. Due to the length of the decision, it is not reprinted here. It is recommended that anyone interested in the use of the *Guides* read this case in its entirety. The court summarized its holding below:

> As we noted earlier in this opinion, in those instances where an agency rule addresses some issue that is already the subject of Legislative action, "[i]f the intention of the Legislature is clear, that is the end of the matter, and the agency's position only can be upheld if it conforms to the Legislature's intent." Syl. pt. 3, in part, *Appalachian Power Co. v. State Tax Department of West Virginia*, 195 W. Va. 573, 466 S.E.2d 424 (1995).
>
> We must apply the same standard to the rule in this case. Thus, we hold that a rule promulgated by the workers' compensation division that mandated the use of a non-legislatively created guide for the examination of certain

injuries is valid only to the extent that the mandated guide does not conflict with the specific dictates of the Legislature as expressed by statute. Those aspects of the mandated guide that are in conflict are invalid.

The DRE Model for the evaluation of spinal injuries conflicts with our law in several areas. The DRE disagrees with statutes that control: the proper time for making an impairment rating, the proper treatment of progressive injuries, the procedure for reopening a claim, and the consideration of a second injury. Any aspect of the *Guides, Fourth* that conflicts with these statutes must fail. Accordingly, we hold, because the Diagnosis-Related Estimate Model for the examination of spine injury claims, as set forth in The American Medical Association's *Guides to the Evaluation of Permanent Impairment* (4th ed. 1993), cannot be reconciled with several specific Workers' compensation statutes promulgated by the West Virginia Legislature, any medical examination conducted in accordance with that model is invalid and unreliable.

Some might argue that the *Guides, Fourth* were adopted in an effort to hold down costs in the Workers' compensation system. In arguments before this Court, counsel for appellants suggested that compensation for back injuries was greatly reduced by the application of the DRE Model. We note that at least one observer suggests that the problems of our workers' compensation system are not the result of overpayment, but rather of under-collection. [footnote deleted] But we take the more charitable view that the Commissioner adopted the *Guides, Fourth* in an effort to determine once and for all "objective" rules or procedures that produce a "fair" result. But only one thing is clear: no matter what sort of guides, rules, procedures, or standards the Legislature or Commissioner may adopt, none can yield an "exact" or "correct" estimate of impairment or disability that is beyond reproach. "The rating of disabilities, regardless of legislative precision or medical expertise, remains an inexact science." *Griffith v. State Workmen's Compensation Comm'r*, 157 W. Va. 837, 843, 205 S.E.2d 157, 161 (1974); *accord, Miracle v. Workers' Compensation Commissioner*, 181 W. Va. 443, 446, 383 S.E.2d 75, 78 (1989); *Lambert v. Workers' Compensation Division*, 211 W. Va. 436, 566 S.E.2d 573 (2002).

Chief Justice Davis composed a strongly worded dissent. He stated:

D. From Magic Words to Magic Tests: The Practical Application of the Majority's Opinion

"The law is a sort of hocus-pocus science." In *Lambert v. Workers' Compensation Division*, 211 W. Va. 436, 446–47, 566 S.E.2d 573, 583–84 (2002), we cautioned against the reliance on buzzwords or magic phrases in the assessment of an injured employee's degree of impairment. Although the majority seemingly echoes this refrain, ironically it does not practice what it preaches. Behind the smoke and mirrors of the Court's decision in the case *sub judice*, the majority nevertheless adopts not magic words but a magic test, the ROM model, for determining the extent of a claimant's work-related disability. Despite the majority's protestations to the contrary, the practical application of its decision will most certainly " 'open the lock' for a claimant seeking compensation." I only hope that the Legislature can uncover this illusion before the Workers' Compensation Fund is depleted to the detriment of future claimants disabled by work-related injuries.

Wagner v. Workers' Compensation Div., 1998 W. Va. LEXIS 219 (W. Va. 1998)

The West Virginia court dealt with a claimant who sustained a lower back injury in January 1993. She had sustained a similar lower back injury in 1982 and had been awarded 22 percent for permanent partial disability. She was rated under the *AMA Guides* (4th ed. 1993) and found to be 15 percent impaired. When her previous impairment of 22 percent was subtracted, she was left with no award and appealed. The claimant argued that because the earlier award was determined under a different, more generous, standard that granted the Workers' Compensation Commissioner discretion to base a permanent partial disability rating on a claimant's true disability, subtracting her earlier percentage of disability from her current percentage of medical impairment unfairly deprived her of disability benefits. Finally, the claimant contended that the Workers' Compensation Division retroactively applied a method of calculating medical impairment or disability that became effective after her date of injury, and this violated her due process rights and resulted in a denial of her substantial rights. The court rejected her appeal. It stated:

> Having determined that Dr. [C.]'s report was unreliable, we next address [claimant]'s contention that subtracting the 22% permanent partial disability award she received in connection with her 1982 injury from the current estimate of her level of medical impairment was unfair because the earlier award considered factors other than mere medical impairment. We are unpersuaded by [claimant]'s argument. While she claims that her percentage of permanent partial disability granted in connection with her 1982 injury included more than mere medical impairment, she has provided nothing but speculation in support of this contention. Moreover, she has provided no clue as to how much of the 22% award was based on factors other than medical impairment.
>
> We have previously explained that while "the general rule in workmen's compensation cases is that the evidence will be construed liberally in favor of the claimant, . . . [that] rule does not relieve the claimant of the burden of proving his [or her] claim by proper and satisfactory proof." *Linville v. State Workmen's Compensation Comm'r*, 160 W. Va. 549, 553–54, 236 S.E.2d 41, 44 (1977) (citation omitted). *Accord Anderson v. State Workers' Compensation Comm'r*, 174 W. Va. 406, 409 n.4, 327 S.E.2d 385, 388 n.4 (1985) (citing *Linville*). Because [claimant] failed to show what portion, if any, of her 22% permanent disability rating arose from factors other than medical impairment, she failed to establish that it was improper to subtract the full 22% from her present percentage of medical impairment.
>
> The only reliable medical evidence regarding her present medical impairment was provided by Dr. [B.]. In his report, Dr. [B.] indicated that

[claimant]'s present percentage of whole person medical impairment is 10% or 15%. In his deposition, Dr. [B.] testified that because the 1982 and 1993 injuries occurred at the same location, the percentage of impairment that resulted from the earlier injury must be subtracted from the current percentage of impairment in order to ascertain the amount of impairment that resulted from the later injury. Dr. [B.] then properly subtracted the 22% permanent disability rating [claimant] had already been awarded from her present percentage of whole person medical impairment and recommended a 0% whole person impairment. Because the only reliable medical evidence recommended 0% whole person impairment, the Commissioner did not apply any law, past or present, to determine disability. Thus, we need not reach [claimant]'s argument that the Commissioner retroactively applied a method of calculating her permanent partial disability that became effective after her date of injury.

1998 W. Va. LEXIS 219, at *14–*17.

Javins v. Workers' Compensation Comm'r, 320 S.E.2d 119 (W. Va. 1984)

In this pneumoconiosis case, the court refers in passing to the use of the *AMA Guides* to "promote uniform procedures and evaluation criteria to obtain reasonably accurate and consistent assessments of pulmonary impairment." *Id.* at 131.

§ 11.38   WISCONSIN

Employers Mut. Liab. Ins. Co. v. Department of Indus., Labor & Human Relations, 214 N.W.2d 587 (Wis. 1974)

The claimant was injured when a steel sliver pierced his eye. One of the issues was whether contact lenses afforded a useful correction for the claimant's injury. The court and the Department of Industry, Labor, and Human Relations referred to the *AMA Guides*.

At the time of review of the findings in the circuit court, the department explained that it relied upon a 1958 article by the American Medical Association's Committee on Medical Rating of Physical Impairment (168 *JAMA* 4:475) for support of its position that contact lenses did not afford "useful" correction. The Wisconsin Supreme Court agreed with the trial judge, an acknowledged authority on the subject of judicial notice, that under the circumstances, judicial notice could not be taken that a correction afforded by a contact lens was not a "useful" correction. 214 N.W.2d at 590.

Lewandowski v. Preferred Risk Mut. Ins. Co., 146 N.W.2d 505 (Wis. 1966)

The *AMA Guides* were excluded from evidence at trial on the grounds of hearsay. This exclusion was affirmed on appeal. The court noted that because the physician did not consult the *AMA Guides*, there was no basis for impeachment.

§11.39   WYOMING

State ex rel. Wyoming Workers' Safety & Com. Div. & FMC Corp., v. Faulkner, 152 P.3d 394 (Wyo. 2007)

The Wyoming Supreme Court dealt with the claimant, Faulkner, who injured his back in 1995 in a non-work-related injury for which he underwent surgery. In 1999, he sustained a work-related back injury for which he had surgery. He had no impairment rating for the 1999 injury. In 2000, he sustained his third and final back injury at work for which he underwent two additional surgeries. He never returned to work.

An IME was done by Dr. Ruttle. He rated the claimant at 23 percent but said the impairment, due to the 2000 injury, "is approximately 1%."

A second evaluation was done by Dr. Dall, and he also came up with the same rating.

The commission rated his impairment at 23 percent and found that apportionment was not authorized under Wyoming Law.

The court upheld the 23 percent rating, finding that the *AMA Guides* did not require apportionment. The court stated:

> In support of their position, the Division and the Employer rely upon language from Section 1.6b of the *AMA Guides* which states: "Apportionment analysis in workers' compensation represents a distribution or allocation of causation among multiple factors that caused or significantly contributed to the injury or disease and resulting impairment. The factor could be preexisting injury, illness, or impairment." Linda Cocchiarella and Gunnar B.J. Andersson, Guides to the Evaluation of Permanent Impairment § 1.6b, at 11 (5th ed. 2001). There is nothing in the language of the *AMA Guides* cited by the Appellants that would lead us to the conclusion that apportionment is mandated by the *AMA Guides*. Other provisions of the *AMA Guides* make it clear that the decision to require or allow apportionment is one that must be made by each state. According to the *AMA Guides*: "Most states have their own customized methods for calculating apportionment. Generally, the most recent permanent impairment rating is calculated, and then the prior impairment rating is calculated and deducted. The remaining impairment rating would be attributed or apportioned to the current injury or condition." Linda Cocchiarella and Gunnar B.J. Andersson, Guides to the Evaluation of Permanent Impairment § 1.6b, at 12 (5th ed. 2001); see also § 1.8, at 13 (recognizing that worker's compensation benefits are a creature of the individual state's specific system and "[d]etermining eligibility of benefits and the extent of disability is specified by statute and case law").

152 P.3d at 399.

In re Pohl, 980 P.2d 816 (Wyo. 1999)

The Wyoming court dealt with a claimant who injured her back. She underwent spinal fusion surgery and accepted a 20 percent permanent partial impairment award. She then moved to Oregon and two years after her surgery requested an impairment rating from her Oregon physician. Although the physician told the claimant that "Oregon physicians don't do [impairment] ratings," the physician supplied a rating. Without including any explanation of how the rating was calculated, the claimant's physician concluded that her whole-body impairment rating had increased to 32 percent. Relying on the 32 percent rating, the claimant petitioned the Worker's Compensation Division for an award for an increase in permanent partial disability pursuant to Wyo. Stat. Ann. § 27-14-605(a) (Michie 1991). The Division disputed the 32 percent rating and arranged for an IME with a second Oregon physician. After examination and testing, the IME examiner concluded that the claimant's impairment rating was 35 percent.

Before rendering a final determination, the Division employed a physician, Dr. M., to conduct a review of the claimant's claim. After reviewing her history and both impairment ratings, Dr. M. concluded that both impairment ratings were invalid under the *AMA Guides* (4th ed. 1993). The Division denied the claimant's claim for an increase in her impairment rating, stating that the "Medical Adjudicator for the Division has reviewed the Impairment Rating and has indicated that you have no additional impairment[;] therefore, additional Permanent Partial Disability benefits will not be awarded."

The court affirmed the validity of the paper review. It stated:

> [Claimant] complains that the Division did not comply with the Workers' Compensation Act when it evaluated her claim for an increase in incapacity under Wyo. Stat. Ann. § 27-14-605(a) (Michie Rpl. June 1991). She contends that the Division acted contrary to Wyo. Stat. Ann. § 27-14-405(m) (Michie 1997) (formerly -405(e) (Rpl. June 1991)) when it employed a physician to perform a "paper review" of [claimant]'s conflicting impairment ratings and later relied on the physician's review in denying benefits. We reject these contentions.
>
> Section 27-14-405(m) provides
>
> > If the percentage of physical impairment is disputed, the division shall obtain a second opinion and if the ratings conflict, shall determine the physical impairment award upon consideration of the initial and second opinion. Any objection to the final determination pursuant to this subsection shall be referred to the medical commission for hearing by a medical hearing panel acting as hearing examiner pursuant to W.S. 27-14-616.
>
> In [claimant]'s case, the Division disputed the percentage of physical impairment and arranged for an IME. After the IME was completed, the Division employed a case review physician, Dr. [M.], to assist in "determin[ing] the physical impairment award upon consideration of the initial and second opinion." Clearly, the Division was within its authority in engaging a medical professional, Dr. [M.], to assist in evaluating the case before it. *See* Wyo. Stat. Ann. § 27-14-801(d) (Michie Rpl. June 1991). Moreover, when

[claimant]'s Oregon physician indicated in a report that "Oregon physicians don't do ratings," closer consideration of the ratings from both Oregon physicians was warranted. After reviewing the impairment ratings, Dr. [M.] concluded that both ratings were invalid due to inaccurate applications of the *AMA Guide*.

In her brief, [claimant] concedes that it is appropriate for the Division to reject evidence which is invalid or erroneous. Nevertheless, she maintains that the Division erred by disregarding the ratings from the Oregon physicians. We disagree. With the accuracy of the impairment ratings challenged, the Division properly denied [claimant]'s claim and left its resolution to the expertise of the Medical Commission. We conclude that the Division's [sic] acted in accordance with Wyo. Stat. Ann. § 27-14-405(m) when it employed Dr. [M.] to evaluate [claimant]'s impairment ratings.

980 P.2d at 820–21.

Clark v. State ex rel. Workers' Div., **934 P.2d 1269 (Wyo. 1997)**

The Wyoming court dealt with a chamber maid who injured her hand at work. An independent medical examination physician assigned her a 66 percent impairment. The hearing officer did not accept this rating because the rating physician did not properly follow the *AMA Guides*. The court affirmed the hearing officer's opinion and stated:

> The hearing examiner did not "revamp and revise" Dr. [V.]'s medical tests, as [claimant] contends. Instead, the hearing examiner appropriately engaged in the process of evaluating the relative value of Dr. [V.]'s testimony. For example, the hearing examiner evaluated the reason Dr. [V.] gave in determining that [claimant] suffered a 66 percent permanent physical impairment:
>
>> [According to the *Guides*,] [i]f a 20% variation in the readings exists, then one may assume the patient is not exerting full effort. If there is suspicion or evidence the subject is exerting less than maximal effort, the grip strength measurements are invalid for estimating impairment (Exhibit E). In this case, the grip strength tests performed by Dr. [V.] (12, 9, 10, 7, and 8) have a variation of approximately 33%. This is a clear indication [claimant] did not exert full effort on the grip strength test. Accordingly, Dr. [V.] should not have considered the grip strength loss and [claimant]'s physical impairment rating should have been 56%. This is 10% less than the amount awarded and paid.
>
> Order Denying Benefits, Findings and Conclusions ¶ 9. The trier of fact may disregard an expert opinion if he finds the opinion unreasonable or not adequately supported by the facts upon which the opinion is based. *Krause*, 803 P.2d at 83; *cf. Rice*, 500 P.2d at 676. In evaluating the medical testimony, the hearing examiner found error within the facts upon which Dr. [V.]'s opinion

was based. Thus, the hearing examiner was well within his discretion when he assigned less weight to that testimony.

934 P.2d at 1271.

Bohren v. Wyoming Workers' Compensation Div., 883 P.2d 355 (Wyo. 1994)

The Wyoming court dealt with a worker who injured her right hip in 1991. She was awarded an 8 percent permanent impairment for chronic pain and limited range of motion in her hip. The claimant then sought an increase in her impairment award due to psychological difficulties from the chronic pain. The court affirmed a denial of additional benefits and stated:

> The original 8% disability rating included an award for chronic pain. The basis of [claimant]'s claim below and here on appeal is that she suffers from psychological injury from her chronic pain. As we have already pointed out, there is no evidence that [claimant] suffered from such an injury. In any event [claimant] was compensated for her chronic pain and limited range of motion in the injured area. That is all the *AMA Guides* call for in setting the impairment rating. Whether chronic pain can cause an impairment greater than the limitations on range of motion is not an accepted part of the *Guides'* rating system.

Id. at 358.

Pacific Power & Light v. Heermann, 872 P.2d 1171 (Wyo. 1994)

The Wyoming Supreme Court dealt with a claimant who was employed as a meter reader. She slipped on snow and ice and injured her hip. She was later diagnosed as having tendinitis. She applied for permanent partial disability and was awarded a 10 percent permanent partial disability.

The appeal of the award was based on the doctor's lack of training in the *AMA Guides*, use of the incorrect edition of the *AMA Guides*, and rating for subjective pain. The court affirmed the award, finding that formal training in the *AMA Guides* is not required. A reevaluation was done with the correct edition.

The court found that the *AMA Guides* allow for an impairment rating for pain when the pain is great enough to cause an impairment. The court stated:

> In *Allen*, both of the physicians who examined the claimant found that her pain did not cause a loss of range of motion. 811 P.2d at 2. Here, the treating physician found that [claimant]'s pain did cause a loss of range of motion. Consistent with our opinion in *Allen*, we hold that subjective pain may support an impairment rating under the *AMA Guides* when that pain reduces the claimant's range of motion. Accord *Sutton v. Quality Furniture Company*, 191 Ga. App. 279, 381 S.E.2d 389 (1989) (subjective pain may support an impairment rating under the *AMA Guides*); *AMA Guides* at 75 ("A grading scheme and procedure for determining impairment of a body part that is affected by pain,

discomfort, or loss of sensation are found in Tables 10a and 10b, respectively"). *See also* Steven Babitsky & Harry Dean Sewall, *Understanding the AMA Guides in Workers' Compensation* Secs. 2.4 at 37 & 5.13 (1992) (describing procedures for rating pain under the *AMA Guides*).

Id. at 1173–74. *See Allen v. Natrona County Sch. Dist. One*, 811 P.2d 1 (Wyo. 1991).

Allen v. Natrona County Sch. Dist. One, 811 P.2d 1 (Wyo. 1991)

The Wyoming Supreme Court dealt with the claimant, a cafeteria worker, who developed bilateral epicondylitis (tennis elbow) from repetitive lifting and stirring. She sought permanent partial disability. The claimant was rated at a 20 percent impairment under the *AAOS Manual* but at a 0 percent impairment under the *AMA Guides*, as there was no loss of motion. The court found that the statute, which requires proof of impairment under the *AMA Guides* before an award can be made for permanent partial impairment, was not unconstitutional. The court stated:

> The issue is whether or not it was reasonable and rational for the legislature to require that claimants present evidence of an impairment pursuant to the *AMA Guide* in order to recover a permanent partial disability and vocational award, and whether or not this requirement, as applied by the administrative hearing officer, constituted a denial of equal protection.
>
> Appellant in this case was not able to recover a permanent partial disability or vocational award because her injury, epicondylitis (tennis elbow), did not rise to the level of being an impairment according to the *AMA Guide*. Appellant had no limitations in either elbow's range of motion, which were full, including flexion, extensions, and pronation/supination. Additionally, there was no evidence of any specific neurological or motor function deficit. Dr. [B.] testified that there was no objective evidence that appellant experienced pain. Since appellant had no limitations on her elbows, despite some subjective complaints of pain, her impairment rating pursuant to the *AMA Guide* was 0 percent. These factors provide substantial evidence to support the administrative hearing officer's determination. It is reasonable for the Wyoming State Legislature to pass a statute that does not allow compensation for only subjective pain, when such pain does not rise to the level of an impairment.

Id. at 4.

§11.40 FEDERAL CASES

Rosa v. Director, Office of Workers' Compensation Programs, 1998 U.S. App. LEXIS 7171 (9th Cir. Apr. 8, 1998)

The U.S. Court of Appeals for the Ninth Circuit dealt with a claimant who appealed a finding of a 16 percent permanent partial disability due to a September

1992 injury to his left leg within the course and scope of his employment. The claimant challenged the ALJ's reliance on the *AMA Guides* (4th ed. 1993). The court held that it was within the ALJ's discretion to rely on the *AMA Guides* (4th ed. 1993). It also rejected the claimant's argument that reliance on the *AMA Guides* (4th ed. 1993) is contrary to the humanitarian nature of the Longshore and Harbor Workers' Compensation Act. The court stated:

> [Claimant] argues that the ALJ erred in relying on the Fourth Edition of the American Medical Association *Guides* (*"Guides"*), in assessing the extent of his knee injury. We disagree.
>
> [Claimant] argues that when an old injury has been rated under a separate edition of the *Guides* and a new injury occurs, the percentage of disability from the new injury is added to the percentage previously determined from the old injury. [Claimant]'s reliance on *DeNoble v. Maritime Transportation Management Inc.*, 12 BRBS 29 (1980), is misplaced.
>
> [Claimant] sustained injuries to his shoulder and foot simultaneously, and was awarded consecutive benefits for permanent partial disability due to "loss of, or loss of use of, more than one member or parts of more than one member," consistent with 33 U.S.C. § 908(c)(22).
>
> In the absence of regulations, the LHWCA does not require adherence to any particular guide or formula to determine disability. *Fisher v. Strachan Fishing Co.*, 8 BRBS 578, 580 (1978). Thus, the ALJ was not bound to apply any particular edition of the *Guides*, nor was he bound by any doctor's opinion. *Mazze v. Frank J. Holleran, Inc.*, 9 BRBS 1053, 1055 (1978). The ALJ found that the Fourth Edition of the *Guides* was more current and medically valid than the Second Edition. In fact, both Dr. [L.] and Dr. [D.] relied on the Fourth Edition of the *Guides* in rating [claimant]'s disability following his 1994 surgery. It was within the ALJ's discretion to rely on a later edition of the *A.M.A. Guides* to determine the extent of [claimant]'s permanent partial disability even though it resulted in a lower disability percentage than had been stipulated to after his 1987 injury.
>
> Both Dr. [L.] and Dr. [D.] rated the extent of [claimant]'s entire disability as it existed after the 1994 surgery. [Claimant] was rated under the *A.M.A. Guides* for a partial medial and lateral meniscectomy. A knee which has undergone that procedure is rated at a 10 percent disability under the Fourth Edition of the *Guides*. Thus, the fact that [claimant] underwent a partial medial meniscectomy previously is irrelevant because the percentage disability from that prior injury and surgery is subsumed in the disability rating for the subsequent surgery.
>
> Doctors [D.] and [L.] rated [claimant]'s disability at 10 percent and 17 percent, respectively. The ALJ concluded that [claimant] exhibited a 16 percent permanent partial disability. The fact that the ALJ rated [claimant]'s disability between the doctors' ratings, and the fact that the ALJ may accept or reject medical testimony all or in part, further attests to the reasonableness of the ALJ's determination.
>
> [Claimant] also argues that the ALJ's reliance on the Fourth Edition of the *A.M.A. Guides* is contrary to the "humanitarian nature" of the LHWCA

because his disability percentage was decreased, rather than increased, following his 1994 surgery.

While the ALJ's decision resulted in a lower rating of [claimant]'s disability, sympathy for the plight of the individual litigant is an insufficient basis for reversing. *Potomac Elec. Power Co. v. Director, OWCP*, 449 U.S. 268, 283, 66 L. Ed. 2d 446, 101 S. Ct. 509 (1980). The LHWCA does not authorize the method of calculating permanent partial disability proposed by [claimant].

The ALJ properly calculated [claimant]'s entitlement to permanent partial disability benefits pursuant to 33 U.S.C. § 908(c)(2) and (19) as $19,589.07. That amount is offset by the $19,360.00 already paid, for a total additional award of $229.07.

AFFIRMED.

1998 U.S. App. LEXIS 7171, at *2–*5.

Battista v. United States, 889 F. Supp. 716 (S.D.N.Y. 1995)

The federal district court dealt with a phone company worker who sued the United States under the Tort Claims Act. The government's expert witness testified that the claimant had no impairment to his leg under the *AMA Guides*. The court noted in dicta that the *AMA Guides* are "an authoritative treatise which sets forth percentages of impairment based upon objective criteria." 889 F. Supp. at 728.

Baker v. Bethlehem Steel Corp., 24 F.3d 632 (4th Cir. 1994)

The Fourth Circuit Court of Appeals dealt with the claimant, who worked for more than 30 years as a shipfitter and was exposed to loud machinery such as handjacks and air hammers. He developed a 30 percent hearing loss in the left ear and was awarded permanent partial disability of 15.6 weeks at $279.24 per week under the Longshore and Harbor Workers' Compensation Act.

The Benefits Review Board reversed and held that the ALJ should have converted the 30 percent monaural loss to a 5 percent binaural hearing impairment under the *AMA Guides* (3d ed. rev. 1990). The board ruled that, pursuant to 33 U.S.C. § 908(C)(13)(B), all monaural hearing loss must be converted to a binaural impairment, on a finding that the formula for calculating monaural hearing loss under 33 U.S.C. § 908(c)(13)(A) cannot be used in cases in which the hearing loss was caused by exposure to noise.

The court of appeals reversed, finding that the *AMA Guides* measure hearing loss but that the Longshore and Harbor Workers' Compensation Act provides how such losses are to be compensated. The court stated:

We see no irreconcilable conflict between the statute's directive that monaural losses be compensated according to the criteria of subsection (A) and the directive of subsection (E) that determinations of hearing loss be made in accordance with the *Guides*. The *Guides* provide the methods employed under the Act for measuring hearing loss, whether monaural or binaural. The statute serves a different function; it provides a formula for determining how such losses should be compensated.

24 F.3d at 634.

Tanner v. Ingalls Shipbuilding, Inc., 2 F.3d 143 (5th Cir. 1993)

The U.S. Court of Appeals for the Fifth Circuit dealt with three claimants who sustained the hearing loss. In each case, the claimant was an employee of the appellee and suffered an employment-related hearing loss. As a result of the hearing tests performed on the claimants, each claimant was diagnosed as having a 0 percent impairment in one ear and measurable impairment in the other ear. Each claimant filed for compensation benefits under the Longshore and Harbor Workers' Compensation Act and was accorded a hearing before an ALJ.

In two of the cases, the ALJ recognized that the claimants had impairment in only one ear (monaural impairment) but concluded that compensation should be calculated as impairment in both ears (binaural impairment), in accordance with 33 U.S.C. § 908(c)(13)(B). The Benefits Review Board affirmed this approach. In the remaining case, the same ALJ awarded compensation on the basis of a monaural impairment in accordance with 33 U.S.C. § 908(c)(13)(A), and the board reversed this decision.

The court found that, although the *AMA Guides* recommend that monaural loss be converted to binaural loss, the statute should prevail, and monaural impairment should be compensated according to the statute. The court stated:

> All three claimants had a measurable hearing loss in only one ear. The statue clearly states that compensation under subsection (A) is for "loss of hearing in one ear" while subsection (B) is for "loss of hearing in both ears." 33 U.S.C. Section 908(c)(13)(A) and (B) (emphasis added). In addition, subsection (C) provides that an audiogram shall be presumptive evidence of the amount of hearing loss. 33 U.S.C. Section 908(c)(13)(C). Therefore, because it is undisputed that the results of an audiogram performed on each claimant showed a zero percent hearing impairment in one ear and measurable impairment in the other, each claimant should be compensated for loss of hearing in one ear as set forth in subsection (A).

2 F.3d at 146.

Rasmussen v. General Dynamics, 993 F.2d 1014 (2d Cir. 1993)

The U.S. Court of Appeals for the Second Circuit dealt with the claimant, who had a 60 percent monaural hearing loss before she took the job with her employer. At work she had been exposed to noise from her own welding work, as well as to noise generated by shearing and bending machines used in the vicinity. The cumulative effect of her preemployment hearing loss and her occupational exposure caused her to suffer a 100 percent hearing loss in her right ear.

The court found that, although the *AMA Guides* recommend that monaural loss be converted to binaural loss, this provision does not override the explicit longshore section providing workers' compensation for monaural hearing loss in the Longshore and Harbor Workers' Compensation Act. The court stated:

> Although the *AMA Guides* recommend that monaural loss be converted to binaural loss, just as the *Guides* recommend that "all impairments should be expressed as impairments of the whole person," this suggestion does not override the explicit statutory subsection providing benefits for victims of monaural hearing loss. The *AMA Guides* prescribe certain methods for calculating hearing loss and for converting monaural to binaural loss; the *Guides* do not, however, determine when such a conversion should be made. . . .
>
> We agree with the Director that the Board's reading is contrary to the language of the statute. If a claimant has a monaural impairment rating under the *AMA Guides* of 0 percent in the better ear, she has a "loss of hearing" within the meaning of Sec. 8(c)(13) in only one ear and is to be compensated accordingly under Sec. 8(c)(13)(A).

993 F.2d at 1017.

Ingalls Shipbuilding v. Director, Office of Workers' Compensation Programs, 991 F.2d 163 (5th Cir. 1993)

The U.S Court of Appeals for the Fifth Circuit dealt with two claimants who filed hearing loss claims under the Longshore and Harbor Workers' Compensation Act (LHWCA).

The court found that despite the fact that the claimants' hearing losses were not severe enough to constitute an "impairment" under the *AMA Guides*, medical benefits were still available to them under the LHWCA. The court stated:

> According to the reports credited by the ALJ, neither [claimant] suffered hearing loss severe enough to constitute an impairment under the *AMA Guides*. As the ALJ held—no impairment means no disability compensation. [Employer] contends that it also means no medical benefits. We do not agree.
>
> Congress inserted the provision requiring use of the *AMA Guides* to measure hearing loss in section 8 of the LHWCA. Section 8 addresses disability compensation. Medical benefits are covered by section 7, which entitles a claimant to reasonable and necessary medical services if he suffers a work-related injury. Section 2(2) defines "injury" as "accidental injury or death arising out of and in the course of employment, and such occupational disease or infection as arises naturally out of such employment or as naturally or unavoidably results from such accidental injury. . . ." Courts have long construed this definition to mean "something go[ne] wrong with the human frame." Had Congress intended to limit hearing loss injuries for which medical benefits were available to those satisfying the *AMA Guides* for permanent impairment, it would have so stated either in the definitions or section 7,

the medical benefits section. Rather, it inserted the *AMA Guides* in section 8. By so doing, it obviously intended an application only to claims governed by section 8, i.e., claims for disability compensation. We so hold.

991 F.2d at 165, 166.

Ingalls Shipbuilding v. Director, Office of Workers' Compensation Programs, 898 F.2d 1088 (5th Cir. 1990)

The claimant sought benefits under the Longshore and Harbor Workers' Compensation Act for hearing losses suffered as a result of exposure to noise at work. The Fifth Circuit Court of Appeals held that the award should have been determined in accordance with the provisions that are applicable to retired workers, but that the imposition of penalties was warranted. The court concluded that the loss to the "whole person" standard established in the *AMA Guides*, which were expressly made applicable to the determination of disability under the LHWCA, was applicable to determine compensation for hearing loss, despite the claim that the applicable standard was hearing loss and that the *AMA Guides* were to be used only to determine the degree of such loss.

The claimant argued that the relevant percentage should be the loss to hearing, and not the loss to the "whole man." The statute, 33 U.S.C.A. § 902(10) (West), states that, when a claim comes under § 910(d)(2), disability means "permanent impairment, determined . . . under the guides to the evaluation of permanent impairment promulgated . . . by the American Medical Association." The *AMA Guides* espouse the philosophy that impairments affect the whole person, and thus any disability should be expressed as a percentage of the whole person. Further, the *AMA Guides* provide a formula and table for evaluating binaural hearing impairment and refer the reader to a table for making the conversion to impairment of the whole person. The claimant contended that the reference to the AMA standards in the statute was meant to ensure uniformity of the compensation awards and that the *AMA Guides* should be used only to evaluate the degree of hearing loss shown by the audiogram. According to the claimant, the statute does not mandate that the disability be converted to impairment of the whole person. *See Cutting v. General Dynamics*, 21 Ben. Rev. Bd. Serv. (MB) 108, 110 (1988). The court of appeals disagreed:

> *Cutting* involved compensation under section 908(c)(13), not under the retiree scheme. In *Cutting*, the Board only addressed the treatment of awards under the [section 908 (c)(1)–(22)] schedule. *Id.* Although the statute does not make specific reference to conversion to whole person impairment we conclude that, under the Department of Labor's interpretation of the statute, the *Guides* should be given full effect. Since the *Guides* clearly convert injuries to impairments of the whole person, that procedure should be followed here.

898 F.2d at 1095.

Jones v. Railroad Retirement Bd., 614 F.2d 151 (8th Cir. 1980)

The case was heard by the Railroad Retirement Board. On appeal, the court looked to the *AMA Guides* for information about epilepsy. A footnote in the court's opinion indicates that, according to the *AMA Guides*, if seizures are controlled, a person can perform most activities of daily life.
See id. at 153 n.2.

E.E. Black, Ltd. v. Marshall, 497 F. Supp. 1088 (D. Haw. 1980)

This case was filed under the Rehabilitation Act of 1973. A claimant with back problems was not hired by a contractor who required a preemployment physical examination. The court sees no basis for the plaintiff's contention that all impairments must be defined by reference to the *AMA Guides*. *Id.* at 1098.

Kelly v. Cohen, 293 F. Supp. 261 (W.D. Pa. 1968)

The court looked to the *AMA Guides* as an interpretative aid. Although the court would have assessed the claimant's impairment as being more severe than the hearing examiner did, the court left the examiner's findings intact.

THE *GUIDES* IN WORKERS' COMPENSATION STATUTES AND REGULATIONS

ALABAMA

Alabama Administrative Code
Alabama Department of Industrial Relations, Workers' Compensation Division
Chapter 480-5-5. Utilization Management and Bill Screening
480-5-5-.35 Impairment Rating Guide.

(1) The American Medical Association *Guides to the Evaluation of Permanent Impairment*, Fourth Edition, shall be the recommended guide used by physicians in determining impairment and/or disability ratings.

******

ALASKA

West's Alaska Statutes Annotated
Title 23. Labor and Worker's Compensation
Chapter 30. Alaska Worker's Compensation Act
Article 5. Computation of Compensation
§ 23.30.190. Compensation for permanent partial impairment; rating guides

(a) In case of impairment partial in character but permanent in quality, and not resulting in permanent total disability, the compensation is $177,000 multiplied by the employee's percentage of permanent impairment of the whole person. The percentage of permanent impairment of the whole person is the percentage of impairment to the particular body part, system, or function converted to the percentage of impairment to the whole person as provided under (b) of this section. The compensation is payable in a single lump sum, except as otherwise provided in AS 23.30.041, but the compensation may not be discounted for any present value considerations.

(b) All determinations of the existence and degree of permanent impairment shall be made strictly and solely under the whole person determination as set out in the American Medical Association *Guides to the Evaluation of Permanent Impairment*, except that an impairment rating may not be rounded to the next five percent. The board shall adopt a supplementary recognized schedule for injuries that cannot be rated by use of the American Medical Association *Guides.*

(c) The impairment rating determined under (a) of this section shall be reduced by a permanent impairment that existed before the compensable injury. If the combination of a prior impairment rating and a rating under (a) of this section would result in the employee being considered permanently totally disabled, the prior rating does not negate a finding of permanent total disability.

(d) When a new edition of the American Medical Association *Guides* described in (b) of this section is published, the board shall, not later than 90 days after the last day of the month in which the new edition is published, hold an open meeting under AS 44.62.310 to select the date on which the new edition will be used to make all determinations required under (b) of this section. The date selected by the board for using the new edition may not be later than 90 days after the last day of the month in which the new edition is published. After the meeting, the board shall issue a public notice announcing the date selected. The requirements of AS 44.62.010–44.62.300 do not apply to the selection or announcement of the date under this subsection.

Alaska Administrative Code
Title 8. Labor and Workforce Development
Part 3. Workers' Compensation
Chapter 45. Compensation, Medical Benefits, and Proceedings before the Alaska Workers' Compensation Board
8 AAC 45.122. Rating of permanent impairment.

(a) The board will give public notice of the edition of the American Medical Association *Guides to the Evaluation of Permanent Impairment* and effective date for using the edition by publishing a notice in a newspaper of general circulation in Anchorage, Fairbanks, and Juneau as well as issue a bulletin for the "Workers' Compensation Manual," published by the department.

(b) It is presumed that the American Medical Association *Guides to the Evaluation of Permanent Impairment* (AMA) address the injury. If the board finds the presumption is overcome by clear and convincing evidence and if the permanent impairment cannot, in the board's opinion, be determined under the AMA guides, then the impairment rating must be based on *The State of Minnesota, Department of Labor and Industry, Permanent Partial Disability Schedule*, effective July 1, 1993, or the *American Academy of Orthopedic Surgeons Manual for Evaluating Permanent Physical Impairments* (AAOS), first edition (1965). If a rating under the *Permanent Partial Disability Schedule* or the AAOS is not of the whole person, the rating must be converted to a whole person rating under the AMA guides.

(c) A rating of zero impairment under AMA guides is a permanent impairment determination and no determination may be made under the *Permanent Partial Disability Schedule* described in (b) of this section or the AAOS.

*****

Alaska Administrative Code
Title 8. Labor and Workforce Development
Part 3. Workers' Compensation
Chapter 45. Compensation, Medical Benefits, and Proceedings before the Alaska Workers' Compensation Board
8 AAC 45.525. Reemployment benefit eligibility evaluations.

. . .

(e) The rehabilitation specialist shall document whether or not a permanent impairment is identified or expected at the time of medical stability. This documentation may be either a physician's rating according to the appropriate edition of the American Medical Association *Guides to the Evaluation of Permanent Impairment*, use of which is directed by AS 23.30.190 or a physician's statement that an impairment rating is or is not expected.

ARIZONA

Arizona Revised Statutes Annotated
Title 23. Labor
Chapter 6. Worker's Compensation
Article 9. Payment of Compensation
§ 23-1065. Special fund; purposes; investment committee

. . .

2. If the commission determines that the employee is entitled to compensation for loss of earning capacity under § 23-1044, subsection C or permanent total disability under § 23-1045, subsection B, the total amount of permanent benefits for which the employer or carrier is solely responsible under paragraph 1 of this subsection shall be expended first, with monthly payments made according to the loss of earning capacity or permanent total disability award. The employer or carrier and the special fund are equally responsible for the remaining amount of compensation for loss of earning capacity under § 23-1044, subsection C or permanent total disability under § 23-1045, subsection B. This paragraph shall not be construed as requiring payment of any benefits under § 23-1044, subsection B in any case in which an employee is entitled to benefits for loss of earning capacity under § 23-1044, subsection C or permanent total disability benefits under § 23-1045, subsection B.

C. In claims involving an employee who has a preexisting physical impairment which is not industrially-related and, whether congenital or due to injury or disease, is of such seriousness as to constitute a hindrance or obstacle to employment or to obtaining reemployment if the employee becomes unemployed, and the impairment equals or exceeds a ten per cent permanent impairment evaluated in accordance with the American medical association guides to the evaluation of permanent impairment, and the employee thereafter suffers an additional permanent impairment not of the type specified in § 23-1044, subsection B, the claim involving the subsequent impairment is eligible for reimbursement, as provided by subsection D of this section, under the following conditions: . . .

4. The employer or carrier and the special fund are equally responsible for the amount of compensation for loss of earning capacity under § 23-1044, subsection C or permanent total disability under § 23-1045, subsection B.

. . .

*****

Title 20. Commerce, Financial Institutions, and Insurance
Chapter 5. Industrial Commission of Arizona
Article 1. Workers' Compensation Practice and Procedure
R20-5-113. Physician's Duty to Provide Signed Reports; Rating of Impairment of Function; Restriction Against Interruption or Suspension of Benefits; Change of Physician

. . .

B. When a physician discharges a claimant from treatment, the physician:

1. Shall determine whether the claimant has sustained any impairment of function resulting from the industrial injury. The physician should rate the percentage of impairment using the standards for the evaluation of permanent impairment as published by the most recent edition of the American Medical Association in Guides to the Evaluation of Permanent Impairment, if applicable; and

2. Shall provide a final signed report to the insurance carrier, self-insured employer, or special fund division that details the rating of impairment and the clinical findings that support the rating.

. . .

CALIFORNIA

West's Annotated California Codes, Labor Code
Division 4. Workers' Compensation and Insurance
Part 2. Computation of Compensation
Chapter 2. Compensation Schedules
Article 3. Disability Payments
§ 4660. Determination of percentages of permanent disability; nature of the physical injury or disfigurement; employee's diminished future earning capacity; schedule; regulations

(a) In determining the percentages of permanent disability, account shall be taken of the nature of the physical injury or disfigurement, the occupation of the injured employee, and his or her age at the time of the injury, consideration being given to an employee's diminished future earning capacity.

(b)(1) For purposes of this section, the "nature of the physical injury or disfigurement" shall incorporate the descriptions and measurements of physical impairments and the corresponding percentages of impairments published in the American Medical Association (AMA) *Guides to the Evaluation of Permanent Impairment* (5th Edition).

(2) For purposes of this section, an employee's diminished future earning capacity shall be a numeric formula based on empirical data and findings that aggregate the average percentage of long-term loss of income resulting from each type of injury for similarly situated employees. The administrative director shall formulate the adjusted rating schedule based on empirical data and findings from the Evaluation of California's Permanent Disability Rating Schedule, Interim Report (December 2003), prepared by the RAND Institute for Civil Justice, and upon data from additional empirical studies.

*****

Barclays Official California Code of Regulations
Title 8. Industrial Relations
Division 1. Department of Industrial Regulations
Chapter 1. Industrial Medical Council
Article 4. Evaluation Procedures
§ 44. Method of Evaluation of Pulmonary Disability.

I. PURPOSE

This document defines the following:

1. Criteria to be used for establishing the presence or absence of respiratory impairment;

2. Criteria for selecting appropriate use of laboratory data and for identifying inappropriate testing;

3. A method for the quantitative and objective assessment of the extent of respiratory disability.

4. Guidelines regarding the content of medical-legal reports for assessing respiratory disability.

II. GENERAL PRINCIPLES

A. Approach

1. Evaluation of subjective (dyspnea) must be subject to collateral evidence and the internal consistency of the history. The dyspnea criteria are used for rough estimates and cannot by themselves establish a level of impairment without one or more of the physiologic determinants listed below in the same class of impairments.

2. In any evaluation, the physician shall progress from the simple to the more complicated. Start with the history and physical examination, follow with basic pulmonary function test, and then proceed as appropriate to more complicated procedures. Some patients will require only spirometry, but most will require determination of diffusing capacity for carbon monoxide (D_{co}), and many will need lung volume measurement. Refer to Chapter 5, "The Respiratory System" in "Guides to the Evaluation of Permanent Impairment" of the American Medical Association, 4th Edition, 1993. These guidelines shall be used in conjunction with the determinants discussed below.

B. Evaluation Tests

1. Spirometry

. . .

d. Compare test results to the tables of predicted normal values in the Chapter 5 of Guides to the Evaluation of Permanent Impairment of the American Medical Association, Fourth Edition, 1993. Where FEV_1 or FVC value is outside the 95% confidence interval, it is considered abnormal. Where FEV_1/FVC value is less than 0.70 or outside the 95% confidence interval, it is considered abnormal.

. . .

Table 2. Impairment Schedule

CLASS 1

. . .

Tests of ventilatory functions (FVC, FEV_1, FEV_1/FVC ratio as percent) above the lower limit of normal for the predicted value is defined by the 95% confidence interval. (See Chapter 5, "The Respiratory System" in Guides to the Evaluation of Permanent Impairment of the American Medical Association, 4th edition, 1993, for methods of calculation.)

. . .

IV.   ASSESSMENT OF IMPAIRMENT AND DISABILITY RATING

A.   General Approach

. . .

Table 2, derived largely from the 1993 AMA Guides to Permanent Impairment, 4th Edition, assigns individuals to physiologic classes. Table 3 interconverts the classes to typical disability impact terms. The data have been derived to be consistent with Workers' Compensation recommendations for cardiac disability in the State of California. For each class, the typical corresponding maximum attainable oxygen consumption measurement is provided. For disability rating it is assumed that 45% of peak attainable oxygen consumption can be sustained throughout the workday. In many cases the sustainable oxygen consumption can be estimated from the bona fide pulmonary function testing. Although lifting ability is not directly determined by lung function, the Workers' Compensation system uses a lifting base terminology. Therefore, a "preclusion equivalent" is included in Table 3. The "preclusion equivalent" is designed to interconvert these ratings to the terminology typically used in Workers' Compensation evaluations.

*****

Barclays Official California Code of Regulations
Title 8. Industrial Relations
Division 1. Department of Industrial Relations
Chapter 4.5. Division of Workers' Compensation
Subchapter 1. Administrative Director—Administrative Rules
Article 5. Predesignation of Personal Physician; Request for Change of Physician;
Reporting Duties of the Primary Treating Physician; Petition for Change of
Primary Treating Physician
§ 9785. Reporting Duties of the Primary Treating Physician.

. . .

(g) When the primary treating physician determines that the employee's condition is permanent and stationary, the physician shall, unless good cause is shown, report within 20 days from the date of examination any findings concerning the existence and extent of permanent impairment and limitations and any need for continuing and/or future medical care resulting from the injury. The information may be submitted on the "Primary Treating Physician's Permanent and Stationary Report" form (DWC Form PR-3 or DWC Form PR-4) contained in section 9785.3 or section 9785.4, or in such other manner which provides all the information required by Title 8, California Code of Regulations, section 10606. For permanent disability evaluation performed pursuant to the permanent disability evaluation schedule adopted on or after January 1, 2005, the primary treating physician's reports concerning the existence and extent of permanent impairment shall describe the impairment in accordance with the AMA Guides to the Evaluation [of] Permanent Impairment, 5th Edition (DWC Form PR-4). Qualified Medical Evaluators and Agreed Medical Evaluators may not use DWC Form PR-3 or DWC Form PR-4 to report medical-legal evaluations.

*****

Barclays Official California Code of Regulations
Title 8. Industrial Relations
Division 1. Department of Industrial Relations
Chapter 4.5. Division of Workers' Compensation
Subchapter 1. Administrative Director—Administrative Rules
Article 7. Schedule for Rating Permanent Disabilities
§ 9805. Schedule for Rating Permanent Disabilities, Adoption, Amendment.

The method for the determination of percentages of permanent disability is set forth in the Schedule for Rating Permanent Disabilities, which has been adopted by the Administrative Director effective January 1, 2005, and which is hereby incorporated by reference in its entirety as though it were set forth below. The schedule adopts and incorporates the American Medical Association (AMA) *Guides to the Evaluation of Permanent Impairment 5th Edition.* The schedule shall be effective for dates of injury on or after January 1, 2005 and for dates of injury prior to January 1, 2005, in accordance with subdivision (d) of Labor Code section 4660, and it shall be amended at least once every five years.

The schedule may be downloaded from the Division of Workers' Compensation website at http://www.dir.ca.gov/dwc/dwcrep.htm

COLORADO

West's Colorado Revised Statutes Annotated
Title 8. Labor and Industry
Labor II—Worker's Compensation and Related Provisions
Worker's Compensation
Article 42. Benefits
§ 8-42-101. Employer must furnish medical aid—approval of plan—fee schedule—contracting for treatment—no recovery from employee—medical treatment guidelines—accreditation of physicians—repeal

. . .

(3)(a)(I) The director shall establish a schedule fixing the fees for which all medical, surgical, hospital, dental, nursing, vocational rehabilitation, and medical services, whether related to treatment or not, pertaining to injured employees under this section shall be compensated, and it is unlawful, void, and unenforceable as a debt for any physician, chiropractor, hospital, person, expert witness, reviewer, evaluator, or institution to contract with, bill, or charge any patient for services, rendered in connection with injuries coming within the purview of this article or an applicable fee schedule, which are or may be in excess of said fee schedule unless such charges are approved by the director. Fee schedules shall be reviewed on or before July 1 of each year by the director, and appropriate health care practitioners shall be given a reasonable opportunity to be heard as required pursuant to section 24-4-103, C.R.S., prior to fixing the fees, impairment rating guidelines, which shall be based on the revised third edition of the "American Medical Association Guides to the Evaluation of Permanent Impairment", in effect as of July 1, 1991, and medical treatment guidelines and utilization standards. Fee schedules established pursuant to this subparagraph (I) shall take effect on January 1. The director shall promulgate rules concerning reporting requirements, penalties for failure to report correctly or in a timely manner, utilization control requirements for services provided under this section, and the accreditation process in subsection (3.6) of this section.

. . .

(III) Notwithstanding the provisions of subparagraph (I) of this paragraph (a), until the impairment rating guidelines and medical treatment guidelines and utilization standards required by subparagraph (I) of this paragraph (a) and subsection (3.5) of this section are adopted and level I accreditation is received, compensation for fees for chiropractic treatments shall not be made more than ninety days after the first of such treatments nor after the twelfth such treatment, whichever first occurs, unless the chiropractor has received level I accreditation.

(b) Medical treatment guidelines and utilization standards, developed by the director, shall be used by health care practitioners for compliance with this section.

. . .

(II) The director shall promulgate rules establishing a system for the determination of medical treatment guidelines and utilization standards and medical impairment rating guidelines for impairment ratings as a percent of the whole person or affected body part based on the revised third edition of the "American Medical Association Guides to the Evaluation of Permanent Impairment," in effect as of July 1, 1991.

(3.5) (b) A medical impairment rating system shall be maintained by the director.

. . .

(3.6) (n) The director shall contract with the medical school of the university of Colorado for the services of a medical director to advise the director on issues of accreditation, impairment rating guidelines, medical treatment guidelines and utilization standards, and case management and to consult with the director on peer review activities as specified in this subsection (3.6) and section 8-43-501. Such medical director shall be a medical doctor licensed to practice in this state with experience in occupational medicine. The director may contract with an appropriate private organization which meets the definition of a utilization and quality control peer review organization as set forth in 42 U.S.C. sec. 1320c-1(1)(A) or (1)(B), to conduct peer review activities under this subsection (3.6) and section 8-43-501 and to recommend whether or not adverse action is warranted.

(o) Except as provided in this subsection (3.6), neither an insurance carrier nor a self-insured employer or injured worker shall be liable for costs incurred for an impairment evaluation rendered by a physician where there is a determination of permanent medical impairment if such physician is not level II accredited pursuant to the provisions of this subsection (3.6).

. . .

(3.7) On and after July 1, 1991, all physical impairment ratings used under articles 40 to 47 of this title shall be based on the revised third edition of the "American Medical Association Guides to the Evaluation of Permanent Impairment," in effect as of July 1, 1991. For purposes of determining levels of medical impairment pursuant to articles 40 to 47 of this title a physician shall not render a medical impairment rating based on chronic pain without anatomic or physiologic correlation. Anatomic correlation must be based on objective findings.

. . .

*****

West's Colorado Revised Statutes Annotated
Title 8. Labor and Industry
Labor II—Workers' Compensation and Related Provisions
Workers' Compensation
Article 42. Benefits
§ 8-42-107. Permanent partial disability benefits—schedule—medical impairment benefits—how determined

(1) Benefits available. (a) When an injury results in permanent medical impairment, and the employee has an injury or injuries enumerated in the schedule set forth in subsection (2) of this section, the employee shall be limited to medical impairment benefits as specified in subsection (2) of this section.

(b) When an injury results in permanent medical impairment and the employee has an injury or injuries not on the schedule specified in subsection (2) of this section, the employee shall be limited to medical impairment benefits as specified in subsection (8) of this section.

. . .

(7)(b)(I) The general assembly finds, determines, and declares that the rating organization that studied the impact of the changes in Senate Bill 91-218, enacted at the first regular session of the fifty-eighth general assembly, assumed that scheduled injuries would remain on the schedule and nonscheduled injuries would be compensated as medical impairment benefits. Therefore, the general assembly finds, determines, and declares that the purpose of changing the provisions of subparagraph (II) of this paragraph (b), as amended by House Bill 99-1157, enacted at the first regular session of the sixty-second general assembly, is to clarify that scheduled injuries shall be compensated as provided on the schedule and nonscheduled injuries shall be compensated as medical impairment benefits, and that, when an injured worker sustains both scheduled and nonscheduled injuries, the losses shall be compensated on the schedule for scheduled injuries and the nonscheduled injuries shall be compensated as medical impairment benefits. The general assembly further determines and declares that mental or emotional stress shall be compensated pursuant to section 8-41-301(2) and shall not be combined with a scheduled or a nonscheduled injury.

(II) Except as provided in subsection (8) of this section, where an injury causes the loss of, loss of use of, or partial loss of use of any member specified in the foregoing schedule, the amount of permanent partial disability shall be the proportionate share of the amount stated in the above schedule for the total loss of a member, and such amount shall be in addition to compensation for temporary disability. Where an injury causes a loss set forth in the schedule in subsection (2) of this section and a loss set forth for medical impairment benefits in subsection (8) of this section, the loss set forth in the schedule found in said subsection (2) shall be compensated solely on the basis of such schedule and the loss set forth in said subsection (8) shall be compensated solely on the basis for such medical impairment benefits specified in said subsection (8).

(III) Mental or emotional stress shall be compensated pursuant to section 8-41-301(2) and shall not be combined with a scheduled or a nonscheduled injury.

(8) Medical impairment benefits—determination of MMI for scheduled and nonscheduled injuries. (a) When an injury results in permanent medical impairment not set forth in the schedule in subsection (2) of this section, the employee shall be limited to medical impairment benefits calculated as provided in this subsection (8). The procedures for determination of maximum medical improvement set forth in paragraph (b) of this subsection (8) shall be available in cases of injuries set forth in the schedule in subsection (2) of this section and also in cases of injuries that are not set forth in said schedule.

. . .

(II) If either party disputes a determination by an authorized treating physician on the question of whether the injured worker has or has not reached maximum medical improvement, an independent medical examiner may be selected in accordance with section 8-42-107.2; except that, if an authorized treating physician has not determined that the employee has reached maximum medical improvement, the employer or insurer may only request the selection of an independent medical examiner if all of the following conditions are met:

. . .

(III) The finding of an independent medical examiner in a dispute arising under subparagraph (II) of this paragraph (b) shall be overcome only by clear and convincing evidence. A hearing on this matter shall not take place until the finding of the independent medical examiner has been filed with the division. (b.5) When an authorized treating physician providing primary care who is not accredited under the level II accreditation program pursuant to section 8-42-101(3.5) makes a determination that an employee has reached maximum medical improvement, the following procedures shall apply:

(I)(A) If the employee is not a state resident upon reaching maximum medical improvement, such physician shall, within twenty days after the determination of maximum medical improvement, determine whether the employee has sustained any permanent impairment. If the employee has sustained any permanent impairment, such physician shall conduct such tests as are required by the revised third edition of the "American Medical Association Guides to the Evaluation of Permanent Impairment" to determine such employee's medical impairment rating and shall transmit to the self-insured employer or insurer all test results and all relevant medical information.

(B) However, if the employee chooses not to have the authorized treating physician perform such tests, or if the information is not transmitted in a timely manner, the self-insured employer or insurer shall arrange and pay for the employee to return to Colorado for examination, testing, and rating, at the expense of the self-insured employer or insurer. If the employee refuses to return to Colorado for examination, no permanent disability benefits shall be awarded.

. . .

(D) If the employee, insurer, or self-insured employer disputes a medical impairment rating, including a finding that there is no medical impairment, made pursuant to sub-subparagraph (A) of this subparagraph (I), the parties to the dispute may select an independent medical examiner in accordance with section 8-42-107.2 to review the rating. The cost of such independent medical examination shall be borne by the requesting party. The finding of such independent medical examiner shall be overcome only by clear and convincing evidence. Any review by an independent medical examiner shall be based on the employee's written medical records only, without further examination, unless a party to the dispute requests that such review include a physical examination by the independent medical examiner. Except when the provisions of section 8-42-107.2(5)(b) apply, the party requesting a physical examination shall pay all additional costs, including, if applicable, the reasonable cost of returning the employee to Colorado.

(II) If the employee is a state resident, such physician shall, within twenty days after the determination of maximum medical improvement, determine whether the employee has sustained any permanent impairment. If the employee has sustained any permanent impairment, such physician shall refer such employee to a level II accredited physician for a medical impairment rating, which shall be based on the revised third edition of the "American Medical Association Guides to the Evaluation of Permanent Impairment". If the referral is not timely made by the authorized treating physician, the insurer or self-insured employer shall refer the employee to a level II accredited physician within forty days after the determination of maximum medical improvement. If the employee, insurer, or self-insured employer disputes the finding regarding permanent medical impairment, including a finding that there is no permanent medical impairment, the parties to the dispute may select an independent medical examiner in accordance with section 8-42-107.2. The finding of any such independent medical examiner shall be overcome only by clear and convincing evidence.

(c) When the injured employee's date of maximum medical improvement has been determined pursuant to paragraph (b) of this subsection (8), and there is a determination that permanent medical impairment has resulted from the injury, the authorized treating physician shall determine a medical impairment rating as a percentage of the whole person based on the revised third edition of the "American Medical Association Guides to the Evaluation of Permanent Impairment," in effect as of July 1, 1991. Except for a determination by the authorized treating physician providing primary care that no permanent medical impairment has resulted from the injury, any physician who determines a medical impairment rating shall have received accreditation under the level II accreditation program pursuant to section 8-42-101. For purposes of determining levels of medical impairment, the physician shall not render a medical impairment rating based on chronic pain without anatomic or physiologic correlation. Anatomic correlation must be based on objective findings. If either party disputes the authorized treating physician's finding of medical impairment, including a finding that there is no permanent medical impairment, the parties may select an independent medical examiner in accordance with section 8-42-107.2. The finding of such independent medical examiner shall be overcome only by clear and convincing evidence. A hearing on this matter shall not take place until the finding of the independent medical examiner has been filed with the division.

. . .

(d) Medical impairment benefits shall be determined by multiplying the medical impairment rating determined pursuant to paragraph (c) of this subsection (8) by the age factor determined pursuant to paragraph (e) of this subsection (8) and by four hundred weeks and shall be calculated at the temporary total disability rate specified in section 8-42-105. Up to ten thousand dollars of the total amount of any such award or scheduled award shall be automatically paid in a lump sum less the discount as calculated in section 8-43-406 upon the injured employee's written request to the employer or, if insured, to the employer's insurance carrier. The remaining periodic payments of any such award, after subtracting the total amount of the lump sum requested by the employee without subtracting the discount calculated in section 8-43-406, shall be paid at the temporary total disability rate but not less than one hundred fifty dollars per week and not more than fifty percent of the state average weekly wage, beginning on the date of maximum medical improvement.

*****

West's Colorado Revised Statutes Annotated
Title 8. Labor and Industry
Labor II—Workers' Compensation and Related Provisions
Workers' Compensation
Article 42. Benefits
§ 8-42-107.2. Selection of independent medical examiner—procedure—time—applicability

(1) This section governs the selection of an independent medical examiner, also referred to in this section as an "IME," to resolve disputes arising under section 8-42-107.

(2)(a)(I) Except as otherwise provided in subparagraph (II) of this paragraph (a), the time for selection of an IME commences as follows, depending on which party initiates the dispute:

(A) For the claimant, the time for selection of an IME commences with the date of mailing of a final admission of liability by the insurer or self-insured employer that includes an impairment rating issued in accordance with section 8-42-107.

. . .

(II) If, as of the date on which the time for selection of an IME would otherwise commence, a medical condition is not yet ratable because of a provision in the medical treatment guidelines or in the revised third edition of the "American Medical Association Guides to the Evaluation of Permanent Impairment," the time for selection of an IME shall commence on the date on which an impairment rating is mailed or physically delivered.

. . .

DISTRICT OF COLUMBIA

District of Columbia Official Code 2001 Edition
Division V. Local Business Affairs
Title 32. Labor
Chapter 15. Workers' Compensation
§ 32-1505. Commencement of compensation; maximum compensation.

(a) No compensation shall be allowed for the first 3 days of the disability, except the benefits provided for in § 32-1507; provided, that in case the injury results in disability of more than 14 days the compensation shall be allowed from the date of the disability.

(b) Compensation for disability or death shall not exceed the average weekly wages of insured employees in the District of Columbia or $396.78, whichever is greater. For any one injury causing temporary or permanent partial disability, the payment for disability benefits shall not continue for more than a total of 500 weeks. Within 60 days of the expiration of the duration of the compensation provided for in this subsection, an employee may petition the Mayor for an extension of up to 167 weeks. The extension shall be granted only upon a finding by an independent medical examiner appointed by the Mayor of continued whole body impairment exceeding 20% under the American Medical Association's Guides to the Evaluation of Permanent Impairment. An injured employee shall have up to 3 years after termination of nonscheduled benefits to re-open his or her case due to changes in condition.

. . .

*****

District of Columbia Official Code 2001 Edition
Division V. Local Business Affairs
Title 32. Labor
Chapter 15. Workers' Compensation
§ 32-1508. Compensation for disability.

Compensation for disability shall be paid to the employee as follows:

(1) In case of total disability adjudged to be permanent, 66⅔% of the employee's average weekly wages shall be paid to the employee during the continuance thereof. Loss of both hands, or both arms, or both feet, or both legs, or both eyes, or of any 2 thereof shall, in the absence of conclusive proof to the contrary, constitute permanent total disability. In all other cases permanent total disability shall be determined only if, as a result of the injury, the employee is unable to earn any wages in the same or other employment;

. . .

(3)(U) In any case in which there shall be a loss of, or loss of use of, more than 1 member or parts of more than 1 member set forth in subparagraphs (A) to (S) of this paragraph, not amounting to permanent total disability, the award of compensation shall be for the loss of, or loss of use of, each such member or part thereof, which awards shall run consecutively, except that where 1 injury affects only 2 or more digits of the same hand or foot, subparagraph (Q) of this paragraph shall apply; and

(U-i) In determining disability pursuant to subparagraphs (A) through (S) of this subsection, the most recent edition of the American Medical Association's Guides to the Evaluation of Permanent Impairment may be utilized, along with the following 5 factors:

(i) Pain;

(ii) Weakness;

(iii) Atrophy;

(iv) Loss of endurance; and

(v) Loss of function.

. . .

FLORIDA

West's Florida Statutes Annotated
Title XXXI. Labor (Chapters 435-453)
Chapter 440. Workers' Compensation
440.15. Compensation for disability

Compensation for disability shall be paid to the employee, subject to the limits provided in § 440.12(2), as follows:

. . .

(3) Permanent impairment benefits.—

(a) Once the employee has reached the date of maximum medical improvement, impairment benefits are due and payable within 14 days after the carrier has knowledge of the impairment.

(b) The three-member panel, in cooperation with the department, shall establish and use a uniform permanent impairment rating schedule. This schedule must be based on medically or scientifically demonstrable findings as well as the systems and criteria set forth in the American Medical Association's Guides to the Evaluation of Permanent Impairment; the Snellen Charts, published by the American Medical Association Committee for Eye Injuries; and the Minnesota Department of Labor and Industry Disability Schedules. The schedule must be based upon objective findings. The schedule shall be more comprehensive than the AMA Guides to the Evaluation of Permanent Impairment and shall expand the areas already addressed and address additional areas not currently contained in the guides. On August 1, 1979, and pending the adoption, by rule, of a permanent schedule, Guides to the Evaluation of Permanent Impairment, copyright 1977, 1971, 1988, by the American Medical Association, shall be the temporary schedule and shall be used for the purposes hereof. For injuries after July 1, 1990, pending the adoption by rule of a uniform disability rating agency schedule, the Minnesota Department of Labor and Industry Disability Schedule shall be used unless that schedule does not address an injury. In such case, the Guides to the Evaluation of Permanent Impairment by the American Medical Association shall be used. Determination of permanent impairment under this schedule must be made by a physician licensed under chapter 458, a doctor of osteopathic medicine licensed under chapters 458 and 459, a chiropractic physician licensed under chapter 460, a podiatric physician licensed under chapter 461, an optometrist licensed under chapter 463, or a dentist licensed under chapter 466, as appropriate considering the nature of the injury.

No other persons are authorized to render opinions regarding the existence of or the extent of permanent impairment.

. . .

*****

Florida Administrative Code Annotated
Title 69. Financial Services
Subtitle 69L. Division of Workers' Compensation
Chapter 69L-7. Workers' Compensation Medical Reimbursement and Utilization Review
69L-7.602. Florida Workers' Compensation Medical Services Billing, Filing and Reporting Rule.

(3) Materials Adopted by Reference. The following publications are incorporated by reference herein:

(h) The American Medical Association's Guide to the Evaluation of Permanent Impairment, as adopted in Rule 69L-7.604, F.A.C.

*****

Florida Administrative Code Annotated
Title 69. Financial Services
Subtitle 69L. Division of Workers' Compensation
Chapter 69L-7. Workers' Compensation Medical Reimbursement and Utilization Review
69L-7.604. Permanent Impairment.

(1) Determination of Physical Impairment Rating. The American Medical Association's Guide to the Evaluation of Permanent Impairment, 3rd Edition, (AMA Guide) (Copyright 1988 by the American Medical Association) is adopted as the schedule for determining the existence and degree of permanent impairment for all injuries prior to July 1, 1990. For injuries occurring on or after July 1, 1990, but before the effective date of the Florida Impairment Rating Guide, the Minnesota Department of Labor and Industry Disability Schedule shall be used unless that schedule does not address an injury, in which case, the AMA Guide shall be used. For injuries occurring on or after its effective date, the Florida Impairment Rating Guide, which is adopted by reference as part of this rule, shall be used. The Florida Impairment Rating Guide shall also be known as the Florida Impairment Rating Schedule, which is the "uniform permanent impairment rating schedule" and the "uniform disability rating schedule" referenced in Section 440.15(3)(a)2., F.S. The impairment rating must always be applied to the body as a whole.

(2) The 1996 Florida Uniform Permanent Impairment Rating Schedule is incorporated into this rule by reference and shall be used for injuries occurring on or after its effective date.

GEORGIA

West's Code of Georgia Annotated
Title 34. Labor and Industrial Relations
Chapter 15. Transfer of Division of Rehabilitation Services to Department of Labor

Appendix Rules and Regulations of the State Board of Workers' Compensation
Rule 263. Determination of Disability Rating

When the employee is no longer receiving weekly benefits under O.C.G.A. § 34-9-261 or § 34-9-262, and a permanent partial disability (PPD) rating has not previously been requested or issued, the employer/insurer shall have thirty days to request, in writing, from an authorized physician, that the employee be rated in accordance with the "Guides to the Evaluation of Permanent Impairment, Fifth Edition," published by the American Medical Association. The employer/insurer shall furnish a copy of the medical report of rating to the employee, and commence payment not later than 21 days after knowledge of the rating. The employer/insurer are presumed to have knowledge of the rating not later than 10 days after the date of the report establishing the rating.

*****

West's Code of Georgia Annotated
Title 34. Labor and Industrial Relations
Chapter 9. Workers' Compensation
Article 7. Compensation Schedules
§ 34-9-263. Income benefits for permanent partial disability

(a) *Definition.* As used in this chapter, "permanent partial disability" means disability partial in character but permanent in quality resulting from loss or loss of use of body members or from the partial loss of use of the employee's body.

(b) *Payment of benefits.*

(1) In cases of permanent partial disability, the employer shall pay weekly income benefits to the employee according to the schedule included within this Code section. These benefits shall be payable without regard to whether the employee has suffered economic loss as a result of the injury, except as herein provided.

. . .

(d) *Impairment ratings.* In all cases arising under this chapter, any percentage of disability or bodily loss ratings shall be based upon Guides to the Evaluation of Permanent Impairment, fifth edition, published by the American Medical Association.

(e) *Loss of more than one major member.* Loss of both arms, hands, legs, or feet, or any two or more of these members, or the permanent total loss of vision in both eyes shall create a rebuttable presumption of permanent total disability compensable as provided in Code Section 34-9-261.

IOWA

Iowa Administrative Code
Agency 876 Workers' Compensation Division
Chapter 2. General Provisions
876-2.4(85) Guides to evaluation of permanent impairment.

The Guides to the Evaluation of Permanent Impairment published by the American Medical Association are adopted as a guide for determining permanent partial disabilities under Iowa Code section 85.34(2). "a" to "s." The extent of loss or percentage of permanent impairment may be determined by use of this guide and payment of weekly compensation for permanent partial scheduled injuries made accordingly. Payment so made shall be recognized by the workers' compensation commissioner as a prima facie showing of compliance by the employer or insurance carrier with the foregoing sections of the Iowa workers' compensation Act. Nothing in this rule shall be construed to prevent the presentations of other medical opinions or guides or other material evidence for the purpose of establishing that the degree of permanent disability to which the claimant would be entitled would be more or less than the entitlement indicated in the AMA guide.

KANSAS

Kansas Statutes Annotated
Chapter 44. Labor and Industries
Article 5. Workers' Compensation
44-510d. Compensation for certain permanent partial disabilities; schedule.

(a) Where disability, partial in character but permanent in quality, results from the injury, the injured employee shall be entitled to the compensation provided in K.S.A. 44-510h and 44-510i and amendments thereto, but shall not be entitled to any other or further compensation for or during the first week following the injury unless such disability exists for three consecutive weeks, in which event compensation shall be paid for the first week. Thereafter compensation shall be paid for temporary total loss of use and as provided in the following schedule, 66⅔% of the average gross weekly wages to be computed as provided in K.S.A. 44-511 and amendments thereto, except that in no case shall the weekly compensation be more than the maximum as provided for in K.S.A. 44-510c and amendments thereto. If there is an award of permanent disability as a result of the injury there shall be a presumption that disability existed immediately after the injury and compensation is to be paid for not to exceed the number of weeks allowed in the following schedule:

. . .

(23) Loss of a scheduled member shall be based upon permanent impairment of function to the scheduled member as determined using the fourth edition of the American Medical Association Guides to the Evaluation of Permanent Impairment, if the impairment is contained therein.

. . .

*****

Kansas Statutes Annotated
Chapter 44. Labor and Industries
Article 5. Workers Compensation
§ 44-510e. Compensation for temporary or permanent partial general disabilities; extent of disability; functional impairment defined; termination upon death from other causes; limitations; other remedies excluded.

(a) If the employer and the employee are unable to agree upon the amount of compensation to be paid in the case of injury not covered by the schedule in K.S.A. 44-510d and amendments thereto, the amount of compensation shall be settled according to the provisions of the workers compensation act as in other cases of disagreement, except that in case of temporary or permanent partial general disability not covered by such schedule, the employee shall receive weekly compensation as determined in this subsection during such period of temporary or permanent partial general disability not exceeding a maximum of 415 weeks. Weekly compensation for temporary partial general disability shall be 66⅔% of the difference between the average gross weekly wage that the employee was earning prior to such injury as provided in the workers compensation act and the amount the employee is actually earning after such injury in any type of employment, except that in no case shall such weekly compensation exceed the maximum as provided for in K.S.A. 44-510c and amendments thereto. Permanent partial general disability exists when the employee is disabled in a manner which is partial in character and permanent in quality and which is not covered by the schedule in K.S.A. 44-510d and amendments thereto. The extent of permanent partial general disability shall be the extent, expressed as a percentage, to which the employee, in the opinion of the physician, has lost the ability to perform the work tasks that the employee performed in any substantial gainful employment during the fifteen-year period preceding the accident, averaged together with the difference between the average weekly wage the worker was earning at the time of the injury and the average weekly wage the worker is earning after the injury. In any event, the extent of permanent partial general disability shall not be less than the percentage of functional impairment. Functional impairment means the extent, expressed as a percentage, of the loss of a portion of the total physiological capabilities of the human body as established by competent medical evidence and based on the fourth edition of the American Medical Association Guides to the Evaluation of Permanent Impairment, if the impairment is contained therein. An employee shall not be entitled to receive permanent partial general disability compensation in excess of the percentage of functional impairment as long as the employee is engaging in any work for wages equal to 90% or more of the average gross weekly wage that the employee was earning at the time of the injury. If the employer and the employee are unable to agree upon the employee's functional impairment and if at least two medical opinions based on competent medical evidence disagree as to the percentage of functional impairment, such matter may be referred by the administrative law judge to an independent health care provider who shall be selected by the administrative law judge from a list of health care providers maintained by the director. The health care provider selected by the director pursuant to this section shall issue an opinion regarding the employee's functional impairment which shall be considered by the administrative law judge in making the final determination. The amount of weekly compensation for permanent partial general disability shall be determined as follows:

. . .

KENTUCKY

Baldwin's Kentucky Revised Statutes Annotated
Title XXVII. Labor and Human Rights
Chapter 342. Workers' Compensation
342.0011 Definitions for chapter

. . .

[(11)](b) "Permanent partial disability" means the condition of an employee who, due to an injury, has a permanent disability rating but retains the ability to work; and

(c) "Permanent total disability" means the condition of an employee who, due to an injury, has a permanent disability rating and has a complete and permanent inability to perform any type of work as a result of an injury, except that total disability shall be irrebuttably presumed to exist for an injury that results in:

1. Total and permanent loss of sight in both eyes;

2. Loss of both feet at or above the ankle;

3. Loss of both hands at or above the wrist;

4. Loss of one (1) foot at or above the ankle and the loss of one (1) hand at or above the wrist;

5. Permanent and complete paralysis of both arms, both legs, or one (1) arm and one (1) leg;

6. Incurable insanity or imbecility; or

7. Total loss of hearing;

. . .

(35) "Permanent impairment rating" means percentage of whole body impairment caused by the injury or occupational disease as determined by "Guides to the Evaluation of Permanent Impairment," American Medical Association, latest available edition; and

(36) "Permanent disability rating" means the permanent impairment rating selected by an administrative law judge times the factor set forth in the table that appears at KRS 342.730(1)(b).

*****

Baldwin's Kentucky Revised Statutes Annotated
Title XXVII. Labor and Human Rights
Chapter 342. Workers' Compensation
342.315 Medical evaluations by university medical schools; procedures; report; payment of costs; performance assessment of medical schools

. . .

(6) Not less often than annually the designee of the secretary of the Cabinet for Health and Family Services shall assess the performance of the medical schools and render findings as to whether evaluations conducted under this section are being rendered in a timely manner, whether examinations are conducted in accordance with medically recognized techniques, whether impairment ratings are in conformity with standards prescribed by the latest edition available of the "Guides to the Evaluation of Permanent Impairment" published by the American Medical Association, and whether coal workers' pneumoconiosis examinations are conducted in accordance with the standards prescribed in this chapter.

*****

Baldwin's Kentucky Revised Statutes Annotated
Title XXVII. Labor and Human Rights
Chapter 342. Workers' Compensation

342.316 Liability of employer and previous employers for occupational disease; claims procedure; time limitations on claims; determination of liable employer; effect of concluded coal workers' pneumoconiosis claim; applicability of consensus procedure

. . .

[(3)(b)]2. Spirometric testing shall be conducted in accordance with the standards recommended in the latest edition available of the "Guides to the Evaluation of Permanent Impairment" published by the American Medical Association and the 1978 ATS epidemiology standardization project with the exception that the predicted normal values for lung function shall not be adjusted based upon the race of the subject. The FVC or the FEV_1 values shall represent the largest of such values obtained from three (3) acceptable forced expiratory volume maneuvers as corrected to BTPS (body temperature, ambient pressure and saturated with water vapor at these conditions) and the variance between the two (2) largest acceptable FVC values shall be either less than five percent (5%) of the largest FVC value or less than one hundred (100) milliliters, whichever is greater. The variance between the two (2) largest acceptable FEV_1 values shall be either less than five percent (5%) of the largest FEV_1 value or less than one hundred (100) milliliters, whichever is greater. Reports of spirometric testing shall include a description by the physician of the procedures utilized in conducting such spirometric testing and a copy of the spirometric chart and tracings from which spirometric values submitted as evidence were taken.

3. The executive director shall promulgate administrative regulations pursuant to KRS Chapter 13A as necessary to effectuate the purposes of this section. The executive director shall periodically review the applicability of the spirometric test values contained in the latest edition available of the "Guides to the Evaluation of Permanent Impairment" published by the American Medical Association and may by administrative regulation substitute other spirometric test values which are found to be more closely representative of the normal pulmonary function of the coal mining population.

. . .

*****

Baldwin's Kentucky Revised Statutes Annotated
Title XXVII. Labor and Human Rights
Chapter 342. Workers' Compensation
342.730 Determination of income benefits for disability; survivors' rights; termination; offsets; notification of return to work

(1) Except as provided in KRS 342.732, income benefits for disability shall be paid to the employee as follows:

. . .

(b) For permanent partial disability, sixty-six and two-thirds percent (66⅔%) of the employee's average weekly wage but not more than seventy-five percent (75%) of the state average weekly wage as determined by KRS 342.740, multiplied by the permanent impairment rating caused by the injury or occupational disease as determined by "Guides to the Evaluation of Permanent Impairment," American Medical Association, latest edition available, times the factor set forth in the table that follows:

AMA Impairment	Factor
0 to 5%	0.65
6 to 10%	0.85
11 to 15%	1.00
16 to 20%	1.00
21 to 25%	1.15
26 to 30%	1.35
31 to 35%	1.50
36% and above	1.70

Any temporary total disability period within the maximum period for permanent, partial disability benefits shall extend the maximum period but shall not make payable a weekly benefit exceeding that determined in subsection (1)(a) of this section. Notwithstanding any section of this chapter to the contrary, there shall be no minimum weekly income benefit for permanent partial disability and medical benefits shall be paid for the duration of the disability.

(c) 1. If, due to an injury, an employee does not retain the physical capacity to return to the type of work that the employee performed at the time of injury, the benefit for permanent partial disability shall be multiplied by three (3) times the amount otherwise determined under paragraph (b) of this subsection, but this provision shall not be construed so as to extend the duration of payments; or

2. If an employee returns to work at a weekly wage equal to or greater than the average weekly wage at the time of injury, the weekly benefit for permanent partial disability shall be determined under paragraph (b) of this subsection for each week during which that employment is sustained. During any period of cessation of that employment, temporary or permanent, for any reason, with or without cause, payment of weekly benefits for permanent partial disability during the period of cessation shall be two (2) times the amount otherwise payable under paragraph (b) of this subsection. This provision shall not be construed so as to extend the duration of payments.

3. Recognizing that limited education and advancing age impact an employee's post-injury earning capacity, an education and age factor, when applicable, shall be added to the income benefit multiplier set forth in paragraph (c)1. of this subsection. If at the time of injury, the employee had less than eight (8) years of formal education, the multiplier shall be increased by four-tenths (0.4); if the employee had less than twelve (12) years of education or a high school General Educational Development diploma, the multiplier shall be increased by two-tenths (0.2); if the employee was age sixty (60) or older, the multiplier shall be increased by six-tenths (0.6); if the employee was age fifty-five (55) or older, the multiplier shall be increased by four-tenths (0.4); or if the employee was age fifty (50) or older, the multiplier shall be increased by two-tenths (0.2).

4. Notwithstanding the provisions of KRS 342.125, a claim may be reopened at any time during the period of permanent partial disability in order to conform the award payments with the requirements of subparagraph 2. of this paragraph.

(d) For permanent partial disability, if an employee has a permanent disability rating of fifty percent (50%) or less as a result of a work-related injury, the compensable permanent partial disability period shall be four hundred twenty-five (425) weeks, and if the permanent disability rating is greater than fifty percent (50%), the compensable permanent partial disability period shall be five hundred twenty (520) weeks from the date the impairment or disability exceeding fifty percent (50%) arises. Benefits payable for permanent partial disability shall not exceed ninety-nine percent (99%) of sixty-six and two-thirds percent (66⅔%) of the employee's average weekly wage as determined under KRS 342.740 and shall not exceed seventy-five percent (75%) of the state average weekly wage, except for benefits payable pursuant to paragraph (c)1. of this subsection, which shall not exceed one hundred percent (100%) of the state average weekly wage, nor shall benefits for permanent partial disability be payable for a period exceeding five hundred twenty (520) weeks, notwithstanding that multiplication of impairment times the factor set forth in paragraph (b) of this subsection would yield a greater percentage of disability.

(e) For permanent partial disability, impairment for nonwork-related disabilities, conditions previously compensated under this chapter, conditions covered by KRS 342.732, and hearing loss covered in KRS 342.7305 shall not be considered in determining the extent of disability or duration of benefits under this chapter.

(2) The period of any income benefits payable under this section on account of any injury shall be reduced by the period of income benefits paid or payable under this chapter on account of a prior injury if income benefits in both cases are for disability of the same member or function, or different parts of the same member or function, and the income benefits payable on account of the subsequent disability in whole or in part would duplicate the income benefits payable on account of the pre-existing disability.

. . .

*****

Baldwin's Kentucky Revised Statutes Annotated
Title XXVII. Labor and Human Rights
Chapter 342. Workers' Compensation
342.7305 Compensability of occupational hearing loss; authority for administrative regulations; rebuttable presumption as to employer liability

(1) In all claims for occupational hearing loss caused by either a single incident of trauma or by repetitive exposure to hazardous noise over an extended period of employment, the extent of binaural hearing impairment shall be determined under the latest available edition of the American Medical Association "Guides to the Evaluation of Permanent Impairment."

(2) Income benefits payable for occupational hearing loss shall be as provided in KRS 342.730, except income benefits shall not be payable where the binaural hearing impairment converted to impairment of the whole person results in impairment of less than eight percent (8%). No impairment percentage for tinnitus shall be considered in determining impairment to the whole person.

*****

Kentucky Administrative Regulations
Title 803. Environmental and Public Protection Cabinet—Department of Labor
Chapter 25. Department of Workers' Claims
803 KAR 25:009. Procedure for adjustment of coal workers' pneumoconiosis claims.

Section 6. Use of American Medical Association's "Guides to the Evaluation of Permanent Impairment" in Coal Workers' Pneumoconiosis Cases.

(1) Predicted normal values for FVC and FEV_1 shall be determined in accordance with the latest edition of the American Medical Association Guideline. Age shall be determined as of the date of the evaluation. Height shall be measured while the plaintiff stands in his stocking feet and shall be rounded to the nearest centimeter. If the plaintiff's height is an odd number of centimeters, the next highest even height in centimeters shall be used.

(2) Formulas established by the guidelines for predicted normal FVC and FEV_1 shall be applied and predicted values computed.

*****

Kentucky Administrative Regulations
Title 803. Environmental and Public Protection Cabinet—Department of Labor
Chapter 25. Department of Workers' Claims
803 KAR 25:160. Charges by medical providers for testimony and reports in workers' compensation claims.

. . .

Section 2. Charges for Medical Reports.

. . .

(2) Medical providers and other health care professionals may charge not more than their usual and customary fee up to a maximum of seventy-five (75) dollars per page, with a maximum up to but not to exceed $200, for the completion of a narrative report containing brief findings resulting from physical or psychological examination, summary of testing performed, diagnosis, records reviewed, impairment rating as determined under the latest available edition of the "Guides to the Evaluation of Permanent Impairment" published by the American Medical Association with appropriate references to the chapter and page number involved, restrictions and limitations noted, if any, and whether the condition is the result of the arousal of a preexisting dormant disabling condition.

. . .

LOUISIANA

West's Louisiana Statutes Annotated
Louisiana Revised Statutes
Title 23. Labor and Workers' Compensation
Chapter 10. Workers' Compensation
Part II. Benefits
Subpart B. Disability Benefits
§ 1221. Temporary total disability; permanent total disability; supplemental earnings benefits; permanent partial disability; schedule of payments

Compensation shall be paid under this Chapter in accordance with the following schedule of payments:

. . .

(4) Permanent partial disability. In the following cases, compensation shall be solely for anatomical loss of use or amputation and shall be as follows:

. . .

(q) No benefits shall be awarded or payable in this Paragraph unless the percentage of the anatomical loss of use or amputation, as provided in Subparagraphs (a) through (*o*) of this Paragraph or the percentage of the loss of physical function as provided in Subparagraph (p) or (s) of this Paragraph is as established in the most recent edition of the American Medical Association's "Guides to the Evaluation of Permanent Impairment."

MAINE

Maine Revised Statutes Annotated
Title 39-A. Workers' Compensation
Part 1. Maine Workers' Compensation Act of 1992
Chapter 3. Workers' Compensation Board
§ 153. Board actions

. . .

8. Impairment guidelines. The following provisions apply regarding impairment guidelines.

A. In order to reduce litigation and establish more certainty and uniformity in the rating of permanent impairment, the board shall establish by rule a schedule for determining the existence and degree of permanent impairment based upon medically or scientifically demonstrable findings. The schedule must be based on generally accepted medical standards for determining impairment and may incorporate all or part of any one or more generally accepted schedules used for that purpose, such as the American Medical Association's "Guides to the Evaluation of Permanent Impairment." Pending the adoption of a permanent schedule, "Guides to the Evaluation of Permanent Impairment," 3rd edition, copyright 1990, by the American Medical Association, is the temporary schedule and must be used for the purposes of this subsection.

B. The board shall collect and analyze data from Maine cases, studies from other states and generally accepted medical guidelines for occupational impairment to examine the feasibility and desirability of establishing an objectively ascertainable functional capacity standard to be used for determining eligibility for benefits under this Act consistent with section 213, subsection 2.

. . .

*****

Code of Maine Rules
90. Independent Agencies
351. Workers Compensation Board
Chapter 7. Utilization Review, Treatment Guidelines, Permanent Impairment
Sec. 6. Permanent Impairment

. . .

2. Permanent impairment shall be determined after the effective date of this rule by use of the American Medical Association's "Guides to the Evaluation of Permanent Impairment," 4th edition, copyright 1993.

MARYLAND

West's Annotated Code of Maryland
Labor and Employment
Title 9. Workers' Compensation
Subtitle 7. Procedures for Claims, Hearings, and Appeals
§ 9-721. LAB. & EMPL. Physician to evaluate permanent impairment; contents of evaluation.

(a) *In general.*— Except as provided in subsection (c) of this section, a physician shall evaluate a permanent impairment and report the evaluation to the Commission in accordance with the regulations of the Commission.

(b) *Contents of evaluation.*—A medical evaluation of a permanent impairment shall include information about:

(1) atrophy;

(2) pain;

(3) weakness; and

(4) loss of endurance, function, and range of motion.

. . .

Code of Maryland Regulations
Title 14. Independent Agencies
Subtitle 09. Workers' Compensation Commission
Chapter 04. Guide for Evaluation of Permanent Impairment
.01 Incorporation by Reference.

Guides to the Evaluation of Permanent Impairment (American Medical Association, Fourth Edition, 1993) is incorporated by reference.

*****

Code of Maryland Regulations
Title 14. Independent Agencies
Subtitle 09. Workers' Compensation Commission
Chapter 04. Guide for Evaluation of Permanent Impairment
.02 General Guidelines.

A. As evidence of permanent impairment, a party may submit a written evaluation of permanent impairment prepared by a physician.

B. When preparing an evaluation of permanent impairment, a physician shall:

(1) Generally conform the evaluation with the format set forth in § 2.2 ("Reports") of the American Medical Association's "Guides to the Evaluation of Permanent Impairment";

(2) Use the numerical ratings for the impairment set forth in the American Medical Association's "Guides to the Evaluation of Permanent Impairment," provided that a physician is not required to use the inclinometer evaluation technique specified in § 3.3, but instead may use the goniometer technique specified in the "Addendum to Chapter 3";

(3) Include the items listed under the heading "Comparison of the results of analysis with the impairment criteria . . ." in § 2.2 ("Reports") of the American Medical Association's "Guides to the Evaluation of Permanent Impairment"; and

. . .

C. A physician preparing an evaluation of permanent impairment may include numerical ratings not set forth in the American Medical Association's "Guides to the Evaluation of Permanent Impairment" for the items listed in § B(4) of this regulation. If the physician does so, the physician shall include in the evaluation the detailed findings that support those numerical ratings.

. . .

F. This regulation shall apply to all evaluations prepared on or after July 1, 1990.

. . .

MASSACHUSETTS

Massachusetts General Laws Annotated
Part I. Administration of the Government (Ch. 1-182)
Title XXI. Labor and Industries (Ch. 149-154)
Chapter 152. Workers' Compensation
Payments
§ 35.Partial incapacity; compensation

. . .

The total number of weeks of compensation due the employee under this section shall not exceed two hundred sixty; provided, however, that this number may be extended to five hundred twenty if an insurer agrees or an administrative judge finds that the employee has, as a result of a personal injury under this chapter, suffered a permanent loss of seventy-five percent or more of any bodily function or sense specified in paragraph (a), (b), (e), (f), (g), or (h) of subsection (1) of section thirty-six, developed a permanently life-threatening physical condition, or contracted a permanently disabling occupational disease which is of a physical nature and cause. Where applicable, losses under this section shall be determined in accordance with standards set forth in the American Medical Association Guides to the Evaluation of Permanent Impairments [sic]. Where the insurer agrees or the administrative judge finds such permanent partial disability as is described in this paragraph, the total number of weeks the employee may receive benefits under both this section and section thirty-four shall not exceed five hundred twenty. Where there has been no such agreement or finding the number of weeks the employee may receive benefits under these sections shall not exceed three hundred sixty-four.

*****

Massachusetts General Laws Annotated
Part I. Administration of the Government (Ch. 1-182)
Title XXI. Labor and Industries (Ch. 149-154)
Chapter 152. Workers' Compensation Payments
§ 36. Specific injuries

(2) Where applicable, losses under this section shall be determined in accordance with standards set forth in the American Medical Association Guides to the Evaluation of Permanent Impairments [sic]. Nothing in this section shall adversely affect the employee's rights to any compensation which is or may become due under the provisions of any other section.

*****

Code of Massachusetts Regulations
Title 452. Department of Industrial Accidents
Chapter 1.00. Adjudicatory Rules
1.07: Claims and Complaints

(2) Pursuant to the provisions of M.G.L. c. 152, § 7G, the following documentation must be attached to a claim for benefits, or complaint for modification or discontinuance of benefits before it will be processed by the Office of Claims Administration:

. . .

[(c)]2. Claims for mileage reimbursement necessarily incidental to the provision of adequate and reasonable medical services shall be accompanied, where applicable, by the following:

. . .

(h) In any claim in which M.G.L. c. 152, § 35A is the only benefit claimed and where dependency is requested for dependents who are conclusively presumed to be dependent under M.G.L. c. 152, § 35A, the claim shall be accompanied, where applicable, by a copy of one or more of the following:

. . .

4. an affidavit by a parent of an unmarried child under the age of 18 attesting to the parent's dependency upon the support of the child.

(i) 1. All claims for functional loss under the provisions of M.G.L. c. 152, § 36 or § 36A shall include a physician's report which indicates that a maximum medical improvement has been reached and which contains an opinion as to the percent of permanent functional loss according to the American Medical Association's guide to physical impairment. There shall also be a statement from the claimant, or the claimant's attorney or other authorized representative indicating the specific monetary value of the benefit award being sought as reflected by the opinion of the physician's accompanying report. No claim for functional loss may be filed sooner than six months following an injury or the latest surgery resulting from the injury.

MINNESOTA

Minnesota Administrative Rules
Chapter 5223. Department of Labor and Industry Disability Schedules
5223.0010 Workers' Compensation Permanent Partial Disability Schedules.

Subp. 4. Rules of construction. The technical terms in this chapter are defined in either part 5223.0020, or by the documents incorporated by reference in this chapter. Documents are incorporated by reference only to the extent necessary for definition or to the extent specifically referenced in a schedule. The documents incorporated by reference are not subject to frequent change, although new editions occasionally may be published. These documents are common medical references and are conveniently available to the public as noted in items A to K. These documents are as follows:

A. Guides to the Evaluation of Permanent Impairment, published by the American Medical Association, Committee on Rating of Mental and Physical Impairment, second edition 1984. This document is also known as the A.M.A. Guides. Available at the University of Minnesota Biomedical Library.

*****

Minnesota Rules, Chapter 5223, Department of Labor and Industry Disability Schedules
5223.0300 Workers' Compensation Permanent Partial Disability Schedules.

Subp. 4. Incorporations by reference. The technical terms in parts 5223.0300 to 5223.0650 are defined either in part 5223.0310 or by the documents incorporated by reference in parts 5223.0300 to 5223.0650. Documents are incorporated by reference only to the extent necessary for definition or to the extent specifically referenced in a schedule. The documents incorporated by reference are not subject to frequent change, although new editions occasionally may be published. These documents are common medical references and are conveniently available to the public at the University of Minnesota, Biomedical Library and are accessible through the Minitex interlibrary loan system. These documents are as follows:

. . .

B. Guides to the Evaluation of Permanent Impairment, published by the American Medical Association, Committee on Rating of Mental and Physical Impairment, 3rd edition, 1988. This document is also referred to as the A.M.A. Guides.

. . .

E. Metropolitan Life Insurance Company Height and Weight Tables, published by the Metropolitan Life Insurance Company, 1983, and reproduced in the A.M.A Guides, 3rd edition, page 178.

MONTANA

Montana Code Annotated
Title 39. Labor
Chapter 71. Workers' Compensation

Part 7. Compensation and Benefits Generally
39-71-703. Compensation for permanent partial disability

(1) If an injured worker suffers a permanent partial disability and is no longer entitled to temporary total or permanent total disability benefits, the worker is entitled to a permanent partial disability award if that worker:

. . .

(b) has a permanent impairment rating that:

(i) is not based exclusively on complaints of pain;

(ii) is established by objective medical findings; and

(iii) is more than zero as determined by the latest edition of the American medical association Guides to the Evaluation of Permanent Impairment.

. . .

(4) A permanent partial disability award granted an injured worker may not exceed a permanent partial disability rating of 100%.

(5) The percentage to be used in subsection (4) must be determined by adding all of the following applicable percentages to the impairment rating:

(a) if the claimant is 40 years of age or younger at the time of injury, 0%; if the claimant is over 40 years of age at the time of injury, 1%;

(b) for a worker who has completed less than 12 years of education, 1%; for a worker who has completed 12 years or more of education or who has received a graduate equivalency diploma, 0%;

(c) if a worker has no actual wage loss as a result of the industrial injury, 0%; if a worker has an actual wage loss of $2 or less an hour as a result of the industrial injury, 10%; if a worker has an actual wage loss of more than $2 an hour as a result of the industrial injury, 20%. Wage loss benefits must be based on the difference between the actual wages received at the time of injury and the wages that the worker earns or is qualified to earn after the worker reaches maximum healing.

(d) if a worker, at the time of the injury, was performing heavy labor activity and after the injury the worker can perform only light or sedentary labor activity, 5%; if a worker, at the time of injury, was performing heavy labor activity and after the injury the worker can perform only medium labor activity, 3%; if a worker was performing medium labor activity at the time of the injury and after the injury the worker can perform only light or sedentary labor activity, 2%.

*****

Montana Code Annotated
Title 39. Labor
Chapter 71. Workers' Compensation
Part 7. Compensation and Benefits Generally
39-71-711. Impairment evaluation—ratings

(1) An impairment rating:

(a) is a purely medical determination and must be determined by an impairment evaluator after a claimant has reached maximum healing;

(b) must be based on the current edition of the Guides to Evaluation of Permanent Impairment published by the American medical association;

(c) must be expressed as a percentage of the whole person; and

(d) must be established by objective medical findings.

(2) A claimant or insurer, or both, may obtain an impairment rating from an evaluator who is a medical doctor or from an evaluator who is a chiropractor if the injury falls within the scope of chiropractic practice. If the claimant and insurer cannot agree upon the rating, the mediation procedure in part 24 of this chapter must be followed.

(3) An evaluator must be a physician licensed under Title 37, chapter 3, except if the claimant's treating physician is a chiropractor, the evaluator may be a chiropractor who is certified as an evaluator under chapter 12.

(4) Disputes over impairment ratings are subject to the provisions of 39-71-605.

*****

Administrative Rules of Montana
Title 24. Department of Labor and Industry
Chapter 126. Board of Chiropractors
Sub-Chapter 9. Impairment Evaluators
24.126.910. Renewal—Denial—Revocation

(1) A minimum of four hours of specialized continuing education relevant to impairment evaluation must be demonstrated every four years, or within one year of a new edition to the American Medical Association's guides to the evaluation of permanent impairment. These hours must be demonstrated in order to qualify for certification renewal. This requirement is in addition to the continuing education hours required for annual renewal of licenses to practice chiropractic in this state.

(2) Persistent deviation from generally accepted standards for impairment evaluation is grounds for denial of renewal of certification and for revocation of the impairment evaluator certificate.

(3) An impairment evaluator must comply with ARM 24.29.1415. These rules can be obtained by contacting the Department of Labor and Industry Workers' Compensation Regulation Bureau.

(4) Impairment evaluator licenses shall be renewed annually.

NEVADA

West's Nevada Revised Statutes Annotated
Title 53. Labor and Industrial Relations
Chapter 616C. Industrial Insurance: Benefits for Injuries or Death
Treatment and Rating of Injured Employees
616C.105. Requirements for designation of chiropractor to rate permanent partial disabilities

The Administrator shall not designate a chiropractor to rate permanent partial disabilities unless the chiropractor has completed an advanced program of training in rating disabilities using the American Medical Association's Guides to the Evaluation of Permanent Impairment which is offered or approved by the Administrator.

West's Nevada Revised Statutes Annotated
Title 53. Labor and Industrial Relations
Chapter 616B. Industrial Insurance: Insurers; Liability for Provision of Coverage
Subsequent Injury Accounts
Self-Insured Employers
616B.557. Payment of cost of additional compensation resulting from subsequent injury of employee of self-insured employer

. . .

3. As used in this section, "permanent physical impairment" means any permanent condition, whether congenital or caused by injury or disease, of such seriousness as to constitute a hindrance or obstacle to obtaining employment or to obtaining reemployment if the employee is unemployed. For the purposes of this section, a condition is not a "permanent physical impairment" unless it would support a rating of permanent impairment of 6 percent or more of the whole man if evaluated according to the American Medical Association's Guides to the Evaluation of Permanent Impairment as adopted and supplemented by the Division pursuant to NRS 616C.110.

. . .

West's Nevada Revised Statutes Annotated
Title 53. Labor and Industrial Relations
Chapter 616B. Industrial Insurance: Insurers; Liability for Provision of Coverage
Subsequent Injury Accounts
Associations of Self-Insured Public or Private Employers
616B.578. Payment of cost of additional compensation resulting from subsequent injury of employee of member of association of self-insured public or private employers

. . .

3. As used in this section, "permanent physical impairment" means any permanent condition, whether congenital or caused by injury or disease, of such seriousness as to constitute a hindrance or obstacle to obtaining employment or to obtaining reemployment if the employee is unemployed. For the purposes of this section, a condition is not a "permanent physical impairment" unless it would support a rating of permanent impairment of 6 percent or more of the whole man if evaluated according to the American Medical Association's Guides to the Evaluation of Permanent Impairment as adopted and supplemented by the Division pursuant to NRS 616C.110.

*****

West's Nevada Revised Statutes Annotated
Title 53. Labor and Industrial Relations
Chapter 616C. Industrial Insurance: Benefits for Injuries or Death
Treatment and Rating of Injured Employees
616C.110. American Medical Association's Guides to the Evaluation of Permanent Impairment: Duty of Division to adopt Guides by regulation; determination of appropriate version of Guides to apply

1. For the purposes of NRS 616B.557, 616B.578, 616B.587, 616C.490 and 617.459:

(a) Not later than August 1, 2003, the Division shall adopt regulations incorporating the American Medical Association's Guides to the Evaluation of Permanent Impairment, 5th edition, by reference. The regulations:

(1) Must become effective on October 1, 2003; and

(2) Must be applied to all examinations for a permanent partial disability that are conducted on or after October 1, 2003, regardless of the date of the injury, until regulations incorporating the 6th edition by reference have become effective pursuant to paragraph (b).

(b) Beginning with the 6th edition and continuing for each edition thereafter, the Division shall adopt regulations incorporating the most recent edition of the American Medical Association's Guides to the Evaluation of Permanent Impairment by reference. The regulations:

(1) Must become effective not later than 18 months after the most recent edition is published by the American Medical Association; and

(2) Must be applied to all examinations for a permanent partial disability that are conducted on or after the effective date of the regulations, regardless of the date of injury, until regulations incorporating the next edition by reference have become effective pursuant to this paragraph.

2. After adopting the regulations required pursuant to subsection 1, the Division may amend those regulations as it deems necessary, except that the amendments to those regulations:

(a) Must be consistent with the edition of the American Medical Association's Guides to the Evaluation of Permanent Impairment most recently adopted by the Division;

(b) Must not incorporate any contradictory matter from any other edition of the American Medical Association's Guides to the Evaluation of Permanent Impairment; and

(c) Must not consider any factors other than the degree of physical impairment of the whole man in calculating the entitlement to compensation.

3. If the edition of the American Medical Association's Guides to the Evaluation of Permanent Impairment most recently adopted by the Division contains more than one method of determining the rating of an impairment, the Administrator shall designate by regulation the method from that edition which must be used to rate an impairment pursuant to NRS 616C.490.

*****

West's Nevada Revised Statutes Annotated
Title 53. Labor and Industrial Relations
Chapter 616C. Industrial Insurance: Benefits for Injuries or Death
Contested Claims
616C.392. Reopening claim: Circumstances under which insurer is required to reopen claim for permanent partial disability

. . .

3. Notwithstanding any specific statutory provision to the contrary, the consideration of whether a claimant is entitled to payment of compensation for a permanent partial disability for a claim that is reopened pursuant to this section must be made in accordance with the provisions of the applicable statutory and regulatory provisions that existed on the date on which the claim was closed, including, without limitation, using the edition of the American Medical Association's Guides to the Evaluation of Permanent Impairment as adopted by the Division pursuant to NRS 616C.110 that was applicable on the date the claim was closed.

*****

West's Nevada Revised Statutes Annotated
Title 53. Labor and Industrial Relations
Chapter 616C. Industrial Insurance: Benefits for Injuries or Death
Compensation for Injuries and Death
Permanent and Temporary Partial Disabilities
616C.490. Permanent partial disability: Compensation

. . .

2. Within 30 days after receiving from a physician or chiropractor a report indicating that the injured employee may have suffered a permanent disability and is stable and ratable, the insurer shall schedule an appointment with the rating physician or chiropractor selected pursuant to this subsection to determine the extent of the employee's disability. Unless the insurer and the injured employee otherwise agree to a rating physician or chiropractor:

(a) The insurer shall select the rating physician or chiropractor from the list of qualified rating physicians and chiropractors designated by the Administrator, to determine the percentage of disability in accordance with the American Medical Association's Guides to the Evaluation of Permanent Impairment as adopted and supplemented by the division pursuant to NRS 616C.110.

. . .

3. If an insurer contacts the treating physician or chiropractor to determine whether an injured employee has suffered a permanent disability, the insurer shall deliver to the treating physician or chiropractor that portion or a summary of that portion of the American Medical Association's Guides to the Evaluation of Permanent Impairment as adopted by the division pursuant to NRS 616C.110 that is relevant to the type of injury incurred by the employee.

. . .

*****

West's Nevada Revised Statutes Annotated
Title 53. Labor and Industrial Relations
Chapter 617. Occupational Diseases
Compensation for Disability and Death
617.459. Determination of percentage of disability resulting from heart or lung diseases

1. The percentage of disability resulting from an occupational disease of the heart or lungs must be determined jointly by the claimant's attending physician and the examining physician designated by the insurer, in accordance with the American Medical Association's Guides to the Evaluation of Permanent Impairment as adopted and supplemented by the division pursuant to NRS 616C.110.

2. If the claimant's attending physician and the designated examining physician do not agree upon the percentage of disability, they shall designate a physician specializing in the branch of medicine which pertains to the disease in question to make the determination. If they do not agree upon the designation of such a physician, each shall choose one physician so specializing, and two physicians so chosen shall choose a third specialist in that branch. The resulting panel of three physicians shall, by majority vote, determine the percentage of disability in accordance with the American Medical Association's Guides to the Evaluation of Permanent Impairment as adopted and supplemented by the division pursuant to NRS 616C.110.

NEW HAMPSHIRE

Revised Statutes Annotated of the State of New Hampshire
Title XXIII. Labor
Chapter 281-A. Workers' Compensation
281-A:23 Medical, Hospital, and Remedial Care.

. . .

V. (b) The commissioner shall develop a form on which health care providers and health care facilities shall report medical, surgical or other remedial treatment. The report shall include, but is not limited to, information relative to the up-to-date medical status of the employee, any medical information relating to the employee's ability to return to work, whether or not there are physical restrictions, what those restrictions are, the date of maximum medical improvement, and, where applicable, the percentage of permanent impairment in accordance with the "Guides to the Evaluation of Permanent Impairment" published by the American Medical Association and as set forth in RSA 281-A:32, and any other information to enable the employer or insurance carrier to determine the benefits, if any, that are due and payable. In addition to the report required under this section, the health care provider shall furnish a statement confirming that the treatment or services rendered were reasonable and necessary with respect to the bodily injury sustained. The statement shall read as follows: "I certify that the narrative descriptions of the principal and secondary diagnosis and the major procedures performed are accurate and complete to the best of my knowledge." The health care provider shall date and sign the statement.

. . .

*****

Revised Statutes Annotated of the State of New Hampshire
Title XXIII. Labor
Chapter 281-A. Workers' Compensation
281-A:31-a Compensation for Permanent Partial Disability.

Where the disability for work resulting from an injury is permanent but partial in nature, the employee has reached maximum medical improvement, is able to return to work, and there is an impairment in accordance with the "Guides to the Evaluation of Permanent Impairment" published by the American Medical Association as set forth in RSA 281-A:32, the employer, or insurance carrier, during such disability shall pay to the injured employee a weekly compensation equal to 60 percent of the difference between his average weekly wage before the injury and the average weekly wage which he is able to earn thereafter. However, in no instance shall the weekly compensation exceed the amounts set forth by the compensation schedule in RSA 281-A:28. Payments shall not continue after the disability ends, nor longer than 262 weeks; and if the partial disability begins after a period of total disability, the period of disability shall be deducted from such total period of 262 weeks.

*****

Revised Statutes Annotated of the State of New Hampshire
Title XXIII. Labor
Chapter 281-A. Workers' Compensation
281-A:32 Scheduled Permanent Impairment Award.

. . .

IX. MORE THAN ONE PERMANENT LOSS. If an injury results in more than one permanent bodily loss specified in paragraphs I-VIII, or if the injury is to the spinal column or the spinal cord, or to the brain, or involves scarring, disfigurement, or other skin impairment resulting from a burn or burns, an award shall be made on the basis of a maximum of 350 weeks with the appropriate number of weeks to be determined in proportion to the maximum in accordance with the percent of the whole person specified for such bodily losses in the most recent edition of "Guides to the Evaluation of Permanent Impairment" published by the American Medical Association. Injury to spinal column or spinal cord shall not be construed to permit an award under this section as a result of soft tissue injury, nor to permit such an award on the basis of more than one permanent loss, unless such injury results in loss of use of upper or lower extremities. For the purposes of this paragraph "injury to the brain" means cerebral or neurological impairment due to central nervous system injury as described in said American Medical Association Guide.

. . .

XIV. RULEMAKING REQUIRED. In order to reduce litigation and establish more certainty and uniformity in the rating of permanent impairment, the commissioner shall adopt rules, under RSA 541-A, incorporating by reference the most recent edition of the American Medical Association's "Guides to the Evaluation of Permanent Impairment" to determine the degree of permanent impairment and on which to base awards under this chapter.

*****

Revised Statutes Annotated of the State of New Hampshire
Title XXIII. Labor
Chapter 281-A. Workers' Compensation
281-A:60 Rulemaking; Powers of the Commissioner.

I. The commissioner shall have the power to adopt rules under RSA 541-A relative to the following:

. . .

(j) Using the most recent edition of the American Medical Association's "Guides to the Evaluation of Permanent Impairment" in accordance with RSA 281-A:32, XIV, and updating such rules as other editions of such guide are published.

. . .

*****

State of New Hampshire, Office of Legislative Services, Division of Administrative Rules
Department of Labor
Chapter Lab 500. Workers' Compensation Claims
Part Lab 508. Responsibilities of Treating Practitioners
Lab 508.01 Medical Reports.

(d) Medical reports submitted in conjunction with assessment of permanent bodily loss under RSA 281-A:32 shall contain affirmation that the findings were determined from Guide [sic] to the Evaluation of Permanent Impairment, the most recent edition, published by the American Medical Association.

*****

State of New Hampshire, Office of Legislative Services, Division of Administrative Rules
Department of Labor
Chapter Lab 500. Workers' Compensation Claims
Part Lab 511. Cases for Departmental Review
Lab 511.04 Permanent Impairment Awards

. . .

(b) The criteria for determination of the permanent impairment award shall be as follows:

(1) The most recent edition of the Guides to the Evaluation of Permanent Impairment, published by the American Medical Association shall be the exclusive determinant for the assessment of permanency awards under RSA 281- A:32, as amended, except where RSA 281-A:32, II is more favorable to the claimant;

(2) Medical evidence regarding permanency evaluations shall contain affirmation from the submitting physician that the findings for permanent bodily loss were determined from the Guides to the Evaluation of Permanent Impairment, the most recent edition;

. . .

*****

State of New Hampshire, Office of Legislative Services, Division of Administrative Rules
Department of Labor
Chapter Lab 500. Workers' Compensation Claims
Part Lab 515. Instructions for Completing Claims Forms
Lab 515.12 The Workers' Compensation Supplemental Medical Report.

(a) The health care provider on form 75WCA-2 shall supply the following information:

. . .

(10) A check in the appropriate box with regard to permanent impairment. If yes, the percent in accordance with the AMA Guide [sic] to the Evaluation of Permanent Impairment in the space provided; and

. . .

NEW MEXICO

West's New Mexico Statutes Annotated
Chapter 52. Workers' Compensation
Article 1. Workers' Compensation
§ 52-1-24. Impairment; definition

As used in the Workers' Compensation Act:

A. "impairment" means an anatomical or functional abnormality existing after the date of maximum medical improvement as determined by a medically or scientifically demonstrable finding and based upon the most recent edition of the American medical association's guide to the evaluation of permanent impairment or comparable publications of the American medical association. Impairment includes physical impairment, primary mental impairment and secondary mental impairment;

. . .

*****

West's New Mexico Statutes Annotated
Chapter 52. Workers' Compensation
Article 1. Workers' Compensation
§ 52-1-25. Permanent total disability

A. As used in the Workers' Compensation Act, "permanent total disability" means:

(1) the permanent and total loss or loss of use of both hands or both arms or both feet or both legs or both eyes or any two of them; or

(2) a brain injury resulting from a single traumatic work-related injury that causes, exclusive of the contribution to the impairment rating arising from any other impairment to any other body part, or any preexisting impairments of any kind, a permanent impairment of thirty percent or more as determined by the current American medical association guide to the evaluation of permanent impairment.

. . .

*****

Code of New Mexico Rules
Title 11. Labor and Workers Compensation
Chapter 4. Workers' Compensation
Part 4. Claims Resolution
11.4.4. Claims Resolution

See full statute for a copy of the actual worksheet.
*****

Code of New Mexico Rules
Title 11. Labor and Workers Compensation
Chapter 4. Workers' Compensation

Part 7. Payments for Health Care Services

11.4.7.7 NMAC Definitions:

. . .

MM. "Physical impairment ratings (PIR)" means an evaluation performed by an MD, DO, or DC to determine the degree of anatomical or functional abnormality existing after an injured or disabled worker has reached maximum medical improvement. The impairment is assumed to be permanent and is expressed as a percent figure of either the body part or whole body, as appropriate, in accordance with the provisions of the Workers' Compensation Act and the most current edition of the American medical association's guides to the evaluation of permanent impairment (AMA guide).

. . .

11.4.7.9 NMAC Procedures for Establishing the Maximum Amount of Reimbursement Due

G. Maximum allowable amount method

. . .

(4) Physical impairment ratings

. . .

(b) Impairment ratings performed for primary and secondary mental impairments shall be billed using CPT code 90899 (unlisted psychiatric service/procedure) and shall conform to the guidelines, whenever possible, presented in the most current edition of the AMA guides to the evaluation of permanent impairment.

. . .

11.4.7.12 NMAC Anesthesia

. . .

B. The "basic unit value" assigned to each procedure in the CPT code series 00100-01999 in the ASA relative value guide adopted by the director in his annual order shall be used when billing.

NORTH DAKOTA

North Dakota Century Code
Title 65. Workforce Safety and Insurance
Chapter 65-05. Claims and Compensation
65-05-12.2 Permanent impairment—Compensation—Time paid.

A permanent impairment is not intended to be a periodic payment and is not intended to reimburse the employee for specific expenses related to the injury or wage loss. If a compensable injury causes permanent impairment, the organization shall determine a permanent impairment award on the following terms:

. . .

6. A doctor evaluating permanent impairment shall include a clinical report in sufficient detail to support the percentage ratings assigned. The organization shall adopt administrative rules governing the evaluation of permanent impairment. These rules must

incorporate principles and practices of the fifth edition of the American medical association's "Guides to the Evaluation of Permanent Impairment" modified to be consistent with North Dakota law, to resolve issues of practice and interpretation, and to address areas not sufficiently covered by the guides. Subject to rules adopted under this subsection, impairments must be evaluated under the fifth edition of the guides.

. . .

10. If the injury causes permanent impairment, the award must be determined based on the percentage of whole body impairment . . .

11.

. . .

The award for the amputation of more than one finger of one hand may not exceed an award for the amputation of a hand. The award for the amputation of more than one toe of one foot may not exceed an award for the amputation of a foot. If any of the amputations or losses set out in this subsection combine with other impairments for the same work-related injury or condition, the organization shall issue an impairment award based on the greater of the permanent impairment multiplier allowed for the combined rating established under the fifth edition of the American medical association's "Guides to the Evaluation of Permanent Impairment" or the permanent impairment multiplier set forth in this subsection.

12. If there is a medical dispute regarding the percentage of an injured employee's permanent impairment, all relevant medical evidence must be submitted to an independent doctor who has not treated the employee and who has not been consulted by the organization in relation to the injury upon which the impairment is based. The organization shall establish lists of doctors who are qualified by the doctor's training, experience, and area of practice to rate permanent impairments caused by various types of injuries. The organization shall define, by rule, the process by which the organization and the injured employee choose an independent doctor or doctors to review a disputed permanent impairment evaluation or rating. The decision of the independent doctor or doctors chosen under this process is presumptive evidence of the degree of permanent impairment of the employee which can only be rebutted by clear and convincing evidence. This subsection does not impose liability on the organization for an impairment award for a rating of impairment for a body part or condition the organization has not determined to be compensable as a result of the injury. The employee bears the expense of witness fees of the independent doctor or doctors if the employee disputes the findings of the independent doctor or doctors.

. . .

*****

North Dakota Administrative Code
Title 92. Workers Compensation Bureau
Article 92-01. General Administration
Chapter 92-01-02. Rules of Procedure—North Dakota Workers' Compensation Act
92-01-02-25. Permanent impairment evaluations and disputes.

1. Definitions:

. . .

c. "Medical dispute" means an employee has reached maximum medical improvement in connection with a work injury and has been evaluated for permanent impairment, and there is a disagreement between doctors arising from the evaluation that affects the amount of the award. It does not include disputes regarding proper interpretation or application of the American medical association guides to the evaluation of permanent impairment, fifth edition.

. . .

2. Permanent impairment evaluations must be performed in accordance with the American medical association guides to the evaluation of permanent impairment, fifth edition, and modified by this section. All permanent impairment reports must include the opinion of the doctor on the cause of the impairment and must contain an apportionment if the impairment is caused by both work-related and non-work-related injuries or conditions.

. . .

5. A permanent impairment award may not include a rating due solely to pain, including chronic pain; chronic pain syndrome; pain that is rated under section 13.8, table 13-22, or chapter 18 of the American medical association guides to the evaluation of permanent impairment, fifth edition; or pain beyond the pain associated with injuries and illnesses of specific organ systems rated under other chapters of the fifth edition.

. . .

6. Permanent mental and behavioral disorder impairment ratings.

a. Any physician determining permanent mental or behavioral disorder impairment shall:

. . .

(2) Use the instructions contained in the American medical association guides to the evaluation of permanent impairment, fifth edition, giving specific attention to:

(a) Chapter 13, "central and peripheral nervous system"; and

(b) Chapter 14, "mental and behavioral disorders"; and

(3) Complete a full psychiatric assessment following the principles of the American medical association guides to the evaluation of permanent impairment, fifth edition, including:

(a) A nationally accepted and validated psychiatric diagnosis made according to established standards of the American psychiatric association as contemplated by the American medical association guides to the evaluation of permanent impairment, fifth edition; and

. . .

*****

North Dakota Administrative Code
Title 92. Workers Compensation Bureau
Article 92-01. General Administration
Chapter 92-01-02. Rules of Procedure—North Dakota Workers' Compensation Act,
Appendix A
Appendix A
Workforce Safety and Insurance
Permanent Mental Impairment Rating Report
Work Sheet

Since the AMA Guides to the Evaluation of Permanent Impairment, Fifth Edition, does not provide a quantified method for assigning permanent impairment percentages under

Chapter 14, "Mental and Behavioral Disorders," the evaluating physician shall utilize this form. When using this form, the evaluating physician shall:

a. Become familiar with the content of the work sheet and develop an understanding of the percentages and categories listed in "I. Level of Permanent Mental Impairment" and Table 14-1 of the AMA Guides to the Evaluation of Permanent Impairment, Fifth Edition;

. . .

d. All permanent impairment reports must include the cause of the impairment and must contain an apportionment if the impairment is caused by both work and non-work injuries or conditions. The various degrees of permanent impairment from "II. Areas of Function" on within this appendix are not added, combined, or averaged. The overall mental rating should be based upon clinical judgment and Table 14-1, and be consistent with other chapters of the AMA guides.

. . .

See full statute for a copy of the actual worksheet.

OKLAHOMA

Oklahoma Statutes Annotated
Title 85. Workers' Compensation
Chapter 1. Definition and General Provisions
§ 3. Definitions

As used in the Workers' Compensation Act:

. . .

19. "Permanent impairment" means any anatomical abnormality after maximum medical improvement has been achieved, which abnormality or loss the physician considers to be capable of being evaluated at the time the rating is made. Except as otherwise provided herein, any examining physician shall only evaluate impairment in accordance with the latest publication of the American Medical Association's "Guides to the Evaluation of Permanent Impairment" in effect at the time of the injury. The Physician Advisory Committee may, pursuant to Section 201.1 of this title, recommend the adoption of a method or system to evaluate permanent impairment that shall be used in place of or in combination with the American Medical Association's "Guides to the Evaluation of Permanent Impairment." Such recommendation shall be made to the Administrator of the Workers' Compensation Court who may adopt the recommendation in part or in whole. The adopted method or system shall be submitted by the Administrator to the Governor, the Speaker of the House of Representatives and the President Pro Tempore of the Senate within the first ten (10) legislative days of a regular session of the Legislature. Such method or system to evaluate permanent impairment that shall be used in place of or in combination with the American Medical Association's "Guides to the Evaluation of Permanent Impairment" shall be subject to disapproval in whole or in part by joint or concurrent resolution of the Legislature during the legislative session in which submitted. Such method or system shall be operative one hundred twenty (120) days after the last day of the month in which the Administrator submits the adopted method or system to the Legislature if the Legislature takes no action or one hundred twenty (120) days after the last day of the month in which

the Legislature disapproves it in part. If adopted, permanent impairment shall be evaluated only in accordance with the latest version of the alternative method or system in effect at the time of injury. Except as otherwise provided in Section 11 of this title, all evaluations shall include an apportionment of injury causation. However, revisions to the guides made by the American Medical Association which are published after January 1, 1989, and before January 1, 1995, shall be operative one hundred twenty (120) days after the last day of the month of publication. Revisions to the guides made by the American Medical Association which are published after December 31, 1994, may be adopted in whole or in part by the Administrator following recommendation by the Physician Advisory Committee. Revisions adopted by the Administrator shall be submitted by the Administrator to the Governor, the Speaker of the House of Representatives and the President Pro Tempore of the Senate within the first ten (10) legislative days of a regular session of the Legislature. Such revisions shall be subject to disapproval in whole or in part by joint or concurrent resolution of the Legislature during the legislative session in which submitted. Revisions shall be operative one hundred twenty (120) days after the last day of the month in which the Administrator submits the revisions to the Governor and the Legislature if the Legislature takes no action or one hundred twenty (120) days after the last day of the month in which the Legislature disapproves them in part. The examining physician shall not follow the guides based on race or ethnic origin. The examining physician shall not deviate from said guides or any alternative thereto except as may be specifically provided for in the guides or modifications to the guides or except as may be specifically provided for in any alternative or modifications thereto, adopted by the Administrator of the Workers' Compensation Court as provided for in Section 201.1 of this title. These officially adopted guides or modifications thereto or alternative system or method of evaluating permanent impairment or modifications thereto shall be the exclusive basis for testimony and conclusions with regard to permanent impairment with the exception of paragraph 3 of Section 22 of this title, relating to scheduled member injury or loss; and impairment, including pain or loss of strength, may be awarded with respect to those injuries or areas of the body not specifically covered by said guides or alternative to said guides. All evaluations of permanent impairment must be supported by objective medical evidence;

20. "Permanent total disability" means incapacity because of accidental injury or occupational disease to earn any wages in any employment for which the employee may become physically suited and reasonably fitted by education, training or experience, including vocational rehabilitation; loss of both hands, or both feet, or both legs, or both eyes, or any two thereof, shall constitute permanent total disability;

21. "Permanent partial disability" means permanent disability which is less than total and shall be equal to or the same as permanent impairment;

. . .

*****

Oklahoma Statutes Annotated
Title 85. Workers' Compensation
Chapter 2. Compensation for Injuries, Basis, Schedules and Claims for Compensation
§ 85-22. Schedule of compensation

The following schedule of compensation is hereby established:

. . .

3. Permanent Partial Disability. (a) With respect to injuries occurring prior to November 4, 1994, in case of disability, partial in character but permanent in quality,

the compensation shall be seventy percent (70%) of the employee's average weekly wages, and shall be paid to the employee for the period named in the schedule, as follows:

. . .

Deafness: Deafness from industrial cause, including occupations which are hazardous to hearing, accident or sudden trauma, three hundred (300) weeks, and total deafness of one ear from industrial cause, including occupations which are hazardous to hearing, accident or sudden trauma, one hundred (100) weeks. Except as otherwise provided herein, any examining physician shall only evaluate deafness or hearing impairment in accordance with the latest publication of the American Medical Association's "Guides to the Evaluation of Permanent Impairment" in effect at the time of the injury. The Physician Advisory Committee may, pursuant to Section 201.1 of this title, recommend the adoption of a method or system to evaluate permanent impairment that shall be used in place of or in combination with the American Medical Association's "Guides to the Evaluation of Permanent Impairment." Such recommendation shall be made to the Administrator of the Workers' Compensation Court who may adopt the recommendation in part or in whole. The adopted method or system shall be submitted by the Administrator to the Governor, the Speaker of the House of Representatives and President Pro Tempore of the Senate within the first ten (10) legislative days of a regular session of the Legislature. Such method or system to evaluate permanent impairment that shall be used in place of or in combination with the American Medical Association's "Guides to the Evaluation of Permanent Impairment" shall be subject to disapproval in whole or in part by joint or concurrent resolution of the Legislature during the legislative session in which submitted. Such method or system shall be operative one hundred twenty (120) days after the last day of the month in which the Administrator submits the adopted method or system to the Legislature if the Legislature takes no action or one hundred twenty (120) days after the last day of the month in which the Legislature disapproves it in part. If adopted, permanent impairment shall be evaluated only in accordance with the latest version of the alternative method or system in effect at the time of injury. Except as otherwise provided in Section 11 of this title, all evaluations shall include an apportionment of injury causation. However, revisions to the guides made by the American Medical Association which are published after January 1, 1989, and before January 1, 1995, shall be operative one hundred twenty (120) days after the last day of the month of publication. Revisions to the guides made by the American Medical Association which are published after December 31, 1994, may be adopted in whole or in part by the Administrator following recommendation by the Physician Advisory Committee. Revisions adopted by the Administrator shall be submitted by the Administrator to the Governor, the Speaker of the House of Representatives and President Pro Tempore of the Senate within the first ten (10) legislative days of a regular session of the Legislature. Such revisions shall be subject to disapproval in whole or in part by joint or concurrent resolution of the Legislature during the legislative session in which submitted. Revisions shall be operative one hundred twenty (120) days after the last day of the month in which the Administrator submits the revisions to the Legislature if the Legislature takes no action or one hundred twenty (120) days after the last day of the month in which the Legislature disapproves them in part. The examining physician shall not follow the guides based on race or ethnic origin. The examining physician shall not deviate from said guides or any alternative thereof except as may be specifically provided for in the guides or modifications to the guides or except as may be specifically provided for in any alternative or modifications thereto adopted by the Administrator of the Workers' Compensation Court as provided for in Section 201.1 of this title. The guides or modifications thereto or alternative system or method of evaluating permanent impairment or modifications thereto shall be the exclusive basis for testimony and conclusions with regard to deafness or hearing impairment.

. . .

(c) With respect to injuries occurring on or after January 1, 2002, through December 31, 2002, in case of disability, partial in character but permanent in quality, the compensation shall be seventy percent (70%) of the employee's average weekly wages, and shall be paid to the employee for the period prescribed by the following schedule:

Deafness: Deafness from industrial cause, including occupations which are hazardous to hearing, accident or sudden trauma, three hundred fifteen (315) weeks, and total deafness of one ear from industrial cause, including occupations which are hazardous to hearing, accident or sudden trauma, one hundred five (105) weeks. Except as otherwise provided herein, any examining physician shall only evaluate deafness or hearing impairment in accordance with the latest publication of the American Medical Association's "Guides to the Evaluation of Permanent Impairment" in effect at the time of the injury. The Physician Advisory Committee may, pursuant to Section 201.1 of this title, recommend the adoption of a method or system to evaluate permanent impairment that shall be used in place of or in combination with the American Medical Association's "Guides to the Evaluation of Permanent Impairment." Such recommendation shall be made to the Administrator of the Workers' Compensation Court who may adopt the recommendation in part or in whole. The adopted method or system shall be submitted by the Administrator to the Governor, the Speaker of the House of Representatives and President Pro Tempore of the Senate within the first ten (10) legislative days of a regular session of the Legislature. Such method or system to evaluate permanent impairment that shall be used in place of or in combination with the American Medical Association's "Guides to the Evaluation of Permanent Impairment" shall be subject to disapproval in whole or in part by joint or concurrent resolution of the Legislature during the legislative session in which submitted. Such method or system shall be operative one hundred twenty (120) days after the last day of the month in which the Administrator submits the adopted method or system to the Legislature if the Legislature takes no action or one hundred twenty (120) days after the last day of the month in which the Legislature disapproves it in part. If adopted, permanent impairment shall be evaluated only in accordance with the latest version of the alternative method or system in effect at the time of injury. Except as otherwise provided in Section 11 of this title, all evaluations shall include an apportionment of injury causation. However, revisions to the guides made by the American Medical Association which are published after January 1, 1989, and before January 1, 1995, shall be operative one hundred twenty (120) days after the last day of the month of publication. Revisions to the guides made by the American Medical Association which are published after December 31, 1994, may be adopted in whole or in part by the Administrator following recommendation by the Physician Advisory Committee. Revisions adopted by the Administrator shall be submitted by the Administrator to the Governor, the Speaker of the House of Representatives and President Pro Tempore of the Senate within the first ten (10) legislative days of a regular session of the Legislature. Such revisions shall be subject to disapproval in whole or in part by joint or concurrent resolution of the Legislature during the legislative session in which submitted. Revisions shall be operative one hundred twenty (120) days after the last day of the month in which the Administrator submits the revisions to the Legislature if the Legislature takes no action or one hundred twenty (120) days after the last day of the month in which the Legislature disapproves them in part. The examining physician shall not follow the guides based on race or ethnic origin. The examining physician shall not deviate from such guides or any alternative thereof except as may be specifically provided for in the guides or modifications to the guides or except as may be specifically provided for in any alternative or modifications thereto adopted by the Administrator of the Workers' Compensation Court as provided in Section 201.1 of this title. The guides or modifications thereto or alternative system or method of evaluating permanent impairment or modifications thereto shall be the exclusive basis for testimony and conclusions with regard to deafness or hearing impairment.

. . .

(d) With respect to injuries occurring on or after January 1, 2003, in case of disability, partial in character but permanent in quality, the compensation shall be seventy percent (70%) of the employee's average weekly wages, and shall be paid to the employee for the period prescribed by the following schedule:

Deafness: Deafness from industrial cause, including occupations which are hazardous to hearing, accident or sudden trauma, three hundred thirty (330) weeks, and total deafness of one ear from industrial cause, including occupations which are hazardous to hearing, accident or sudden trauma, one hundred ten (110) weeks. Except as otherwise provided herein, any examining physician shall only evaluate deafness or hearing impairment in accordance with the latest publication of the American Medical Association's "Guides to the Evaluation of Permanent Impairment" in effect at the time of the injury. The Physician Advisory Committee may, pursuant to Section 201.1 of this title, recommend the adoption of a method or system to evaluate permanent impairment that shall be used in place of or in combination with the American Medical Association's "Guides to the Evaluation of Permanent Impairment." Such recommendation shall be made to the Administrator of the Workers' Compensation Court who may adopt the recommendation in part or in whole. The adopted method or system shall be submitted by the Administrator to the Governor, the Speaker of the House of Representatives and President Pro Tempore of the Senate within the first ten (10) legislative days of a regular session of the Legislature. Such method or system to evaluate permanent impairment that shall be used in place of or in combination with the American Medical Association's "Guides to the Evaluation of Permanent Impairment" shall be subject to disapproval in whole or in part by joint or concurrent resolution of the Legislature during the legislative session in which submitted. Such method or system shall be operative one hundred twenty (120) days after the last day of the month in which the Administrator submits the adopted method or system to the Legislature if the Legislature takes no action or one hundred twenty (120) days after the last day of the month in which the Legislature disapproves it in part. If adopted, permanent impairment shall be evaluated only in accordance with the latest version of the alternative method or system in effect at the time of injury. Except as otherwise provided in Section 11 of this title, all evaluations shall include an apportionment of injury causation. However, revisions to the guides made by the American Medical Association which are published after January 1, 1989, and before January 1, 1995, shall be operative one hundred twenty (120) days after the last day of the month of publication. Revisions to the guides made by the American Medical Association which are published after December 31, 1994, may be adopted in whole or in part by the Administrator following recommendation by the Physician Advisory Committee. Revisions adopted by the Administrator shall be submitted by the Administrator to the Governor, the Speaker of the House of Representatives and President Pro Tempore of the Senate within the first ten (10) legislative days of a regular session of the Legislature. Such revisions shall be subject to disapproval in whole or in part by joint or concurrent resolution of the Legislature during the legislative session in which submitted. Revisions shall be operative one hundred twenty (120) days after the last day of the month in which the Administrator submits the revisions to the Legislature if the Legislature takes no action or one hundred twenty (120) days after the last day of the month in which the Legislature disapproves them in part. The examining physician shall not follow the guides based on race or ethnic origin. The examining physician shall not deviate from such guides or any alternative thereof except as may be specifically provided for in the guides or modifications to the guides or except as may be specifically provided for in any alternative or modifications thereto adopted by the Administrator of the Workers' Compensation Court as provided in Section 201.1 of this title. The guides or modifications thereto or alternative system or method of evaluating permanent impairment or modifications thereto shall be the exclusive basis for testimony and conclusions with regard to deafness or hearing impairment.

. . .

*****

Oklahoma Statutes Annotated
Title 85. Workers' Compensation
Chapter 9. Abusive Practices
§ 201.1. Physician Advisory Committee

. . .

B. The Committee shall:

. . .

3. After public hearing, review and make recommendations for acceptable deviations from the American Medical Association's "Guides to the Evaluation of Permanent Impairment" using appropriate and scientifically valid data. Those recommendations may be adopted, in part or in whole, by the Administrator to be used as provided for in paragraph 11 of Section 3 and Section 22 of this title;

4. After public hearing, review and make recommendations for an alternative method or system to evaluate permanent impairment that shall be used in place of or in combination with the American Medical Association's "Guides to the Evaluation of Permanent Impairment." Appropriate and scientific data shall be considered. The alternative method or system to evaluate permanent impairment may be adopted, in part or in whole, by the Administrator to be used as provided for in paragraph 11 of Section 3 and Section 22 of this title. Revisions, deviations and alternatives to the American Medical Association's "Guides to the Evaluation of Permanent Impairment" shall become effective as provided in paragraph 11 of Section 3 and Section 22 of this title;

. . .

*****

Oklahoma Statutes Annotated
Title 85. Workers' Compensation
Chapter 4—Appendix. Rules of the Workers' Compensation Court
Appendix A. Text of Former Rule 37
Rule 37. Hearing impairment

The following criteria for measuring and calculating monaural and binaural hearing impairment has been prepared by the Workers' Compensation Court from information provided by the American Academy of Ophthalmology and Otolaryngology, the 1977 edition of the American Medical Association's "Guides to the Evaluation of Permanent Impairment" and local physicians. The Court is grateful for the use of this material and such assistance.

The Workers' Compensation Act provides, in 85 O.S. § 22(3), that hearing impairment is a scheduled member loss and specific provision is made for compensating binaural hearing impairment. That Section states that deafness in one ear shall be based upon the claimant's percentage of monaural hearing impairment multiplied by 100 weeks of compensation; while deafness in both ears shall be based upon the claimant's percentage of binaural hearing impairment multiplied by 300 weeks of compensation. Therefore, any computation or conversion either of monaural or binaural hearing impairment to the whole man (as done by the "Guides") is clearly incorrect according to Oklahoma law.

In using these criteria, certain abbreviations and definitions should be kept in mind.

. . .

4. Estimated hearing level for speech is the simple average of hearing levels at five frequencies, 500, 1,000, 2,000, 3,000 and 4,000 Hz. Note that this method includes the hearing level at 3,000 and 4,000 Hz which were not included in the 1977 edition of the "Guides." Therefore, the tables on pages 105 and 106 of the "Guides" cannot be used.

. . .

TO DETERMINE HEARING IMPAIRMENT

. . .

2. As previously noted, the tables in the "Guides" cannot be used because they do not use a decibel loss at 3,000 Hz and 4,000 Hz. Therefore, the Court has adopted the original mathematical formula used by the "Guides" but has modified it only so as to reflect the measurement of hearing at five levels rather than three. That formula is as follows:

. . .

*****

Oklahoma Statutes Annotated
Title 85. Workers' Compensation
Chapter 4—Appendix. Rules of the Workers' Compensation Court
Rule 21. AMA Guides

A. Except as provided in Rules 22 and 23, a physician's evaluation of the extent of permanent impairment shall be prepared in compliance with the appropriate edition of the AMA Guides to the Evaluation of Permanent Impairment, including approved deviations and exceptions to the Guides in effect on the date of injury, as set forth in this rule.

B. The Third Edition of the AMA Guides shall be used to rate permanent impairment as a result of injuries occurring on or after January 1, 1989.

C. The Third Edition Revised of the AMA Guides shall be used to rate permanent impairment as a result of injuries occurring on or after May 1, 1991.

D. The Fourth Edition of the AMA Guides shall be used to rate permanent impairment as a result of injuries occurring on or after November 1, 1993. When applicable, the 4th Edition of the Guides shall apply to examinations conducted through June 19, 1994.

E. The 4th Edition of the Guides with the following deviation shall apply to all examinations conducted on or after June 20, 1994: When determining spinal impairment, a physician shall not utilize the Injury or Diagnosis Related Estimates (DRE) models, including the DRE Tables, as set forth in Chapter Three, "The Musculoskeletal System."

F. The 5th Edition of the Guides, except for the Diagnosis-Related Estimates (DRE) Method and the DRE tables set forth in Chapter 15, "The Spine," shall be used to rate permanent impairment as a result of injuries occurring on or after June 28, 2001.

G. The examining physician shall not follow the guides based on race or ethnic origin.

H. The provisions of subsections A, B, C, D, E, F and G of this rule shall not apply to scheduled members enumerated in 85 O.S., Section 22.

I. Injuries occurring prior to January 1, 1989 are to be evaluated by the following editions of the Guides:

Injuries occurring prior to July 1, 1978 are to be evaluated based upon the claimant's ability to perform "ordinary manual labor."

Injuries occurring on or after July 1, 1978 through October 31, 1984—First Edition.

Injuries occurring on or after November 1, 1984 through December 31, 1988—Second Edition.

J. Evaluations of permanent impairment which are prepared in support of a Motion for Change of Condition shall be performed in compliance with the edition of the AMA Guides, including approved deviations and exceptions thereto, in effect on the date of injury.

******

Oklahoma Statutes Annotated
Title 85. Workers' Compensation
Chapter 4—Appendix. Rules of the Workers' Compensation Court
Rule 22. Hearing impairment

A. The "Guides to the Evaluation of Permanent Impairment" of the American Medical Association shall be used to evaluate permanent impairment caused by hearing loss where the last exposure occurred on or after June 1, 1987. Prior to that date, former "Rule 37," as set out in Appendix "A" to the Court Rules shall be used to evaluate hearing loss.

B. Hearing loss in only one ear shall be rated under the AMA Guides as a monaural hearing loss. Hearing loss in both ears shall be rated under the AMA Guides as a binaural hearing loss and shall not be converted to a whole person rating.

*****

Oklahoma Statutes Annotated
Title 85. Workers' Compensation
Chapter 4—Appendix. Rules of the Workers' Compensation Court
Rule 23. Eye impairment

The State Industrial Court previously published the Snellen Chart as the criteria for measuring and calculating the percentage of eye impairment in a single eye. This method of rating eye injuries has been accepted and approved by the Ophthalmological Section of the American Medical Association. Physicians may continue to use these criteria in the future. The Workers' Compensation Act provides, in 85 O.S., Section 22(3), that eye impairment is a scheduled member loss. That section states that loss of an eye shall be compensated by the payment of a specified number of weeks of permanent partial disability benefits. However, industrial blindness, in both eyes, according to 85 O.S., Section 3(20), means the claimant is permanently and totally disabled by statutory definition regardless of claimant's capacity to earn any wages in any occupation. Therefore, any computation or conversion of any loss of vision in one eye into the whole man (as done by the American Medical Association's "Guides to the Evaluation of Permanent Impairment") is clearly incorrect according to Oklahoma law. However, partial loss of vision in both eyes may be combined into the whole man provided that the physician states the evaluation of the loss of each eye separately and then evaluates the combination.

The physician should consult with the "Guides" regarding the equipment necessary to test the function of eyes and for the methods of evaluation. The following Snellen Chart may then be used for computing the percentage of visual efficiency. It should be noted that all measurements shall be based upon uncorrected vision.

. . .

OREGON

Oregon Administrative Rules Compilation
Chapter 125. Department of Administrative Services
Division 160. Administration and Benefits of the Inmate Injury System
125-160-0010 Definitions

. . .

(15) "Disability rating" means the attending physician's determination from objective medical findings of claimant's percent of permanent disability due solely to the covered injury. The rating shall conform to the following:

(a) If the claimant has no pre-existing disabilities or disability awards, the disability rating shall be the claimant's permanent impairment. It shall be found according to the 3rd Revised, or later, edition of the AMA Guides to the Evaluation of Permanent Impairment. The physician shall identify the edition used. The disability rating shall be expressed as a percentage of a whole person. If more than one organ system is rated, the percentage of impairment of the whole person shall be combined using the combined values chart in the AMA Guides.

(b) If the claimant has pre-existing disabilities or disability awards, the maximum disability from all sources and causes shall not exceed 100 percent. The Department or the physician shall combine the current disability rating for the covered injury with all prior disabilities and disability awards from any source. The combined values chart in the AMA Guides shall be used. If the combined disability rating exceeds 100 percent, the disability rating for the covered injury shall be reduced to lower the total to 100 percent. The Department shall convert a disability award from any other system to an impairment rating of a whole person when necessary.

******

Oregon Administrative Rules Compilation
Chapter 436. Department of Consumer and Business Services, Workers'
Compensation Division
Division 35. Disability Rating Standards
436-035-0007 General Principles

. . .

(10) Except as otherwise required by these rules, methods used by the examiner for making findings of impairment are the methods described in the AMA Guides to the Evaluation of Permanent Impairment, 3rd Ed., Rev. 1990, and are reported by the physician in the form and format required by these rules.

(11) Range of motion is measured using the goniometer as described in the AMA Guides to the Evaluation of Permanent Impairment, 3rd Edition (Revised), 1990, except when measuring spinal range of motion; then an inclinometer must be used.

(12) Validity is established for findings of impairment according to the criteria noted in the AMA Guides to the Evaluation of Permanent Impairment, 3rd Ed., Rev., 1990, unless the validity criteria for a particular finding is not addressed in this reference, is not pertinent to these rules, or is determined by physician opinion to be medically inappropriate for a particular worker. Upon examination, findings of impairment which are determined to be ratable under these rules are rated unless the physician determines the findings are invalid and provides a written opinion, based on sound medical principles, explaining why the findings are invalid. When findings are determined invalid, the findings receive a value of zero. If the validity criteria are not met but the physician determines the findings are valid, the physician must provide a written rationale, based on sound medical principles, explaining why the findings are valid. For purposes of this rule, the straight leg raising validity test (SLR) is not the sole criterion used to invalidate lumbar range of motion findings.

. . .

*****

Oregon Administrative Rules Compilation
Chapter 436. Department of Consumer and Business Services, Workers'
Compensation Division
Division 35. Disability Rating Standards
436-035-0011 Determining Percent of Impairment

. . .

(6) Except as otherwise noted in these rules, impairment values to a given body part, area, or system are combined according to the method outlined on pages 254–256 by the

AMA Guides to the Evaluation of Permanent Impairment, 3rd Ed. (Revised), 1990, as follows:

. . .

(7) To determine impairment due to loss of strength, the 0 to 5 international grading system and 0 to 5 method as noted in the AMA Guides to the Evaluation of Permanent Impairment, 3rd Ed. Revised, 1990 are used. The grade of strength is reported by the physician and assigned a percentage value from the table in subsection (a) of this section. The impairment value of the involved nerve is multiplied by this value. Grades identified as "++" or "−−" are considered either a "+" or "−", respectively.

. . .

(b) When a physician reports a loss of strength with muscle action (e.g. flexion, extension, etc.) or when only the affected muscle(s) is identified, current anatomy texts or the AMA Guides to the Evaluation of Permanent Impairment, 3rd Ed. (Revised), 1990, the 4th Ed., 1993, or the 5th Ed., 2001, may be referenced to identify the specific muscle(s), peripheral nerve(s) or spinal nerve root(s) involved.

. . .

*****

Oregon Administrative Rules Compilation
Chapter 436. Department of Consumer and Business Services, Workers'
Compensation Division
Division 35. Disability Rating Standards
436-035-0110 Other Upper Extremity Findings

(1) Loss of palmar sensation in the hand, finger(s), or thumb is rated according to the location and quality of the loss, and is measured by the two point discrimination method, as noted by the AMA Guides, 3rd Ed. Rev., 1990.

. . .

PENNSYLVANIA

Purdon's Pennsylvania Statutes and Consolidated Statutes
Title 77 P.S. Workers' Compensation
Chapter 1. Interpretation and Definitions
Definitions § 25.5. Impairment Guides

The term "Impairment Guides," as used in this act, means the American Medical Association's Guides to the Evaluation of Permanent Impairment, Fourth Edition (June 1993).

*****

Purdon's Pennsylvania Statutes and Consolidated Statutes
Title 77 P.S. Workers' Compensation
Chapter 5. Liability and Compensation
Schedules of Compensation
§ 511.2. Medical examination; impairment rating

(1) When an employee has received total disability compensation pursuant to clause (a) [FN1] for a period of one hundred four weeks, unless otherwise agreed to, the employee

shall be required to submit to a medical examination which shall be requested by the insurer within sixty days upon the expiration of the one hundred four weeks to determine the degree of impairment due to the compensable injury, if any. The degree of impairment shall be determined based upon an evaluation by a physician who is licensed in this Commonwealth, who is certified by an American Board of Medical Specialties approved board or its osteopathic equivalent and who is active in clinical practice for at least twenty hours per week, chosen by agreement of the parties, or as designated by the department, pursuant to the most recent edition of the American Medical Association "Guides to the Evaluation of Permanent Impairment."

(2) If such determination results in an impairment rating that meets a threshold impairment rating that is equal to or greater than fifty per centum impairment under the most recent edition of the American Medical Association "Guides to the Evaluation of Permanent Impairment," the employee shall be presumed to be totally disabled and shall continue to receive total disability compensation benefits under clause (a). If such determination results in an impairment rating less than fifty per centum impairment under the most recent edition of the American Medical Association "Guides to the Evaluation of Permanent Impairment," the employee shall then receive partial disability benefits under clause (b): [FN2] Provided, however, That no reduction shall be made until sixty days' notice of modification is given.

. . .

(4) An employee may appeal the change to partial disability at any time during the five hundred-week period of partial disability; Provided, That there is a determination that the employee meets the threshold impairment rating that is equal to or greater than fifty per centum impairment under the most recent edition of the American Medical Association "Guides to the Evaluation of Permanent Impairment."

(5) Total disability shall continue until it is adjudicated or agreed under clause (b) that total disability has ceased or the employee's condition improves to an impairment rating that is less than fifty per centum of the degree of impairment defined under the most recent edition of the American Medical Association "Guides to the Evaluation of Permanent Impairment."

. . .

(7) In no event shall the total number of weeks of partial disability exceed five hundred weeks for any injury or recurrence thereof, regardless of the changes in status in disability that may occur. In no event shall the total number of weeks of total disability exceed one hundred four weeks for any employee who does not meet a threshold impairment rating that is equal to or greater than fifty per centum impairment under the most recent edition of the American Medical Association "Guides to the Evaluation of Permanent Impairment" for any injury or recurrence thereof.

(8)(i) For purposes of this clause, the term "impairment" shall mean an anatomic or functional abnormality or loss that results from the compensable injury and is reasonably presumed to be permanent.

(ii) For purposes of this clause, the term "impairment rating" shall mean the percentage of permanent impairment of the whole body resulting from the compensable injury. The percentage rating for impairment under this clause shall represent only that impairment that is the result of the compensable injury and not for any preexisting work-related or nonwork-related impairment.

******

Purdon's Pennsylvania Statutes and Consolidated Statutes
Title 77 P.S. Workers' Compensation
Chapter 5. Liability and Compensation
Schedules of Compensation
§ 513. The following schedule of compensation is hereby established:

For all disability resulting from permanent injuries of the following classes, the compensation shall be exclusively as follows:

. . .

(8)(i) For permanent loss of hearing which is medically established as an occupational hearing loss caused by long-term exposure to hazardous occupational noise, the percentage of impairment shall be calculated by using the binaural formula provided in the Impairment Guides. The number of weeks for which compensation shall be payable shall be determined by multiplying the percentage of binaural hearing impairment as calculated under the Impairment Guides by two hundred sixty weeks. Compensation payable shall be sixty-six and two-thirds per centum of wages during this number of weeks, subject to the provisions of clause (1) of subsection (a) of this section.

(ii) For permanent loss of hearing not caused by long-term exposure to hazardous occupational noise which is medically established to be due to other occupational causes such as acoustic trauma or head injury, the percentage of hearing impairment shall be calculated by using the formulas as provided in the Impairment Guides. The number of weeks for which compensation shall be payable for such loss of hearing in one ear shall be determined by multiplying the percentage of impairment by sixty weeks. The number of weeks for which compensation shall be payable for such loss of hearing in both ears shall be determined by multiplying the percentage of impairment by two hundred sixty weeks. Compensation payable shall be sixty-six and two-thirds per centum of wages during this number of weeks, subject to the provisions of clause (1) of subsection (a) of this section.

(iii) Notwithstanding the provisions of subclauses (i) and (ii) of this clause, if there is a level of binaural hearing impairment as calculated under the Impairment Guides which is equal to or less than ten per centum, no benefits shall be payable. Notwithstanding the provisions of subclauses (i) and (ii) of this clause, if there is a level of binaural hearing impairment as calculated under the Impairment Guides which is equal to or more than seventy-five per centum, there shall be a presumption that the hearing impairment is total and complete, and benefits shall be payable for two hundred sixty weeks.

. . .

*****

Pennsylvania Administrative Code
Title 34. Labor and Industry
Part VIII. Bureau of Workers' Compensation
Chapter 123. General Provisions—Part II
Subchapter B. Impairment Ratings
§ 123.103. Physicians.

. . .

(d) In addition to the requirements of subsections (a) and (b), physicians designated by the Department to perform IREs shall meet training and certification requirements which may include, but are not limited to, one or more of the following:

(1) Required attendance at a Departmentally approved training course on the performance of evaluations under the AMA "Guides to the Evaluation of Permanent Impairment."

(2) Certification upon passage of a Departmentally approved examination on the AMA "Guides to the Evaluation of Permanent Impairment."

. . .

*****

Pennsylvania Administrative Code
Title 34. Labor and Industry
Part VIII. Bureau of Workers' Compensation
Chapter 123. General Provisions—Part II
Subchapter B. Impairment Ratings
§ 123.105. Impairment rating determination.

(a) When properly requested under § 123.102 (relating to IRE requests), an IRE shall be conducted in all cases and an impairment rating determination must result under the most recent edition of the AMA "Guides to the Evaluation of Permanent Impairment."

(b) To ascertain an accurate percentage of the employee's whole body impairment, when the evaluating physician determines that the compensable injury incorporates more than one pathology, the evaluating physician may refer the employee to one or more physicians specializing in the specific pathologies which constitute the compensable injury. Any physician chosen by the evaluating physician to assist in ascertaining the percentage of whole body impairment shall possess the qualifications as specified in § 123.103(a) and (b) (relating to physicians). The referring physician remains responsible for determining the whole body impairment rating of the employee.

(c) The physician performing the IRE shall complete Form LIBC-767, "Impairment Rating Determination Face Sheet" (Face Sheet), which sets forth the impairment rating of the compensable injury. The physician shall attach to the Face Sheet the "Report of Medical Evaluation" as specified in the AMA "Guides to the Evaluation of Permanent Impairment." The Face Sheet and report shall be provided to the employee, employee's counsel, if known, insurer and the Department within 30 days from the date of the impairment evaluation.

. . .

RHODE ISLAND

West's General Law of Rhode Island Annotated
Title 28. Labor and Labor Relations
Chapter 29. Workers' Compensation—General Provisions
§ 28-29-2. Definitions

In chapters 29–38 of this title, unless the context otherwise requires:

. . .

[(3)](ii) As used under the provisions of this title, "functional impairment" means an anatomical or functional abnormality existing after the date of maximum medical improvement as determined by a medically or scientifically demonstrable finding and based upon the most recent edition of the American Medical Association's Guide to the Evaluation of Permanent Impairment or comparable publications of the American Medical Association.

*****

West's General Laws of Rhode Island Annotated
Title 28. Labor and Labor Relations
Chapter 33. Workers' Compensation—Benefits
§ 28-33-18. Weekly compensation for partial incapacity

. . .

(c)(1) Earnings capacity determined from degree of functional impairment pursuant to § 28-29-2(3) shall be determined as a percentage of the whole person based on the most recent addition [sic] of the American Medical Association Guides To The Value [sic] Of Permanent Impairment.

. . .

SOUTH CAROLINA

Code of Laws of South Carolina 1976, Annotated Regulations
Chapter 67. South Carolina Workers' Compensation Commission
Article 11. Scheduled Losses
67-1101. Total or Partial Loss or Loss of Use of a Member, Organ, or Part of the Body.

. . .

B. This schedule of organs, members, and bodily parts lists prominent parts of the anatomy subject to occupational injury and is not complete. The value of an organ, member, or bodily part not included may be determined in accordance with the American Medical Association's "Guide to the Evaluation of Permanent Impairment," or any other accepted medical treatise or authority. Compensation shall be payable for total loss, permanent partial loss, or loss of use of a member, organ, or part of the body when compensation is not otherwise payable.

. . .

*****

Code of Laws of South Carolina 1976, Annotated Regulations
Chapter 67. South Carolina Workers' Compensation Commission
Article 11. Scheduled Losses
67-1102. Loss of Hearing.

A. The method for determining hearing impairment is based on the American Academy of Otolaryngology "Guide for Evaluation of Hearing Handicap," copyright 1979, which is based upon the American Medical Association's "Guides to the Evaluation of Permanent Impairment," copyright 1977.

. . .

*****

Code of Laws of South Carolina 1976, Annotated Regulations
Chapter 67. South Carolina Workers' Compensation Commission
Article 11. Scheduled Losses
67-1105. Loss of Vision.

. . .

B. The following table, derived from the Snellen Notation, is used to determine the percentage of impairment to vision. The physician also may rely upon the American Medical Association's "Guide to the Evaluation of Permanent Impairment" and any other accepted medical authority or treatise in deriving an impairment rating.

. . .

SOUTH DAKOTA

South Dakota Codified Laws
Title 62. Workers' Compensation
Chapter 62-1. Definitions and General Provisions
62-1-1.2. Impairment defined

For the purposes of this chapter, impairment shall be determined by a medical impairment rating, expressed as a percentage to the affected body part, using the Guides to the Evaluation of Permanent Impairment established by the American Medical Association, fourth edition, June 1993.

South Dakota Codified Laws
Title 62. Workers' Compensation
Chapter 62-7. Claims Procedure
62-7-39. Determining partial or permanent total disability compensation

An employee, employer, employer's insurer, or self-insured employer shall be permitted to use the results of post-offer base line testing or a functional capacity assessment, as utilized by Guidelines to the Evaluation of Permanent Impairment established by the American Medical Association, fourth edition, June 1993, performed during the course of employment, or other medical evidence of impairment for the purpose of determining permanent partial or permanent total disability compensation due to an employee.

TENNESSEE

West's Tennessee Code Annotated
Title 50. Employer and Employee
Chapter 6. Workers' Compensation
Part I—General Provisions
§ 50-6-102. Definitions

As used in this chapter, unless the context otherwise requires:

. . .

(2) "AMA Guides" means the most recent edition of the American Medical Association Guides to the Evaluation of Permanent Impairment, American Medical Association. In the event of a release of a new edition of the publication in a given year, the new edition shall be deemed to be the most recent edition on January 1 of the year following its release. The edition that is in effect on the date the employee is injured is the edition that shall be applicable to the claim;

. . .

*****

West's Tennessee Code Annotated
Title 50. Employer and Employee
Chapter 6. Workers' Compensation
Part 1—General Provisions
§ 50-6-133. Continuing education

It shall be the duty of the administrative office of the courts, in consultation with the advisory council on workers' compensation, to develop and provide appropriate continuing education programs on topics related to workers' compensation at each annual meeting. Such continuing education shall include both generalized applications of the provisions of this chapter and the use of the AMA Guides. The program shall also address any specific variances in the application of the provisions of this chapter throughout the state.

*****

West's Tennessee Code Annotated
Title 50. Employer and Employee
Chapter 6. Workers' Compensation
Part 2—Claims and Payment of Compensation
§ 50-6-204. Medical care and treatment; burial expenses; physical examinations

. . .

(3)(A) To provide uniformity and fairness for all parties in determining the degree of anatomical impairment sustained by the employee, a physician, chiropractor or medical practitioner who is permitted to give expert testimony in a Tennessee court of law and who has provided medical treatment to an employee or who has examined or evaluated an employee seeking workers' compensation benefits shall utilize the applicable edition of the AMA Guides as established in § 50-6-102 or in cases not covered by the AMA Guides an impairment rating by any appropriate method used and accepted by the medical community.

(B) No anatomical impairment or impairment rating, whether contained in a medical record, medical report, including a medical report pursuant to § 50-6-235(c), deposition or oral expert opinion testimony shall be accepted during a benefit review conference or be admissible into evidence at the trial of a workers' compensation matter unless the impairment is based on the applicable edition of the AMA Guides or in cases not covered by the AMA Guides an impairment rating by any appropriate method used and accepted by the medical community.

(C) The administrator of the division of workers' compensation shall determine the date on which the most recent edition of the AMA Guides became effective for purposes of this subdivision (d)(3) and the administrator shall maintain the full title of the most recent edition and the date it became effective on the division's website.

. . .

*****

West's Tennessee Code Annotated
Title 50. Employer and Employee
Chapter 6. Workers' Compensation
Part 2—Claims and Payment of Compensation
§ 50-6-241. Maximum permanent partial disability award; reconsideration of industrial disability

(a)(1) For injuries arising on or after August 1, 1992, and prior to July 1, 2004, in cases where an injured employee is eligible to receive any permanent partial disability benefits, pursuant to § 50-6-207(3)(A)(i) and (F), and the pre-injury employer returns the employee to employment at a wage equal to or greater than the wage the employee was receiving at the time of injury, the maximum permanent partial disability award that the employee may receive is two and one-half (2 ½) times the medical impairment rating determined pursuant to the provisions of the American Medical Association Guides to the Evaluation of Permanent Impairment (American Medical Association), the Manual for Orthopedic Surgeons in Evaluating Permanent Physical Impairment (American Academy of Orthopedic Surgeons), or in cases not covered by either of these, an impairment rating by any appropriate method used and accepted by the medical community. In making determinations, the court shall consider all pertinent factors, including lay and expert testimony, employee's age, education, skills and training, local job opportunities, and capacity to work at types of employment available in claimant's disabled condition.

(2) In accordance with this section, the courts may reconsider, upon the filing of a new cause of action, the issue of industrial disability. Such reconsideration shall examine all pertinent factors, including lay and expert testimony, employee's age, education, skills and training, local job opportunities, and capacity to work at types of employment available in claimant's disabled condition. Such reconsideration may be made in appropriate cases where the employee is no longer employed by the pre-injury employer and makes application to the appropriate court within one (1) year of the employee's loss of employment, if such loss of employment is within four hundred (400) weeks of the day the employee returned to work. In enlarging a previous award, the court must give the employer credit for prior benefits paid to the employee in permanent partial disability benefits, and any new award remains subject to the maximum established in subsection (b).

(b) Subject to the factors provided in subsection (a), in cases for injuries on or after August 1, 1992, and prior to July 1, 2004, where an injured employee is eligible to receive permanent partial disability benefits, pursuant to § 50-6-207(3)(A)(i) and (F), and the pre-injury employer does not return the employee to employment at a wage equal to or greater than the wage the employee was receiving at the time of injury, the maximum permanent partial disability award that the employee may receive is six (6) times the medical impairment rating determined pursuant to the provisions of the American Medical Association Guides to the Evaluation of Permanent Impairment (American Medical Association), the Manual for Orthopedic Surgeons in Evaluating Permanent Physical Impairment (American

Academy of Orthopedic Surgeons), or in cases not covered by either of these, an impairment rating by any appropriate method used and accepted by the medical community. In making such determinations, the court shall consider all pertinent factors, including lay and expert testimony, employee's age, education, skills and training, local job opportunities, and capacity to work at types of employment available in claimant's disabled condition.

. . .

*****

Tennessee Rules and Regulations
0800. Tennessee Department of Labor and Workforce Development
0800-2. Division of Workers' Compensation
Chapter 0800-2-20. Medical Impairment Rating Registry Program
0800-2-20-.02. Purpose and Scope.

(1) Purpose. The purpose of the Medical Impairment Rating Registry Program is to comply with and implement Tenn. Code Ann. § 50-6-204(d)(5) and (6) (Repl. 2005) by establishing a resource to resolve disputes regarding the degree of permanent medical impairment ratings for injuries or occupational diseases to which the Act is applicable. In order to ensure high-quality independent medical impairment evaluations, the Department establishes these Rules for parties and physicians. MIR Registry physicians shall provide evaluations in a manner consistent with the standard of care in their community and in compliance with these Rules, as well as issue opinions based upon the applicable edition of the AMA Guides to the Evaluation of Permanent Impairment or other appropriate method pursuant to the Act.

*****

Tennessee Rules and Regulations
0800. Tennessee Department of Labor and Workforce Development
0800-2. Division of Workers' Compensation
Chapter 0800-2-20. Medical Impairment Rating Registry Program
0800-2-20-.04. Requisite Physician Qualifications for Inclusion on Medical Impairment Rating Registry.

. . .

(c) Have successfully completed a training course, approved by the Commissioner, dedicated to the proper application of the applicable edition of the American Medical Association Guides to the Evaluation of Permanent Impairment (hereafter the "AMA Guides") in impairment evaluations and furnish satisfactory evidence thereof; and

. . .

*****

Tennessee Rules and Regulations
0800. Tennessee Department of Labor and Workforce Development
0800-2. Division of Workers' Compensation
Chapter 0800-2-20. Medical Impairment Rating Registry Program
0800-2-20-.05. Application Procedures for Physicians to Join the Registry.

. . .

(2) Physicians seeking appointment to the MIR Registry shall complete an "Application for Appointment to the MIR Registry," available upon request or on-line at

www.state.tn.us/labor-wfd/mainforms.html, certify to and, upon approval of the application, comply with the following conditions:

(a) Conduct all MIR evaluations based on the guidelines in the applicable edition of the AMA Guides and submit the original "MIR Impairment Rating Report" with all attachments to the Program Coordinator. In cases not covered by the applicable AMA Guides, any impairment rating allowed under the Act shall be appropriate;

. . .

*****

Tennessee Rules and Regulations
0800. Tennessee Department of Labor and Workforce Development
0800-2. Division of Workers' Compensation
Chapter 0800-2-20. Medical Impairment Rating Registry Program
0800-2-20-.07. Payments/Fees.

. . .

(2) The evaluation fee includes normal record review, the evaluation, and production of a standard "MIR Impairment Rating Report." All non-routine test(s) for an impairment rating essential under the applicable edition of the AMA Guides to the Evaluation of Permanent Impairment shall have been performed prior to the evaluation. Routine tests necessary for a complete evaluation, such as range of motion or spirometry tests, should be performed by the MIR Registry physician as part of the evaluation at no additional cost.

*****

Tennessee Rules and Regulations
0800. Tennessee Department of Labor and Workforce Development
0800-2. Division of Workers' Compensation
Chapter 0800-2-20. Medical Impairment Rating Registry Program
0800-2-20-.11. Requirements for the "MIR Impairment Rating Report."

. . .

(2) If, after reviewing the records, taking a history from the claimant and performing the evaluation, the MIR Registry physician concurs with the attending doctor's determination of MMI, the report shall, at a minimum, contain the following:

. . .

(d) An impairment rating consistent with the findings and utilizing a standard method as outlined in the applicable AMA Guides, calculated as a total to the whole person if appropriate. In cases not covered by the AMA Guides, an impairment rating by any appropriate method used and accepted by the medical community is allowed, however, a statement that the AMA Guides fails to cover the case as well as a statement of the system on which the rating was based shall be included;

(e) The rationale for the rating based on reasonable medical certainty, supported by specific references to the clinical findings, especially objective findings and supporting documentation including the specific rating system, sections, tables, figures, and AMA

Guides page numbers, when appropriate, to clearly show how the rating was derived; and

(f) A true or electronic signature and date by the MIR physician performing the evaluation certifying to the following:

1. "It is my opinion, both within and to a reasonable degree of medical certainty that, based upon all information available to me at the time of the MIR impairment evaluation and by utilizing the relevant AMA Guides or other appropriate method as noted above, the claimant has the permanent impairment so described in this report. I certify that the opinion furnished is my own, that this document accurately reflects my opinion, and that I am aware that my signature attests to its truthfulness. I further certify that my statement of qualifications to serve on the MIR Registry is both current and completely accurate."

. . .

*****

Tennessee Rules and Regulations
0800. Tennessee Department of Labor and Workforce Development
0800-2. Division of Workers' Compensation
Chapter 0800-2-20. Medical Impairment Rating Registry Program
0800-2-20-.12. Peer Review.

(1) All MIR Impairment Rating Reports are subject to review for appropriateness and accuracy by an individual or organization designated by the Commissioner at any time. Failure to properly apply the AMA Guides in determining an impairment rating, as determined by the Medical Director, may result in penalties up to and including removal from the MIR Registry

*****

Tennessee Rules and Regulations
0800. Tennessee Department of Labor and Workforce Development
0800-2. Division of Workers' Compensation
Chapter 0800-2-20. Medical Impairment Rating Registry Program
0800-2-20-.13. Removal of a Physician from the Registry.

(1) The Commissioner, upon the advice of the Medical Director, may remove a physician from the MIR Registry permanently or temporarily. In doing so, the Commissioner shall first notify the physician in writing that he or she is at risk of being removed from the MIR Registry. The procedures followed for removal under this section shall follow the same procedures as those set forth below in Rule 0800-2-20-.13(2) and (3). The Commissioner may remove a physician from the MIR Registry permanently or temporarily based upon any of the following grounds:

. . .

(c) Refusal or substantial failure to comply with the provisions of these Rules, including, but not limited to, failure to determine impairment ratings correctly using the AMA Guides, as determined by the Medical Director;

. . .

TEXAS

Vernon's Texas Statutes and Codes Annotated
Labor Code
Title 5. Workers' Compensation
Subtitle A. Texas Workers' Compensation Act
Chapter 408. Workers' Compensation Benefits
Subchapter G. Impairment Income Benefits
§ 408.124. Impairment Rating Guidelines

(a) An award of an impairment income benefit, whether by the commissioner or a court, must be based on an impairment rating determined using the impairment rating guidelines described by this section.

(b) For determining the existence and degree of an employee's impairment, the division shall use "Guides to the Evaluation of Permanent Impairment," third edition, second printing, dated February 1989, published by the American Medical Association.

(c) Notwithstanding Subsection (b), the commissioner by rule may adopt the fourth edition of the "Guides to the Evaluation of Permanent Impairment," published by the American Medical Association, or a subsequent edition of those guides, for determining the existence and degree of an employee's impairment.

*****

Texas Administrative Code
Title 28. Insurance
Part 2. Texas Department of Insurance, Division of Workers' Compensation
Chapter 130. Impairment and Supplemental Income Benefits
Subchapter A. Impairment Income Benefits
§ 130.1. Certification of Maximum Medical Improvement and Evaluation of
Permanent Impairment

(c) Assignment of Impairment Rating.

(1) An impairment rating is the percentage of permanent impairment of the whole body resulting from the current compensable injury. A zero percent impairment may be a valid rating.

(2) A doctor who certifies that an injured employee has reached MMI shall assign an impairment rating for the current compensable injury using the rating criteria contained in the appropriate edition of the AMA Guides to the Evaluation of Permanent Impairment, published by the American Medical Association (AMA Guides).

(A) The appropriate edition of the AMA Guides to use for all certifying examinations conducted before October 15, 2001 is the third edition, second printing, dated February, 1989.

(B) The appropriate edition of the AMA Guides to use for certifying examinations conducted on or after October 15, 2001 is:

(i) the fourth edition of the AMA Guides (1st, 2nd, 3rd, or 4th printing, including corrections and changes as issued by the AMA prior to May 16, 2000). If a subsequent printing(s) of the fourth edition of the AMA Guides occurs, and it contains no substantive changes from the previous printing, the commission by vote at a public meeting may authorize the use of the subsequent printing(s); or

. . .

(C) This subsection shall be implemented to ensure that in the event of an impairment rating dispute, only ratings using the appropriate edition of the AMA Guides shall be considered. Impairment ratings assigned using the wrong edition of the AMA Guides shall not be considered valid.

(3) Assignment of an impairment rating for the current compensable injury shall be based on the injured employee's condition as of the MMI date considering the medical record and the certifying examination. The doctor assigning the impairment rating shall:

. . .

(D) compare the results of the analysis with the impairment criteria and provide the following:

. . .

(ii) A description of how the findings relate to and compare with the criteria described in the applicable chapter of the AMA Guides. The doctor's inability to obtain required measurements must be explained.

. . .

(4) After September 1, 2003, if range of motion, sensory, and strength testing required by the AMA Guides is not performed by the certifying doctor, the testing shall be performed by a health care practitioner, who within the two years prior to the date the injured employee is evaluated, has had the impairment rating training module required by § 180.23 (relating to Commission Required Training for Doctors/Certification Levels) for a doctor to be certified to assign impairment ratings. It is the responsibility of the certifying doctor to ensure the requirements of this subsection are complied with.

. . .

(5) If an impairment rating is assigned in violation of subsection (c)(4), the rating is invalid and the evaluation and report are not reimbursable. A provider that is paid for an evaluation and/or report that is invalid under this subsection shall refund the payment to the insurance carrier.

. . .

(d) Reporting.

(1) Certification of MMI, determination of permanent impairment, and assignment of an impairment rating (if permanent impairment exists) for the current compensable injury requires completion, signing, and submission of the Report of Medical Evaluation and a narrative report.

(B) The Report of Medical Evaluation includes an attached narrative report. The narrative report must include the following:

. . .

(vii) the edition of the AMA Guides that was used in assigning the impairment rating (if the injured employee has permanent impairment) . . .

. . .

*****

Texas Administrative Code
Title 28. Insurance
Part 2. Texas Department of Insurance, Division of Workers' Compensation
Chapter 180. Monitoring and Enforcement
Subchapter B. Medical Benefit Regulation
§ 180.21. Commission Designated Doctor List

. . .

(d) To be on the DDL on or after January 1, 2007, the doctor shall at a minimum:

(3) have successfully completed Division-approved training and examination on the assignment of impairment ratings using the currently adopted edition of the American Medical Association Guides, medical causation, extent of injury . . .

. . .

*****

Texas Administrative Code
Title 28. Insurance
Part 2. Texas Department of Insurance, Division of Workers' Compensation
Chapter 180. Monitoring and Enforcement
Subchapter B. Medical Benefit Regulation
§ 180.23. Commission Required Training for Doctors/Certification Levels

. . .

(i) This subsection governs authorization relating to certification of MMI, determination of permanent impairment, and assignment of impairment ratings in the event that a doctor finds permanent impairment exists when the examination of the employee occurs on or after September 1, 2003.

(2) Full authorization to assign an impairment rating and certify MMI in an instance where the employee is found to have permanent impairment requires a doctor to receive commission certification by successfully completing the commission-prescribed Impairment Rating Training Module and passing the test. To remain certified, a doctor is required to successfully complete follow-up training and testing every four years.

(3) A doctor who has not completed the commission-prescribed training under subsection (i)(2) of this section but who has had similar training in the AMA Guides from a commission-approved vendor within the prior two years may submit the syllabus and training materials from that course to the commission for review. If the commission determines that the training is substantially the same as the commission-prescribed training and the doctor passes the commission-prescribed test, the doctor is fully authorized under this subsection. The ability to substitute training only applies to the initial training requirement, not the follow-up training.

. . .

*****

Texas Administrative Code
Title 28. Insurance
Part 2. Texas Department of Insurance, Division of Workers' Compensation
Chapter 180. Monitoring and Enforcement
Subchapter B. Medical Benefit Regulation
§ 180.26. Doctor and Insurance Carrier Sanctions

(c) Except as provided by subsection(e) of this section, the Medical Advisor (as defined by Texas Labor Code § 413.05(1) shall recommend deletion of a doctor from the ADL if any of the following occurs:

(4) having a significant (uncorrected or willful) pattern of [sic] practice relating to the delivery or evaluation of health care that the commission finds is not fair and reasonable or that the commission determines does not meet professionally recognized standards of health care including, but not limited to:

. . .

(G) certifying maximum medical improvement (MMI) and/or assigning impairment ratings in violation of the Statute and Rules, including, but not limited to, not complying with the applicable AMA Guides when assigning an impairment rating;

. . .

UTAH

Utah Administrative Code
Labor Commission
R612. Industrial Accidents
R612-7. Impairment Ratings for Industrial Injuries and Diseases

. . .

R612-7-3. Method for rating

A. For rating all impairments, which are not expressly listed in Section 34A-2-412, the Commission incorporates by reference "Utah's 2006 Impairment Guides" as published by the Commission for all injuries rated on or after July 11, 2006. For those conditions not found in "Utah's 2006 Impairment Guides," the American Medical Association's "Guides to the Evaluation of Permanent Impairment, Fifth Edition" are to be used.

VERMONT

West's Vermont Statutes Annotated
Title Twenty-One. Labor
Chapter 9. Employer's Liability and Workers' Compensation
§ 648. Permanent partial disability benefits

. . .

(b) Any determination of the existence and degree of permanent partial impairment shall be made only in accordance with the whole person determinations as set out in the most recent edition of the American Medical Association Guides to the Evaluation of Permanent Impairment. The commissioner shall adopt a supplementary schedule for injuries that are not rated by the most recent edition of the American Medical Association Guides to the Evaluation of Permanent Impairment.

(c) Notwithstanding the provisions of subsections (a) and (b) of this section, for the purposes of determining the payment period for any permanent partial impairment to the spine, the percentage of impairment shall be determined in accordance with rules adopted by the commissioner according to which an injury to the spine which is evaluated as a 60 percent impairment of the whole person shall provide 330 weeks of compensation.

(d) An impairment rating determined pursuant to this section shall be reduced by any previously determined permanent impairment for which compensation has been paid, but if the combination of the prior impairment rating and the rating determined pursuant to this section would result in the employee being considered permanently totally disabled, the prior rating shall not negate a finding of permanent total disability.

*****

West's Vermont Statutes Annotated
Title Twenty-One. Labor
Chapter 9. Employer's Liability and Workers' Compensation
§ 667. Examination by independent medical examiners

   . . .

(b) A pool of independent medical examiners shall be established to perform independent medical examinations. Representatives of management and labor from the governor's advisory council on workers' compensation, if available, otherwise other representatives of management and labor shall each submit a list of health care providers as proposed members of the pool. The commissioner shall select the common names from both lists. If, in the opinion of the commissioner, the number of independent medical examiners in the pool is not sufficient for any reason, or does not adequately represent a range of health care providers, the commissioner shall select additional health care providers or request additional names. All health care providers in the pool shall receive training about the nature and purpose of workers' compensation and shall follow the guidelines developed by rule by the commissioner. Where a dispute involves a determination of the degree of permanent partial disability, the independent medical examiner shall use the most recent edition of the American Medical Association Guides to the Evaluation of Permanent Impairment or the supplement provided by the commissioner.

   . . .

WASHINGTON

Washington Administrative Code
Title 296A. (Ch. 1-59) Labor and Industries, Department of
Chapter 296-20. Medical Aid Rules
296-20-220. Special rules for evaluation of permanent bodily impairment.

(1) Evaluations of permanent bodily impairment using categories require uniformity in procedure and terminology. The following rules have been enacted to produce this

uniformity and shall apply to all evaluations of permanent impairment of an unspecified nature.

. . .

(q) The rating of impairment due to total joint replacement shall be in accordance with the limitation of motion guidelines as set forth in the "Guides to the Evaluation of Permanent Impairment" of American Medical Association, with department of labor and industries acknowledgement of responsibility for failure of prostheses beyond the seven year limitation.

*****

Washington Administrative Code
Title 296A. (Ch. 1-59) Labor and Industries, Department of
Chapter 296-20. Medical Aid Rules
296-20-370. Respiratory impairments.

(1) Rules for evaluation of permanent respiratory impairments:

(a) Definitions.

(i) "FEV_1" means the forced expiratory volume in 1 second as measured by a spirometric test performed as described in the most current American Thoracic Society Statement on Standardization of Spirometry, and using equipment, methods of calibration, and techniques that meet American Thoracic Society (ATS) criteria including reproducibility. The measurement used must be taken from a spirogram which is technically acceptable and represents the patient's best effort. The measurement is to be expressed as both an absolute value and as a percentage of the predicted value. The predicted values are those listed in the most current edition of the American Medical Association (AMA) Guidelines for rating permanent respiratory impairment.

. . .

*****

Washington Administrative Code
Title 296A. (Ch. 1-59) Labor and Industries, Department of
Chapter 296-20. Medical Aid Rules
296-20-2010. General rules for impairment rating examinations by attending doctors and consultants.

. . .

(2) Whenever an impairment rating examination is made, the attending doctor or consultant must complete a rating report that includes, at a minimum, the following:

. . .

(d) An impairment rating consistent with the findings and a statement of the system on which the rating was based (for example, the AMA Guides to the Evaluation of Permanent Impairment and edition used, or the Washington state category rating system—refer to WAC 296-20-19000 through 296-20-19030 and WAC 296-20-200 through 296-20-690); and

. . .

*****

Washington Administrative Code
Title 296A. (Ch. 1-59) Labor and Industries, Department of
Chapter 296-20. Medical Aid Rules
296-20-19030. To what extent is pain considered in an award for permanent partial disability?

The categories used to rate unspecified disabilities incorporate the worker's subjective complaints. Similarly, the organ and body system ratings in the AMA Guides to the Evaluation of Permanent Impairment incorporate the worker's subjective complaints. A worker's subjective complaints or symptoms, such as a report of pain, cannot be objectively validated or measured. There is no valid, reliable or consistent means to segregate the worker's subjective complaints of pain from the pain already rated and compensated for in the conventional rating methods. When rating a worker's permanent partial disability, reliance is primarily placed on objective physical or clinical findings that are independent of voluntary action by the worker and can be seen, felt or consistently measured by examiners. No additional permanent partial disability award will be made beyond what is already allowed in the categories and in the organ and body system ratings in the AMA guides.

For example:

• Chapter 18 of the 5th Edition of the AMA Guides to the Evaluation of Permanent Impairment attempts to rate impairment caused by a patient's pain complaints. The impairment caused by the worker's pain complaints is already taken into consideration in the categories and in the organ and body system ratings in the AMA guides. There is no reliable means to segregate the pain already rated and compensated from the pain impairment that Chapter 18 purports to rate. Chapter 18 of the 5th Edition of AMA Guides to the Evaluation of Permanent Impairment cannot be used to calculate awards for permanent partial disability under Washington's Industrial Insurance Act.

*****

Washington Administrative Code
Title 296A. (Ch. 1-59) Labor and Industries, Department of
Chapter 296-23. Radiology, Radiation Therapy, Nuclear Medicine, Pathology, Hospital, Chiropractic, Physical Therapy, Drugless Therapeutics and Nursing—
Drugless Therapeutics, etc
Independent Medical Examination
296-23-377. If an independent medical examination (IME) provider is asked to do an impairment rating examination only, what information must be included in the report?

(1) If, after reviewing the records, taking a history from the worker and performing the examination, the IME provider concurs with the attending doctor's determination of MMI, the impairment rating report must, at a minimum, contain the following:

. . .

(d) An impairment rating consistent with the findings and a statement of the system on which the rating was based (for example, the AMA Guides to the Evaluation of Permanent

Impairment and edition used, or the Washington state category rating system—refer to WAC 296-20-19000 through 296-20-19030 and WAC 296-20-200 through 296-20-690); and

. . .

WEST VIRGINIA

West Virginia Code of State Rules
Title 85. Workers' Compensation Rules of the West Virginia Insurance
Commissioner, Exempt Legislative Rule (Ser. 20)
Series 20. Medical Management of Claims, Guidelines for Impairment Evaluations,
Evidence, and Ratings, and Ranges of Permanent Partial Disability Awards
§ 85-20-3. Definitions.

. . .

3.8.

"Guides Fourth" means the "Guides to the Evaluation of Permanent Impairment," (4th ed. 1993), as published by the American Medical Association.

. . .

3.10.

"Permanent impairment" means a permanent alteration of an individual's health status and is assessed by medical means and is a medical issue. An impairment is a deviation from normal in a body part or organ system and its functioning. An injured worker's degree of permanent whole body medical impairment is to be determined in keeping with the determination of whole person permanent impairment as set forth in the applicable Guides. For the purposes of this Rule, the Guides' use of the term "whole person" impairment is the equivalent of the term "whole body" impairment.

. . .

*****

West Virginia Code of State Rules
Title 85. Workers' Compensation Rules of the West Virginia Insurance
Commissioner, Exempt Legislative Rule (Ser. 20)
Series 20. Medical Management of Claims, Guidelines for Impairment Evaluations,
Evidence, and Ratings, and Ranges of Permanent Partial Disability Awards
§ 85-20-12. Psychiatric compensability, treatment and impairment ratings.
(Effective Date: January 20, 2006.)

12.2. Definitions.

As used in these rules, the following terms have the stated meanings unless the context of a specific use clearly indicates another meaning is intended.

. . .

b. "Causation legal standard" means a physical, chemical, or biologic factor contributed to the occurence of a medically identifiable condition. A medical determination is required to confirm the feasibility of the contributing factor could result in the occurrence of the condition (AMA Guides 4th Ed., Glossary).

c. "Aggravation, legal standard" means a physical, chemical, biological or medical condition significantly contributing to the worsening of a condition in such a way that the degree of permanent impairment increased by more than 3%. (AMA Guides 4th Ed., Glossary). For the impact to merit allocation of permanent impairment, the ultimate increase of impairment at MMI must at least be 3%.

. . .

g. "Permanent partial psychiatric impairment" means impairment that is assigned a percentage of impairment rating from the W. Va. Workers' Compensation Impairment Guidelines for Psychiatric Impairment (Exhibit B).

. . .

12.3. Evidentiary Requirements.

The evidentiary weight to be given to a report will be influenced by how well it demonstrates that the evaluation was conducted in accordance with the rule and three attached Exhibits (Exhibit A, Exhibit B, and Exhibit C). Exhibit A lists disorders and conditions not significantly contributed to by a work-related injury. Exhibit B is a guideline for providing impairment ratings. Exhibit C is a report outline for psychiatric independent medical evaluations. The evaluator must address and memorialize each bold face section found in Exhibit C.

*****

West Virginia Code of State Rules
Title 85. Workers' Compensation Rules of the West Virginia Insurance
Commissioner, Exempt Legislative Rule (Ser. 20)
Series 20. Medical Management of Claims, Guidelines for Impairment Evaluations,
Evidence, and Ratings, and Ranges of Permanent Partial Disability Awards
§ 85-20-53. Long-Term Opioid Therapy Guideline.

. . .

53.12 Continuation of Long-Term OMA:

b. Complete analgesia is not the goal of long-term OMA. The efficacy of the therapy is measured not only by reduction in pain but also by improvement in physical and social function. Therefore, documentation of pain and function is essential to monitor the success of the therapy. Functional tool: Table 18.3 of the AMA Guides, Fifth Edition, or a comparable tool.

. . .

*****

West Virginia Code of State Rules
Title 85. Workers' Compensation Rules of the West Virginia Insurance
Commissioner, Exempt Legislative Rule (Ser. 20)
Series 20. Medical Management of Claims, Guidelines for Impairment Evaluations,
Evidence, and Ratings, and Ranges of Permanent Partial Disability Awards
§ 85-20-65. Adoption of Standards

65.1. Except as provided for in section 66 of this Rule, on and after the effective date of this rule all evaluations, examinations, reports, and opinions with regard to the degree of permanent whole body medical impairment which an injured worker has suffered shall be conducted and composed in accordance with the "Guides to the Evaluation of Permanent Impairment," (4th ed. 1993), as published by the American Medical Association. If in any particular claim, the examiner is of the opinion that the Guides or the section 64 substitutes cannot be appropriately applied or that an impairment guide established by a recognized medical specialty group may be more appropriately applied, then the examiner's report must document and explain the basis for that opinion. Deviations from the requirements of the Guides or the section 6 substitutes shall not be the basis for excluding evidence from consideration. Rather, in any such instance such deviations shall be considered in determining the weight that will be given to that evidence. An example of an acceptable recognized medical specialty group's own guides is the "Orthopedic Surgeons Manual in Evaluating Permanent Physical Impairment."

65.2. These revised rules are not applicable to any permanent impairment rating examination performed prior to the effective date of these revised rules. Accordingly, the revised rules are not applicable to any reports or opinions based upon those examinations, in whole or in part, which are submitted either before or after the effective date of these revised rules.

. . .

*****

West Virginia Code of State Rules
Title 85. Workers' Compensation Rules of the West Virginia Insurance
Commissioner, Exempt Legislative Rule (Ser. 20)
Series 20. Medical Management of Claims, Guidelines for Impairment Evaluations,
Evidence, and Ratings, and Ranges of Permanent Partial Disability Awards
Exhibit B

EXHIBIT B WEST VIRGINIA WORKERS' COMPENSATION DIVISION IMPAIRMENT GUIDELINE FOR RATING PSYCHIATRIC IMPAIRMENT

Exhibit B shall be used to determine a claimant's psychiatric impairment rating using the classification consistent with the AMA Guides to the Evaluation of Permanent Impairment, Fifth Edition, in conjunction with the Axis V Global Assessment of Functioning Scale (GAF, DSM-IV-TR 2000, page 34), the claimant's treatment needs, and functional status. Axis V refers only to psychological, occupational, and social functioning and the examiner must NOT include impairment in functioning as a result physical limitations in the formulation of the GAF (GAF, DSM-IV-TR 2000).

Disorders believed to have resulted from brain injury, such as cognitive disorders, should NOT be rated using this guideline, but should be evaluated according to relevant sections of Chapter 4 of the AMA Guides to the Evaluation of Permanent Impairment, Fourth Edition.

The diagnoses of Pain Disorder and Dissociative Disorder, NOS, while important in the presentation and treatment of the underlying physical condition, should not receive an impairment rating.

. . .

*****

WYOMING

West's Wyoming Statutes Annotated
Title 27. Labor and Employment
Chapter 14. Workers' Compensation
Article 4. Employee Benefits
§ 27-14-405. Permanent partial disability; benefits; schedule; permanent
disfigurement; disputed ratings

. . .

(f) An injured employee suffering an ascertainable loss may apply for a permanent partial impairment award as provided in this section.

(g) An injured employee's impairment shall be rated by a licensed physician using the most recent edition of the American Medical Association's guide to the evaluation of permanent impairment. The award shall be paid as provided by W.S. 27-14-403 for the number of months determined by multiplying the percentage of impairment by forty-four (44) months.

. . .

*****

Wyoming Rules and Regulations
Department of Employment
Workers' Compensation Division
Chapter 7. Benefits
Section 1. Awards of Compensation.

. . .

(b) Computation of Impairment Award. The calculation of the award pursuant to W.S. § 27-14-405(g) will be based upon the percentage of whole body impairment as determined by the most recent edition of the American Medical Association Guides to the Evaluation of Physical [sic] Impairment or its successor publication.

. . .

*****

Wyoming Rules and Regulations
Department of Employment
Workers' Compensation Division
Chapter 10. Miscellaneous Medical Protocols
Section 14 Impairment Ratings—Requirements

(a) Any physician determining permanent physical impairment shall:

(i) have a current, active, and unrestricted license to practice medicine, issued by a state medical board; and

(ii) use the most recent edition of the American Medical Association's Guide to the Evaluation of Permanent Impairment; and

(iii) use the instructions and complete all required measurements referencing all tables contained in the American Medical Association's Guide [sic] to the Evaluation of

Permanent Impairment. The Division requires impairment ratings to be submitted in the same format as the forms contained within that publication; and

(iv) A physician who is providing a physical impairment rating to an individual who has undergone multiple level fusion of the spine may utilize either the Range of Motion (ROM) and/or the DRE (Diagnosis Related Estimate) Method, or both, as the rating physician sees fit to provide the most appropriate physical impairment rating for the injured worker.

(v) Impairment Rating reports will be reviewed by Division medical staff and monitored for compliance with the most recent edition of the American Medical Association's Guide to the Evaluation of Permanent Impairment, including quality, timeliness, ability to convey and substantiate medical opinions and conclusions concerning injured workers. The Division may not pay for ratings not performed using the criteria set forth in this section and in the American Medical Association's Guide [sic] to the Evaluation of Permanent Impairment.

FEDERAL STATUTES AND REGULATIONS

United States Code Annotated
Title 33. Navigation and Navigable Waters
Chapter 18. Longshore and Harbor Workers' Compensation
§ 902. Definitions

When used in this chapter—

(10) "Disability" means incapacity because of injury to earn the wages which the employee was receiving at the time of injury in the same or any other employment; but such term shall mean permanent impairment, determined (to the extent covered thereby) under the guides to the evaluation of permanent impairment promulgated and modified from time to time by the American Medical Association, in the case of an individual whose claim is described in section 910(d)(2) of this title.

*****

United States Code Annotated
Title 33. Navigation and Navigable Waters
Chapter 18. Longshore and Harbor Workers' Compensation
§ 908. Compensation for disability

(c) Permanent partial disability: In case of disability partial in character but permanent in quality the compensation shall be 66⅔ per centum of the average weekly wages, which shall be in addition to compensation for temporary total disability or temporary partial disability paid in accordance with subsection (b) or subsection (e) of this section, respectively, and shall be paid to the employee, as follows:

(13) Loss of hearing:

. . .

(E) Determinations of loss of hearing shall be made in accordance with the guides for the evaluation of permanent impairment as promulgated and modified from time to time by the American Medical Association.

(23) Notwithstanding paragraphs (1) through (22), with respect to a claim for permanent partial disability for which the average weekly wages are determined under section 910(d)(2) of this title, the compensation shall be 66⅔ per centum of such average weekly wages multiplied by the percentage of permanent impairment, as determined under the guides referred to in section 902(10) of this title, payable during the continuance of such impairment.

United States Code Annotated
Title 42. The Public Health and Welfare
Chapter 84. Department of Energy
Subchapter XVI. Energy Employees Occupational Illness Compensation Program
Part E. Contractor Employee Compensation
§ 7385s-2. Compensation schedule for contractor employees

(2) Wage loss

(b) Determination of minimum impairment rating

For purposes of subsection (a) of this section, a minimum impairment rating shall be determined in accordance with the American Medical Association's Guides to the Evaluation of Permanent Impairment.

FEDERAL STATUTES AND REGULATIONS

Code of Federal Regulations
Title 20. Employees' Benefits
Chapter III. Social Security Administration
Part 404. Federal Old-Age, Survivors and Disability Insurance (1950-   )
Subpart P. Determining Disability and Blindness
Appendices [Editorially Supplied]
Appendix 1 to Subpart P of Part 404—Listing of Impairments

. . .

101.00 Musculoskeletal System

. . .

G. Measurements of joint motion are based on the techniques described in the chapter on the extremities, spine, and pelvis in the current edition of the "Guides to the Evaluation of Permanent Impairment" published by the American Medical Association.
*****

Code of Federal Regulations
Title 20. Employees' Benefits
Chapter I. Office of Workers' Compensation Programs, Department of Labor
Subchapter B. Federal Employees' Compensation Act
Part 10. Claims for Compensation Under the Federal Employees' Compensation Act as Amended
Subpart D. Medical and Related Benefits, Medical Reports
§ 10.333 What additional medical information will OWCP require to support a claim for a schedule award?

To support a claim for a schedule award, a medical report must contain accurate measurements of the function of the organ or member, in accordance with the American Medical Association's Guides to the Evaluation of Permanent Impairment. These measurements may include: The actual degree of loss of active or passive motion or deformity; the amount of atrophy; the decrease, if any, in strength; the disturbance of sensation; and pain due to nerve impairment.

*****

Code of Federal Regulations
Title 20. Employees' Benefits
Chapter I. Office of Workers' Compensation Programs, Department of Labor
Subchapter B. Federal Employees' Compensation Act
Part 10. Claims for Compensation Under the Federal Employees' Compensation Act as Amended
Subpart E. Compensation and Related Benefits
Compensation for Disability and Impairment
§ 10.404 When and how is compensation for a schedule impairment paid?

Compensation is provided for specified periods of time for the permanent loss or loss of use of certain members, organs and functions of the body. Such loss or loss of use is known as permanent impairment. Compensation for proportionate periods of time is payable for partial loss or loss of use of each member, organ or function. OWCP evaluates the degree of impairment to schedule members, organs and functions as defined in 5 U.S.C. 8107 according to the standards set forth in the specified (by OWCP) edition of the American Medical Association's Guides to the Evaluation of Permanent Impairment.

. . .

*****

Code of Federal Regulations
Title 20. Employees' Benefits
Chapter I. Office of Workers' Compensation Programs, Department of Labor
Subchapter C. Energy Employees Occupational Illness Compensation Program Act of 2000
Part 30. Claims for Compensation Under the Energy Employees Occupational Illness Compensation Program Act of 2000, as Amended
Subpart F. Survivors; Payments and Offsets; Overpayments, Payment of Claims and Offset for Certain Payments
§ 30.509 Under what circumstances may a survivor claiming under Part E of the Act choose to receive the benefits that would otherwise be payable to a covered Part E employee who is deceased?

. . .

(c) OWCP only makes impairment determinations based on rationalized medical evidence in the case file that is sufficiently detailed and meets the various requirements for the many different types of impairment determinations possible under the AMA's Guides. Therefore, OWCP will only make an impairment determination for a deceased covered Part E employee pursuant to this section if the medical evidence of record is sufficient to satisfy the pertinent requirements in the AMA's Guides and subpart J of this part.

*****

Code of Federal Regulations
Title 20. Employees' Benefits
Chapter I. Office of Workers' Compensation Programs, Department of Labor
Subchapter C. Energy Employees Occupational Illness Compensation Program Act of 2000
Part 30. Claims for Compensation Under the Energy Employees Occupational Illness Compensation Program Act of 2000, as Amended
Subpart J. Impairment Benefits Under Part E of EEOICPA
General Provisions
§ 30.901 How does OWCP determine the extent of an employee's impairment that is due to a covered illness contracted through exposure to a toxic substance at a DOE facility or a RECA section 5 facility, as appropriate?

. . .

(b) The minimum impairment rating shall be determined in accordance with the current edition of the American Medical Association's Guides to the Evaluation of Permanent Impairment (AMA's Guides). In making impairment benefit determinations, OWCP will only consider medical reports from physicians who are certified by the relevant medical board and who satisfy any additional criteria determined by OWCP to be necessary to qualify to perform impairment evaluations under Part E, including any specific training in use of the AMA's Guides, specific training and experience related to particular conditions and other objective factors.

. . .

*****

Code of Federal Regulations
Title 20. Employees' Benefits
Chapter I. Office of Workers' Compensation Programs, Department of Labor
Subchapter C. Energy Employees Occupational Illness Compensation Program Act of 2000
Part 30. Claims for Compensation Under the Energy Employees Occupational Illness Compensation Program Act of 2000, as Amended
Subpart J. Impairment Benefits Under Part E of EEOICPA
Medical Evidence of Impairment
§ 30.905 How may an impairment evaluation be obtained?

(a) Except as provided in paragraph (b) of this section, OWCP may request that an employee undergo an evaluation of his or her permanent impairment that specifies the percentage points that are the result of the employee's covered illness or illnesses. To be of any probative value, such evaluation must be performed by a physician who meets the criteria OWCP has identified for physicians performing impairment evaluations for the pertinent covered illness or illnesses in accordance with the AMA's Guides.

. . .

*****

Code of Federal Regulations
Title 20. Employees' Benefits
Chapter I. Office of Workers' Compensation Programs, Department of Labor
Subchapter C. Energy Employees Occupational Illness Compensation Program Act of 2000
Part 30. Claims for Compensation Under the Energy Employees Occupational Illness Compensation Program Act of 2000, as Amended
Subpart J. Impairment Benefits Under Part E of EEOICPA
Ratable Impairments
§ 30.910 Will an impairment that cannot be assigned a numerical percentage using the AMA's Guides be included in the impairment rating?

(a) An impairment of an organ or body function that cannot be assigned a numerical impairment percentage using the AMA's Guides will not be included in the employee's impairment rating.

(b) A mental impairment that does not originate from a documented physical dysfunction of the nervous system, and cannot be assigned a numerical percentage using the AMA's Guides, will not be included in the impairment rating for the employee. Mental impairments that are due to documented physical dysfunctions of the nervous system can be assigned numerical percentages using the AMA's Guides and will be included in the rating.

*****

Code of Federal Regulations
Title 20. Employees' Benefits
Chapter VI. Employment Standards Administration, Department of Labor
Subchapter A. Longshoremen's and Harbor Workers' Compensation Act and Related Statutes
Part 702. Administration and Procedure
Subpart D. Medical Care and Supervision
Hearing Loss Claims
§ 702.441 Claims for loss of hearing.

. . .

(d) In determining the loss of hearing under the Act, the evaluators shall use the criteria for measuring and calculating hearing impairment as published and modified from time-to-time by the American Medical Association in the Guides to the Evaluation of Permanent Impairment, using the most currently revised edition of this publication. In addition, the audiometer used for testing the individual's threshold of hearing must be calibrated according to current American National Standard Specifications for Audiometers. Audiometer testing procedures required by hearing conservation programs pursuant to the Occupational Safety and Health Act of 1970 should be followed (as described at 29 CFR 1910.95 and appendices).

*****

Code of Federal Regulations
Title 20. Employees' Benefits
Chapter VI. Employment Standards Administration, Department of Labor
Subchapter A. Longshoremen's and Harbor Workers' Compensation Act and Related Statutes
Part 702. Administration and Procedure
Subpart F. Occupational Disease Which Does Not Immediately Result in Death or Disability
§ 702.601 Definitions.

. . .

(b) Disability. With regard to an occupational disease for which the time of injury, as defined in § 702.601(a), occurs after the employee was retired, disability shall mean permanent impairment as determined according to the Guides to the Evaluation of Permanent Impairment which is prepared and modified from time-to-time by the American Medical Association, using the most currently revised edition of this publication. If this guide does not evaluate the impairment, other professionally recognized standards may be utilized. The disability described in this paragraph shall be limited to permanent partial disability. For that reason they are not subject to adjustments under section 10(f) of the Act, 33 U.S.C. 910(f).

. . .

IMPAIRMENT CASE LAW DECISIONS

Impairment	State	Citation
Ankle	FL	*Decor Painting & Iowa Mut. Ins. Co. v. Rohn*, 401 So. 2d 899 (Fla. Dist. Ct. App. 1981)
	LA	*Captain v. Sonnier Timber Co.*, 503 So. 2d 689 (La. Ct. App. 1987)
Arm	AZ	*Dark v. Industrial Comm'n*, 705 P.2d 957 (Ariz. Ct. App. 1985)
	AZ	*Dutra v. Industrial Comm'n*, 659 P.2d 18 (Ariz. 1983)
	DC	*Negussie v. District of Columbia Dep't of Employment Servs.*, 915 A.2d 391 (D.C. 2007)
	FL	*Jones Mahoney Corp. v. Hutto*, 421 So. 2d 703 (Fla. Dist. Ct. App. 1982)
	IA	*Christensen v. Snap-On Tools Corp.*, 602 N.W.2d 199 (Iowa Ct. App. 1999)
	LA	*Lanoue v. All Star Chevrolet*, 867 So. 2d 755 (La. App. 1st Cir. 2003)
	MT	*Hall v. State Comp. Ins. Fund*, 708 P.2d 234 (Mont. 1985)
	OK	*Oklahoma State Penitentiary v. Weaver*, 809 P.2d 1324 (Okla. Ct. App. 1991)
	OK	*Texas Okla. Express v. Sorenson*, 652 P.2d 285 (Okla. 1982)
	RI	*Molony & Rubien Constr. Co. v. Segrella*, 373 A.2d 816 (R.I. 1977)
	TN	*Thomas v. Magna Seating Sys. of Am., Inc.*, 2003 Tenn. LEXIS 711 (Tenn. Spec. Workers' Comp. App. Panel Aug. 15, 2003)
	TN	*Jackson v. Goodyear Tire & Rubber Co.*, 2001 WL 303509 (Tenn. Spec. Workers' Comp. App. Panel Mar. 29, 2001)
Back	AL	*Municipality of Anchorage v. Leigh*, 823 P.2d 1241 (Alaska 1992)
	AR	*Jones v. Wal-Mart Stores, Inc.*, 2007 WL 2713381 (Ark. Ct. App. 2007)
	AR	*Mays v. Alumnitec*, 64 S.W.3d 772 (Ark. Ct. App. 2001)
	AR	*Ouachita Marine & Indus. Corp. v. Morrison*, 428 S.W.2d 216 (Ark. 1969)
	AZ	*Tucson Steel Div. v. Industrial Comm'n*, 744 P.2d 462 (Ariz. Ct. App. 1987)
	AZ	*Cassey v. Industrial Comm'n*, 731 P.2d 645 (Ariz. Ct. App. 1987)
	AZ	*Chavez v. Industrial Comm'n*, 575 P.2d 340 (Ariz. Ct. App. 1977)
	AZ	*Smith v. Industrial Comm'n*, 522 P.2d 1198 (Ariz. Ct. App. 1976)

Impairment	State	Citation
	CO	*Wilson v. Industrial Claim Appeals Office of State of Colo.*, 91 P.3d 1117 (Colo. Ct. App. 2003)
	CO	*Wackenhut Corp. v. Industrial Claim Appeals Office of State of Colo.*, 17 P.3d 202 (Colo. Ct. App. 2000)
	CO	*McLane W., Inc. v. Industrial Claim Appeals Office of State of Colo.*, 996 P.2d 263 (Colo. Ct. App. 1999)
	CO	*Lambert & Sons, Inc. v. Industrial Claim Appeals Office*, 1998 Colo. App. LEXIS 168 (Colo. Ct. App. July 9, 1998)
	CO	*Askew v. Industrial Claim Appeals Office of State of Colo.*, 927 P.2d 1333 (Colo. 1996)
	CO	*Askew v. Sears, Roebuck & Co.*, 914 P.2d 416 (Colo. Ct. App. 1995)
	CO	*Metro Moving & Storage Co. v. Gussert*, 914 P.2d 411 (Colo. Ct. App. 1995)
	DE	*Turbitt v. Blue Hen Lines, Inc.*, 711 A.2d 1214 (Del. 1998)
	FL	*Bishop v. Baldwin Acoustical & Drywall*, 696 So. 2d 507 (Fla. Dist. Ct. App. 1997)
	FL	*Glisson v. State Dep't of Mgmt. Servs.*, 621 So. 2d 543 (Fla. Dist. Ct. App. 1993)
	FL	*Kessler v. Community Blood Bank*, 621 So. 2d 539 (Fla. Dist. Ct. App. 1993)
	FL	*Wilson v. Harris Corp.*, 557 So. 2d 50 (Fla. Dist. Ct. App. 1989)
	FL	*Rodriguez v. Dade County Sch. Bd.*, 511 So. 2d 712 (Fla. Dist. Ct. App. 1987)
	FL	*Patterson v. Wellcraft Marine*, 509 So. 2d 1195 (Fla. Dist. Ct. App. 1987)
	FL	*Kenney v. Juno Fire Control Dist.*, 506 So. 2d 449 (Fla. Dist. Ct. App. 1987)
	FL	*Martin County Sch. Bd. v. McDaniel*, 465 So. 2d 1235 (Fla. Dist. Ct. App. 1984)
	FL	*Hunt-Wilde Corp. v. Kitchen*, 452 So. 2d 2 (Fla. Dist. Ct. App. 1984)
	FL	*Coca-Cola Co. Foods Div. v. Hawk*, 451 So. 2d 1025 (Fla. Dist. Ct. App. 1984)
	FL	*Whitehall Corp. v. Davis*, 448 So. 2d 47 (Fla. Dist. Ct. App. 1984)
	FL	*Storage Tech. Corp. v. Philbrook*, 448 So. 2d 42 (Fla. Dist. Ct. App. 1984)
	FL	*Brandon v. Hillsborough County Sch. Bd.*, 447 So. 2d 982 (Fla. Dist. Ct. App. 1984)
	FL	*Universal Corp. v. Lawson*, 447 So. 2d 293 (Fla. Dist. Ct. App. 1984)
	FL	*Rich v. Commercial Carrier Corp.*, 442 So. 2d 1011 (Fla. Dist. Ct. App. 1982)
	FL	*Florida Sheriffs Youth Fund v. Harrell*, 438 So. 2d 450 (Fla. Dist. Ct. App. 1983)
	FL	*Tampa Bay Moving Sys. v. Frederick*, 433 So. 2d 628 (Fla. Dist. Ct. App. 1983)

Impairment	State	Citation
	FL	*Refrigerated Transp. Co. v. Edmond*, 428 So. 2d 338 (Fla. Dist. Ct. App. 1983)
	FL	*Morrison & Knudsen/Am. v. Scott*, 423 So. 2d 463 (Fla. Dist. Ct. App. 1982)
	FL	*Cowick v. State*, 419 So. 2d 779 (Fla. Dist. Ct. App. 1982)
	FL	*State v. Campbell*, 417 So. 2d 1156 (Fla. Dist. Ct. App. 1982)
	FL	*Dade Am. Host Supply v. Perez*, 417 So. 2d 296 (Fla. Dist. Ct. App. 1982)
	FL	*Cumberland Farm Food Stores v. Meier*, 408 So. 2d 700 (Fla. Dist. Ct. App. 1982)
	FL	*Buro v. Dino's Southland Meats*, 354 So. 2d 874 (Fla. Dist. Ct. App. 1978)
	HI	*Duque v. Hilton Hawaiian Vill.*, 98 P.2d 640 (Haw. 2004)
	ID	*Poss v. Meeker Mach. Shop*, 712 P.2d 621 (Idaho 1985)
	ID	*Pomerinke v. Excel Trucking Transp.*, 859 P.2d 337 (Idaho 1993)
	KS	*Carrizales v. Winsteads Rests.*, 82 P.3d 875 (Kan. Ct. App. 2004)
	KY	*Adams v. Coastal Coal Co.*, 2005 WL 2674978 (Ky. Oct. 20, 2005)
	KY	*Brasch-Barry Gen. Contractors v. Jones*, 175 S.W.3d 81 (Ky. 2005)
	KY	*Finley v. DBM Techs.*, 217 S.W.3d 261 (Ky. Ct. App. 2007)
	KY	*Firemen's Fund Ins. Co. v. Weeks*, 2007 WL 4460608 (Tex. App.—El Paso, 2007)
	KY	*Thornton v. Volt Servs. Group*, 2005 WL 1412530 (Ky. June 16, 2005)
	KY	*George Humfleet Mobile Homes v. Christman*, 125 S.W.3d 288 (Ky. 2004)
	KY	*Napier v. Middlesboro Appalachian Reg'l Hosp.*, 2003 WL 538123 (Ky. Mar. 18, 2004)
	KY	*Appalachian Racing, Inc. v. Blair*, 2003 WL 21355872 (Ky. June 12, 2003)
	KY	*Kentucky River Enters., Inc. v. Elkins*, 107 S.W.3d 206 (Ky. 2003)
	KY	*Shaffer v. Lourdes Hosp.*, 2000 WL 1763242 (Ky. Ct. App. Dec. 1, 2000)
	KY	*Ball v. Big Elk Creek Coal Co.*, 1999 WL 1086306 (Ky. Ct. App. Nov. 19, 1999)
	KY	*Whittaker v. Johnson*, 987 S.W.2d 181 (Ky. 1993)
	KY	*Newberg v. Garrett*, 858 S.W.2d 181 (Ky. 1993)
	KY	*Newberg v. Thomas Indus.*, 858 S.W.2d 339 (Ky. Ct. App. 1993)
	KY	*Cook v. Paducah Recapping Serv.*, 694 S.W.2d 684 (Ky. Ct. App. 1985)
	ME	*Bourgoin v. J.P. Levesque & Sons*, 726 A.2d 201 (Me. 1999)
	MD	*Sears, Roebuck & Co. v. Ralph*, 666 A.2d 1239 (Md. 1995)
	NV	*Maxwell v. SIIS*, 849 P.2d 267 (Nev. 1993)
	NH	*Appeal of Cote*, 781 A.2d 1006 (N.H. 2001)

Impairment	State	Citation
	NM	*Chavarria v. Basin Moving & Storage*, 976 P.2d 1019 (N.M. Ct. App. 1999)
	NM	*Montez v. J&B Radiator*, 779 P.2d 129 (N.M. Ct. App. 1989)
	NM	*Toynbee v. Mimbres Mem'l Nursing Home*, 833 P.2d 1204 (N.M. Ct. App. 1992)
	ND	*Coleman v. North Dakota Workers' Comp. Bureau*, 567 N.W.2d 853 (N.D. 1997)
	ND	*Hoyem v. North Dakota Workers' Comp. Bureau*, 578 N.W.2d 117 (N.D. 1998)
	ND	*Feist v. North Dakota Workers' Comp. Bureau*, 569 N.W.2d 1 (N.D. 1997)
	ND	*McCabe v. North Dakota Workers' Comp. Bureau*, 567 N.W.2d 201 (N.D. 1997)
	ND	*McCollum v. Workers' Comp. Bureau*, 567 N.W.2d 811 (N.D. 1997)
	OK	*Spangler v. Lease-Way Auto. Transp.*, 780 P.2d 209 (Okla. Ct. App. 1989)
	OK	*Perliner v. J.C. Rogers Constr. Co.*, 753 P.2d 905 (Okla. 1988)
	OK	*Special Indem. Fund v. Stockton*, 653 P.2d 194 (Okla. 1982)
	TN	*Rowland v. Northbrook Health Care Ctr.*, 2001 WL 873475 (Tenn. Spec. Workers' Comp. App. Panel July 30, 2001)
	TN	*Short v. Dietz Mobile Home Transp.*, 2001 WL 370317 (Tenn. Spec. Workers' Comp. App. Panel Apr. 16, 2001)
	TN	*Harless v. Huntsville Manor Nursing Home*, C.A. No. 7258 (Ch. Ct., Scott County, Tenn., Aug. 31, 1994)
	TN	*Henson v. City of Lawrenceburg*, 851 S.W.2d 809 (Tenn. 1993)
	TN	*Elmore v. Travelers Ins. Co.*, 824 S.W.2d 541 (Tenn. 1992)
	TN	*Harness v. CNA Ins. Co.*, 814 S.W.2d 733 (Tenn. 1991)
	TN	*Lyle v. Exxon Corp.*, 746 S.W.2d 694 (Tenn. 1988)
	TN	*Earls v. Sompo Japan Ins. Co. of Am.*, 2006 Tenn. LEXIS 295 (Tenn. Spec. Workers' Comp. App. Panel at Nashville, Apr. 11, 2006)
	TN	*Morrow v. International Mill Servs., Inc.*, 2004 WL 1064299 (Tenn. Spec. Workers' Comp. App. Panel, 2004)
	TN	*Humphrey v. David Witherspoon, Inc.*, 734 S.W.2d 315 (Tenn. 1987)
	TX	*Barrigan v. MHMR Servs. for Concho Valley*, 2007 WL 27732 (Tex. App.—Austin 2007)
	TX	*Lara v. Pacific Employers Ins. Co.*, 2003 WL 21517857 (Tex. App.—El Paso, 2003)
	TX	*Brookshire Bros., Inc. v. Lewis*, 997 S.W.2d 908 (Tex. App.—Beaumont 1999)
	TX	*Old Republic Ins. Co. v. Rodriguez*, 966 S.W.2d 208 (Tex. App. 1998)
	UT	*Jacobson Constr. v. Hair*, 667 P.2d 25 (Utah 1983)
	VT	*Stamper v. University Apartments, Inc.*, 522 A.2d 227 (Vt. 1986)
	VT	*Bishop v. Town of Barre*, 442 A.2d 50 (Vt. 1982)
	WV	*Repass v. Workers' Comp. Div.*, 569 S.E.2d 162 (W. Va. 2002)

Impairment	State	Citation
	WV	*Wagner v. Workers' Comp. Div.*, 1998 W. Va. LEXIS 219 (W. Va. Dec. 11, 1998)
	WY	*In re Pohl*, 980 P.2d 816 (Wyo. 1999)
	WY	*State of Wyo. ex. rel. Wyoming Workers' Safety & Comp. Div. v. Faulkner*, 152 P.3d 394 (Wyo. 2007)
Back shoulder	DE	*Wykpisz v. Steel*, 2001 WL 755376 (Del. Sup. Ct. 2001)
Bakers' asthma	FL	*Coq v. Fuchs Baking Co.*, 507 So. 2d 138 (Fla. Dist. Ct. App. 1987)
	KY	*Lanter v. Kentucky State Police*, 171 S.W.3d 45 (Ky. 2005)
	MN	*Deschampe v. Arrowhead Tree Serv.*, 428 N.W.2d 795 (Minn. 1988)
	NH	*Petition of Blackford*, 635 A.2d 501 (N.H. 1993)
Bronchial hypersensitivity	AZ	*Hunter v. Industrial Comm'n*, 633 P.2d 1052 (Ariz. Ct. App. 1981)
Carpal tunnel syndrome	AR	*Reeder v. Rheem Mfg. Co.*, 832 S.W.2d 505 (Ark. Ct. App. 1992)
	NM	*Torres v. Plastech Corp.*, 947 P.2d 154 (N.M. 1997)
	TN	*Reece v. J.T. Walker Indus., Inc.*, 2007 WL 4322003 (Tenn. Spec. Workers' Comp. App. Panel 2007)
	TN	*Jaske v. Murray Ohio Mfg. Co.*, 750 S.W.2d 150 (Tenn. 1988)
	TN	*White v. United Indus. Syndicate*, 742 S.W.2d 635 (Tenn. 1987)
Contact dermatitis	CT	*Misenti v. International Silver Co.*, 729 CRD-6-88-9 (Oct. 1989)
	FL	*Dayron Corp. & Claims Ctr. v. Morehead*, 509 So. 2d 930 (Fla. 1989)
	FL	*OBS Co. v. Freeney*, 475 So. 2d 947 (Fla. Dist. Ct. App. 1985)
Cranial nerves	AR	*Swift-Eckrich, Inc. v. Brock*, 975 S.W.2d 857 (Ark. Ct. App. 1998)
Cumulative trauma	OK	*Moore v. Uniroyal Goodrich*, 959 P.2d 1193 (Okla. Ct. App. 1997)
deQuervain's tendonitis	TN	*Reece v. J.T. Walker Indus., Inc.*, 2007 WL 4322003 (Tenn. Spec. Workers' Comp. App. Panel 2007)
Disk	SD	*Caldwell v. John Morrel & Co.*, 489 N.W.2d 353 (S.D. 1992)
Disfigurement	NV	*Maxwell v. SIIS*, 849 P.2d 267 (Nev. 1993)
Ear	OK	*Green v. Glass*, 920 P.2d 1081 (Okla. Ct. App. 1996)
	Fed.	*Baker v. Bethlehem Steel Corp.*, 24 F.3d 632 (4th Cir. 1994)
	Fed.	*Tanner v. Ingalls Shipbuilding, Inc.*, 2 F.3d 143 (5th Cir. 1993)
	Fed.	*Rasmussen v. General Dynamics*, 993 F.2d 1014 (2d Cir. 1993)
	Fed.	*Ingalls Shipbuilding v. Director, OWCP*, 991 F.2d 163 (5th Cir. 1993)
Elbow	FL	*McCray v. Murray*, 423 So. 2d 559 (Fla. Dist. Ct. App. 1982)
	GA	*Sutton v. Quality Furniture*, 381 S.E.2d 389 (Ga. Ct. App. 1989)
	LA	*Wise v. Lapworth*, 614 So. 2d 728 (La. Ct. App. 1993)
	KY	*Williams v. FEI Installation*, 2005 WL 3488386 (Ky. Ct. App. 2005)
Eye	CO	*Advanced Component Sys. v. Gonzales*, 935 P.2d 24 (Colo. Ct. App. 1996)

Impairment	State	Citation
	IA	*Coffman v. Kind & Knox Gelatine, Inc.*, 2006 Iowa App. LEXIS 784 (Iowa Ct. App. 2006)
	OH	*Dunn v. Eaton Corp.*, 1999 Ohio App. LEXIS 1758 (Ohio Ct. App. Mar. 31, 1999)
Fibromyalgia	TX	*Rogers v. Morales*, 975 F. Supp. 856 (N.D. Tex. 1997)
Finger	IA	*Robbennolt v. Snap-On Tools Corp.*, 555 N.W.2d 229 (Iowa 1996)
Foot	FL	*Clay Hyder Trucking v. Persinger*, 419 So. 2d 900 (Fla. Dist. Ct. App. 1982)
	NM	*Barela v. Midcon of N.M. Inc.*, 785 P.2d 271 (N.M. Ct. App. 1989)
	SC	*Dunmore v. Brooks Veneer Co.*, 149 S.E.2d 766 (S.C. 1966)
	TN	*Long v. Mid-Tenn. Ford Truck Sales, Inc.*, 160 S.W.3d 505 (Tenn. 2005)
Groin	CO	*Dillard v. Industrial Claim Appeals Office*, 134 P.3d 407 (Colo. Dec. 18, 2006)
	TN	*Gates v. Jackson Appliance Co.*, 2001 WL 720624 (Tenn. Spec. Workers' Comp. App. Panel June 27, 2001)
Hand	FL	*Shaw v. Publix Supermarkets, Inc.*, 609 So. 2d 683 (Fla. Dist. Ct. App. 1992)
	FL	*Gainesville Coca-Cola v. Young*, 596 So. 2d 1278 (Fla. Dist. Ct. App. 1992)
	FL	*G&W Wood Prods. v. Parrott*, 447 So. 2d 407 (Fla. Dist. Ct. App. 1984)
	FL	*Genelus v. Boran, Craig, Schreck Constr Co.*, 438 So. 2d 964 (Fla. Dist. Ct. App. 1983)
	FL	*Rhaney v. Dobbs, Inc.*, 415 So. 2d 1277 (Fla. Dist. Ct. App. 1982)
	NE	*Jacob v. Columbia Ins. Group*, 511 N.W.2d 211 (Neb. Ct. App. 1994)
	NH	*Petition of Blake*, 623 A.2d 741 (N.H. 1993)
	OK	*Oklahoma Tax Comm'n v. Evans*, 827 P.2d 183 (Okla. Ct. App. 1992)
	TN	*Scruggs v. Wal-Mart Stores, Inc.*, 2000 WL 371198 (Tenn. Spec. Workers' Comp. App. Panel Apr. 4, 2000)
	UT	*Jacobson Constr. v. Hair*, 667 P.2d 25 (Utah 1983)
	WY	*Clark v. State ex rel. Workers' Div.*, 934 P.2d 1269 (Wyo. 1997)
Head	FL	*Philpot v. City of Miami*, 541 So. 2d 680 (Fla. Dist. Ct. App. 1989)
Head/Neck	AK	*Polk County v. Jones*, 74 Ark. App. 159, 47 S.W.3d 904 (Ark. Ct. App. 2001)
	OK	*Wheat v. Heritage Manor*, 784 P.2d 74 (Okla. 1989)
Headaches	FL	*Whitehall Corp. v. Davis*, 448 So. 2d 47 (Fla. Dist. Ct. App. 1984)
Hearing	AK	*Yoder v. Alaska*, No. 4FA-84-1315 (Alaska Super. Ct. Jan. 30, 1985)
	AZ	*Pacific Fruit Express v. Industrial Comm'n*, 735 P.2d 820 (Ariz. 1987)
	AZ	*Adams v. Industrial Comm'n*, 552 P.2d 764 (Ariz. 1976)

Impairment	State	Citation
	CO	*City of Aurora v. Vaughn*, 824 P.2d 825 (Colo. Ct. App. 1991)
	CO	*Jefferson County Sch. v. Headrick*, 734 P.2d 659 (Colo. Ct. App. 1986)
	FL	*Peck v. Palm Beach County Bd. of County Comm'rs*, 442 So. 2d 1050 (Fla. Dist. Ct. App. 1983)
	KY	*Knott Floyd Land Co. v. Fugate*, 2007 WL 4462301 (Ky. 2007)
	KY	*AK Steel Corp. v. Johnston*, 153 S.W.3d 837 (Ky. 2005)
	KY	*Palmore v. Allgood*, 767 S.W.2d 328 (Ky. Ct. App. 1989)
	OK	*Special Indem. Fund v. Choate*, 847 P.2d 796 (Okla. 1993)
	OK	*Houston v. Zebco*, 821 P.2d 367 (Okla. 1991)
	OK	*Williams v. Vickers*, 799 P.2d 421 (Okla. 1990)
	OK	*Peabody Galion Corp. v. Workman*, 643 P.2d 312 (Okla. 1982)
	PA	*Richcreek v. WCAB (York Int'l Corp.)*, 786 A.2d 1054 (Pa. Commw. Ct. 2001)
	PA	*LTV Steel Co. v. WCAB (Mozena)*, 562 Pa. 205, 754 A.2d 666 (Pa. 2000)
	PA	*Rockwell Int'l v. W.C.A.B. (Meyer)*, 741 A.2d 835 (Pa. Commw. Ct. 1999)
	PA	*Washington Steel Corp. v. W.C.A.B. (Waugh)*, 734 A.2d 81 (Pa. Commw. Ct. 1999)
	Fed.	*Ingalls Shipbuilding v. Director, OWCP*, 898 F.2d 1088 (5th Cir. 1990)
Heart	AZ	*Department of Corr. v. Industrial Comm'n*, 894 P.2d 726 (Ariz. Ct. App. 1995)
	FL	*Jamar Sportswear, Inc. v. Miller*, 413 So. 2d 811 (Fla. Dist. Ct. App. 1982)
	ID	*Johnson v. Amalgamated Sugar*, 702 P.2d 803 (Idaho 1985)
	LA	*Brossett v. State ex rel. Department of Transp.*, 467 So. 2d 121 (La. Ct. App. 1985)
	NV	*Rosser v. State ex rel. State Indus. Ins. Sys.*, 113 Nev. 1125, 946 P.2d 185 (1997)
Hematoma	FL	*Quality Petroleum Corp. v. Mihm*, 424 So. 2d 112 (Fla. Dist. Ct. App. 1982)
Hepatitis	OR	*In re Compensation of Bohnke*, 640 P.2d 685 (Or. Ct. App. 1982)
Hernia	TN	*Corcoran v. Foster Auto GMC, Inc.*, 746 S.W.2d 452 (Tenn. 1988)
Herniated disk	AZ	*W.A. Krueger v. Industrial Comm'n*, 722 P.2d 234 (Ariz. 1986)
Hip	FL	*Shop & Go, Inc. v. Dunigan*, 463 So. 2d 585 (Fla. Dist. Ct. App. 1985)
	FL	*Trindade v. Abbey Road Beef 'N Booze*, 443 So. 2d 1007 (Fla. Dist. Ct. App. 1983)
	FL	*Ravensword-Griffin Volunteer Fire Dep't v. Newman*, 442 So. 2d 321 (Fla. Dist. Ct. App. 1982)
	FL	*Mathis v. Kelly Constr. Co.*, 417 So. 2d 740 (Fla. Dist. Ct. App. 1982)
	IA	*Lauhoff Grain Co. v. McIntosh*, 395 N.W.2d 834 (Iowa 1986)
	LA	*Durbin v. State Farm Fire & Cas. Co.*, 558 So. 2d 1257 (La. Ct. App. 1990)

Impairment	State	Citation
	LA	*Sumrall v. Crown Zellerbach Corp.*, 525 So. 2d 272 (La. Ct. App. 1990)
	LA	*Anderson v. Aetna Cas. & Sur. Co.*, 505 So. 2d 199 (La. Ct. App. 1987)
	LA	*Hughes v. General Motors Guide Lamp Div.*, 469 So. 2d 369 (La. Ct. App. 1985)
	NV	*Ransier v. State Indus. Ins. Sys.*, 766 P.2d 274 (Nev. 1988)
	ND	*Kroeplin v. North Dakota Workers' Comp. Bd.*, 415 N.W.2d 807 (N.D. 1987)
	OK	*Tulsa County v. Roberts*, 738 P.2d 969 (Okla. Ct. App. 1987)
	OK	*Altus House Nursing v. Roberts*, 646 P.2d 9 (Okla. Ct. App. 1982)
	OK	*B.F. Goodrich v. Hilton*, 634 P.2d 1308 (Okla. 1981)
	UT	*Kaiser Steel Corp. v. Industrial Comm'n*, 709 P.2d 1168 (Utah 1975)
	WY	*Bohren v. Wyoming Workers' Comp. Div.*, 883 P.2d 355 (Wyo. 1994)
Jaw	HI	*Cabatbat v. County of Haw., Dep't of Water Supply*, 78 P.3d 756 (Haw. 2003)
Kidney	ID	*Hite v. Kulhenak Bldg. Contractor*, 524 P.2d 531 (Idaho 1974)
Knee	AZ	*Vargas v. Industrial Comm'n*, 926 P.2d 533 (Ariz. Ct. App. 1996)
	AZ	*Slover Masonry, Inc. v. Industrial Comm'n*, 761 P.2d 1035 (Ariz. 1988)
	AZ	*Alsbrooks v. Industrial Comm'n*, 578 P.2d 159 (Ariz. 1978)
	FL	*McCabe v. Bechtel Power Corp.*, 510 So. 2d 1056 (Fla. Dist. Ct. App. 1987)
	FL	*Allen v. Gordon*, 429 So. 2d 369 (Fla. Dist. Ct. App. 1983)
	IA	*Second Injury Fund v. Bergeson*, 526 N.W.2d 543 (Iowa 1995)
	NH	*Hausen v. Seabrook Clam Co.*, 623 A.2d 225 (N.H. 1993)
	NM	*Toynbee v. Mimbres Mem'l Nursing Home*, 833 P.2d 1204 (N.M. Ct. App. 1992)
	TN	*Brown v. Nissan N. Am., Inc.*, 2006 Tenn. LEXIS 1138 (Tenn. Spec. Workers' Comp. App. Panel at Nashville, July 24, 2006)
	TN	*Pesce v. Aerostructures/Vought Aircraft Indus.*, 2007 WL 906707 (Tenn. Spec. Workers' Comp. App. Panel 2007)
	TX	*Old Republic Ins. Co. v. Rodriguez*, 966 S.W.2d 208 (Tex. App. 1998)
Leg	AZ	*Gomez v. Industrial Comm'n*, 716 P.2d 22 (Ariz. Ct. App. 1985)
	AR	*Milburn v. Concrete Fabricators*, 709 S.W.2d 822 (Ark. Ct. App. 1986)
	DE	*Butler v. Ryder M.L.S.*, 1999 Del. Super. LEXIS 29 (Del. Super. Ct. Feb. 1, 1999)
	FL	*Buro v. Dino's Southland Meats*, 354 So. 2d 874 (Fla. Dist. Ct. App. 1978)
	IA	*Caylor v. Employers Mut. Cas. Co.*, 337 N.W.2d 890 (Iowa Ct. App. 1983)
	IA	*Graves v. Eagle Iron Works*, 331 N.W.2d 116 (Iowa 1983)
	MS	*Smith v. Jackson Constr. Co.*, 607 So. 2d 1119 (Miss. 1992)

Impairment	State	Citation
	MT	*Hall v. State Comp. Ins. Fund*, 708 P.2d 234 (Mont. 1985)
	OK	*Special Indem. Fund v. Stockton*, 653 P.2d 194 (Okla. 1982)
	TN	*Reagan v. Tennessee Mun. League*, 751 S.W.2d 842 (Tenn. 1988)
	Fed.	*Rosa v. Director, Office of Workers' Comp. Programs*, 1998 U.S. App. LEXIS 7171 (9th Cir. Apr. 8, 1998)
Leg/Foot	OR	*In re Compensation of Clemons*, 169 Or. App. 231, 9 P.3d 123 (Or. Ct. App. 2000)
Loss of strength	AZ	*Mountain Shadows Resort Hotel v. Industrial Comm'n*, 710 P.2d 1066 (Ariz. Ct. App. 1985)
	AZ	*Dutra v. Industrial Comm'n*, 659 P.2d 18 (Ariz. 1983)
Lung	AR	*Excelsior Hotel v. Squires*, 2005 WL 2375225 (Ark. Ct. App. Sept. 28, 2005)
		Excelsior Hotel v. Squires, 115 S.W.3d 83 (Ark. Ct. App. Div. IV 2003)
	KY	*Newberg v. Price*, 868 S.W.2d 92 (Ky. 1994)
	KY	*Varney v. Newberg*, 860 S.W.2d 752 (Ky. 1993)
	KY	*Newberg v. Garrett*, 858 S.W.2d 181 (Ky. 1993)
	KY	*Blue Diamond Coal/Scotia Coal v. Beale*, 847 S.W.2d 61 (Ky. Ct. App. 1993)
	KY	*Beale v. Highwire, Inc.*, 843 S.W.2d 898 (Ky. Ct. App. 1993)
	KY	*Wright v. Hopwood Mining*, 832 S.W.2d 884 (Ky. 1992)
	KY	*Newberg v. Reynolds*, 831 S.W.2d 170 (Ky. 1992)
	KY	*Newberg v. Wright*, 824 S.W.2d 843 (Ky. 1992)
	KY	*Newberg v. Chumley*, 824 S.W.2d 413 (Ky. 1992)
	NM	*Yeager v. St. Vincent Hosp.*, 973 P.2d 850 (N.M. Ct. App. 1998)
	OK	*Special Indem. Fund v. Choate*, 847 P.2d 796 (Okla. 1993)
	OK	*Lacy v. Schlumberger Well Serv.*, 839 P.2d 157 (Okla. 1992)
	OK	*Weyerhaeuser Co. v. Washington*, 838 P.2d 539 (Okla. Ct. App. 1992)
	OK	*Parks v. Blue Circle, Inc.*, 832 P.2d 11 (Okla. 1992)
	OK	*Kropp v. Goodrich*, 829 P.2d 33 (Okla. 1992)
	OK	*Davis v. B.F. Goodrich*, 826 P.2d 587 (Okla. 1992)
	OK	*Hollytex Carpet Mills, Inc. v. Hinkle*, 819 P.2d 289 (Okla. Ct. App. 1991)
	SD	*Cantalope v. Veterans of Foreign War Club of Eureka*, 2004 SD 4, 674 N.W.2d 329 (S.D. 2004)
Lung disease	NC	*Parrish v. Burlington Indus., Inc.*, 321 S.E.2d 492 (N.C. Ct. App. 1984)
Mental	KY	*Lanter v. Kentucky State Police*, 171 S.W.3d 45 (Ky. 2005)
Mold hypersensitivity	DE	*Pekala v. E.I. DuPont de Nemours & Co.*, 2007 WL 1653496 (Del. Super. Ct. 2007)
Muscle weakness	FL	*Brice S., Inc. v. Cancino*, 447 So. 2d 367 (Fla. Dist. Ct. App. 1984)
Neck	AZ	*Salt River Project v. Industrial Comm'n*, 837 P.2d 1212 (Ariz. Ct. App. 1992)
	AZ	*Desert Insulations, Inc. v. Industrial Comm'n*, 654 P.2d 296 (Ariz. Ct. App. 1982)

Impairment	State	Citation
	AK	*Hapney v. Rheem Mfg. Co.*, 342 Ark. 11, 26 S.W.3d 777 (Ark. 2000)
	DE	*Simmons v. Delaware State Hosp.*, 660 A.2d 384 (Del. 1995)
	FL	*Walker v. Gulf & W. Food Prods.*, 461 So. 2d 993 (Fla. Dist. Ct. App. 1984)
	FL	*Deseret Ranches v. Crosby*, 461 So. 2d 295 (Fla. Dist. Ct. App. 1985)
	FL	*Frank's Fine Meats v. Sherman*, 443 So. 2d 1055 (Fla. Dist. Ct. App. 1984)
	FL	*Buro v. Dino's Southland Meats*, 354 So. 2d 874 (Fla. Dist. Ct. App. 1978)
	ID	*Poss v. Meeker Mach. Shop*, 712 P.2d 621 (Idaho 1985)
	KY	*Newberg v. Thomas Indus.*, 852 S.W.2d 339 (Ky. Ct. App. 1993)
	ND	*Saari v. North Dakota Workers' Comp. Bureau*, 598 N.W.2d 174 (N.D. 1999)
	OK	*Norwood v. Lee Way Motor Freight, Inc.*, 646 P.2d 2 (Okla. Ct. App. 1982)
	TN	*Chapman v. Bekaert Steel Wire Corp.*, 2003 Tenn. LEXIS (Tenn. Spec. Workers' Comp. App. Panel Oct. 16, 2003) *Bolton v. CNA Ins. Co.*, 821 S.W.2d 932 (Tenn. 1991)
	WI	*Lewandowski v. Preferred Risk Mut. Ins. Co.*, 146 N.W.2d 505 (Wis. 1966)
Pain	AZ	*Simpson v. Industrial Comm'n*, 942 P.2d 1172 (Ariz. Dist. Ct. App. 1997)
	FL	*Maggard v. Simpson Motors*, 451 So. 2d 529 (Fla. Dist. Ct. App. 1984)
	FL	*Muniz v. Glades County Sugar Growers*, 443 So. 2d 351 (Fla. Dist. Ct. App. 1983)
	FL	*Tallahassee Mem'l Reg'l Med. Ctr. v. Snead*, 400 So. 2d 1016 (Fla. Dist. Ct. App. 1981)
	LA	*Breaux v. Ralph Crais Oil Corp.*, 485 So. 2d 575 (La. Ct. App. 1986)
	NH	*Appeal of Rainville*, 1999 N.H. LEXIS 6 (N.H. Feb. 8, 1999)
	UT	*Gardner v. Edward Gardner Plumbing & Heating*, 693 P.2d 678 (Utah 1984)
Pneumoconiosis	WV	*Javins v. Workers' Comp. Comm'r*, 320 S.E.2d 119 (W. Va. 1984)
Prior surgery	AZ	*Chavez v. Industrial Comm'n*, 575 P.2d 340 (Ariz. Ct. App. 1978)
Psychiatric	FL	*Public Gas Co. v. Shaw*, 464 So. 2d 1243 (Fla. Dist. Ct. App. 1985)
	FL	*Vannice Constr. Co. v. Silverman*, 419 So. 2d 369 (Fla. Dist. Ct. App. 1982)
	FL	*Racz v. Chennault*, 418 So. 2d 413 (Fla. Dist. Ct. App. 1982)
	FL	*Cumberland Farm Food Stores v. Meier*, 408 So. 2d 700 (Fla. Dist. Ct. App. 1982)
	KS	*Adamson v. Davis Moore Datsun, Inc.*, 868 P.2d 546 (Kan. Ct. App. 1994)

Impairment	State	Citation
	MT	*S.L.H. v. State Comp. Mut. Ins. Fund*, 15 P.3d 948, 2000 MT 362 (Mont. 2000)
	OH	*State ex rel. Dresser v. Industrial Comm'n*, 652 N.E.2d 1020 (Ohio 1995)
	OK	*Oklahoma State Penitentiary v. Weaver*, 809 P.2d 1324 (Okla. Ct. App. 1991)
	NM	*Peterson v. Northern Health Care*, 912 P.2d 831 (N.M. Ct. App. 1996)
	TN	*Blanton v. CVS Tenn. Distrib., Inc.*, 2006 Tenn. LEXIS 197 (Tenn. 2006)
Psychological	GA	*General Motors Corp. v. Summerous*, 317 S.E.2d 318 (Ga. Ct. App. 1984)
	NV	*Maxwell v. SIIS*, 849 P.2d 267 (Nev. 1993)
	OK	*General Tool & Supply v. Somers*, 737 P.2d 581 (Okla. Ct. App. 1987)
	OK	*Montgomery Ward & Co. v. Johnson*, 645 P.2d 1051 (Okla. Ct. App. 1982)
	UT	*Northwest Carriers v. Industrial Comm'n*, 639 P.2d 138 (Utah 1981)
Reflex sympathetic dystrophy	KS	*Thompson v. U.S.D.*, No. 512, 2007 WL 2580530 (Kan. Ct. App. 2007)
Reproductive system	OK	*General Tool & Supply v. Somers*, 737 P.2d 581 (Okla. Ct. App. 1987)
Respiratory disease	CT	*Piscitelli v. Connecticut Coke/Eastern Gas & Fuel Assocs.*, 575 CRD-3-87 (Workers' Comp. Comm'n Jan. 1989)
	OK	*Zebco v. Houston*, 800 P.2d 245 (Okla. 1990)
	OK	*Gaines v. Sun Refinery & Mktg.*, 790 P.2d 1073 (Okla. 1990)
	OK	*Orrell v. B.F. Goodrich*, 787 P.2d 848 (Okla. 1990)
	OK	*Edwards v. Amoco*, 776 P.2d 566 (Okla. Ct. App. 1989)
	OK	*King v. Razien Oil Co.*, 768 P.2d 385 (Okla. Ct. App. 1989)
Ribs	AK	*Excelsior Hotel v. Squires*, 2005 WL 2375225 (Ark. App. Sept. 28, 2005)
Ruptured disk	FL	*Christian v. Greater Miami Acad.*, 541 So. 2d 701 (Fla. Dist. Ct. App. 1989)
	OK	*LaBarge v. Zebco*, 769 P.2d 125 (Okla. 1988)
	TN	*Davenport v. Taylor Feed Mill*, 784 S.W.2d 923 (Tenn. 1990)
Seizures	Fed.	*Jones v. Railroad Ret. Bd.*, 614 F.2d 151 (8th Cir. 1980)
Shoulder	AZ	*Low v. Industrial Comm'n*, 680 P.2d 188 (Ariz. App. Ct. 1984)
	CO	*Strauch v. PSL Swedish Healthcare Sys.*, 917 P.2d 366 (Colo. Ct. App. 1996)
	CO	*Walker v. Jim Fuoco Motor Co.*, 942 P.2d 1390 (Colo. Ct. App. 1997)
	FL	*Walker v. Gulf & W. Food Prods.*, 461 So. 2d 993 (Fla. Dist. Ct. App. 1984)
	ID	*Poss v. Meeker Mach. Shop*, 712 P.2d 621 (Idaho 1985)
	KS	*Durham v. Cessna Aircraft Co.*, 945 P.2d 8 (Kan. Ct. App. 1997), *review denied*, No. 96-77514-AS (Kan. Dec. 23, 1997)
	KY	*Napier v. Middlesboro Appalachian Reg'l Hosp.*, 2004 WL 538123 (Ky. Mar. 18, 2004)
	MD	*Getson v. W.M. Babcorp*, 694 A.2d 961 (Md. 1997)

Impairment	State	Citation
	NH	*In re Wal-Mart Stores*, 765 A.2d 168 (N.H. 2000)
	ND	*Saari v. North Dakota Workers' Comp. Bureau*, 598 N.W.2d 174 (N.D. 1999)
	OH	*State ex rel. Lucente v. Industrial Comm'n*, 472 N.E.2d 718 (Ohio 1984)
	TN	*Key v. Savage Zinc, Inc.*, No. M 200000306WCR3CV, 2001 WL 758736 (Tenn. Spec. Workers' Comp. App. Panel July 6, 2001)
	TN	*Cain v. Whirlpool Corp.*, 2001 WL 873459 (Tenn. Spec. Workers Comp. App. Panel 2001)
Skin	FL	*Paradise Fruit Co. v. Floyd*, 425 So. 2d 9 (Fla. Dist. Ct. App. 1982)
Speech discrimination	AK	*Yoder v. Alaska*, No. 4FA-84-1315 (Alaska Super. Ct. Jan. 30, 1985)
Thumb	AZ	*CAVCO Indus. v. Industrial Comm'n*, 631 P.2d 1087 (Ariz. 1981)
Vascular	AZ	*Pena v. Industrial Comm'n*, 668 P.2d 900 (Ariz. Ct. App. 1983)
	FL	*Hulbert v. Avis Rent-A-Car Sys.*, 469 So. 2d 235 (Fla. Dist. Ct. App. 1985)
	FL	*Taylor v. International Paper Co.*, 404 So. 2d 808 (Fla. Dist. Ct. App. 1981)
Vision	FL	*Recon Paving, Inc. v. Cook*, 439 So. 2d 1019 (Fla. Dist. Ct. App. 1983)
	ND	*Kavonius v. North Dakota Workmen's Comp. Bureau*, 306 N.W.2d 209 (N.D. 1981)
	WI	*Employers Mut. Liab. Ins. Co. v. Department of Indus., Labor & Human Relations*, 214 N.W.2d 587 (Wis. 1974)
Wrist	AZ	*Perez v. Industrial Comm'n*, 685 P.2d 154 (Ariz. Ct. App. 1984)
	AZ	*Reno v. Industrial Comm'n*, 750 P.2d 852 (Ariz. 1988)
	FL	*SpringAir Mattress Co. v. Cox*, 413 So. 2d 1265 (Fla. Dist. Ct. App. 1982)
	IA	*Simbro v. Delong's Sportswear*, 332 N.W.2d 886 (Iowa 1983)
	NH	*Appeal of Fournier*, 786 A.2d 854 (N.H. 2001)
	KS	*Martinez v. Excel Corp.*, 79 P.2d 230 (Kan. Ct. App. 2003)
Wrist and shoulder	TN	*Russell v. Bill Heard Enters., Inc.*, 2001 WL 721062 (Tenn. Spec. Workers' Comp. App. Panel June 26, 2001)

THE 15 MOST IMPORTANT CHANGES IN THE *AMA GUIDES* (4TH ED. 1993)

This appendix discusses the 15 most important changes between the fourth edition and the third edition of the *AMA Guides*.[1] These changes are:

1. There is a new definition of *permanent impairment.*

2. Physicians may now express an opinion concerning disability in certain circumstances.

3. Additional information is required in medical reports.

4. There are numerous new and useful examples; some of the old examples now yield different ratings than their counterparts from the previous edition.

5. Spine evaluations are now generally performed under the new injury model of impairment evaluation.

6. There is a new approach to lower extremity evaluation.

7. Modified impairment criteria and ranges are utilized in many chapters.

8. Specific instruction is now included to ensure accurate spirometry during lung impairment evaluation.

9. There are expanded and modified lists of objective procedures useful in evaluating impairment.

10. There are new directions for evaluating skin disfigurement.

11. Documentation of mental disorders is now permitted via reports from new sources.

12. There is a new chapter on pain.

13. Glossary definitions of many key terms are modified; many new terms are defined for the first time.

14. The background on the Americans with Disabilities Act (ADA)[2] is provided, with a comparison and contrast to the terms of the *AMA Guides.*

---

[1] For changes between the fourth and fifth editions, see Chapter 4.

[2] 42 U.S.C. §§ 12101 *et seq.*

15. There is new treatment of predicted normal spirometry values for non-Whites.

1. There is a new definition of *permanent impairment.* The *AMA Guides* (3d ed. rev. 1990) defined *permanent impairment* as an impairment to which "the clinical findings determined over a period of time, usually 12 months, indicate that the condition is static and well stabilized."[3]

The *AMA Guides* (4th ed. 1993) defines a *permanent impairment* as "an adverse condition that is stable and unlikely to change."[4]

2. Physicians may now express an opinion concerning disability in certain circumstances. The *AMA Guides* (3d ed. rev. 1990) carefully avoided the issue of whether a physician could express an opinion on the ultimate issue in many workers' compensation cases, that is, disability. This edition talked in terms of employability and then concluded that "[d]isability results when the individual lacks the characteristics of employability."[5]

The *AMA Guides* (4th ed. 1993) recognizes that physicians may, under certain circumstances, directly express an opinion on disability. This edition specifically states: "If the physician is well acquainted with the patient's activities and needs, he or she may also express an opinion about the presence or absence of a disability or handicap."[6]

3. Additional information is required in medical reports. The *AMA Guides* (4th ed. 1993) makes the following changes to the model report form found in the *AMA Guides* (3d ed. rev. 1990):[7]

1. Requires the date of the report.

2. Changes item no. 4b from "The degree of impairment is not likely to change by more than 3 percent within the next year"[8] to "The degree of impairment is not likely to change substantially within the next year."[9]

3. Adds the words *including occupation* to the list of daily activities and asks the doctors to list the types of daily activities affected in item no. 5.[10]

4. Includes the following sentence in item no. 6: "Each organ system impairment estimate should be expressed in terms of percent impairment of the whole person and by adding a column for percent impairment of the whole person."[11]

---

[3] American Medical Association (AMA), Guides to the Evaluation of Permanent Impairment (3d ed. rev. 1990) (hereinafter *AMA Guides* (3d ed. rev. 1990)) at 6.

[4] AMA, Guides to the Evaluation of Permanent Impairment (4th ed. 1993) (hereinafter *AMA Guides* (4th ed. 1993)) at v.

[5] *AMA Guides* (3d ed. rev. 1990) at 2.

[6] *AMA Guides* (4th ed. 1993) at 2.

[7] *See AMA Guides* (3d ed. rev. 1990) at 11–12.

[8] *Id.* at 8.

[9] *AMA Guides* (4th ed. 1993) at 11.

[10] *Id.* at 12.

[11] *Id.*

5. Adds items no. 7 through no. 9: "Requiring the final estimated whole-person impairment, the dates of treatment or evaluation and a statement of consistency or inconsistency in the history, physical examination and laboratory findings."[12]

4. There are numerous new and useful examples; some of the old examples now yield different ratings than their counterparts from the previous edition. The *AMA Guides* (4th ed. 1993) contains many new examples of impairment evaluation. In addition, because of changes in this edition, some of the examples retained from the *AMA Guides* (3d ed. rev. 1990) now yield different impairment ratings.

5. Spine evaluations are now generally performed under the new injury model of impairment evaluation. The previous editions of the *AMA Guides* used the range of motion (ROM) model for spine evaluation. Under the ROM model, system evaluations were performed by determining the patient's degree of spine motion and then assigning the appropriate impairment percentage. The authors of the *AMA Guides* (4th ed. 1993) point out the following major problems associated with this evaluation technique.

1. A disregard of clinical data and diagnostic information

2. Problems with accuracy and reproducibility of mobility measurements

3. A failure to take into account the effects of aging.[13]

The authors of the *AMA Guides* (4th ed. 1993) attempted to address these concerns through the development of the injury model of spine impairment evaluation.[14] The injury model involves assigning a patient to one of eight categories called diagnosis-related estimates (DREs) based on objective clinical findings.[15] Each DRE category has been assigned a corresponding impairment percentage, with the lowest impairment rating for category I and the highest for category VIII. The ROM model is to be used only when no categories from the injury model are "applicable" or in close cases to help an evaluator place a patient in the appropriate injury model category.[16]

It is important for counsel to be aware that the ROM model is now disfavored and may be used only in the two previous situations mentioned. Also, the evaluators may not combine the ROM and the injury methods or use the ROM method when the patient clearly fits into an injury model DRE category.

---

[12] *Id.*

[13] *Id.* at 94.

[14] The authors of the *AMA Guides* (4th ed. 1993) do not claim to have created a perfect model. "It is acknowledged that the [injury model] approach is different from that of previous *Guides* editions and that future developments may lead to refinement or a different recommendation altogether." *Id.*

[15] *AMA Guides* (4th ed. 1993) at 94.

[16] *Id.* at 94, 99.

All persons evaluating impairments according to *Guides* criteria are cautioned that either one *or* the other approach should be used in making the final impairment estimate. If one component were used according to *Guides* recommendations, then a final impairment estimate using the other component usually would not be pertinent or germane.[17]

6. There is a new approach to lower extremity evaluation. The *AMA Guides* (3d ed. rev. 1990) based impairment evaluation of the lower extremity on ROM and amputation. The approach used in *AMA Guides* (4th ed. 1993) utilizes "anatomic, diagnostic, and functional methods" to evaluate permanent impairment of the lower extremity.[18] The crucial innovation of the *AMA Guides* (4th ed. 1993) is that the physician is given the discretion to select the appropriate method of evaluation. A physician may now select from among the following methods:

1. Limb length discrepancy
2. Gait derangement
3. Muscle atrophy
4. Manual muscle testing
5. Range of motion
6. Joint ankylosis
7. Arthritis
8. Amputation
9. Diagnosis-based estimates
10. Skin loss

The *AMA Guides* (4th ed. 1993) also allows a combination of two or three methods in some instances. It states that the physician should use "judgment and experience" in selecting the method or methods.[19] It is crucial to note that the fourth edition does not provide specific guidelines for the physician to follow when selecting an evaluation method or methods. The only guidance provided is in several examples.[20] Those examples illustrate how the physician selected the best approach for evaluating the impairment *in that particular case.*

A major issue concerning lower extremity evaluation will most likely be whether the evaluator selected the best approach for evaluating an impairment.

---

[17] *Id.* at 94 (emphasis in original).

[18] *Id.* at 75.

[19] *Id.*

[20] *See id.* The comment for this example states that a physician properly chose one method over three possible because that method "best reflected the basic pathological process."

In cases similar to those examples in the *AMA Guides* (4th ed. 1993), the evaluator should use the same method as the physician in the example.[21]

Some language in the *AMA Guides* (4th ed. 1993) suggests that there is usually no "wrong" method to use in evaluating impairment.[22] For example, the *AMA Guides* (4th ed. 1993) states that the physician should select the "best" or "optimal" approach.[23] Logically, an evaluation method that is not optimal may still be acceptable, reliable, and valid. It is necessary for counsel to be aware of this distinction. This argument is buttressed by other language. For example, in one comment to an example,[24] the *AMA Guides* (4th ed. 1993) states that a certain method of evaluation would be "more appropriate" than another in that case.[25] Implicit in this language is the idea that both methods are appropriate.

7. Modified impairment criteria and ranges are utilized in many chapters. Many of the organ systems in the *AMA Guides* (4th ed. 1993) are rated for impairment according to criteria that have been modified from the criteria found in the *AMA Guides* (3d ed. rev. 1990). In addition, many of the categories of impairment for the various organ systems in the fourth edition contain different ranges of impairment than were found in the third edition. Counsel must carefully verify that the proper criteria and the proper ranges of impairment are being used.

8. Specific instruction is now included to ensure accurate spirometry during lung impairment evaluation. The *AMA Guides* (4th ed. 1993) contains specific directions to follow to ensure acceptable spirometry.[26] The measurements are to be performed at least three times.[27] The results of the two best forced vital capacity (FVC) efforts should be within 5 percent of each other.[28] Special instructions are provided when wheezing is heard or the FEV_1/FVC ratio is below. 70.[29]

9. There are expanded and modified lists of objective procedures useful in evaluating impairment. These expanded lists, provided for most organ systems, reflect the progress in medical knowledge since the publication of the *AMA Guides* (3d ed. rev. 1990).

10. There are new directions for evaluating skin disfigurement. Unfortunately, the *AMA Guides* (4th ed. 1993) is somewhat inconsistent as to how skin

---

[21] *See AMA Guides* (4th ed. 1993) at 81. This example states that, in the example, evaluating for mal-positioning and ankylosis is more appropriate than using the impairment for an intraarticular ankle fracture.

[22] It is important for counsel to be aware that in several situations the *AMA Guides* (4th ed. 1993) specifically states that a certain evaluation method would be inappropriate. In these cases, there would be a "wrong" method. *See id.* at 78 for a comment specifying when not to use the muscle atrophy method.

[23] *Id.* at 75.

[24] *Id.* at 81.

[25] The "*more* appropriate" (emphasis added) language is also found at *id.* at 84. *See also id.* at 77 for a comment discussing the "better" approach.

[26] *Id.* at 159–60.

[27] *Id.* at 159.

[28] *Id.* at 159–60.

[29] *Id.* at 160.

disfigurement should be rated.[30] First, it states that disfigurement impairment should be evaluated under Chapter 14, "Mental and Behavioral Disorders."[31] This is because disfigurement may cause "social rejection, or an unfavorable self-image with self-imposed isolation, life-style alteration, or other behavioral changes."[32] In the very next paragraph, however, the *AMA Guides* (4th ed. 1993) states that disfigurement impairment should be evaluated under Table 2 on page 280.[33] Under the *AMA Guides* (3d ed. rev. 1990), disfigurements were to be evaluated only under Chapter 14, and not through Table 2.[34]

In the *AMA Guides* (4th ed. 1993), counsel should note that Table 2 does not use behavior as a criterion for impairment; however, it does use limitations on daily activities to govern impairments.[35] This latter paragraph probably means that the physician is to take into account behavioral changes due to disfigurement when judging the limitations upon daily activities.

In light of the previous discussion, there appear to be three possible ways in the *AMA Guides* (4th ed. 1993) to rate a disfigurement impairment. A physician may use only Table 2, only Chapter 14, or both Table 2 and Chapter Example 5[36] and Example 4[37] seem to favor assessment of the disfigurement portion of the impairment under Chapter 14.[38] A careful reading of Examples 5 and 4 will show counsel that they do not reconcile the previously mentioned inconsistency. Counsel may therefore have a very good chance of success when challenging a disfigurement impairment.

Finally, counsel must note that the last two paragraphs of this section in the *AMA Guides* (4th ed. 1993) provide guidelines for rating and reporting disfigurement impairments.[39] Disfigurement impairments that are not in conformity with these guidelines may be subject to question.

11. Documentation of mental disorders is now permitted via reports from new sources. The *AMA Guides* (4th ed. 1993) permits documentation of a mental disorder by the use of reports of new sources. These sources may include psychiatric nurses, psychiatric social workers, and health professionals in hospitals and clinics.

12. There is a new chapter on pain. The *AMA Guides* (3d ed. rev. 1990) contained an appendix entitled "Pain and Impairment." The editors of the *AMA Guides* (3d ed. rev. 1990) concentrated on chronic pain, finding that it was endemic in our society and that the understanding of pain "lacks a measure of precision and

---

[30] *Id.* at 279.
[31] *Id.*
[32] *Id.*
[33] *Id.* at 278.
[34] *AMA Guides* (3d ed. rev. 1990) at 224.
[35] *AMA Guides* (4th ed. 1993) at 280.
[36] *Id.* at 284.
[37] *Id.* at 288.
[38] *Id.* at 284.
[39] *Id.* at 279.

confidence which might be desirable."[40] The editors reviewed the basic concepts and categories of pain, pain management and impairment, and concluded that

> [s]ince chronic pain by definition is primarily a perceptual, maladaptive behavioral problem, since pain per se cannot be validated objectively or quantitated [sic], and since the underlying substrate of somatic pathology is minimal or nonexistent, it follows that little, if any, impairment exists in most instances of the chronic pain syndrome.[41]

The editors of the *AMA Guides* (4th ed. 1993) completely rewrote and expanded the appendix dealing with pain. The fourth edition contains new sections on pain, impairment and disability, classification and models, clinical assessment, and headaches.

13. Glossary definitions of many key terms are modified; many new terms are defined for the first time. The following terms were modified in the *AMA Guides* (4th ed. 1993):

1. Apportionment

2. Intensity

3. Aggravation

4. Causation

5. Activities of daily living

6. Documentation

7. Employability

The following terms were newly defined in the *AMA Guides* (4th ed. 1993):

1. Recurrence

2. New injury

14. The background on the Americans with Disabilities Act (ADA) is provided, with a comparison and contrast to terms of the *AMA Guides*. The editors of the *AMA Guides* (4th ed. 1993) added a detailed new section to the glossary. This section explains the background, the definitions, and the terms *disability* and *accommodation* in the Americans with Disabilities Act.[42]

15. There is new treatment of predicted normal spirometry values for non-Whites. The *AMA Guides* (4th ed. 1993) contains information concerning the

---

[40] *AMA Guides* (3d ed. rev. 1990) at 247.

[41] *Id.* at 252.

[42] 42 U.S.C. §§ 12101 *et seq.*

average or predicted values used in the impairment evaluation process.[43] These predicted values for White males and females are provided in Tables 2, 3, 4, 5, 6, and 7.[44] Counsel should note that because Blacks have lower spirometric values than corresponding Whites, an adjustment must be made to the predicted values in Tables 4, 5, 6, and 7 when a Black patient is evaluated for pulmonary impairment.[45] (Under the *AMA Guides* (3d ed. rev. 1990), a similar adjustment was made for Asians.[46]) This adjustment is made by multiplying the predicted FVC and the predicted FEV_1 by .88 and multiplying the predicted diffusing capacity by .93.[47]

The *AMA Guides* further notes that evidence exists that Hispanics, Native Americans, and Asians have lower lung function than Whites in North America. Because the cause and magnitude of this difference has not yet been well established, no adjustment for this difference is made by the *AMA Guides* (4th ed. 1993). In cases involving Asians, Native Americans, and Hispanics, counsel may be able to question the validity of the *AMA Guides* because of the failure or inability of the *AMA Guides* to take these differences into account.

---

[43] *See* Ky. Rev. Stat. Ann. § 342.316 (Baldwin), which instructs the Kentucky Workers' Compensation Board to review the *AMA Guides* test spirometry values and adopt new ones if these can be found to be more closely representative of the coal mining population.

[44] *AMA Guides* (4th ed. 1993) at 158–60. These tables provide predicted normals only for even-numbered heights and ages. *See* Ky. Admin. Regs. 25:011, which provides explicit instructions on calculating the predicted spirometry values when the examinee has an odd-numbered height or age.

[45] *AMA Guides* (4th ed. 1993) at 160.

[46] *AMA Guides* (3d ed. rev. 1990) at 120.

[47] *AMA Guides* (4th ed. 1993) at 160.

APPENDIX D

KEY POINTS IN THE *AMA GUIDES* (4TH ED. 1993)

This Appendix presents summary discussion of the 14 key points in the *AMA Guides* (4th ed. 1993):

1. Impairment versus disability

2. Permanent impairment

3. Two or more impairments

4. Rounding off

5. Pain

6. Activities of daily living

7. Mental impairment

8. Disfigurement

9. Symptom frequency and intensity

10. Causation

11. Apportionment

12. Aggravation

13. Hearing loss

14. Spinal impairment.

If a physician does not understand these points or fails to follow these rules, his or her impairment evaluation could be easily challenged.

The key points contained in the *AMA Guides* (5th ed. 2000) and the most significant differences between the fourth edition and the fifth edition of the *Guides* are discussed in Chapter 4 of this volume. The sixth edition of the *AMA Guides* is discussed in Chapter 5.

1. Impairment versus disability. The terms *impairment* and *disability* are neither synonymous nor interchangeable. *Impairment* under the *AMA Guides* is defined as an alteration in an individual's health status; it is a medical issue assessed by medical means.[1] *Disability* is defined as an alteration of "an

---

[1] *AMA Guides* (4th ed. 1993) at 1.

individual's capacity to meet personal, social, or occupational demands, or statutory or regulatory requirements, because of an impairment. Disability may be thought of as the gap between what a person can do and what the person needs or wants to do."[2]

2. Permanent impairment. Only permanent impairment can be evaluated under the *AMA Guides*. A *permanent impairment* is an impairment "that has become static or stabilized during a period of time sufficient to allow optimal tissue repair, and is unlikely to change in spite of further medical or surgical therapy."[3]

3. Two or more impairments. Generally, when two or more impairments exist, the value of each impairment is determined separately. These values are not simply added together but are converted to the whole-person concept by using the combined values chart.[4] There are, however, significant exceptions to this rule. For example, when evaluating the impairment of a hand, the impairment values of the involved digits are added and not combined.[5] It is important to note that combining impairments always results in a lower value than if the impairments were added together.

4. Rounding off. The final impairment whole-person percentage, whether it is based on the evaluation of one organ system or several organ systems, may be rounded to the nearer of the two nearest values ending in 0 or 5.[6] Rounding off may not be allowed in some jurisdictions.[7]

5. Pain. The percentages of impairments for pain are not given in the chapter of the *AMA Guides* devoted to pain. Pain is classified under the *AMA Guides* according to its intensity (minimal, slight, moderate, or marked) and its frequency (intermittent, occasional, frequent, or constant).[8] The proper question to ask when rating pain is not, Does this daily activity cause pain? but rather, Can the patient perform this daily activity?[9]

In *Chavarria v. Basin Moving & Storage*,[10] the court remanded the case for failure of the WCJ to consider medical evidence of impairment for chronic pain under the *AMA Guides*. In the case of *Hoyem v. North Dakota Workers' Compensation Bureau*,[11] the court held that the denying of a rating and evaluation for pain was proper.

6. Activities of daily living. *Impairments* are defined under the *AMA Guides* as conditions that interfere with a person's activities of daily living

---

[2] *Id.* at 2.
[3] *Id.* at 279.
[4] *See id.* at 322–24.
[5] *Id.* at 1.
[6] *Id.* at 9.
[7] *See* Alaska Stat. § 23.30.190.
[8] *AMA Guides* (4th ed. 1993) at 310.
[9] *Id.* at 309.
[10] 976 P.2d 1019 (N.M. Ct. App. 1999).
[11] 578 N.W.2d 117 (N.D. 1998).

(ADLs). These activities include self-care and personal hygiene, communication, physical activity, sensory function, hand function, travel, sexual function, sleep, and social and recreational activities.[12]

   7. Mental impairment. The percentages of impairment are not provided by the *AMA Guides* (4th ed. 1993) because "no data exist to show the reliability" of impairment percentages in this area.[13] Mental impairment is evaluated by analyzing the patient's ADLs, social function, concentration, and adaptation and by placing the patient in one of five classes of impairment detailed in the *AMA Guides* (4th ed. 1993). These classes of impairment are no impairment, mild impairment, moderate impairment, marked impairment, and extreme impairment.[14] At least one court has held that the trial judge should assign the numerical rating based on the physician's testimony about the category of impairment because no impairment percentages are given for mental impairments.[15] A state statute may require that an award be based on a rating expressed as a percentage, and this requirement may conflict with an evaluation of mental impairment based on the *AMA Guides* because no percentages of impairment are provided in the *AMA Guides*.[16] The court in *S.L.H. v. State Compensation Mutual Insurance Fund*[17] dealt with a Montana statute that required a percentage of impairment but also required that the *AMA Guides* be used. *S.L.H.* held that since the *AMA Guides* do not provide percentages, the case should be remanded so the workers' compensation court can assign a percentage based on the evidence in the record. North Dakota regulations provide a form for evaluators to use to transform *AMA Guides* ratings into percentages of impairment.[18]

---

[12] *Id.* at 1, 317.

[13] *Id.* at 301.

[14] *Id.* at 300–01. It is important to note that impairment percentages for mental disorders were provided in the *AMA Guides* (3d ed. 1988).

[15] Peterson v. Northern Health Care, 912 P.2d 831 (N.M. Ct. App. 1996).

[16] The court in Knott County Nursing Home v. Wallen, 2001 WL 629401 (Ky. Ct. App. June 8, 2001), states the problem: "We believe that the argument raised by counsel in this case highlights the fact that often the legal community and the medical community are simply not operating on the same page. In order for there to be an award of permanent partial disability, the ALJ is bound to the formula contained in KRS 342. In order to accomplish this, the ALJ must have in hand a functional impairment rating. The current edition of the *AMA Guides* on the other hand, state [sic] that there is no empiric evidence to support any method for assigning a percentage of impairment of the whole person. It seems to us it would border on absurdity to allow an ALJ to award permanent total disability in an injury case where there is also a psychiatric/psychological component wherein the medical expert testifies as to classification of impairment as opposed to percentages of impairment, and to deny another claimant a permanent partial disability award because there is a classification of impairment but no corresponding finding of a percentage of impairment. What remains is that we are left with clinical judgments which may not be based on empirical evidence but made of necessity." 2001 WL 629401, at *2.

[17] 15 P.3d 948, 2000 MT 362 (Mont. 2000).

[18] N.D. Admin. Code § T.92, art. 1, ch. 2, app. A.

8. Disfigurement. *Disfigurement* is defined as an altered or abnormal color, shape, or structure of a visible body part.[19] Disfigurement may produce impairment by causing social rejection or an unfavorable self-image with self-imposed isolation, lifestyle alteration, or other behavioral changes. Disfigurement may also result in impairment.[20] Disfigurement that does not result in functional impairment may not be compensable in some jurisdictions.[21]

9. Symptom frequency and intensity. The frequency and intensity of the occurrence of symptoms are graded. Symptom frequency is graded into four categories: intermittent, occasional, frequent, and constant. These gradations are defined in the following manner:

1. Intermittent—The symptoms or signs have been medically documented to occur less than one-fourth of the time that the patient is awake.
2. Occasional—The symptoms or signs have been medically documented to occur more than one-fourth of the time but less than one-half of the time that the patient is awake.
3. Frequent—The symptoms or signs have been medically documented to occur between one-half and three-fourths of the time that the patient is awake.
4. Constant—The symptoms or signs have been medically documented to occur between three-fourths and all of the time that the patient is awake.[22]

Symptom intensity is also graded into four categories: minimal, slight, moderate, and marked. These gradations are defined in the following manner:

1. Minimal—The symptoms or signs are annoying but have not been documented medically to cause appreciable diminution in an individual's capacity to carry out daily activities.
2. Slight—The symptoms or signs are tolerated by the individual and have been medically documented to cause some diminution in the individual's capacity to carry out the ADLs.
3. Moderate—The symptoms or signs have been documented medically to cause serious diminution in the individual's capacity to carry out the ADLs.
4. Marked—The symptoms or signs preclude carrying out ADLs.[23]

10. Causation. Causation may be difficult to document when the impairment's etiology is environmental or occupational and not traumatic.[24] A physician must review an extensive amount of information when making a causation determination.[25]

---

[19] *AMA Guides* (4th ed. 1993) at 316.

[20] *Id.* at 279.

[21] *See, e.g.,* Advanced Component Sys. v. Gonzales, 935 P.2d 24 (Colo. Ct. App. 1996).

[22] *AMA Guides* (4th ed. 1993) at 316.

[23] *Id.*

[24] *Id.*

[25] *Id.* at 317.

11. Apportionment. *Apportionment* is defined as the estimate of the degree to which each of the various occupational or nonoccupational factors may have caused or contributed to a particular impairment.[26] When apportioning a preexisting impairment, accurate information and data on both impairments are needed.[27] Apportionment should be considered a medical question of fact.[28]

An appeals court in Arizona held that the proper way to apportion preexisting impairments is as follows: "[A] claimant's total post-industrial injury impairment should be determined first. The preexisting nonindustrial impairment should then be determined and deducted. The remaining impairment, measured as a percentage of the whole impairment, is attributable to the industrial injury and should be the basis for the award."[29] When a preexisting degenerative condition is asymptomatic before a work-related injury, apportionment out of the preexisting condition may not be allowed by the court.[30]

The court, in *Bourgoin v. J.P. Levesque & Sons*,[31] citing the *AMA Guides*, held that apportionment is appropriate where a claimant has preexisting diabetes that is not work related. Apportionment may not be appropriate when a claimant is issued a medical impairment rating for a previous injury and before the second injury the claimant's condition improves to the point that he or she is asymptomatic.[32] It has been held to be permissible to apportion out a rating based on a more generous system when rating a recent injury under the *AMA Guides* (4th ed. 1993).[33]

The court upheld a rating where apportionment was not done.[34] The claimant in *Wackenhut Corp.* had previously injured his left sacroiliac joint, and his latest injury was to his right sacroiliac joint. The court in *Wackenhut Corp.* found no error

---

[26] *Id.* at 315.

[27] *Id.* at 10.

[28] Askew v. Sears, Roebuck & Co., 914 P.2d 416 (Colo. Ct. App. 1995).

[29] Vargas v. Industrial Comm'n, 926 P.2d 533 (Ariz. Ct. App. 1996).

[30] *See* Askew v. Industrial Claim Appeals Office, 927 P.2d 1333 (Colo. 1996).

[31] 726 A.2d 201 (Me. 1999).

[32] *See* Lambert & Sons, Inc. v. Industrial Claim Appeals Office, 1998 Colo. App. LEXIS 168 (Colo. Ct. App. July 9, 1998). Similarly, in Wackenhut Corp. v. Industrial Claim Appeals Office of State of Colo., 17 P.3d 202 (Colo. Ct. App. Oct. 26, 2000), the claimant injured his back. The treating physician apportioned the entire injury rating to a preexisting back injury, but the independent medical examination (IME) physician found that apportionment was not appropriate and gave the claimant a 14 percent whole-person rating. He testified that he relied upon a medical note from a chiropractor that the treatment for claimant's prior back injury was for a left thoraco-costal sprain injury, involving the left sacroiliac and left cervical area, and stated that in contrast, the claimant's current injury involved the right sacroiliac area. The court noted that the claimant was able to work out regularly and jog and that he did not have any problems with his back after being placed at maximum medical improvement from his first injury, and he was asymptomatic at time of his second injury. It affirmed the award based on the 14 percent nonapportioned rating.

[33] Wagner v. Workers' Comp. Div., 1998 W. Va. LEXIS 219 (W. Va. Dec. 11, 1998).

[34] Wackenhut Corp. v. Industrial Claim Appeals Office of State of Colo., 17 P.3d 202 (Colo. Ct. App. 2000).

in the ALJ's conclusion that the IME physician's rating was performed consistently with the requirements of the *AMA Guides*.[35]

12.   Aggravation.   This term means that a preexisting medical condition or infirmity has worsened in such a way that the degree of permanent impairment has increased by more than 3 percent.[36]

13.   Hearing loss.   The *AMA Guides* do not take into account the effects of aging on hearing loss. Accepting an age-related deduction based on the International Standard for 1999 of the International Organization for Standardization (ISO 1999) is reversible error.[37] *LTV Steel Co., Inc. v. W.C.A.B. (Mozena)*[38] held that "[b]ecause there is no way to distinguish, scientifically or mathematically, the amount of hearing loss caused by acoustic trauma from that caused by the aging process, and [the Act] provides for no standard to measure presbycusis, we find that [the Act] does not permit a deduction from a claimant's total binaural hearing impairment for that portion of the impairment caused by presbycusis."

14.   Spinal impairment.   The range-of-motion model cannot be used to resolve a disagreement between two physicians. It is to be used when a single physician needs to decide for himself or herself which diagnosis-related estimates category is suitable for the examinee.[39] In the case of *Carrizales v. Winsteads Restaurants*,[40] the court upheld a rating physician's findings of radiculopathy to support a DRE rating despite the fact that there was no evidence of loss of reflexes or atrophy, and the rating physician did not administer any electrodiagnostic tests.

---

[35] *Id.* at 204.

[36] *AMA Guides* (4th ed. 1993) at 316.

[37] Rockwell Int'l v. W.C.A.B. (Meyer), 741 A.2d 835 (Pa. Commw. Ct. 1999).

[38] 562 Pa. 205, 754 A.2d 666 (Pa. July 19, 2000).

[39] Ball v. Big Elk Creek Coal Co., 1999 WL 1086306 (Ky. Ct. App. Nov. 19, 1999).

[40] 82 P.3d 875 (Kan. Ct. App. 2004).

TABLE OF CASES

[References are to section numbers and appendixes.]

C

F

Farm Fresh, Inc. v. Bucek, 895 P.2d 719 (Okla. 1995), 1.04, 11.28

Feist v. North Dakota Workers Comp. Bureau, 1997 ND 177, 569 N.W.2d 1 (N.D. 1997), 11.26, App. B

Ferris, State ex rel., v. Comm'n, Franklin App. No. 85AP-599 (Ohio May 20, 1986), 11.27

Finley v. DBM Techs., 217 S.W.3d 261 (Ky. Ct. App. 2007), 11.14, App. B

Fireman's Fund Ins. v. Weeks, 2007 WL 4460608 (Tex. App.—El Paso 2007), 1.07, 11.33, App. B

Flanigan's Enters., Inc. v. Pont, 395 So. 2d 1217 (Fla. Dist. Ct. App. 1981), 11.08

Florida Mining & Materials v. Moore, 443 So. 2d 328 (Fla. Dist. Ct. App. 1983), 11.08

Florida Sheriffs Youth Fund v. Harrell, 438 So. 2d 450 (Fla. Dist. Ct. App. 1983), 1.12, 11.08, App. B

Foote v. State Pers. Comm'n, 116 N.H. 145, 355 A.2d 412 (1976), 11.23

Fournier, Appeal of, 786 A.2d 854 (N.H. 2001), 1.13, 4.02[L], 11.23, App. B

Foxx v. American Transp., 924 S.W.2d 814 (Ark. Ct. App. 1996), 1.04, 11.03

Frank's Fine Meats v. Sherman, 443 So. 2d 1055 (Fla. Dist. Ct. App. 1984), 11.08, App. B

Freeman v. VF Corp., Kay Windsor Div., 675 S.W.2d 710 (Tenn. 1984), 2.03

G

Gaines v. Sun Refinery & Mktg., 790 P.2d 1073 (Okla. 1990), 1.13, 6.02, 11.28, App. B

Gainesville Coca-Cola v. Young, 596 So. 2d 1278 (Fla. Dist. Ct. App. 1992), 1.12, 11.08, App. B

Garcia v. Eagle Pass Auto Elec., Inc., No. 90-11-10301-CV (Tex. Dist. Ct. Maverick County Dec. 31, 1990), 11.33

Gardner v. Edward Gardner Plumbing & Heating, 693 P.2d 678 (Utah 1984), App. B

Gates v. Jackson Appliance Co., 2001 WL 720624 (Tenn. Spec. Workers' Comp. App. Panel June 27, 2001), 1.08, 2.03, 11.32, App. B

Genelus v. Boran, Craig, Schreck Constr Co., 438 So. 2d 964 (Fla. Dist. Ct. App. 1983), App. B

General Chem. Div. Allied Chem. & Dye Corp. v. Fasano, 47 Del. 546, 94 A.2d 600 (Del. Super. Ct. 1953), 11.06

General Motors Corp. v. Summerous, 317 S.E.2d 318 (Ga. Ct. App. 1984), 11.09, App. B

General Tool & Supply v. Somers, 737 P.2d 581 (Okla. Ct. App. 1987), 11.28, App. B

George Humfleet Mobile Homes v. Christman, 125 S.W.3d 288 (Ky. 2004), 1.08, 11.14, App. B

Getson v. WM Babcorp, 694 A.2d 961 (Md. 1997), 1.02, 11.17, App. B

Gilpatric, Petition of, 639 A.2d 267 (N.H. 1994), 11.23

Glass v. Edens, 233 Ark. 786, 346 S.W.2d 685 (1961), 11.03

Glisson v. State Dep't of Mgmt. Servs., 621 So. 2d 543 (Fla. Dist. Ct. App. 1993), 11.08, App. B

Golden Animal Hosp. v. Horton, 897 P.2d 833 (Colo. 1995), 11.04

Gomez v. Industrial Comm'n, 148 Ariz. 565, 716 P.2d 22 (Ariz. 1986), 11.02

Gomez v. Industrial Comm'n, 148 Ariz. 575, 716 P.2d 32 (Ct. App. 1985), 1.01, 1.12, 11.02, App. B

Goodrich v. Hilton, 634 P.2d 1308 (Okla. 1981), 11.28

Graul, State v., 181 Ga. App. 573, 353 S.E.2d 70 (1987), 11.09

Graves v. Eagle Iron Works, 331 N.W.2d 116 (Iowa 1983), 11.12, App. B

Gray v. Administrative Dir. of the Court, State of Haw., 84 Haw. 138, 931 P.2d 580 (1997), 11.10

Green v. Glass, 920 P.2d 1081 (Okla. Ct. App. 1996), 3.04, 11.28, App. B

Griffith v. State Workmen's Comp. Comm'r, 157 W. Va. 837, 205 S.E.2d 157 (1974), 11.37

G&W Wood Prods. v. Parrott, 447 So. 2d 407 (Fla. Dist. Ct. App. 1984), App. B

H

Hailsen v. Seabrook Clam Co., 623 A.2d 225 (N.H. 1993), 11.23

Hall v. State Comp. Ins. Fund, 708 P.2d 234 (Mont. 1985), App. B

Hapney v. Rheem Mfg. Co., 342 Ark. 11, 26 S.W.3d 777 (2000), 11.03, App. B

Hapney v. Rheem Mfg. Co., 341 Ark. 548, 26 S.W.3d 771 (2000), 11.03

Harless v. Huntsville Manor Nursing Home, C.A. No. 7258 (Tenn. Ch. Ct. Scott County Aug. 31, 1994), 1.12, 3.04, 11.32, App. B

Harness v. CNA Ins. Co., 814 S.W.2d 733 (Tenn. 1991), 1.08, 11.32, App. B

Hausen v. Seabrook Clam Co., 623 A.2d 225 (N.H. 1993), App. B

Hayes v. Wal-Mart Stores Inc., 71 Ark. App. 207, 29 S.W.3d 751 (2000), 11.03

Henley v. Roadway Express, 699 S.W.2d 150 (Tenn. 1985), 2.03

Henry v. Smith, 742 P.2d 35 (Okla. Ct. App. 1987), 11.28

Henson v. City of Lawrenceburg, 851 S.W.2d 809 (Tenn. 1993), 11.32, App. B

Hise Constr. v. Candelaria, 98 N.M. 759, 652 P.2d 1210 (1982), 11.24

Hite v. Kulhenak Bldg. Contractor, 524 P.2d 531 (Idaho 1974), 11.11, App. B

Hollytex Carpet Mills, Inc. v. Hinkle, 819 P.2d 289 (Okla. Ct. App. 1991), 11.28, App. B

Houston v. Zebco, 821 P.2d 367 (Okla. 1991), 6.02, 11.28, App. B

Hoyem v. North Dakota Workers Comp. Bureau, 578 N.W.2d 117 (N.D. 1998), 11.26, App. B, App. C

Huffman v. General Motors Corp., 811 P.2d 106 (Okla. Ct. App. 1991), 11.28

Hughes v. General Motors Guide Lamp Div., 469 So. 2d 369 (La. Ct. App. 1985), App. B

Hulbert v. Avis Rent-A-Car Sys., 469 So. 2d 235 (Fla. Dist. Ct. App. 1985), App. B

Humphrey v. David Witherspoon, Inc., 734 S.W.2d 315 (Tenn. 1987), 2.03, 11.32, App. B

Hunter v. Industrial Comm'n, 130 Ariz. 59, 633 P.2d 1052 (Ct. App. 1981), 1.12, 11.02, App. B

Hunt-Wilde Corp. v. Kitchen, 452 So. 2d 2 (Fla. Dist. Ct. App. 1984), 11.08, App. B

I

Ingalls Shipbuilding v. Director, Office of Workers' Comp. Programs, 991 F.2d 163 (5th Cir. 1993), 11.40, App. B

Ingalls Shipbuilding v. Director, Office of Workers' Comp. Programs, 898 F.2d 1088 (5th Cir. 1990), 11.40, App. B

Injured Workers Ass'n v. Department of Labor, 630 So. 2d 1189 (Fla. Dist. Ct. App. 1994), 11.08

Insurance Co. of Pa. v. Martinez, 18 S.W.3d 844 (Tex. App.—El Paso 2000), 11.33

International Bhd. of Elec. Workers, Local 1357 v. Hawaiian Tel. Co., 68 Haw. 316, 713 P.2d 943 (1986), 11.10

Ives v. South Buffalo Ry. Co., 201 N.Y. 271, 94 N.E. 431 (1911), 1.01

Ivey v. Trans Global Gas & Oil, 3 S.W.3d 441 (Tenn. 1999), 11.32

J

Jackson v. Goodyear Tire & Rubber Co., 2001 WL 303508 (Tenn. Spec. Workers' Comp. App. Panel Mar. 29, 2001), 1.07, 11.32, App. B

Jacob v. Columbia Ins. Group, 511 N.W.2d 211 (Neb. Ct. App. 1994), 1.06, 11.21, App. B

Jacobson Constr. v. Hair, 667 P.2d 25 (Utah 1983), 11.34, App. B

Jamar Sportswear, Inc. v. Miller, 413 So. 2d 811 (Fla. Dist. Ct. App. 1982), 11.08, App. B

Jaske v. Murray Ohio Mfg. Co., 750 S.W.2d 150 (Tenn. 1988), 11.32, App. B

Javins v. Workers' Comp. Comm'r, 320 S.E.2d 119 (W. Va. 1984), 1.01, 11.37, App. B

Lambert v. Workers' Comp. Div., 211 W. Va. 436, 566 S.E.2d 573 (2002), 11.37

Lambert & Sons, Inc. v. Industrial Claim Appeals Office, 1998 Colo. App. LEXIS 168 (Colo. Ct. App. July 9, 1998), 11.04, App. B, App. C

Landry v. Graphic Tech., Inc., 2 P.3d 758 (Kan. 2000), 6.04

Langton v. Rocky Mountain Health Care Corp., 937 P.2d 883 (Colo. Ct. App. 1996), 11.04

Lanoue v. All Star Chevrolet, 867 So. 2d 755 (La. Ct. App. 1st Cir. 2003), 1.07, 11.15, App. B

Lanter v. Kentucky State Police, 171 S.W.3d 45 (Ky. 2005), 4.04[K], 11.14, App. B

Lara v. Pacific Employers Ins. Co., 2003 WL 21517857 (Tex. App.—El Paso July 3, 2003), 11.33, App. B

Lauhoff Grain Co. v. McIntosh, 395 N.W.2d 834 (Iowa 1986), 11.12, App. B

Leaseway Motor Co. Transp. v. Cline, 2007 WL 858834 (Ky. 2007), 11.14

Lewandowski v. Preferred Risk Mut. Ins. Co., 146 N.W.2d 505 (Wis. 1966), 11.38, App. B

Light v. Frontier Health, Inc., No. E1999-00256-SC-WCM-CV, 2000 Tenn. LEXIS 671 (Tenn. Spec. Workers' Comp. App. Panel Dec. 5, 2000), 2.03

Linville v. State Workmen's Comp. Comm'r, 160 W. Va. 549, 236 S.E.2d 41 (1977), 11.37

Long v. Mid-Tennessee Ford Truck Sales, Inc., 160 S.W.3d 504 (Tenn. 2005), 11.32, App. B

Low v. Industrial Comm'n, 680 P.2d 188 (Ariz. Ct. App. 1984), 11.02, App. B

LTV Steel Co. v. WCAB (Mozena), 562 Pa. 205, 754 A.2d 666 (Pa. 2000), 1.07, 11.30, App. B, App. C

Lucente, State ex rel., v. Industrial Comm'n, 472 N.E.2d 718 (Ohio 1984), App. B

Lucero v. Smith's Food & Drug Ctrs., Inc., 1994 NMCA 079, 118 N.M. 35, 878 P.2d 353 (1994), 11.24

Lyle v. Exxon Corp., 746 S.W.2d 694 (Tenn. 1988), 11.32, App. B

Lyson v. N.D. Workmen's Comp. Bureau, 129 N.W.2d 351 (N.D. 1964), 11.26

M

Madrid v. St. Joseph Hosp., 1996 NMSC 64, 122 N.M. 524, 928 P.2d 250 (1996), 1.01, 1.08, 1.12, 3.04, 11.24, 11.31

Maggard v. Simpson Motors, 451 So. 2d 529 (Fla. Dist. Ct. App. 1984), 1.12, 11.08, App. B

Martin County Sch. Bd. v. McDaniel, 465 So. 2d 1235 (Fla. Dist. Ct. App. 1984) (*on reh'g en banc*), *appeal and cross-appeal dismissed*, 478 So. 2d 54 (Fla. 1985), 1.12, 11.08, App. B

Martinez v. Excel Corp., 79 P.2d 230 (Kan. Ct. App. 2003), 2.01, 11.13, App. B

Martinez v. Meharry Med. Coll., 673 S.W.2d 141 (Tenn. 1984), 11.32

Mathis v. Kelly Constr. Co., 417 So. 2d 740 (Fla. Dist. Ct. App. 1982), 1.12, 11.08, App. B

Maxwell v. SIIS, 849 P.2d 267 (Nev. 1993), 1.06, 11.22, App. B

Mays v. Alumnitec, 64 S.W.3d 772 (Ark. Ct. App. 2001), 1.06, 4.02[I], 11.03, App. B

Mazze v. Frank J. Holleran, Inc., 9 Ben. Rev. Bd. Serv. (MB) 1053 (1978), 11.40

McCabe v. Bechtel Power Corp., 510 So. 2d 1056 (Fla. Dist. Ct. App. 1987), 1.08, 11.08, App. B

McCabe v. North Dakota Workers Comp. Bureau, 567 N.W.2d 201 (N.D. 1997), 1.08, 3.04, 11.26, App. B

McCollum v. North Dakota Workers Comp. Bureau, 1997 ND 163, 567 N.W.2d 811 (N.D. 1997), 11.26, App. B

McCray v. Murray, 423 So. 2d 559 (Fla. Dist. Ct. App. 1982), App. B

McCubbin v. Walker, 256 Kan. 276, 886 P.2d 790 (1994), 11.13

McDaniel v. CSX Transp., Inc., 955 S.W.2d 257 (Tenn. 1997), 11.32

McLane W. Inc. v. Industrial Claim Appeals Office, 996 P.2d 263 (Colo. Ct. App. 1999), 1.05, 2.01, 11.04, App. B

McLean, State ex rel., v. Industrial Comm'n, 25 Ohio St. 3d 90, 495 N.E.2d 370 (1986), 11.27

McNutt Constr./First Gen. Servs. v. Scott, 40 S.W.3d 854 (Ky. 2001), 11.14

Melcher v. Drummond Mfg. Co., 312 Ky. 588, 229 S.W.2d 52 (1950), 11.14

Second Injury Fund v. Bergeson, 526 N.W.2d 543 (Iowa 1995), 11.12, App. B
Second Injury Fund v. Fraser-Owens, 17 Ark. App. 58, 702 S.W.2d 828 (1986), 11.03
Second Injury Fund v. Yarbrough, 19 Ark. App. 354, 721 S.W.2d 686 (1986), 11.03
Shaffer v. Lourdes Hosp., 2000 WL 1763242 (Ky. Ct. App. Dec. 1, 2000), 1.07, 11.14, App. B
Shaver v. Kopp, 545 N.W.2d 170 (N.D. 1996), 11.26
Shaw v. Publix Supermarkets, Inc., 609 So. 2d 683 (Fla. Dist. Ct. App. 1992), 11.08, App. B
Shipley v. Ala Moana Hotel, 83 Haw. 361, 926 P.2d 1284 (1996), 11.10
Shop & Go, Inc. v. Dunigan, 463 So. 2d 585 (Fla. Dist. Ct. App. 1985), App. B
Shop & Go, Inc. v. Hart, 537 So. 2d 667 (Fla. Dist. Ct. App. 1989), 11.08
Short v. Dietz Mobile Home Transp., 2001 WL 370317 (Tenn. Spec. Workers' Comp. App. Panel
   Apr. 16, 2001), 11.32, App. B
Silva v. Kaiwiki Milling Co., 24 Haw. 324 (Terr. 1918), 11.10
Simbro v. Delong's Sportswear, 332 N.W.2d 886 (Iowa 1983), App. B
Simmons v. Delaware State Hosp., 660 A.2d 384 (Del. 1995), 6.02, 11.06, App. B
Simpson v. Industrial Comm'n of Ariz., 942 P.2d 1172 (Ariz. Ct. App. 1997), 1.12, 11.02, App. B
Singleton v. Kenya Corp., 961 P.2d 571 (Colo. Ct. App. 1998), 11.04
S.L.H. v. State Comp. Mut. Ins. Fund, 2000 MT 362, 15 P.3d 948 (Mont. Dec. 28, 2000), 2.03,
   11.20, App. B, App. C
Slover Masonry, Inc. v. Industrial Comm'n of Ariz., 158 Ariz. 131, 761 P.2d 1035 (1988), 11.10, App. B
Slover Masonry, Inc. v. Industrial Comm'n, 155 Ariz. 211, 745 P.2d 958 (Ct. App. 1987), 11.02
Smith v. City of Albuquerque, 105 N.M. 125, 720 P.2d 1379 (Ct. App. 1986), 11.24
Smith v. Dixie Fuel Co., 900 S.W.2d 609 (Ky. 1995), 11.14
Smith v. Gerber Prods., 54 Ark. App. 57, 922 S.W.2d 365 (1996), 11.03
Smith v. Industrial Comm'n, 113 Ariz. 304, 552 P.2d 1198 (1976), 1.12, 11.02, 11.26, App. B
Smith v. Jackson Constr. Co., 607 So. 2d 1119 (Miss. 1992), 11.19, App. B
Spangler v. Lease-Way Auto. Transp., 780 P.2d 209 (Okla. Ct. App. 1989), 11.28, App. B
Spaugh v. Munyan Painting Contractors, 444 So. 2d 1100 (Fla. Dist. Ct. App. 1984), 11.08
Special Fund v. Francis, 708 S.W.2d 641 (1986), 11.14
Special Indem. Fund v. Choate, 847 P.2d 796 (Okla. 1993), 1.02, 1.11, 6.04, 11.28, App. B
Special Indem. Fund v. Stockton, 653 P.2d 194 (Okla. 1982), 11.28, App. B
Spring Air Mattress Co. v. Cox, 413 So. 2d 1265 (Fla. Dist. Ct. App. 1982), 11.08, App. B
Stamper v. University Apartments, Inc., 522 A.2d 227 (Vt. 1986), 1.11, 11.35, App. B
State Highway Comm'n, State ex rel., v. Bassett, 81 N.M. 345, 467 P.2d 11 (1970), 11.24
Storage Tech. Corp. v. Philbrook, 448 So. 2d 42 (Fla. Dist. Ct. App. 1984), App. B
Stovall v. Great Flame Coal Co., 684 S.W.2d 3 (Ky. Ct. App. 1984), 11.14
Strauch v. PSL Swedish Healthcare Sys., 917 P.2d 366 (Colo. Ct. App. 1996), 1.02, 11.04, App. B
Strickland v. Coca-Cola Bottling Co., 760 P.2d 793 (N.M. Ct. App. 1988), 11.24
Stroud v. Morrison Nursery, 806 So. 2d 133 (La. Ct. App. 3d Cir. 2001), App. A
Sumrall v. Crown Zellerbach Corp., 525 So. 2d 272 (La. Ct. App. 1st Cir. 1988), 11.15, App. B
Sunland Hosp. v. Garrett, 415 So. 2d 783 (Fla. Dist. Ct. App. 1982), 11.08
Sutton v. Quality Furniture Co., 191 Ga. App. 279, 381 S.E.2d 389 (1989), 1.12, 11.09, 11.24,
   11.39, App. B
Swift-Eckrich, Inc. v. Brock, 975 S.W.2d 857 (Ark. Ct. App. 1998), 11.03, App. B
Symington v. North Dakota Workers Comp. Bureau, 545 N.W.2d 806 (N.D. 1996), 11.26

T

Tafoya v. Kermac Nuclear Fuels, Corp., 71 N.M. 157, 376 P.2d 576 (1962), 11.24
Tallahassee Mem'l Reg'l Med. Ctr. v. Snead, 400 So. 2d 1016 (Fla. Dist. Ct. App. 1981), 11.08,
   App. B

W

W.A. Krueger Co. v. Industrial Comm'n, 150 Ariz. 66, 722 P.2d 234 (1986), 11.02, App. B

Wackenhut Corp. v. Industrial Claim Appeals Office of Colo., 2000 CJ C.A.R. 5916, 17 P.3d 202 (Colo. Ct. App. 2000), 11.04, App. B, App. C

Waddell v. Industrial Claim Appeals Office, 964 P.2d 552 (Colo. Ct. App. 1998), 11.04

Wagner v. Workers' Comp. Div., 1998 W. Va. LEXIS 219 (W. Va. Dec. 11, 1998), 11.37, App. B, App. C

Walker v. Gulf & W. Food Prods., 461 So. 2d 993 (Fla. Dist. Ct. App. 1984), 11.08, App. B

Walker v. Jim Fuoco Motor Co., 942 P.2d 1390 (Colo. Ct. App. 1997), 1.02, 3.04, 11.04, App. B

Wal-Mart Stores, In re, 145 N.H. 635, 765 A.2d 168 (2000), 1.12, 11.10, 11.23, App. B

Wal-Mart Stores, Inc. v. Keel, 817 So. 2d 1 (La. 2002), App. A

Wal-Mart Stores, Inc. v. Williams, 2000 WL 528252 (Ark. Ct. App. May 3, 2000), 1.07, 11.03

Washington Steel Corp. v. Workers' Comp. Appeal Bd. (Waugh), 734 A.2d 81 (Pa. Commw. Ct. 1999), 1.07, 11.30, App. B

Weiss v. Industrial Comm'n, 87 Ariz. 21, 347 P.2d 578 (1959), 11.02

Weyerhaeuser Co. v. Washington, 838 P.2d 539 (Okla. Ct. App. 1992), 11.28, App. B

Wheat v. Heritage Manor, 784 P.2d 74 (Okla. 1989), 6.02, 11.28, App. B

White v. Georgia-Pacific Corp., 339 Ark. 474, 6 S.W.3d 98 (1999), 11.03

White v. United Indus. Syndicate, 742 S.W.2d 635 (Tenn. 1987), 11.32, App. B

Whitehall Corp. v. Davis, 448 So. 2d 47 (Fla. Dist. Ct. App. 1984), App. B

Whitener v. South Cent. Solid Waste Auth., 773 P.2d 1248 (Okla. 1989), 6.02, 11.28

Whiteside v. Smith, 67 P.3d 1240 (Colo. 2003), 11.04

Whittaker v. Johnson, 987 S.W.2d 320 (Ky. 1999), 1.04, 11.14, App. B

Whittaker v. Reeder, 30 S.W.3d 138 (Ky. 2000), 11.14

Williams v. FEI Installation, 2005 WL 3488386 (Ky. Ct. App. Dec. 22, 2005), 1.07, 10.05, 11.14, App. B

Williams v. Vickers, Inc., 799 P.2d 621 (Okla. 1990), 11.28, App. B

Williamson v. Aetna Cas. & Sur. Co., 101 Ga. App. 220, 113 S.E.2d 208 (1960), 11.26

Wilson v. Harris Corp., 557 So. 2d 50 (Fla. Dist. Ct. App. 1989), 11.08, App. B

Wilson v. Industrial Claim Appeals Office of Colo., 81 P.3d 1117 (Colo. Ct. App. 2003), 1.07, 1.13, 11.04, App. B

Wise v. Lapworth, 614 So. 2d 728 (La. Ct. App. 1993), 11.15, App. B

Woods v. TRW Inc., 557 S.W.2d 274 (Tenn. 1977), 11.32

Wright v. Hopwood Mining, 832 S.W.2d 884 (Ky. 1992), 11.14, App. B

Wykpisz v. Steel, 2001 WL 755376 (Del. 2001), 11.06, App. B

Wyoming Workers' Safety & Comp. Div. & FMC Corp., State of Wyo. ex rel., v. Faulkner, 152 P.3d 394 (Wyo. 2007), 11.39, App. B

Y

Yader v. State of Alaska, No. 4FA-84-1315 (Alaska Super. Ct. Jan. 30, 1985), 11.01

Yeager v. St. Vincent Hosp., 973 P.2d 850 (N.M. Ct. App. 1998), 2.03, 11.24, App. B

Yoder v. Alaska, No. 4FA-84-1315 (Alaska Super. Ct. Jan. 30, 1985), 1.06, App. B

York v. Burgess-Norton Mfg. Co., 803 P.2d 697 (Okla. 1990), 11.28

Z

Zavatsky v. Stringer, 56 Ohio St. 2d 386, 384 N.E.2d 693 (1978), 11.27

Zebco v. Houston, 800 P.2d 245 (Okla. 1990), 6.02, 7.02, 11.28, App. B

INDEX

J

K

L